AVIATION THEORY

Basic Aeronautical Knowledge

including Human Factors

Name ....

Address ....

....

....

ARN .... Date of Birth ....

Telephone ....

Mobile ....

Email ....

Aviation Theory Centre

Disclaimer
Nothing in this text supersedes any operational documents issued by the Civil Aviation Safety Authority (Australia) or its equivalent in any country, the aircraft, engine and avionics manufacturers or the operators of aircraft throughout the world.

First Edition June 1999
Revised June 2000
Revised July 2001
Second Edition January 2003
Revised February 2004
Reprinted February 2005
Reprinted June 2006
Revised and reprinted in colour September 2007 & 2009
Reprinted February 2011
Reprinted June 2013, December 2013

Third Edition & First e-dition - December 2014

Published by:
Aviation Theory Centre Pty Ltd
ABN: 24 088 462 873

Graphics & Typesetting: Aviation Theory Centre

Websites: www.aviationtheory.net.au
Email: aviationtheory@msn.com.au

ISBN: 978-1-875537-57-0

Printed in China through Asia Pacific Offset Ltd

Editorial

David Robson tp

David is a career aviator having been nurtured on balsa wood, dope and tissue paper. He learnt to fly in Chipmunks and made his first solo flight shortly after his seventeenth birthday. His first job was as a junior draftsperson at the Commonwealth Aircraft Corporation in Port Melbourne.

He joined the Royal Australian Air Force in 1965 and served for twenty-one years as a fighter pilot and test pilot. He flew over 1,000 hours on Mirages and 500 on Sabres. He completed the Empire Test Pilots' course at Boscombe Down in 1972, flying everything from gliders to the Hunter, Lightning and Argosy. He completed a tour in Vietnam as a forward air controller, flying the O-2A and directing air strikes in support of the Australian Task Force. He was a member of the Mirage formation aerobatic team, the *Deltas*, which celebrated the RAAF's 50th anniversary.

After retiring from the Air Force he became a civilian instructor and lecturer and spent over ten years with the Australian Aviation College. During 1986–88 he was the editor of the *Aviation Safety Digest* (the "crash comic"), which won the Flight Safety Foundation's international award. He was awarded the Australian Aviation Safety Foundation's Certificate of Air Safety.

He has recently been introduced to recreational aircraft to ensure that ATC books can continue to contribute to all facets of aviation training from the ground up. Next step: UAVs?

Preface

This edition of *Basic Aeronautical Knowledge* (BAK) addresses the many changes that have taken place in aviation in the past few years. While many of the training aircraft are the same, there are, at last, several novel designs available. We have included reference to some of these.

The airspace, the procedures, the licences, the examinations, the traffic density, medical standards, the radio calls and the level of knowledge about ourselves have changed significantly. Further, on the 1st of September 2014, Civil Aviation Safety Regulation (CASR) Part 61 was made law. This new regulation has made significant changes to the pilot licensing system in Australia. These changes are explained in Chapter 5.

For the student pilot there is little effect in getting started apart from a reduced minimum medical standard. Then the training proceeds towards a Recreational Pilots Licence (RPL). This replaces the previous General Flying Progress Test (GFPT). Students with a pass in the GFPT or holding a Recreational Pilots Certificate, may be granted a RPL - after a flight test.

The theory for the RPL is similar to the well established BAK examination, but with the addition of the PPL Human Factors level of knowledge. This is also included in this book.

For flying training, there is a range of schools and many different aircraft types available. Training can be started on an approved recreational aircraft and gliding is also a good way to be introduced to flying. Choose your school and especially your instructor, carefully.

As you proceed with your flying training, you will receive "long briefings" on each flight exercise. These exercises and the content of the briefings, which are fully explained in the *Flying Training Manual*, will be less than an hour - because your instructor will assume that you have the necessary background knowledge for understanding the content of the briefing. The structure of this book is designed to assist this process.

There are also formal examinations at set milestones in your training:

- a *pre-solo test*, which may be an oral or written test that focuses on your aircraft, local rules and procedures and your airfield;
- a *pre-area solo test*, which is a written examination including theoretical knowledge and operations within your training area; and
- the *Basic Aeronautical Knowledge* examination - expanded to include more emphasis on Human Factors.

This book contains the theoretical study associated with the first stages of pilot training up to the BAK/HF examination. These studies are the most important you will ever do as a pilot, because they form the foundation for all subsequent training.

The Civil Aviation Safety Authority (CASA) specifies elements of study which must be conducted before your first solo flight, your first solo to the training area and the *RPL*. The level of knowledge for each stage of your training is specified in the CASA *Day VFR Syllabus* and now, the *CASR Part 61 Manual of Standards (MOS)*, with which you should become familiar.

Thank you for choosing an Aviation Theory Centre publication. We wish you every success with your studies and your flying training.

David Robson

Summary of CASR Part 61

As of 01SEP2014 the regulations regarding Flight Crew Licensing in Australia were changed. The new regulations are contained in CASR Part 61, extracts of which are contained herein. Please visit the CASA web-site for more comprehensive information.

http://www.casa.gov.au/scripts/nc.dll?WCMS:PWA::pc=PARTS061

Regulations relating to the conduct of flight training for these licences, ratings and endorsements, is contained in CASR Part 141 - which came into effect on the same date.

Summary of Changes

The new legislation introduces a new *licence* - the Recreational Pilots Licence (RPL) in addition to the PPL, CPL and ATPL. (Pilots who are current holders of a Recreational Pilots Certificate or have passed the GFPT, may be issued with the RPL after completing a flight review).

Each licence then relates to an aircraft *category* (e.g. aeroplane or helicopter). Within these primary categories, the licence reflects the pilot's competencies by the addition of an aircraft *class rating* or *type rating* (e.g. single-engine, piston or a specified aircraft type). Then there are *operational ratings* such as IR, PIFR and flight instructor.(The previous Command Instrument rating becomes simply an Instrument Rating, (IR).

Each operational rating is then '*endorsed*', e.g. IR for a single-engine aeroplane (SEA) or Low Level rating (LL) for a helicopter (H).

Additionally, there are *design feature endorsements* for items such as a retractable undercarriage or tailwheel and *flight activity endorsements* for operations such as glider towing, aerobatics or formation flying.

The aircraft class or type rating, operational ratings and endorsements are all displayed on the new licence rather than in the Pilots Log Book. Existing records will be transferred from the log book to the new licence when renewed.

CASR Part 61 is sub-divided into Subparts and the Subparts into Divisions as described in Chapter 5.

Aviation
Theory
Centre

Contents

Introduction

This book is designed to provide you with all of the information specified in the Day (VFR) Syllabus/Part 61 Manual of Standards - for the BAK examination plus Human Factors. While it contains all the *need-to-know* elements, it also contains additional knowledge to enable you to actually understand what it's all about. This is important not only for greater safety, but also to act as the foundation stone for advancement to PPL and CPL studies. The study that you complete at this early stage is the most important that you will ever complete. It is the basis for all that follows. It is vital that it be well and truly understood.

This study is not about passing examinations. It is about forming the basis of understanding so that you can progress with the flying lessons. The examinations are a means of sampling your knowledge. They are not the end result; the end result is successful completion of training and recognition as a safe and competent pilot. You will especially find that the chapter on the theory of flight is more comprehensive than the minimum required by CASA.

The most important lessons you will ever learn are these early ones. Understanding what is happening to the aircraft, and why, makes the flying lessons more effective, better understood, better retained and more valuable. What you learn and remember in these first few exercises will lay the ground rules for all future flying. You will progress more quickly if you put a little more effort into this background theory now. Besides it's a fascinating subject in its own right.

Why study theory at all? There are three reasons:

- to learn the "rules of the road";
- to learn from others who have learnt the hard way; and
- to provide a basic understanding of the principles before applying them in the air.

The book is written in plain language and is superbly illustrated. Our strong belief is that illustration considerably helps comprehension.

The book covers two main flying training phases:

- Firstly, it covers the information that should be understood and remembered prior to your first solo flight – whether in the circuit or the training area. (While the CASA requires only a brief oral or written test before first solo and a written test before the first area solo, the level of knowledge for both is similar. It is our view that it is better to cover the total knowledge and that it be treated as one test before the first solo circuit.)
- Secondly, it covers the broader introduction to weather, aircraft performance, navigation and loading. This is "enabling" information which exceeds the BAK syllabus requirements. It introduces the flying operations and human factors as related to flying.

Human factors is not a theoretical subject. It is about us: what strengths we have and what weaknesses. We are human, after all, and humans make mistakes. We can be misled, distracted, tired, stressed, confused and misinformed. Understanding our own human nature will hopefully reduce the probability and the seriousness of potentially hazardous situations.

We also learn by example. We are programmed that way. The instructor we follow through these basic stages is an important human factor in establishing our habit patterns and our attitude to safety, thoroughness, professionalism and accuracy. If you feel that your instructor is not setting a standard that you believe is appropriate, ask for a change.

We urge you to cultivate a professional attitude to your flying and accept nothing less.

Of all the knowledge contained in this volume, we ask especially that you retain one piece of information or message for the remainder of your flying career. That message is that you ultimately decide your own fate.

You choose, consciously or unconsciously, to be unsafe (short-lived), marginally safe, thoroughly safe, consistently safe, reliably safe, or predictably safe. You decide how accurately you fly, how much you study and how professional you want to be.

Your personal attitude, together with the attitude of the aircraft, are the most important factors in deciding the fate of the aircraft and its contents.

When you have become a pilot and earned the right to fly in command, you join a select group and can be justifiably proud.

When you fly alone, you have a responsibility not to collide with another aircraft and not to fall on someone's person or property. However, if you carry a passenger, you have a legal, ethical and social duty-of-care – a professional responsibility to do everything reasonably within your power to carry and deliver them in absolute safety. There should never be the slightest doubt about it. If there is, then you must not proceed until the doubt is removed. Their lives are literally in your hands. They could be on the operating table and you, the surgeon.

Further, you can make your passenger's memories of the flight enjoyable or horrific. If you carry someone, take the care to help them enjoy the experience. They will not thank you if you make them sick or frightened.

Enjoy your flying.There is no better way to see this country and indeed, to broaden your personal as well as physical horizons. We sincerely hope that you will continue beyond this first step and remain active as a pilot, whether professional or private – until a ripe old age.

Happy landings.

1 - What is an Aircraft?

Aviation
Theory
Centre

Introduction

What is an aircraft? Essentially, an aircraft is an aerial vehicle – a vehicle for carrying people and freight safely and efficiently through the medium of the air. An aircraft is classified by how it flies and how it is powered:

- fixed-wing or rotary-wing (helicopter);
- powered or glider (or sailplane);
- piston or turbine; and
- single or multi-engine.

At this stage, we will consider only the piston-powered, single-engine, fixed-wing aircraft that you will fly. To better understand why it is the way it is, let's see how the designer conceived our aircraft and how the design of the aircraft evolved.

Let's say we need an aircraft for private use and for training, to accommodate up to four people and some baggage on short day flights from our local airfield.

Figure 1-1 Precious cargo.

Firstly, the pilot and passengers need to be seated and protected, and they need to be able to see. They also need access.

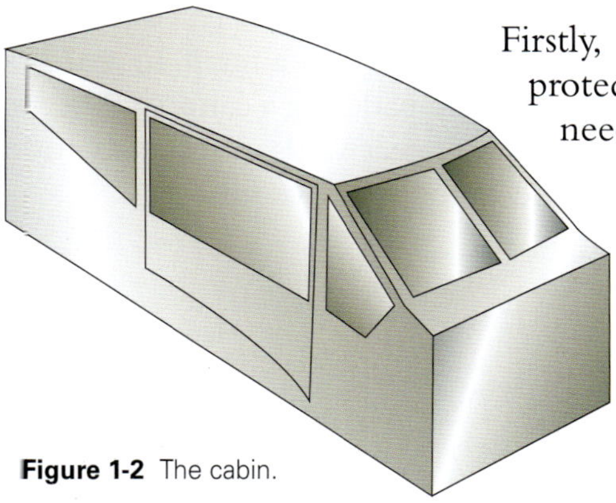

Figure 1-2 The cabin.

Figure 1-3 Added comforts.

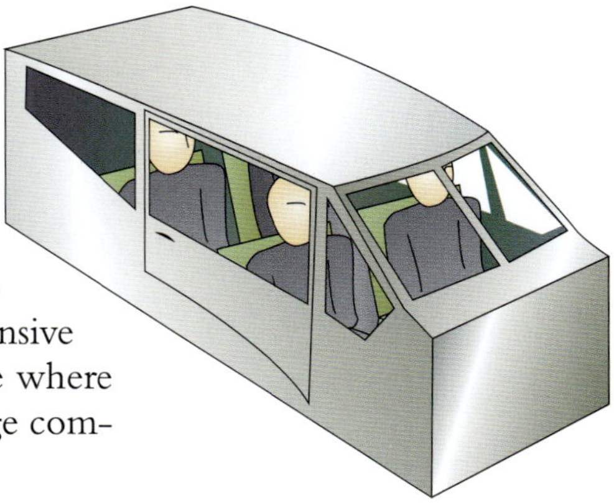

So, we now have a cabin, seats, windows (the front one is called the windscreen as it is in a car) and doors. We add seat belts, some ventilation (or even air conditioning in more expensive and complex aircraft) and space for the baggage where it doesn't interfere with the passengers (a baggage compartment – like the boot of a car).

To overcome the force of gravity, the first essential is a pair of wings to lift the vehicle into the air. This makes it an *air*craft.

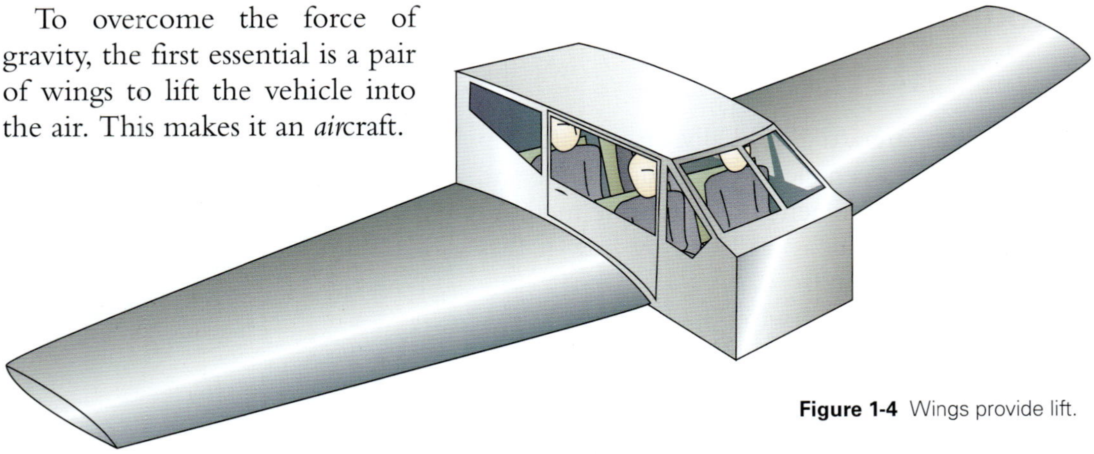

Figure 1-4 Wings provide lift.

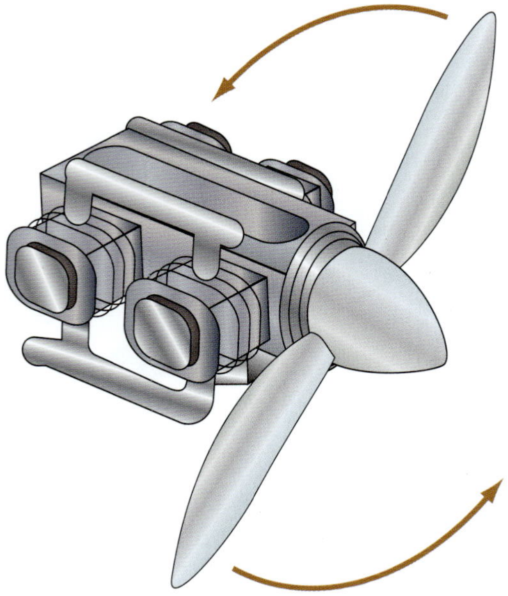

Figure 1-5 Propulsion.

To go anywhere, the cabin needs to be propelled, and, to provide lift, the wings need to be moved through the air. A helicopter moves its wings (rotor blades) without having to move the cabin, and so it can hover. However, we have to move forwards through the air to produce the necessary lift to carry us against the force of gravity. So we add an engine and a propeller. The propeller could be at the front, the back or on the wings, but generally it is positioned in front of the cabin.

The *propulsion* or *thrust* (push) is caused by the propeller pushing air rearwards, and the reaction causes the aircraft to go forwards – just like paddling a canoe where we push the water rearwards and the reaction causes the canoe to move forwards.

Figure 1-6
Action causes a reaction.

Let's now have a closer look at the medium through which we travel.

What is Air?

To appreciate how an aircraft flies, we need to examine the characteristics of the environment in which it operates. The earth's atmosphere, while invisible, has particular features which allow an air-breathing, heavier-than-air object to fly. Let's examine these characteristics. What we call *air* is a gas with many elements. The air we breathe consists of 78% nitrogen, 21% oxygen and the remaining 1% is a cocktail of many substances. We, animals and the aircraft's engine can breathe because of the oxygen. Our aircraft can fly because air has mass (substance), weight (due to gravity), density (weight vs volume), temperature and pressure (static pressure due to altitude and dynamic pressure due to movement). Because air has mass, and therefore weight, the stack of air above the earth causes the lower levels to be squashed. Thus the air nearest the surface of the earth (lower altitudes) is thicker, warmer and at a higher static pressure than the air at higher altitudes. The air near the surface has an average temperature of +15°C, a density of 1,225 g/m^3 and a pressure of 1,013.2 hPa (mb). Because the air has mass, we can stretch it, we can squash it, we can heat it and we can cool it. Thus air is the life force of the engines, the aircraft, the wings, as well as the passengers and the crew.

The engine functions by sucking in the air, mixing it with fuel, igniting the mixture (with the oxygen in the air) and using the temperature rise and consequent expansion to generate a force. This force pushes the piston which rotates the crankshaft which, in turn, rotates the attached propeller.

The aeroplane flies because the wings are shaped to compress the air underneath and to reduce the pressure of the air above. The combination of these effects lifts the aeroplane into the air and sustains it above the earth. Many people, including myself, still marvel at how a massive aircraft can possibly fly on a cushion of "thin", invisible air.

The essence of all motion was identified by mathematician Issac Newton. His *laws of motion* describe, and allow us to calculate, the motion of all bodies. In space, it is relatively simple; in our atmosphere, it's a little more complicated because of the air itself. Yet, as we know, this very substance makes flight possible. Air has mass. It is this fact that allows us to fly. Air is wonderful stuff; it is thick enough to carry us, we can see through it and, with some resistance, it is thin enough to let us pass through.

How Engines Provide Thrust

To accelerate, a body must be pushed by an *external* force. If you stand on a scooter and push against its base, it will not move. The only way to get it to move is to push backwards against the ground. The reaction to that rearwards push causes the scooter to move forwards. The external force is the ground pushing back against the sole of our shoe due to friction. If it was slippery, or gave way, we wouldn't move.

Figure 1-7
An external force.

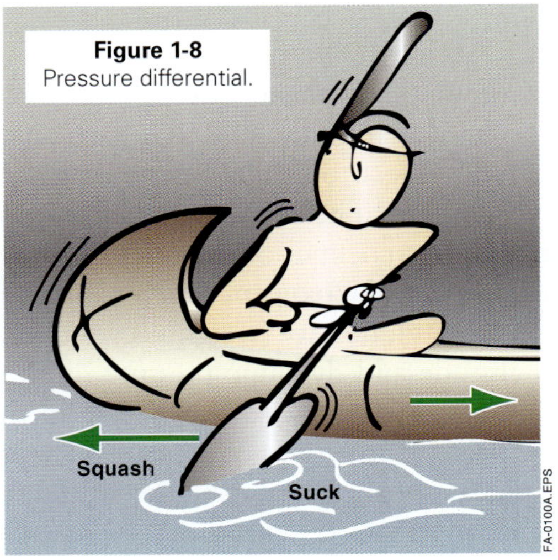

Figure 1-8
Pressure differential.

To move forwards in our canoe, we push water rearwards with the paddle. If we look more closely at the paddle, we will see that it *compresses* and *pushes* the water behind, causing increased pressure, and also causes an area of *suction,* or reduced pressure, in the water in front of the paddle. The difference in pressure, between the rear and front surfaces of the blade, produces the thrusting force and propels us.

Of course we could push air instead of water – like the airboats of the Florida Everglades.

Figure 1-9 Air is pushed and shoved.

The fact remains that, if we are to move forwards, something must be pushed rearwards. All motion through the air and all force generated by the aircraft whether to accelerate, lift, turn or manoeuvre is by sucking, squashing, squeezing and blowing. This science is called *aerodynamics*.

The engine and propeller act like a continuous pump. The engine turns the propeller, which sucks the air from in front, squashes it and squeezes it against the air behind.

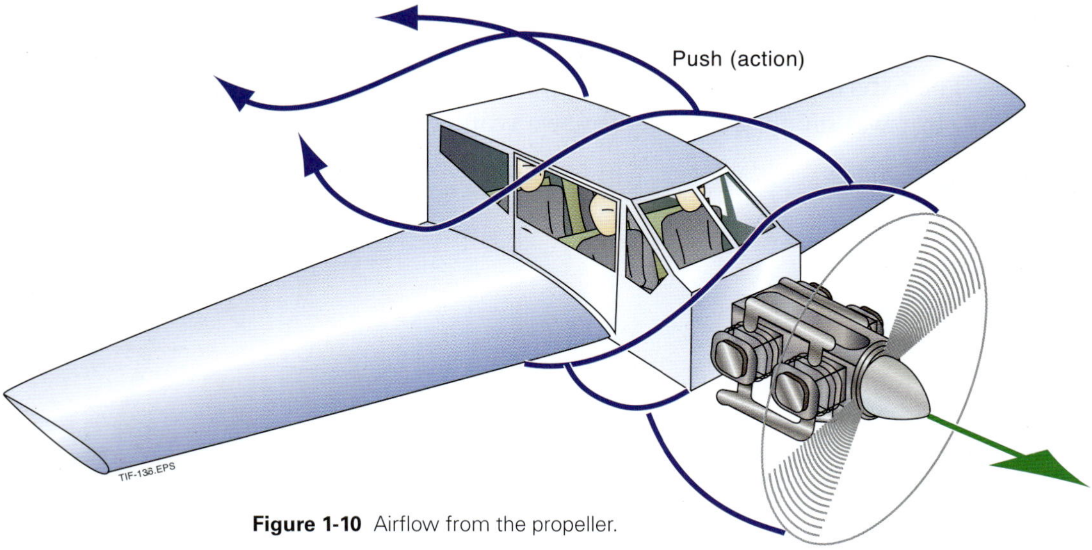

Figure 1-10 Airflow from the propeller.

It's similar to those big electric fans. Have you seen one fall over backwards when it's at maximum speed? That is the reaction on the electric fan caused by the action of the blades (the pushing the air). The reaction is called *thrust*.

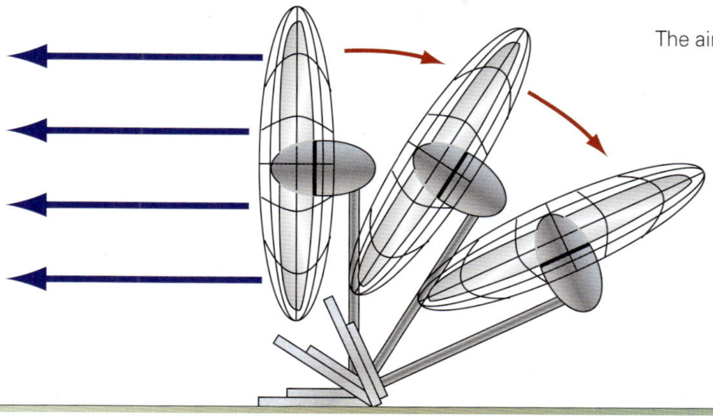

Figure 1-11
The air pushes back (reacts).

Wings & Wheels

Our engine needs fuel and, fortunately, we can use spare space in the wings for the fuel tanks. To manoeuvre on the ground and to accelerate to flying speed we need some wheels and, to stop, we need brakes. The *undercarriage* or *landing gear* is the name used for the wheels, brakes and the legs on which they are mounted. These may be retractable (for higher speed) or fixed (for lower speed, less weight and cost). If the aircraft has a wheel at the front (a *nosewheel*), then it has a tricycle undercarriage.

We also need to be able to steer the aircraft on the ground. Generally, the steering is via the nosewheel being connected to pedals on the floor of the cockpit. Left foot forward turns the aircraft left and right foot forward turns the aircraft to the right. The brakes are normally operated by depressing the toe pedals, and they can be operated independently or simultaneously.

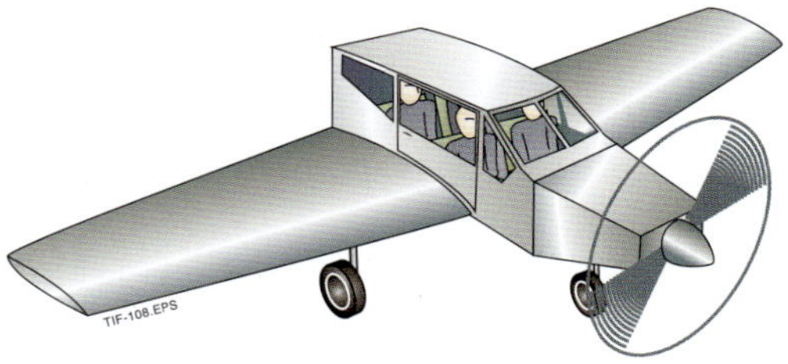

Figure 1-12 Tricycle undercarriage.

nosewheel advantage:
better visibility
better directional contron
better deceleration

Figure 1-13 Tricycle undercarriage.

Figure 1-14 Tail wheel undercarriage.

Some aircraft have a *tailwheel* instead of a nosewheel and this may also be steerable or castoring. Why do older aircraft have tailwheels? Because they are usually operated from grass fields, and a nosewheel is vulnerable to damage on uneven surfaces.

However, the tailwheel configuration is more difficult to manage on the ground and during take-off and landing, especially with a crosswind, and so of course they used to always take-off into the wind. The tailwheel is also lighter and offers less wind resistance or drag. You will mostly only see a tailwheel on agricultural aircraft (which use unprepared runways) or aerobatic aircraft (to reduce weight and drag). You will use smooth prepared runways that may have crosswinds, therefore you will stick to the tricycle undercarriage configuration.

Figure 1-15 High wing.

The wings can be mounted on the top of the cabin, the bottom, or in-between. If the aircraft was to be used for scenic flights, we would put wings on the top (*high wing*). Aircraft for farmers are also configured this way since the wings are less vulnerable to stone damage, they can clear fences, and it is easier to load and unload freight from their utility.

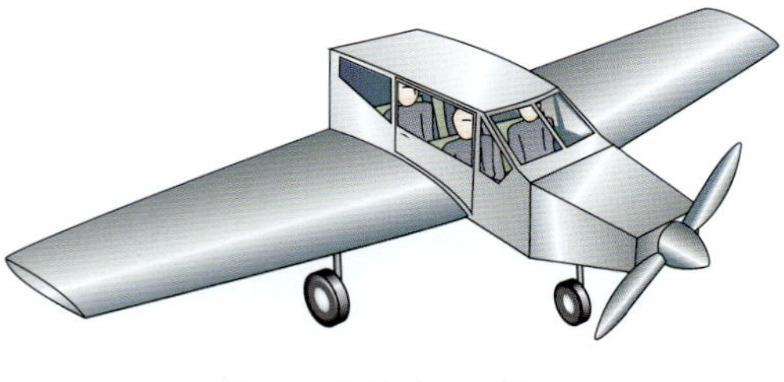

Figure 1-16 Low wing.

However, it is less easy to see when you are turning as the high wing obstructs the view towards the centre of the turn. Therefore, for training and operations in busy areas or for manoeuvring near the ground, the preference may be for a *low wing*.

Figure 1-17 Mid-wing.

A *mid-wing* configuration is less common because the *spar* of the wing interferes with the cabin space, and it is complex to transfer the flight loads without a continuous spar.

Streamlining

Let's make our aircraft more efficient. Because we have to push it through the air and because the wings have to generate lift to overcome weight, we need to make the aircraft as streamlined as possible and as light as possible. We may add *fairings* (structures designed to reduce drag) to blend where the wing meets the fuselage. We minimise and streamline the antenna. We add *fairings* to the wheels and undercarriage legs, and we add *cowls* (covers) to the engine.

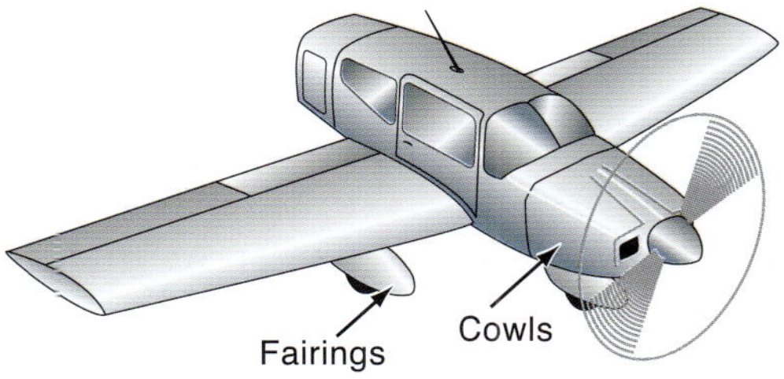

Figure 1-18 Cowls and fairings.

Figure 1-19 Fairing.

But something is still missing.

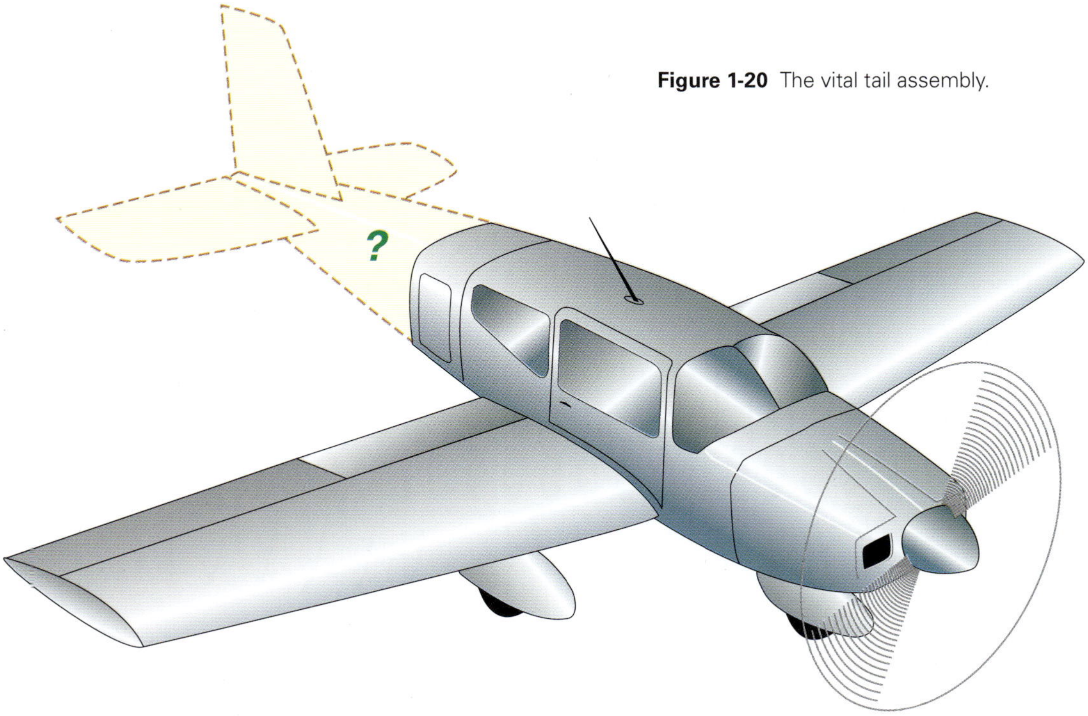

Figure 1-20 The vital tail assembly.

Before we finish building our aircraft, we'll have a closer look at how wings function. We are going to talk about how an aircraft is able to stay up in the air – how the wings *lift*.

How an Aircraft is Lifted

All aerial vehicles reduce the pressure of the air above and increase the pressure of the air below. This pressure differential builds the cushion on which they are supported. A hovercraft sucks the air from above, squashes it and squeezes it out underneath. Thus, it creates downwash and floats on a cushion of air.

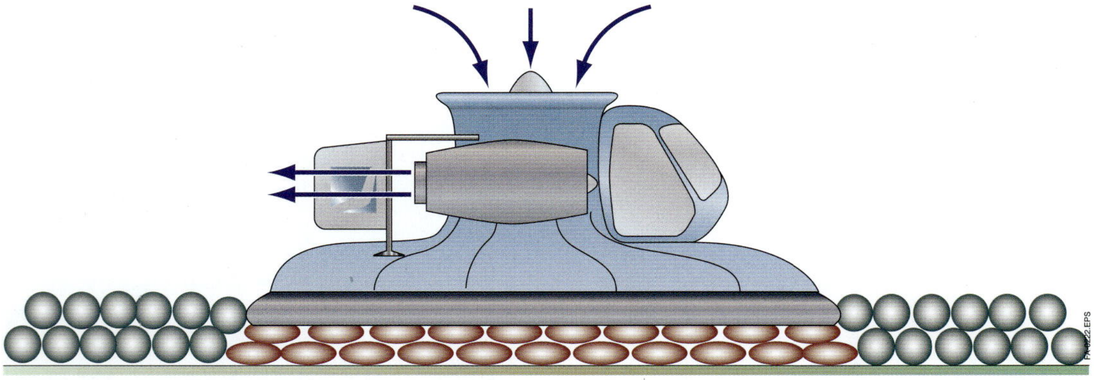

Figure 1-21 Hovercraft.

Figure 1-22 A helicopter lifting and thrusting.

A helicopter sucks air from above, squashes it and squeezes it out below. If we remove the ground surface, the squash is reduced, but there can still be enough to fly. It just takes more effort.

The rotor blades function as wings to generate lift and, when the rotor disc is tilted, also provide thrust.

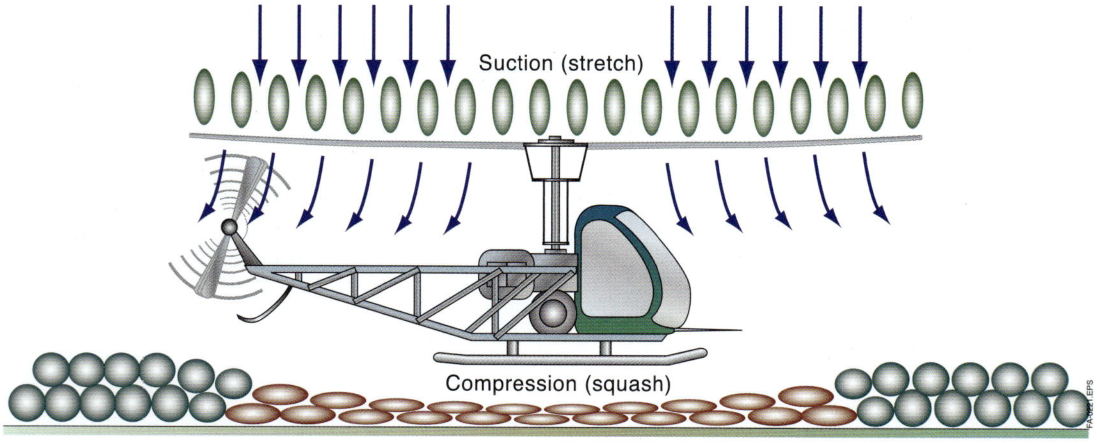

Figure 1-23 Air through the rotor.

A wing also sucks air from above, squashes it and squeezes it downwards in a very unique way. (The rotor blade is a wing.)

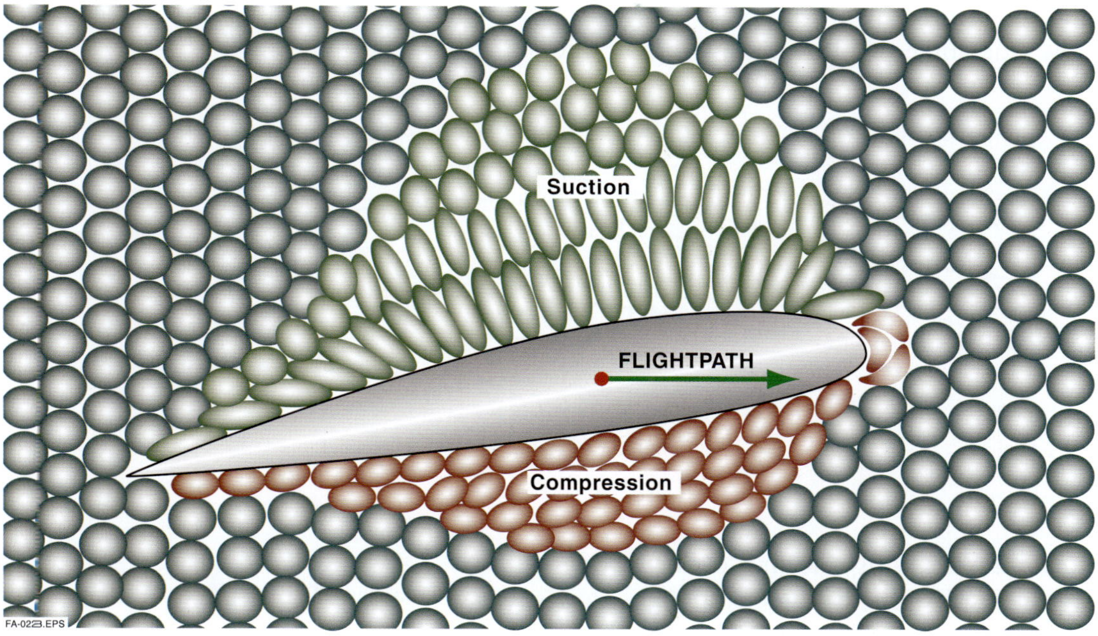

Figure 1-24 The shape and angle of the wing affects the air.

As the wing moves through the air, it compresses the air molecules in front and below and creates an area of reduced pressure suction, or partial vacuum, above and behind. If you put your hand horizontally out of the window of a moving car and twist it to cause an *angle of attack* to the airflow, the reaction causes the hand to be pushed upwards and rearwards.

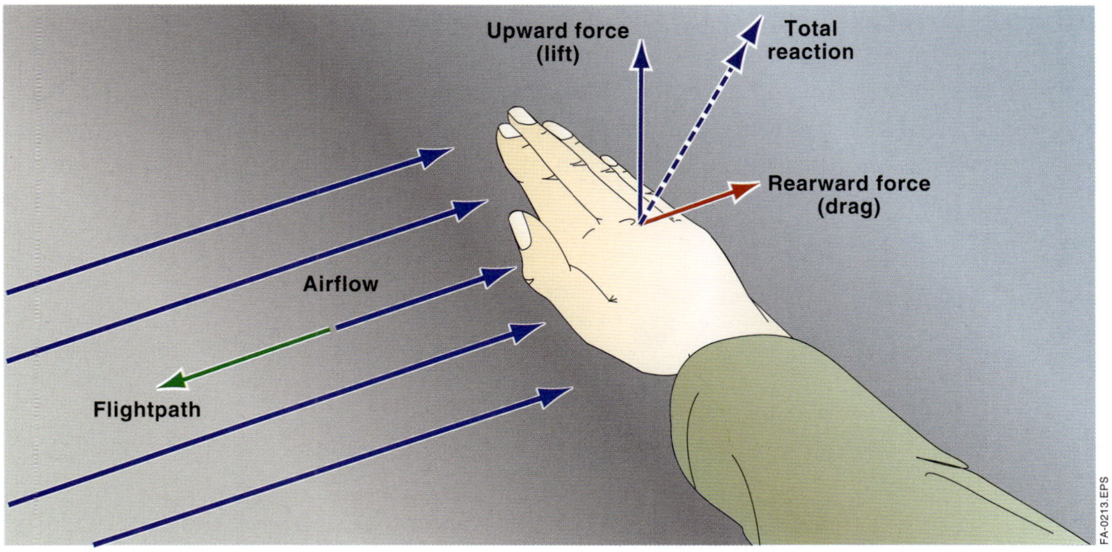

Figure 1-25 The hand feels the force (reaction) of the moving air.

The wing is no different, just more efficient. We have mentioned that the wings generate lift to overcome the force of gravity and lift the aircraft off the ground. We mentioned also that the engine and propeller combine to produce thrust to accelerate the aircraft and propel it through the air. This forward speed causes the air to move over and under the wing. Because of the shape and the angle of the wing to the relative airflow (the angle of attack), the wing produces a lifting force.

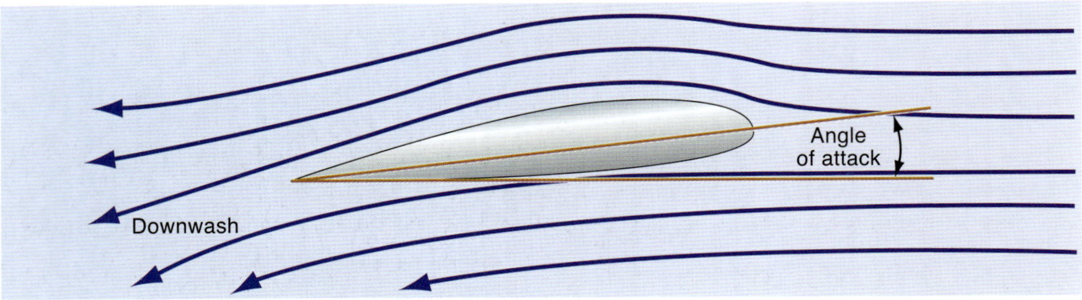

Figure 1-26 Angle of attack.

Behind the wing, the air is deflected downwards. Just like the canoe's paddle, the downward deflection of the air causes a reaction. The total reaction can be simplified into two elements or components:

- vertical force called *lift*, which acts through its centre of pressure; and
- a rearward component called *induced drag*, which is the unavoidable drag caused (induced) by the process of generating lift.

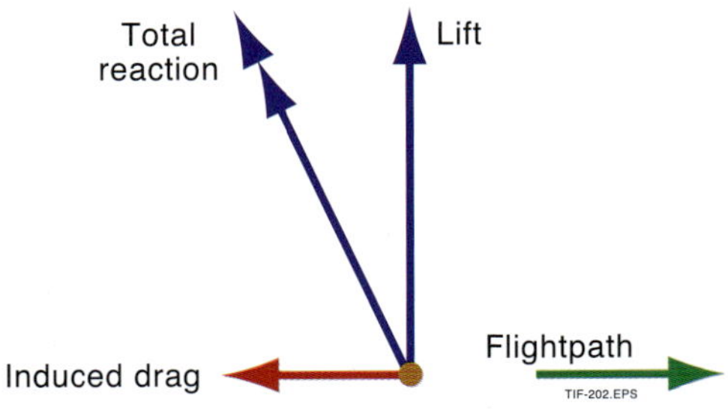

Figure 1-27 Total reaction.

In a wind tunnel, it is possible to measure what is happening to the wing and the effect on the surrounding air. The pressure reduction in the air above the wing is about twice as much as the pressure increase below the wing. Thus two thirds of the wing's total reaction is generated by the upper surface and one third is generated by the lower surface. Both elements are necessary and inseparable. The total reaction is caused by a combination of the amount of pressure differential and the area of the wing.

The amount of the pressure differential is dependent on the speed of the wing through the air and the angle of attack of the wing to the air. Note the *tilt* of the total reaction. Part of the reaction is lift and part is drag – called *induced drag* – a form of drag that is inevitably induced in the production of lift.

Figure 1-28 The shape of a section of the wing is called an aerofoil.

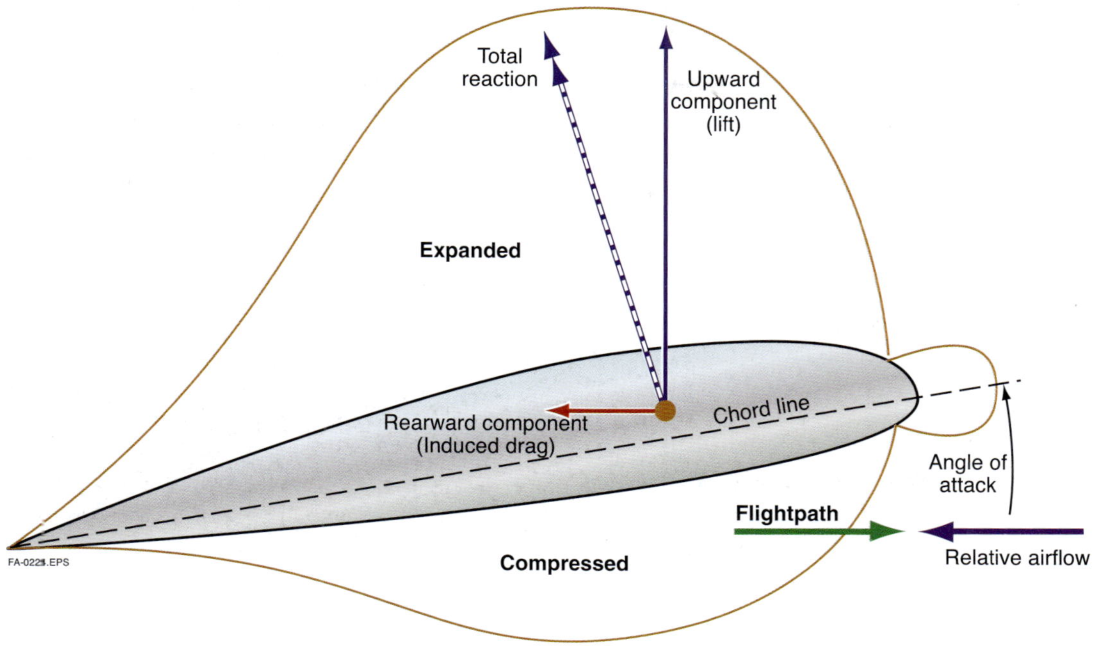

Figure 1-29 A wing at work.

In a wind tunnel, you would notice the following:

- reduced pressure and an increased rush (velocity) of air over the upper surface of the wing;
- compression and a forward push of the air under the surface of the wing;
- disturbance to the smooth flow of the air around the rear part of the wing's surface; and
- a degree of *downwash* or downward deflection of the air behind the wing as a result of the passage of the wing, where the reaction to this downwash is the *total reaction*.

The amount of lift, and drag, is dependent on four elements:

- the thickness of the air (called *air density*);
- the speed of the wing through the air (called *airspeed*);
- the size of the wing (called *wing area*); and
- the efficiency of the wing (called *lift coefficient*), which is dependent on the *angle of attack* of the wing and the cross-sectional shape of the wing.

The angle of attack is the angle that the wing presents to the air. It is measured between the direction of the path of the wing through the air (the *flightpath*, which is the exactly opposite direction of the air flowing past the wing, called the *relative airflow*) and the chord line of the wing. The chord line is a straight line from the leading edge to the trailing edge of the wing section.

Returning to our own aircraft, we now have propulsion to overcome drag, and wings to provide lift. But before we can fly, we must add four more important features:

- *stability* so our vehicle remains upright, straight and doesn't tumble;
- *control* so we can decide the flightpath and speed of the aircraft;
- *instruments and navigation aids* (navaids) to give information on the progress of the flight, the performance of the aircraft, its geographic position and the correct functioning of the systems; and
- *communications equipment* to talk and listen to the control tower and other aircraft.

Stability & Control

Stability is provided by the *fin*, *tailplane* and the *rear fuselage* (called *keel surfaces*).

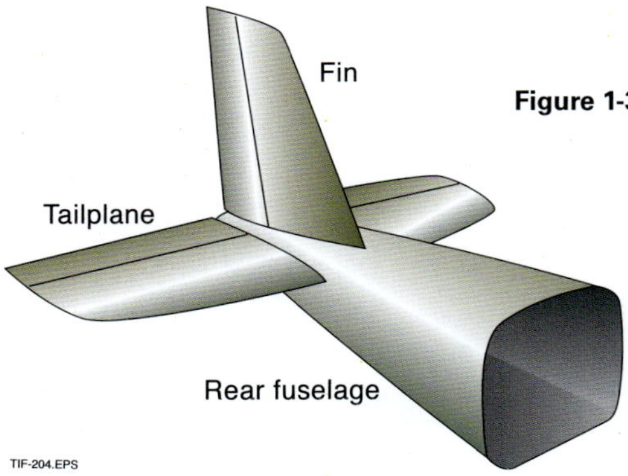

Figure 1-30 (Left) Keel surfaces.

Figure 1-31 (Right) Fin and rudder.

Control is via the *control surfaces* (the *elevators*, *ailerons* and *rudder*) which overcome stability to allow the aircraft to be manoeuvred.

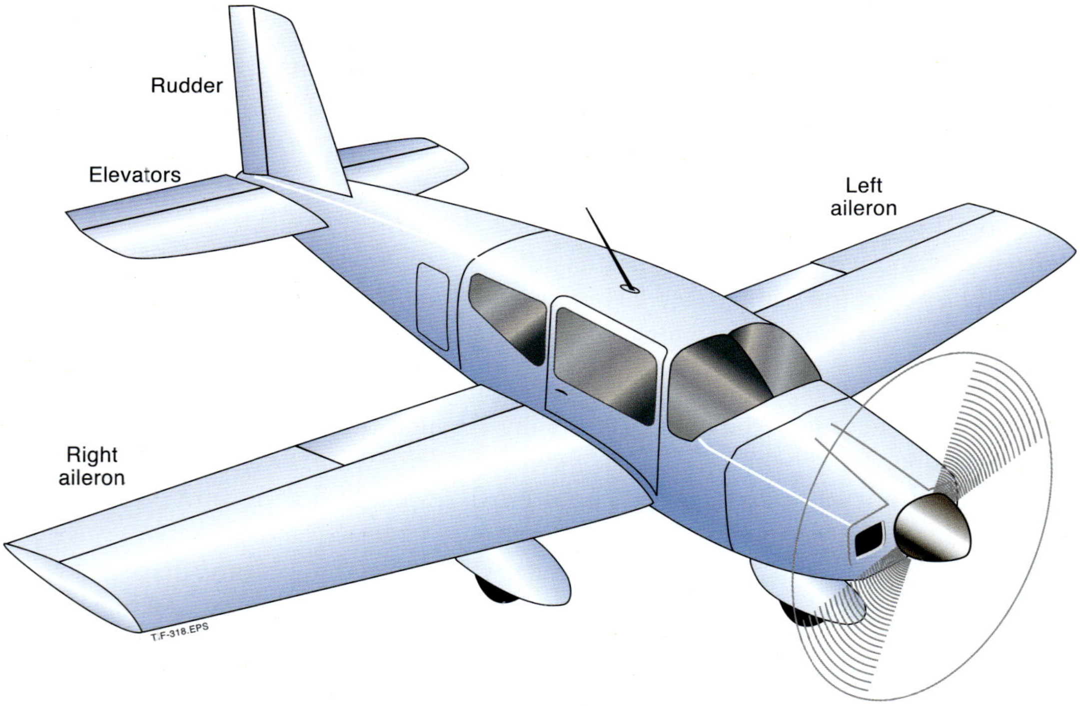

Figure 1-32 Control surfaces.

Let's see how control and stability interact.

What is Stability?

Stability is the natural tendency of the aircraft to maintain its direction through the air. You will be familiar with a dart or an arrow. Stability is its tendency to fly straight and not diverge or tumble. The arrow and dart achieve stability by the presence of flights or tail feathers. An arrow, if fired straight up, will fall backwards and then swap ends to point into the new direction it's going. See how the arrow always points into the *relative airflow*. The *flightpath* and the *relative airflow* are always equal and opposite to each other.

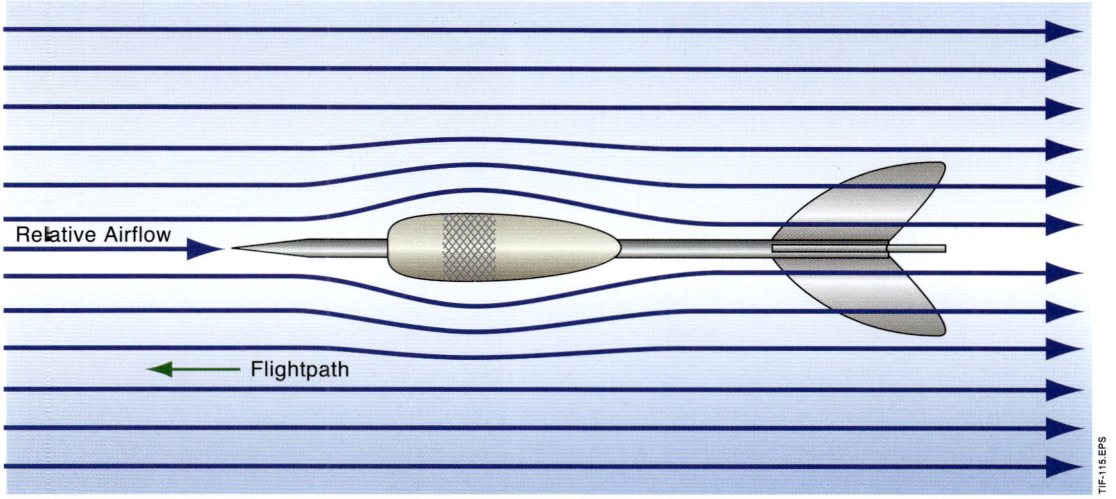

Figure 1-33 Airflow causes stability.

If we balance the dart on a pin and push the air past it with a fan, we'll be able to see stability. The balance point is called the *centre of gravity* (CG) – its position is *critical*.

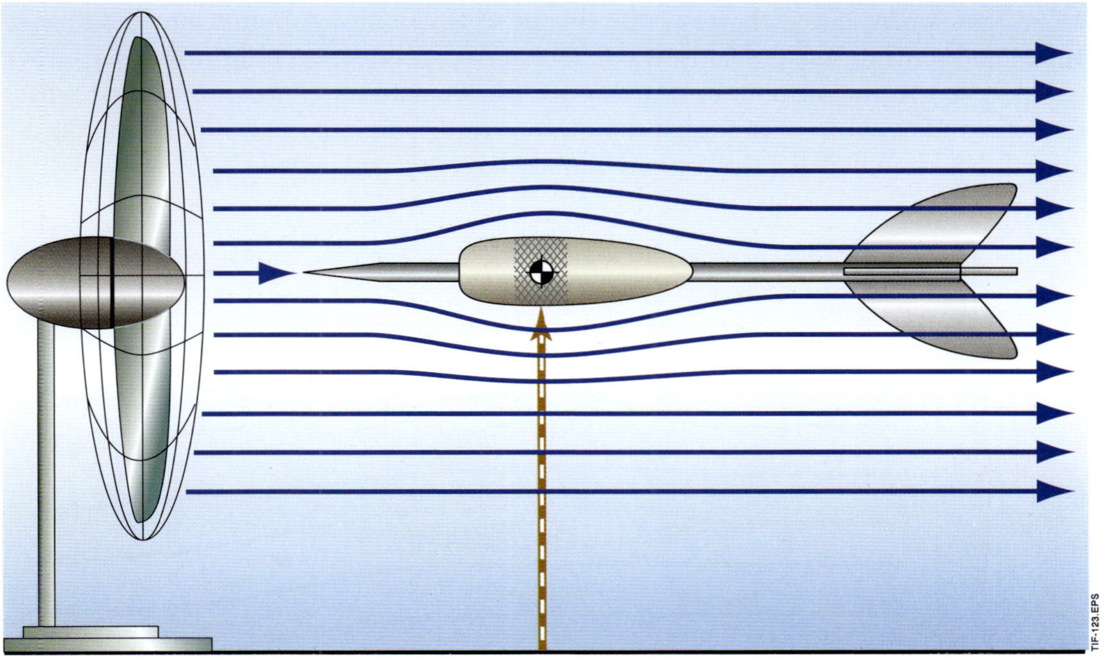

Figure 1-34 Centre of gravity.

The fan is causing the air to blow past the dart with exactly the same effect as if the dart were moving through the air; it's just easier this way to see what's happening. Wherever we move the fan – up, down, left, right – the dart will point at it.

Level airflow – level flightpath (figure 1-35).

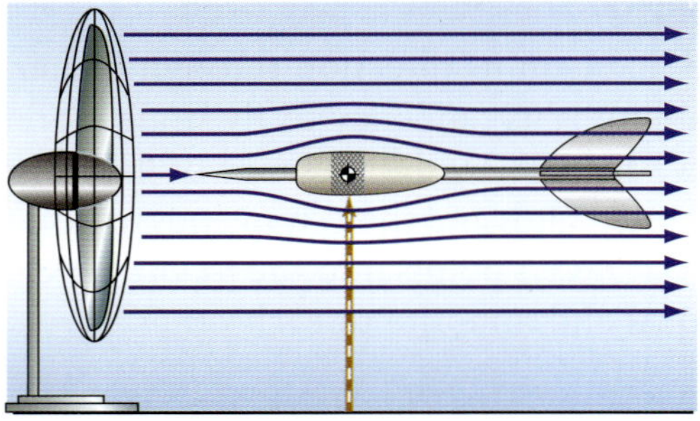

Figure 1-35 Level airflow – level flightpath.

Downward airflow – upward flightpath (figure 1-36).

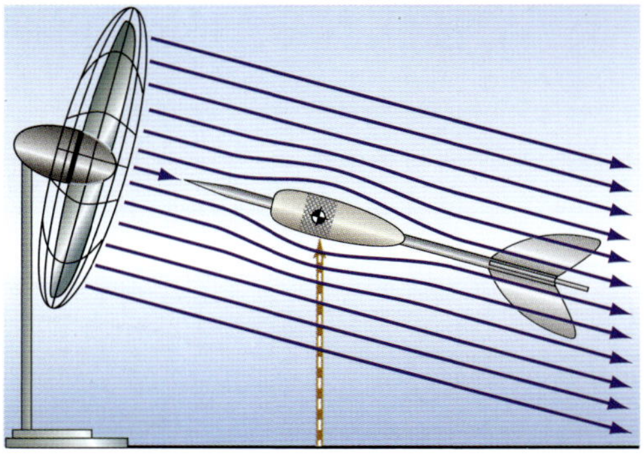

Figure 1-36 Downward airflow – upward flightpath

Upward airflow – downward flightpath (figure 1-37).

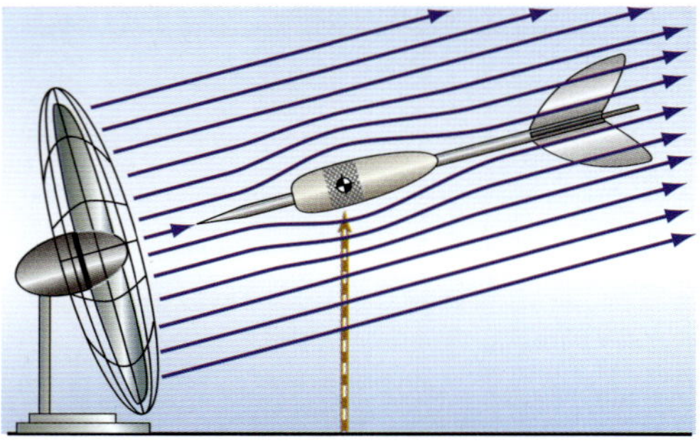

Figure 1-37 Upward airflow – downward flightpath

Let's put similar tail feathers on our aircraft so that it always points into the relative airflow and remains stable; that is, it will return to that direction if disturbed. Again we will balance the aircraft on a pole and move the air with a fan – so we can see what's happening. We will have to forego the bottom feather because it would scrape on the ground, but we will make the top one slightly larger to compensate.

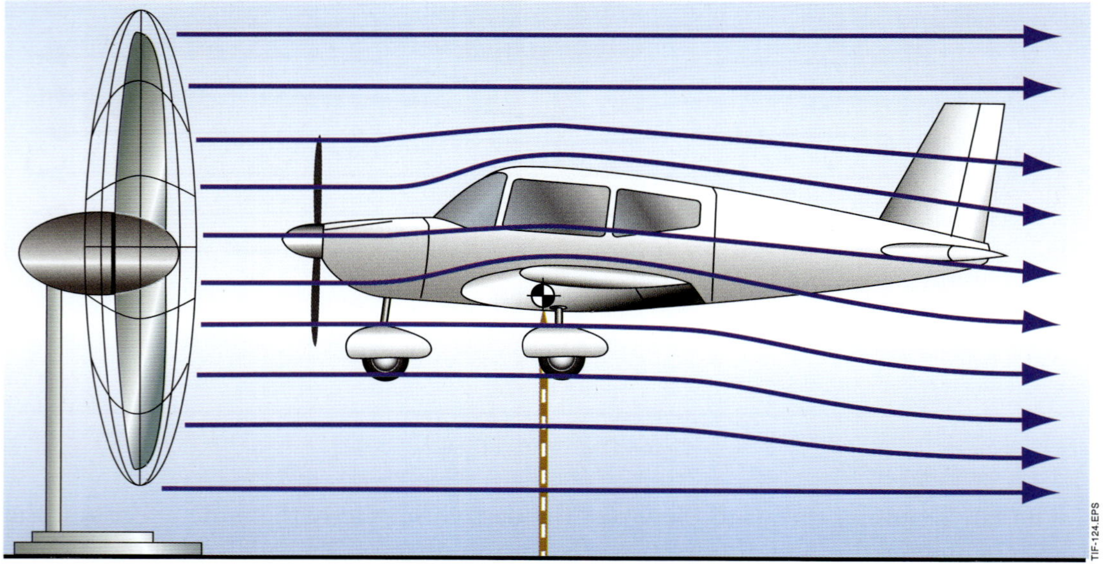

Figure 1-38 The aircraft's tail feathers.

Like the dart, the aircraft will now always point into the relative airflow. This means it is *stable – it does not tend to deviate from its flightpath.*

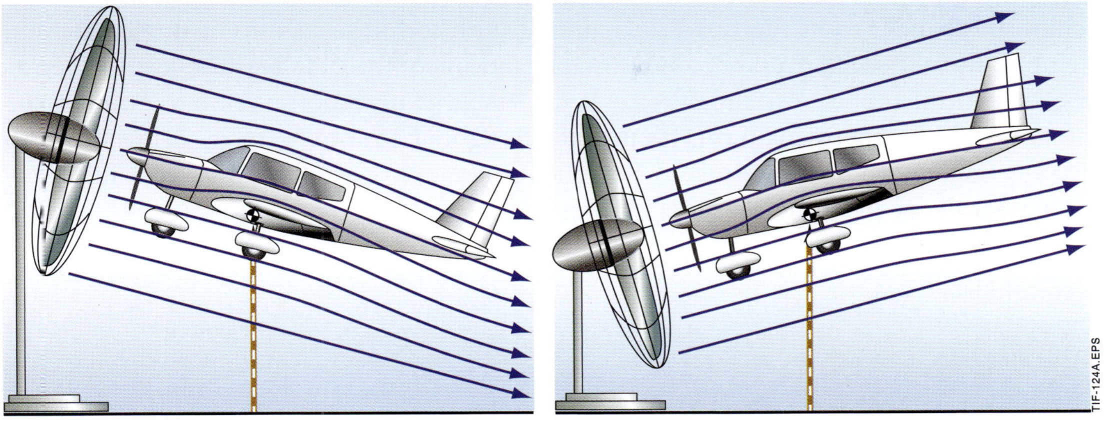

Figure 1-39 Stability points the aircraft.

More, or Less, Stability?

The length, width and depth of the arrow in front of the CG compared to the length, width and depth behind the CG determines how stable it is, i.e. how powerful the tendency is to point into the direction of the relative airflow and how quickly it returns. We can add weight to the front which moves the CG forwards and effectively lengthens the tail. We can add a longer and lighter tail shaft so there is stronger stability. We can also increase the size of the tail feathers. All of these increase stability.

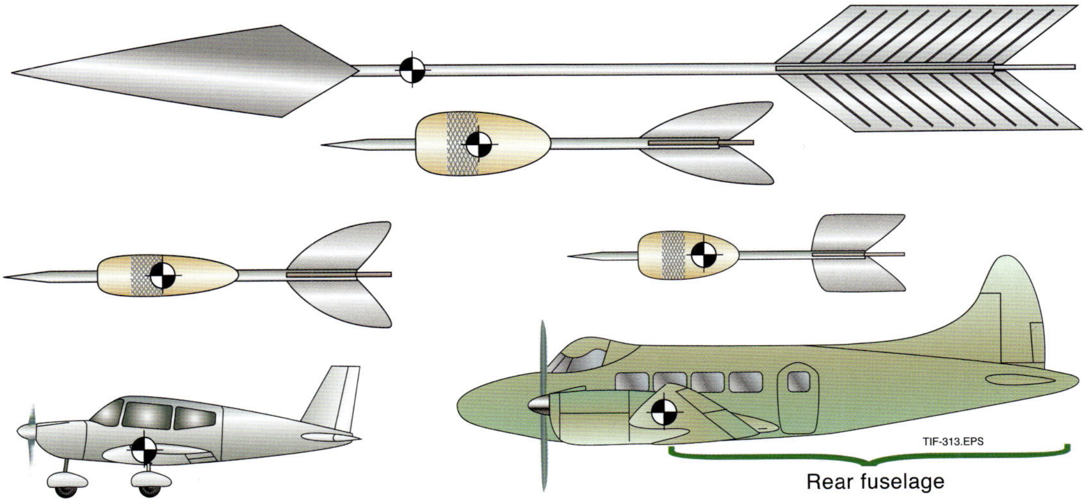

Figure 1-40 Keel surface area changes with CG position.

An aircraft is exactly the same. It is easy to ensure that our aircraft is very stable by having large fixed tail surfaces and a longer and larger area of rear *fuselage* (this includes the cabin as well as the tail support structure behind the point of balance – the CG). The area ahead of the CG opposes stability as it tends to promote deviations. *Thus the degree of stability for any aircraft is very dependent on the position of the centre of gravity.*

Stability Versus Control

So we have achieved stability, but there is a catch. If we have too much stability, we have too little control. Control is the ability to change our flightpath. We wish to be able to change direction, altitude and speed in flight. The more stable the aircraft, the more it will resist changes to its flightpath. An aircraft with too little stability is unpleasant and tiring to fly and could even become unstable and uncontrollable because it is too sensitive to control inputs. An aircraft that is too stable is unresponsive. So we design the aircraft to find a happy medium. It's just like designing a motor vehicle. A bus needs to be very stable with firm controls. A Formula One racing car needs to be very manoeuvrable with very light and sensitive controls.

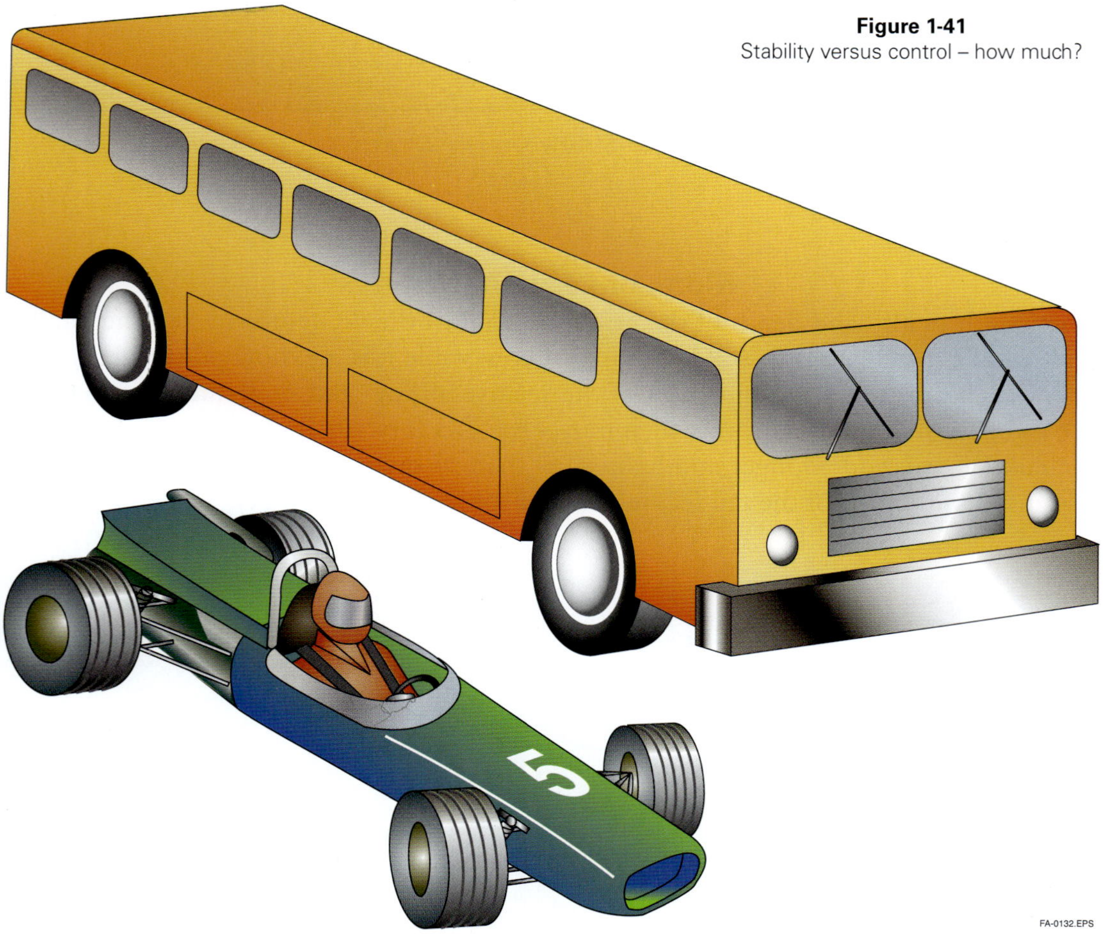

Figure 1-41
Stability versus control – how much?

The designer considers the purpose of the aircraft and balances the amount of stability versus the degree of control. A fighter aircraft is almost unstable but very manoeuvrable, and a passenger aircraft is very stable but less manoeuvrable. In our training aircraft, we want a medium amount of stability and control so the aircraft is easy to fly, neither demanding nor tiring, and can be manoeuvred without excessively high control forces.

Figure 1-42 Elevator and trim tab.

Let's see how we can control the flightpath of our aircraft. Look again at our dart. It will always point into the relative airflow. What if we deflect the rear part of the two *horizontal* tail feathers upwards? The tail will fall until the downward push on the deflected area is balanced by the upward force on the forward part. See how the bent part of the tail tries to raise the point of the dart but that the rest of the tail is now being pushed by the airflow in the opposite direction.

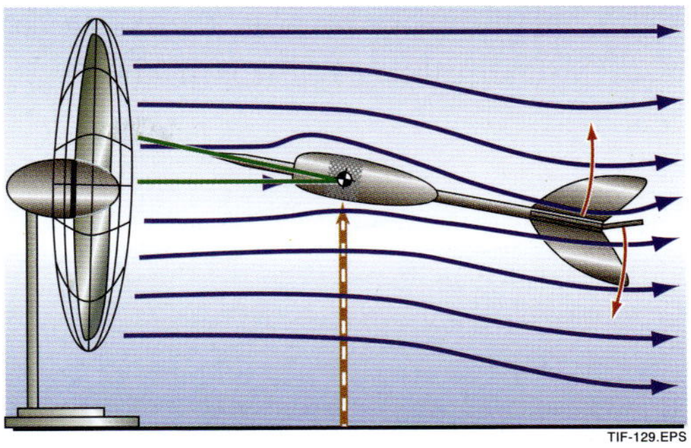

Figure 1-43 Deflected feathers.

The dart will stop in a position at a slight angle to the relative airflow and will stay there as long as the tail feathers remain deflected. This angle is called the *angle of attack*. It doesn't matter which way through the air the dart is flying. The deflected part of the dart will maintain that same relative angle to the relative airflow – the same angle of attack.

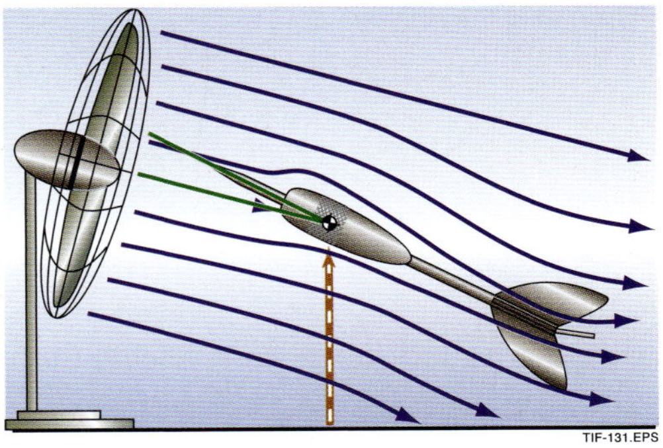

Figure 1-44 Same angle of attack.

If we do the same thing to our aircraft by hinging the rear of the *horizontal stabiliser* (or *tailplane*), we can achieve the same effect.

Look at the aircraft below. It is balanced in the air. The nose attitude is held up because the elevator (the moveable surface at the rear) is deflected. Because of this angle of attack, the wing is generating enough lift to carry the weight of the aircraft. We can now remove the pole. A propeller provides the thrust to move the aircraft through the air which generates airflow over the wings. Therefore, we can also remove the fan.

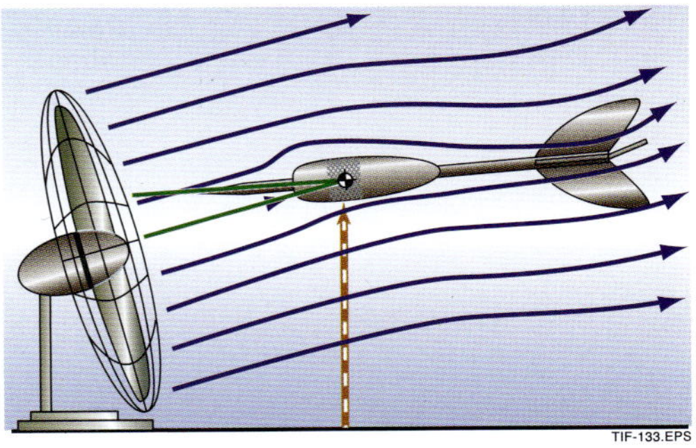

Figure 1-45 Same angle of attack.

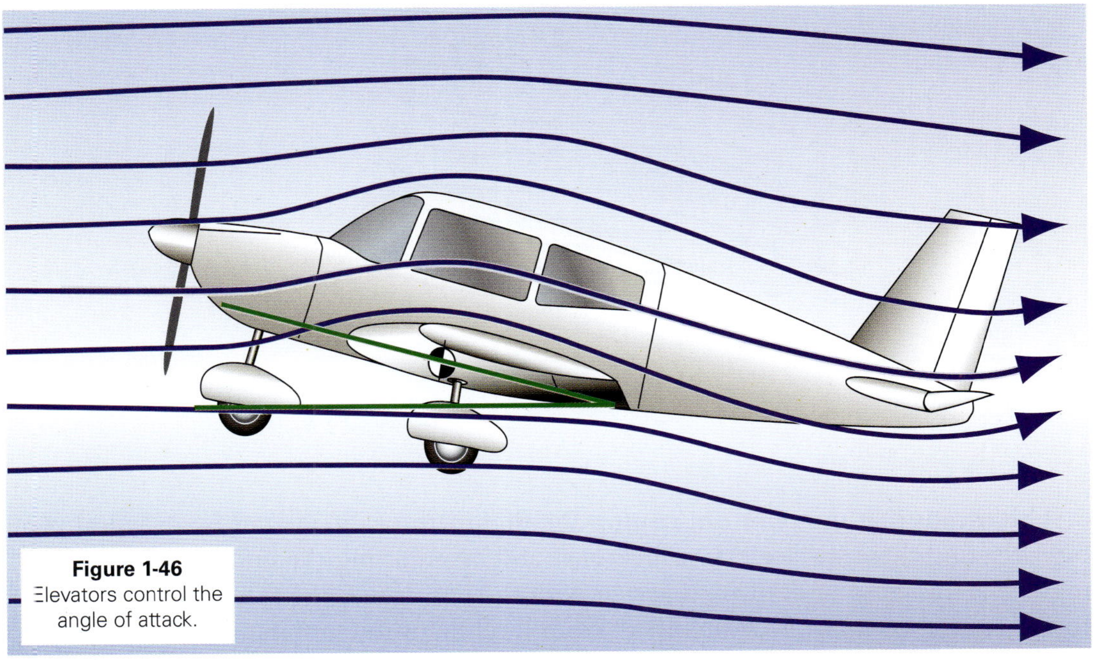

Figure 1-46
Elevators control the angle of attack.

It's very important now to realise that the same angle of attack with full power will result in a climbing flightpath. . .

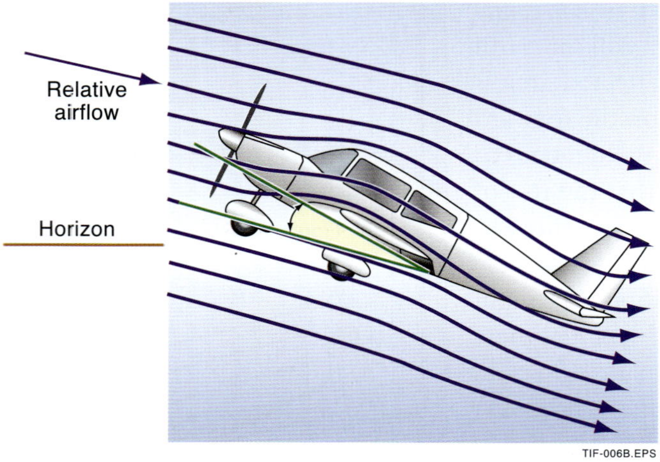

Figure 1-47
Same angle of attack.

. . .with medium power, a level flightpath, and . . .

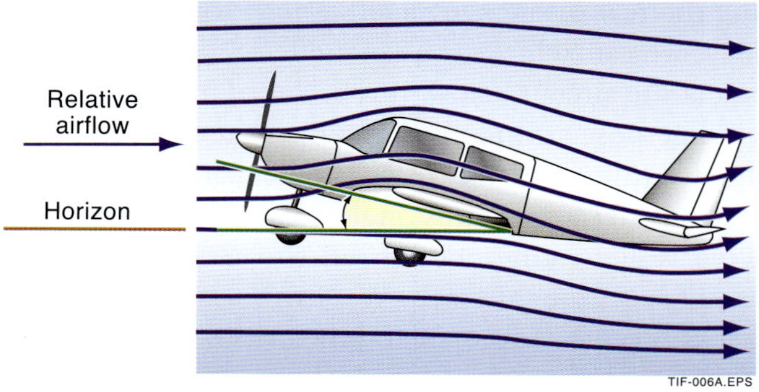

Figure 1-48
Same angle of attack.

. . .with low power, a descending flightpath.

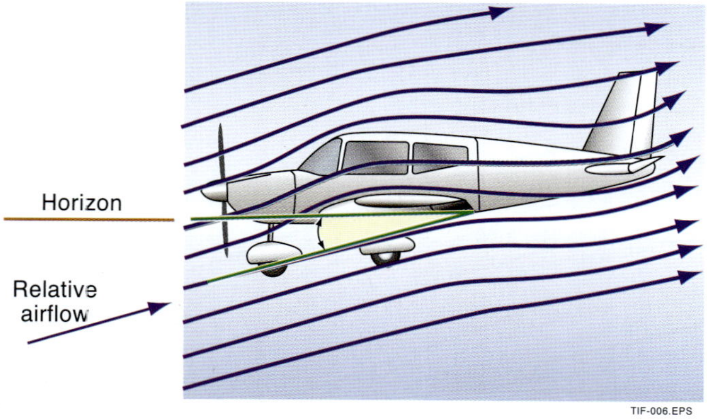

Figure 1-49
Same angle of attack.

This means that the pilot can control the flightpath of the aircraft in a vertical plane by deflecting these surfaces we call *elevators* and by adjusting the engine power accordingly. It is this elevator control, together with the power setting of the engine, that gives the pilot total control of the flightpath from level flight to climbing or descending.

So we have achieved control of the flightpath in a vertical direction. Now what about turning? An aircraft is turned just like a motorcycle – by *banking*. To achieve a change of direction in a balanced and effective way, the aircraft is banked and the wings cause the force that changes the direction. The more you tilt the aircraft, the tighter the turn – just like on a motorcycle.

It is a part (component) of the wing's lifting force that causes the aircraft to turn when the wings are tilted even a small amount – the more tilt, the tighter the turn.

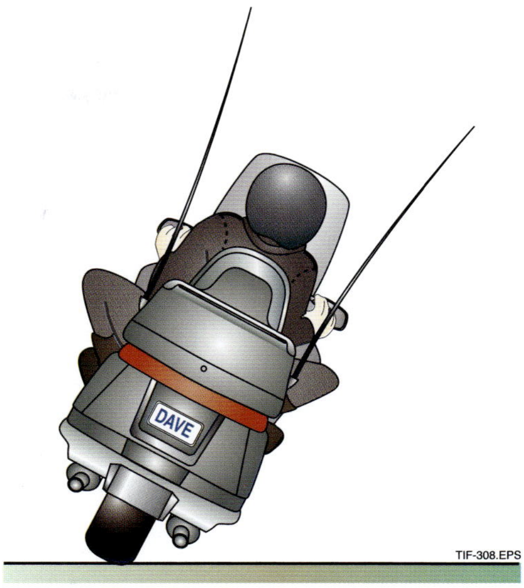

Figure 1-50 Banking to turn.

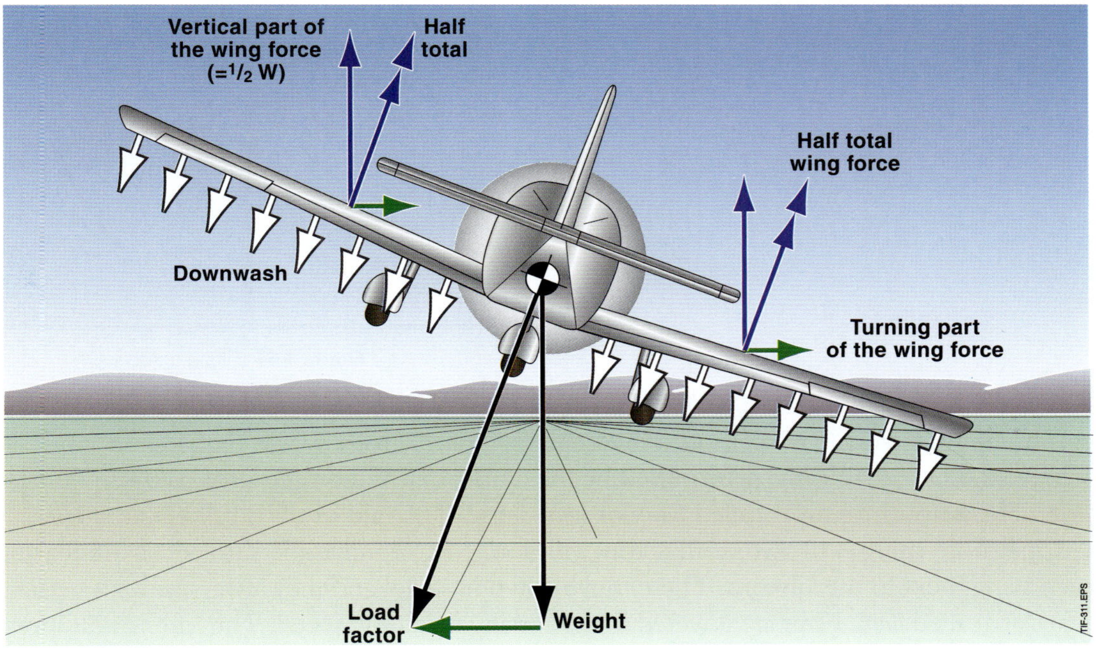

Figure 1-51 Banking to turn.

To achieve this tilt, the rear outer section of each wing is hinged. These surfaces, called *ailerons*, roll the aircraft into the turn.

Figure 1-52 Aileron.

One goes up and the other goes down and the aircraft rolls or rotates – just as a dart does when you deflect one feather up and its opposite feather down.

We can tilt left. . .

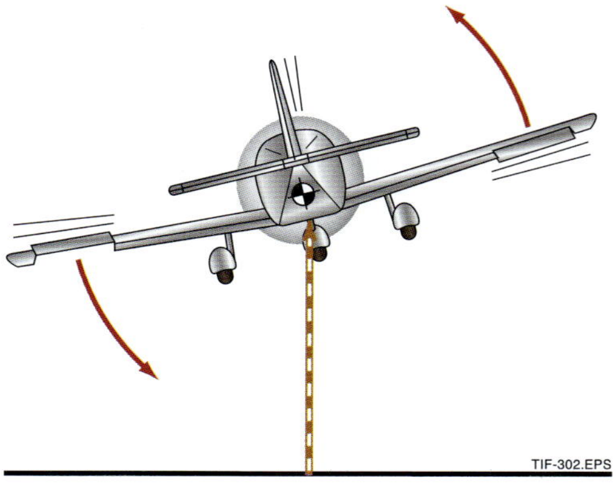

Figure 1-53 Tilting left.

. . . and right.

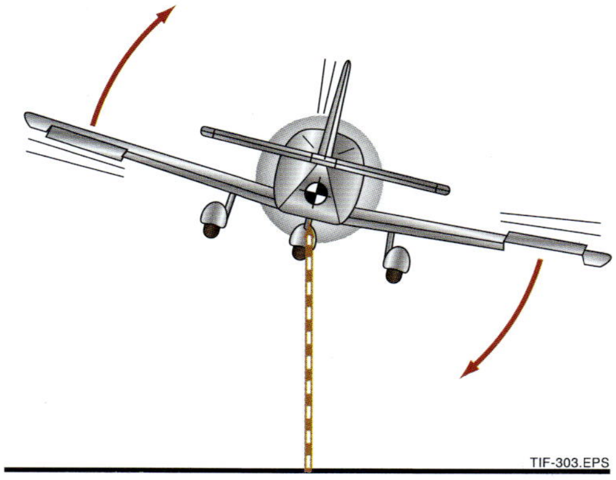

Figure 1-54 Tilting right.

The amount of tilt is controlled by centring the ailerons when the desired angle is achieved. The rate of tilt is determined by the amount of aileron (control column) deflection. The amount of tilt is called *bank* or *bank angle*. The rate of tilt is called *rate of roll*.

One more thing – or two, really. You will notice extra moveable surfaces at the rear of each wing, next to the ailerons. These move down in stages and they always move together. They are called *flaps*. Flaps are lowered for increasing lift at low speed. They are very important for landing as they allow the aircraft to fly more slowly and to descend more steeply while at the same time giving a good view of the runway because the nose attitude is lower.

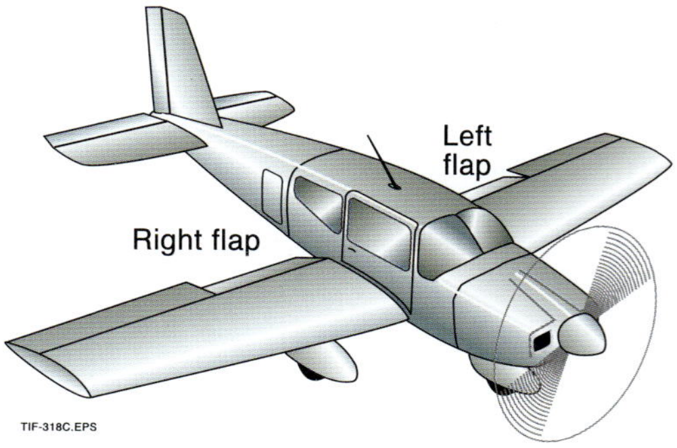

Figure 1-55 (Above and left) Flaps.

We'll next look at the pilot's working environment – the *cockpit*, where it all comes together under the hands and mind of the pilot. In the cockpit are contained the control column, rudder pedals, engine controls, instruments, navigation aids and radios.

But, before we go inside, let's note the names of the major parts of the aircraft.

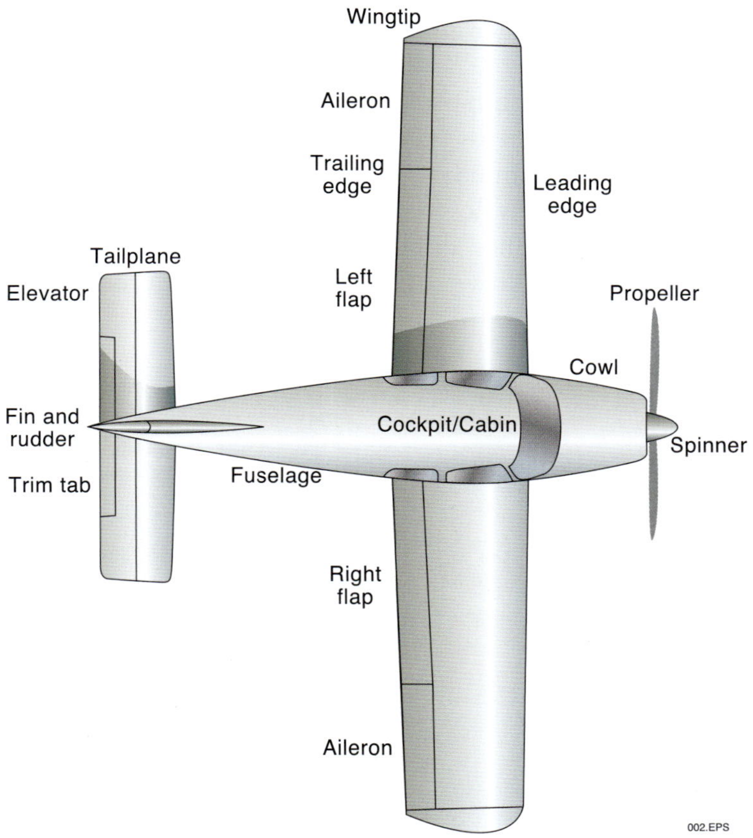

Figure 1-56 Parts of an aeroplane.

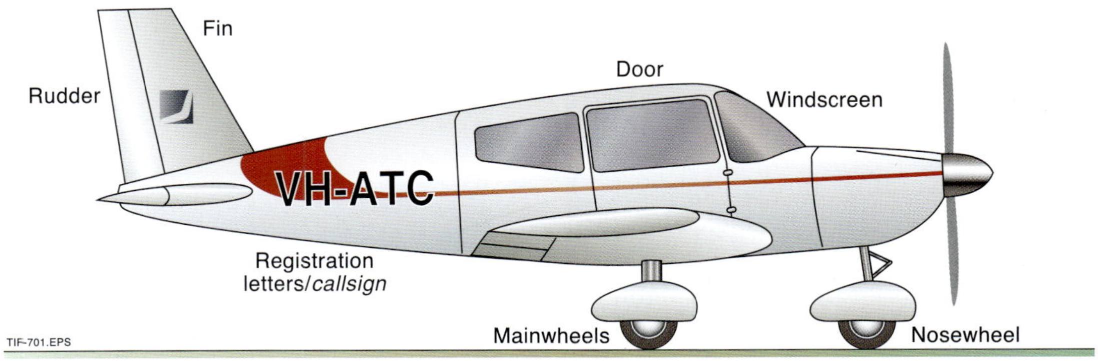

Figure 1-57 Parts of an aeroplane.

Not a bad result for a first attempt at designing an aircraft. Let's now have a look inside.

The Cockpit

Figure 1-58 Cockpit with joysticks.

Why the place that the pilot occupies is called the *cockpit* no one seems sure. Certainly in WWI the name was apt because it was like the place where fighting cocks tore each other to pieces – but it is believed that the name was coined before then. It is still in common use although on larger aircraft it is known as the *flightdeck*.

The design of the cockpit is important. Unfortunately, not all cockpits are the same and not all are equally well organised. Ultimately, how well an aircraft is flown depends on not only the pilot but also on how well designed the controls, switches, displays and instruments are for convenience, clear interpretation and ease-of-use. This is a typical cockpit layout for a training aircraft:

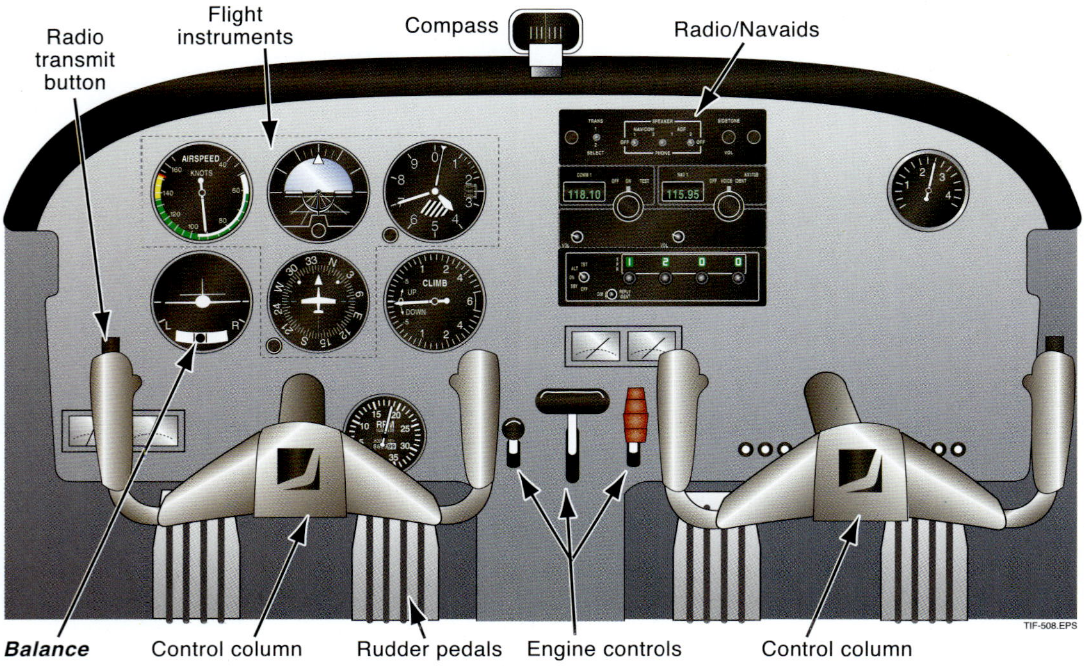

Figure 1-59 Controls and instruments.

From the cockpit, the pilot controls the flightpath of the aircraft. The pilot can accelerate by increasing thrust, decelerate by reducing thrust, climb by increasing thrust and changing the flightpath upwards, descend by reducing thrust and by changing the flightpath downwards, and turn by rolling the aircraft to a bank angle and maintaining that angle. The pilot's references are the *attitude* of the aircraft – this is simply the position of the nose in relation to the horizon – together with the power that is set.

Figure 1-60 Attitude.

The control of attitude plus power is the essence of piloting and the most important lesson to remember. It is the crux of all types of flying in all types of aircraft.

Always remember:

Attitude and power, together, control the flightpath and speed of the aircraft.

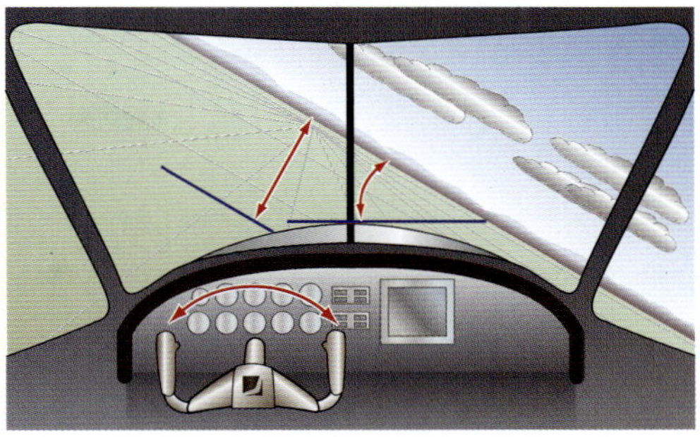

Figure 1-61 Attitude in a turn.

To vary, adjust or restore the attitude, the pilot moves the *control surfaces* by applying pressure to the *control column* – backwards, forwards, left or right or together.

To operate the controls against the pressure of the airflow, the pilot must apply a force or pressure in order to achieve the desired attitude. It's easy to remember which way to move it – the nose, tail or wingtip will always move away from the control column (only the rudder has a different effect).

Forward pressure on the control column causes the elevators to move downwards. . . (figure 1-62)

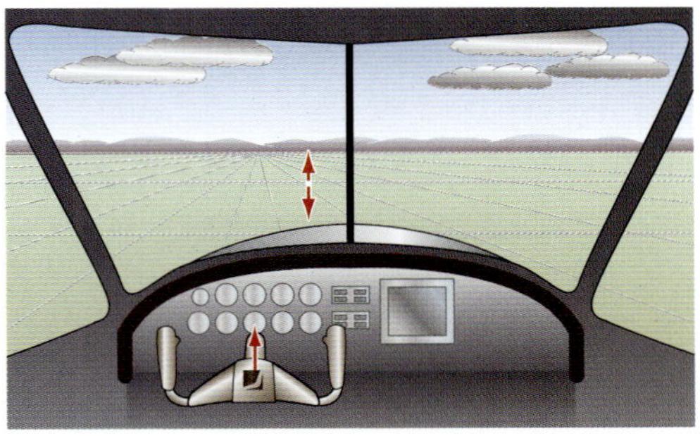

Figure 1-62 Forward pressure.

. . . and therefore the nose of the aircraft moves downwards (the nose moves away) (figure 1-63).

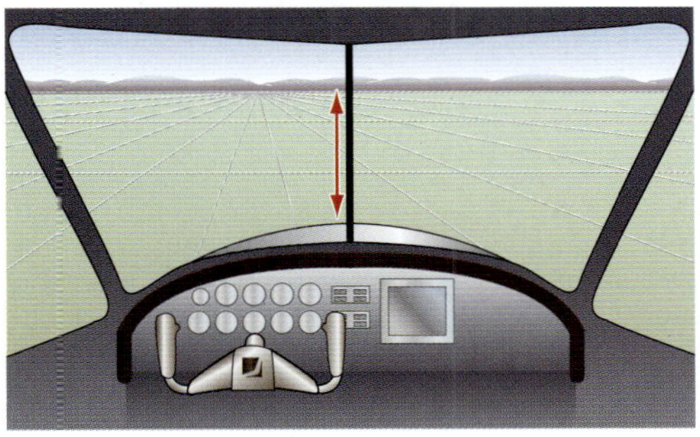

Figure 1-63 Lowered nose.

Rearward pressure on the control column raises the elevators. . . (figure 1-64)

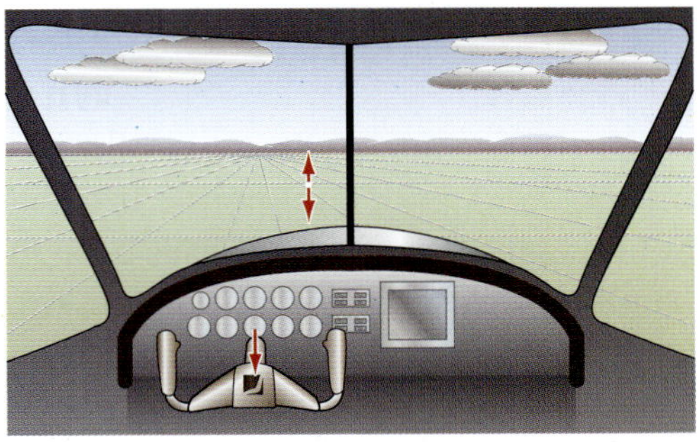

Figure 1-64 Rearward pressure.

. . . and therefore the nose moves upwards (the tail moves away) (figure 1-65).

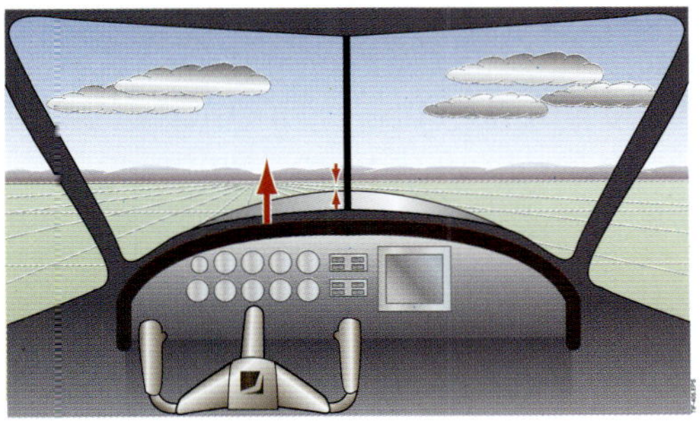

Figure 1-65 Raised nose.

Left pressure. . .(figure 1-66)

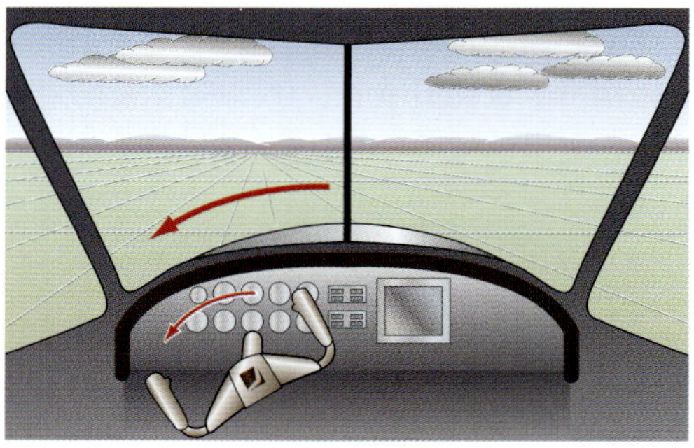

Figure 1-66 Left roll.

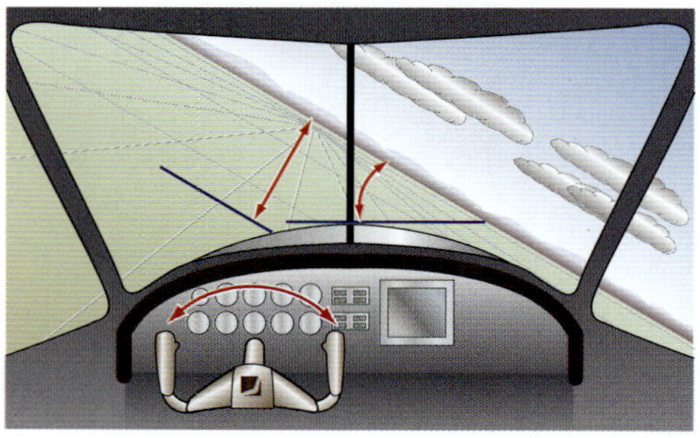

Figure 1-67 Left bank.

. . . rolls the aircraft to the left (the left wingtip moves away) (figure 1-67).

Right aileron pressure. . .(figure 1-68)

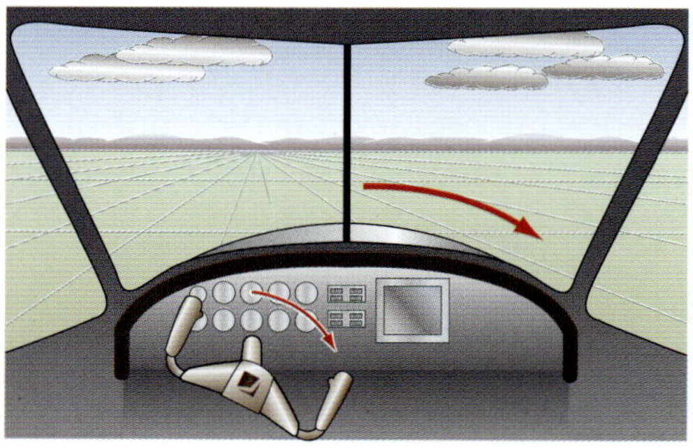

Figure 1-68 Right roll.

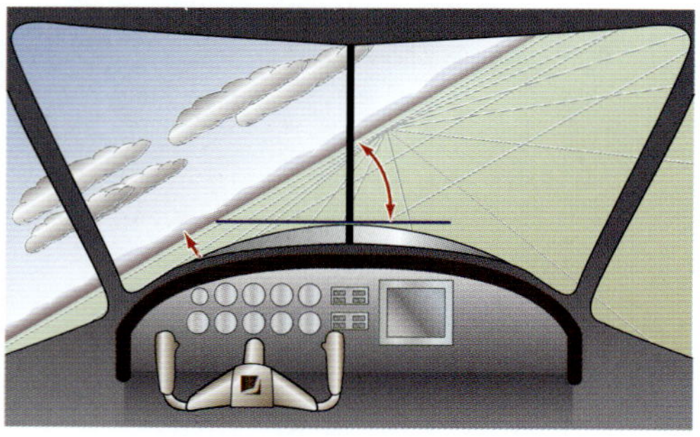

Figure 1-69 Right bank.

. . . rolls the aircraft to the right (figure 1-69).

Who has Control?

Almost every aircraft has two pilots – whether a captain and first officer, student and instructor, or pilot and spouse. It is vital to know all the time who is flying the aircraft. Sounds self-evident? There have been many, many instances of both pilots having had their hands on their control column and, for example, the aircraft having bounced severely on landing – the instructor thinking that the student had control and the student thinking that the instructor was demonstrating. For this reason, there is now a universal method of handing over control of the aircraft. It is important to learn this from the very beginning.

Some schools have used the expressions *handing over* and *taking over* respectively, but the standardised procedure is now:

- To hand over control, say, "*You have control*"– the other pilot will say, "*I have control*" and will waggle the controls.
- To take over control, say, "*I have control*" and waggle the controls – the other pilot will say, "*You have control*".

Flight Instruments

The pilot controls the flightpath and speed with the controls, but he/she then has to know what is happening to the aircraft. How does the pilot tell if the aircraft is going up or down and how fast? The pilot refers to the flight instruments.

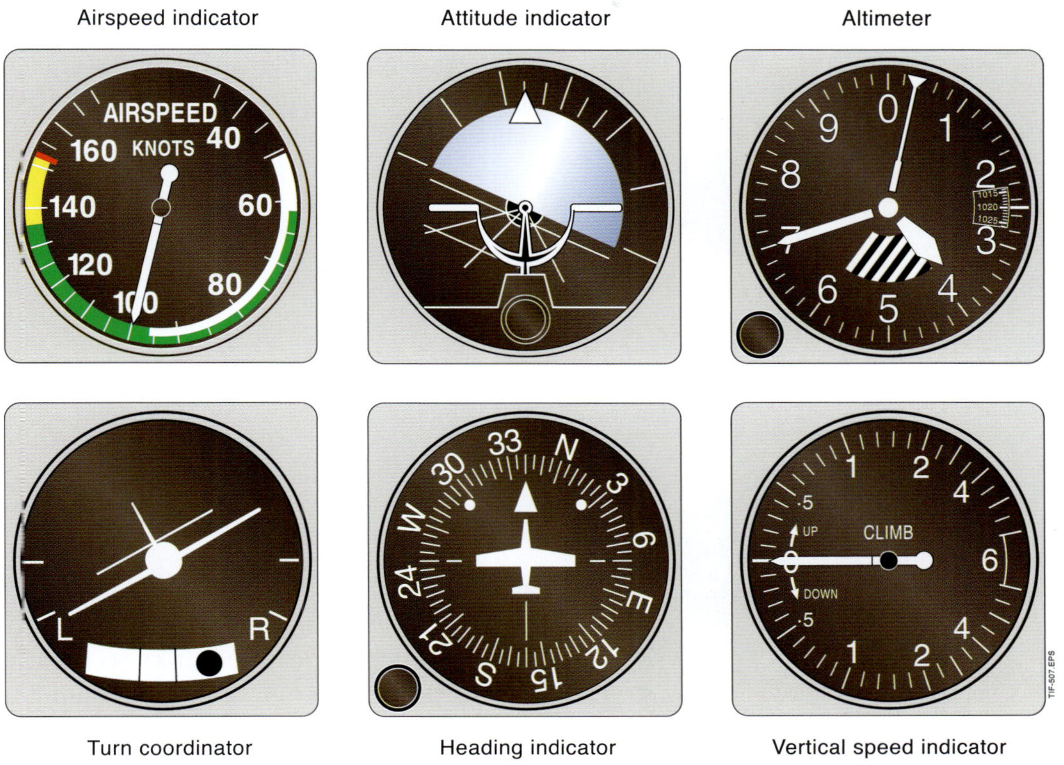

Figure 1-70 Flight instruments.

Figure 1-71 Flight instruments.

The most important instruments are grouped together directly in front of the pilot – on the left side of the panel. These standard six instruments are known as the *primary flight instruments* and are similar in all aircraft – even the Jumbo – and even in modern electronic displays.

The flight instruments include the following.

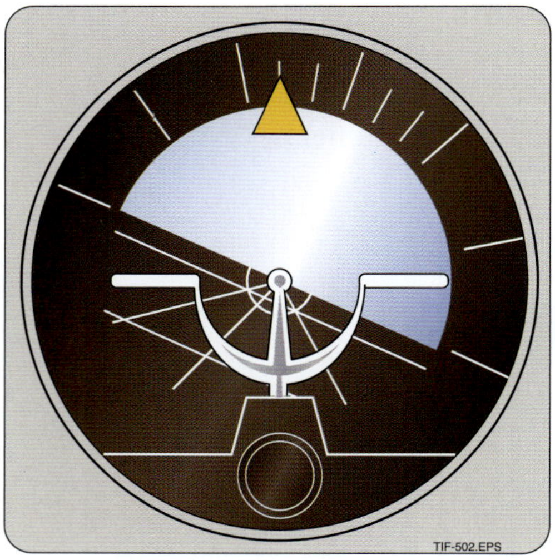

Figure 1-72 Attitude indicator.

The *attitude indicator* (AI) accurately represents the horizon and shows if the nose is up or down and whether the wings are level or banked. *This one is showing a level pitch attitude with 20° of left bank.*

Figure 1-73 Airspeed indicator.

The *airspeed indicator* (ASI) displays airspeed, which is measured in knots (nautical miles per hour). A knot is roughly 2 km/hour. *This ASI shows 128 kt (about 250 km/hour).*

Figure 1-74 Altimeter.

The *altimeter* displays the altitude measured in thousands and hundreds of feet (a foot is 0.3 metres). The instrument reads like an analogue clock. *This one shows three thousand and seven hundred feet (3,700 ft).*

The *heading indicator* (HI), sometimes called a *directional gyro* (DG), displays the aircraft's direction in degrees relative to magnetic north. *This one shows 340° (20° left, or west) of north.* (North is 0° or 360° as there are 360 degrees in a circle but is always called *three six zero* degrees.) Some indicators are automatically aligned to north. Others have to be set manually and realigned regularly (every 15 minutes or so). *It is important to note that heading is where the aircraft is pointing not necessarily where it is going – because wind has an added effect causing the aircraft to drift.*

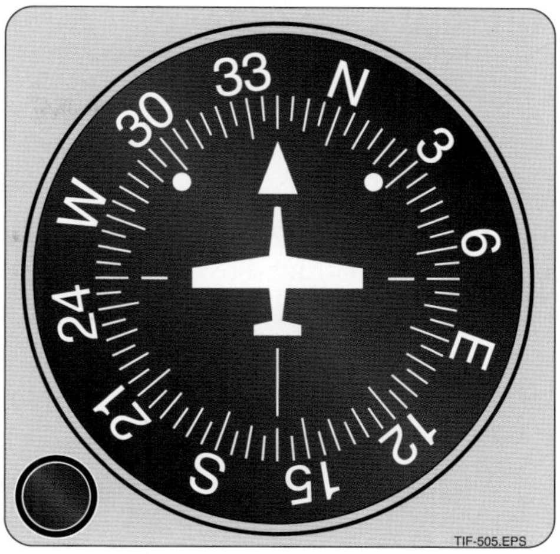

Figure 1-75 Heading indicator.

The *turn coordinator* (below left) and *turn and balance indicator* (below right) show two items of information: the rate at which the aircraft is turning (rate one is 180° in 1 minute) and whether the aircraft is balanced (not slipping or skidding). The ball at the bottom is called the *balance ball* (*skid ball* in slang). To balance the aircraft, the pilot presses on the rudder pedal on the side that the ball is displaced – the pilot *steps on the ball.* Both of these indicators are showing rate one and balanced flight. On the turn coordinator, you will notice a sign which says "*2 MIN TURN*" (which is rate one, or 360° in 2 minutes) and "*No Pitch Information*" which is to prevent the pilot being misled into using the instrument in place of the attitude indicator.

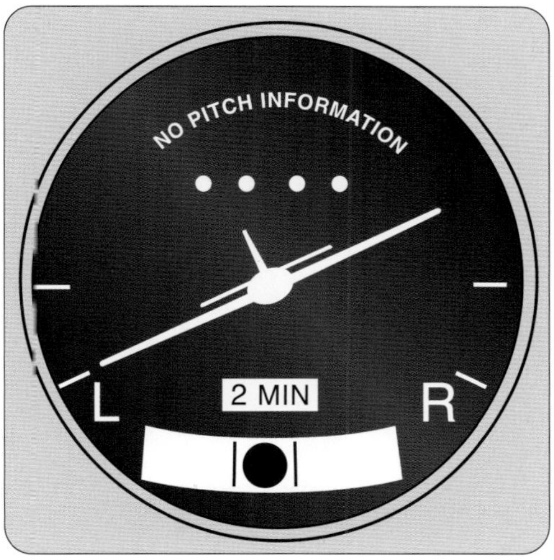

Figure 1-76 (Above) turn coordinator; (above right) turn and balance indicator and (opposite) vertical speed indicator.

The *vertical speed indicator* (VSI) uses the changes in air pressure as the aircraft changes altitude and the rate of pressure change is reflected as a rate of climb or descent in feet per minute. This one shows level flight.

There is an additional important instrument that the pilot uses to control the aircraft's flightpath – although it is not considered a flight instrument. It is the power or rpm indicator which shows engine/propeller speed. In some aircraft, there is also a manifold pressure gauge as we'll discuss later.

Review 1

Pre-Solo Level of Knowledge

1. What is air?
2. How is thrust produced?
3. What is produced as a result of a physical action?
4. Which foot is moved forwards to turn the aircraft to the left on the ground?
5. What is one advantage of having a high-wing configuration?
6. What is a disadvantage of a tailwheel undercarriage?
7. An undercarriage that folds up is called a . . . . . undercarriage.
8. What is the name of the smoothly shaped panels that cover the engine?
9. The path of the aircraft through the air is called its . . . . .
10. The pressure of the air above the wing is . . . . . than below.
11. The angle of the wing to the airflow is called the angle of . . . . .
12. Which part of the aircraft is the fuselage?

13. What is the name of the fixed vertical surface that is attached to the rear of the fuselage?
14. The picture that the pilot sees through the windscreen is called the . . . . .
15. Specifically, this picture is a measure of the position of the nose or the bottom edge of the windscreen in relation to the . . . . .
16. What causes the aircraft to turn?
17. Why do the ailerons move in opposite directions?
18. Why don't the flaps also move in opposite directions?
19. What are they for?
20. Which way does the nose move when the control column is pressed forwards?
21. What if the aircraft is upside down?
22. What do you say when you wish to hand over control of the aircraft to the instructor?
23. What is a knot?
24. There are two elements to this picture: . . . . . and . . . . .

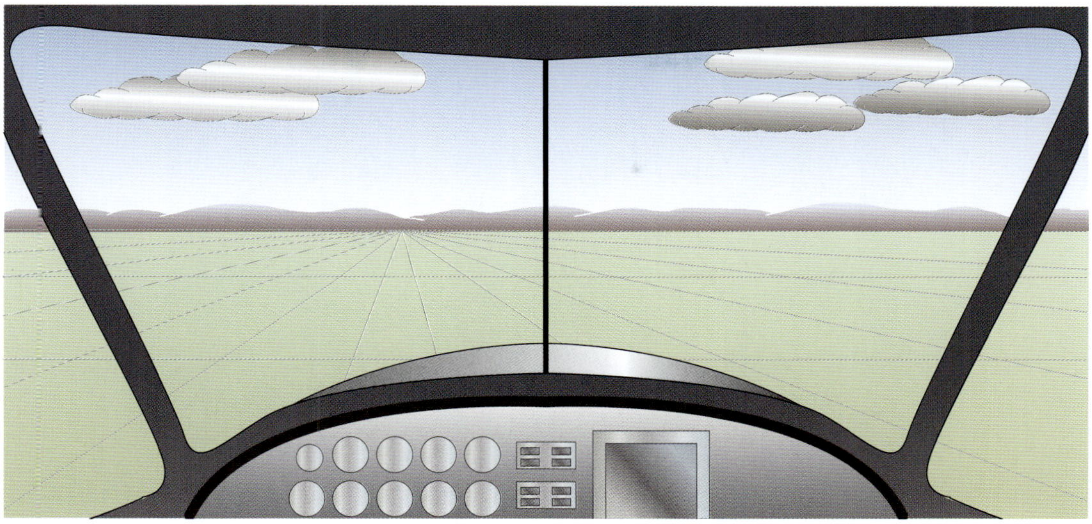

25. Name the six primary flight instruments.

BAK Level of Knowledge

26. The angle of attack is measured between the chord line of the wing and the . . . . .

27 Thrust is caused by converting the heat from burning the fuel to compression of the pistons in the engine which turns the . . . . . which then pushes the . . . . . . rearwards.

28 The total force produced as a result of the aerofoil moving through the air is called the . . . . .

29. This force has two components called . . . . . and . . . . .

30. Name three things that determine the amount of total reaction?

31. What sort of drag is the essential penalty of producing lift?

32. What is downwash?

33. What is stability?

34. What is the name of the balance point of an aircraft?

35. Can an aircraft to have too much stability?

36. What is the name of the control surfaces that determine the angle of attack of the wing?

37. Attitude, together with the power from the engine, determines the . . . . . of the aircraft.

38. To cause a turn, a force is required to change the direction of flight. How is this force produced?

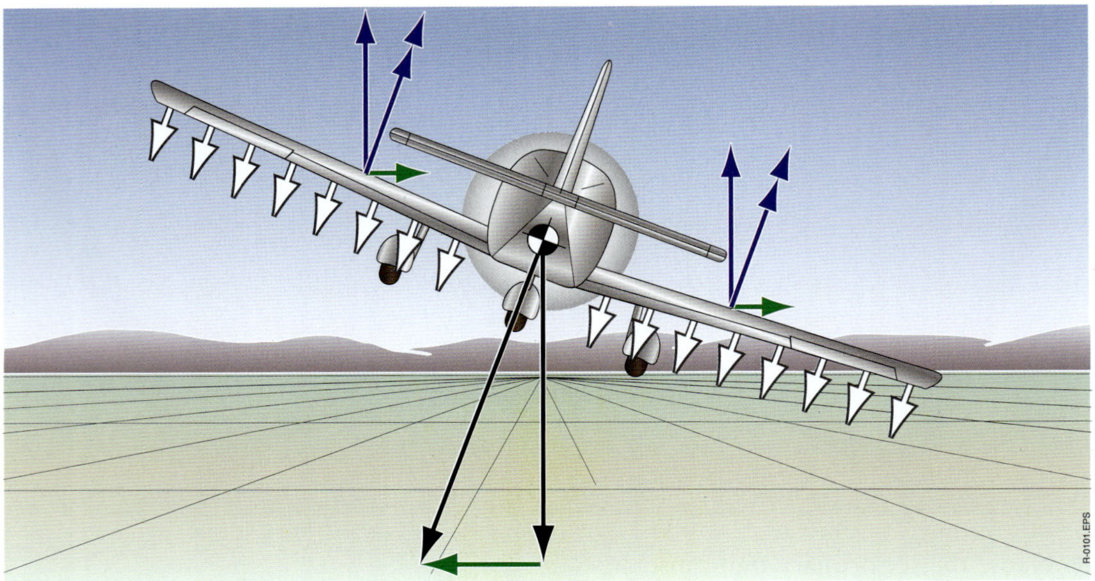

39. The very front of the wing is called the . . . . .
40. The rear of the wing is called the . . . . .
41. . . . . . and . . . . . together control the flightpath of the aircraft.
42. What is shown on the turn coordinator?
43. What is magnetic heading?
44. What is a foot?
45. Why is the sign “2 MIN TURN” shown on the turn coordinator?
46. Which rudder pedal is depressed to centre the balance ball when it is to the right?
47. Why is airspeed said to be the most important piece of information a pilot needs?
48. What is the name of the lever that controls the power of the engine?
49. What is meant by navaids?

50. The point at the very front of the aircraft is called the . . . . .
51. What is meant by a *component* of lift?

2 - Communications

Introduction

You will probably hear the expression, "*aviate, navigate, communicate*". It is a guide for the priorities that a pilot establishes to ensure that the important things are addressed before the less important ones. We must retain control of the aircraft and maintain situational awareness, but, having said that, we must not downgrade the importance of communications.

In most of our operations, we are on a see-and-be-seen basis. Much of what we are trying to avoid cannot be easily seen early enough to avoid conflict; so we have to forewarn our senses. This we do by forming a mental picture of where the traffic is and where it will be in relation to ourselves, as we proceed. The mental plot is a significant part of our ability to detect and avoid other traffic, and it relies totally on our ability to communicate. We must provide our own separation.

Communication is that important, and, I would add, not only communication but annunciation and articulation. We must be clearly understood, and it must be clearly understood that we clearly understood what was said to us. Now we are communicating!

With the introduction of *International Civil Aviation Organisation* (ICAO) radio procedures, there has been an increased requirement for the readback of clearances and instructions. This is understandable since it provides confirmation that what was instructed was correctly received and understood. However, in our more congested airspace, the need for the transmissions to be clear, concise and correct the first time has become essential.

There is another significant factor. A driver of a mini can be as good a driver as the professional driver of a semi-trailer. It's a matter of how the task is approached. Flying is no different, except that most of the time we are out of sight. So for the most part, our professionalism is measured by the quality of our radio transmissions – both the technical quality of the radio and the clarity and content of the message. Whether we are flying a B747 or a Cessna 150, the rest of the world only hears the radio calls. On that, we are judged – and on that alone. A trainee pilot can be just as professional as the Jumbo captain and his/her radio can be equally well maintained. It is a matter of professional pride – as it should be. And money is no excuse. We can practise aloud in the shower – at no cost:

> *"Hot Shower, this is Mike India Kilo Echo, request a straight-in approach?" "Mike India Kilo Echo you are cleared to land. The surface wind is light and variable. The temperature is two three. There is significant precipitation over the runway!"*

This may sound a little childish, but it works. It's the same as an actor learning his or her lines. It's not only the words but hearing yourself say them and how you say them that is important. What clarity, what intonation, what ease of understanding. We are no different to actors – it's just that our role has an immediate real world effect and how we play the role directly affects others in the same "theatre" of operations. We have a responsibility to play our part well. It plays a leading role in being a competent pilot.

Radio: What it is, What is Said & How to Use it

Radio voice communications in aviation are known as *radio telephony* (RTF or R/T), hence the name of the licence you obtain in the course of your pilot training is the *flight radiotelephone operator's licence*.

Figure 2-1 Antennas.

Communication by Pressure Waves

When a person speaks, his or her vocal chords causes vibrations in the air. A flow of air is required through the voice box to generate these pressure waves, the particular nature of which depend upon the person's muscle control over their voice box. Air (or some other medium, e.g. water) must be present to carry these slight fluctuations of pressure to the ear of the listener. At the receiving end, the sound waves impinge upon the ear drums, causing them to vibrate at the same frequency. The mechanism in each ear converts these vibrations into signals that are sent to the brain.

It is quite easy to cause minor variations in the atmospheric pressure surrounding you. For example, if you take a steel ruler, hold it on the edge of a table and cause it to vibrate, your ears will pick up the sound waves. By varying the length of the ruler that is allowed to vibrate, you can alter the frequency of these vibrations (i.e. the number of vibrations or oscillations per second) and, as a consequence, a different pitch of sound is heard.

The average human hearing can detect frequencies between approximately 20 and 20,000 *cycles* (waves or oscillations) per second. One cycle per second is called one *hertz* (Hz). One thousand cycles per second is called one *kilohertz* (kHz). One million cycles per second is one *megahertz* (MHz). In general aviation, we operate in part of the *very high frequency* (VHF) band, usually within the range of 110–140 MHz.

Like ripples on a pond, energy is *attenuated* (dissipated) quite quickly as the sound waves travel further from the source. The maximum range at which the signal can be heard is determined by the frequency of the signal (pitch) and the power of the transmitter (loudness of the voice/shouting). Loud, deep voices travel furthest – as do powerful, low frequency, transmitters.

Wave motion can be described by its shape and frequency. As you may have noticed when swimming, the normal waveshape is a smooth symmetrical shape (called a *sine wave* or sine curve).

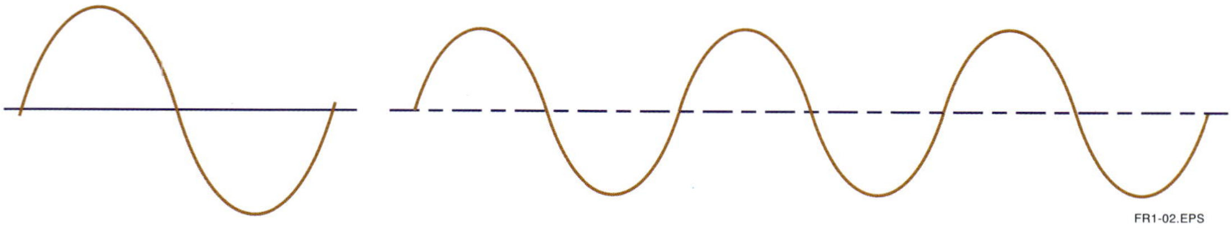

Figure 2-2 The normal shape of energy waves is symmetrical (often described as sine waves).

Waves in water consist of water molecules moving up and down (and around) in a regular pulse as the energy passes. They don't actually move along; they just transmit the pressure wave. Similarly, sound waves passing through the air consist of the air being compressed and expanded (i.e. pressure variations) in a regular manner but the air does not move along. It's like watching a Mexican wave at the footy. No one changes seats but the wave moves around the stadium. The time from the top of one wave to the next is its *frequency*. The height of the arms at the top measured from the depth at their lowest point is called the *amplitude*.

Radio waves use excitement of electromagnetic waves to provide an intelligent message to the medium on which they travel. They need neither air nor water, and they can travel through space where there is none.

Using Radio Waves to Carry Voice Messages

Radio waves consist of regular variations in the strength of electric and magnetic fields. They can travel through a vacuum, through outer space and even through walls. However, like sound waves, the energy in radio waves is attenuated by dense, rigid material such as the earth and large buildings.

Sound waves are pressure waves and travel at what is called the speed of sound (approximately 340 m/second, depending upon air temperature). Radio waves are electromagnetic waves, and they travel much faster, at the speed of light (300 million m/second).

As well as travelling long distances with very little attenuation, radio waves have the advantage of being able to be tuned. Unlike the various pressure vibrations in the audio range (which our ears hear as a blend of sounds all mixed together), we can actually tune a radio receiver to one particular frequency allowing it to receive messages on that frequency alone. All unwanted radio frequencies, and the information being transmitted on them, are automatically screened out. If our desired signal on the selected frequency predominates over unwanted weak signals or noise, then we have good radio reception.

Radio Frequencies

Radio communications frequencies for light aircraft fall into two frequency bands.

Frequency Band	Designator	Frequency Range	Use
High Frequency	HF	3–30 MHz	HF COM
Very High	VHF	30–300 MHz	VHF COM VHF NAV

Table 2-1 Radio frequency bands.

VHF Radio

Many aeroplanes are equipped with at least one VHF radio, usually called VHF COM. Sometimes a second set is fitted so the radios are called COM 1 and COM 2. Most aeroplanes also have a VHF navigation radio which is called VHF NAV.

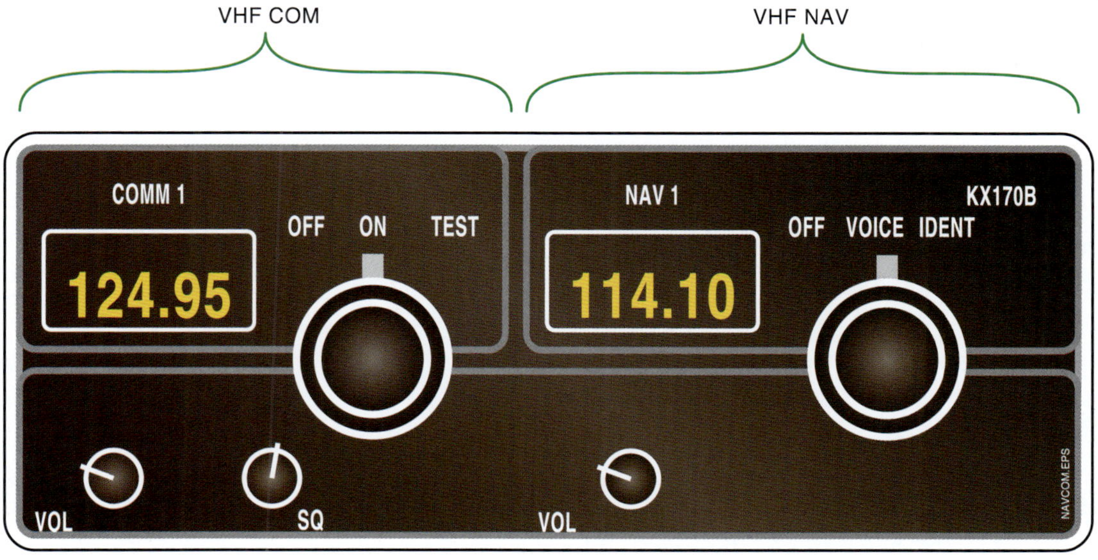

Figure 2-3 Combined VHF NAV/COM receiver.

Figure 2-4 Central radio/navaid stack.

Because VHF transmissions are direct, straight-line (*line-of-sight*) beams, like TV transmissions, their effectiveness depends upon the distance to the other station and whether or not there are obstructions between the two stations.

The following table is a guide to the approximate coverage of VHF radio between an aeroplane and a ground station. The higher we go above the ground, the further we can see and receive radio signals.

Aircraft altitude (feet)	VHF coverage (nautical miles)
below 5,000 ft	60 nm
5,000 to 10,000 ft	90 nm

Table 2-2 VHF radio coverage guide.

Local terrain may shield VHF transmissions.

In recent years, automatic relay equipment located on the ground and in satellites has enabled long-range, high-quality communications using VHF (line-of-sight) frequencies.

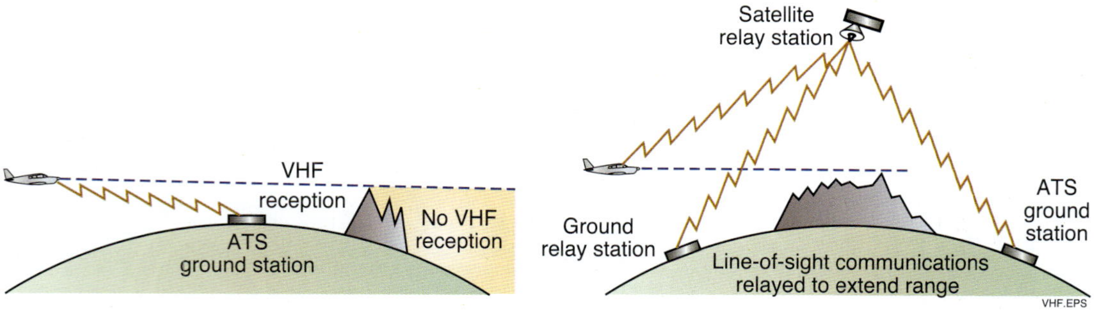

Figure 2-5 Satellite relay.

For other than local transmissions, the aeronautical communications network uses satellite and ground repeater (automatic relay) stations to two primary air traffic centres (located at Brisbane and Melbourne). There is no time delay in the process.

Radio Installation in the Cockpit

Connected to the radios are:

- sockets for the headset or spare microphone;
- speaker and hand-held microphone when not using a headset;
- electronic *intercom* (for internal cockpit communications);
- a press-to-transmit or press-to-talk (PTT) button on the control yoke (the hand-held mike has its own); and
- a selector panel (in some aircraft) to connect the NAV and COM radios to the headsets, speaker or microphone.

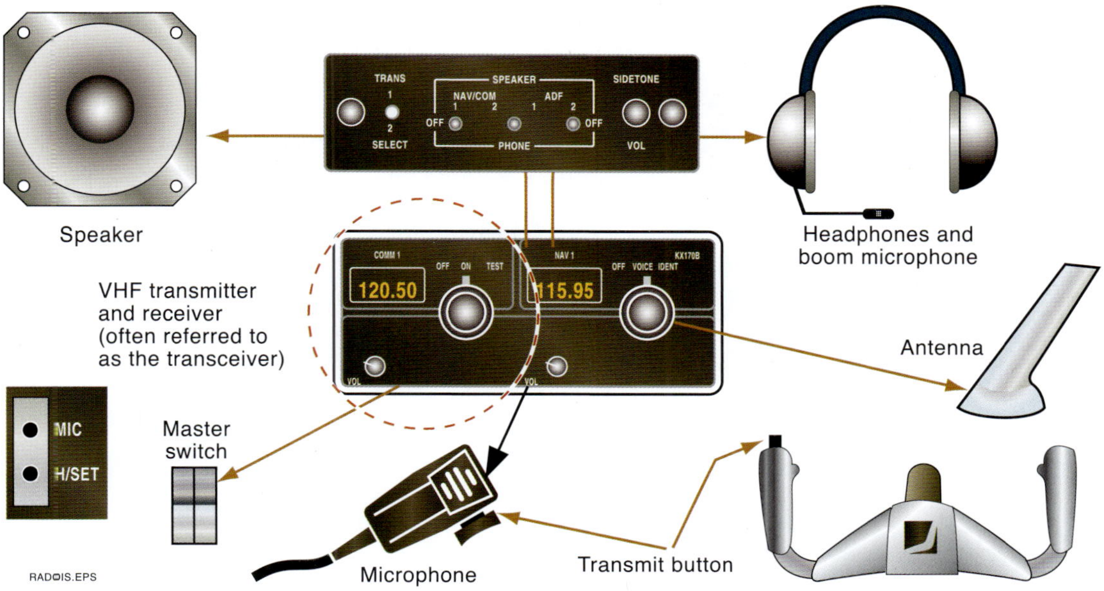

Figure 2-6 Schematic of cockpit radio set-up.

When the engine is running, the electrical power to the radio is supplied by the alternator. When the engine is not running, the electrical power is supplied by the battery. Power is supplied to the radios via the *battery master switch* and, in some cases, an *avionics master switch*. *Avionics* is an abbreviated term for aviation electronics which encompasses both radios and navigation aids. You will also hear the terms *navaids* and *radio-navaids*.

Microphones

The headset carries its own microphone on a small boom and allows hands-free operation because the press-to-talk (PTT) button (for transmissions outside the aircraft) is on the control yoke and can be operated by the thumb. The intercom operates continuously and not via the PTT. There is a spare hand-held mike for back-up use, but it must be held while transmitting. The mechanics of a microphone are similar to the way in which an ear converts sound waves into electrical impulses to the brain. The microphone takes the same pressure waves produced by your voice and converts the sound into electrical signals. These signals add the voice message (modulation) which is carried by the transmitted radio wave, called the *carrier wave*. If you hear a hiss over the radio it can mean that someone is transmitting but their microphone is not working. You are hearing the carrier wave only.

Headset & Intercom

The connection between your voice and the radio is via a headset which contains the boom microphone for speaking, and earphones for listening. The headset has two plugs which are connected to a socket on the instrument panel or the centre console. All training aeroplanes are required to have headsets and an electronic intercom for communications within the aircraft. There will be a small intercom control panel with two knobs – one for volume and one for squelch.

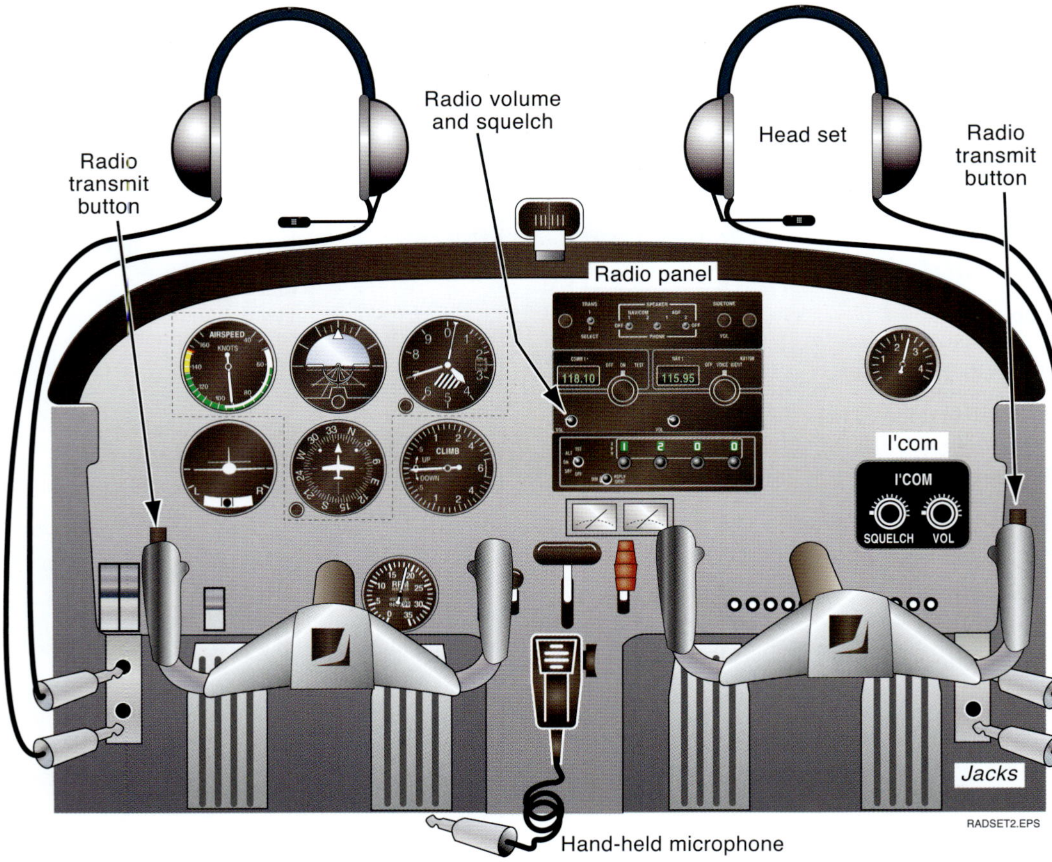

Figure 2-7 Communications system components.

The squelch controls the sensitivity of the microphones. If the squelch is turned down, the background noise is removed, but the first word you speak may be clipped because the intercom goes to a passive (*quiescent*) mode when it hears no voices. Too much squelch and the background noise will keep the intercom active but may be distracting. Some headsets also have individual volume controls on the ear-piece, so if everything is quiet it may have been turned down on one or both sides.

When not under training, you may dispense with the headset and instead use a hand-held microphone and the loudspeaker in the roof of the cabin. This is not the best arrangement as there is no internal communications other than shouting, and the pilot's hand is occupied with the microphone instead of controlling the aircraft.

Use of the VHF COM

Switching on the Radio

The sequence for switching on the radio is as follows:

- Check the master switch on (and avionics power switch if applicable).
- Switch the radio on.
- Select the desired frequency. (It is digital and there is no need to fine-tune the station.)
- On the audio panel, select the appropriate radio switches to speaker or phones as desired.
- Adjust volume to desired level and adjust squelch control (if fitted) to cut out undesired background noise.
- Select transmitter to desired radio, i.e. COM 1 or COM 2.

Figure 2-8 Simple radio/navaids.

Squelch Control

There is also a squelch control on the radio, which may be an added function (pull out to operate) of the volume control. Correct setting is a matter of finding the right balance. Set it so you can just hear a continuous hiss and your first word is not clipped. The function of squelch is to eliminate unwanted weak signals that cause background noise (static or hash). Noise makes it difficult to hear the desired stronger signals. Some squelch controls are automatic and others are manual.

To adjust the manual squelch control:

- turn the squelch up high (i.e. clockwise) until strong background noise or hash is heard; then
- rotate the squelch knob anticlockwise until the noise just disappears (or is at least at an acceptably low level).

Turning the squelch down too far may also cut out the signal that we want to hear, as well as the unwanted noise.

What if the Radio Doesn't Work?

If the radio doesn't work, carry out the following checks:

- If there is no noise in the headset, check earphone volumes and plug connections, check intercom on and volume and squelch is up.
- If you hear the instructor okay but not yourself, check the microphone plug is fully in.
- If you have to puff to trigger voice, the intercom squelch is set too low.
- If the intercom works okay but there is no radio reception, select the audio selector panel to phones and correct radio. Check radio is on, avionics master is on, radio on correct frequency, radio squelch is set.
- If still no reception, check second radio on same frequency.
- If the reception is weak, check squelch and volume and try other radio.
- If there is no reply to your transmissions, note if there is a side-tone, which is a change in the nature of your voice and a slight hiss as you talk with the transmit button depressed. If no side-tone and the intercom is normal, try the second radio. If you can only receive the intercom then use the hand-held mike to talk to the tower.

Communicating

With the headset comfortably fitted, check that the earphone volumes are up and connect the two plugs. As soon as the battery master switch is turned on, the intercom will be active and can be set, however, it is better to set the levels of squelch and volume after the engine is started. After engine start when the radio or avionics master switch is turned on, the main selector panel will be active and the radios themselves can be tuned and set.

The intercom works purely in a voice activation mode. It is triggered when you speak and the sensitivity is controlled by the squelch. There is no need to press any transmit button. Transmissions outside the aircraft are initiated by pressing the transmit button on the control column or on the side of the hand-held microphone.

Set the boom mike or hold the hand-held mike directly in front of your mouth so that your lips are puckered as for a kiss. Speak normally but avoid the tendency to rush the call or to shout. Speak positively and concisely – just as if you were giving directions rather than chatting.

The microphone is like a telephone with the important following distinctions:

- the transmit button must be depressed for you to transmit;
- while transmitting, most radio sets are unable to receive; and
- only one transmission from one station within range can occur on the frequency in use without interference. *While you are transmitting, no one else can.*

Your radio will continue to transmit as long as the transmit button is depressed. Even if you are not speaking, the carrier wave will continue to be transmitted, blocking out other stations that are trying to call on that particular frequency. So, at the end of your transmission ensure that the PTT is released.

Before transmitting, there are some basic rules which you must always follow:

- Listen out on the frequency to be used and avoid interference with other transmissions. If another station, be it another aircraft or an air traffic services (ATS) unit, is transmitting and if a response to its call is awaited do not interrupt. Be particularly aware of this in the rare situation of hearing a distress (*Mayday*) call, or an urgency (*pan-pan*) call. Of course, if you wish to transmit a distress or urgency call then you are entitled to interrupt any transmissions of lower priority.
- Decide what you want to say. For most communications, we use a standard radio phraseology which is easily learnt. This simplifies things for both the person transmitting and the person receiving. Avoid long silences and hesitation sounds (ah, um, er, etc.) during your transmission but do use pauses where appropriate. Don't use slang and don't clutter the frequency with social chat.
- Have the wording of your intended transmission clearly in your mind (or even written down) prior to pressing the transmit button will help you to avoid hesitation.

When using a microphone, make sure of the following:

- Actuate the press-to-talk (PTT) switch before commencing to talk, and do not release it until after your message is completed.
- Speak with the microphone close to or just touching your upper lip.
- Do not significantly vary the distance between your lips and the microphone.
- Speak directly into the microphone.
- Speak a little slower than normal, but at normal volume – do not raise your voice or shout, and do not speak in a whisper.
- Pronounce each word clearly and ensure that you clearly annunciate the end of the word. Running words together, or slurring them, may make reception difficult.
- Pause briefly before and after the transmission of numbers.

Standard Words & Phrases

The most important aspect of radio communication is that the message gets across clearly and quickly and that the frequency is not blocked unnecessarily. In aviation, English is the internationally accepted language for radio communications and a standard phraseology is used.

Pronunciation of Letters

The *phonetic alphabet* is used to ensure correct understanding of transmitted letters. Instead of saying "A" or "B", which, over the radio, can be confused with "I" and "C", we say "Alfa" and "Bravo". In transmitting individual letters the following standard words are used. Stress the syllables that are printed in capital letters. Thus, in the word *November,* the second syllable "VEM" is emphasised so that it is pronounced *no-VEM-ber.*

Letter	Word	Pronounced	Letter	Word	Pronounced
A	ALFA	AL-fah	N	NOVEMBER	no-VEM-ber
B	BRAVO	BRAH-voh	O	OSCAR	OSS-kah
C	CHARLIE	CHAR-lee	P	PAPA	pa-PAH
D	DELTA	DELL-tah	Q	QUEBEC	key-BECK
E	ECHO	ECK-OH	R	ROMEO	ROW-meoh
F	FOXTROT	FOKS-trot	S	SIERRA	see-AIR-ah
G	GOLF	GOLF	T	TANGO	TANG-go
H	HOTEL	ho-TELL	U	UNIFORM	YOU-nee-form
I	INDIA	IN-deeah	V	VICTOR	VICK-ta
J	JULIETTE	JEW-lee-ETT	W	WHISKEY	WISS-key
K	KILO	KEY-loh	X	X-RAY	ECKS-ray
L	LIMA	LEE-mah	Y	YANKEE	YANG-key
M	MIKE	MIKE	Z	ZULU	ZOO-loo

Table 2-3 Phonetic alphabet.

Callsigns of Aircraft

The most common use of the phonetic alphabet is for aircraft callsigns. Each Australian civil aircraft has a registration that consists of VH-. . . followed by three letters. The VH is an international designation for Australian civil aircraft. The UK uses G- for Great Britain and the US uses N- for North America (the US also uses a combination of letters and numerals because there are so many aircraft, e.g. N-4175L).The registration is also its radio *callsign* – its identification code. While operating within Australia, it is usual to use only the last three letters of the registration.

Registration	Callsign
VH-ABC	AL-fah BRAH-voh CHAR-lee
VH-POQ	pa-PAH OSS-kah key-BECK

Table 2-4 Callsigns of aircraft.

On some occasions the aircraft type is also included in the transmitted information, for example:

"*Warrior,* [pause] *ROW-meoh TANG-go ZOO-loo*",
or "*WISS-key OSS-kah ZOO-loo,* [pause] *a Pitts*", as appropriate.

The phonetic alphabet may also be used whenever it is thought necessary to spell a word to ensure correct understanding of a message (such as the names of towns in position reports), if radio reception is poor, or if any confusion arises. An easy way to learn the phonetic alphabet is, as you drive your car, to practise aloud saying the registration numbers of passing cars or street signs.

Pronunciation of Numbers

If you are transmitting single digits then you should use the following words, stressing the syllables in capitals.

Number or Numeral Element	Pronunciation
0	ZE-RO
1	WUN
2	TOO
3	TREE (or THREE)
4	FOUR
5	FIFE
6	SIX
7	SEV-en
8	AIT
9	NIN-er
decimal	DAY-SEE-MAL
hundred	HUN-dred
thousand	TOU-SAND (or THOUSAND)

Table 2-5 Pronunciation of numbers.

It is especially important to differentiate between 5 (pronounced FIFE) and 9 (pronounced NIN-er) because, when spoken normally, they are often confused. If there is a decimal point in the number then it is indicated by the word *DAY-SEE-MAL*. For example, an instruction to VH-AKB to change frequency to 118.3 MHz would be transmitted as:

"AL-fa KEY-loh BRAH-voh, [pause]
contact Alice Tower on WUN WUN AIT, DAY-SEE-MAL, THREE."

You can now extend your practice using car registration numbers to include the numerals. ETV 309 would be pronounced:

"ECK-OH TANG-go VICK-ta, TREE ZE-RO NIN-er."

Transmission of Numbers

All numbers are transmitted by pronouncing each numeral separately (e.g. 10 is WUN ZE-RO, 236 is TOO TREE SIX), except for:

- whole hundreds (e.g. 500 is FIFE HUN-dred);
- whole thousands (e.g. 7,000 is SEV-en TOU-SAND); and
- combinations of thousands and whole hundreds (e.g. 7,500 is SEV-en TOU-SAND, FIFE HUN-dred).

In aviation, the way of expressing cloud cover is in eighths of the sky covered. Eighths in radio transmissions is expressed as *oktas*. A little over half the sky covered, say five eights, would be expressed as *FIFE OK-tas*.

Transmission of Time

Because aeroplanes are continually moving from one time zone to another, it is standard practice in aviation to use a specific time reference known as *Zulu* (Z). *Zulu time* is the the code for *Greenwich mean time* (GMT) and *coordinated universal time* (UTC).

When transmitting locally, it is usual only to say the minutes of the hour.

However, if there is any possibility of a misunderstanding or if your ETA is after the next "o'clock", then the hour, in Zulu time, should also be included.

In aviation, we use the 24-hour clock, the day beginning at 0000 and ending 24 hours later at 2400 (which is of course 0000 for the next day). For example:

- 8:30 am is 0830 hr (*oh eight thirty*).
- 10 am is 1000 hr (*ten hundred hours*).
- Midday (12 noon) is 1200 hr (*twelve hundred hours*).
- One hour later, 1 pm, is 1300 hr (i.e. 1200 plus 1 hour) (*thirteen hundred hours*).
- 4:30 pm is 1630 (i.e. 1200 plus 4:30) (*sixteen thirty hours*).
- 8 pm is 2000 hr (i.e. 1200 plus 0800) (*twenty hundred hours*).
- 8:17 pm is 2017 hr (*twenty, seventeen*).
- Midnight is *twenty four hundred hours*.

The above terms are common use for relating time using the twenty four hour clock. However, in radio transmissions, *Zulu* time is expressed as individual numerals, spoken phonetically. Eight-thirty am (in Greenwich) is 0830 hr (*oh eight thirty hours*) – *and it is the same time for all ships and aircraft, everywhere in the world*. However it is transmitted as, "*ZE-RO AIT THREE ZE-RO, Zulu*". For local use the hour and the word *Zulu* can be deleted.

Time	Transmitted as
0815	WUN FIFE (or ZE-RO AIT WUN FIFE)
1720	TOO ZE-RO (or WUN SEV-en TOO ZE-RO)
2300	TOO THREE ZE-RO ZE-RO (or twenty-three hundred)
0400	ze-ro four ze-ro ze-ro (or oh four hundred)

Table 2-6 Transmission of time.

Relationship of Australian Standard Times to UTC

Use the following to convert local standard time to coordinated universal time:

- UTC = EST (Eastern Standard Time) *minus* 10 hours.
- UTC = ESuT (Eastern Summer Time) *minus* 11 hours.
- UTC = CST (Central Standard Time) *minus* 9 hours 30 minutes.
- UTC = CSuT (Central Summer Time) *minus* 10 hours 30 minutes.
- UTC = WST (Western Standard Time) *minus* 8 hours.

For example:

- 1500 EST = 0500 UTC;
- 1600 ESuT = 0500 UTC; and
- 1430 UTC = 2230 WST = 2400 CST = 0030 EST.

There is a trap here in the case of CST and CSuT. Note the relationship is not a whole hour. Local time of 12<u>55</u> hr is 03<u>25</u>Z. Thus reading the minute hand of your watch does not give the correct Zulu time in minutes. We have to deduct 30 minutes. Time 55 local, becomes time 25 Zulu (i.e. *five five* is actually *two five*). Simply imagine a *tail* on the minute hand and read from that – or set UTC on the aircraft's clock.

Standard Words & Phrases

The most important result in communication is for your message to be received and clearly understood. For this reason you should use plain English and simple words and phrases. To make radio communications uniform, some standard words and phrases have been devised. Their meanings are clear. They are brief and so occupy less air time. Whenever possible you should use this standard phraseology.

If you cannot recall the appropriate standard phraseology for your particular situation, or if there is no standard phrase for the information that you wish to convey, then just go ahead and use plain, concise English.

Word/Phrase	Meaning
Acknowledge	Let me know that you have received and understood this message.
Affirm	Yes.
Approved	Permission for proposed action granted.
Break	I hereby indicate the separation between portions of the message (to be used where there is no clear distinction between the text and other portions of the message).
Break break	I hereby indicate separation between parts of a message directed to different aircraft in a very busy environment.
Cancel	Annul the previously transmitted clearance.
Check	Examine a system or procedure (no answer is normally expected).
Cleared	Authorised to proceed under the conditions specified.
Confirm	Have I correctly received the following . . . ? or Did you correctly receive this message?
Contact	Establish radio contact with . . .

Table 2-7 Standard words and phrases.

Correct	That is correct.
Correction	An error has been made in this transmission (or message indicated) the correct version to . . .
Disregard	Consider that transmission as not sent.
Go ahead	Proceed with your message.
How do you read?	What is the readability of my transmission? The readability scale is: 1. Unreadable. 2. Readable now and then. 3. Readable but with difficulty. 4. Readable. 5. Perfectly readable.
I say again	I repeat for clarity or emphasis.
Monitor	Listen out on (frequency).
Negative	"No" or "permission is not granted" or "That is not correct".
Over	My transmission is ended and I expect a response from you (not normally used in VHF communication).
Out	My transmission is ended and I expect no response from you (not normally used in VHF communication).
Read back	Repeat all, or the specified part, of this message back to me exactly as received.
Re-cleared	A change has been made to your last clearance and this new clearance supersedes your previous clearance or part thereof.
Report	Pass me the following information.
Request	I should like to know or I wish to obtain.
Roger	I have received all of your last transmission (under NO circumstances to be used in reply to a question requiring READ BACK or a direct answer in the affirmative or negative).
Say again	Repeat all or the following part of your last transmission.
Speak slower	Reduce your rate of speech.
Standby	Wait and I will call you.
Verify	Check and confirm with originator.
Words twice	1. As a request: Communication is difficult. Please send every word or group of words twice. 2. As information: Since communication is difficult every word or group of words in this message will be sent twice.

Table 2-7 Standard words and phrases.

The ADF

The *automatic direction finder* (ADF) consists of a navigation receiver which is connected electronically to an instrument in the cockpit. The ADF receives signals from a *non-directional beacon* (NDB), which is a transmitter on the ground or, in some cases, a commercial radio station, that transmits in all directions (*non-directional* means not in one direction only). The needle on the instrument points directly towards the station, but you must consider the face of the instrument as a plan view, like the clock-code.

The ADF is tuned to the frequency of the particular beacon. Typical frequencies for the NDB are between 200 and 430 kHz.

Voice transmissions and the ATIS (*automatic terminal information service*) can be received on the ADF, but you cannot reply. The ADF can also be used to receive transmissions from any AM broadcast station which transmits on frequencies between 200 and 1,655 kHz, although their use for navigation has to be treated with caution.

Radar

Radar is an abbreviation for *radio detection and ranging*. It was a wartime invention which used the reflection of a direct pulse of electromagnetic energy to detect the presence and to establish the bearing, distance and, nowadays, altitude of an aircraft from a ground transmitter. The transmitter sends a pulse in a very accurate direction and starts a clock. If an *echo* is received, the time taken gives the distance to the target, and the direction, and tilt of the antenna, gives the direction and height. This echo is called a *skin paint* and the system is called *primary radar*.

Primary Radar

A *primary radar* is a device which transmits a pulse and relies on part of that energy to be reflected back to a receiver which converts the time and angle information into bearing and distance. This type of system is used for weather radar.

Secondary Radar

A further invention, to be used with radar, was called IFF (identification, friend or foe). When a friendly aircraft was painted (illuminated) by a radar pulse, a device called a *transponder* (transmitting-responder) sent another pulse back on the same frequency. This return pulse was coded to say that the aircraft was friendly. This system had the following advantages:

- the return pulse had new energy and so could respond to the radar at greater distances; and
- the return signal could be encoded to show the actual altitude of the aircraft and its individual identification.

To confuse the enemy, the IFF was referred as the *parrot* and the controller would tell the pilot to turn on the IFF by saying "*squawk*". To cancel the signal he would say "*strangle your parrot!*" To this day the controller will ask you to *squawk code 1247* – or whatever.

A ground-based radar that relies on the response from a transponder is called a *secondary surveillance radar* (SSR). This system is now in general use, and all aircraft operating in controlled airspace (all except Class G) must carry a transponder. In the air traffic control centre, the controller can see the aircraft, its callsign, altitude and speed and can better sequence and separate aircraft from each other.

A transponder has several operating modes (see table 2-8).

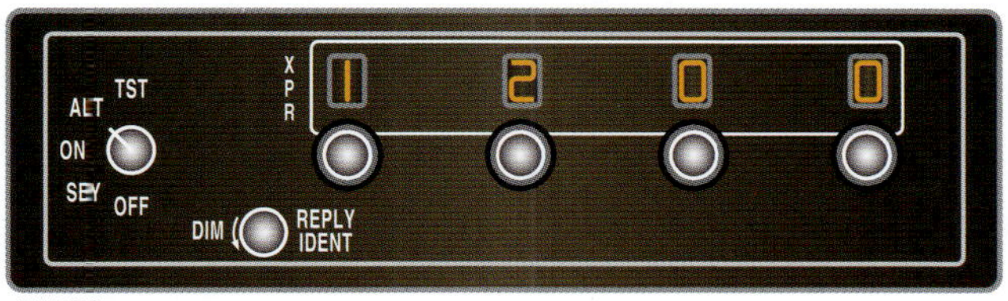

Figure 2-9 Transponder control panel.

OFF	Power is off.
SBY	Standby, power on, ready to operate.
ON	Transmits the set code when interrogated.
ALT	Transmits the set code and the aircraft altitude when interrogated.
TST	Checks function, transmits code once.
IDENT	Symbol flashes on ATC radar screen.

Table 2-8 Transponder operating modes.

Transponder Codes

Air traffic control will assign you a discrete transponder code when required. The code for VFR aircraft not participating in radar information services (RIS) is 1200. Other than the 1200 code, at this stage you need only remember two other codes:

- 7600, which will indicate to the ATC that you have a radio failure; and
- 7700, which indicates a further serious emergency.

Incidentally, the transponder code is a *readback item*, so if assigned a code, you must repeat it to the controller.

Transponder Response

The transponder is normally operated in the ALT mode. This means that when it is interrogated, its transmitted response is the code that is set and the aircraft altitude. The air traffic controller will see the code and altitude on a screen which is then marked with your callsign. This gives the controller a complete three dimensional picture of the aircraft range, bearing and altitude from the radar site. If the controller is not receiving a correct response from your aircraft, you might be requested to *reselect code*, *recycle transponder* or *squawk ident*. To transmit (squawk) without being interrogated, simply select TST momentarily on the mode switch.

Some GA aircraft are fitted with a *traffic collision alerting device* (TCAD). TCAD provides warning of other traffic as follows:

- an audio alert;
- range to the other aircraft; and
- altitude difference from other aircraft as a plus or minus.

TCAD relies on the ground radar illuminating both aircraft and triggering their transponders. So it will work near major radars but not in the bush. RPT aircraft are being fitted with a *traffic alert and collision avoidance system* (TCAS). The TCAS does not need radar illumination as it has its own interrogator to trigger other transponders.

Summary

If a transponder is fitted to your aircraft, turn it on for all flight operations as follows:

- In the circuit area, set code 1200 and SBY.
- In the training area and outside controlled airspace (Class G), squawk 1200 and ALT.
- In controlled airspace, squawk the code included in the airways clearance and ALT.

When changing codes always select SBY first and then reselect ALT after new code is set.

Emergency Radio Procedures

It is very important that you are familiar with emergency radio procedures (these are contained in ERSA). Request assistance whenever you have any serious doubt regarding the safety of a flight. Transmission should be slow and distinct, with each word pronounced clearly so that there is no need for repetition. This of course should apply to all radio transmissions, but it is more important in emergency situations. If you do find yourself in real difficulty, waste no time in requesting assistance from an ATS unit or on the appropriate CTAF frequency. Timely action may avoid an even more serious emergency.

What is Considered to be an Emergency?

It is impossible for us to cover all the possibilities. The declaration of an emergency by the pilot in command is an area for your operational judgement. Emergencies can be classified according to the urgency and to the degree of seriousness of the consequences. As the pilot, you decide, but always err on the safe side. Some categories might be as follows:

- No urgency of time but needing assistance, such as being uncertain of position and unable to confirm direction to proceed, but having plenty of fuel and remaining daylight.
- Some urgency of time, such as being uncertain of position and having fuel reserves or remaining daylight at less than an hour or so.
- Some urgency and potential for serious consequences, such as a loss of oil pressure or a rough running engine or fuel depletion that may be insufficient to reach an airfield.
- Potential seriousness but not yet developed, such as having some doubt about the serviceability of the aircraft or systems or the medical condition of the pilot.
- Potential seriousness but no urgency, such as the loss of the primary attitude indicator over eight oktas of cloud but with plenty of fuel and daylight.
- Potentially catastrophic and urgent, such as risk of a loss of control due to reduced visibility or risk of controlled flight into terrain due to rising ground and lowering cloudbase.

It is impossible to set hard-and-fast rules. If in doubt, tell someone what the potential problem is and do it early rather than late – when there is still plenty of time, fuel and daylight. If there is any urgency, formally declare an emergency – at least a pan-pan. If there is any risk of loss of control or injury, declare a mayday.

Declaring an Emergency

If an emergency arises it is your responsibility as pilot in command to assess just how serious the emergency is (or could be) and to take appropriate safety action. *The pilot has the ultimate responsibility for the safety of the aircraft.*

Many emergencies require your immediate attention and occupy you fully for some moments, but it is advisable at the first opportune moment to tell someone. Radio can play a vital role when assistance is required; however, in an emergency, remember always the first priority is to control and position the aircraft. Remember: *Aviate, navigate, communicate.*

There are three degrees of emergency, and as pilot in command you should prefix your radio call with one of the following:

- *mayday* (repeated three times) for a *distress* call;
- *pan-pan* (repeated three times) for an *urgency* call; or
- *security* (repeated three times) for a *safety* call.

Distress Message (*Mayday* Call)

A mayday call has priority over all others, and the word *mayday* should force everyone else into immediate radio silence. *Mayday* is the anglicised (English) spelling with the same phonetic pronunciation as the French expression *m'aidez* which means *help me!*

If you require immediate assistance or are threatened by grave or imminent danger:

- The mayday distress message should be transmitted on the current frequency.
- If you are using a CTAF frequency and receive no response to your distress call, if you have time, repeat the call on the FIS frequency.
- If still no response, and if time permits, repeat the call on 121.5 MHz (the international emergency frequency usually monitored by airliners and some ground stations).
- Squawk code 7700. If you are in a radar environment, this causes a special symbol to on the ATC radar screen, and rings an alarm bell to alert the radar controllers.

For example:
Mayday, mayday, mayday
Foxtrot Papa Delta
two zero miles west of Gilldoola at this time
altitude four thousand
Cessna one eight two
engine failure
forced landing in open paddock
one person on board

Urgency Message (*Pan-Pan* Call)

The urgency or pan-pan message is made over the air–ground frequency in use, or the relevant FIS frequency if considered more prudent, when an emergency exists but does not require immediate assistance.

Typical situations when a pan-pan message is appropriate include the following:

- if you are experiencing navigational difficulties and require the urgent assistance of ATC or flight service;
- if you have a passenger on board that has become seriously ill and will require urgent attention;
- if you see another aeroplane or a ship the safety of which is threatened and urgent action is perhaps needed; and
- if you are making an emergency change of level in controlled airspace and you may conflict with traffic below.

For example:
Pan-pan, pan-pan, pan-pan
Adelaide
Alfa Charlie Echo
two zero miles south of Broken Hill at three zero
heading two five zero
airspeed nine zero knots
three thousand feet
Piper Warrior
experiencing severely reduced visibility in dust storm
descending to land on agricultural strip

Loss of Radio Contact

In the event of a total loss of radio contact, there will be a procedure for you to return safely to your aerodrome for landing, and there is a standby system of light signals used for communications to and from the aerodrome control tower.

Light Signal	Aircraft in Flight	Aircraft on the Ground
Steady green	Authorised to land if you are satisfied that no collision risk exists	Authorised to take-off if you are satisfied no collision risk exists
Steady red	Give way to other aircraft and continue circling	Stop – where you are
Green flashes	Return for immediate landing	Authorised to taxi if you are satisfied that no collision risk exists
Red flashes	Aerodrome unsafe – do not land	Taxi clear of landing area in use
White flashes	No meaning	Return to starting point on aerodrome

Table 2-9 Light signals to aircraft.

Emergency Locator Transmitter (ELT)

If you have never seen an *emergency locator transmitter* (ELT) before, ask your flying instructor if you could examine one and have your instructor go through the procedures for its activation. This will make this section more meaningful.

The emergency locator transmitter is also known by other names:

- VHF survival beacon (VSB); and
- emergency locator beacon (ELB).

The ELT is a VHF radio transmitter capable of sending a signal simultaneously on the international distress frequencies: 121.5 and 243 MHz. Each unit has its own power source (battery), so before setting out on a flight where the carriage of an ELT is required, *check that the battery recharge date (stamped on the ELT) has not expired.*

When activated, emergency locator transmitters transmit on the international standard emergency frequencies of 121.5 MHz and 243 MHz. Since 121.5 MHz lies within the frequency band receivable by VHF COM radios, it is recommended that pilots listen to this frequency once or twice on each long flight and report any signals heard. This will ensure that an early report of an ELT activation, and therefore detection of a possible emergency situation, is received by a *rescue coordination centre.*

ELTs can easily be activated unintentionally, possibly causing unnecessary rescue action to be commenced and putting other people at risk. For this reason, you should ensure that your ELT is not inadvertently activated. As a check, it is a good idea to monitor the VHF COM radio briefly on 121.5 MHz prior to leaving the taxiing area at the commencement of a flight and also when taxiing back to the parking area at the completion of the flight. If an ELT signal is detected, check the status of your own ELT and if the signal is from another ELT, report reception of the signal to the nearest air traffic services unit.

Emergency Light Signals

Generally, if you encounter any form of emergency, you will have the use of your radio to alert air traffic control, a ground station or traffic in your area. If, however, you do not have the use of your radio, you may also use light signals to attract attention, such as flashing the landing lights.

If you do not have any light signals available to you, then use any means at your disposal to attract attention (e.g. mobile phone).

Review 2

Pre-Solo Level of Knowledge

1. What is meant by RTF (or R/T)?
2. Why was the phonetic alphabet created? Fill out the table below.

Letter	Word	Transmitted as	Letter	Word	Transmitted as
A			N		
B			O		
C			P		
D			Q		
E			R		
F			S		
G			T		
H			U		
I			V		
J			W		
K			X		
L			Y		
M			Z		

3. The VHF radio frequency band is from . . . . . to . . . . . MHz.
4. What is MHz?
5. What is amplitude?
6. Should the squelch be set at minimum or maximum or somewhere in between?
7. Why have a transmit button on the control column?
8. Is the transmit button the same as the PTT?
9. What significance does the word *mayday* have?
10. Say ATC in phonetics.
11. What transponder mode do you set for circuit operations?
12. If the radio fails completely in the circuit area, what would you do?
13. What do the letters ELT stand for?

BAK Level of Knowledge

14. What is the significance of VHF COM versus VHF NAV?
15. About how far can you expect to receive VHF transmissions from an altitude below 5,000 feet?
16. What are the pros and cons of a hand-held microphone versus a headset?
17. Say IHTFP in phonetics.
18. If another aircraft says "*how do you read me*" and the transmission is feint and the clarity is blurred, what numbers, in regard to readability, would you choose?
19. Why should we select STBY when changing transponder codes?

20. If the oil pressure drops slowly, would you declare and emergency and, if so, what call would you make?

21. If the radio fails completely in the training area, what would you do?

22. In the event of no noise whatsoever in your headset, what actions/checks would you undertake?

23. What is the international VHF distress frequency?

24. If an aircraft is called to be in your *left, seven o'clock high*. Where exactly is it?

25. What do you do if you are on final and see a red light from the control tower?

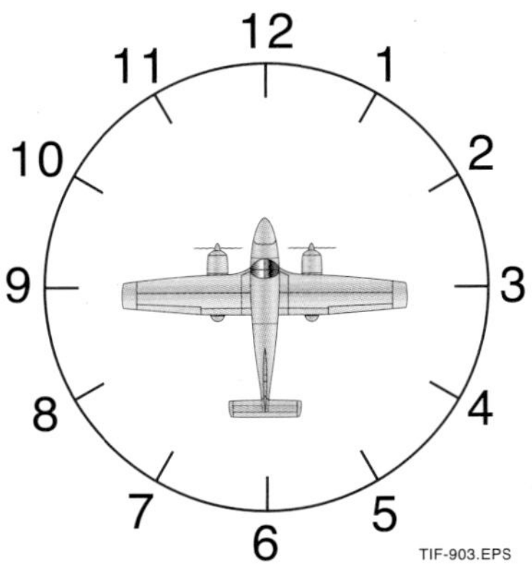

3 - Aviation Terminology, Abbreviations, Units & Rules of Thumb

Aviation
Theory
Centre

Terminology

In a short time you will become familiar with the unique terminology and abbreviations associated with aviation.

alpha (α): Greek symbol used universally to represent angle of attack.

beta (β): angle of sideslip.

arrivals: Aircraft joining the circuit.

attitude: (*The most important word in flying.*) The nose position – up or down (and how much), and wings level or banked (left or right, and how much) – in relation to the visual horizon or the attitude indicator.

AVGAS/Avgas: Aviation gasoline, petroleum – fuel.

circuit: The flightpath of the aircraft around the aerodrome when taking off and landing.

clock code: Remember the movie, *Twelve O'Clock High?* The title refers to a way of describing where something is in relation to the nose of the aircraft. Twelve o'clock high means straight ahead and above you.

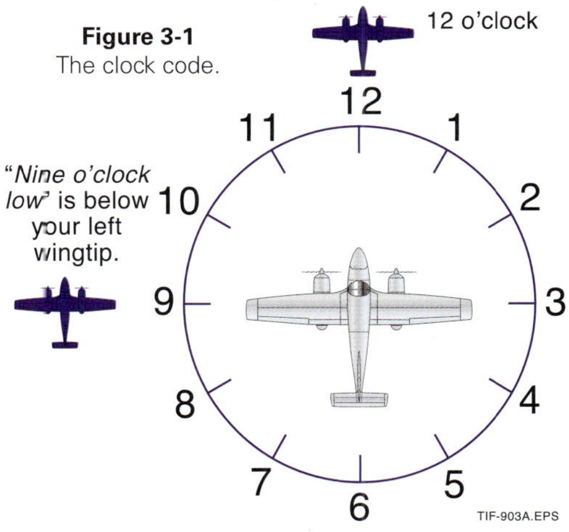

Figure 3-1
The clock code.

coaming (or glareshield): Overhanging lip above the instrument panel to reduce reflections.

departure: Leaving the circuit area. Alternatively, loss of control – departure from controlled flight.

hangar: The aircraft garage.

headset: Earphones and boom microphone set.

holding point: Take-off waiting point near the runway.

intercom: Internal communications system – an electronic system for talking inside the cockpit.

knot: A speed of one nautical mile per hour.

maintenance release: The document that tells the pilot that the aircraft is serviceable for the flight.

numbers: The numbers show the runway direction to the nearest 10°.

okta: ⅛ of the sky (4 oktas of cloud means ½ the area of the sky is obscured).

squelch: Adjustment knob to reduce background noise on the intercom and radio.

tarmac: The aircraft parking area.

threshold: The beginning of the runway marked with spaced white lines called *piano keys.*

Unicom: During the period that normal air traffic services are not available, a Unicom service may be provided on CTAF frequencies. It is a general broadcast frequency for use by pilots. Services on this frequency for fuel, parking, transport have lower priority than services for the purpose of traffic warning and separation.

wake turbulence: The disturbed air behind a large aircraft – be very careful of this.

wind velocity: The speed and direction from which the wind is blowing expressed in knots and degrees magnetic for the ATIS and degrees true for the area forecast.

windshear: Varying wind speed and direction at different heights – *be very careful of this.*

Abbreviations

AAL: above aerodrome level.
AGL: above ground level.
AI or AH: attitude indicator or artificial horizon.
AIP: Aeronautical Information Publication (a comprehensive series of operational documents for VFR and IFR pilots).
AMSL: above mean sea level – the altitude indicated by the altimeter when QNH is set on the subscale.
ARFOR: area forecast.
ASI: airspeed indicator.
ATC: air traffic control.
AVGAS: aviation gasoline.
BAK: basic aeronautical knowledge.
CASA: Civil Aviation Safety Authority.
CAVOK: ceiling and visibility OK.
CFI: chief flying instructor.
CG: centre of gravity.
CHT: cylinder head temperature.
CPL: commercial pilots licence.
CTA: control area/controlled airspace.
CTAF: common traffic advisory frequency.
CTR: aerodrome control zone.
DA: density altitude.
DAMP: drugs and alcohol management plan.
DI or DG: direction indicator or directional gyro.
EGT: exhaust gas temperature.
ELT or ELB: emergency location/locator transmitter.
ERSA: En Route Supplement Australia (an aerodrome directory and useful reference publication).
ETA: estimated time of arrival.
FIR/FIA/FIS: flight information region/area/service.
FPM: feet per minute (for rate of climb or descent).
GA: general aviation.
GFPT: General Flying Progress Test.
GMT: Greenwich mean time – same as UTC and Z.
GPS: global positioning system.
GS: Groundspeed – the speed of the aircraft relative to a point on the ground. It is the resultant (combination) of true airspeed and wind velocity.
IAS: indicated airspeed, the speed of the aircraft as shown on the airspeed indicator.
IFR: instrument flight rules.
ILS: instrument landing system.
IMC: instrument meteorological conditions (IMC exists if VMC do not).
ISA: International Standard Atmosphere.
kHz: kilohertz, radio frequency expressed in thousands of cycles per second.
KIAS: knots, indicated airspeed.
KTAS: knots, true airspeed.
L/D: lift/drag ratio.
LAME: licensed aircraft maintenance engineer.
LMT: local mean time.
LSALT: lowest safe altitude.
MAP: manifold absolute pressure (this is measured in inches of mercury – in./Hg). Together with rpm, MAP gives a measure of engine power.
MET: meteorology – generally refers to weather conditions and forecasts.
MP: manifold pressure (same as MAP); more common usage than MAP.
MHz: megahertz – radio frequency in millions of cycles per second.
MULTICOM: general comms frequency.
NDB: non-directional beacon.
NOTAM: notice to airmen advising status of airspace, navigation aids, hazards, procedure changes.
NVFR: night visual flight rules (expressed as night VFR – same usage as NVMC).
OCTA: outside controlled airspace (same as Class G airspace).
PAX: passengers.
PIC: pilot in command.
POB: persons on board.
POH: pilot's operating handbook – also flight manual.
PPL: private pilots licence.
PRD: prohibited, restricted and danger areas.
PSI: pounds per square inch – pressure.
PTT: press to talk (or transmit) – button for external radio transmissions.

PVT: private category flight (as distinct from charter, airwork, RPT).
QNH: altimeter pressure datum to show vertical distance above local mean sea level.
RA: recreational aviation or aircraft
RIS: radar information service.
RBI: relative bearing indicator = clock code in degrees.
RMI: radio magnetic indicator.
ROC: rate of climb.
ROD: rate of descent.
RPM, rpm: revolutions per minute.
RPT: regular public transport.
RWY: runway.
SARTIME: time after which search begins.
SARWATCH: monitoring of a flight to activate emergency services if not cancelled by a specified time.
SIGMET: significant weather warning.
SMC: surface movement control – the aerodrome traffic control agency for all ground operations, including vehicles.
TAF: terminal area forecast.
TAS: true airspeed.
TR: track over the ground.
TWR: control tower.
Unicom: universal communications, a secondary function of some CTAF frequencies.
USG: US gallon.
UTC: universal coordinated time – same as GMT or Z.
VFG: Visual Flight Guide (a compendium of useful information for VFR pilots).
VFR: visual flight rules.
VHF: very high frequency – radio.
VMC: visual meteorological conditions – good weather.
VSI: vertical speed indicator – rate of climb or descent indicator in units of hundreds of feet per minute.
VNC: visual navigation chart, scale 1:500,000.
VTC: visual terminal chart, scale 1:250,000.
W/V: wind velocity – direction from and speed.
WAC: World Aeronautical Chart – universal topographical chart – scale of 1:1,000,000.
WX: weather.
XW or, more commonly, X-wind: crosswind.

Units of Measurement

Direction

Heading

Heading is the direction in which the longitudinal axis (the nose) of the aeroplane is pointed. It is usually expressed as a three-figure group with reference to a particular datum, usually *magnetic north*. There are 360 degrees in the full circle. For instance, an aeroplane pointing 45° east of magnetic north has a heading of 045°M. You will become familiar with the *cardinal compass points* of east, south, west and north, being 090, 180, 270 and 360 degrees respectively.

The indicator in figure 3-2 shows a *compass heading* of 188°. Compass heading is what is shown on the instrument (which has small errors). *Magnetic heading* is your actual heading (after correcting for compass errors).

Figure 3-2 Heading indicator.

Bearing & Track

Bearing and track are expressed in the same way as heading. While *heading* is where the aircraft is pointing, *track* is where it is going and *bearing* is the direction to or from a feature or navigation aid. The bearing from a point is also called a *radial*, e.g. the aircraft is on the 180-degree radial. Bearing can also be expressed relative to the nose of the aircraft via the clock code or as a number of degrees.

Runway Direction

Runway direction is rounded off to the nearest 10° and the three-figure group reduced to a two-figure group by deleting the final 0. For instance, a runway with a direction of 038°M would be called Runway 04, and its reciprocal would be called Runway 22.

Relative Position

Relative position, with reference to a pilot sitting in the cockpit, is often expressed using the *clock code*, with 12 o'clock being straight ahead, 3 o'clock 90 degrees to the right, 6 o'clock behind (180 degrees) and 9 o'clock out to the left (270 degrees). For instance, air traffic control could warn you of conflicting traffic using words such as "*Cessna in your right 2 o'clock position travelling right to left, confirm when sighting*". Equally, the bearing to a feature might be 30 degrees right of the nose or on a relative bearing of 030 degrees (relative to the nose of the aircraft – *not 030°M*, which is relative to magnetic north).

Distance, Speed & Velocity (Velocity Includes Both Speed & Direction)

The *unit for distance* for en route navigation is the *nautical mile*, which is a traditional navigational unit. It is equivalent to 1,852 metres. The *unit for speed* is the *knot* – one knot being one nautical mile per hour. *Wind velocity* is described in terms of the direction from which the wind is blowing and its speed in knots. For instance, a wind velocity of 020°/30 is a wind blowing from direction 020° at a speed of 30 kt. *Visibility* (how far we can see) is expressed in metres, for distances less than 5,000 m, and kilometres, for longer distances. Runway length is expressed in metres. For instance, Runway 36 might have a length of 1,300 m and the visibility might be 8 km, the wind might be 23 kt and the airfield might be 10 nm away. You may have 190 litres of fuel and require a 2, 000 ft runway to land safely! Be very careful with units of measurement.

Vertical Distance

The unit for vertical distance is the *foot,* which is approximately one-third of a metre. There are very specific meanings for terms relating to vertical distance above a particular reference level (datum).

- *Altitude* is the vertical distance of the aircraft *above mean sea level (QNH is set).*
- *Elevation* is the vertical distance of the aerodrome reference *above mean sea level.*
- *Height* is the vertical distance of the aircraft *above the ground.* This is called *above ground level* (AGL) or *above aerodrome level* (AAL) depending on the reference. The aircraft's altitude minus the airfield elevation gives the height of the aircraft above the airfield.

On aeronautical charts the elevation of all objects (terrain, hills and permanent masts, etc) is expressed as AMSL (above mean sea level). An aircraft at an altitude of 1,200 ft AMSL (QNH set) is 1,100 ft above terrain that has an elevation of 100 ft. It is 1,100 ft above ground level (AGL). The local ground or aerodrome level is used as the datum. If an obstruction is less than 100 m high above ground it may not appear on the WAC.

The same reference, AAL, is also used for cloudbase in an aerodrome forecast to show how much clearance there is between the cloud and the ground. In an area forecast (ARFOR), the cloud levels are AMSL, however, because the aircraft will be flying with reference to AMSL (i.e. on area QNH altimeter setting).

Time

Universal Time

The time reference used in aviation is *coordinated universal time* (UTC), also known as *Greenwich mean time* (GMT) and abbreviated as *Zulu time* (Z). The reference is the actual time at the Royal Observatory in Greenwich, Greater London, which is also the reference for world navigation (the zero meridian).

Local Time

Local time is the time on your watch or TV news program. *Eastern Standard Time* (EST) is 10 hours ahead of Zulu time. Local time varies according to state and season (see page 411).

Flight Times

Various times and time intervals are used for both flight and in-flight times:

- *airborne time* is the time from takeoff to touchdown (also called *flightswitch* or *airswitch*);
- *engine running time* is used for maintenance schedules; and
- *estimated elapsed time* (EET) is the estimated time to complete a leg of a flight.

Also used are *estimated time of arrival* (ETA), *actual time of arrival* (ATA), *estimated time of departure* (ETD) and *actual time of departure* (ATD).

Time Coding

Time is usually expressed as a four-figure group based on the 24-hour clock or locally as minutes past the hour. For instance, if the present standard time in Greenwich, England, is 8:12 am (GMT, UTC or Zulu), then the time in Zulu time all around the world is 0812Z (*zero eight one two, Zulu*). Within a local area, time will be simply expressed in two digits, e.g. *time, two seven*, representing minutes only past the hour.

Date can be brought into it also, using an eight-figure group if you want to mention the month as well as the day and time, or as a six-figure group if the month is not relevant. For instance, December 25 at 1542Z could be written as 12251542Z (the 12th month, 25th day, 15th hour and 42nd minute UTC) or, without the month, as 251542Z.

Weight/Mass

The standard unit for weight is the *kilogram* (kg), but you may see the term *pound* (lb) used in American books. 1 kg is 2.2 lb. You will have to convert fuel quantity to weight (litres to kilograms) for performance calculations.

Temperature

Degrees Celsius (°C) are the standard units for temperature, but you may see *degrees Fahrenheit* (°F) used in American books. The freezing point of water (at standard pressure) is 0°C (which equals +32°F) and the boiling point of water at standard pressure is 100°C (which equals 212°F). The Celsius scale has 100 units to the Fahrenheit scale of 180 units.

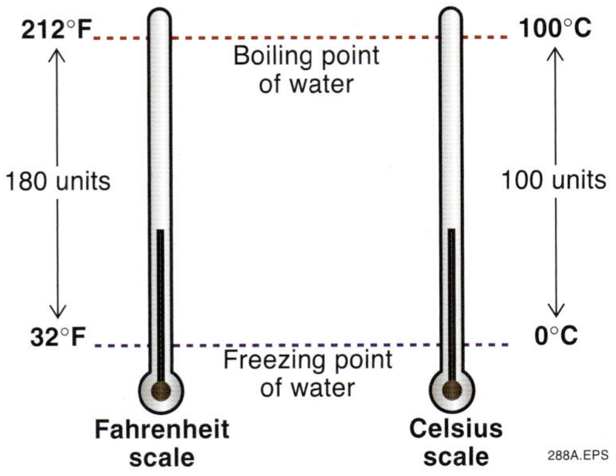

Figure 3-3
Fahrenheit and Celsius temperature scales.

Pressure

The standard unit for atmospheric pressure is the *hectopascal* (hPa) used on meteorological charts and heard on the automatic terminal information service (ATIS) which is a recorded broadcast of current aerodrome information.

Inches of mercury (in. Hg) is used in the US for atmospheric pressure. It is also used for engine manifold pressure (power set by the throttle) on engines with constant-speed propellers. Tyre pressures are expressed in pounds per square inch (psi) or kilopascals (kPa).

Fuel/Oil Volume

The standard unit for fuel quantity is the *litre*, but you may also see the term *US gallon* (USG) used on fuel gauges in American-built aeroplanes. You may also encounter *Imperial gallons*, as previously used in British Commonwealth countries. Nowadays, litres are in standard use for fuel quantities in most parts of the world except the US where it is still US gallons. 1 USG = 3.8 litres.

To convert volume to weight, you need to know the specific gravity (SG) of the fluid. AVGAS has a specific gravity of 0.71, i.e. one litre weighs 0.71 kg. Oil quantity may be measured in US quarts (quarter gallons).

Rules of Thumb

Conversion Factors

To Convert	To	Multiply by
Celsius	Fahrenheit	1.8 and add 32
centimetres	inches	0.394
feet	metres	0.305
Fahrenheit	Celsius	Subtract 32 and multiply by $^5/_9$ (0.556)
horse power	kilowatts	0.7458
Imperial gallons	US gallons	1.200
Imperial gallons	litres	4.546
inches	centimetres	2.540
kilograms	pounds	2.205
kilometres	nautical miles	0.539
kilometres	statute miles	0.621
kilopascals	pound/square inch	0.145
litres	Imperial gallons	0.220
litres	US gallons	0.264
metres	feet	3.281
metres	yards	1.094
pounds	kilograms	0.454
pounds/square inch	kilopascals	6.895
nautical miles	kilometres	1.853
nautical miles	metres	1853
nautical miles	statute miles	1.151
statute miles	kilometres	1.609
statute miles	nautical miles	0.868
US gallons	Imperial gallons	0.833
US gallons	litres	3.79
yards	metres	0.914

Table 3-1 Conversion factors.

Metric/Imperial

To convert	To	Do the following	Example
millimetres	inches	Multiply by 4 and divide by 100	25 mm × 4 = 100 ÷ 100 = 1 in
metres	feet	Multiply by 3 and add 10% of the result	300 metres = 900 + 90 = 990 ft
kilograms	pounds	Multiply by 2 and add 10%	200 kg = 400 + 40 = 440 lb

Table 3-2 Converting metric to imperial.

Temperature

To Convert	To	Do the following	Example
Celsius	Fahrenheit	Double it and add 30 for temperatures below 20°C; double it and add 25 for temperatures above 20°C:	15°C = (15 × 2) + 30 = 60°F (actual is 59°F) 25°C = (25 × 2) + 25 = 75°F (actual is 77°F).
Fahrenheit	Celsius	Subtract 30 and half for temperatures below 70°F; subtract 25 and half for temperatures above 70°F:	60°F = (60 – 30) ÷ 2 = 15°F (actual is 15.5°C) 85°F = (85 – 25) ÷ 2 = 30°F (actual is 33.3°C).

Table 3-3 Temperature conversions.

Time/Distance/Speed

- 60 kt groundspeed is 1 nm/minute – so time equals distance.
- 90 kt is 1½ nm/minute so multiply distance by ⅔ to find time to go.
- 120 kt is 2 nm/minute so divide distance by 2 to find time.
- 150 kt is 2½ nm/minute – instead of trying to divide by 2½, multiply distance by 4 and divide by 10 to find time, e.g. 40 nm will take (40 × 4) ÷ 10 = 160 ÷ 10 = 16 minutes.
- 180 kt is 3 nm/minute.

Specific Gravities

The specific gravity of a liquid is effectively the weight in kilograms of one litre of that liquid:

- Water 1.0.
- AVGAS 0.71.
- AVTUR 0.8.
- Oil 0.89.

Ball-Park Figures

Always do a rough mental check to keep the electronics honest:

- 1 USG is roughly 4 litres.
- 1 litre of AVGAS is roughly ¾ kg.
- 1 USG of AVGAS weighs roughly 3 kg.
- 1 nm is roughly 2 km.
- 60 kt is roughly 100 ft per second.
- 1 metre is roughly 3 ft plus 10 percent (1 metre = 3.3 ft; 100 metres = 300 + 30 ft = 330 ft).
- 1 kt is roughly 2 kph (actually 1.8) and roughly ⅔ metre per second.
- 90 kt is roughly 45 metres per second:

$$\frac{45\text{m/s} \times 60\text{ s} \times 60\text{ min}}{1{,}000} = 162\text{ kph}$$

$$\text{and } \frac{162}{1.8} = 90\text{ kt}$$

Review 3

Pre-Solo Level of Knowledge

1. What is meant by the symbol α (*alpha*)?
2. What is a maintenance release and why is it vital to flight safety?
3. What are the *numbers*?
4. Define the following abbreviations: ASI, IAS, VFR, VMC, VSI, CFI, RPM, MAP, AVGAS and GFPT.
5. What is magnetic north?

BAK Level of Knowledge

6. What is meant by the symbol β (*beta*)?
7. Define the term *wake turbulence*.
8. Define the following abbreviations: AMSL, TAS, NDB, LAME, NOTAM, VTC, WAC, CAVOK and AGL.
9. What is a radial?

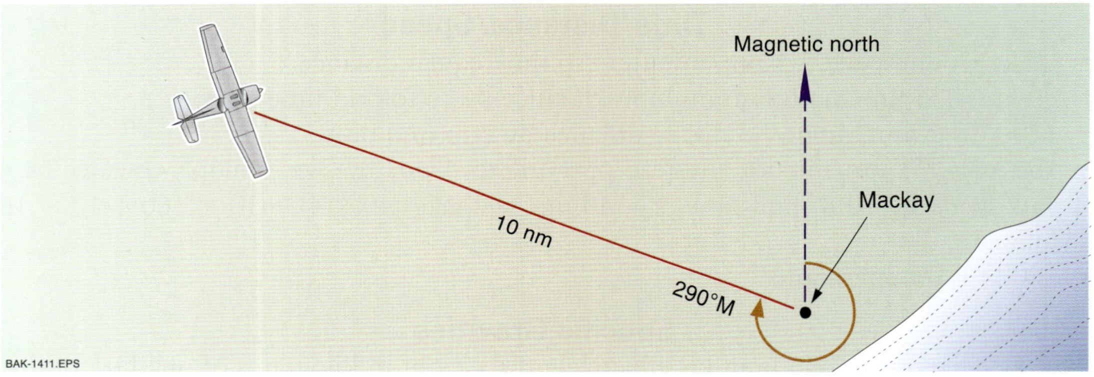

10. The difference between true north and magnetic north is called . . . . .
11. What significance does this difference have?
12. What is the time difference between Australian EST and UTC?
13. What is Zulu time?
14. What is the difference between altitude and height?
15. What is groundspeed?
16. What is drift?
17. What is the specific gravity of AVGAS?

4 - Aircraft General Knowledge

Aviation
Theory
Centre

Airframe Structure

Primary Structure

The primary structure of the aircraft (the *airframe*) includes the *cockpit* and *cabin*, the *wings*, the *tail assembly*, the *engine compartment(s)*, and the *fuselage* which joins it all together.

Ultimately, the purpose of the structure is to transfer the lift from the wings to support the weight of the structure and load, and to protect its payload (passengers and cargo). As well as the forces caused by the lift (both lifting and twisting), it has to have strength in reserve for turbulence, wind gusts and air currents (thermals). It also has to carry the thrust from the propeller to pull the aircraft through the air (via the *prop shaft*, *engine*, *engine mounts* and *airframe structure*). The *tail surfaces* are attached to provide stability. The *control surfaces* allow the pilot to override the stability to change the flightpath of the aircraft. On the ground the airframe is supported by the *undercarriage*.

The airframe has to provide both strength and stiffness. When the control surfaces are deflected by the pilot, the air loads try to twist the wing. This force is carried by the internal structure or by external bracing wires. In very early aircraft, this twisting of the wings was used to roll the aircraft, but ailerons later proved more effective.

Figure 4-1
The structure of the aircraft is called the airframe.

The configuration of the airframe can take two primary forms. The first form is the very common aluminium or composite fibreglass structure with a main spar inside the wing, enclosed fuselage and no external bracing wires – although some high-wing aircraft have a bracing strut between the wing and the fuselage.

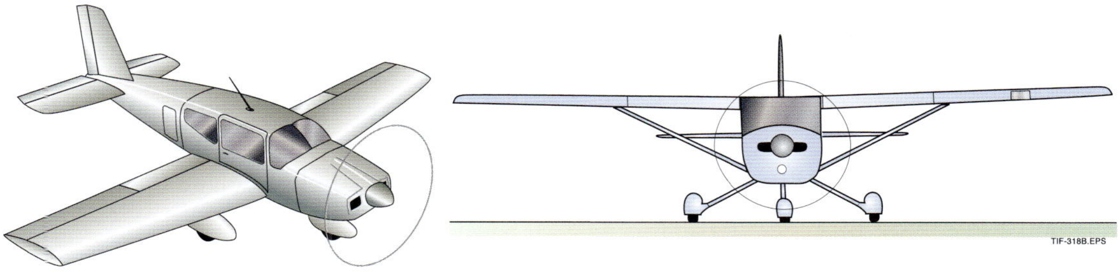

Figure 4-2 Low wing and high wing with struts.

The second form is a fabric-covered structure where the skin only carries the lift from the air and does not contribute to the strength and stiffness of the primary structure. This type will usually have some external bracing wires and struts.

Figure 4-3 Drifter.

Figure 4-4 Fabric covered structure.

For aerodynamic and engineering reasons (a compromise between low drag, stability, control and ease of manufacture), the tail may be placed ahead of the wing (a *canard*) or behind.

There may be one or more wing sets – these may be above and below or ahead and behind.

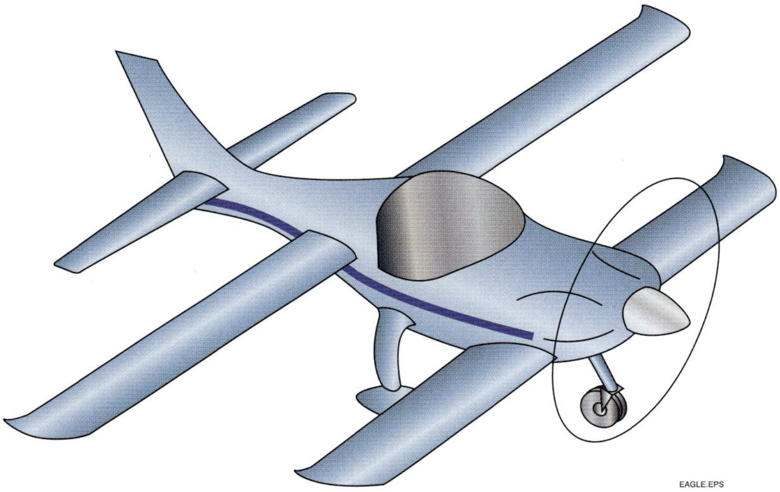

Figure 4-5 Multiple lifting surfaces.

The engine may be positioned to push the aircraft or to pull the aircraft along (in both cases it moves because the propeller pushes the air rearwards), there could be one or more engines (or none in the case of a glider), and it may have a single fuselage or booms, or a totally open fuselage structure.

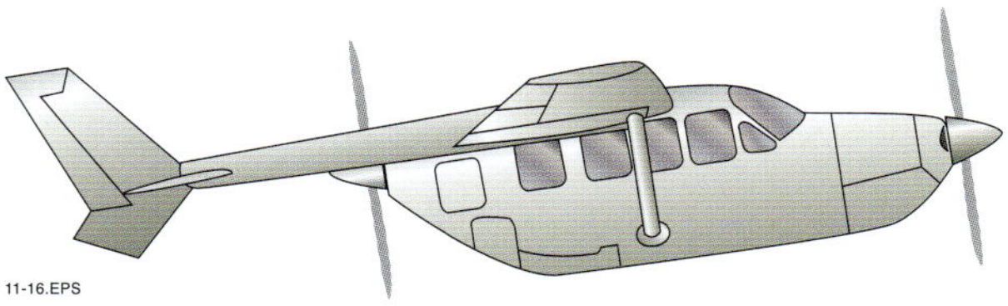

Figure 4-6 Tandem engines, centreline thrust.

Figure 4-7 Pusher propeller.

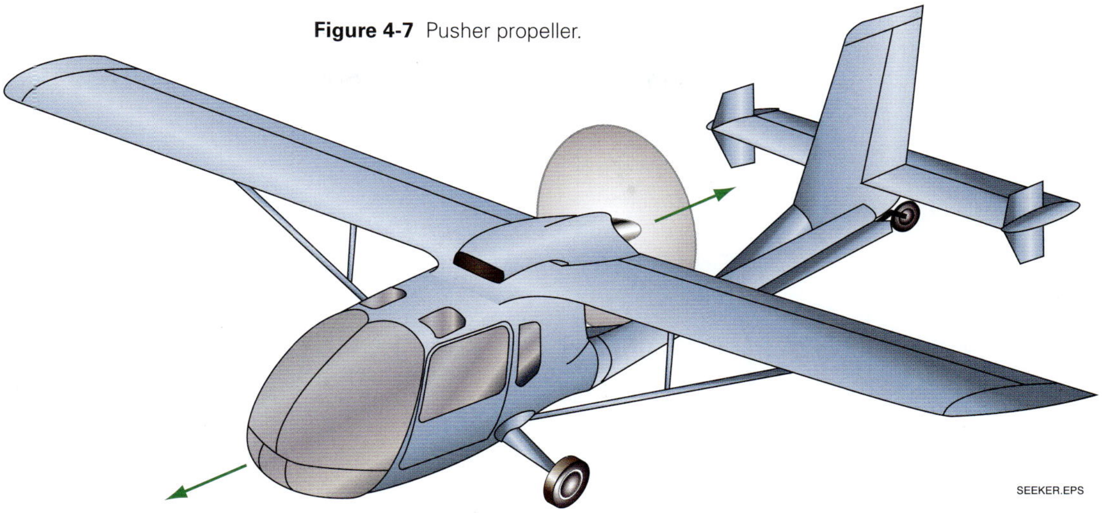

The wings may be mounted on the top, middle or bottom of the fuselage and they may be straight, tapered, square shaped, long and slim or short and deep.

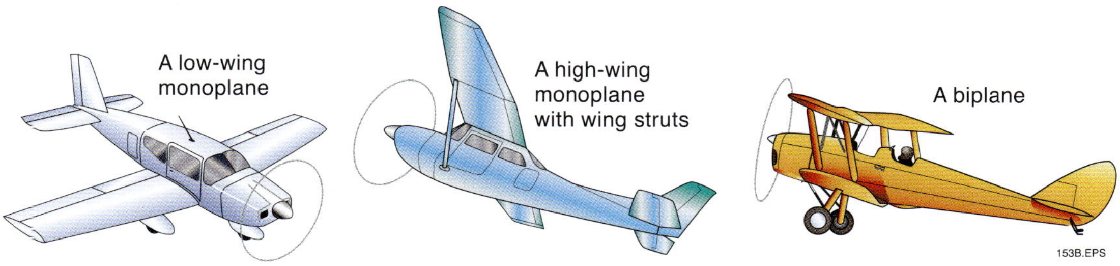

Figure 4-8 Low- and high-wing monoplanes and a biplane.

Each structure has advantages and disadvantages depending on the purpose and flight envelope (speed, altitude and range) of the aircraft. Let's look more closely at two types:

- the aluminium (or composite) structure of a typical general aviation (GA) aircraft; and
- the externally braced, fabric-covered structure of the antique or ultralight aircraft.

The structure which has no external bracing usually uses the skin to carry some of the bending and twisting forces. This is called a *monocoque* structure. However, like an aluminium drink can, it is easily weakened by any slight damage to the skin and so it is generally supported by some internal structure. In the case of the wing, this is called the *main spar* and there may be several additional *spars* and external *struts*.

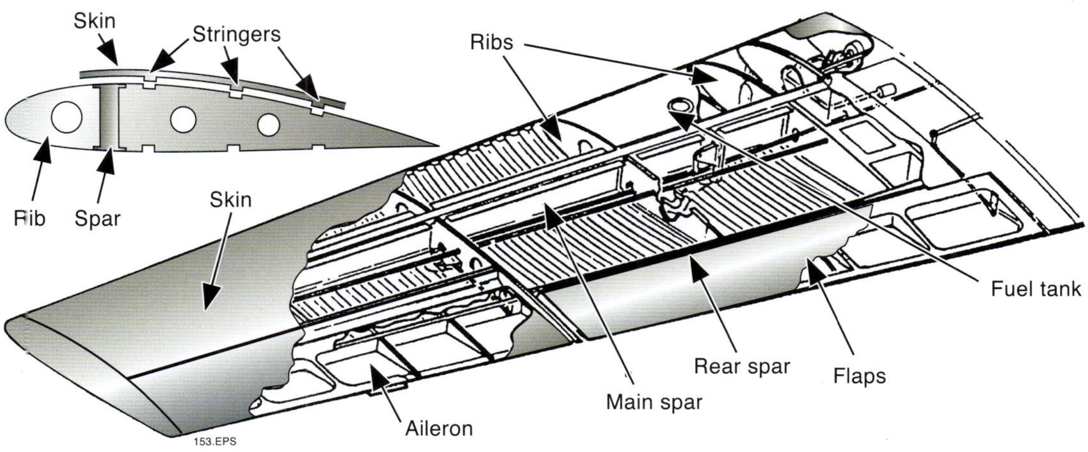

Figure 4-9 Spars, ribs and stringers in the wing.

In the fuselage there will be *frames* and *longerons* together with an *outer, load-bearing skin*. This structure is a *semi-monocoque*, stressed-skin construction.

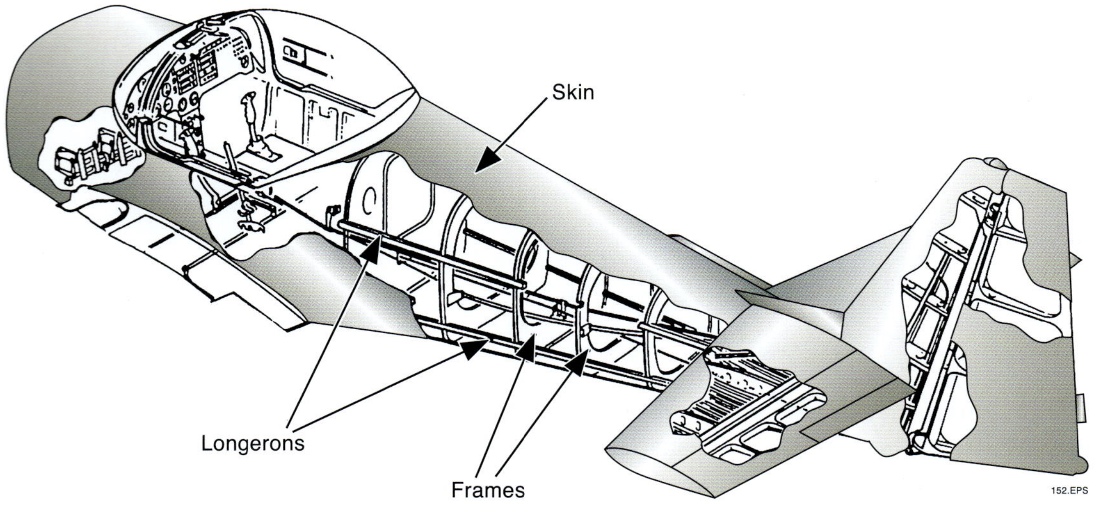

Figure 4-10 Semi-monocoque construction.

The *composite* material may be a plastic foam, shell, or honeycomb-filled to increase strength and rigidity. The structure is designed to allow some flexing as a rigid structure will transfer every bump to the cabin and is very uncomfortable for the passengers. (Ever looked at the wing of a Jumbo during take-off? It flexes to absorb the loads.)

In the case of the externally braced structure, the skeleton carries all of the loads and so has to be stronger and heavier than the stressed skin construction. It is easier to de-rig for storage and it is easier and cheaper to manufacture and to repair however. It is also vulnerable to damage and rigging error. It is an unacceptable risk to fly with any damaged, corroded, frayed, stretched or missing cables as the loading can be disproportionately high and a catastrophic failure may result. The externally braced structure also has the penalty of extra drag due to the struts and cables. There are two types of *external bracing*:

- the *flying wires* or struts which carry the flight loads; and
- the *landing wires* which carry the weight of the structure on the ground, any negative g-loads or gusts and ground loads due to taxiing, take-off and landing.

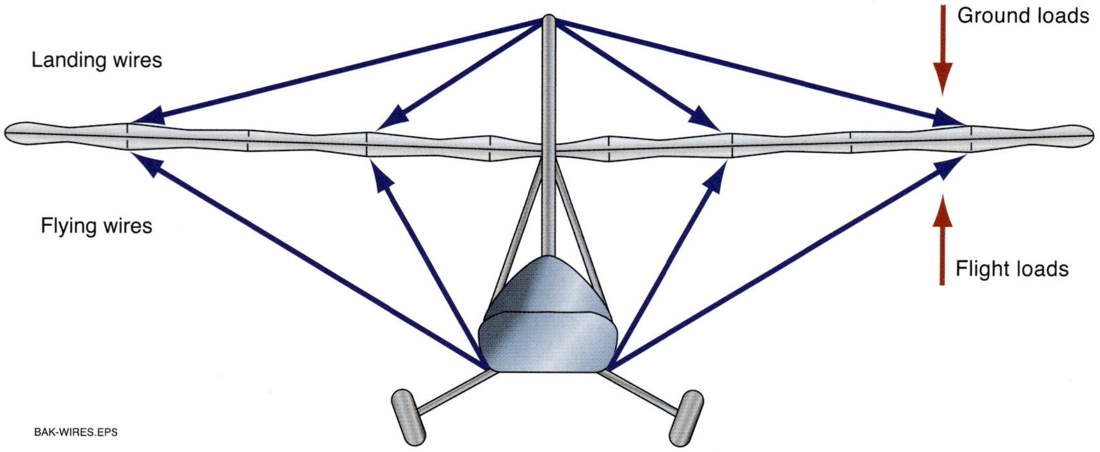

Figure 4-11 External bracing wires.

For normal flight, the flying wires carry the loads. In some aircraft the wires are actually finely shaped metal aerofoils. Have you looked closely at the rigging of the beautiful De Havilland Tiger Moth?

Rigger's Angle of Incidence

The wing and the tailplane are set at a specific angle to the axis of the fuselage. The angle is called the *rigger's angle of incidence.* This angle is critical and must not be altered.

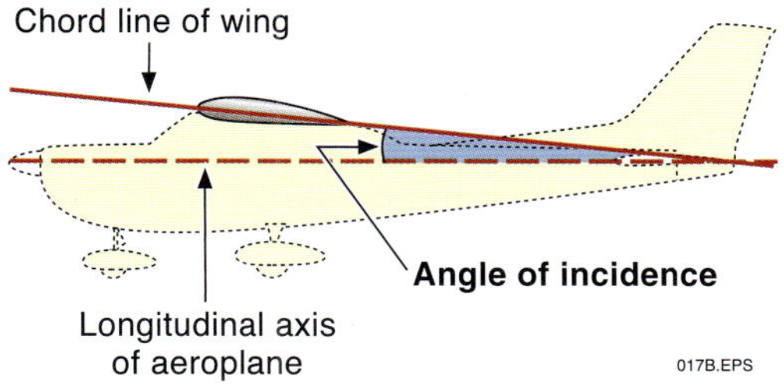

Figure 4-12
Rigger's angle of incidence.

Flight Controls

The flight control system includes the control surfaces (*ailerons*, *elevator* and *rudder*), the cockpit controls (*control column* and *rudder pedals*) and all of the *linkages* between them.

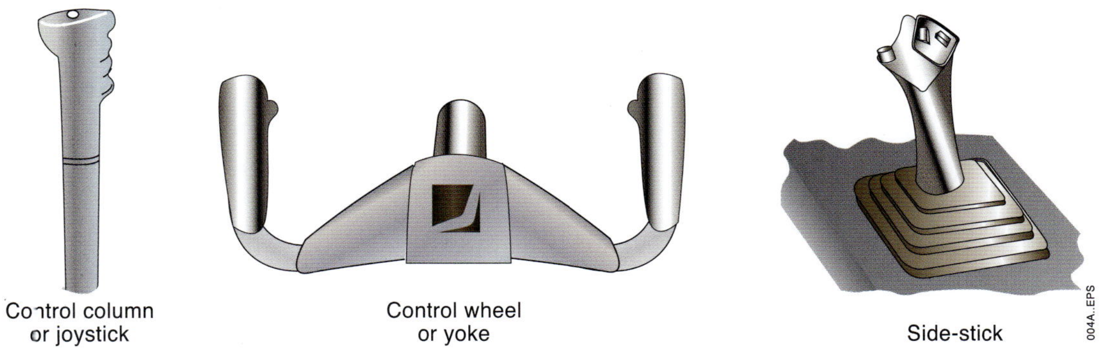

Figure 4-13 Types of control columns.

The control surfaces on most modern light aircraft are all metal or composite fibre. Many older aircraft, ultralights and aerobatic aircraft use fabric-covered control surfaces to reduce mass and to improve balancing. The linkages are by means of cables and pulleys or rigid push–pull rods. The system will include an elevator trim system and perhaps rudder trim.

The control surfaces are designed to tolerate aerodynamic loads that try to keep them *streamlined.* They are vulnerable to reverse loads caused by wind gusts on the ground. There may be *control locks* to protect the system when the aircraft is parked, but it is important to restrain the controls at all times when on the ground. Sometimes the seat harness can be used, or if taxiing, hold the controls firmly by hand.

You can survive almost any eventuality in flight if you can retain control of the aircraft's flightpath. For this reason, the flight control system is the most important element of each and every preflight inspection. Have them checked also after any flight where the flight controls may have been subjected to higher than normal, or reverse, loads.

Tailplane

The *tailplane* may be fitted with a hinged, one- or two-piece *elevator*, or the whole tailplane may pivot on two bearings. This surface is called a *stabilator* or *all moving tail*.

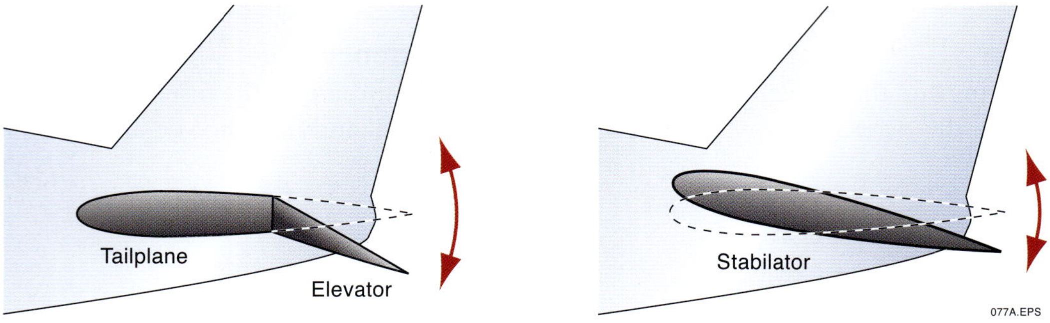

Figure 4-14 (Left) Fixed tailplane and moving elevator and (right) stabilator.

Flaps

There are various designs for *flaps*; each has particular advantages.

Figure 4-15 Flaps.

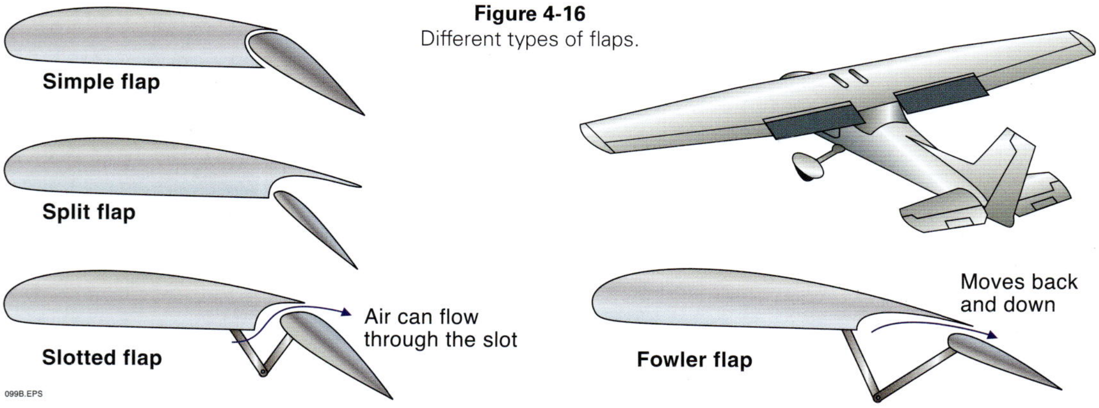

Figure 4-16
Different types of flaps.

Undercarriage

The *undercarriage* allows movement of the aircraft on the ground. It will be either a *tricycle* configuration with the nosewheel at the front (*trike*) or a *tailwheel* configuration with two mainwheels and a smaller tailwheel. The nosewheel may be steerable via the rudder pedals, while the tailwheel will castor with the rudder or side loads. The tailwheel will probably have a centring spring. The trike is easier to control especially in a crosswind, but the nosewheel is vulnerable to damage on rough surfaces. The tailwheel undercarriage has less weight and less drag.

The undercarriage is chosen according to the role of the aircraft. Agricultural and aerobatic aircraft will generally have tailwheel undercarriages and touring or training aircraft a tricycle configuration. The design of the undercarriage is critical as it has to match the landing attitude of the aircraft. The mainwheels of the taildragger must be of sufficient length to allow the aircraft to touch down at the landing attitude without landing tailwheel first.

The Slepcev Storch, which has slats to allow the slowest possible touchdown speed, has to have very long legs to allow the aircraft to touch down on all wheels at the highest possible landing attitude equating to the lowest possible landing speed.

Figure 4-17 Slepcev Storch.

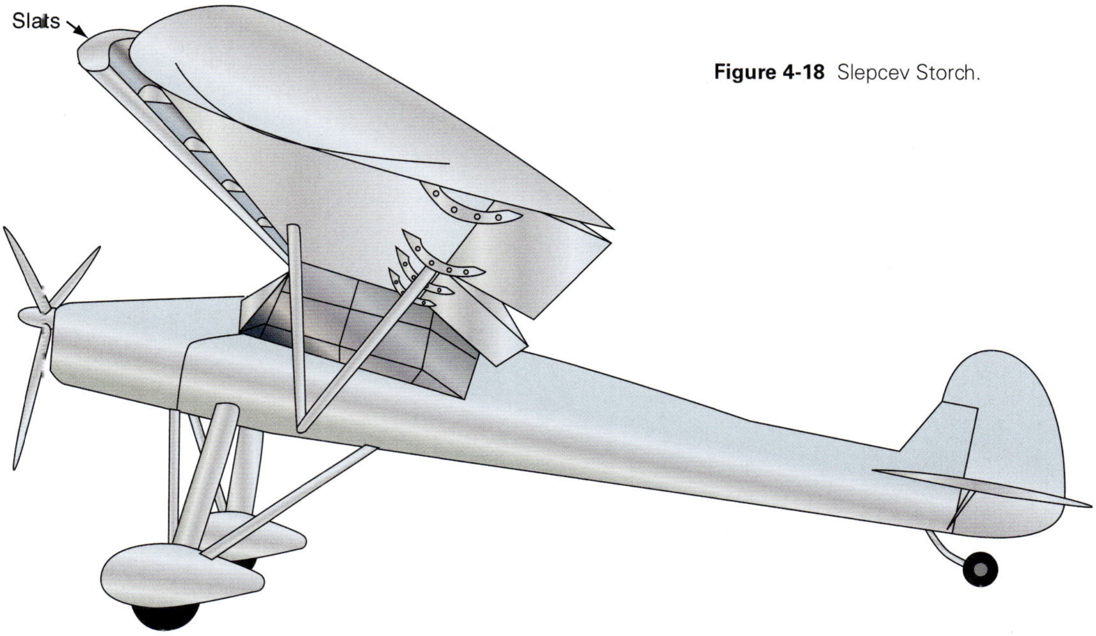

Figure 4-18 Slepcev Storch.

Conversely, the nosewheel of the trike is equally critical. If the leg is too extended or the landing speed is excessive (especially with full flap) then the nosewheel will touch down first and *wheelbarrowing* may occur. Under these circumstances directional control is difficult and the nosewheel may even collapse. This is another reason why correct landing speed is so important.

Figure 4-19 Wheelbarrowing.

Brakes

The brakes will be *mechanically* or *hydraulically* operated. They are *differential* (left or right or both) to assist with manoeuvring in strong winds or tight spaces. They are operated through toe pedals. The park brake is symmetrical and operated by a lever or valve.

To operate the rudder pedals:

- place your feet on the floor; and
- slide one foot forward.

To operate the brakes:

- place feet on the pedal; and
- depress the toes.

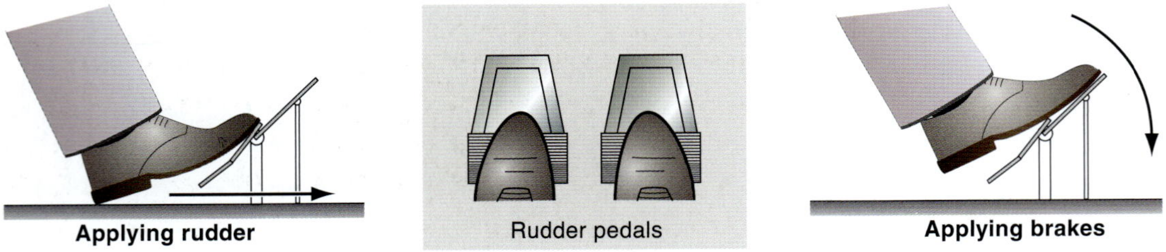

Figure 4-20 Using rudder and toe brakes.

The tyres are pneumatic (filled with air or nitrogen). The tyre pressure is important, as soft or deflated tyres can add considerably to friction on the ground, seriously extend the take-off distance and affect steering. The undercarriage transfers ground loads to the aircraft's structure and this can be an area for regular maintenance and inspection.

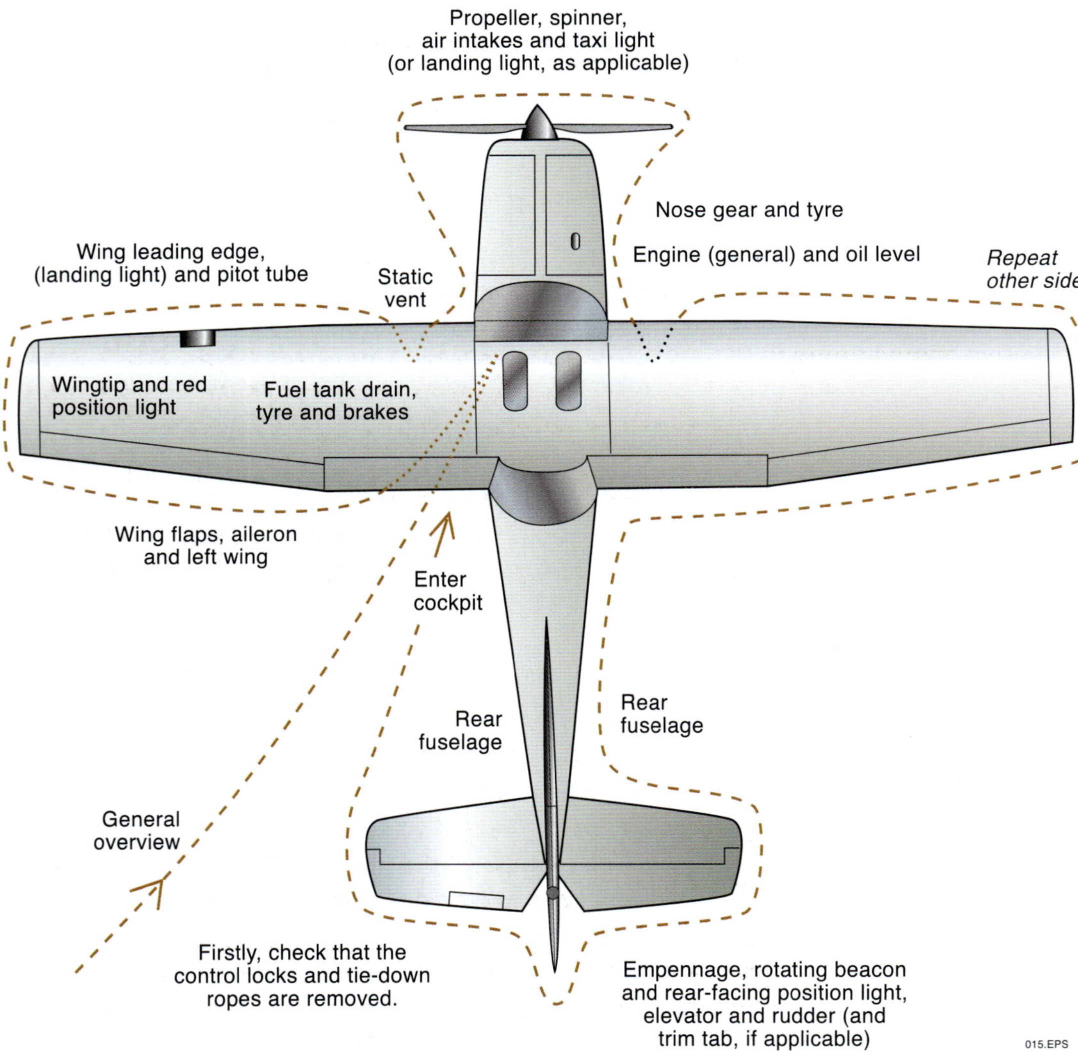

Figure 4-21 A typical walkaround for the external check.

Aircraft Propulsion

The aircraft is propelled by the *engine–propeller* combination. The engine is sometimes called the *powerplant*. High-speed aircraft use *gas turbine* (jet) engines. Smaller aircraft use *piston* engines (like a motor vehicle). The piston engine could be:

- four-stroke petrol;
- two-stroke petrol;
- four-stroke diesel; or
- two-stroke diesel.

Figure 4-22 Radial engine.

We will focus on the more common four-stroke petrol engine.

There have been many engine configurations tried in the search for greater power and fuel efficiency, and reduced weight and drag. Some were aircooled and some were liquid cooled. Some had many cylinders. Some had few. Some pushed. Some pulled.

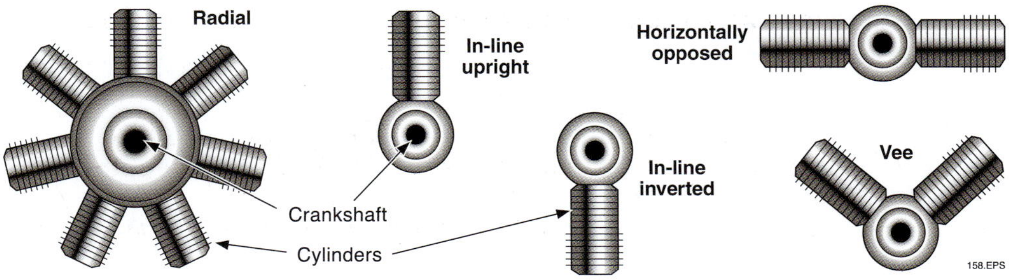

Figure 4-23 Common cylinder layouts in aircraft engines.

The Four-Stroke Engine

The usual engine found in the modern light aeroplane is a petrol-burning, air-cooled, reciprocating (up-and-down) piston engine, with the cylinders (4, 6 or 8 of them) laid out in a horizontally opposed manner. For these standard US engines, the propeller rotates in a clockwise direction when viewed from the cockpit.

Figure 4-24 Six cylinder engine.

Basic Principles of the Piston Engine

The reciprocating engine has a number of cylinders within which pistons move up and down (hence the name *reciprocating* engine as distinct from a *rotary* engine). In each cylinder a fuel–air mixture is burned, the heat energy causing the gases to expand increasing the pressure and push the piston down the cylinder. A two-stage energy conversion process is therefore involved, whereby chemical energy (in the fuel) is converted to heat energy in the cylinder, and then finally converted to mechanical energy via the action of the piston.

The piston is connected by a rod to a crankshaft, which it turns. This connecting rod converts the up-and-down motion of the piston into a rotary motion of the *crankshaft*, which transmits the power generated by the engine to the propeller.

Advantage of boxer engine : light and small

Most light aeroplanes have the propeller directly coupled to the crankshaft, that is, the crankshaft is also the propeller shaft. The speed of rotation in revolutions per minute (rpm) is indicated in the cockpit on the *tachometer.* The propeller produces the thrust force necessary for powered flight. The pilot can alter the power output of the engine by moving the *throttle lever.*

- The *piston* moving within the cylinder forms one of the walls of the combustion chamber. The piston has rings which seal the piston in the cylinder, preventing any loss of power around the sides of the piston and passage of the oil into the combustion chamber.
- The *crankshaft* and *connecting rod* change the straight-line motion of the piston to a rotary turning motion. The crankshaft also absorbs the power from all the cylinders and transfers it to the propeller.
- The *connecting rod* forms a link between the piston and the crankshaft.
- An *inlet valve* lets the fuel–air mixture into the cylinder.
- The *cylinder* forms part of the chamber in which the fuel–air mixture is compressed and burned.
- An *exhaust valve* lets exhaust gases out of the cylinder after the combustion process.
- *Spark plugs* ignite the compressed fuel–air mixture.

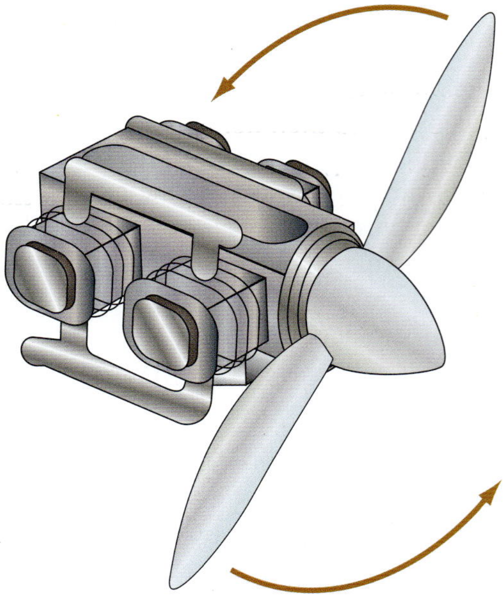

Figure 4-25 The engine drives the propeller.

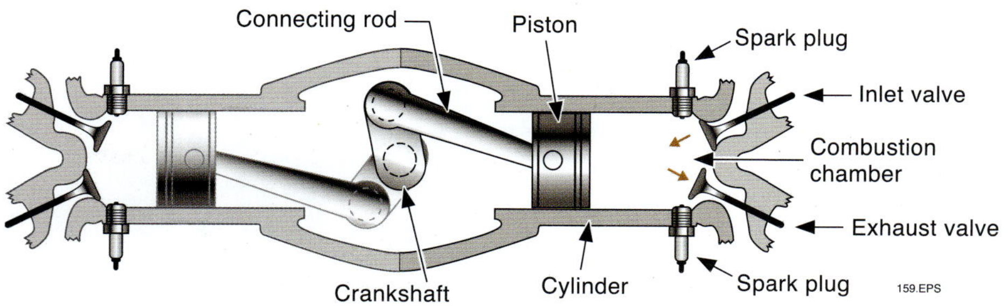

Figure 4-26 Basic parts of an opposed reciprocating engine.

The throttle lever is connected directly to a *butterfly valve* in the *carburettor,* and when pushed forward, it progressively opens the butterfly valve allowing more air into the inlet manifold. The extra airflow sucks more fuel from the main jet, and the increase in the fuel–air mixture causes a power increase. The more forward, the more power, the more rapid the movement, the more sudden the increase – but the engine may hesitate. In the case of a fixed-pitch propeller, an increase in power shows as an rpm increase on the tachometer. Engines fitted with a variable-pitch propeller have a manifold pressure gauge, like the vacuum gauge in some cars, which would show an increase in *manifold absolute pressure* (MAP). It is now more usual to refer to this as *manifold pressure* (MP). Manifold pressure is measured in inches of mercury (in. Hg). When MP increases, the increased airflow also increases the fuel flow, and the engine power increases. The engine rpm is kept constant by the propeller's governor mechanism, but the thrust is increased because the propeller blade angle is increased and it can now *bite* more air.

One complete cycle of the four-stroke engine comprises four strokes of the piston travelling within the cylinder. A stroke is one movement of the piston from the top to bottom of its travel or vice versa. The four-stroke cycle includes four movements: down, up, down and then up. These four movements make one complete cycle – and then the next cycle begins. Hence the name of *four-stroke* engine (four strokes in one cycle).

The German engineer, Nicholas Otto, developed this engine so the four-stroke cycle is also known as the *Otto cycle*. The four strokes are called the following:

- *intake* (or *induction*) (down);
- *compression* (up);
- *power* (or *expansion*) (down); and
- *exhaust* (up).

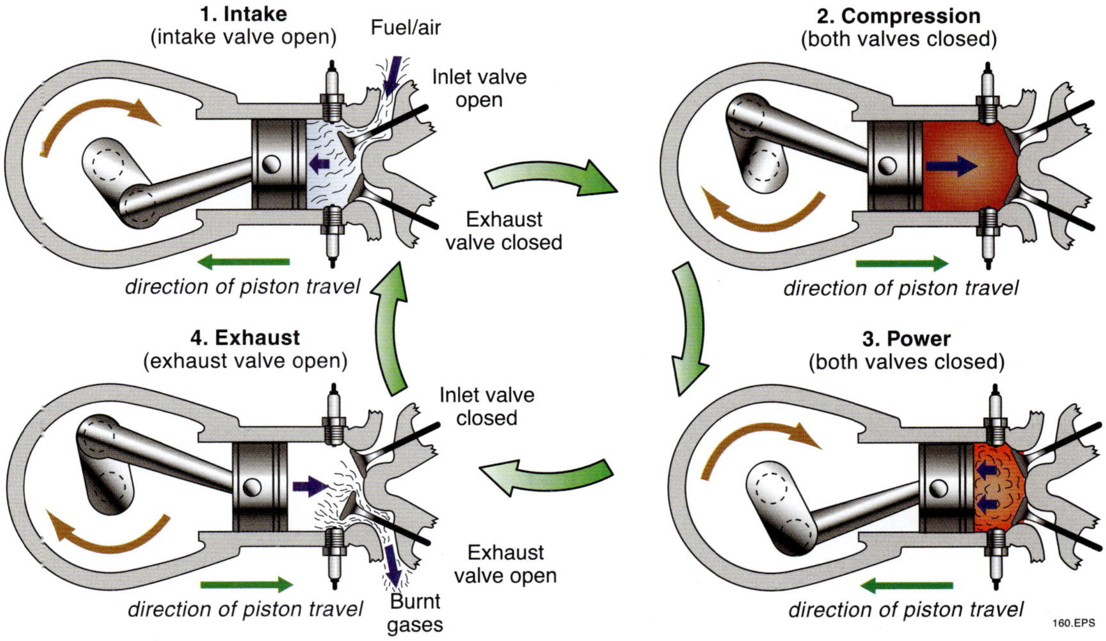

Figure 4-27 The four-stroke cycle.

The four strokes form a complete cycle which then becomes continuous – intake, compression, power, exhaust, intake, compression, etc. This is happening within each cylinder. Modern aircraft engines use the *modified Otto cycle*, which adjusts both the ignition timing and the valve timing to achieve a higher and more reliable power output from the engine. The valve timing is achieved through provision of a *camshaft*, which opens the inlet and exhaust valves at the best time to allow increased fuel–air induction and improved exhaust. The ignition starts about 25° *before top dead centre* (BTDC) and the peak pressure is made to occur about 30° *after top dead centre* (ATDC). This gives the optimum angle for the piston and connecting rod to push onto the crankshaft. (Note that ignition and valve timing is always referenced to degrees of crankshaft rotation.)

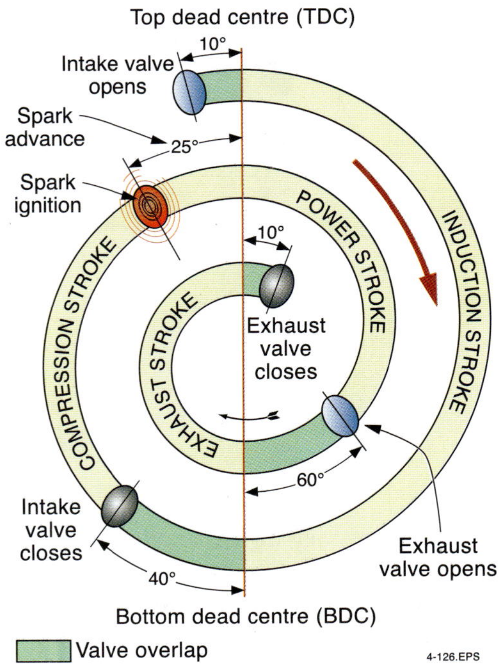

Figure 4-28 Typical valve timing of a four-stroke engine – modified Otto cycle.

Ignition System

The purpose of the ignition system is to provide a spark that will ignite the fuel–air mixture in the combustion chamber at the appropriate moment. This is achieved by producing a high voltage (or high tension) that causes an electric current to jump across the electrodes of the spark plug. The spark is timed to occur just prior to the piston reaching top dead centre (Ý25° BTDC) on the compression stroke. This timing of the spark is vital. It is slightly in advance to enable a controlled flame-front to start moving through the fuel–air mixture that is being compressed in the cylinder on the compression stroke. The burning gases expand and exert a very high pressure on the piston, at about 30° ATDC, to produce the power stroke.

Aircraft engines have dual (independent and parallel) ignition systems with the magneto of each ignition system supplying one of the two spark plugs per cylinder.

Dual ignition systems have the following advantages:

- they offer safety in the event of failure of one ignition system; and
- they result in more efficient fuel combustion when both are active.

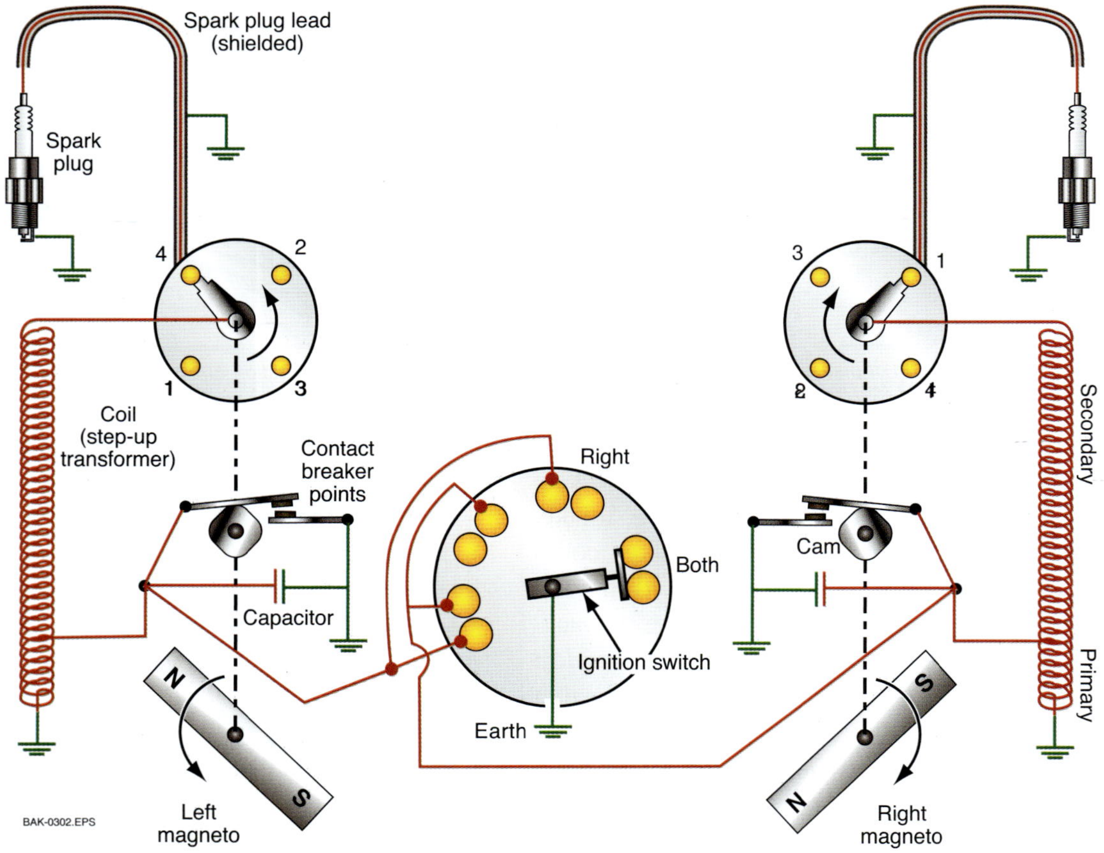

Figure 4-29 Dual ignition system.

The necessary *high-tension* (HT) electrical energy for the spark plugs comes from self-contained generation and distribution units, the *magnetos*, which are totally independent of the battery and the electrical system. Each of the dual ignition systems has its own magneto. The engine mechanically drives the rotating shaft of each magneto. This drive rotates the magnet in the magneto and operates the contact breaker points thus distributing the HT pulse to the correct spark plug at the correct time.

Figure 4-30 Ignition system.

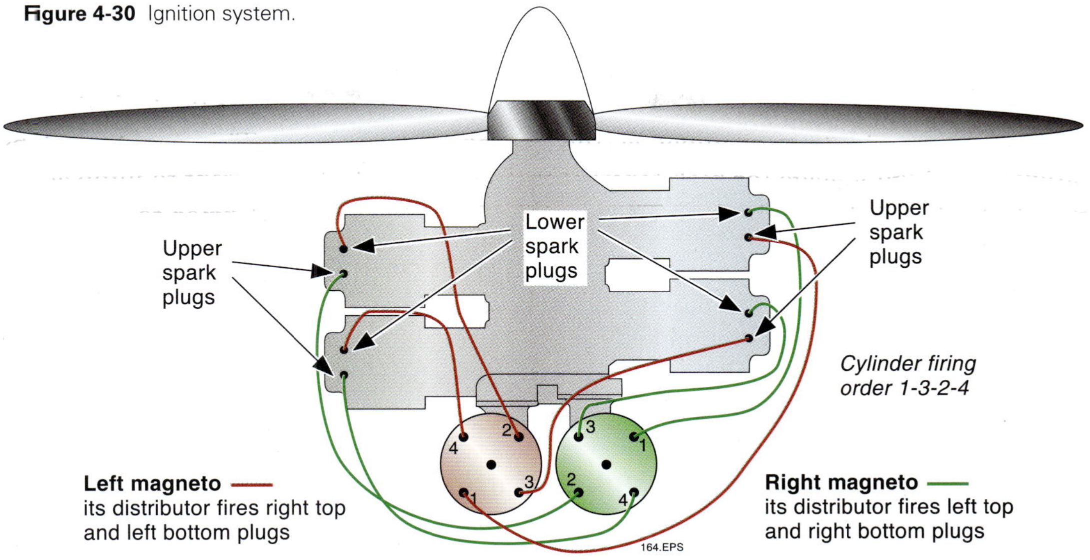

Use of the Ignition Switch Words

Some aeroplanes have separate switches for each magneto, while most modern aeroplanes have rotary switches operated by the ignition key. With these, you can select the left system (L), the right system (R), or both. Both are selected for normal engine operation. Aeroplanes with a separate starter button or key are usually started on the left magneto only.

The engine will run on one magneto, but not as smoothly as on two, and with a slight drop in rpm. With one spark instead of two, there will be only one flame-front advancing through the fuel–air mixture in the cylinder instead of two. This increases the time required for full combustion. Full combustion may not occur as a small part of the mixture is too far away from the spark plug. This reduces combustion efficiency and energy is lost from the engine thereby decreasing the rpm. In flight, an engine temperature increase is noticeable because of the late composition; *rough running* may also occur.

If L is selected, only the left magneto system supplies a spark. The R magneto is grounded (or earthed), that is, its primary current runs to ground and no spark is generated.

Therefore, going from BOTH to L should cause a drop in rpm and possibly slightly less smooth running. If no drop in rpm occurs, then either the R system is still supplying a spark or else the R magneto was not working previously when BOTH was selected.

Figure 4-31
Independent magneto switches.

Figure 4-32 Ignition/start switch.

Ignition Checks

Piston engine aircraft generally have two ignition systems. To check if they are both functioning correctly, you must conduct an ignition or magneto check. This is done by running the engine at a set rpm of 1,500–2,000, depending on what is specified in the pilot's operating handbook for your aircraft. To check a magneto, select one by grounding the other. If you turn the ignition key to R, the right magneto is selected and the left magneto is grounded. A drop in engine rpm will generally occur. This is known as a *mag check* or *mag drop*, and the same is done to the other magneto. If the engine does not run on one of the magnetos or runs roughly, the ignition system is not functioning normally and should be checked. If the engine does not experience a magneto drop, this indicates that the spark plugs or magnetos need to be inspected by an engineer before flight.

Prior to shutdown, the magnetos are checked to ensure that neither of them is still live. This is done by performing a *dead cut*. A dead cut is performed by ensuring the power is barely above idle and moving the ignition momentarily to the off position, noting the engine stops firing, and quickly on. The checking action should be smooth and brief, otherwise excess fuel will lie in the exhaust to be reignited when ignition is back on, causing risk of damage to the exhaust system.

Engine Starting

To start an engine fitted with a magneto ignition system, we simply have to rotate the engine. It is common to use an electrical starter motor powered from the battery. Other methods of providing the rotation include *hand swinging*. Some very small engines have *pull starters*, like a motor mower.

When we rotate the engine for start, it turns at a rate of only 300–400 rpm. This causes us two problems. Firstly, the magnet in the magneto cannot move fast enough to create a strong primary current so the spark is produced is too weak. Secondly, we have the ignition timing set for about 25° BTDC, which is perfect for an engine rotating at 2,400 rpm but much too early for a slow engine. To overcome both these problems, we fit a starting device called an *impulse coupling*. The impulse coupling assists starting by providing:

- a delayed (retarded) spark; and
- a stronger (hotter) spark.

Note: Prolonged use of the starter motor will drain the battery and overheat the starter. If the battery is severely discharged, it can explode. If the battery is weakened, it can no longer provide a back up for the alternator. Prolonged use of the starter motor could also cause it to overheat and possibly ignite. Allow the system to cool for several minutes if the starter has been operated for more than 30 seconds (cumulative total).

Firing Sequence

For all engines, the ignition timing is designed not only to achieve optimum burning in each cylinder, but also to ensure that a certain firing sequence is achieved. This sequence is chosen to minimise vibration, internal stresses and peak loads on the engine mounts and to ensure smooth continuous power.

Horizontally Opposed Engine

For the typical Lycoming four-cylinder horizontally-opposed engine the sequence is 1, 3, 2, 4, and for a six cylinder Continental engine it is 1,6,3,2,5,4.

Note: Lycoming and Continental number their cylinders differently even though the firing sequence is the same.

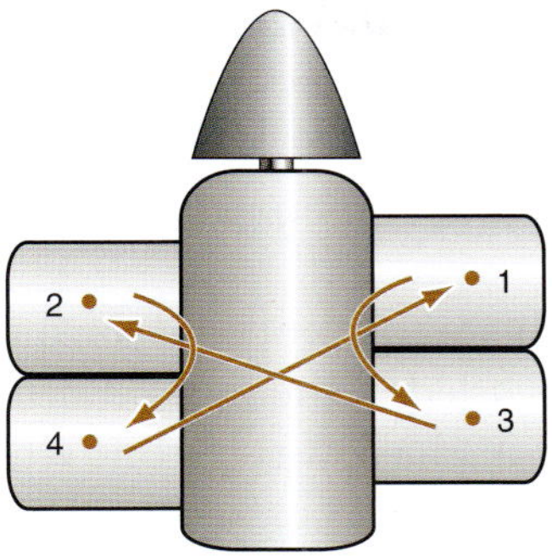

Figure 4-33 Firing sequence - Lycoming four cylinder engine

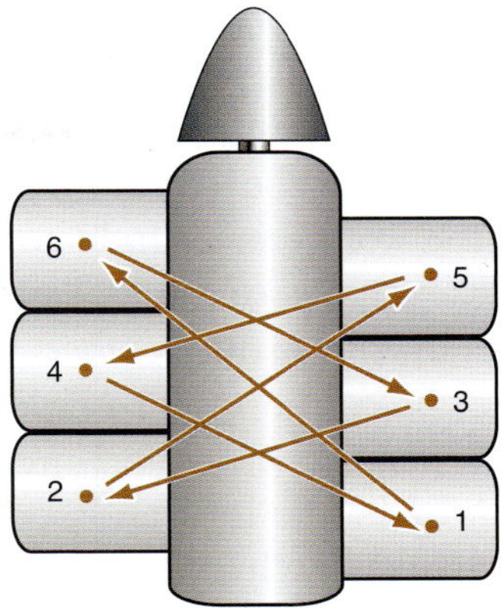

Figure 4-34 Firing sequence - Continental six cylinder engine

Radial Engine

As mentioned earlier, there was another traditional engine layout, the radial, which, for a long time, was out of production. It was common in military and civil aircraft subsequent the time of the rotary engines of WW I to the introduction of the turbo-prop and pure jet engines in the 'fifties and 'sixties. For heavy transport and airline aircraft, the radial continued in service until the new millennium.

Recently, an Australian company, ROTEC, has resurrected the radial as a small engine for homebuilt aircraft. Each engine is a work of art.

Since the radial engine is a conventional petrol, four-stroke engine, we do not need to discuss the strokes and the valve timings. However, the firing order of the cylinders is important.

The radial engine has its cylinders arranged in a circle around a central shaft. There may be one or two rows, or ***banks***, of cylinders. There must be an odd number of cylinders in each row and you will understand why, when we describe the firing order of the cylinders. There is one master connecting rod and several articulated rods. The crank had its centre (big end) offset from the propeller shaft and so exerts a twisting force (torque) to turn the propeller.

The crank turns two full rotations for the four strokes of its four-stroke cycle. The figure shows the top cylinder from the time immediately after the spark plug has ignited the mixture and the cylinder is at TDC.

After the top cylinder, the next cylinder to ignite is two cylinders away and then the next is two cylinders after that. Hence the need for an odd number of cylinders - so it skips to the odd numbered cylinders on the second rotation of the crankshaft.

Thus the firing sequence is 1,3, 5, 7, 9, 2, 4, 6,8, 1, 3, 5.....

The significant advantage of the radial is that the cylinders firing in

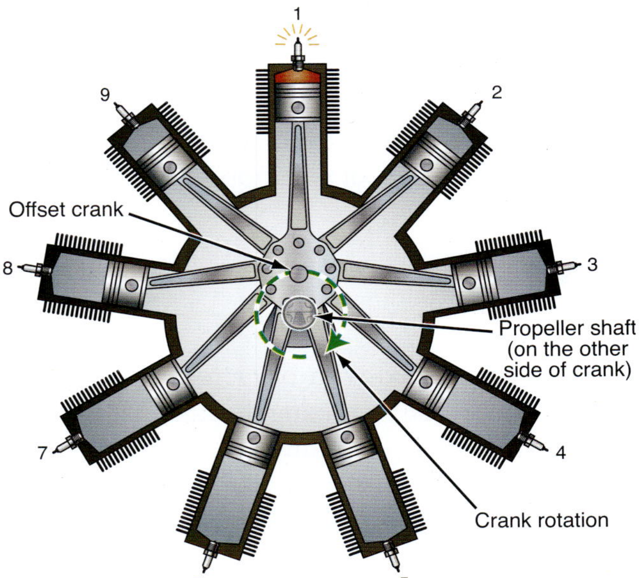

Figure 4-35 Firing Sequence - Single row nine cylinder radial engine

sequence provide very smooth and continuous power and high torque. The radial can turn a larger coarser pitch propeller at lower RPM, and hence deliver the same thrust for reduced fuel consumption. Also, each cylinder is equally cooled by the airflow. (In a twin-row engine the second cylinders are staggered so they collect the air passing between the front row cylinders).

The disadvantage of the radial is large frontal area and consequent drag but, for lower speed aircraft, this is outweighed by the advantages.

Another precaution with a radial is the need to rotate the propeller during pre-flight. This is to open the valves and circulate oil that has settled in the bottom cylinders - and to prevent hydraulic lock and consequent stressing of the lower pistons when starting. This also explains why there is considerable smoke form the exhaust as a radial engine is started, Residual oil in the cylinders is being burnt.

Note that most US radial engines rotate clockwise as viewed from the cockpit, and thus the aircraft tends to swing to the right on take-off - opposite to aircraft fitted with US horizontally-opposed engines, which rotate anti-clockwise as viewed from the cockpit and tend to swing to the left.

Engine Exhaust System

The purpose of the exhaust system is to quickly remove the waste gases from the engine and without back pressure. The more efficient the exhaust system, the more fresh fuel–air mixture that can be put into the engine and the more engine power that can be produced. Black exhaust smoke indicates that the fuel–air mixture is too rich (i.e. a significant amount of fuel is being exhausted without being completely burned). White smoke, which is very difficult to see, is an indication that the mixture is set too lean. Blue exhaust smoke indicates a significant amount of oil is getting past the piston rings and is being burned in the combustion chamber along with the fuel–air mixture. This suggests a loss of compression and therefore power.

On four-stroke engines the exhaust system is very open – just a pipe coming straight from the exhaust manifold. Two-stroke engines often have tuned exhaust systems. These systems create a back pressure at the right moment to make the incoming charge hesitate so that more of the charge is kept in the cylinder. This reduces wastage of the charge and increases engine power.

It is important that there is no leakage of exhaust fumes into the cabin because they contain carbon monoxide, a colourless and odourless gas that is difficult to detect but which can cause loss of consciousness and death.

Carburettor

Fuel must be mixed with oxygen in the correct ratio in order to burn properly. The oxygen is provided by mixing the fuel with air so that the fuel–air ratio is kept reasonably correct at about 1 part of fuel to 10 parts of air by weight. The device commonly used to mix fuel with air in an engine is called the *carburettor.*

The carburettor works on the *venturi* principle. Airflow through the throat of the carburettor has its pressure reduced. The atmospheric pressure in the float chamber is greater, causing the fuel to flow through the main metering jet and into the throat of the carburettor. The fuel vaporises and mixes with the air. The fuel–air mixture then flows through to the cylinders in preparation for burning. The pilot can vary the airflow (and therefore the fuel flow) by adjusting the throttle butterfly in the throat of the carburettor by moving the throttle lever in the cockpit. The fuel–air ratio can also be varied, for optimum power or fuel economy, by using the mixture control.

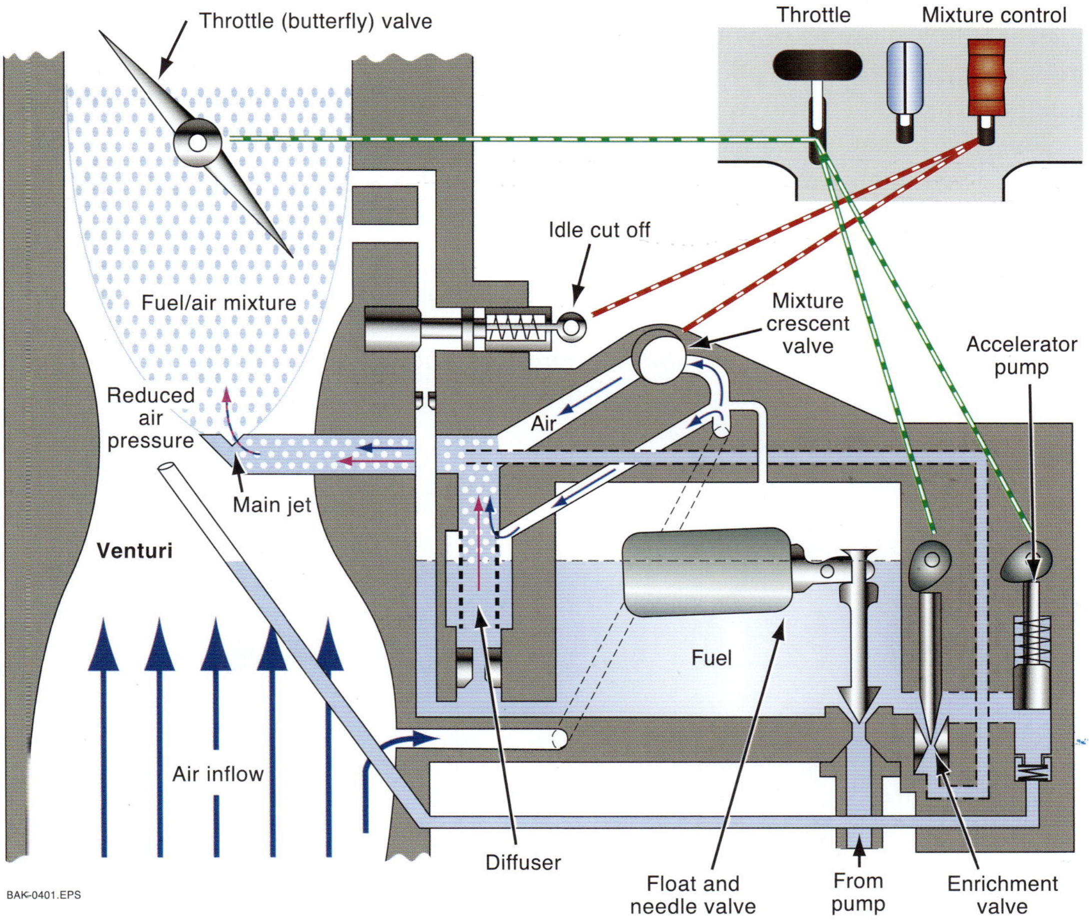

Figure 4-36 Cross section of a simple float-type carburettor.

The throttle varies the quantity of the fuel–air mixture (the charge) reaching the cylinders. The mixture control varies the fuel/air ratio of the charge. If the mixture is rich, there is excess fuel and, after combustion, some unburned fuel will remain, i.e. rich = excess fuel. If the mixture is lean, there is a shortage of fuel in the sense that, after all of the fuel has burned, there will still be some oxygen remaining, i.e. lean = not enough fuel and excess oxygen. A lean mixture results in a hotter burn but less power.

A carburettor has a venturi through which the amount of airflow is controlled by the throttle valve (butterfly). The venturi has fuel jets positioned in it so that the correct amount of fuel by weight is metered into the airflow. The butterfly valve is controlled by the pilot moving the throttle lever in the cockpit. It is important that you move the throttle smoothly so that unnecessary stress is not placed on the many moving parts in the engine. To open or close the throttle fully should take about three seconds (the same time as a 1-and-2-and-3 count).

Using the Mixture Control

The fuel–air ratio is the ratio between the weight of fuel and the weight of air mixed together and entering the cylinders, where the combustion process is to occur. Although we say fuel–air ratio, we really mean the ratio of air to fuel such as 10:1.

The carburettor is the device used to mix the fuel and the air, and it is designed in its most basic form to function best under mean sea-level conditions at the standard temperature of +15°C. Under other conditions when the air density is significantly less, such as at high altitudes or with high temperatures, the basic operation of the carburettor must be modified by the pilot to maintain a suitable fuel–air ratio. This is achieved by using the mixture control in the cockpit.

The mixture control is usually in the full rich position for take-off, unless you are operating at a very high-elevation aerodrome, possibly with a high temperature, where the air density as a consequence is very low. Usually, the mixture control is left in the full rich position for the climb, unless it is an extended climb to altitudes well above 5,000 ft. As you climb with the mixture control in this position, the excess fuel, available from the richening fuel–air mixture, acts as a cooling agent for the cylinder walls and piston tops assisting in avoiding detonation. Some more sophisticated aero engines require leaning during the climb, but for training aeroplanes this is not generally the case.

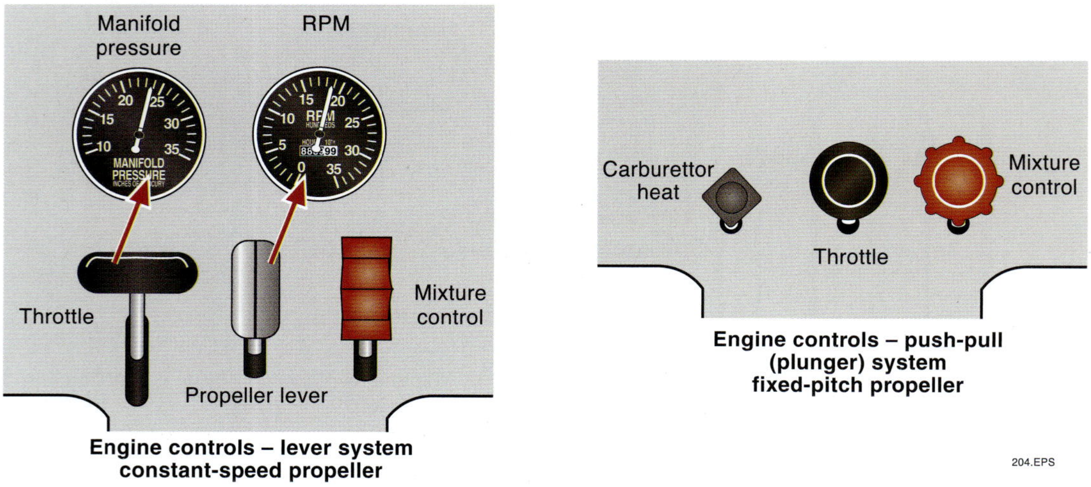

Figure 4-37 Engine controls.

Leaning the Mixture

During the early stages of flight training, the mixture control is kept in the full rich position. This provides the engine with a 10:1 ratio of air to fuel in the mixture, which is suitable for circuit practice and training area operations. You will not become fully conversant with engine leaning until the navigation phase of your training. There are some small penalties for operating full rich. One is the fuel consumption rate is increased and another is that during taxi or low-power operations spark plug fouling can occur.

To lean the mixture, slowly move the mixture control back towards the lean position. As the chemically correct ratio is reached (15:1), the peak exhaust gas temperature (EGT) will be reached. With further leaning, the engine will show signs of running a little roughly. The mixture control should then be gently moved forwards a small amount to regain the peak EGT (indicating a chemically correct mixture) and smoother running. The mixture control is then moved further in to a slightly richer position, to ensure that the engine is operating on the rich side of the chemically correct mixture. This must be repeated when either the cruise altitude or the power setting is changed. During take-off (and landing, when high power for a go-around may be required), the mixture control should normally be in the full rich position. Mixture is also set to the full rich position at top of descent. Note the following:

- Different engines require different methods of leaning. Refer to the pilot's operating handbook for your training aeroplane.
- Some aeroplanes are equipped with an exhaust gas temperature (EGT) gauge which indicates peak EGT when there is the chemically correct mixture (CCM), and this can assist you in leaning the mixture correctly.
- There are two common methods of leaning: (1) move the mixture control rearwards until rough running occurs, then push the control forward until smoother running is achieved; and (2) find peak EGT and set the mixture control slightly richer, about 3 divisions on the gauge Ý 60° cooler.

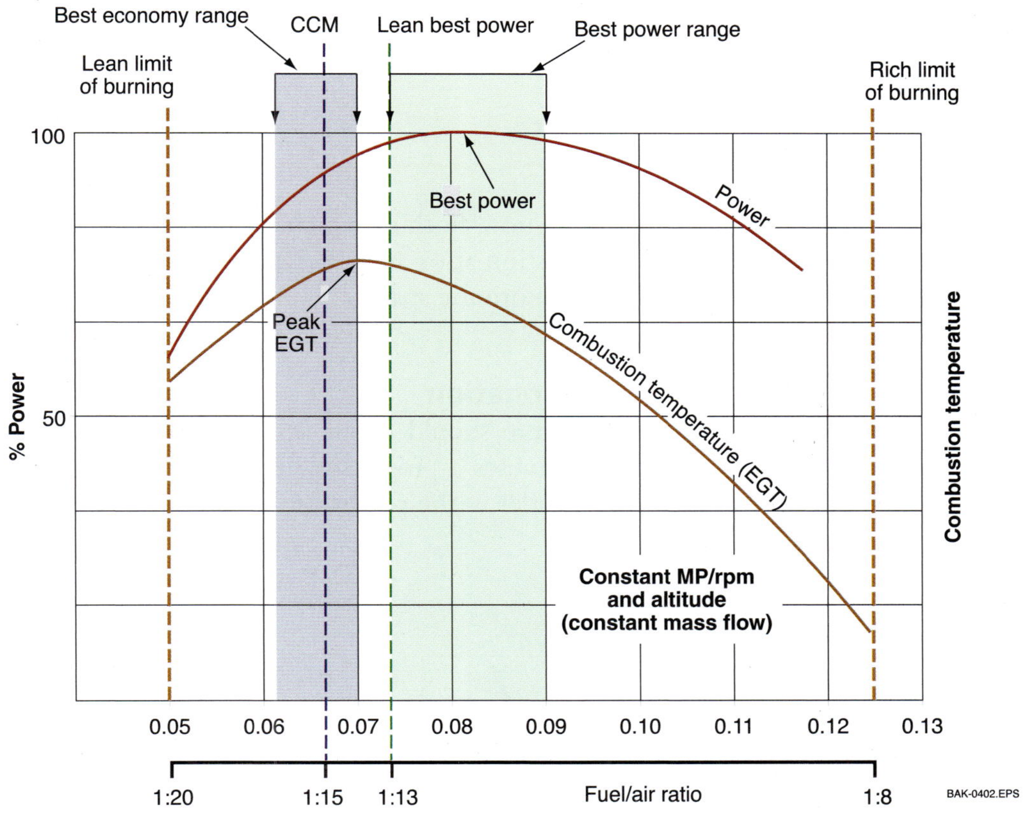

Figure 4-38 Fuel-to-air ratio versus power graph.

Consequences of Rich & Lean Mixtures

The mixture is usually slightly rich to provide some internal fuel cooling to protect against detonation and overheating in the cylinders. Detonation is more likely to occur at power settings above 75% maximum continuous power. At normal cruise power and above 5,000 ft altitude, leaning is advisable. At power settings above 75%, the mixture control should be in the full rich position.

An *overrich mixture* can cause a loss of power, rough running, high fuel consumption, fouling of the spark plugs and possibly formation of lead deposits (from unburnt fuel) on the cylinder heads and valves. An *overlean mixture* at high power settings will cause excessively high cylinder head temperatures, leading to detonation (explosive combustion in the cylinders).

Severe detonation can damage an engine very quickly. The pilot is then faced with a loss of power and quite possibly complete engine failure.

If you suspect that conditions are conducive to detonation, richen the mixture and check engine temperatures. A high cylinder head temperature could be an indication of detonation. A slightly rich mixture is preferable to a too lean mixture.

Idle Cut-Off (ICO)

The idle cut-off position of the mixture control is the normal means of shutting down (stopping) the engine. When the mixture control is moved fully rearward to the idle cut-off position by the pilot, a small valve moves to cut off the fuel supply to the idle circuit. The engine will continue running until all of the fuel–air mixture in the inlet manifold and the cylinders is burned. This leaves no combustible fuel–air mixture anywhere in the system, which would not be the case if the engine was stopped simply by turning the ignition off.

Abnormal Combustion

There are two kinds of abnormal combustion, both of which should be avoided:

- detonation, which is explosive combustion at or after the spark; and
- pre-ignition, which is early ignition before the spark.

Detonation

Progressive burning of the fuel–air mixture should occur as the flame-front advances through the combustion chamber. This causes a progressive increase in pressure which smoothly forces the piston down the cylinder in the power stroke. The normal burn rate is about 80 ft/second.

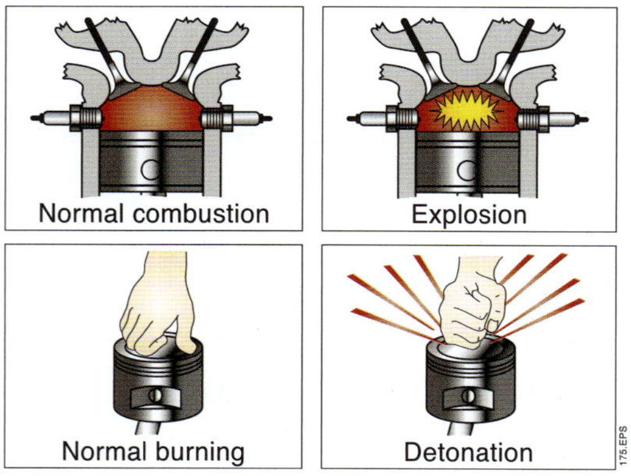

Figure 4-39
A comparison between normal combustion and detonation.

When a gas is compressed, it experiences a rise in temperature (you can feel this if you hold your finger over the outlet of a bicycle pump during the compression stroke). If the pressure and the temperature rise is too great, there will be a spontaneous explosive combustion. (Instead of maximum pressure occurring when the piston is going down, the pressure occurs against the rising piston.) This explosive increase in pressure is called *detonation* and can cause severe damage to the pistons, valves and spark plugs, as well as causing a decrease in power and quite possibly complete engine failure.

The burn rate during detonation is in excess of 1,000 ft/second. Mild detonation may not be detected by a pilot, although an excessively high cylinder head temperature indicated on the CHT gauge and rough running are warnings that detonation may be occurring. The unnecessary use of carburettor heat, particularly with high ambient temperatures and/or high power settings, will further raise the fuel–air mixture temperature to dangerous levels and may precipitate the onset of detonation.

Other contributory factors are the following:

- a time-expired fuel;
- fuel with a lower than recommended octane rating;
- overlean mixture at high power settings;
- excessive manifold pressure; and/or
- an overheated engine.

Aeroplane engines are normally operated a little on the rich side, the extra fuel acting as a coolant to prevent the mixture becoming too hot and to cool the cylinder walls by evaporation. If detonation conditions exist or are expected, for instance by an excessively high cylinder head temperature, you should do the following:

- richen the mixture;
- reduce pressures in the cylinders (throttle back); and/or
- increase airspeed to assist cooling the engine.

Pre-Ignition

Pre-ignition, while involving a progressive combustion of the fuel–air mixture, is a premature ignition that commences before the spark from the plug. This early ignition (or pre-ignition) can be caused by a hot-spot in the cylinder (e.g. a carbon deposit) becoming red-hot and igniting the mixture before the spark plug fires, causing peak pressure in the cylinder far too early in the cycle.

The following are the results of pre-ignition:

- rough running;
- possible back-firing;
- sudden rise in the cylinder head temperature; and/or
- possible engine damage such as a burnt piston, broken cylinder head, scuffed cylinder wall, and damage to valves and spark plugs.

Pre-ignition can be caused by the following:

- hot spots in the cylinder (carbon deposits, damaged head gasket);
- using high power when the mixture is too lean (overheating the cylinders); and/or
- overheated spark plugs (possibly as a result of detonation).

Pre-ignition may occur in one cylinder only when a hot spot is the cause. Detonation is more likely to occur in all cylinders. Pre-ignition is a function of the condition of a particular cylinder (e.g. a hot spot) whereas detonation is a function of the fuel or temperature. Detonation may start in one cylinder, but the rapid heating can quickly cause it to effect the other cylinders.

Carburettor & Induction Icing

As air accelerates through the carburettor venturi, a pressure decrease is generated (to draw the fuel in), and consequently a significant temperature drop occurs. Even quite warm air can cool to below zero, and if it contains moisture, ice will form.

The first sign of carburettor ice is rough running and a gradual loss of rpm on an aircraft with a fixed-pitch propeller. An aircraft with a variable-pitch propeller system would experience rough running and a loss of manifold pressure. Progressive throttle increments to maintain the same rpm may indicate that ice is forming in the carburettor and is restricting the airflow. Unless the carburettor ice is removed, full power will not be available and the engine may even stop. There are three types of induction icing.

Impact Ice

Impact ice will occur when supercooled water droplets (i.e. water droplets below freezing point) impact on the filter or the metal surfaces of the inlet air scoop and ducting to the carburettor, immediately forming ice. Impact ice can occur when the outside air temperature is near or below zero and the aeroplane is in cloud, rain or sleet, i.e. in visible moisture, with water droplets at or below zero, or if the inlet surfaces themselves are below zero – for example, if the aeroplane is on descent from high altitudes, where the temperature is below the freezing level, into areas of visible moisture.

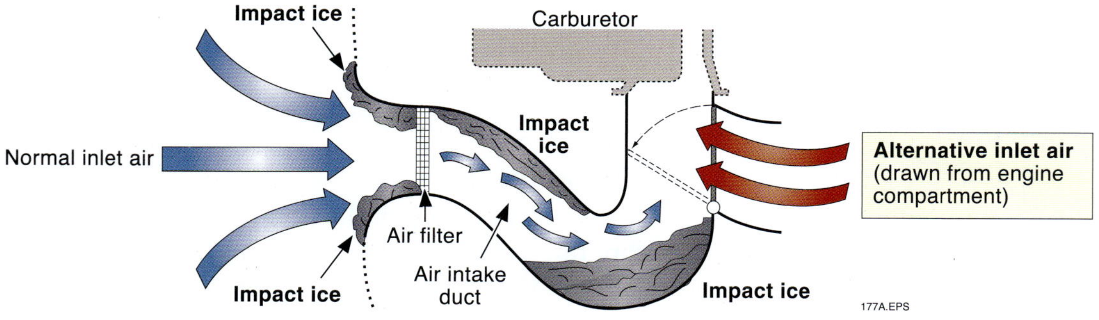

Figure 4-40 Impact ice.

Fuel Evaporation Ice

When fuel is introduced into the carburettor airstream, the temperature of the resulting fuel–air mixture is lowered substantially due to the latent heat absorption that occurs during fuel vaporisation. You can feel this effect when water or perspiration evaporates off your skin on a hot day. Fuel ice will form downstream of the metering jet in the throat of the carburettor if the temperature of the fuel–air mixture drops to between 0 °C and –8 °C. The water will precipitate from the incoming air (if it is moist) and freeze onto any surface it encounters, such as the inlet manifold walls and the throttle butterfly valve. This ice will seriously restrict the airflow and thus reduce the engine's power output. Fuel ice can occur in ambient air temperatures well above freezing, even as high as 30 °C when the relative humidity exceeds about 50%. Fuel ice is sometimes called *refrigeration ice* since it is caused by the vaporising of a liquid – the same process that is used in most refrigerators.

Throttle Ice

The collective temperature drop in the carburettor is significant. If moisture is present, ice can form on the throttle valve. The resulting temperature drop is greatest at small throttle openings. The throttle butterfly restricts the airflow at low power settings, creating a substantial pressure drop. The small opening is easier to block or disrupt the flow, so there is a greater likelihood of carburettor ice at low throttle settings.

Visible moisture is not necessary for the formation of throttle ice. Be warned: *carburettor ice can occur when the outside air temperature is HIGH!*

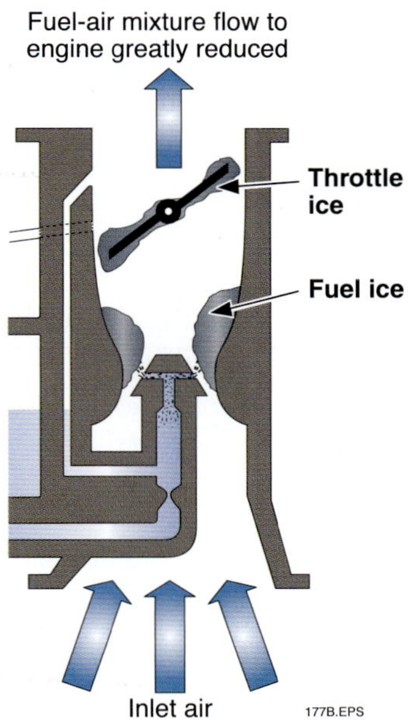

Figure 4-41 Fuel and throttle ice.

Both fuel ice and throttle ice can occur even when the outside air temperature is high. Any time the outside air temperature is within the approximate range −10°C to +20°C and especially if the relative humidity is high, you should remain alert for signs of carburettor ice caused by cooling in the carburettor venturi. Any of this carburettor ice can have a very serious effect on the running of the engine. The size and shape of the carburettor passages are altered by the ice, the airflow is disturbed, and the ratio of the fuel–air mixture ratio is affected – all leading to rough running, a loss of power and possibly a total stoppage of the engine unless prompt corrective action is taken.

Typical symptoms of carburettor ice forming are the following:

- rough running; and
- a power loss shown by a drop in rpm for a fixed-pitch propeller, resulting in poorer performance (a loss of airspeed or a poorer rate of climb).

Icing Probability

Carburettor ice can form quickly at a *relative humidity* (RH) above 50% in *outside air temperatures* (OAT) below 20°C.

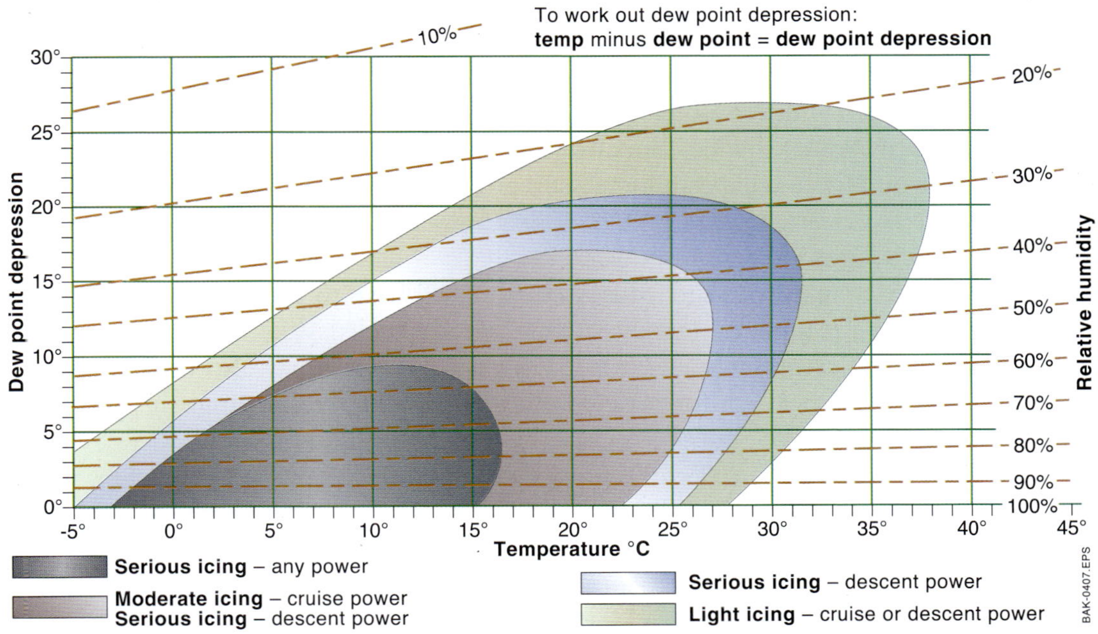

Figure 4-42 Probability of carburettor icing.

Carburettor Heat

Different aircraft vary in their susceptibility to carburettor icing. It is vital that you know the procedures for your aircraft to detect, deter and defy carburettor icing.

Most modern aeroplanes have a carburettor heat system to counteract ice. This usually involves heating the induction air prior to intake into the carburettor by passing the air close to the (hot) exhaust system of the engine. The density of this heated air passing through the carburettor will be less, so the initial effect of applying carburettor heat will be to decrease the power from the engine (seen as an initial drop in rpm for a fixed-pitch propeller) possibly by as much as 10%. If there is no initial drop in rpm, then the carburettor heat may not be functioning. Under these circumstances, you should not fly the aircraft.

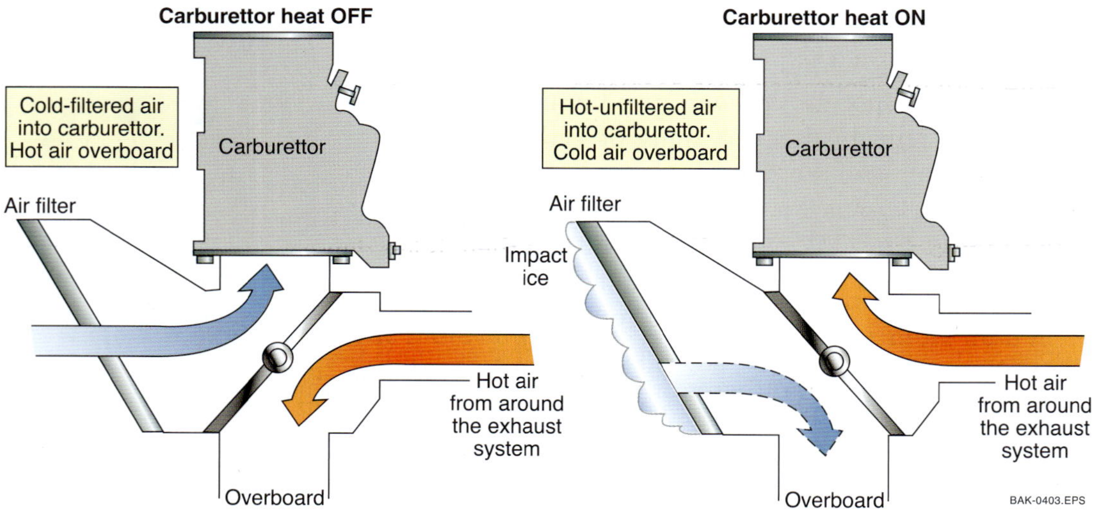

Figure 4-43 Application of carburettor heat.

The carburettor heat control is usually located near the throttle in the cockpit. By pulling it fully out (rearwards), heated air is passed into the carburettor. It is usual, if carburettor ice is suspected, to apply full carburettor heat. As the hot air passes through the carburettor venturi, it will melt the ice. If there has been a large ice build-up in the carburettor, the engine may run extremely roughly, especially as the melted ice (now water) passes through the cylinders along with the fuel–air mixture, but this roughness will quickly disappear. When the ice clears from the carburettor, the engine will begin running smoother and there will be an increase in power. The rpm of a fixed-pitch propeller will rise as the ice clears. Carburettor heat may now be removed, at which time there will be a further slight increase in power.

If carburettor ice re-forms, then this operation will have to be repeated. Full carburettor heat must be reapplied until the carburettor ice melts. When carburettor heat is required to remove carburettor ice, it is known as *de-icing*. It may also be necessary to leave the carburettor heat on for long periods to prevent ice forming; this process is known as *anti-icing*.

Some aircraft are fitted with a carburettor air temperature gauge (CAT gauge), which may be used to keep the carburettor air temperature out of the icing range. It may allow you to use only partial carburettor heat to prevent further formation of ice once the initial ice has been removed with full carburettor heat. If carburettor ice still forms, immediately reapply full carburettor heat to remove it, and then try a higher setting of partial heat to increase the air temperature sufficiently to prevent further ice formation.

Be aware of the following:

- Partial use of carburettor heat may raise the temperature of the induction air into that temperature range which is most conducive to the formation of carburettor ice, thereby increasing the risk of ice build-up rather than decreasing it. Monitor the engine power gauges and be alert for any rough running. If in doubt, use full or no carburettor heat.
- On descent with low power, particularly in high humidity, it is usual to apply carburettor heat to ensure that no carburettor ice forms. The small throttle butterfly openings needed for low power increase the chance of carburettor ice forming.
- On short final approach to land, the carburettor heat is usually returned to the cold position, just in case full power is required in the event of a go-around.
- Avoid using carburettor heat on the ground because the hot air is (in most aeroplanes) taken from around the engine exhaust manifold and, unlike the normal inlet air, is unfiltered. This will avoid introducing dust and grit into the carburettor and the engine.

Note: Use of carburettor heat decreases engine power.

The carburettor heat system provides hot air to the engine for the purpose of de-icing or anti-icing. As hot air is less dense than cold air there are two very subtle side effects:

- the mixture becomes a little richer than it was; and
- the engine power decreases slightly because there is less dense air reaching the engine.

Preflight Checks of Carburettor Heat

To check if the carburettor heat system is working, set the recommended rpm and select the carburettor heat to HOT. The tachometer will indicate a decrease in rpm if it is working, due to the hot air being less dense than the cold filtered air. Leave the carburettor heat in the HOT position for a few seconds to ensure it is running smoothly, and then push it back to the COLD position; rpm should increase.

Carburettor ice may form on the ground as well as in the air. If you do have carburettor ice, the engine will run rough when you select the carburettor heat to the HOT position (if it is not already doing so). Once the ice is melted, it will run smoothly again, and the rpm will increase. Then select the carburettor heat to the COLD position, and rpm will increase slightly further.

Fuel-Injection Systems

Many sophisticated engines have fuel metered into the induction manifold and then into the cylinders without using a carburettor. This is known as fuel injection. Most basic training aeroplanes are not fuel injected.

In fuel-injection systems, a venturi system is still used to sense the pressure differential. This is coupled to a *fuel control unit* (FCU), from which metered fuel is piped to the fuel manifold unit (fuel distributor). From there, a separate fuel line carries fuel to the discharge nozzle in each cylinder head, or into the inlet port near the inlet valve. With fuel injection, each individual cylinder is provided with a correct mixture by its own separate fuel line. (This is unlike the carburettor system, which supplies the fuel–air mixture to all cylinders, requiring a slightly richer-than-ideal mixture to be supplied to most of the cylinders by the carburettor to ensure that the leanest-running cylinder does not run too lean.)

As fuel-injection systems do not have a carburettor, they do not have carburettor heat. However, if impact ice forms on the air inlet, a source of alternate air to the engine is available. There is a selection in the cockpit – perhaps under the instrument panel.

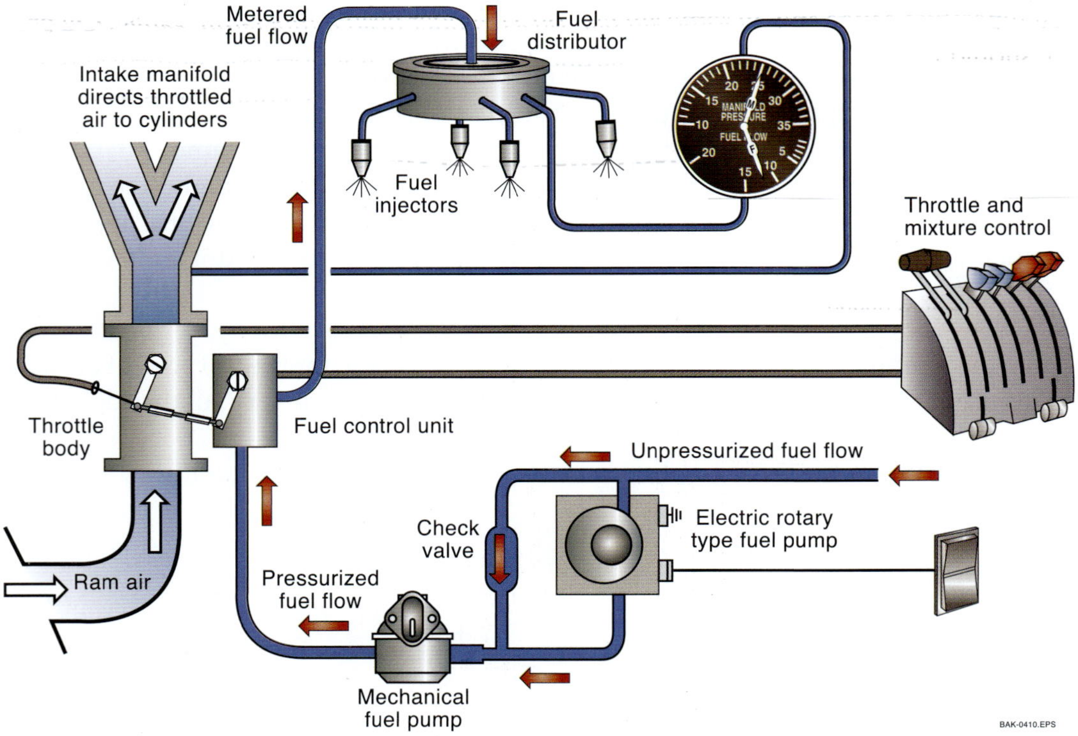

Figure 4-44 Fuel-injection system.

The following are some advantages of fuel-injection systems when compared to carburettor systems:

- Fuel induction icing problems are almost eliminated.
- More uniform delivery of the fuel–air mixture to each cylinder.
- Improved control of fuel–air ratio.
- Instant acceleration of the engine after idling with no tendency for it to stall, i.e. instant response.
- Increased engine efficiency.

Some disadvantages of fuel-injection systems are as follows:

- Starting an already hot engine that has a fuel-injection system may be difficult due to vapour locking in the fuel lines. Electric boost pumps that pressurise the fuel lines can help alleviate this problem.
- Having very fine fuel lines, fuel-injected engines are more susceptible to any fuel contamination such as dirt or water.
- Surplus fuel provided by a fuel-injection system will pass through a return line which may be routed to only one of the fuel tanks. If the pilot does not retain an awareness of where the surplus fuel is being returned to, it may result in uneven fuel loading in the tanks or fuel being vented overboard (thus reducing flight fuel available).

Engine Lubrication

Sufficient quantity of oil of the correct grade is essential. An oil dipstick to check oil quantity is generally found under a small cowl door above the engine, along with an oil filling point. Always check that the oil filler cap has been firmly replaced prior to flight. Indication of correct operation of the oil system is provided in the cockpit by an oil pressure gauge, an oil temperature gauge and, in some aircraft, on a cylinder head temperature gauge. Oil pressure should rise within 30 seconds of starting the engine – if it does not, immediately shut down the engine before damage occurs (by retarding the mixture control to ICO).

Five Functions of Oil

Lube	Lubricates (reduces friction) between the moving parts so that they can move smoothly
Cool	Assists cooling the engine by carrying heat generated by combustion away from the piston heads
Clean	Cleans by carrying away contaminants which can then be removed by the oil filter
Seal	Provides a seal between the cylinder walls, the pistons and the piston rings, to more effectively trap the pressure from the combustion process. Also absorbs wear and movement in bearings
Protect	Protects the metal parts from corrosion by excluding air from the working surfaces

Table 4-1 Five functions of oil.

Oil lubricates the moving parts. If a thin film of oil separates two metal surfaces, it will allow them to slide over each other without actually touching. There will be low friction forces, and consequently, not much heat or stress is generated in this part of the engine. Without oil there would be high friction forces, generating very high temperatures to develop quickly in the metal causing expansion of the metal parts resulting in extreme wearing of the metal surfaces and, very likely, subsequent mechanical failure.

Oil cools the hot sections of the engine. The pistons absorb a lot of heat from the combustion process and are cooled by oil splashed or sprayed onto them from below (i.e. from the pump). The heat absorbed from the hot sections of the engine is removed by the oil continually being circulated. The hot oil is carried away and cooled in a component known as the oil cooler, which is exposed to the airflow. Correct oil quantity is important to the cooling process. If the amount of oil in the sump is low, the ability to cool is reduced.

Oil cleans away contaminants. Oil circulating through an engine can carry away dirt and other foreign material, thereby reducing abrasive wear on the moving parts of the engine. This contamination is removed from the oil as it passes through the oil filter. If the filter is not kept clean (by correct maintenance or replacement at the recommended service intervals) it may become blocked, causing dirty oil to bypass the filter and circulate within the engine's lubrication system. Dirty oil has poorer cooling and lubricating qualities and so the engine will suffer – there will be an increased wear rate which will shorten the life of the engine.

Oil seals and cushions. Oil also provides a seal between the cylinder walls, the piston rings and the pistons as they move up and down within the cylinders, preventing the high pressure combustion gases escaping past the piston rings into the crankcase, and so increasing the effectiveness of converting the fuel energy into mechanical energy. Engine components subjected to high loads, such as the bearings at either end of the connecting rods, especially the crankshaft (or big end) bearings, need to be cushioned by a layer of oil so that the mechanical shock on them is reduced.

Oil protects the engine parts. When metal is allowed to remain uncovered in the presence of moisture or some of the chemicals that contaminate the air, rust or other surface corrosion will form. This is especially true of steel surfaces such as cylinder walls or crankshaft, which have been hardened by the process of nitriding. A thin film of oil covering these surfaces will prevent the oxygen reacting with the metal and pitting it.

Properties of Oil

Oil must be sufficiently viscous over the operating temperature range of the engine – it must flow freely, but not be too thin. An oil of high viscosity (stickiness) flows slowly; an oil of low viscosity flows more easily. High temperatures make oil less viscous and cause it to flow more freely. *Excessively high temperatures affect the lubricating qualities of oil, impairing its effectiveness, so keep an eye on the oil temperature gauge.*

The oil must remain sufficiently viscous under the wide range of operating temperatures and bearing pressures found in aviation engines. The owner or operator of the aeroplane may decide to use an oil of lower viscosity than normal in a severely cold climate. Likewise, an oil of higher viscosity could be used if the aeroplane is to be operated in a continually hot climate. Engine oils are generally compatible so mixing oils will not have an adverse effect on your engine in the short term. Remember: it is better to operate with mixed or dirty oil than to risk operating with no oil.

Multigrade Oils

Multigrade oils are light base oils which have an additive to prevent them from thinning too much as the oil warms up. They are a blend of synthetic and mineral-based stocks. Multigrade oils are produced to operate over a range of temperatures. A typical multigrade rating, which you read off the bottle, may be *15W50*. This indicates that the oil is a 15-weight oil and will not thin any more than a 50-weight oil when it gets hot. If the temperature is any lower, then the oil will be too viscous and therefore resistant to flow. The proper viscosity is the single most important criterion of lubricating oil.

Multigrade oils are thinner at start-up, making startup easier and providing less drag on the starter motor. This means that multigrade oils pump through the system better than single-grade oils at cold temperatures, and they provide better protection. The mineral-base stocks aid in flushing out the lead by-products of combustion. They also have anti-corrosion additives to help protect engines of low usage or in high humidity climates.

An anti-wear additive is also added to the system to provide protection to high wear components such as the camshaft and filters. A 15W50 oil may be used in four-stoke piston aircraft engines and is an alternative to SAE 50 oils.

A Typical Oil System

After doing its work in the engine, the oil returns to a *sump* which is a reservoir, usually in the lower part of the engine casing. This is called a *wet sump*. Most light aircraft engines are wet sump engines (as are motor vehicles).

A *dry sump engine* has scavenge pumps that pump the oil from the collection cavities in the engine to a tank that is separate from the engine. It is usual to have a dry sump on aerobatic aeroplanes for continuous lubrication in extreme attitudes and inverted flight.

An engine-driven pump supplies oil from the sump or the tank through oil lines, passages and galleries to the moving parts of the engine. Within the oil pump is a pressure regulator, which is a spring-loaded pressure relief valve (PRV). If the pressure set on the pressure relief valve is exceeded, it will open and relieve the pressure by allowing oil to be returned to the pump inlet. In this way, the oil pressure is maintained between 60 and 100 psi. An *oil pressure gauge* in the cockpit indicates the oil pressure provided by the oil pump. The oil pressure sensor is situated after the oil pump and before the oil does its work in the engine.

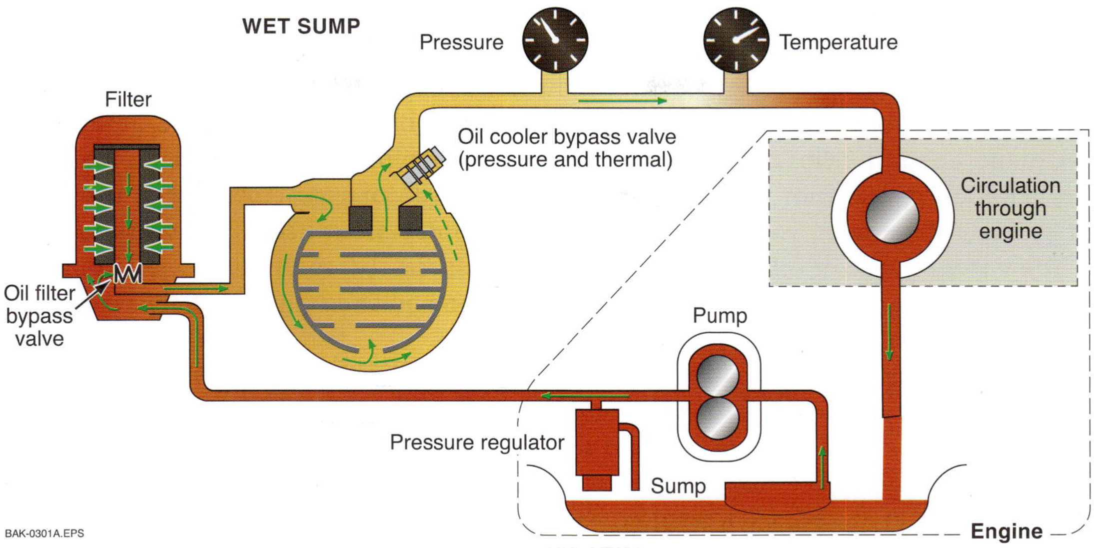

Figure 4-45 A typical wet sump oil system.

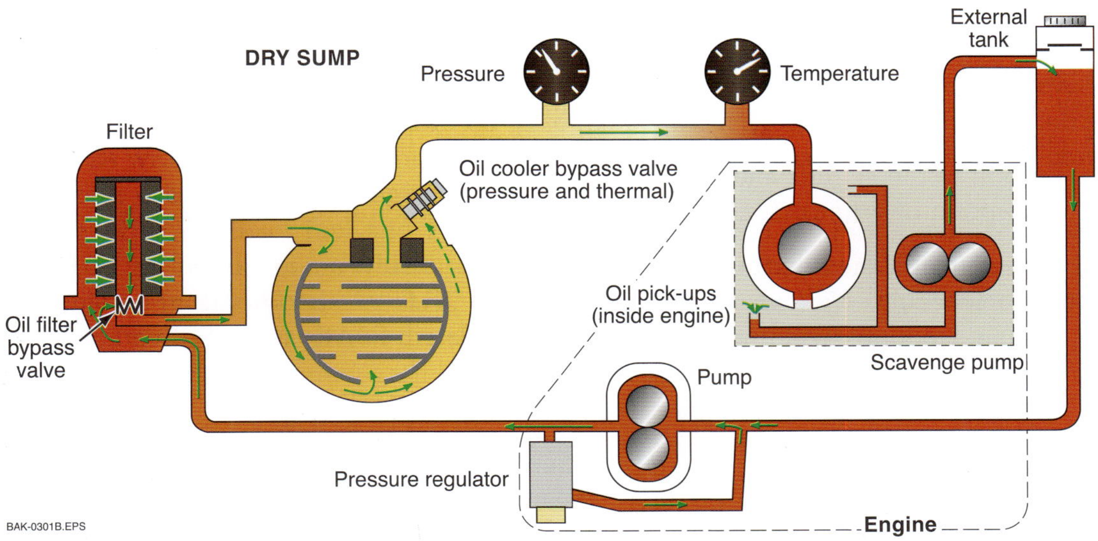

Figure 4-46 A typical dry sump oil system.

Oil filters and screens are placed in the system to remove any foreign matter such as dirt or carbon particles in the circulating oil. The oil filters should be inspected and replaced at regular intervals, as required in the maintenance schedule. The foreign matter collected may give an indication of the condition of the engine – for instance, small metal particles might indicate an impending engine failure. Within the oil filter housing is the oil-filter bypass valve. This permits the oil to bypass the filter in the event of the filter becoming clogged. Dirty and contaminated oil is preferable to no oil at all.

The oil circulates around the moving parts and through the engine, lubricating, cooling and cleaning as it goes, and is then returned to the wet sump by gravity, or to a separate oil tank by scavenge pumps (dry sump system). Because the oil absorbs engine heat, the cooling that occurs in the sump is often insufficient and so most engines have an oil cooler. The oil is pumped from the sump through the oil filter to the oil cooler. Often oil coolers have both a thermal and pressure bypass system.

If the oil is already cool, a thermally operated valve allows it to bypass the oil cooler, as further cooling is unnecessary. If the oil is hot (as it is when the engine has warmed-up), the thermally operated valve directs the oil through the cooler. Should the cooler become blocked, a pressure bypass valve allows the oil to bypass the cooler. Collecting the oil in the sump helps cool the oil a little, the oil then passes through the oil cooler for further cooling just prior to entering the main parts of the engine. As part of your daily or preflight inspection, you should check the oil cooler system to ensure the following:

- the system is free of oil leakage or fatigue cracks; and
- the air passages are clear (birds have been known to build nests in just a few hours).

An oil temperature gauge is placed in the cockpit. It is connected to a temperature probe that senses the temperature of the oil after the oil has passed through the oil cooler and before its use within the hot sections of the engine. Also, some aeroplanes have a cylinder head temperature (CHT) gauge to provide another indication of engine temperature to the pilot. *Oil pressure is one of the best indications of sufficient quantity and correct function of your oil system. Most piston engines operate in a pressure range of 60 to 100 psi.*

Periodic Oil Changes are Necessary

Since the same oil in an engine is continually circulated, over a period of time it will become contaminated because the filters cannot clean it perfectly. Chemical changes will also occur in the oil in the following form:

- oxidation caused by contamination from some of the by-products of the fuel combustion in the engine; and
- absorption of water that condenses in the engine when it cools after shutdown.

Consequently the oil must be changed at regular intervals, as required by the maintenance schedule. *Use only recommended type and grade of oils.* The aeroplane's pilot's operating handbook will usually show the oil grade as an SAE rating (Society of Automotive Engineers); however, commercial aviation oil has a commercial aviation number which is double the SAE rating:

80 grade oil – SAE 40
100 grade oil – SAE 50

There are different types of oils designed for different operating conditions. Use only the correct type of oil as directed in the pilot's operating handbook and do not use turbine (jet) oil in piston engines.

Problems with the Oil System

Incorrect Oil Type

The incorrect type of oil will possibly cause poor lubrication, poor cooling and engine damage.

Incorrect Oil Quantity

The oil level should be checked prior to flight. There will be an oil dipstick in the tank for this purpose. The dipstick is calibrated to show maximum and minimum oil quantities. If the oil quantity is below the minimum, then you will find that the oil overheats and/or the oil pressure is too low or fluctuates. If the oil quantity is too great, then the excess oil may be forced out through various parts of the engine, such as the front shaft seal.

The oil quantity needs to be checked before each flight, because it gradually decreases for the following reasons:

- being burned with the fuel–air mixture in the cylinders;
- being lost as a mist or spray through the oil breather; and
- leaks.

Low Oil Pressure

At normal power, a low oil pressure may indicate a lack of oil and an impending engine failure. Low oil pressure could mean the following:

- insufficient oil in the system;
- a leak in the oil tank or oil lines;
- a failure of the oil pump;
- a problem in the engine, such as failing bearings; and/or
- the oil pressure relief valve (PRV) stuck open.

On start-up, the oil pressure gauge should indicate a rise within 30 seconds. For some engines in very cold climates, this time may be extended to 60 seconds. Refer to the manufacturer's handbook.

High Oil Temperature

Too little oil being circulated will also be indicated by a high oil temperature, that is, a rising oil temperature may indicate a decreasing oil quantity. Prolonged operation at excessive cylinder head temperatures will also give rise to a high oil temperature indication. This would be most likely to occur in situations of high power, low airspeed (climbing), especially in high ambient air temperatures. Pilot action to reduce oil temperature could be the following:

- reduce power;
- lower the nose to increase airspeed; and/or
- open cowl flaps (if fitted).

Faulty Oil Pressure Gauge

A low oil pressure indication may be recognised as a faulty gauge – and not a genuine low pressure – by noting that the oil temperature remains normal over a period of time. Keep your eye on both gauges.

High Oil Pressure

A pressure relief valve in the system should ensure that the oil does not reach an unacceptably high oil pressure. A high oil pressure may cause some part of the system to fail, rendering the whole oil system inoperative.

Low or Fluctuating Oil Pressure

Where an indication of low or fluctuating oil pressure occurs and is associated with a rise in oil temperature while in flight – play it safe and land as soon as possible, as it could indicate a serious problem in the lubrication system, including low oil quantity.

Gradual Loss of Oil

If the engine is gradually losing oil, then the oil temperature will gradually rise due to less oil having to do the same amount of work – cooling and lubricating the engine. In such a situation, the oil pressure will probably be maintained, but with the oil temperature rising until the oil quantity reaches a critically low level when a sudden drop in oil pressure (and consequent engine problems) could occur.

If you suspect a problem concerning oil, then you should plan a landing before the problem becomes serious. This is a matter of judgement for the pilot, but land safely as soon as possible.

Engine Cooling

Air Cooling

Most modern light aeroplane engines are air-cooled by exposing the cylinders and their cooling fins to an airflow. The fins increase the exposed surface area to allow better cooling.

As the airflow passes around a cylinder, it may become turbulent and break away in such a manner that uneven cooling occurs, forming local hot-spots. To avoid this uneven cooling, cowling ducts at the front of the engine capture air from the high-pressure area behind the propeller, and then baffles distribute it as evenly as possible around the cylinders. After cooling the engine, the air flows out through cowl vents, which are sometimes controlled by cowl flaps, at the back of the engine bay.

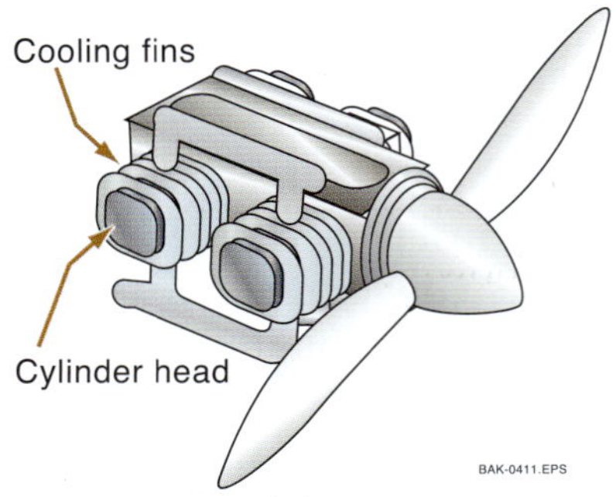

Figure 4-47 Air cooling.

Air cooling is least effective at high power and low airspeed, for instance, on take-off, climb or go-around. The high power produces a lot of heat, and the low airspeed provides a reduced cooling airflow. Conversely, at high airspeed and low power, for instance, on descent, the cooling might be too effective.

Some aeroplanes have adjustable cowl flaps that can be operated (electrically or manually) from the cockpit, giving the pilot more control over the cooling of the engine.

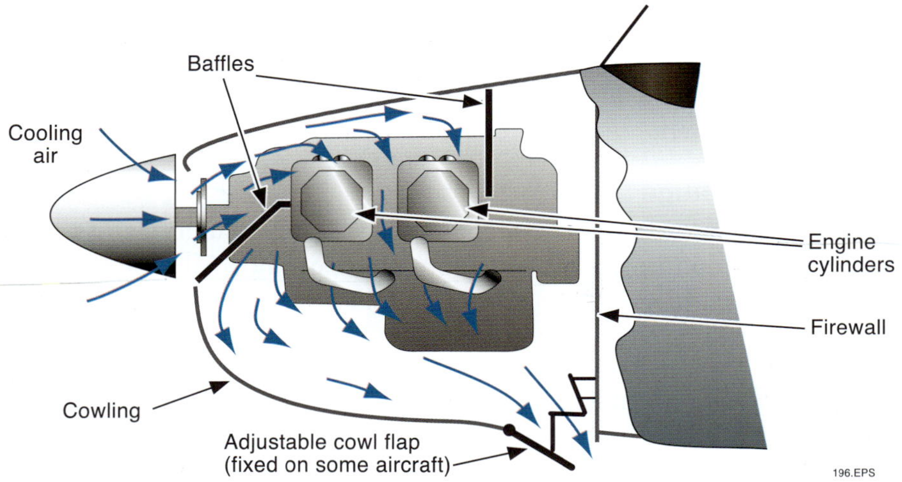

Figure 4-48 Cowl flaps control cooling of the engine.

On some aeroplanes the propeller spinner is part of the airflow director for the cooling air, and so these aeroplanes should not be operated without the spinner installed. If you find yourself in such a situation, reference to the flight manual or a maintenance engineer will establish what is allowable for your aeroplane.

Liquid Cooling

Liquid cooling (like most cars) of aircraft engines until recently tended to increase the complexity and weight of an engine and decrease its reliability. With advancements in technology and improved engineering practices, the more efficient heat removal of liquid cooling systems have allowed many small, high-powered engines to take to the air. Developments in "sport aircraft" engines have permitted high revving two-stroke engines to become very efficient, reliable and popular.

The Two-Stroke Engine

The two-stroke engine is much simpler than the four-stroke engine, because it does not have *poppet valves*, *camshafts* or *pushrods*. Instead, the cylinder walls have special ports which act like valves as the piston moves up and down. The area below the piston, always a dry sump on normally aspirated engines, is used to accept the incoming mixture as the piston moves up on the compression stroke. Part of the intake stroke and compression stroke are combined.

After ignition the piston moves down on the powerstroke, the mixture which is now underneath the piston is compressed slightly then forced out of the sump and into the cylinder, pushing the exhaust gases out through the exhaust port. The intake stroke is complete and the exhaust stroke occurs at the same time the power stroke takes place. The energy pulse generated at the power stroke is less than the equivalent four-stroke engine. But that doesn't matter because a two-stroke engine produces twice as many power strokes.

Figure 4-49 Two-stroke engine.

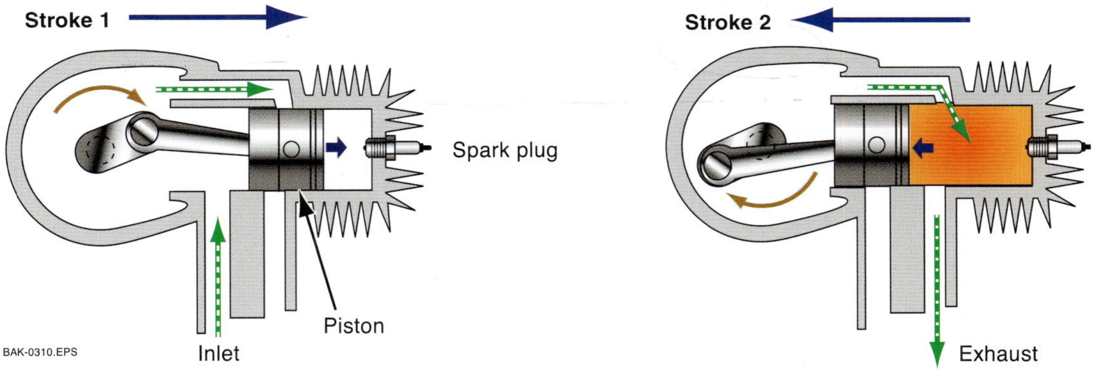

Figure 4-50 The two-stroke cycle.

Ignition

The typical gasoline-powered two-stroke engine has an ignition system just as a four-stroke engine does. Dual magneto systems are used on light aircraft because of their efficiency, reliability and safety. *Capacitive discharge ignition systems* (CDI) are also very efficient at producing a hot spark at the correct time without using points. They use a magnetic sensor. Some sports aircraft use CDIs (dual systems) which are very light, compact and reliable, but they are reliant on the electrical system. To function, they need a battery, especially during start.

Exhaust

The engine ports are shaped to allow some of the pressure pushing the piston down to initiate exhaust outflow. This means that, as the intake gases push in, the exhaust gases have already started to move out. Exhaust systems on two-stroke engines are tuned to create a slight depression at the exhaust port at the bottom of the power stroke and slight compression at the start of the compression stroke. This helps scavenge to exhaust gases and reduces wastage of the intake gases. Two-stroke engines are very noisy. It is difficult to *muffle* all the exhaust noise without interfering with the exhaust back pressure. To help reduce noise, sometimes *intake silencers* are provided.

Induction System

Often the carburettor used on a two-stroke engine is a very simple *sidedraught* device. Mostly cable and spring operated, they use a slide and needle valve to regulate the air and fuel induction. Like *updraught* float-type carburettors, the sidedraught carburettor has a float and an idle jet to allow low rpm. This carburettor is usually fitted with a *choke* but not an acceleration/priming pump. For starting, the main venturi is choked a little to reduce the amount of air going to the engine, causing a rich mixture to be available. After start when smooth running is established, the choke should be put off.

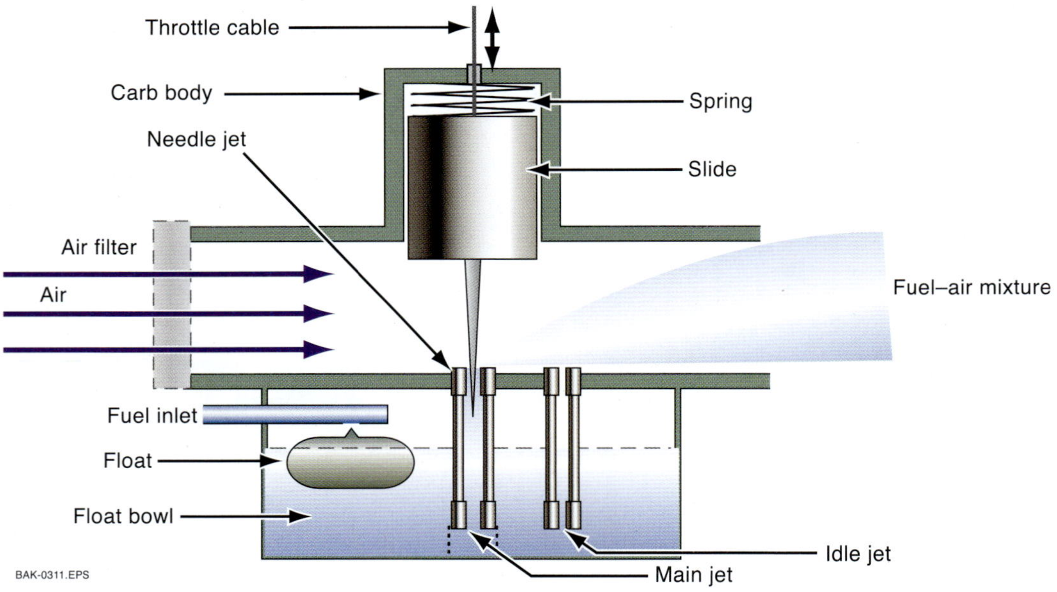

Figure 4-51 Sidedraught carburettor.

Lubrication

The crankcase of small two-stroke engines is a *dry sump*. The practice was for oil to be mixed with the fuel (at a ratio of 25:1 – 25 parts fuel to one part oil). This arrangement allowed the cylinder walls and the small and big end bearings to be lubricated satisfactorily. However, adding oil to the fuel also had its limitations. The carburettor had to be adjusted to allow for the thicker mixture and there was a tendency to oil up the spark plugs. It was easy to misdiagnose engine problems too: if the engine was running hot, people would often add more oil to the mix, changing the ratio from 25:1 to 20:1. Unfortunately, the greater quantity of oil simply displaced the fuel, and instead of making the engine run cooler with the additional oil, it actually ran hotter because of the leaner fuel–air mixture. The downside of using a fuel-oil mix is that most of the oil ends up in the combustion chamber and is burnt. This also pollutes the atmosphere with blue smoke.

Modern two-strokes use an external oil tank and feed the oil directly to the cylinder walls and engine bearings. To keep the engine simple and light, this oil is not *scavenged* (recovered). This type of dry sump system is known as a *total loss* system. When operating this engine, the oil tank needs to be refilled between flights.

Cooling

Traditionally, two-stroke engines have been air cooled, however, liquid cooling has become increasingly popular (as it has on motorcycles). Liquid cooling while adding weight and complexity to the engine, has several advantages when compared to air cooling. It provides for a more uniform heat transfer from the engine to the water jacket. This maintains a lower and more even temperature than air cooling. Liquid cooling minimises hot spots in the engine. All this results in the reduction of the operating range of temperature. This allows the engine to be manufactured to finer tolerances which result in a stronger, more efficient and more powerful engine.

Propeller and Drive

Small two-stroke petrol engines have a fairly narrow *power band* that occurs at a much higher rpm than for comparable four-stroke engines – typically between 5,000 and 7,000 rpm. A lightweight, three- or four-blade propeller can be suited to a 3,000 rpm shaft, but, without ducting, it becomes very inefficient at 6,000 rpm. A reduction gear box is the answer. Sports aviation permits belt-and-pulley reduction devices, but many modern two-stroke engines have a built-on sealed gearbox providing a step-down ratio of between 2:1 and 2.6:1.

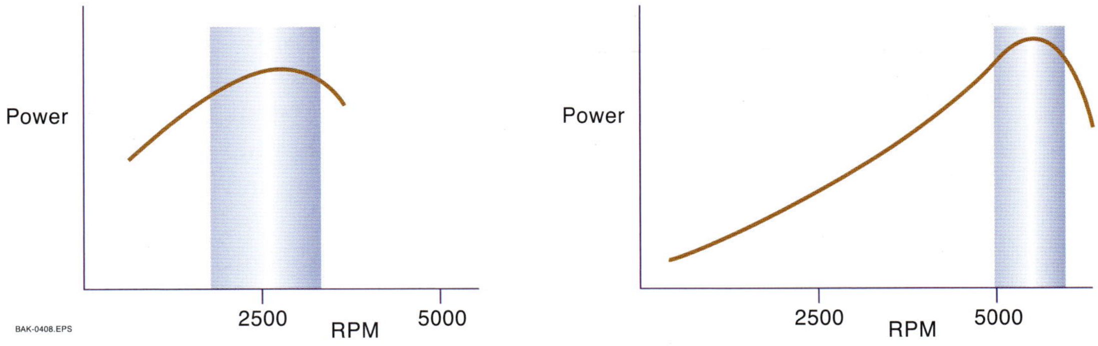

Figure 4-52 Power bands – geared (left) and direct drive (right).

Starting

There are several ways to rotate a small engine for starting. Once priming is completed, choke and brakes are set, and the ignition is on, we can "hand prop" to start. Caution: specific training is necessary to hand start aircraft engines. Of course, electric starters are available. Another method is to have a pull cord like those used on some lawn mowers. Rewind starters are also used. They utilise the stored energy of a heavy spring, also as with some lawn mower.

Aircraft Diesel Engines

Why Diesel?

Aviation gasoline is not only expensive, it contains lead, a potentially serious source of environmental pollution. Compared to motor fuel, AVGAS is made in small batches and is a *narrow-cut,* specialised fuel, subject to tight quality assurance processes. It is more refined and more expensive than other fuels and may not be available into the future. Diesel fuel has been refined only one or two stages from *fuel oil,* which is not far removed from crude oil, and, like aviation turbine fuel (AVTUR), it is a *wide-cut* fuel. Thus diesel fuel is significantly cheaper than AVGAS. Diesel engines are also more economical, offer greater torque at lower rpm and are more reliable than petrol engines. Until today, diesel engines have been too heavy for aviation applications. They are heavier because the engine has to cope with much higher internal pressures.

Note: The engine is named 'diesel' after its inventor, Rudolf Diesel.

When diesel engines are mentioned, we may think of the big, slow-turning engines of the past. They have chugged along reliably for days, weeks, months - even years. Perhaps we think of those big diesel-electric motors in locomotives. Indeed, large diesel engines have powered the world's locomotives and ships for many decades. They power the generators on the farm or the tarmac, the school bus, a road train or a ship. We are used to the reliable, ground-based diesel engine. Smaller lightweight, turbocharged diesels are now common in four-wheel drive vehicles, most heavy trucks and some cars. Now they are competitive for aviation applications.

The diesel engine can be a two- or four-stroke engine. Model aircraft diesel engines are little two-strokes; full-sized aircraft may be either.

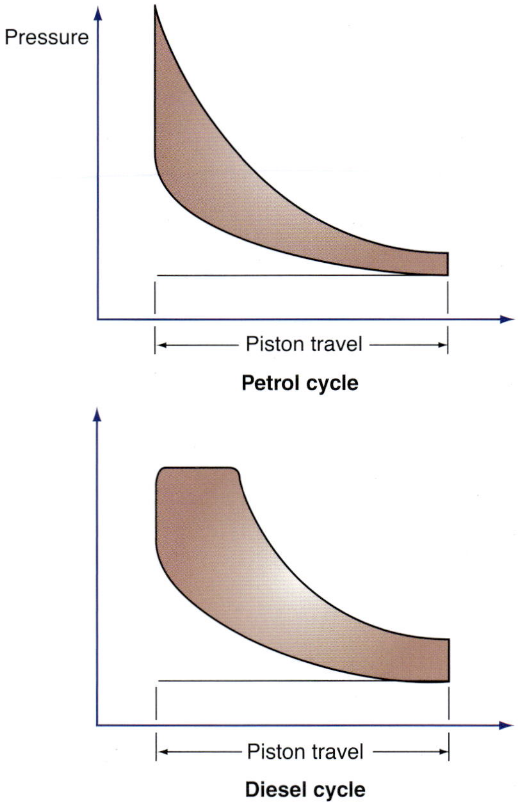

Figure 4-53 Comparison of the petrol cycle and the diesel cycle.

Diesel Operation

The diesel engine relies on spontaneous ignition - which results from the temperature rise due to compression of the fuel/air mixture. In this way, the diesel avoids the complexity and potential unreliability of an electrical ignition system. (Some may use a glow plug or pre-heating to start the cycle but, once they are up and running, they are self-igniting).

Diesels can use less refined fuel but this fuel does not vaporise as readily as AVGAS and, as a result, carburettors are not adequate. Petrol vaporises (converts to gas) relatively easily and mixes with air in the throat of the carburetter. Diesel fuel must be atomised (converted from liquid to a fine spray and then mixed with air). Modern diesel engines therefore use fuel injection. Fuel is injected at the start of the power stroke and, unlike the petrol engine, the fuel charge is injected directly into the cylinders. Power output is controlled by changing the duration of the fuel pulse.

Assuming the fuel/air mixture is correct and the charge has reached the cylinder, the piston rises with the valves closed and the charge is compressed. Diesel engines have very high compression ratios, (about 12:1). This compression ratio causes the fuel to detonate (self ignite). Such a late self-ignition combustion process could cause peak pressures in a petrol engine but, in a diesel engine, the burn rate of the compressed charge is such that the power pulse occurs just after top dead centre and the piston pushes away from the top on its power stroke. It is a more controlled burn and a more even power stroke.

The diesel engine does not have spark plugs, ignition harness nor magnetos. This reduces weight. The fuel-injected aircraft diesel engine can also remove the valves, rockers, push-rods and camshaft.

Without an induction manifold, the engine needs positive inlet air pressure - provided by an external compressor. A particularly efficient way to do this is to turbocharge the engine. That is, use the exhaust gases to drive a turbine which drives the compressor to provide induction air. However, the turbocharger doesn't run well at low rpm because there is insufficient exhaust gas flow to power the compressor. At the risk of adding weight, we also fit a supercharger. This is a compressor, driven mechanically by the engine which caters for the low rpm regime.Thus they may have a turbo-supercharger.

A diesel engine still needs to be very strong to tolerate the high combustion pressures. Advances in metallurgy have provided much of the strength without a significant weight increase. Also, a liquid cooling system is usually fitted.

The aero super-turbocharged two-stroke diesel will not be a small engine. However, compared to a common reliable 200 HP gasoline engine it should gain its airworthiness approvals with about 20% weight advantage and a 30% maintenance and operating cost advantage over the gasoline engine.

The price of diesel fuel and aviation turbine fuel (AVTUR) is about the same. AVTUR is a light kerosene which is compatible with diesel engines. AVTUR is already available on most airports. AVTUR is not acceptable for a gasoline engine but is most likely to be the fuel for aircraft diesel engines.

Propellers

Fixed-Pitch Propellers

Before approaching a propeller, always ensure the magneto switch is off and avoid touching or moving through the propeller arc. Propellers are made of wood, aluminium or composite material such as carbon fibre (actually carbon fibre-reinforced resin). Propellers are either fixed pitch, where the blade angle cannot be changed, or variable pitch, in which case the blade angle is changed. The blade angle responds to a speed-sensing (rpm) governor that is commonly called a constant-speed unit (CSU).

Light training aircraft are usually fitted with a fixed-pitch propeller. The purpose of the propeller is to convert engine power to thrust. The propeller is an aerofoil, which generates lift. This lift is used to propel the aircraft through the air, and when used with respect to a propeller, this lift is termed *thrust*.

Figure 4-54 Constant-speed propeller.

Number of Blades

Figure 4-55 Five-blade propeller.

Propellers can have 2, 3, 4 and sometimes 5 or more blades. While the radius of the propeller arc may be determined by ground clearance, more often it is a function of propeller rpm. If we turn a long two-blade propeller at very high rpm, the propeller tips could become supersonic and lose thrust. With a shorter three- or four- blade propeller, we can produce a similar amount of thrust without losing efficiency. Engine and propeller matching occurs at the design stage of producing an aeroplane. Where very high rpm engines are required, a reduction gear box is used to allow the engine to operate efficiently at its best rpm and the propeller to operate efficiently at its best rpm. This is known as *indirect drive* and is seen often on ultralight aircraft and turbo-prop aircraft.

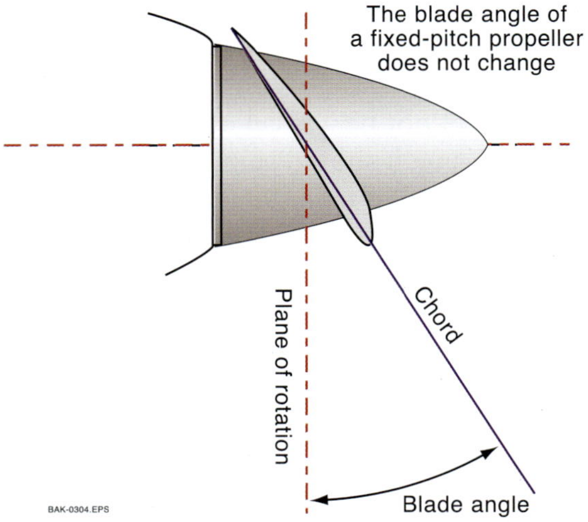

Figure 4-56 Propeller blade angle.

Blade Angle

Blade angle refers to the angle between the plane of rotation and the chord of the propeller section. The blade angle of a fixed-pitch propeller does not change.

If the blade angle is stated for a particular propeller, it is at a standard reference point, which is at 75% of blade length measured from the hub.

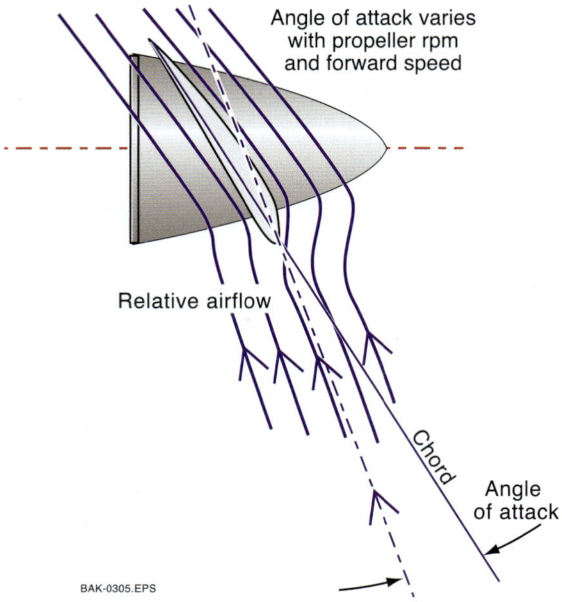

Figure 4-57 Blade angle of attack.

Angle of Attack

Angle of attack denotes the angle between the chord of the propeller section and the relative airflow.

As the direction of the relative airflow changes with engine (propeller) rpm and aircraft forward speed (IAS), the angle of attack changes with rpm and IAS variations.

Vectors Relating to RPM & Forward Speed (IAS)

As fixed-pitch propellers have a fixed-blade angle, the optimum angle of attack is achieved only at one rpm and airspeed combination for each propeller. Many light training aircraft have fixed-pitch propellers with a blade angle providing a compromise between best take-off performance and best cruise performance.

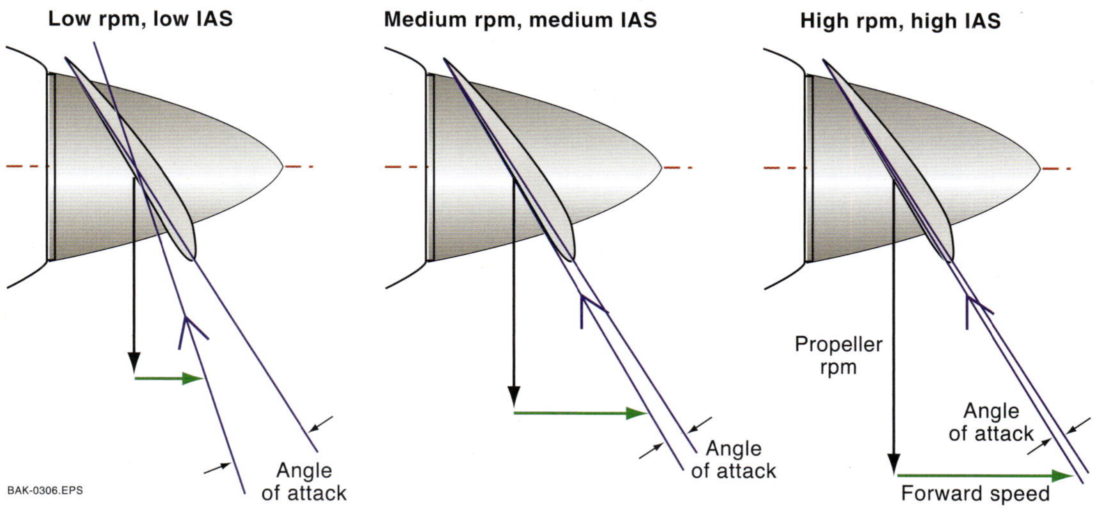

Figure 4-58 Angle of attack variation.

Power Control – Fixed-Pitch Propeller

The throttle is the only engine power control on an engine fitted with a fixed-pitch propeller. The throttle causes an increase in engine power and a proportional increase in rpm. As MP and rpm are both representative of power, on an engine fitted with a fixed-pitch propeller usually only one power instrument is provided.

Constant-Speed Propeller

A constant-speed propeller really means a system using a constant-speed unit (CSU) and a variable-pitch propeller. This is a constant rpm system that permits the pilot to select the propeller speed, and therefore engine speed, needed for any situation. This system then automatically maintains that rpm under varying conditions of airspeed and power.

Propeller RPM Control

As the blade angle of a propeller is decreased, the torque required to spin the propeller is reduced, and for any given power setting, the rpm of the engine will tend to increase. Conversely, if the blade angle increases, the torque required increases, and the engine and the propeller would tend to slow down. By changing the blade angle (pitch) of the propeller, the rpm will change. The propeller lever permits the pilot to set a desired rpm. When maximum power at low airspeed is required, as for take-off, the pilot pushes the propeller lever fully forward to the rpm full increase position. With full throttle, the maximum set rpm is achieved by the reduction of propeller pitch. For cruising, the pilot sets the MP with the throttle then eases back on the propeller control. This influences the constant-speed unit (CSU), which increases the propeller pitch, and the engine speed settles to the desired rpm for cruise conditions. The rpm automatically stays set until the propeller level is again moved.

Oil pressure (hydraulic action) is used to change the propeller pitch (blade angle). In the propeller hub, oil pressure acting on a piston produces a force that is opposed by the natural centrifugal twisting moment of the blades. To increase the propeller blade angle, high pressure oil is directed to the propeller. This moves the piston back. Motion of the piston is transmitted to the blades through the actuating links moving the blades toward high pitch.

When the opposing forces are equal, oil flow to the propeller stops, and the piston will stop. The piston will remain in this position, holding the pitch of the blades constant until the constant-speed unit (CSU) directs oil flow to or from the propeller.

Besides the propeller, the other major component of the system is the constant-speed unit or governor. The engine drives the governor gear-type oil pump and the flyweight assembly. The oil pump boosts engine oil pressure to provide quick and positive response by the propeller. The rotational speed of the flyweight assembly varies directly with engine speed and controls the position of the pilot valve. Depending on its position, the pilot valve will direct oil flow to the propeller, allow oil to flow back from the propeller, or assume a neutral position with no oil flow. These oil flow conditions correspond to increased pitch, decreasing pitch or constant pitch of the propeller blades.

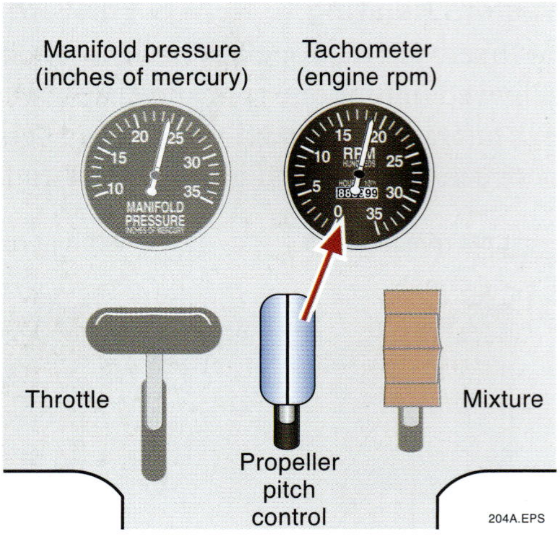

Figure 4-59 Propeller rpm selector (sometimes called the pitch lever).

Setting RPM

When the cockpit propeller lever is moved forward, rpm increases, applying pressure to the speeder spring in the CSU. This means that the flyweights must spin faster to raise the pilot valve, which results in a higher engine rpm setting. When the propeller lever is pulled back, rpm decreases, reducing the pressure on the speeder spring. This reduces the speed necessary for the flyweights to move the pilot valve and produces a lower rpm setting.

Constant RPM

Movement of the propeller lever sets the speeder spring pressure. The flyweights position the pilot valve to direct oil to or from the propeller. This, in turn, positions the propeller blades at a pitch that absorbs the engine power at the rpm selected. When the moment of rpm balance occurs, the force of the flyweights equals the speeder spring load. The pilot valve is in the constant rpm position, with no oil flowing to or from the propeller. This balance represents a constant rpm, and can be any rpm within the system operating range. This is the *on speed* condition.

Figure 4-60 On speed.

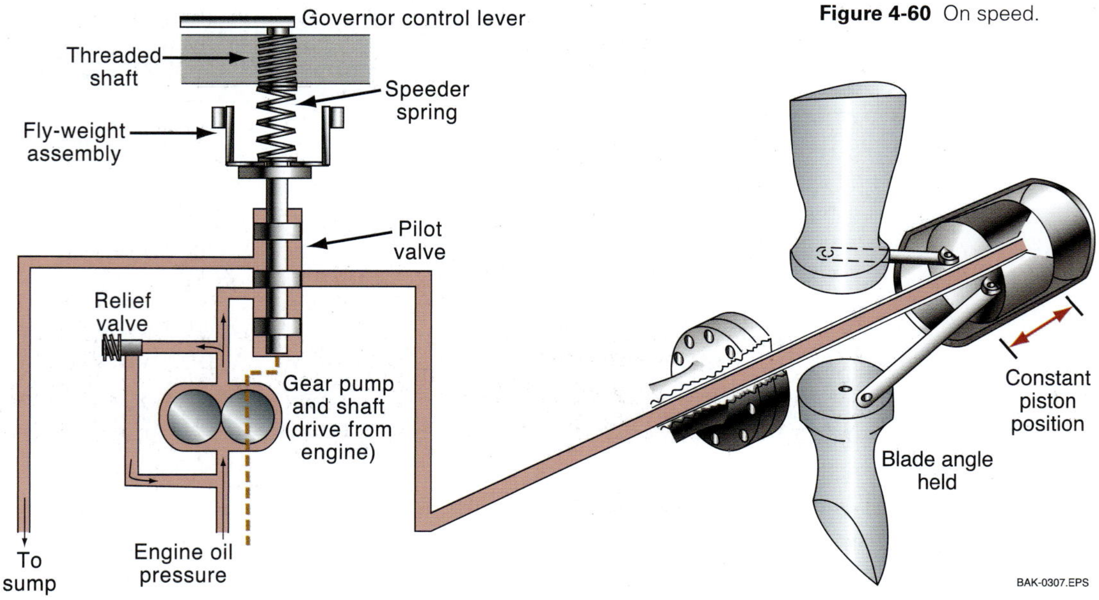

Underspeed

A constant rpm, if the aircraft begins to climb or engine power is reduced, a temporary underspeed occurs. Airspeed reduces and rpm tends to decay (the angle of attack of the blades increases). The instant this happens, the flyweights will droop, causing the pilot valve to move down. Then oil flows from the propeller, reducing the pitch of the blades. This reduces the induced drag on the blades and allows the available engine power to restore the set rpm.

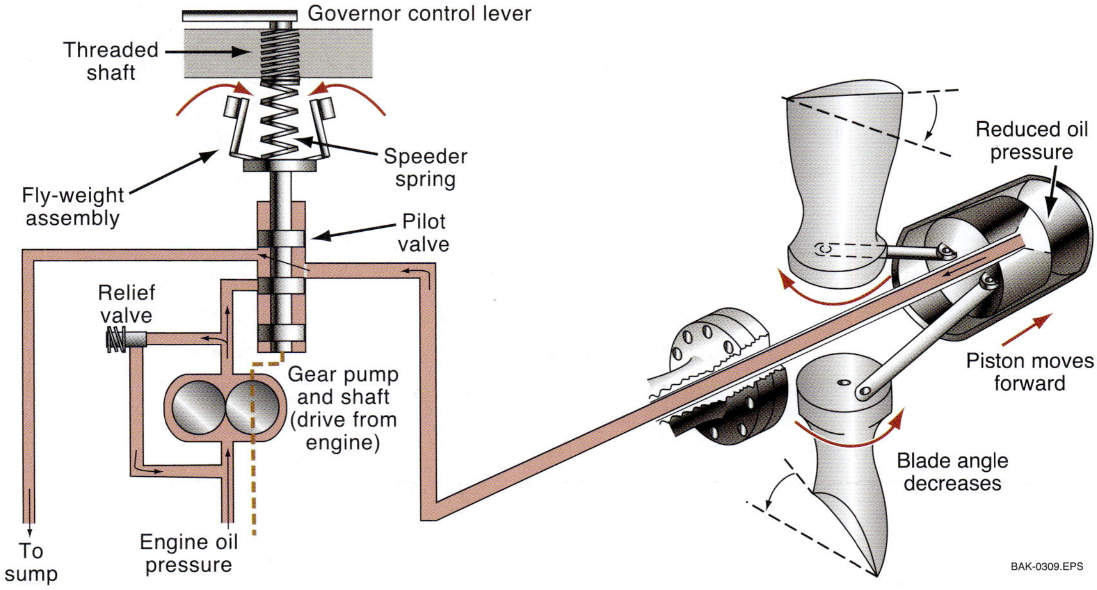

Figure 4-61 Underspeed tendency.

Overspeed

If the aircraft is put into a descent or engine power increased, there is a tendency to overspeed. Airspeed increases and rpm tends to increase (the angle of attack of the blades decreases). The instant this happens, the flyweights move out and raise the pilot valve, which causes oil to flow to the propeller, increasing the pitch of the blades, increasing propeller torque (drag). The engine speed then slows down to restore the original rpm setting.

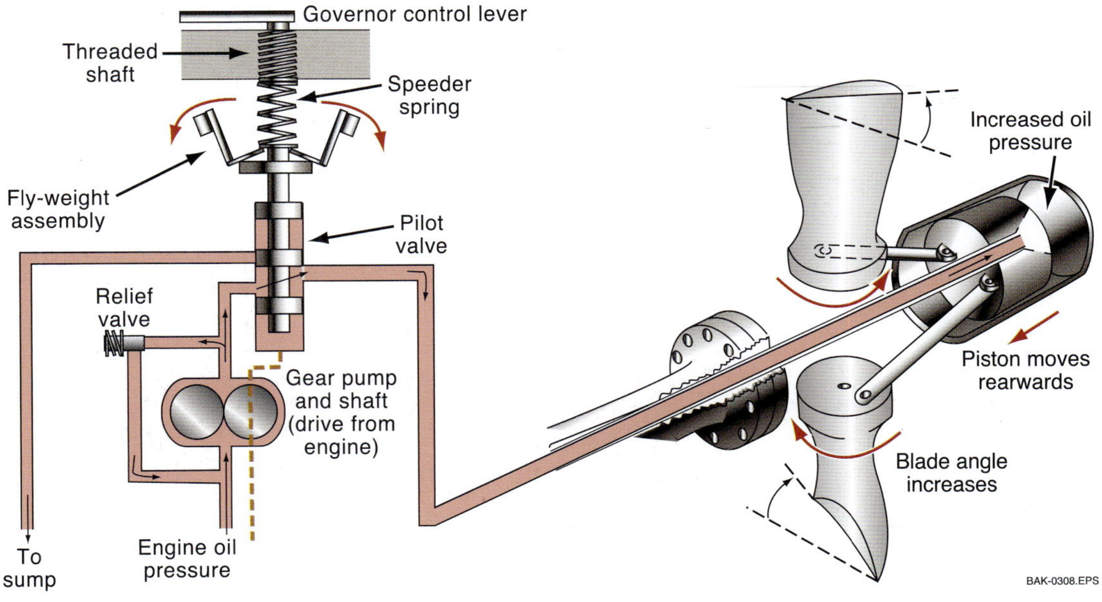

Figure 4-62 Overspeed tendency.

Pitch Stops

Mechanical stops are installed in the propeller to limit blade travel in both the coarse and fine pitch directions. If the blade is driven to the fine pitch position, it contacts the fine pitch stop. If the blade is driven to the coarse pitch position, it will contact the coarse pitch stop.

Power Control

An aircraft engine fitted with a variable-pitch propeller and CSU uses both a throttle and propeller lever to control engine power. Consequently, a *manifold pressure gauge* and a *tachometer* is provided. The CSU will maintain the engine at the set rpm within the operating range of the variable-pitch propeller. While within this operating range the throttle changes MP, which alters power for that set rpm.

If the propeller has reached an operating limit, the course or fine pitch stops, the throttle will then alter both MP and rpm.

During start up, taxi and engine run up, the propeller is out of its operating range and is resting on the fine pitch stop. This means that, as the throttle is moved to increase MP, the rpm increases. During the magneto check, some engine power is lost – as the propeller is not yet in its operating range – and the rpm decreases.

The propeller check involves moving the propeller lever from the full increase position, governing speed approximately 2,700 rpm, rearwards to a position, which changes the set rpm to below 2,000 rpm. This is why the engine rpm decreases during this check.

The CSU (governor) will change the propeller pitch to maintain a constant engine rpm. The pilot can use the propeller lever to select any rpm within the operating range, providing the engine is producing enough power to turn the propeller at the governing rpm.

The CSU uses engine oil at an increased pressure to hydraulically control the propeller. On a single-engine aircraft (non-counter-weight propeller), if the oil pressure was lost the forces on the rotating propeller blades would twist them to the fine pitch position.

The CSU is no longer functional, the aircraft will not cruise efficiently but the aircraft can be recovered to the nearest suitable field. Most important, because the propeller is in fine pitch, full power would be available if required during the landing.

Setting Power

The saying *rev-up, throttle back* may help you to remember the correct sequence for adjusting the engine power.

- When increasing power, select rpm (revs) then MP.
- When reducing power, select MP then rpm.

The blade angle is changed to keep a constant rpm. In doing so, this also keeps a fairly constant, efficient angle of attack. The blade angle automatically changes, to maintain a fairly constant and efficient angle of attack at all power, rpm and airspeed combinations.

Effects of the Engine-Propeller

Because the engine rotates the propeller in a particular direction and because the airflow from the propeller has a spiral path as well as the rearward push, then there are effects on the behaviour of the aircraft, particularly on take-off and especially if it has a tail-wheel undercarriage.

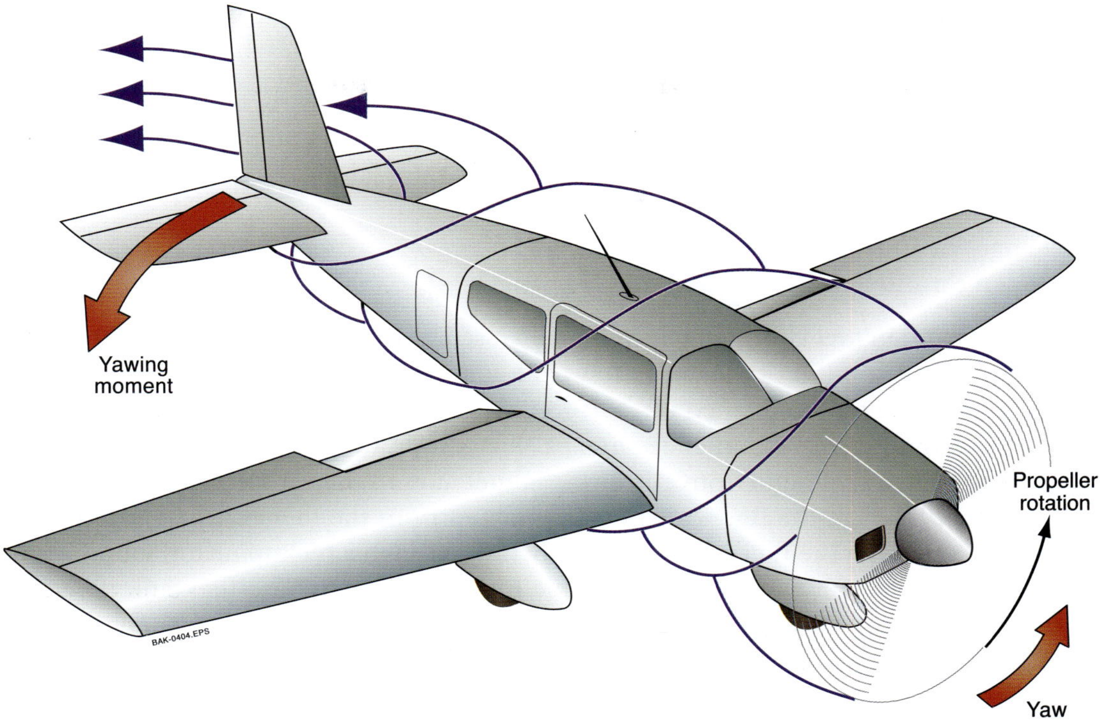

Figure 4-63 Slipstream effect.

Whenever the power is increased there will be a nose-up pitching moment and a yawing moment to the left (for most US-built engines). The yaw is caused by a combination of the following:

- slipstream effect on the fin;
- torque effect since the engine feels a reaction to the torque of turning the propeller;
- gyroscopic effect as the angle of attack is changed on raising the tail or rotation for lift-off (gyroscopic precession causes the pitch change to become a yawing moment); and
- asymmetric blade effect if there is a significant angle of attack, e.g. a tailwheel configuration.

Figure 4-64 Down-going blade produces more thrust with the tail on the ground.

Note: All of these effects are cumulative, i.e. all tend to yaw the aircraft to the left.

Fuel System & Fuels

The function of a fuel system is to store fuel and deliver it to the carburettor (or fuel-injection system) in adequate quantities at the proper pressures. It should provide a continuous flow of fuel under positive pressure for all normal flight conditions, including the following:
- changes of altitude;
- changes of attitude; and
- sudden throttle movements and power changes.

Fuel is stored in fuel tanks, which are usually installed in the wing. A sump and a drain point at the lowest point of the tank allows heavy impurities (such as water or sediment) to gather, so they can be drained off.

The fuel supply line commences higher than the bottom of the sump to prevent impurities (water or sludge) from entering the fuel lines to the carburettor, even though there is a fuel filter in the line to remove impurities from the fuel as it passes down the supply line. Because the fuel enters the supply line through a pickup near the bottom of the tank, there will always be some unusable fuel in the tanks. The fuel tank is vented to the atmosphere so that the air pressure above the fuel in the tank remains the same as outside, as altitude is changed. Reduced pressure in the tank due to ineffective venting could reduce the rate of fuel flow to the engine and could cause the engine to stop.

Fuel vents should be checked in the preflight external inspection to ensure that they are not blocked or damaged. The vents often act as overflow drains to prevent excessive pressure building up if fuel volume increases due to full tanks being warmed in the sun.

A *high-wing aeroplane* with the tanks in the wings will generally allow the fuel to be gravity-fed to the carburettor without the need for a fuel pump, though most modern aircraft have both a mechanical pump and an electric boost pump.

In a *low-wing aeroplane*, the tanks, being lower than the engine, need a fuel pump to lift the fuel to the carburettor. Prior to start-up, an electric auxiliary (boost) pump is used to provide the pressure to prime the engine and to purge any vapour from the fuel line. Once the engine is started, the engine-driven mechanical fuel pump takes over. Correct functioning of the pump can be monitored on the fuel pressure gauge.

Some aircraft have a low-pressure fuel light. These are uncommon in light aircraft but common in turbine aircraft. This light will come on when the fuel pressure is still adequate but below acceptable levels. This may also occur if you have filter icing or some blockage of the filter. In this case, the light is indicating the onset of restricted fuel flow. The pressure switch for the low-pressure light is usually located downstream of the boost pump(s) and upstream of the engine-driven pump(s).

For many aeroplanes, the pilot's operating handbook recommends that the electric fuel pump be switched on for critical manoeuvres such as take-off, landing and low flying. This will prevent fuel starvation in the event of the engine-driven mechanical fuel pump failing.

On low-wing aeroplanes with fuel carried in tanks below the level of the engine, it is important that the fuel strainer drain valve is checked closed during the preflight external inspection. If it is not closed, the engine-driven fuel pump may not be able to draw sufficient fuel into the engine (sucking air instead), and the engine may be starved of fuel unless the electric fuel pump is used.

Priming

Priming the engine is especially useful when starting a cold engine on a cold day, when the fuel in the carburettor is reluctant to vaporise. On some aircraft, priming is achieved by an electric boost pump and the accelerator pump, which is part of the normal throttle operation, or by a manual priming pump.

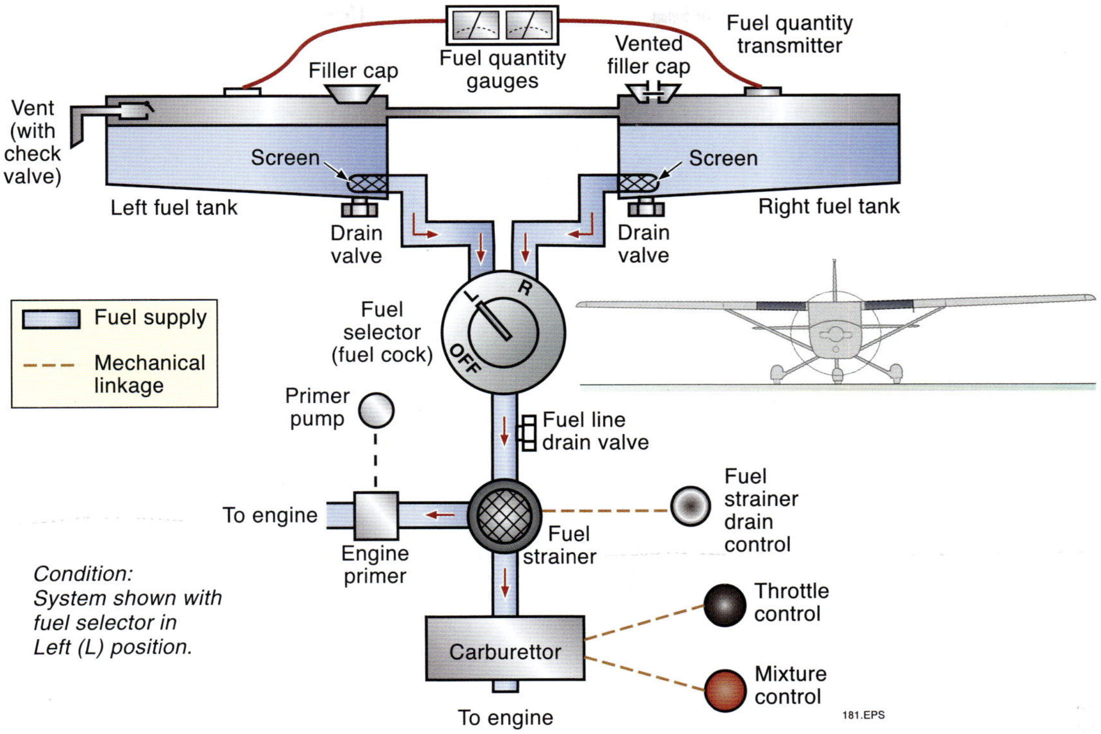

Figure 4-65 High-wing aircraft often use a simple gravity-feed fuel system.

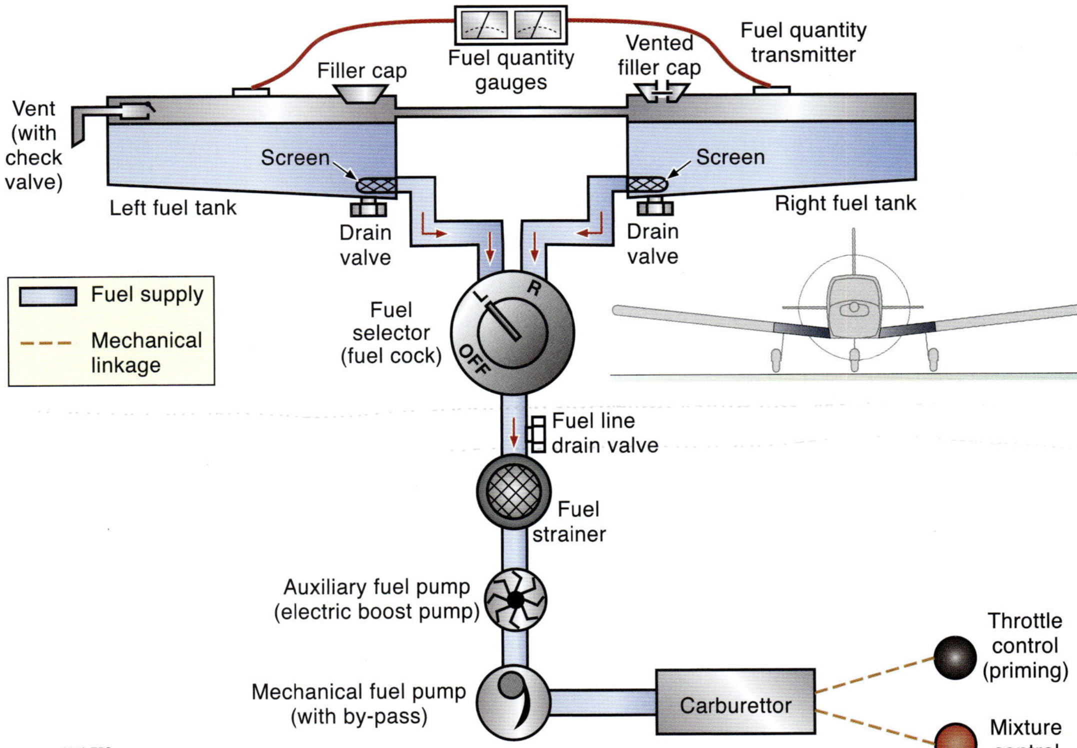

Figure 4-66 Low-wing aircraft use a pressure-feed system.

When a hand-operated pump is fitted, the pilot uses it to pump fuel into the induction system of the engine in preparation for engine start-up. This fuel does not pass through the carburettor but is hand-pumped directly into the inlet manifold just before the cylinders. The primer must be locked off when the engine is running to avoid excessive fuel being drawn through the priming line into the cylinders, especially at low power settings, which could stop the engine due to the fuel–air mixture being too rich. This is not common but is known as a *rich mixture cut*.

Fuel Tank Selection by the Pilot

A fuel line runs from each tank to a selector valve in the cockpit, which the pilot uses to select the tank from which fuel will be taken or to shut the fuel off. Incorrect fuel tank selection can result in fuel starvation, and has been the cause of many accidents – so study your pilot's operating handbook very closely on this matter. The sounds of silence while you still have fuel in one tank, but not the tank that you have incorrectly selected, can be very loud indeed! You should not run a tank dry in flight before switching tanks, because the fuel pump may draw air into the fuel lines, causing a vapour lock which may stop the fuel flow, even from another tank, into the engine. Once a vapour lock has formed, it may be very difficult to restart the engine.

It is advisable when changing tanks to switch on the boost pump to guarantee fuel pressure to the carburettor, and then to positively monitor the fuel pressure as the tanks are changed. Any sudden and unexpected loss of power should bring two possible causes immediately to mind:

- lack of fuel to the engine; or
- carburettor icing.

If the problem relates to fuel, your actions should include the following:

- close the throttle (to avoid a sudden surge of power as the engine restarts);
- set the mixture control to the full rich position;
- turn the electric fuel boost pump on; and
- check fuel tank selection and tank quantity.

If the problem is carburettor ice, apply full carburettor heat; then reapply the throttle.

Fuel Gauges

Most light aeroplanes have electrically operated fuel gauges in the cockpit, and so the master switch will have to be on for them to register. Some older aeroplanes have direct-reading fuel gauges which do not require electrical power. Do not trust the fuel gauges, since they can read quite inaccurately, especially when the aeroplane is not straight and level. Always carry out a visual check of the contents in the fuel tanks during the pre-flight external inspection by removing the fuel caps, visually checking the contents of the tanks, and then replacing the caps securely. The fuel consumption rate specified in the pilot's operating handbook assumes correct leaning of the mixture that, if not done, could lead to a fuel burn 20% in excess of the "book figures", and the fuel gauges consequently reading much less than expected because of excessive fuel burn.

Fuelling/Refuelling

Reference: CAO 20.9.

Putting fuel into the aircraft is variously called *fuelling* or *refuelling*. There are stringent regulations covering the fuelling of aircraft, and these are detailed in the above reference and described in a subsequent chapter of this manual. When refuelling, the aeroplane must be positioned well away from other aeroplanes and from buildings. The engine must not be running, and the ignition switches should be in the off position.

The location of any firefighting equipment should be noted in case it is needed. No smoking is allowed and passengers must be kept well clear.

To prevent the possibility of a spark of static electricity igniting the fuel vapour, you must connect ground-earthing wires between the aeroplane and the refuelling nozzle. You must also earth the aircraft and the refuelling equipment to ensure that they have the same electrical potential. This must be done before refuelling, even before you remove the fuel caps, since fuel vapour could be released into the atmosphere.

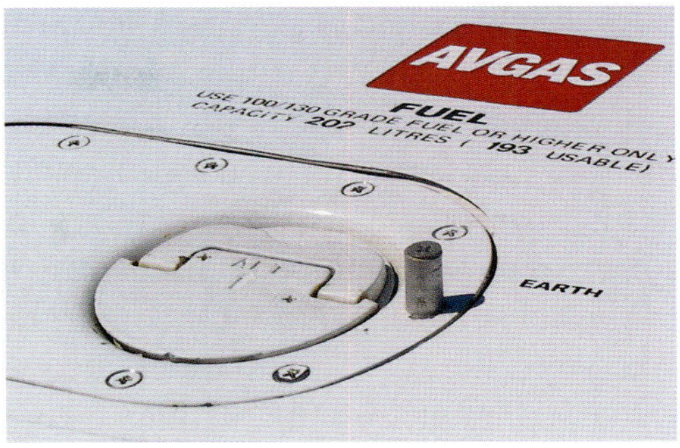

Figure 4-67 Earthing tab next to filler cap.

Fuel Grades

Aviation gasoline (AVGAS) possesses anti-detonation (or anti-knock) qualities which are described by their octane rating or performance numbers. The higher the rating or grade, the greater the compression that the fuel–air mixture can take without detonating. The high-octane fuels have lead added to improve their anti-detonation qualities.

The higher number is an indicator of a rich mixture detonation (when compared with the standard reference fuel). The lower number is an indicator of lean mixture detonation (when compared with the standard reference fuel). If you use fuel that is date-expired, the octane rating may have decreased with age, allowing detonation to occur even at normal operation high power settings, with a consequent loss of power and possible engine damage.

The grades of aviation gasoline (AVGAS) for use in piston engines are colour coded. Normal fuel for light aeroplanes is 100LL (low lead) which is coloured blue or 100/130 octane, coloured green.

Fuel Grade	Colour
100 LL	Blue (low lead)
100/130	Green

Table 4-2 Fuel grades.

The most important thing is to ensure that you are using the correct fuel type for your particular aircraft. Remember: *gasoline* (AVGAS) is required for piston engines; *aviation turbine fuel* (AVTUR) is used in gas turbine engines (jets). AVTUR is kerosene and is straw-coloured or clear, has a distinctive smell, and must not be used in gasoline piston engines. Also, the fuelling equipment has colour-coded labelling:

- jet-fuel decals have a black background with white letters showing the grade (AVTUR);
- AVGAS decals have a red background with white letters, e.g. 100/130 or AVGAS.

There are additional small labels on the fuel hoses or nozzles coloured the same as the fuel grade decals for both AVGAS and jet fuel.

Never use AVTUR (kerosene) in piston engines (except perhaps diesel engines).

Cautions Regarding the Use of a Motor Fuel

AVGAS comes in batches which are subject to stringent quality control. Ordinary motor fuel from petrol stations, sometimes called *motor gasoline* (MOGAS), does not have such tight quality control. MOGAS has a different octane rating system and burning characteristics to AVGAS. It is more volatile. In an aeroplane engine, automobile fuel would cause a lower power output, fouling of the spark plugs, possible vapour locks and a strong possibility of detonation. *Never use MOGAS in an aeroplane engine unless it is specifically authorised. (There are specific approvals for some types of aircraft engines to use MOGAS.)*

Fuel Checks (for Water & Other Contaminants)

Fuel should be checked for contamination before refuelling. The most common contamination is water. It can leak into ground fuel tanks and from there be loaded into the fuel truck and into the tanks of an aeroplane. Water can also get into the tanks through the fuel caps if not secured tightly or if their seals are worn.

Fuel naturally contains a small amount of water and this can condense out, say with a drop in temperature, contaminating the fuel system and causing a loss of engine power or possibly engine failure. Of course the failure is most likely when high power is set for take-off. There are certain fuel test pastes and fuel test papers available which react when water is present, and the fuelling agent will use these on a regular basis to guarantee the purity of the fuel in the storage tanks. Other impurities besides water can also cause problems in the fuel. Rust, sand, dust and micro-organisms can cause similar problems to water. Filtering or straining the fuel should indicate the presence of these and hopefully remove them prior to fuelling. Be especially cautious when fuelling from drums because they may have been standing for some time. Always check drum fuel with water-detection paste and check the release note for date of expiry and for correct grade of fuel. Filter the fuel through a chamois cloth if the drum pump has no filter.

Checking the Aircraft Fuel System for Contamination

Water is more dense than fuel and will sink to the low points in the fuel system. After fuelling has been completed, a small quantity of fuel should be drained from the bottom of each tank and from the fuel strainer drain valve to check for impurities, especially water which will sink to the bottom of the glass. Fuel drains are usually spring-loaded valves at the bottom of each fuel tank, and the fuel strainer drain is usually found at the lowest point in the whole fuel system.

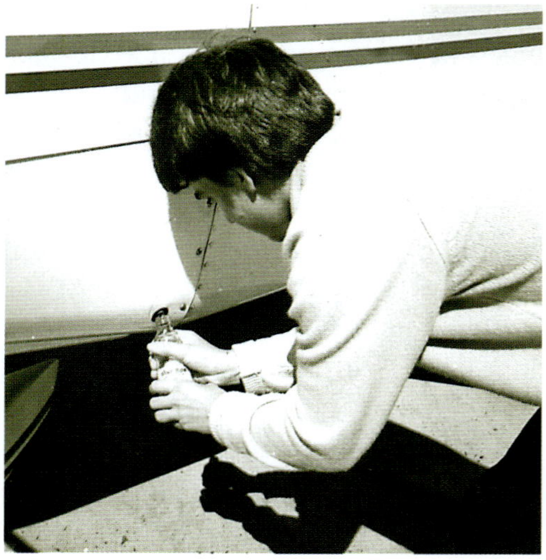

Figure 4-68 Check for contaminants.

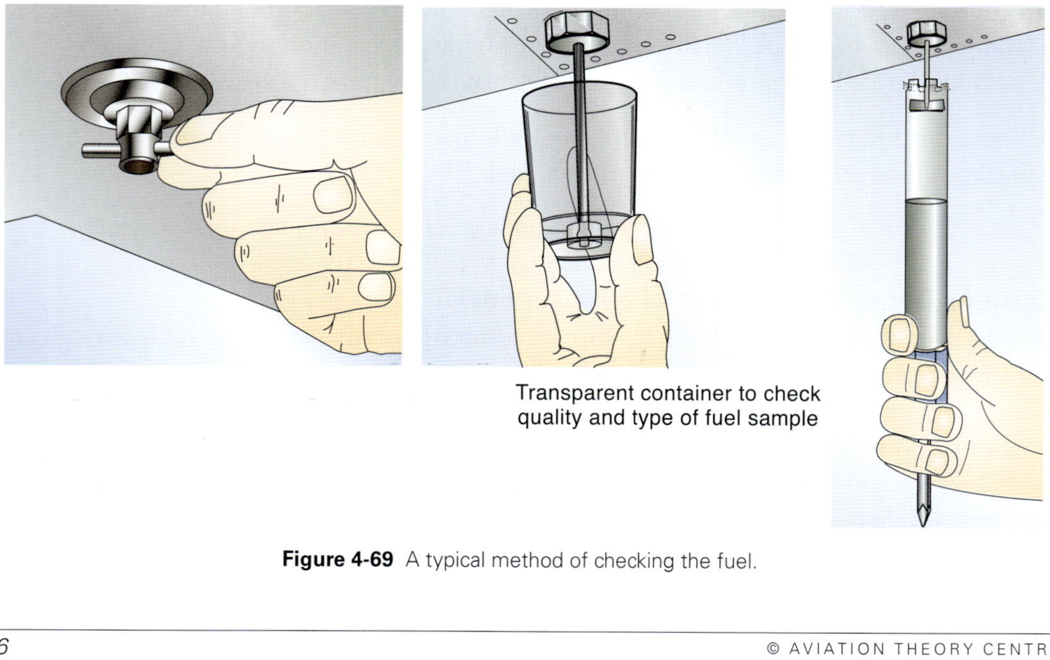

Figure 4-69 A typical method of checking the fuel.

Full Tanks Minimise Overnight Condensation

There is usually a drop in air temperature at night and, if the airspace above the fuel in the aeroplane's fuel tanks is large (i.e. the fuel level is fairly low), the fuel tank walls will become cold, and there will be much more condensation than if the tanks were full of fuel. The water, as it condenses out of the air, will run down the walls and accumulate at the bottom of the fuel tanks. If the tanks are kept full when the aeroplane is not being used for some days, or overnight if low temperatures are expected, this will help minimise condensation.

However, consider the following:

- If the aeroplane has a take-off weight restriction the following day, it may have to be partially defuelled to reduce the weight or adjust the balance.
- If the tanks are full and the temperature rises, the fuel will expand and some could vent from the tank, creating a possible fire hazard on the tarmac.

Carry out a check for water in the aeroplane's fuel system at the following times:

- prior to the first flight of the day;
- following each fuelling; and
- any time you suspect fuel contamination.

If you find any water in the tanks, do the following:

- repeat the draining process until all the water has been removed;
- positively rock the wing to allow any other water to gravitate to the water trap;
- drain off more fuel and check for water at all drain points; and
- inform a maintenance engineer if the fuel doesn't clear.

Fuel System Management

Be familiar with, and follow, the procedures recommended in the pilot's operating handbook for your aeroplane. Understand the fuel system, especially the functioning of the fuel selector valves. Before take-off, you must check your fuel system:

- Ensure that the aeroplane has the correct grade of fuel on board and that it is free of impurities.
- Ensure that sufficient fuel for the flight plus an adequate reserve is on board. Do not rely only on the fuel gauges as they are often inaccurate. Calculate the fuel required and be sure to check the tanks visually prior to flight for sufficient fuel. Remember that some of the fuel in the tanks will be unusable fuel.
- Carry out a fuel drain if required or if you think it is advisable.
- Ensure that there are no leaks, that fuel caps are replaced, and that tank vents are unobstructed. Fuel tank caps are usually on the upper surface of the wing, which is a low-pressure area in normal flight. Fuel can be siphoned out very quickly in flight if the tank caps are not secured.

Do not change tanks immediately prior to take-off or landing, or at low altitude. If possible, verify prior to take-off that fuel is being drawn from the appropriate tank(s). If operation is possible from more than one tank at the one time, this is usually preferred for operations near the ground. If boost pumps are installed, their use for take-off is advised. Refer to your pilot's operating handbook for correct procedures. Turn the boost pump on before changing tanks (check that there is fuel in the tank before you select it). Monitor fuel pressure during and after changing tanks, and as you switch off the boost pump.

Listen to the engine note and if there is a change, turn the boost pump back on and consider returning to the previous tank selection.

Electrical System

The electrical system powers such items as cabin lights, landing lights, instrument lights, navigation lights, rotating beacons or anti-collision lights, starter motors, electric flaps, radios, radar, pitot heaters, fuel gauges, fuel boost pumps, electrically retractable landing gear and so on. Your pilot's operating handbook will contain information on the electrical system of your particular aeroplane. A typical modern light aeroplane has a *direct current* (DC) electrical system. The electric power is produced by an *alternator* when the engine is running (the *alternating current* is converted to *direct current)*, or provided from a battery or external power source when the engine is not running.

The alternator output, either 14 or 28 volts DC, is connected by wire directly to the *bus bar* (which distributes the current to the electrical services). The current flows through this equipment (motor or light), does its work there, then flows through a wire attached to the aircraft metal structure. The aircraft structure forms the *earth return* path for the electrical current.

Main Components of the Electrical System

Bus Bar

The bus bar is the main conductor and the distribution centre in the electrical system. Electrical power from the alternator (or generator) and a battery is supplied to the bus bar, which is essentially a large number of interconnected terminals, from where it is distributed to the circuits and electrical components that require power. There is usually a primary bus bar and a secondary bus bar.

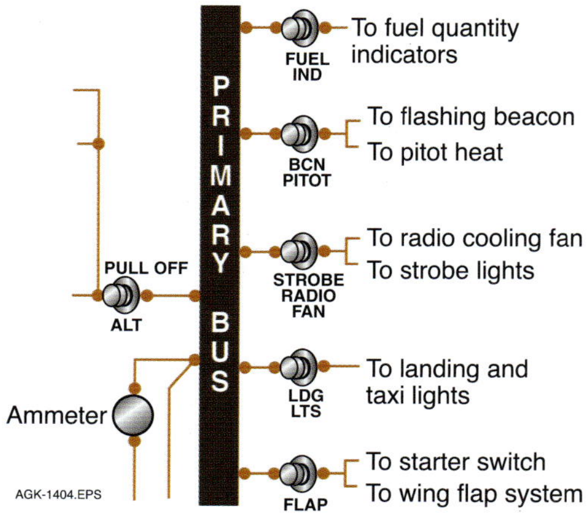

Figure 4-70 Bus bar.

Battery

The battery provides the initial electrical power to rotate the engine with an electric starter motor. It also provides back-up or emergency electrical power. During starting, the battery is also required to provide the direct current (DC) to excite the alternator magnetic fields. Once the engine is running, it is self-sustaining and no longer needs electrical power from the battery – in fact, the alternator provides current to recharge the battery after the engine has been started. ***Do not start a flight with a battery in poor condition*** – it could result in having no electrical power in flight if the alternator fails. If the battery is discharged, replace it or have it recharged before flight. ***Do not start the engine with radios and other unnecessary electrical equipment switched on.*** Large voltage fluctuations may occur when the starter is engaged and may damage sensitive electronic circuits. Turn on this ancillary electrical equipment after the engine is started, and after you have checked that the alternator is charging the battery. For the same reasons, turn off ancillary electrical equipment before shutting down the engine.

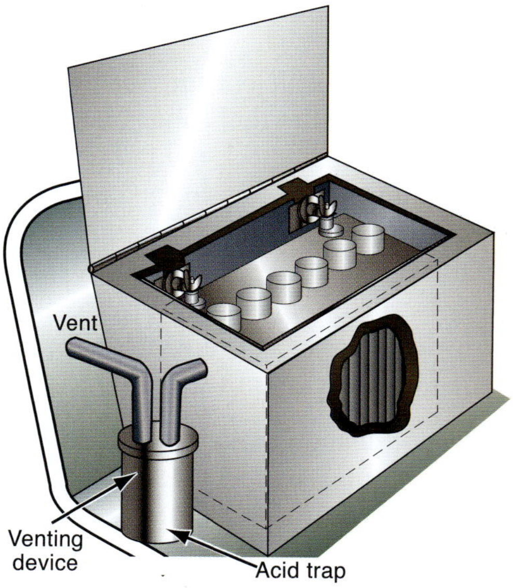

Figure 4-71 Typical battery cells and container.

Alternator

An alternator is an electrical generating device that generates alternating current (AC). Most small aircraft only need DC, and diodes are used to rectify the AC to produce DC. The electrical power in most modern light aeroplanes is usually supplied by an engine driven alternator. As well as providing the power for lights, radios and other services, a very important function of the alternator is to recharge the battery. The output from the alternator is known as the *system voltage* and is either 14 volts or 28 volts DC. Note that some older aircraft have a DC generator rather than an alternator to produce electrical power.

Overvoltage Protection

Some aeroplanes have *overvoltage protectors* (or overvoltage relays) to prevent equipment damage if the voltage regulator fails. There may also be a voltmeter to indicate the voltage, with perhaps an overvoltage light. If the overvoltage light illuminates, you should turn the alternator switch off, reduce the electrical load by switching off non-essential services, and land as soon as possible (because the battery will be solely supplying electrical power and will not be charging).

Ammeters

The ammeter indicates the electrical current (called *amperes*, or *amps*). There are two quite distinct types of ammeter presentation and, as a pilot, you should be familiar with both types.

Load-Type Ammeter

A load (*left-zero*) ammeter measures only the output of the alternator. It is graduated from zero amperes on the left end of the scale and increases in amperes to the right end of the scale, or it may be shown as a percentage of the alternator's rated load (many Piper aircraft use this type).

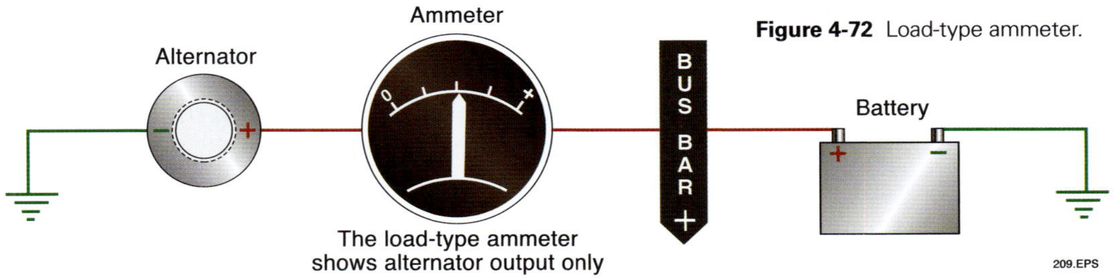

Figure 4-72 Load-type ammeter.

As the load-type ammeter indicates the electrical load on the alternator, this type of ammeter can be referred to as loadmeter. With the battery switch on and the engine not running, or, with the engine running and the alternator switch off, the ammeter will show zero. If the engine is started and the alternator is turned on, the ammeter will then show the alternator output current.

During start-up, the battery discharges electrical power, so immediately after start-up the ammeter indication will be quite high during the initial battery recharging. When the battery is fully charged, and the alternator is operating, the ammeter should show a reading slightly above the zero graduation if all the other electrical circuits are switched off. As these extra circuits are switched on (lights, radios, etc.), the ammeter reading will increase.

If the ammeter reading drops to zero in flight, it probably means an alternator failure. Some electrical systems have a red warning light that illuminates when the alternator fails to supply electrical power. You should be familiar with the procedures for electrical failure in your pilot's operating handbook, which may allow you to restore electrical power. Generally, it is advisable to reduce electrical load to a minimum if the alternator fails, since only the battery will be supplying electrical power. Land as soon as practicable to have the problem corrected.

Centre-Zero Ammeter

The centre-zero ammeter measures the flow of current (amperage) to and from the battery. Current into the battery is a charge, with the ammeter needle deflected right of centre. Current out of the battery is a discharge, with the ammeter needle deflected left of centre. No current flow (either into or out of the battery) is shown by the needle being in the centre-zero position.

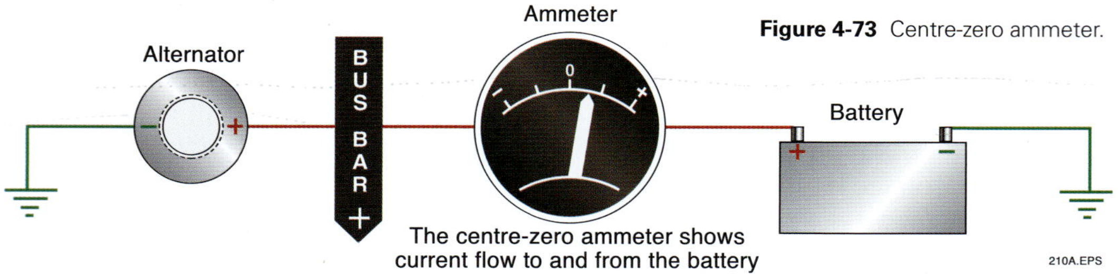

Figure 4-73 Centre-zero ammeter.

- With the battery switch on and no alternator output, the ammeter will indicate a discharge from the battery, that is, the battery is providing current for the electrical circuits that are switched on. The ammeter needle is to the left (discharge) side of centre-zero.
- With the alternator on and supplying electrical power, if the electrical load required to power the circuits switched on is less than the capability of the alternator, the ammeter will show a charge, that is, there will be a flow of current to the battery.
- If the alternator is on, but incapable of supplying sufficient power to the electrical circuits, the battery must make up the balance and there will be some flow of current from the battery. The ammeter will show a discharge. If this continues, the battery could be discharged or flattened, so reduce the load on the electrical system by switching off unnecessary electrical equipment until the ammeter indicates a charge, i.e. a flow of current from the alternator into the battery.

Voltmeter

The *voltmeter* indicates positive charge of the alternator and the state of the battery if you have an alternator failure. For a 28-volt system, the voltmeter will indicate around 27.5 volts, and for a 14-volt system it will indicate around 13.75 volts. You should check the manufacturers figures for the aircraft you're flying. Any voltage outside the parameters specified by the manufacturer should be reported to an engineer.

If you suffer an alternator failure on a 28-volt system, the voltage will drop to approximately 25 volts. The voltmeter will now be indicating the charge of the battery. As the voltage drops to 24 volts, the battery will be almost drained.

Master Switch (Battery Switch/Alternator Switch)

The master switch controls the aeroplane's electrical system. The master switch needs to be on for the bus bar to receive power or for the battery to be recharged when the engine is running. It should be turned off after stopping the engine, to avoid the battery discharging by powering electrical equipment connected to it.

Figure 4-74
Master switch.

In aeroplanes with an alternator installed, the master switch is a split switch (with two halves that can be switched on and off separately):

- one half operates the battery switch (or master relay for the electrical systems), that connects battery power to the bus bar (electrical load distribution point or bar);
- the other half, the alternator switch, is for energising the alternator by connecting the alternator field to the bus bar, thus providing the alternator with battery power for field excitation.

Both switches must be on for normal operation of the electrical system. If either switch has to be turned off in flight then you should consider terminating the flight as soon as possible. They can be switched on separately, but only the alternator can be switched off separately – switching the battery off will automatically switch the alternator off as well.

Fuses, Circuit Breakers & Overload Switches

Fuses, circuit breakers and overload switches are provided to protect the equipment from any electrical current overload. If there is an electrical overload or short-circuit, a fuse-wire will melt or a circuit breaker (CB) will pop, i.e. pop out, and break the circuit so that no current can flow through it. It may prevent the circuit from overheating, smoking or catching fire.

As most circuit breakers use bimetal thermal sensors, it is recommended that a 90-second waiting period is observed to allow the element to cool after it operates. Before attempting a reset, if the equipment causing the fault can be turned off, it should be. It is normal procedure (provided there is no "dark brown" smell or other sign of burning or overheating) to reset a circuit breaker once only, by pushing it back in or resetting it. If a circuit breaker pops again, you can be fairly sure there is an electrical problem, and so it should not be reset a second time. Overload switches are combined on/off switches with a built-in circuit breaker. Overload switches will switch themselves off if they experience an electrical overload. The pilot can switch them back on like a resettable circuit breaker.

Engine Start Circuit

Some engines have push button start switches, while many others have a "start" contact added to the magneto switch. This diagram shows that the very large current required for starting runs through a heavy-duty relay or solenoid and is not seen on the ammeter.

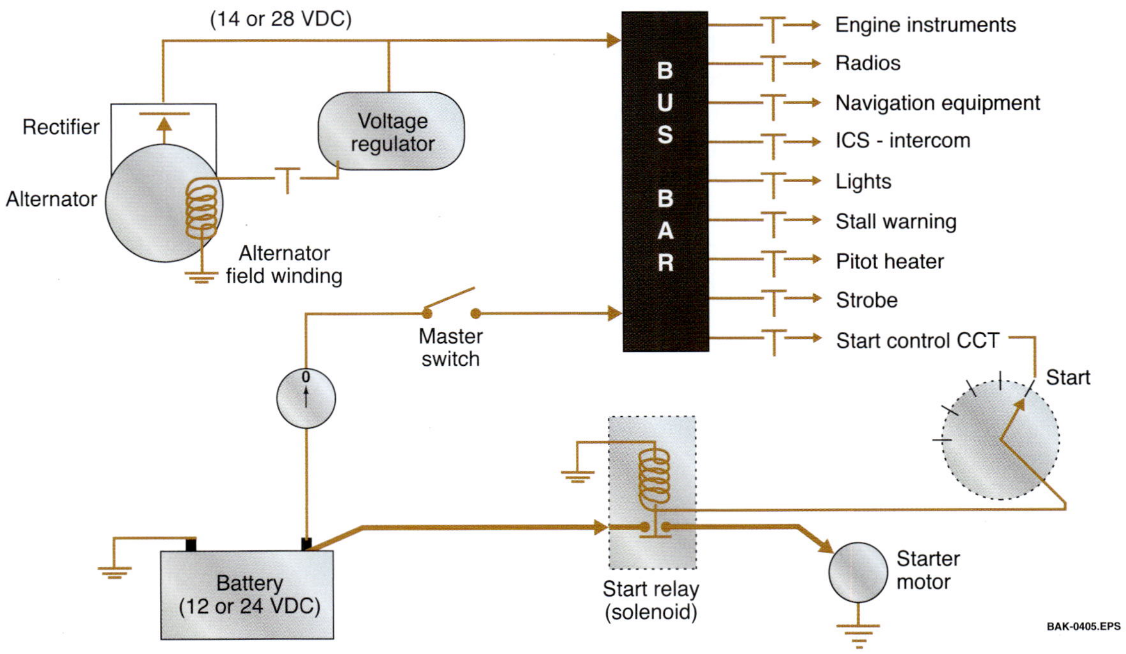

Figure 4-75 Engine starter circuit.

Normal Electrical System Operation

The engine cannot be started unless the master switch is on. The bus bar is powered during preflight by turning the master switch on. Although the start switch is built into the magneto switch, the start circuit is an electrical system and not part of the ignition system. The high starting current is not seen on the ammeter because it takes a direct path through thick, low-resistance wires via the starter solenoid to the starter motor.

Should the alternator fail, the battery automatically powers the bus bar so all equipment will continue to operate normally for some time. However, if the battery power was then consumed, all electrical equipment would be lost, including the radios, transponder, electric flaps and, in some aircraft, engine instruments. The loss of rpm indications will cause concern but the engine will continue to function normally.

Abnormal Electrical System Operation

An electrical overload will normally cause a circuit breaker to pop. This protects the affected circuit. Allow 90 seconds to cool and, if no indication of smoke, fire or burning, reset the circuit breaker – but reset once only. If the CB pops again, do not reset a second time.

The ammeter should be checked when the engine is running to ensure that the alternator is supplying sufficient current (amps) for the electrical services and to recharge the battery. A centre-zero ammeter indicates the rate at which current is flowing into the battery and recharging it. With the engine running, the ammeter can indicate two faults:

- insufficient current to charge the battery; and
- too much current.

With too much current, an excessive charge rate, the battery could overheat and the electrolyte, which is usually dilute sulphuric acid, could evaporate, possibly damaging the battery. The cause of the excessive current charging is likely to be a faulty voltage regulator, and equipment such as the radios could be adversely affected. Many aeroplanes have an overvoltage sensor that would, in these circumstances, automatically disconnect the alternator and illuminate a red warning light in the cockpit to alert the pilot.

If the alternator (or generator) fails – indicated in most aeroplanes by either the load-type ammeter indication dropping to zero (or centre-zero ammeter showing a discharge) and a red warning light – the battery will act as an emergency source of electrical power. To extend the period for which the battery can supply power following failure of the alternator the electrical load should be reduced. This can be done by switching off non-essential services such as unnecessary lights and radios. Consideration should be given to terminating the flight at the nearest suitable aerodrome while electrical power is still available.

Engine & Systems Abnormal Operations Indications

If there are *any* unusual engine noises, vibrations or indications on the ground, *do not fly that aircraft*. In the air, observe the following:

- *Oil pressure* – if the oil pressure drops, turn towards the nearest airfield and maintain altitude until you are within gliding distance. Minimise throttle changes.
- *Oil temperature* – if the temperature increases, keep an eye on the pressure, and be ready to turn for home or to land. Reduce power and increase airspeed.
- *Cylinder head temperature* (CHT) – if the CHT increases to an abnormally high value, it may mean that the mixture is too lean. Select full rich and reduce power. Also increase airspeed.
- *Fuel pressure* – if the fuel pressure drops, immediately turn on the boost pump and head for the nearest airfield. If you have just changed fuel tanks, make sure you have selected the correct one, or go back to the previous selection. Avoid high-power demands.
- *Propeller rpm* – if you have exceeded the maximum permissible rpm and time limits, reduce power and return for landing. Report the overspeed in the maintenance release. If the propeller rpm drops or oscillates with a set throttle, consider carburettor icing (select hot), fuel selection (empty tank) and check the oil pressure. Head for home.
- *Electrical current* – if the ammeter/loadmeter shows abnormal indications, turn off the services you don't need, remain in VMC and complete the flight or return home. If the voltmeter shows a discharge, minimise use of electrical services and be prepared for a no-radio arrival.

Hydraulic Systems

Undercarriage

Some general aviation aeroplanes have a hydraulically operated, retractable, undercarriage. The hydraulic pump is driven by an electric motor. Larger aircraft may also have hydraulically operated flaps, and high-speed aircraft have hydraulic flight controls. It is entirely separate from the foot-operated hydraulic brake system. A basic hydraulic system includes a pump, regulator, reservoir, relief valve, filters, plumbing, oil and various control valves, actuators, and an accumulator. To operate a hydraulic service, the pilot moves a control valve (or electric switch which moves the valve) that directs hydraulic fluid to an actuator – like turning on a tap. The pressure exerted by the hydraulic fluid then moves an actuator, which mechanically operates the service.

Figure 4-76 Retractable undercarriage.

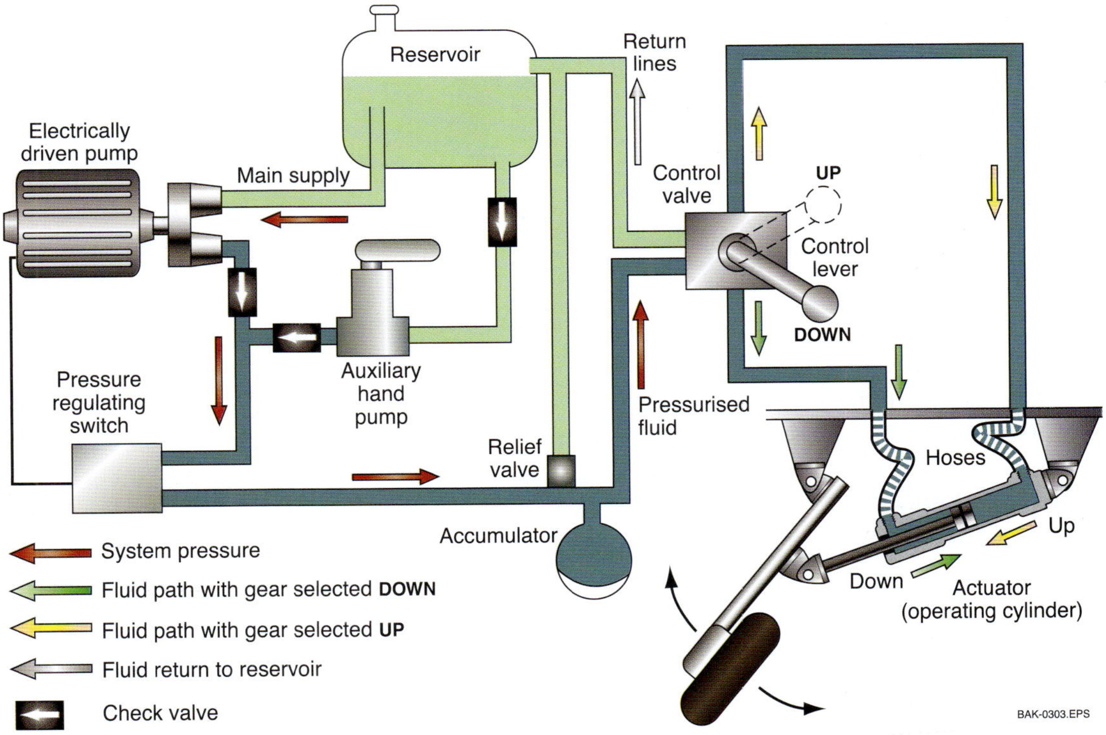

Figure 4-77 Hydraulic system with an electric pump.

Wheel Brakes

The wheel brakes are usually disc brakes. They are hydraulically operated by rotating the rudder pedal (by depressing the top, like a car's accelerator pedal). Pressing the left toe brake will apply the left wheel brake, and pressing the right toe brake will apply the right wheel brake.Used separately, they provide *differential* braking, which is used to supplement nosewheel steering for tight manoeuvring and to brake when turning; brakes used together provide straight-line braking.

A typical wheel-brake system utilises a master cylinder containing hydraulic fluid for each brake system. As an individual toe brake is pressed, this toe pressure is transmitted by the hydraulic fluid to a slave cylinder which causes callipers to clamp the brake pads onto the disc. The brake disc, which is part of the wheel assembly, is thus slowed down. When the toe pedal is released, the pressure is released allowing the wheel to rotate freely again.

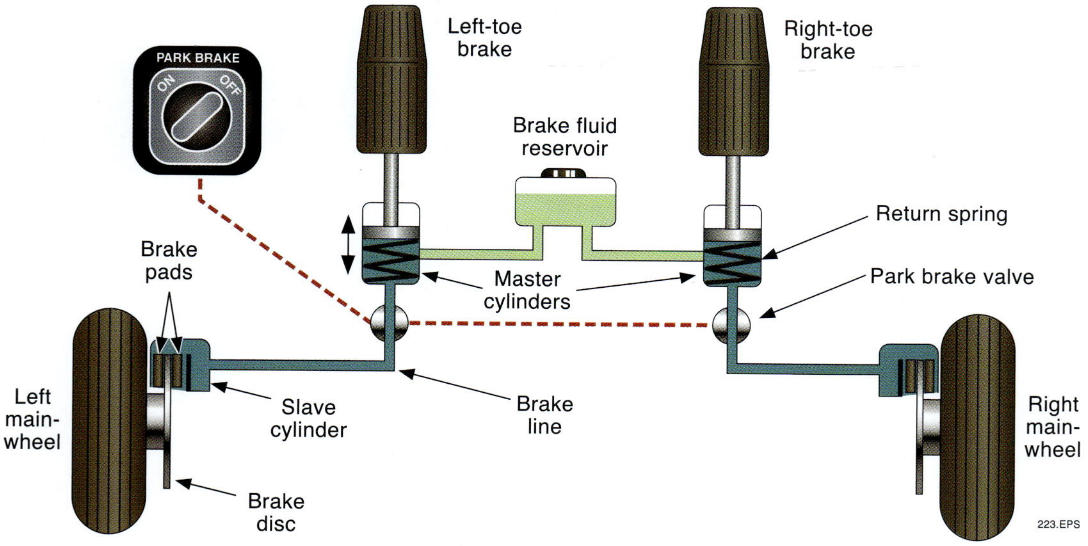

Figure 4-78 A typical light aircraft brake system.

The park brake may be a lever with ratchet detents – like an antique car or truck or a valve which retains system pressure to lock the wheels. Application of this parking brake requires two actions:

- pressurise the system by applying toe pressure; and
- selecting the park brake valve on.

Simply selecting the park brake on *does not* lock the wheels. Pumping the toe pedals supplies the pressure for the callipers to clamp the discs. This pressure can be applied before or after the park brake is selected to on. Releasing the park brake valve is a single action which releases the pressure and frees the wheels to rotate.

Braking – Operating Problems

Check your brakes as soon as the aircraft begins to move forwards thus ensuring the brakes are working before the aircraft has built significant momentum. If fluid leaks from the system or is empty, the pedal may depress to the floor with little or no effective braking. A more common problem is air leaking into the system and a pedal feeling spongy. Note that the left and right systems are not connected and usually only braking on one side is lost. Spongy brakes reduce braking capacity and directional control in a crosswind so should be fixed before flight even of you can pump up the pressure by pumping the pedals. A spongy pedal is a symptom of a leak somewhere, and the brake may not be available for landing.

Hydraulic Fluids

Two types of fluids are available. One is mineral based; the other vegetable based. They are colour coded. The mineral-based oil is red, and the vegetable-based oil is blue. Since mineral-based hydraulic fluid attacks natural rubber, synthetic rubber packings must be used in a system using mineral-based fluid. Vegetable-based fluid can be used with either natural rubber or synthetic rubber packings. The hydraulic system reservoir filler cap is clearly marked to show the type of fluid used in the system. If the two types of hydraulic fluids are mixed, a heavy gum will result which will be deposited throughout the system and may cause many of the units to become inoperative. Use of mineral-based fluid in a system having natural rubber packings will result in serious leakage and eventual failure of the system.

Cockpit Heating & Ventilation

Fresh air is available to the cabin from external airscoops, which are usually forward of the doors. Fresh air can be fed directly to the pilots and also to the mixer box.

Warm air is provided in most single-engine aircraft by circulating fresh air around the exhaust system then feeding it to the mixer box. The levers in the cabin allow the pilot to select the appropriate temperature for the cabin and to demist the wind shield as required.

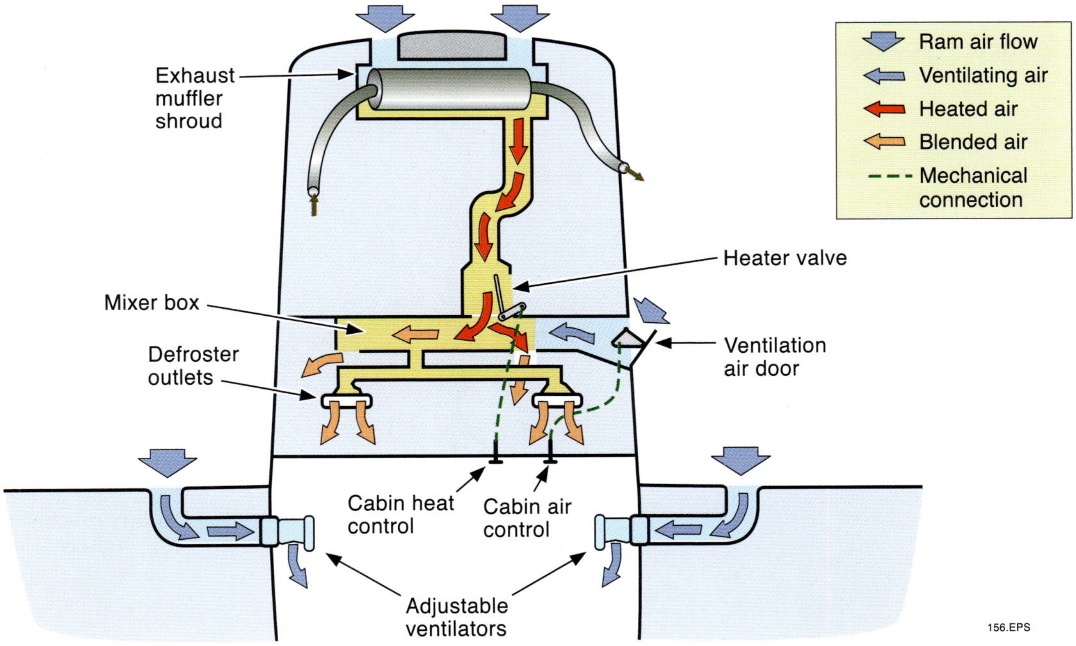

Figure 4-79 Heating/ventilation system.

CAUTION: *Because the exhaust system heats the cabin air, there is a slight risk of carbon monoxide entering the cabin. For this reason, the exhaust system must be kept in good condition.*

Flight Instruments

The first impression most people have of the cockpit or flight deck is of the complexity and number of instruments. When you analyse the instrument panels of even the largest jet transport aeroplanes, however, you will find that the instrumentation is not complicated. In fact, the basic instruments will be very similar to those found in the smallest training aeroplane. Aeroplane flight instruments fall into three basic categories:

- pressure instruments, which use variations in atmospheric air pressure;
- gyroscopic instruments using the properties of gyroscopes; and
- compass systems that sense the earth's magnetic field.

Pressure Instruments

The basic flight instruments informing the pilot of airspeed (airspeed indicator), altitude (altimeter) and rate of change of altitude (vertical speed indicator) are pressure instruments.There are two aspects of air pressure that need to be considered: static pressure and dynamic pressure.

Static Pressure

In the atmosphere at any point, static pressure is exerted equally in all directions. It is the result of the weight of all the air molecules above that point pressing down, due to gravity. Static pressure decreases with altitude and is exerted on all points on an aircraft, inside and out, except when the aircraft is specially sealed.

As its name implies, static pressure does not involve relative movement of the air. Static pressure is sampled on the surface of an aircraft by a static vent, then directed to a barometer type device to be measured.

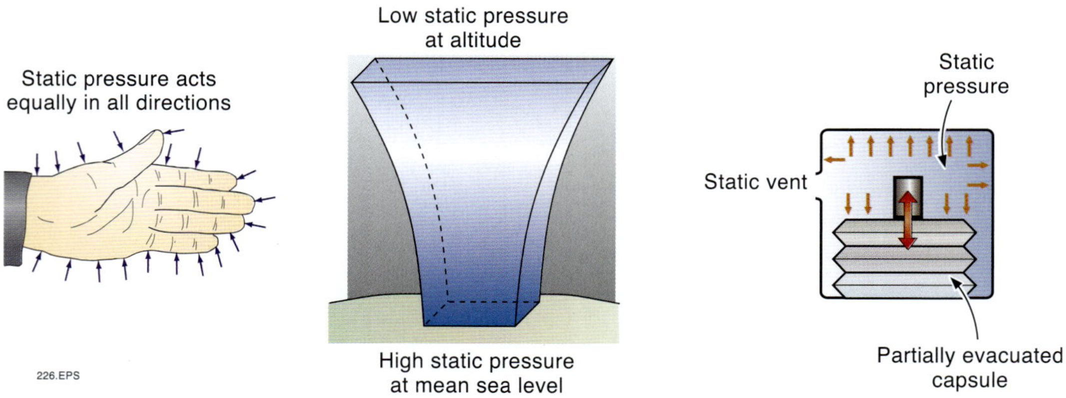

Figure 4-80 Static pressure.

Dynamic Pressure

If you hold your hand up in a strong wind or out of the window of a moving car, then an extra wind pressure is felt due to the air impacting your hand. This extra pressure (above the static pressure), which is always present, is called dynamic pressure or pressure due to relative movement. It is felt by a body which is moving relative to the air, that is, it could be moving through the air or the air could be flowing past it.

Dynamic pressure depends upon two factors. The first factor is the speed of the body relative to the air. The faster the car moves or the stronger the wind blows, then the stronger the dynamic pressure that you feel on your hand. This is because of the greater number of air molecules that impact upon it per second.

The second factor is the density of the air. In outer space, no matter how fast you travelled, you would not feel this dynamic pressure because there are practically no molecules to impact upon you. At sea level, where the atmosphere is most dense, your hand would be struck by many molecules per second, certainly many more than in the upper levels of the atmosphere. So, although travelling at the same speed, you will feel a much lower dynamic pressure in the higher, less dense regions of the atmosphere.

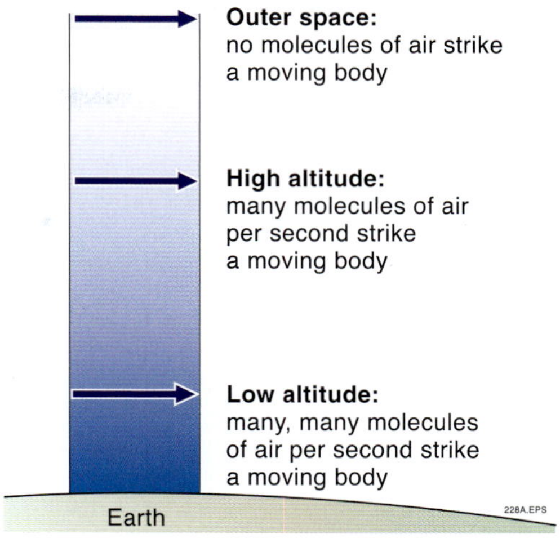

Figure 4-81 Dynamic pressure.

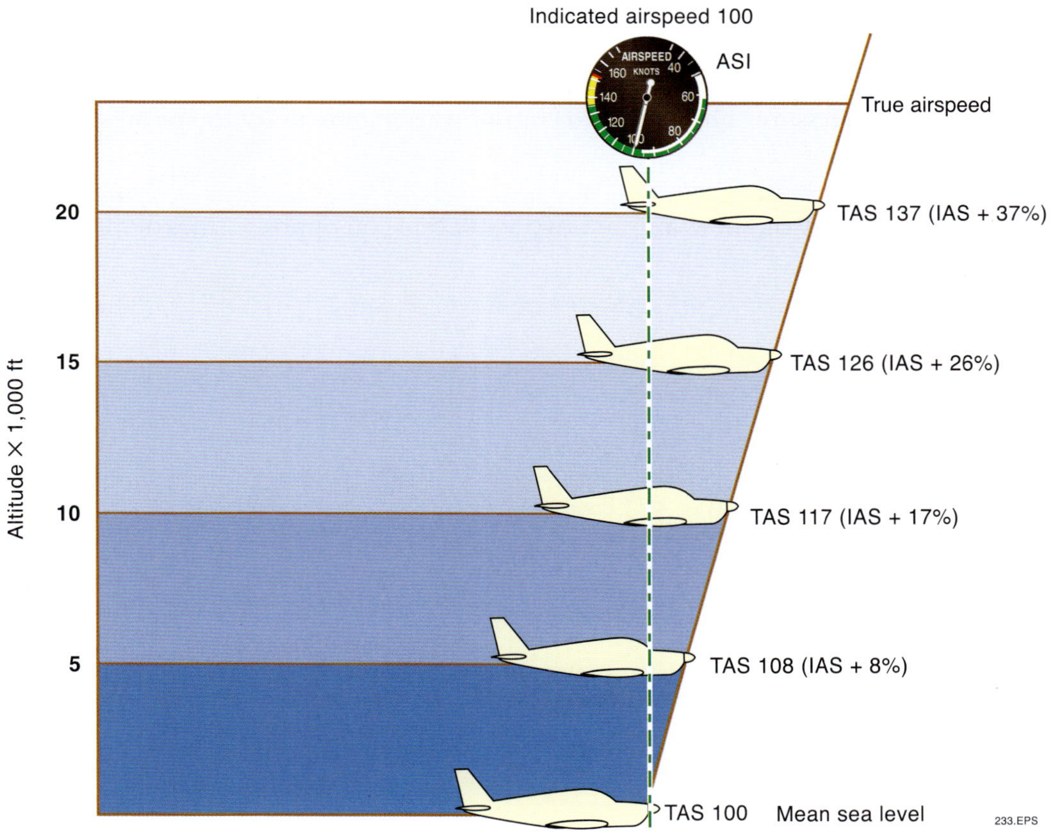

Figure 4-82 With a constant indicated airspeed, true airspeed increases with increased altitude.

Total Pressure (Pitot Pressure)

Static pressure is always exerted, but, for dynamic pressure to be present, there must also be motion of the body relative to the air. Total pressure consists of static pressure plus dynamic pressure. Total pressure is also known as *pitot* pressure (pronounced *pee-toe*). The airspeed indicator (ASI) senses dynamic pressure (i.e. the difference between total pressure and static pressure) and its scale is calibrated to read in units of speed (knots).

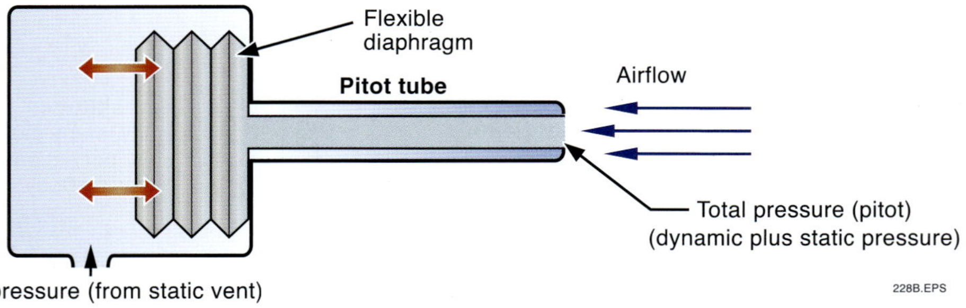

Figure 4-83 Principle of airspeed measurement.

Pitot-Static System

The three pressure flight instruments that make use of the pitot and/or static pressures are:

- the altimeter, which senses static pressure to indicate altitude;
- the vertical speed indicator, which relates the rate of change of static pressure to a rate of climb or descent; and
- the airspeed indicator, which determines the difference between total pressure and static pressure giving the dynamic pressure, to provide indicated airspeed.

The pitot tube senses total pressure and the aeroplane's static vent provides the measurement of static pressure. There are two common arrangements of the pitot–static sensing system:

- a combined pitot–static head; or
- a pitot tube, usually on the wing, and two static vents on opposite sides of the fuselage.

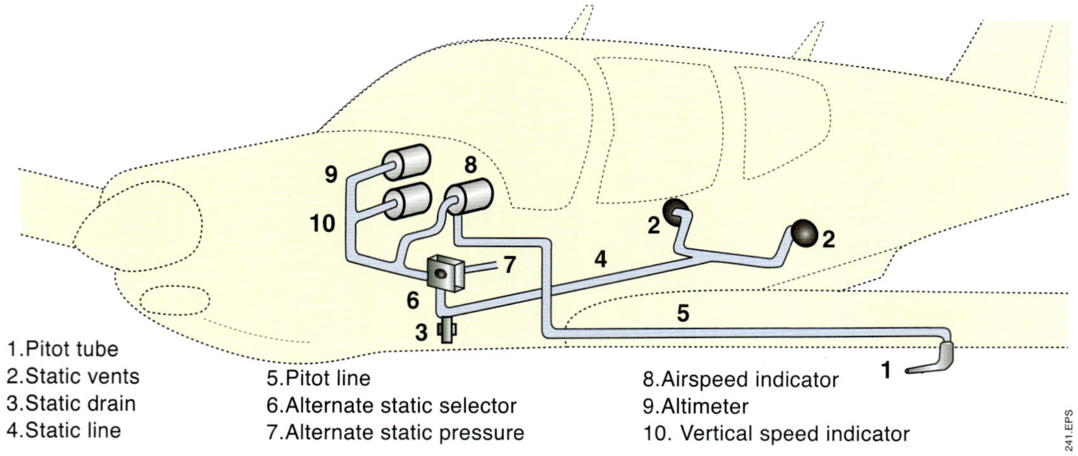

Figure 4-84 Pitot–static system.

The pitot tube must be positioned where the airflow is not greatly disturbed, often forward of or beneath the outer section of one wing. Otherwise the airspeed indicator system will suffer from significant errors. Most aeroplanes have two static vents, one on each side of the fuselage, so that the reading for static pressure, when evened out, is more accurate, especially if the aeroplane is slipping or skidding This is known as a *balanced static system*.

It is vital that the pitot tube and static vent(s) are not damaged or obstructed, otherwise false readings from the relevant flight instruments could degrade the safety of the flight. They should be carefully checked in the preflight external inspection. The pitot cover and static covers used to prevent water or insects accumulating in the tubes must be removed before flight.

To counter a blocked or iced static vent, there is an alternate source of static air from within the aircraft.There is no alternative pitot pressure. Instead, the head is heated.

Alternate Static Source

Generally, on non-pressurised aircraft, the alternate static source is located in the cabin or inside the engine bay. When used, this source introduces some error in the instruments, because the cabin air pressure is lower than the outside air pressure due to airflow over the cabin. Airspeeds and altitudes read higher than normal. The vertical airspeed indicator shows a momentary climb as the alternate static source is opened, followed by stabilisation and normal readings thereafter.

Be careful not to confuse the alternate static source with *alternate air*, which is an alternative source of air for the engine induction system in a fuel-injected engine. The controls for each are sometimes close to each other.

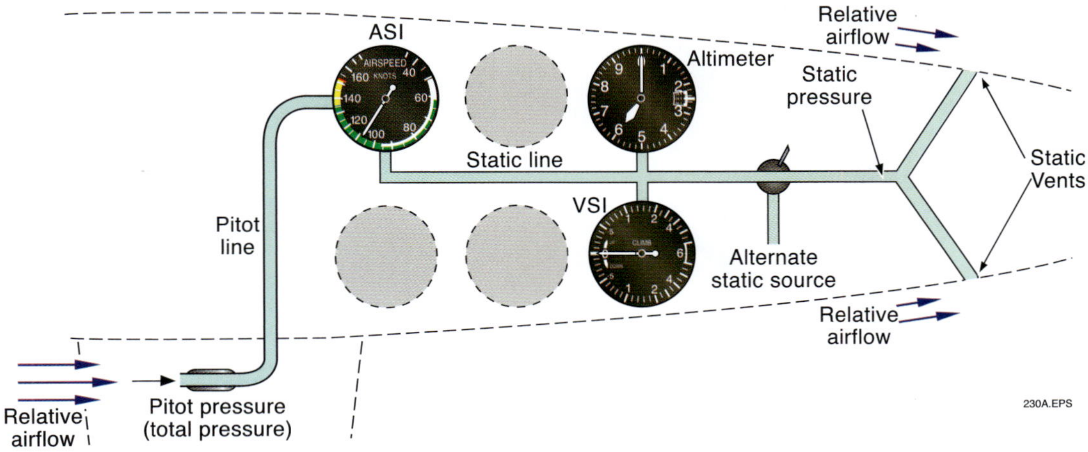

Figure 4-85 Pressure instruments.

Pitot Heat

It is possible that the pitot tube could be blocked by ice. There is usually only one pitot head, and it is fitted with an electric heater. This is checked during preflight and should be turned on when rain is encountered, in cloud or if there is a risk of ice or frost.

Pitot heat is rarely used on the ground (because it may overheat). Generally, it is only checked on the ground as part of the preflight inspection to ensure it is operating.

Airspeed Indicator (ASI)

The airspeed indicator shows *indicated airspeed* (IAS). It is a measure of dynamic pressure. We can find dynamic pressure by subtracting the static pressure from the pitot tube measurement. This is simply done by having a diaphragm with total pressure from the pitot tube being fed onto one side of it and static pressure being fed onto the other side.

The diaphragm in the ASI system will position itself according to the difference between the two. A pointer is connected to it and shows the magnitude of dynamic pressure against a circular scale calibrated in knots.

As airspeed increases, the dynamic pressure increases but the static pressure remains the same. The difference gives us a measure of the dynamic pressure (indicated airspeed).

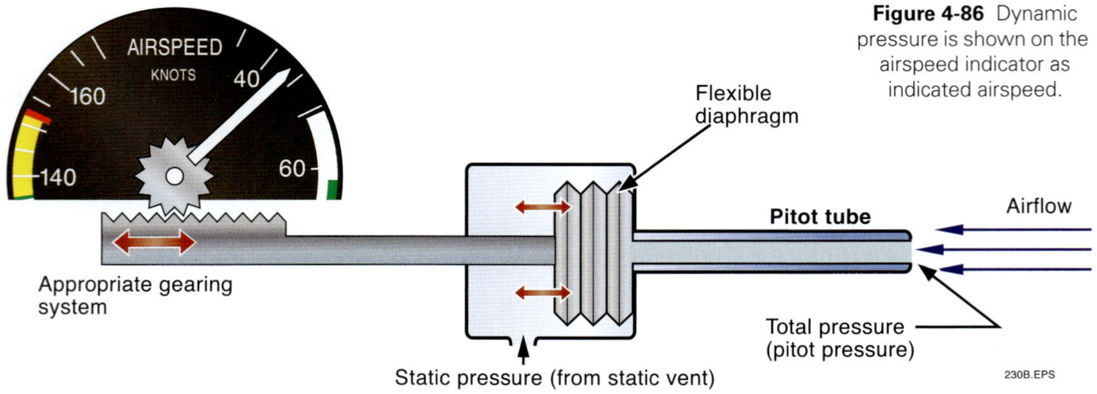

Figure 4-86 Dynamic pressure is shown on the airspeed indicator as indicated airspeed.

Colour Coding on the ASI

To assist quick reading of aircraft limitations ASIs have certain sectors (speed ranges) and certain specific speeds marked according to a colour code.

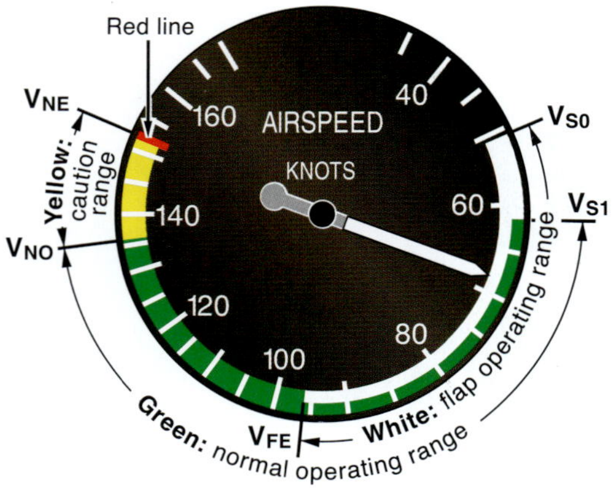

V_{S0}	*Stall speed at max weight, landing gear down, flaps down, power off*
V_{S1}	*Stall speed at max weight, landing gear up (if retractable), flaps up, power off*
V_{FE}	*Maximum speed, flaps extended*
V_{NO}	*Maximum structural cruising speed (for normal operations)*
V_{NE}	*Never-exceed speed (max speed, all ops.)*

277B.EPS

Figure 4-87 Airspeed indicator colour coding.

- *Green arc* denotes the normal-operating speed range, from stalling speed V_{S1} at maximum gross weight (flaps up, wings level) up to V_{NO} (normal-operating limit speed or maximum structural cruise speed), which should not be exceeded except in smooth air. Operations at indicated airspeeds in the green arc should be safe in normal flying conditions.
- *Yellow arc* denotes the caution range, which extends from V_{NO} (normal-operating limit speed) up to V_{NE} (never-exceed speed).
- *White arc* denotes the flaps operating range, from stall speed at maximum gross weight in the landing configuration V_{S0} (full flaps, landing gear down, wings level, power-off) up to V_{FE} (maximum flaps-extended speed).
- *Red radial line* denotes V_{NE}, the never-exceed speed. If gusts are encountered at speeds above V_{NE}, even in smooth air, design load factors may be exceeded.

ASI Readings with a Blocked Static Vent or Pitot Tube

A blockage or ice-buildup of either the static vent or pitot tube will cause the pressure to be trapped in that particular line to the pressure instruments. If you are climbing and the static vent ices over, then the static pressure trapped in the line will be higher than the actual static pressure where the aeroplane has climbed to. The measured difference between pitot (total) pressure and static pressure will be less than actual, therefore the ASI will underread, i.e. show a lower indicated airspeed than actual.

On a descent, the reverse is true: a blocked static vent would cause the ASI to over-read, i.e. show an indicated airspeed higher than actual. This is a dangerous situation if the pilot does not recognise it and reduces the speed, because the aeroplane will actually be flying at a speed less than that indicated.

If you commence a take-off with a completely blocked pitot tube, only the static pressure trapped in the pitot tube will be fed to the ASI, to be compared to the static pressure from the static vent. The ASI will indicate zero. Of course, with zero indicated airspeed, you would not take-off. If the pitot tube and its drain holes ice over, then the total pressure in the pitot tube will stay constant. In a climb, the outside static pressure reduces, hence the airspeed indicator will overread. Conversely, on descent below the altitude where icing occurred, the ASI will underread.

Errors in the ASI

There are some small errors associated with the airspeed indicator system:

- Instrument error is usually no more than one or two knots and applied to IAS to give calibrated airspeed (CAS); in practice, this correction is so small in light aircraft that it is usually disregarded.
- The airspeed indicator is calibrated to read correctly at sea level (in standard conditions of temperature and pressure). If air density is less than at sea level (which is the case at altitude) the airspeed indicator will indicate an airspeed that is less than the true airspeed (TAS). Some ASIs have a small rotatable scale that allows an adjustment for the density error. If the correct altitude and temperature is manually set, the pilot can read the TAS as well as the IAS.

Altimeter

Unlike a car, an aeroplane must be positioned in three dimensions. It must be navigated vertically as well as horizontally. The altimeter is the most important instrument for vertical navigation. The reference point for vertical navigation and for charts is *mean sea level* (MSL). *Mean* refers to the *average* height of the sea surface calculated from hourly tide readings taken over many years. The altimeter relates the static pressure at the level of the aeroplane to an equivalent height in the *International Standard Atmosphere* (ISA), a theoretical standard atmosphere which acts as a common reference point.

The main purpose of the International Standard Atmosphere is to provide a standard against which pressure instruments can be calibrated and aircraft performance data compared. ISA static pressure at mean sea level (MSL) is 1,013.2 hPa.

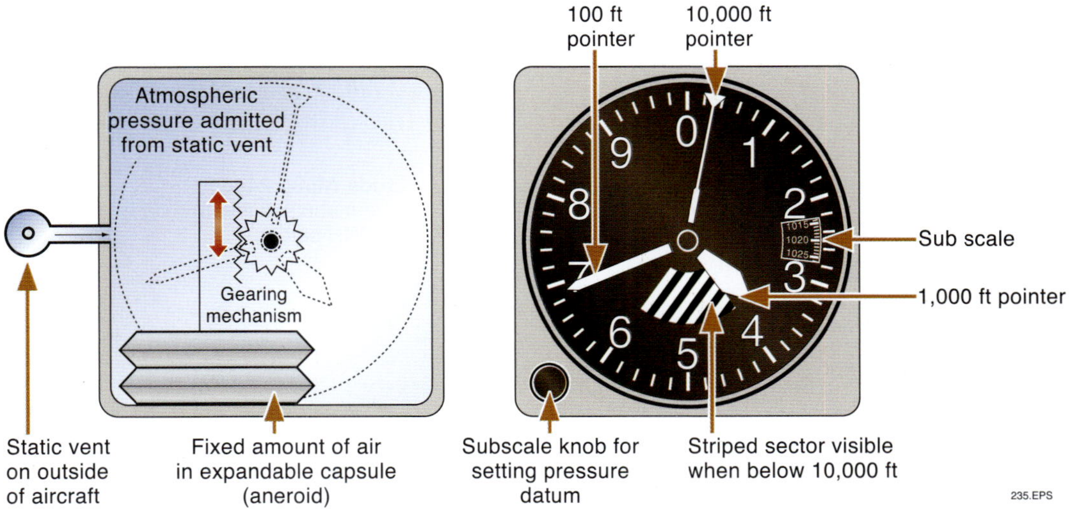

Figure 4-88 Altimeter.

A change of 1 hPa of pressure at sea level will produce an altimeter change of 28 ft. At 20,000 ft, a 1 hPa change represents 67 ft change in altitude. A useful guide is that the static pressure reduces by 1 hPa for each 30 ft gain in altitude in the lower levels of the atmosphere (up to about 5,000 ft). For instance, if the pressure falls by 15 hPa, the altimeter will indicate a 450 ft gain in altitude and, at 3,000 ft altitude, the atmospheric pressure is 100 hPa below the mean sea-level value.

How the Altimeter Works

The altimeter contains a sealed, flexible capsule called an *aneroid* that contains air. The outside of the aneroid is exposed within the sealed instrument case to the ambient static pressure sensed at the static port. As the aeroplane climbs and static pressure decreases, the sealed capsule expands and drives pointers, via a mechanical linkage. The pointers on the altimeter's face indicate the increasing height above the reference point.

Altimeter Subscale Settings

The altimeter has been designed so that a range of pressure values, datum pressures, can be set on a subscale, using the rotatable knob attached to the instrument. The altimeter will display the vertical distance above whatever pressure datum has been set on the subscale. In Australia, all operations below 10,000 ft *above mean sea level* (AMSL) use mean sea level as the reference datum and so the MSL pressure is always set on the subscale. This pressure setting is referred to as the *QNH.*

With QNH set, the datum is mean sea level – for the atmospheric pressure that exists at the time. Remember pressure changes with weather patterns too. Height above mean sea level is called *altitude.* Height above the ground is called *height.*The advantage of flying with QNH set is that we can immediately use the altimeter reading to determine our vertical clearance above the ground, radio masts, obstructions, aerodromes, etc., because these are all marked on aeronautical charts as *elevations*, i.e. height above MSL. We also know that all other aircraft in the area are using the same setting.

For local operations, the *local QNH* of the aerodrome is set on the subscale prior to take-off. The altimeter should then show close to the aerodrome elevation. At controlled aerodromes, local QNH is available from the automatic terminal information service (ATIS), or from the control tower. At non-towered aerodromes, you can simply wind the altimeter until it indicates aerodrome elevation – the subscale will then read the local QNH. If you set the altimeter to zero the subscale reading is called QFE. – 高海拔和低於sea level的机場

When departing your airfield you will need to set the *area QNH* for your region. This can be up to 5 hPa (150 ft) different from the local aerodrome QNH.

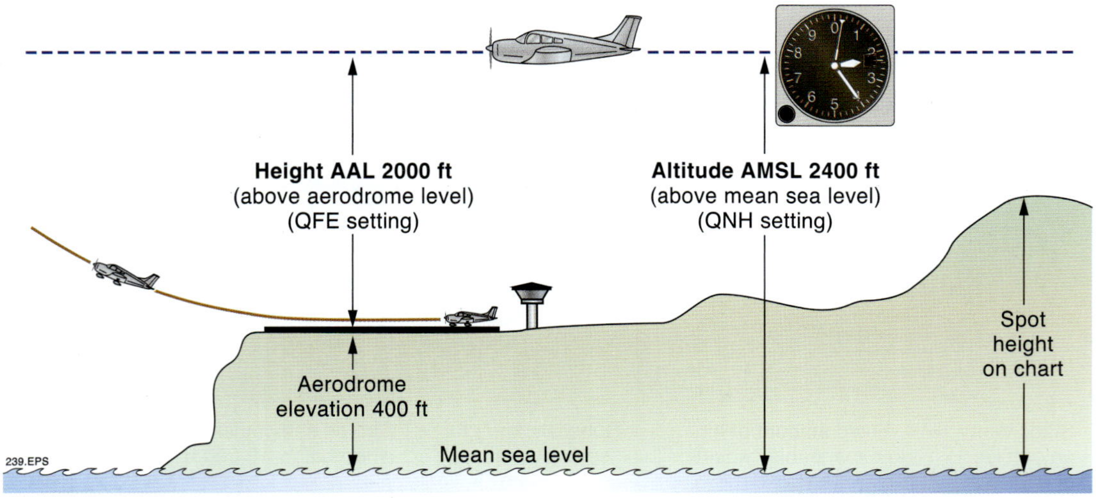

Figure 4-89 Height, elevation and altitude.

High elevation airport : >5000'

Pressure ALT: altimeter setting 1013 = 30×(1013 − QNH) + field elevation

Up to about 5,000 ft, 1 hPa is approximately equal to 30 ft. If the QNH is set in error by 2 hPa, then the altimeter reading will be in error by 60 ft. For example, if flying at 5,000 ft, as indicated by the altimeter, and the subscale is set to 1,026 hPa instead of the true value, 1,028, then the aircraft's actual altitude will be 5,000 + 60 = 5,060 ft. *If the subscale setting is too low, the altimeter will read low. If the subscale setting is too high, the altimeter will read high.*

Blockages of the Static Vent

If ice or insects (or anything) block the static vent completely, then that static pressure will remain fixed in the line to the altimeter. A constant altitude will be indicated, even though the aeroplane may be changing altitude, because there is no pressure differential between the inside and outside of the aneroid.

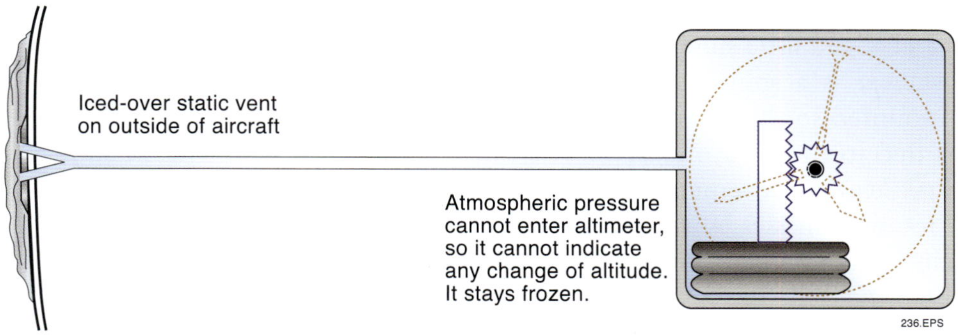

Figure 4-90 A blocked static vent – altimeter reads constant irrespective of the aircraft altitude.

Vertical Speed Indicator

Figure 4-91 Vertical speed indicator.

The vertical speed indicator (VSI) is a pressure instrument also based on the principle that static pressure decreases with altitude. The VSI presents rate of change of static pressure to rate of change of altitude, in hundreds (or thousands) of feet per minute (fpm). The VSI is sometimes called the *rate of climb and descent indicator* (RCDI).

If you begin a descent, the aeroplane will be moving into air with a progressively increasing static pressure. The new and higher pressure at the lower level is fed directly from the static vent into a flexible capsule. The same pressure is also fed into the casing that surrounds this capsule, but via a *choke capillary* (a small hole) that introduces a slight delay in the change of pressure. The capsule therefore expands and drives a pointer on the VSI scale to indicate a rate of descent, e.g. 500 fpm. The faster the climb or descent, the more the metered air, trying to pass through the small hole, has to "catch up", and the more the rate of climb or descent that is indicated. Clever isn't it?

However, it also takes some seconds before a stabilised rate is indicated, due to the inherent lag (or delay) in the VSI. Its design feature is also its limitation; however, you'll get to know and allow for its behaviour just as you will all of the instruments.

Blocked Static Vent

If the static vent became iced over or blocked, then the two pressure areas (inside the capsule and surrounding it) would equalise and the VSI would read zero, even though the aeroplane's altitude might be changing.The alternate static source fixes the problem.

Gyroscopic Instruments

It is difficult to appreciate the enormous importance of the invention of the gyroscope to aviation. Ancient history shows children playing with spinning tops, but little practical use was made of their unique characteristics. The aeronautical applications of the gyroscope in the form of the instruments of the turn indicator and then the attitude indicator (artificial horizon) were developed in the US to allow the mail planes to fly in all weathers. The attitude indicator and the turn coordinator have changed little since that time.

A *gyroscope* is a spinning wheel (called a *rotor*), mounted so that its spin axis (pivot or axle) is free to move in one or more planes (called *freedoms* of movement). A characteristic of rotating masses is their tendency to maintain their original alignment in space (called *rigidity*). The heavier the mass and the faster it is rotating, the greater the rigidity and the greater the resistance to change.

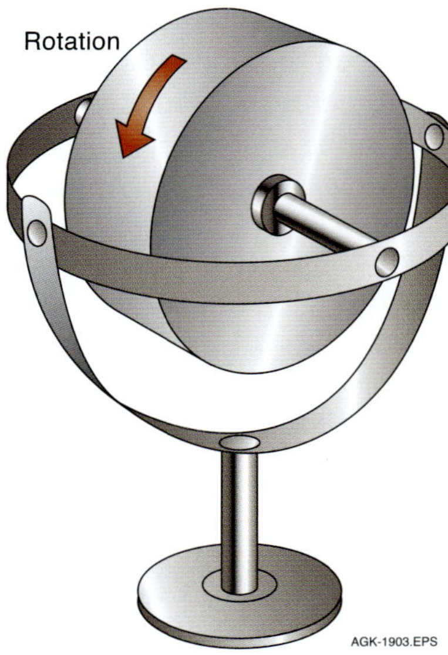

Figure 4-92 Simple gyroscope.

This means that a gyro axis, which is free to move, tries to point at a fixed datum in space while the aeroplane, in which it is mounted, moves around it. Gyroscopes are therefore invaluable as the basis for instruments that remain aligned to a set datum in direction (heading) or verticality (pitch and roll attitude).

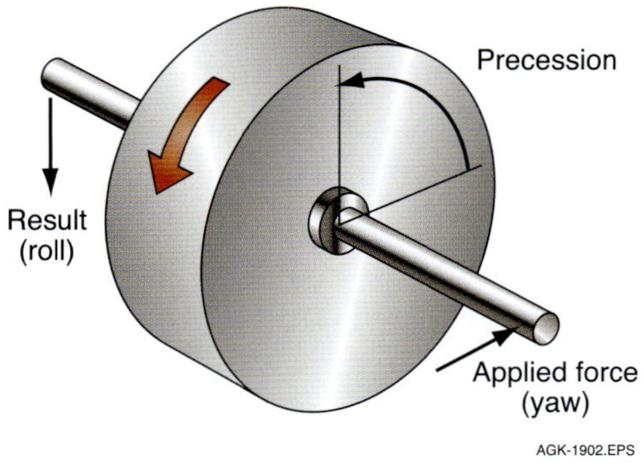

Figure 4-93 Precession.

A gyro that is correctly aligned drifts after a period of 15–20 minutes due to friction within the bearings. The heading indicator must be realigned to the magnetic compass every 15 minutes or so. The attitude indicator has a gravity sensor (mercury switch) to keep realigning it to the vertical. The gyroscopic flight instruments are as follows:

- the attitude indicator;
- the heading indicator; and
- a turn indicator or a turn coordinator.

Vacuum System

A gyro rotor may be spun electrically or by a stream of high-speed air directed onto buckets cut into the perimeter of the rotor. The vacuum system (which draws, or inducts, this high-speed air into the gyro instrument cases and onto the gyro rotors, causing them to spin very fast) needs a little explaining.

Vacuum Pump

Most modern vacuum systems use an engine-driven suction pump. This evacuates the air from the cases of the gyroscopic-driven instruments creating a vacuum (low pressure). The required suction is typically 4.5 to 5.4 in. Hg indicated in the cockpit on a suction gauge.

Filtered air is continuously drawn in at high speed through a nozzle directed at the gyro buckets, causing the gyro to spin at high rpm, often in excess of 20,000 rpm. This air is continuously being sucked out by the suction pump and exhausted into the atmosphere.

If the filter blocks, or the vacuum system fails, a lower reading, i.e. below about 4.5 in. Hg, will be indicated on the suction gauge. The reduced airflow may allow the gyroscopes to run down gradually and the air-operated instruments will behave erratically, incorrectly, or sluggishly.

Failure of the vacuum pump will be indicated by a zero reading on the suction gauge. It may be that the gyroscopes have sufficient speed to allow the instruments to read correctly for a minute or two before the gyros run down following failure of the vacuum pump. If the reading on the suction gauge is too high, i.e. greater than about 5.4 in. Hg, the gyro rotors may spin too fast and suffer mechanical damage. To prevent this, a vacuum relief valve (or vacuum regulator) in the system will admit air from the atmosphere to reduce the excessive vacuum.

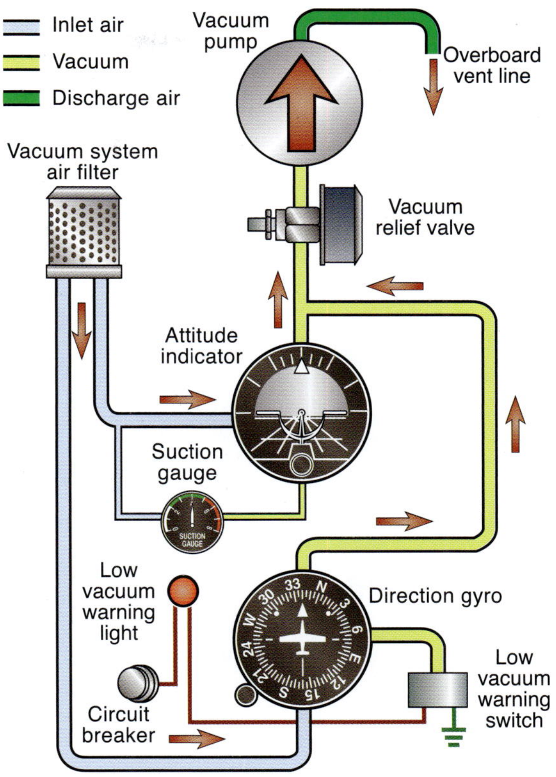

Figure 4-94 Vacuum system.

Vacuum Provided by a Venturi Tube

Some aeroplanes (especially older ones) have their vacuum system operated by a venturi-shaped tube on the outside of the airframe, rather than by an engine-driven vacuum pump. When air flows through the venturi tube, and speeds up due to the shape of the venturi, the static pressure decreases (Bernoulli's principle). This low-pressure area, if connected to the gyro instrument cases, will draw air through each instrument via an internal filter and spin the gyroscopes, as does the engine-driven vacuum system.

Before the venturi-powered vacuum system can work, there must be an appreciable airflow through the venturi tube. This is normally created by the forward motion of the aeroplane through the air – sufficient airflow is provided at flying speeds. It may be several minutes after take-off before the gyroscopes spin fast enough for the instrument indications to be reliable and before they can be aligned. This is a significant disadvantage compared with the engine-driven system. Other disadvantages include the increased drag caused by the externally mounted venturi tube, and the possibility of ice affecting it (like in a carburettor, where the reduced pressure causes a reduced temperature).

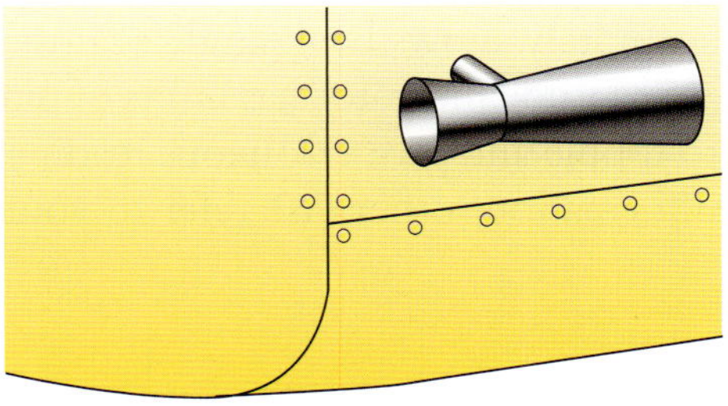

Figure 4-95 Venturi tube.

Attitude Indicator (Artificial Horizon)

The attitude of the aeroplane to the real horizon is accurately represented by the artificial horizon line attached to the gyro and a by small symbolic aeroplane attached to the instrument dial. This symbolic aeroplane is the miniature or *index* aeroplane.

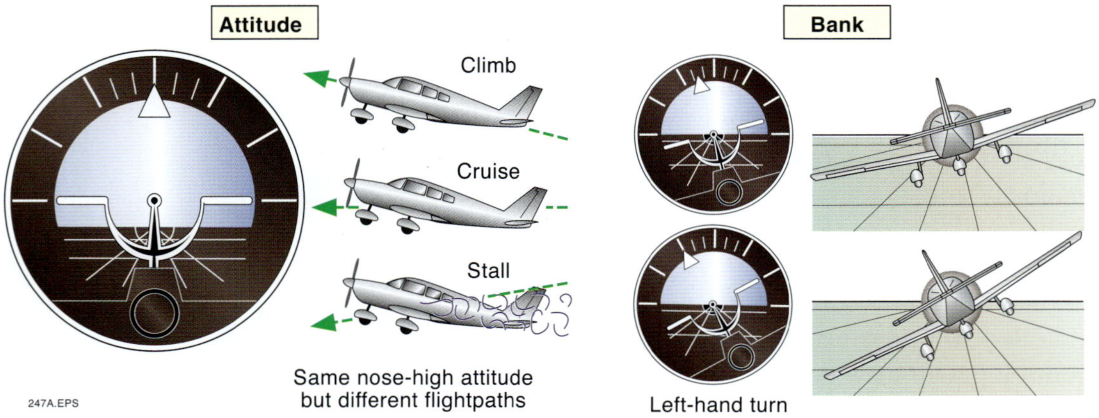

Figure 4-96 Pitch attitude displayed on the attitude indicator does not reflect climb/descent performance.

The attitude indicator shows pitch attitude and bank angle. Pitch attitude is indicated by the position of the centre dot of the miniature aeroplane relative to the artificial horizon bar. Better instruments have pitch attitude marks at 5- and 10-degree increments above and below the horizon. Bank attitude is indicated by the relationship of the wings of the miniature aeroplane to the artificial horizon. There is also a sky pointer which accurately shows bank angle against an outer scale on the upper case of the instrument. An attitude indicator has limits of pitch and bank which, if exceeded, may cause the gyro to topple and give erroneous readings (your pilot's operating handbook may contain this information, otherwise refer to your flight instructor).

Heading Indicator (Directional Gyro)

The magnetic compass is the primary reference for direction. However, it is difficult to read in turbulence, and it is subject to acceleration and turning errors. The heading indicator (HI) is a gyroscopic instrument that must be kept aligned with the magnetic compass in flight. Although it takes its directional reference from the compass, it is not subject to acceleration and turning errors (making accurate turns and heading-keeping possible) and is easy to read in turbulence. It does gradually lose alignment due to the transport errors and friction. You can correct for this simply by realigning the HI with the magnetic compass.

Figure 4-97 Heading indicator.

Procedure for Aligning Heading Indicator with Magnetic Compass

The HI has a knob that enables the pilot to align the HI with the magnetic compass. This should be done every 15 to 20 minutes – about a 3° drift is acceptable over this time.

- Fly steady, accurate, straight and level.
- Read the magnetic compass heading (when the compass is steady).
- Adjust the HI to read the same heading as the magnetic compass.

Toppling

The term *toppling* indicates the movement of the gyro in an unstable, erratic or tumbling motion. This can be caused through performing extreme manoeuvres. Once a gyro has toppled, it will not indicate correctly unless it is realigned or re-erected. Some older gyros have a caging device which holds the gimbals in place. The instrument should be caged during aerobatic manoeuvres, and it will not topple if it is caged. Newer gyros have a self-erecting mechanism. Therefore, they do not require caging but may take time to restore accurate indications.

Turn & Balance Indicator

The turn indicator uses a *rate gyroscope* set to sense change only about the vertical axis of the aircraft. This instrument has clear *rate-one* markers to indicate turns of 180 degrees per minute. Turn indicators function as an emergency back-up to the attitude indicator and so must have a separate source of power, Since the AI is vacuum driven, the turn indicator is electrically driven (DC). The rotor can be heard spinning up after turning the master switch on during preflight, and there is usually an off flag. A balance ball is part of the same instrument. This is a simple inclinometer in which the ball moves to a position consistent with the forces applied to the aircraft as reflected by the ball being left behind (to one side). The balance ball is not connected to the gyro.

Figure 4-98
Turn indicator.

Turn Coordinator

The turn coordinator uses an electrically driven rate gyro similar to the turn indicator but has its gimbal tilted up at the forward end to an angle of 37°. This means that the turn coordinator will sense both yaw and roll rates. It was developed as a useful device to indicate wings-level if the AI failed. As the presentation of the turn coordinator is similar to the attitude indicator, the aeroplane symbol could be misinterpreted, and hence its warning – *no pitch information* – to avoid confusion and indicate that the instrument is without pitch reference. Far better to have a standby attitude indicator.

Most light aircraft have a turn coordinator which is electrically powered. With a loss of electrical power, the turn coordinator will no longer provide bank information. The wings will stay level, indicating zero bank. Some turn coordinators have a red flag which pops up, indicating a loss of electrical supply.

The turn coordinator also incorporates a balance ball. An electrical failure will not affect the balance ball. *Either a turn indicator or a turn coordinator is fitted – not both.* Alternatively, modern aircraft have a standby attitude indicator – the balance ball being incorporated under the primary attitude indicator. This is a much safer combination.

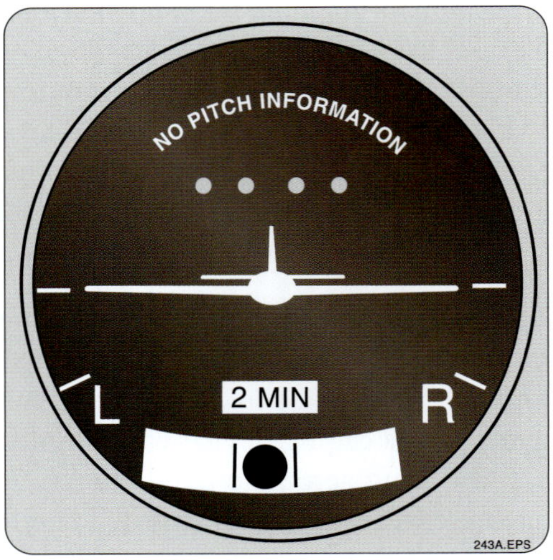

Figure 4-99 Turn coordinator.

Balance Ball

The *balance ball* is not a gyroscopic device. Rather, it is a very simple, and very useful, mechanical device that indicates the direction of the g-forces, that is, the combined effect of the earth's gravity force and any turning force acting on the aeroplane. The balance ball has no power source. It is also known as the *slip–skid indicator* or *skid-ball.*

The balance ball is simply a small spherical mass, free to move like a pendulum bob, except that it moves in a curved tube filled with a damping fluid. In balanced flight, it will appear in the middle, at the lowest point in the curved cylinder (like a pendulum bob hanging straight down or the bubble in a spirit-level). If the ball is central between two marks (like the spirit-level), the aeroplane is in balance – it is neither slipping nor skidding, and the centreline of the aircraft is pointing directly into the relative airflow.

If there is any slip or skid, the ball will move to one side in the same way as a pendulum bob would swing out. Similarly, you would feel a force pushing you out, usually through the seat of your pants or your shoulders leaning out or into the cockpit.

If the ball is out to the right, the pilot applies right rudder pressure to centre it.

Same-side rudder pressure is used to centre the ball (step on the ball to balance).

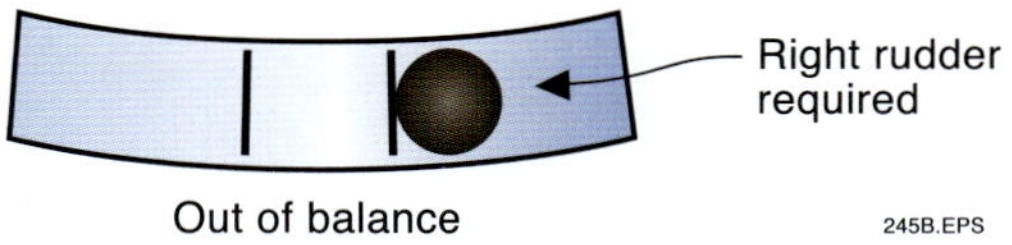

Figure 4-100 Balance indicator – out of balance.

In a coordinated turn, the pilot will feel no sideways forces; nor will the ball, which will remain centred. Any sideways force (either a slip in toward the turn or a skid out of the turn) will be shown by the ball (and felt in the seat of your pants).

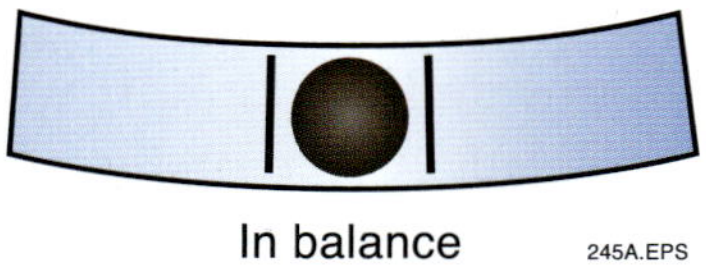

Figure 4-101 Balance indicator – in balance.

Compass Instruments

Magnetic Compass

The magnetic compass, also called the *direct-indicating compass*, is the primary source of directional information, to which the heading indicator is aligned. The magnetic heading of the aeroplane is read from the compass card under the *lubber line* on the face of the instrument.

Magnetic compass readings will not be accurate while the aeroplane is accelerating or turning, or when entering a climb or descent; nor will they be accurate if magnetic, electrical, battery or iron objects are placed near the compass.

The modern aeroplane has a direct-reading compass filled with a liquid in which a float supporting a bar magnet is pivoted.

The liquid supports some of the weight, decreases the friction on the pivot and, most importantly, dampens (decreases) the oscillations of the magnet and float during flight. This allows the compass to give a steadier indication and makes it easier to read.

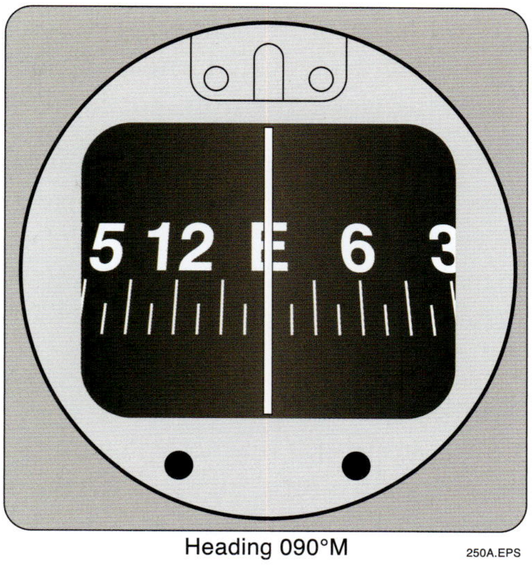

Figure 4-102 Magnetic compass display.

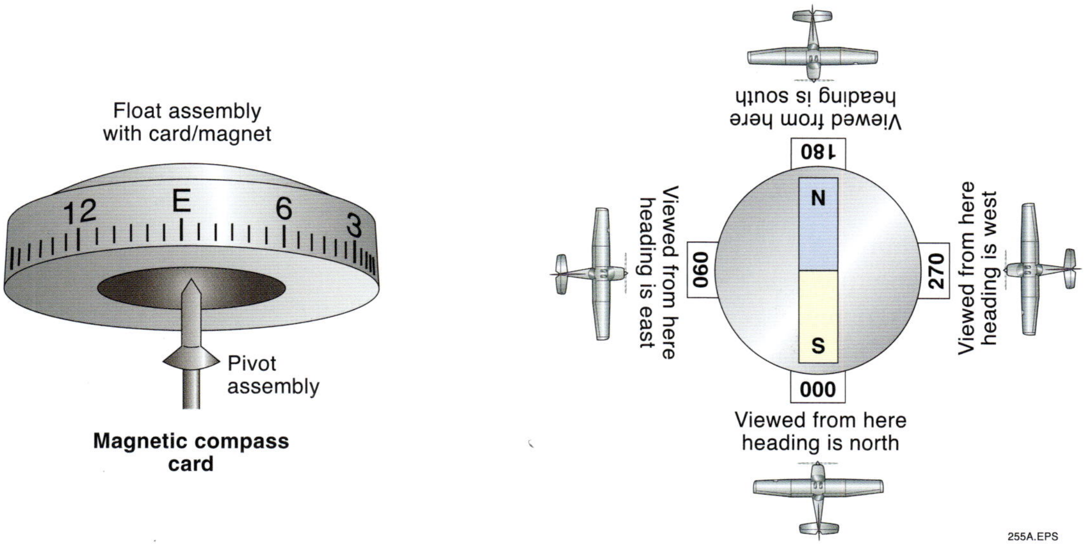

Figure 4-103 Magnetic compass.

Attached to the pivot assembly is a compass card, graduated in degrees. This can be read by the pilot against a reference marker, known as the lubber line, attached to the bowl of the compass, and therefore attached to the rest of the aeroplane. Remember that it is the aeroplane that turns around the magnet inside the compass. Ideally, the compass magnet points magnetic north and south at all times. As the aeroplane changes direction, the compass magnet does not.

Direction

There are two common ways to describe direction:

- using the *cardinal points* (the four primary directions of north, south, east and west); or
- by using a graduated circle of 360° increasing clockwise from north.

When using a compass, the units are always degrees magnetic, because the compass senses the earth's magnetic field and so is referenced to magnetic north. Direction is always expressed as a three-figure group (e.g. 070°M).

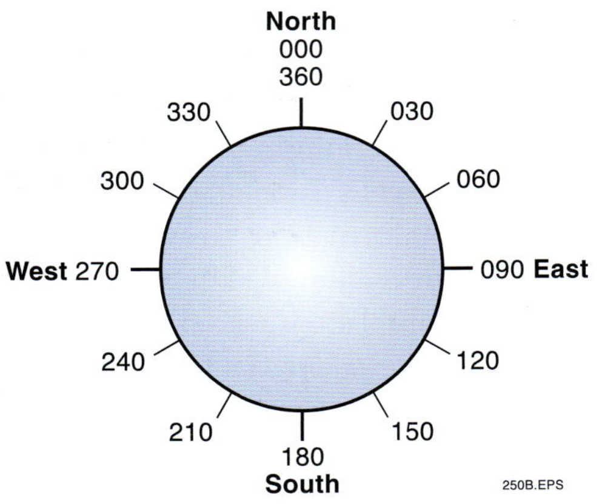

Figure 4-104 Direction.

Earth's Magnetic Field

A freely suspended magnet will swing so that its axis points north–south. The end of the magnet that points toward the earth's north magnetic pole is called the north-seeking pole of the magnet. The magnet is an ancient means of determining direction, and it is still used in almost every aeroplane flying. The earth acts like a very large and weak magnet.

The surface of the earth is surrounded by a weak magnetic field, consisting of lines of magnetic force that begin deep within the earth near Hudson Bay in Canada and flow toward a point deep within the earth near South Victoria Land in Antarctica. Because of their proximity to the north and south geographical poles (which are known as true north and true south, and are on the earth's axis of rotation), the magnetic poles are referred to as the north magnetic pole and the south magnetic pole.

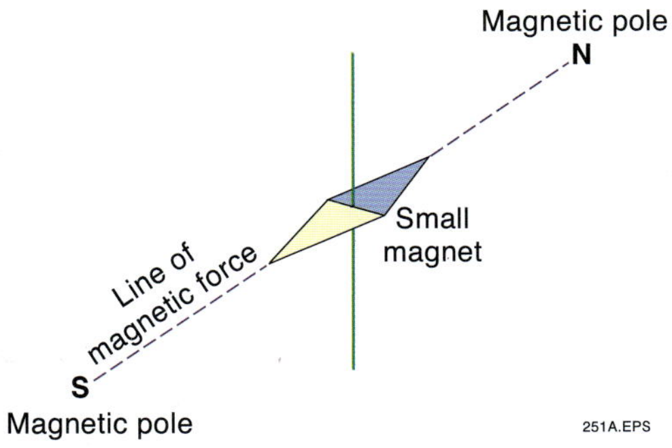

Figure 4-105 A simple bar magnet.

Magnetic Variation

The latitude–longitude grid shown on maps is based on the geographical poles – true north and true south. Our small compass magnet, however, points towards the north magnetic pole. The angular difference between true north and magnetic north at any particular point on the earth is called magnetic variation – if the magnet points east of true north, then the variation is said to be east. If the compass points to the west of true north, then the variation is west. Magnetic variation is the same for all aircraft in a given vicinity. Isogonals are lines on maps joining places which have the same magnetic variation.

Understanding magnetic variation is not important at this stage of your flying training; it will be covered again in chapter 12.

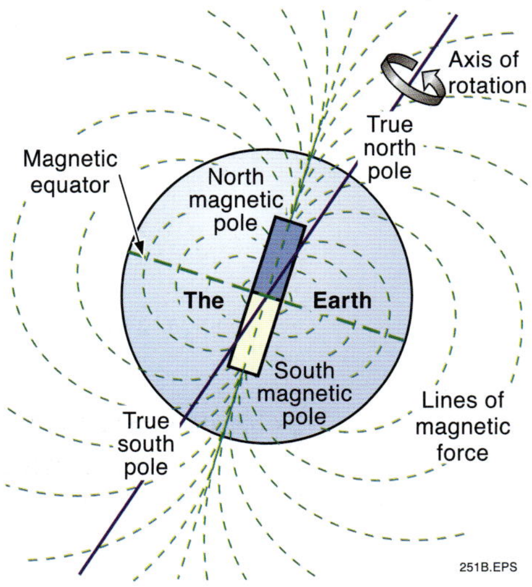

Figure 4-106 The earth's magnetic field.

Magnetic Deviation

If the magnet in the aeroplane's compass is affected only by the earth's magnetic field, it would be very accurate. However, an aeroplane is made up of metal, rotating parts of the engine, radios etc., all of which generate their own magnetic field.

The combined effect that all of these fields in a particular aeroplane has on the magnetic compass is an error called *magnetic deviation*. Deviation causes the compass to deviate, or deflect, from indicating the aircraft magnetic heading.

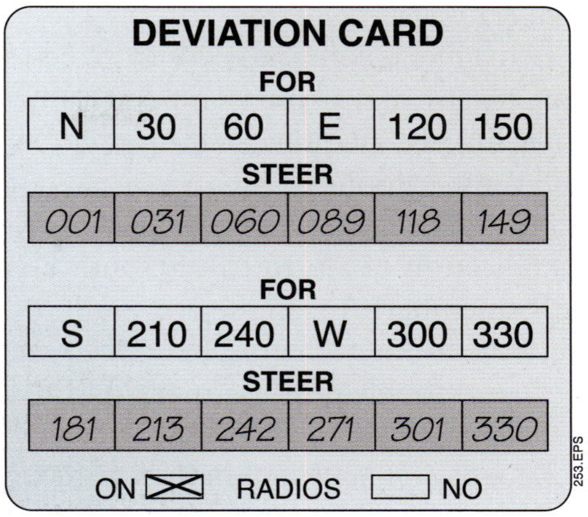

Figure 4-107 Simple deviation card.

The amount of deviation can only be established once the compass is installed in the particular aeroplane and test measurements made with the engine running and electrical equipment on (known as swinging the compass).

In each aeroplane a small placard, known as the *deviation card*, is mounted, usually on or near the compass. The card shows the heading that the pilot will need to steer in order to achieve a main heading. The amount of deviation is different for each aeroplane and will vary depending upon the approximate heading of the aeroplane.

Precautions When Carrying Magnetic or Metal Goods

The deviation card is filled out by a licensed engineer who has actually checked the compass in that particular aeroplane. This deviation correction card allows only for the magnetic influences in the aeroplane that were present when the compass was tested.

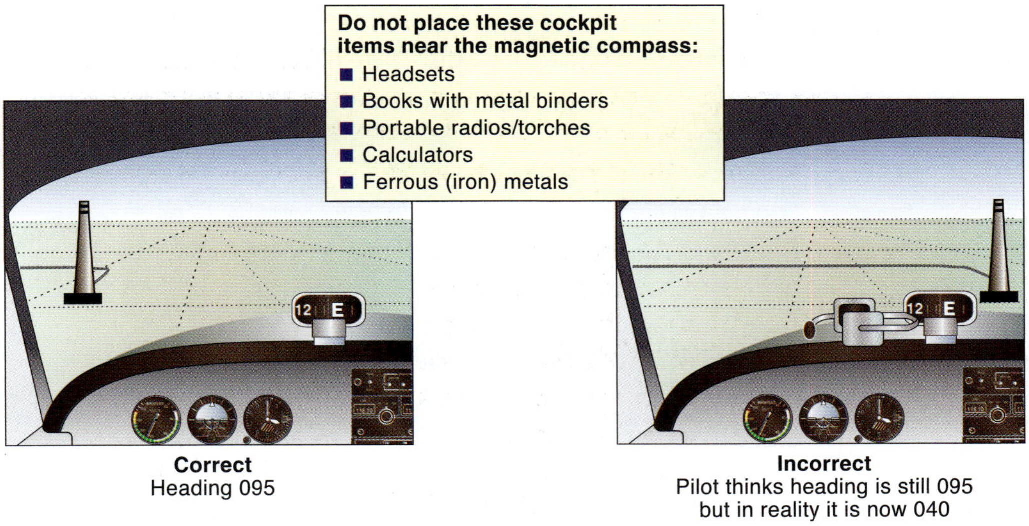

Figure 4-108 Keep foreign objects away from the magnetic compass.

Any other magnetic influences that may later be introduced into the aeroplane will not be allowed for, even though they can significantly affect the compass. Therefore, as pilot, ensure that no metal or magnetic materials, such as metal pens, clipboards, books with metal binders, key rings, headphones, electronic calculators or transistor radios, are placed anywhere near the compass. Magnetic or metal materials placed near the compass may introduce large and unpredictable errors. Many pilots have become lost as a result of random deviations in the compass readings caused by these extraneous magnetic fields.

Turn & Acceleration Errors

The magnetic compass is constructed to minimise errors. However, the suspension system means that if the compass is anywhere other than at the magnetic equator, the combined gravitational and magnetic forces will not act through the compass pivot and will cause errors.

- In the southern hemisphere, if accelerating on east or west, acceleration error is an indication of a turn to the south. There is no acceleration error for north or south. Remember: Apparent turn south.
- In the southern hemisphere, the compass behaviour is such that it rotates too fast as a turn through north is made and too slow for a turn through south. There are no turning errors through east or west. To simplify turning error, the compass is said to be *nippy on north and sluggish on south*. This means that, to minimise the error when flying, the pilot must *overshoot north and undershoot south* (ONUS).

These errors are complex and are covered in greater depth in private and commercial pilot manuals. Talk to your flying instructor. A more accurate method of making turns without a HI is to make a timed rate-one (3°/second) turn using the turn coordinator.

Serviceability Checks

Before flight, check that the compass is serviceable. The liquid in which the magnet is suspended should be free of bubbles and should not be discoloured. The glass should not be broken, cracked or discoloured, and it should be secure. *Check the deviation card. Check that the compass indication is approximately correct.* Runways are named according to their magnetic direction; for example, a runway pointing 183° magnetic is called Runway 18, so when pointing in the same direction as this runway, your compass should indicate within 10°.

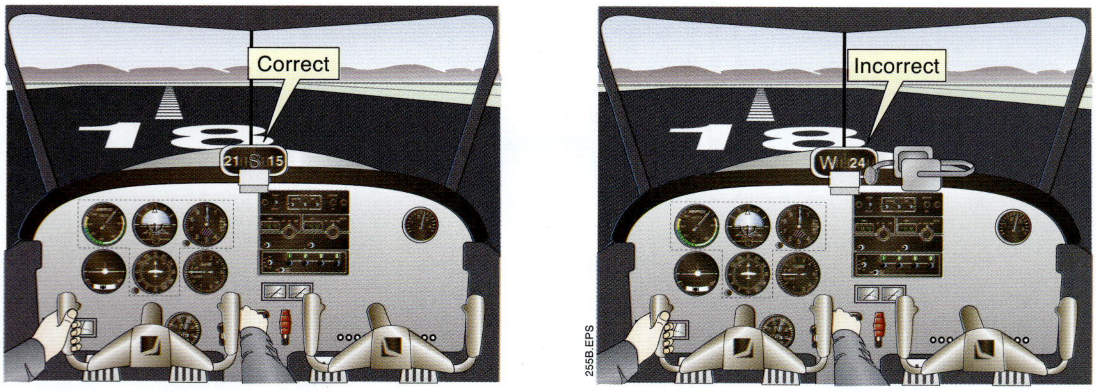

Figure 4-109 Always cross-check compass direction.

While taxiing out prior to take-off, when you turn the aeroplane left and right to check the operation of the turn coordinator and heading indicator, you can also check the response of the magnetic compass. Remember that the compass remains in the same direction and the aeroplane turns around it, that is, it seems backward.

A typical litany is:

Turning left, skidding right, wings level, compasses decreasing. . .

and

Turning right, skidding left, wings level, compasses increasing.

Review 4

Pre-Solo Level of Knowledge

1. What is the main purpose of the aircraft's structure?
2. What do the tail surfaces do?
3. A biplane has . . . . . wings?
4. What is a yoke?
5. What is a trike?
6. How do you apply pressure to the rudder without applying the brakes?
7. Which way does the propeller of your aircraft rotate – when viewed from the cockpit?
8. Why is an engine lubricated?
9. What provides this lubrication?
10. What oil system item does the pilot need to check?
11. What type of oil does your engine use?
12. Why have two magnetos?
13. Why fly on both?
14. Why keep the mixture full rich for all circuit operations?
15. What if the propeller has dents/chips in the leading edge?
16. Why does the pilot drain fuel before flight?
17. Is this done before every flight?
18. How is it done?
19. What do you look for?
20. When do you use carburettor heat?
21. What happens if the pitot cover is left on for take-off?
22. What is indicated by the white arc on the ASI?
23. How often should you check the alignment of the heading indicator (HI)? With what?

BAK Level of Knowledge

24. What is a canard?
25. A pusher has the propeller pushing the air whereas a conventional tractor configuration pulls the aircraft along? Explain or argue.
26. Explain the rigger's angle of incidence.
27. What is a stabilator?
28. What is the main feature of a Fowler flap?
29. What is a chock?
30. What happens to the ignition if the alternator fails?
31. With an RH above 50% and the OAT at 20°C, carburettor icing can readily occur . . . . . .
32. Carburettor heat is usually used to . . . . . . the carburettor after ice has formed.
33. What does the carburettor do?
34. What does the mixture control do?
35. Why have both the throttle and the mixture control?
36. Why reduce the throttle before the propeller rpm when reducing power?
37. What causes and aircraft with a single propeller to want to veer on take-off?

38. Why does the aircraft's fuel system have a boost pump?
39. Which aircraft do not and why not?
40. If the brake pedal has no resistance and, when you apply the brake, the pedal goes to the floor what would you do?
41. Explain the difference between pitot, total, static and dynamic pressures.
42. How is air pressure used to indicate airspeed?
43. Why is it not always accurate?
44. Why is it used to indicate angle of attack and how so?
45. What does the altimeter read in a climb if the static port is blocked?
46. What would the VSI read under the same circumstances?
47. Why use a vacuum system to drive the gyros?
48. Why not pressure rather than vacuum?
49. Why have electric standby instruments?
50. Why does the magnetic compass read backwards?

5 - Air Law: Rules & Procedures of Flight

Aviation Theory Centre

Introduction

Until now, we have considered how an aircraft flies, how its systems are operated and what effect weather may have. If we were alone in the sky, we could now relax – but we are never alone. Protection is provided by defining the rules-of-the-road, airspace boundaries, air routes, reporting points, procedures, surveillance, warning devices and last but not least, looking out for each other. Above all else, it depends on each of us being responsible about how we operate our aircraft – something we call *airmanship.*

Aviation Regulations & Procedures

Aircraft operate within a regulatory and procedural framework which is designed to protect pilots, passengers and the general public. The rules and procedures are contained in the following documents:

- Civil Aviation Regulations (CAR1988) and Civil Aviation Safety Regulations (CASR);
- Civil Aviation Orders (CAO);
- Aeronautical Information Publication (AIP) which is in two parts - General (GEN) and En Route (ENR);
- Civil Aviation Advisory Publications (CAAP);
- En Route Supplement Australia (ERSA);
- NOTAMs; and
- Aeronautical Information Circulars (AIC).

All operational documents are subject to a frequent, regular amendment service.

Civil Aviation Regulations & Civil Aviation Safety Regulations

The purpose of the Civil Aviation Safety Regulations is to provide rules for the safe operation of aircraft within Australian airspace.The older regulations are contained in CAR 1988. The newer regulations were called CAR 1998 and are now to be known as Civil Aviation Safety Regulations (CASRs). CARs are being progressively phased out.

The CARs and CASRs contain regulations on:

- the registration and marking of aircraft;
- airworthiness requirements;
- maintenance of aircraft;
- aircraft documentation;
- flight crew qualifications;
- personal log books;
- radio systems;
- aerodromes;
- Air Traffic Services and other services;
- conditions of flight;
- rules of the air; and
- signals for the control of air traffic.

Civil Aviation Orders (CAOs)

The Civil Aviation Orders (CAOs) contain instructions, directions or notifications by CASA, regarding the following:
- air service operations;
- pilot licences and ratings;
- flight crew standards;
- flight time limitations; and
- use of aerodromes.

Aeronautical Information Publication (AIP)

The AIP consolidates relevant preflight information and inflight procedures of a lasting nature into a primary publication containing:
- general information;
- aerodrome and ground aids;
- communications;
- meteorology;
- search and rescue;
- air traffic rules and services;
- operations; and
- departure and approach procedures.

Civil Aviation Advisory Publication (CAAP)

The CAAP contains advice on operational matters relating to civil aviation. Its general contents include recommendations for:
- a training syllabus;
- maintenance;
- registration;
- fuel policy and planning requirements; and
- aerodromes.

En Route Supplement Australia (ERSA)

The En Route Supplement Australia is an aerodrome and facility directory with information on air traffic services and frequencies, including:
- aerodrome information and local procedures;
- facilities provided;
- prohibited, restricted and danger (PRD) areas;
- location codes;
- aircraft type designators;
- flight plan requirements;
- special procedures not associated with an aerodrome;
- preflight information services;
- forecast and weather codes; and
- emergency procedures.

NOTAM (Notices to Airmen)

NOTAMs provide information that is of direct operational significance and which may immediately affect aircraft operations, such as obstructions, navaid unserviceabilities, and aerodrome and airspace restrictions. They may be generally applicable (central office NOTAMs), area related or aerodrome specific.

Its contents include:

- location identification;
- NOTAM number;
- subject reported;
- date and time of issue;
- time of commencement of information;
- time of cessation of information;
- times of period of activity;
- plain language text; and
- lower and upper limits.

Aeronautical Information Circular (AIC)

The AIC is used to disseminate aeronautical information to aircrew. Usually the information is of an administrative nature and not directly concerned with the present conduct of airborne operations, but it may have implications for the future.

Visual Meteorological Conditions

Reference: AIP ENR 1.2 para 2.

There are two sets of rules under which an aircraft can operate, *visual flight rules* (VFR) and *instrument flight rules* (IFR). To be able to operate under visual rules, the conditions must be equal to or better than, minimum *visual meteorological conditions* (VMC). If VMC does not exist, the aircraft must operate under IFR and the pilot and aircraft must be approved for IFR operations. An IFR aircraft may also choose to operate under IFR procedures in VFR conditions – where it may give added separation or priority. For now, we can only fly under VFR or, in some areas, under a dispensation known as *special VFR*.

Minimum conditions for visual flight are defined in terms of flight visibility and vertical and horizontal distances from cloud. They are called the *visual meteorological conditions* (VMC). They have been designed to ensure that you have sufficient visual cues outside the cockpit to control the attitude of your aeroplane by visual reference to the horizon, to allow you to see and avoid other traffic, and to be able to navigate visually by reference to the ground.

Airspace	Airspace Dimension	Visibility	Distance from Cloud	
			Vertical	Horizontal
Controlled Airspace Class A	IFR aircraft only			
Controlled Airspace Class C	At or about 10,000 ft AMSL	8 km	1,000 ft	1,500 m
	Below 10,000 ft AMSL	5,000 m	1,000 ft	1,500 m
Controlled Airspace Class D	Within Class D CTR	5,000 m	1,000 ft above 500 ft below	600 m
Controlled Airspace Class E	as for Class C except no special VFR			
Non Controlled Airspace Class G	>10,000 ft AMSL	8 km	1,000 ft	1,500 m
	<10,000 ft AMSL	5,000 m	1,000 ft	1,500 m
	≤3,000 ft AMSL or 1,000 ft AGL – whichever is higher	5,000 m	Clear of cloud and in sight of ground or water	Clear of cloud and in sight of ground or water

Table 5-1 Visual Meteorological Conditions.

Note: Special VFR may be available in Class C & D airspace.

Below 10,000 ft altitude, you must have a visibility of at least 5,000 m and you must stay clear of cloud by 1,500 m horizontally and 1,000 ft vertically. In Class G, below 3,000 ft (or 1,000 ft above ground) you must simply remain clear of cloud and in sight of ground or water. In Class D you must remain 600m horizontally from cloud and at least 1,000 feet above or 500 feet below. Be wary if you are above cloud as the amount can increase quite rapidly. If in doubt, don't chance it. For example, if, while flying in the training area, weather conditions appear to be about to change for the worse, even though your flying instructor has approved you to fly on this day, it is your responsibility to ensure that you don't fly in conditions below the VMC.

Visual Flight Rules

Reference: AIP ENR 1.2

If VMC exists, you may fly under *visual flight rules* (VFR). These are described below.

You must remain in VMC and you must be:

- subsonic; and
- able to navigate by visual reference to the ground or water when operating at or below 2,000 ft AGL.

If you are in controlled airspace and navigating visually, you must notify ATC if you find yourself more than 1 nm off track.

If you fly over broken cloud (BKN), i.e. a total coverage of 4/8 or more, you must:

- continue to maintain VMC;
- be able to visually fix your position at least every 30 minutes; and
- ensure from met reports and forecasts that you will be able to maintain VMC during the descent and throughout the flight to your destination or alternate aerodrome.

If a TAF or other forecast is not available for your destination, particularly in remote areas, call a local authority such as police, post office or pilots for actual weather conditions.

Special VFR

Reference: AIP ENR 1.2 para 1.2

Air traffic control may authorise flight under special VFR rules in controlled airspace (C or D only), on pilot request, provided:

- it will not delay an IFR flight;
- you will remain clear of cloud (reduced separation from VFR);
- the visibility is not less than 1.6 km or 800 metres for helicopters; and
- you remain above 500 ft AGL or, if over a populated area, 1,000 ft AGL.

Rights of Way

Reference: CAR 161 to 163

- Power-driven aircraft must give way to airships, gliders and balloons and to aircraft towing gliders, banners or other objects.
- If approaching an aircraft head-on, turn right.
- Give way to aircraft on your right, when on the ground and in the air.
- If on a converging heading at approximately the same height, the aircraft on the right has right of way.

- An aircraft being overtaken has right of way.
- While overtaking, make all turns to the right.
- Do not overtake an aircraft by climbing or diving.

  Note: An overtaking aircraft is an aircraft approaching from behind within an area which forms an angle of less than 70° with the line of symmetry (longitudinal axis) of the aircraft being overtaken.

- Give way to an aircraft landing or on final approach.
- Give way to an aircraft that must land as a matter of urgency.
- When approaching to land, give way to aircraft below you (e.g. landing ahead of you or taking off).
- Although the aircraft at a lower height has right of way, this rule may not be used to cut-in on an aircraft on final or landing.
- Do not take-off if there is any risk of collision.

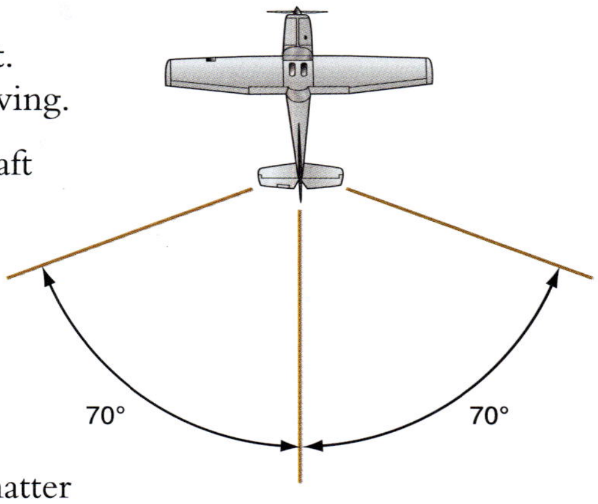

Figure 5-1 Overtaking zone.

The thirteenth commandment: "If in doubt, give way".

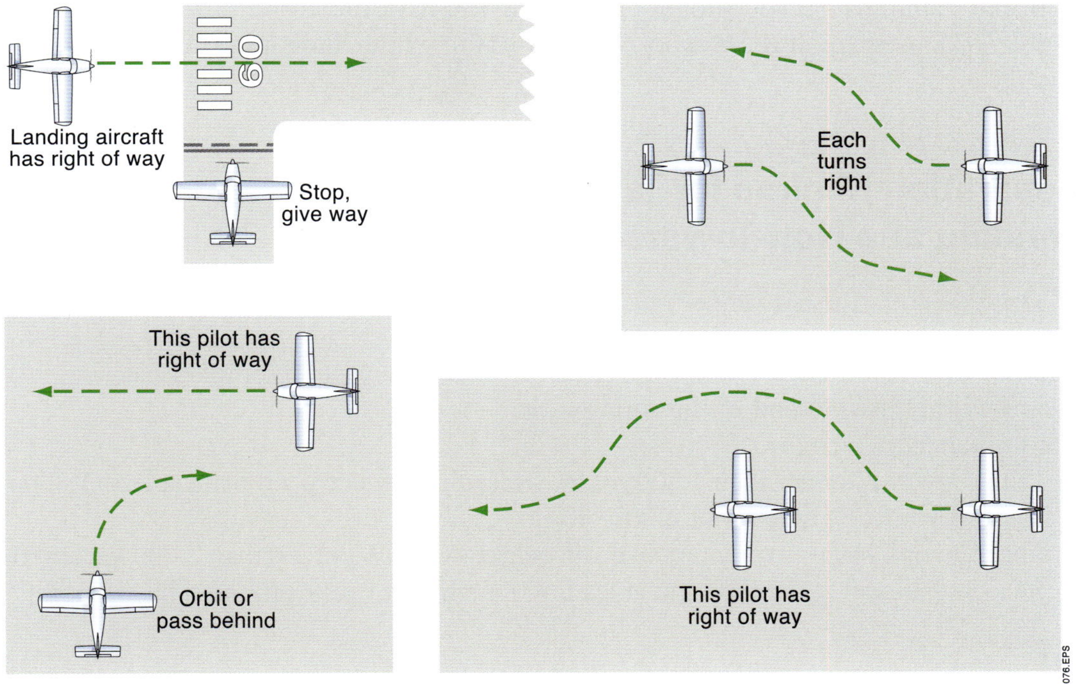

Figure 5-2 Rights of way.

Note: Although the aircraft on the right has right of way, it also must communicate and, if necessary, take action to avoid a collision.

Operating near other Aircraft

You must not fly so close to another aircraft as to create a collision hazard, or manoeuvre on the ground in such a manner as to create a hazard to your aircraft or another aircraft. Although the regulations do not specify minimum distances between aircraft in flight, minimum distances of 600 metres horizontally and 500 feet vertically would be reasonable.

Vertical Separation

Reference: AIP ENR 1.7

To ensure vertical separation, all aircraft set their pressure altimeters to a common datum for the area in which they are operating. This setting is called the ***QNH***.

Altimetry Procedures (Flights Below 10,000 ft AMSL)

In Australia, flights below 10,000 ft, are conducted with reference to *mean sea level* (MSL), which is a standard reference for all aircraft. On start-up at the departure aerodrome, the altimeter subscale is set to local mean sea-level pressure, known as *local QNH*. When this is set the altimeter will read the elevation of the aerodrome, i.e. its height above sea level. If departing from an aerodrome in a control zone, the local QNH can be obtained from the automatic terminal information service (ATIS), or from the tower controller when ready to taxi.

Outside controlled airspace, local QNH is available from flight service, or you can find a practical value by winding the altimeter until it shows the altitude equal to the aerodrome elevation. The subscale will then show the local QNH which can be left for the flight. On a local training flight, you will have the altimeter set to the aerodrome QNH for the whole flight or there may be a QNH for the training area (area QNH). If you are operating from an aerodrome which has air traffic control then, when returning from the training area, you should ensure that you have the current QNH by listening to the ATIS message. If there is no ATIS, air traffic will include it in their reply to your initial call.

Separation Minima for Take-Off & Landing at a Non-Towered Aerodrome

Take-Off

You may not commence a take-off until an aircraft taking off before you has:
- crossed the upwind end of the runway; or
- commenced a turn; or
- if the runway is longer than 1,800 m, the preceding aircraft is airborne at least 1,800 m ahead of your proposed point of lift-off; or
- if both aircraft have a maximum take-off weight (MTOW) of less than 2,000 kg, and the preceding aircraft is airborne and at least 600 m ahead of your proposed lift-off point.

Landing

You must not continue your approach to land beyond the approach threshold unless:
- an aircraft landing before you on the same runway is airborne and:
  - has commenced a turn; or
  - is beyond the point at which you would complete your landing roll, and should you need to go around, there is sufficient distance to allow you to manoeuvre safely; or
- an aircraft using the same runway has landed, vacated and is taxiing away from the runway in use; or
- an aircraft using another runway has crossed or landed and is holding short of the runway you are landing on.

Seeing & Being Seen – What it's all About

In the circuit area, there could be several aircraft on different runways. In the training area, there are always other aircraft. In open skies, there will always be someone else – seen or unseen. Australia is a big country, but on frequently used, direct tracks and around aerodromes where aircraft converge and descend (like "*flies around the honey-pot*"), we are all at risk. Further, every aircraft has a blind spot. In some cases, a considerable area of view is obscured by the wings, cockpit roof and door frames.

How to Detect and Remain Clear of Other Aircraft

Lookout is an integrated process which applies all of our sensors, communications and procedures. For the most part, our separation is on a see-and-be-seen basis. This can be a good thing but also carries some risk. The onus is on each of us to actively maintain safe clearance from other traffic and this takes some focus (pardon the pun).

The most important sensors are the pilot's eyes and we can supplement them with other aids. A very important aspect of looking, seeing, detecting, noticing and observing is the mental processing that goes with looking.

We all arbitrarily look for other aircraft but are we really seeing? Remember the eyes relax to focus only a metre or two ahead. So focusing has to be a conscious control. Scanning is taught but there is no one pattern that caters for all situations. Remember how we were taught to cross the road? "*Look right, look left, and look right again*". Sometimes you will hear the same directions in the air. Before turning right, "*Clear right, clear left, clear right again, turning right*". After a while, the formality and speaking aloud is not required but we have set a habit pattern that we will follow automatically. That's the purpose of repetitive training.

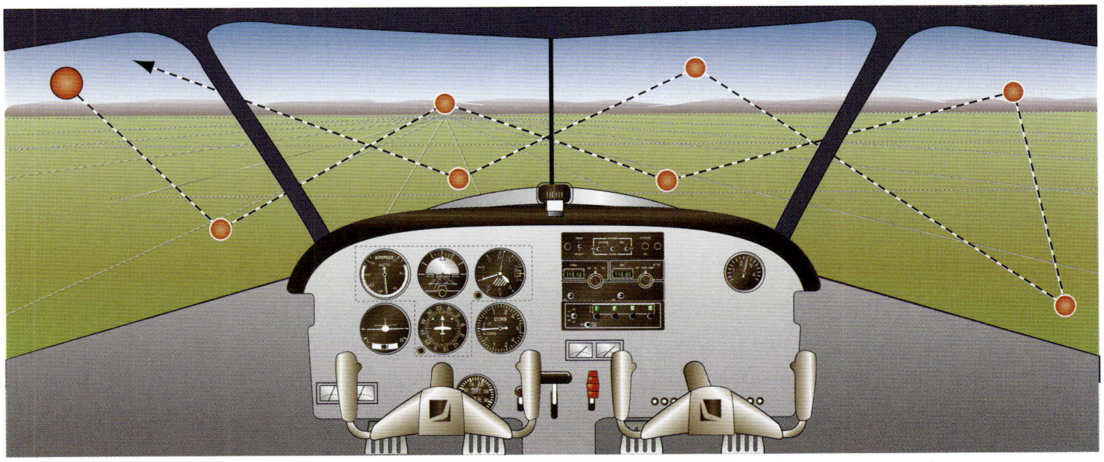

Figure 5-3 Methodical scan – called the *saccade–fixation* cycle.

A methodical scan is hard to maintain, and soon the mind and eyes go into neutral. The head may turn, the mouth may speak, the eyes may look but no one is seeing. A regular cycle of a quick all-round scan followed by slower examination of more important areas (in the direction of our intended flightpath), followed by another quick all-round scan, and then back to the slow-directed scan seems to be an effective way.

Alerted See-and-Avoid

The best way to see something is to know where to look. By mentally picturing the relative position of other aircraft from their radio broadcasts and expected trend, you can reduce the visual scan area and focus your attention to the aircraft that is most likely to conflict and its relative direction. This is known as the *alerted see-and-avoid* technique.

Will I See them Coming – in Time?

The human eye has wonderful discrimination and will detect an object the size of a light aircraft at a distance of several miles. This is plenty of time to take avoiding action. At any early stage, only a small flightpath change is necessary to avoid conflict. We notice objects by movement, colour, contrast, size, shape, texture – but most of all by movement. Have you ever watched eagles or hawks hovering, looking for prey – above all, they notice the slightest movement. The mouse and the rabbit freeze as soon as they sense danger. An aircraft on a collision course has no relative movement – except towards you. As a result, it just grows in size. A speck on the windscreen becomes an aircraft.

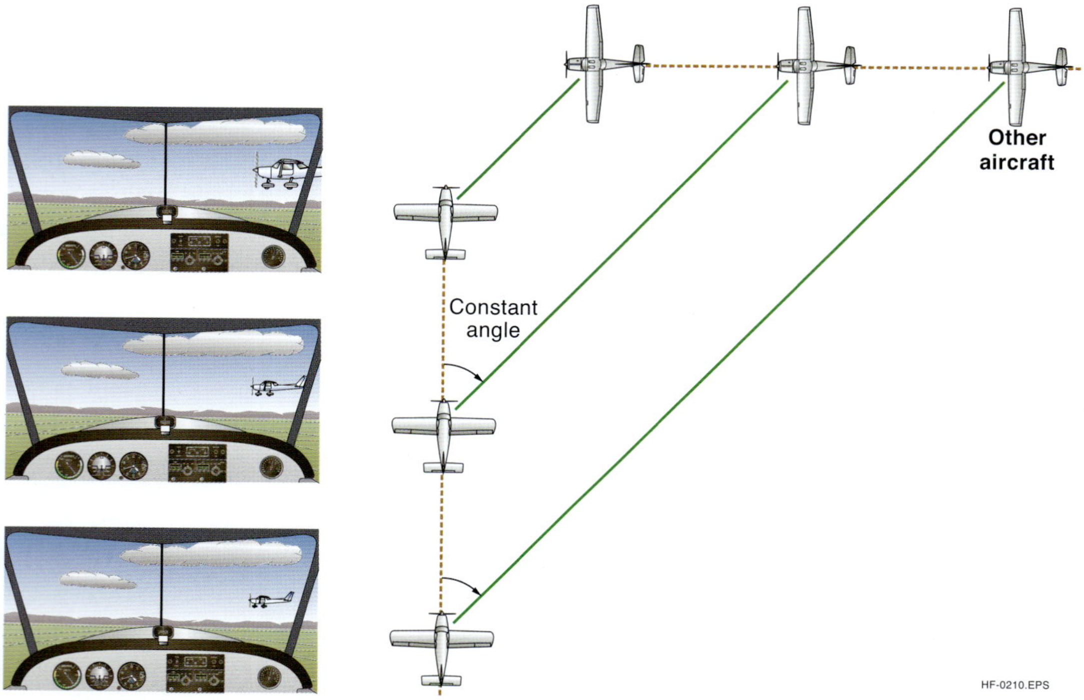

Figure 5-4 Constant relative line of position (LOP) = collision course.

When an aircraft is on a collision course there will be no relative movement. It will stay in the same place on the windscreen. Changing attitude and heading clears blind spots and also increases relative motion. Note the areas of vision that are obscured by your aircraft - especially in the climb, descent and circuit area.

Transponders & TCAS

Some light aircraft and many RPT aircraft are fitted with a *traffic alert and collision avoidance system* (TCAS). The complex ones give the pilot flight direction to avoid possible conflict. The basic ones give relative position and distance to the other aircraft to help you find it visually. The most important aspect as far as we are concerned, is that even if we are not fitted with a TCAS, at least other aircraft and radars will see us if we have the transponder turned on. Always fly with the transponder On.

Select the transponder to standby (SBY) only if requested by air traffic services; or when changing code.

Situational Awareness

As you learn to fly, you will become conscious of your position in space. This is a most important awareness to encourage. Ask yourself (in addition to which way is up? and how high am I?):

- *Which way is the aerodrome?*
- *Roughly how far?*
- *How long will it take to get there?*
- *How much fuel will I need?*
- *Where is a safe alternate aerodrome?*
- *Where is high ground?*
- *Where is the conflicting traffic?*
- *Where is controlled airspace?*

Having a continuing awareness of where you are you will further develop what is called situational awareness. In addition to position, the most important part of safe separation is building a mental picture of where the other traffic is, in relation to you and your intended flightpath. Is there a conflict or is there going to be a conflict? This mental picture including the position and status of your aircraft and the weather is called *situational awareness* and is more important than just flying the aircraft – which ultimately becomes unconscious and automatic, like riding a bicycle.

As you gain experience and the task of flying the aircraft becomes second nature, then you will broaden your situational awareness to include information regarding time, fuel state, engine health, weather. Your instructor will introduce checklists and work-cycles to develop your situational awareness. They are very valuable practices.

Airmanship

A good pilot is in total control of the aircraft, in command of the situation and considerate of other airspace users and passengers. This C^3 is usually called *airmanship*.

Like much of aviation, airmanship has its roots in the sea: *aeronautical*, *captains*, *port* and *starboard*, *east* and *west*, *nautical miles*, *windward*, *leeward*, *squadrons*, *echelon* and even the word *pilot* are all terms that we have inherited from the naval profession. Airmanship is derived from seamanship. The term tends to mean different things to different people but the core principles hold true. With the pleasure and rewards of the profession of aviation comes responsibility.

In the profession of aviation we value and recognise certain attributes:

- awareness and compliance with the rules of the air;
- courtesy and sensitivity to other users of the sky, especially visitors and learners;
- safe and responsible operation of the aircraft;
- situational awareness, anticipation and safe decision-making;
- care and consideration for passengers, whether fare-paying or not;
- integrity and reliability to contain one's emotions and temptations;
- the honesty to assess one's own ability, limitations, weaknesses and readiness;
- the dedication and assertiveness to place standards and reputation ahead of financial gain and to have the courage to say no;
- the self-discipline and motivation to develop one's professional skills and knowledge;
- the pride to be part of the profession; and
- respect for those who have gone before and for those who fly with us.

Airspace

Reference: AIP ENR 1.4 para 1

How Airspace is Organised

Particular types of airspace have established rules and procedures for entry and transit. Aircraft are monitored by radar, transponders and collision alerting systems. To enter this airspace, a clearance is required - so air traffic control can monitor and guide us. IFR traffic is monitored, and given warnings of other traffic with potentially conflicting flightpaths. Class C controlled airspace where high-speed traffic and regular public transport (RPT) aircraft are operating is most protected.

Airspace is classified on an international scale according to the degree of control and traffic density. Some Australian oceanic approaches are declared *Class A airspace* and these are for IFR aircraft only. There is no *Class B airspace* in Australia. Australian capital city aerodromes, such as Sydney, Melbourne and Perth, have *Class C airspace*, which requires prior permission (a *clearance*) to operate within. It is under the positive control of the approach or departure controllers. *Class D airspace* is airspace around major regional aerodromes and capital city general aviation aerodromes. It consists of a control zone of defined dimensions and requires a clearance to enter. Class D airspace is generally below 4,500 ft AMSL (above mean sea level). *Class E* defines some corridors and has some monitoring and reporting requirements for instrument flights, but visual flights are responsible for their own separation. VFR flights in Class E, do not require a clearance.

Control Zones

A *control zone* (CTR) is defined as controlled airspace around an aerodrome extending upwards from the surface of the earth to a specified upper limit. As with the CTA, vertical limits and lateral dimensions are shown on the en-route charts (ERC-L) and VTCs.

Civil Control Zones (Civil CTR)

Civil control zones are all CTRs other than a military CTR. The majority of regular public transport CTRs are within Class C airspace,

Class D CTRs have been established at Albury, Coffs Harbour, Tamworth and Wagga Wagga. In all civil CTRs, Class C airspace procedures apply, and at Class D CTRs specific rules for ATC separation and clearances apply

Capital city Class D aerodromes are Jandakot (Perth), Parafield (Adelaide), Camden (near Sydney), Moorabbin (Melbourne) and Bankstown (Sydney). Local procedures apply. These are specified in ERSA.

Military Control Zones

Military control zones have been established at certain aerodromes, e.g. Pearce (WA), Edinburgh (SA), Richmond, Williamtown (NSW), Amberley (QLD) and Tindal (NT). Civil flights in military CTRs and other military administered airspace may be authorised subject to military activity, weather and any special procedures for the control of civil aircraft which have been agreed and published.

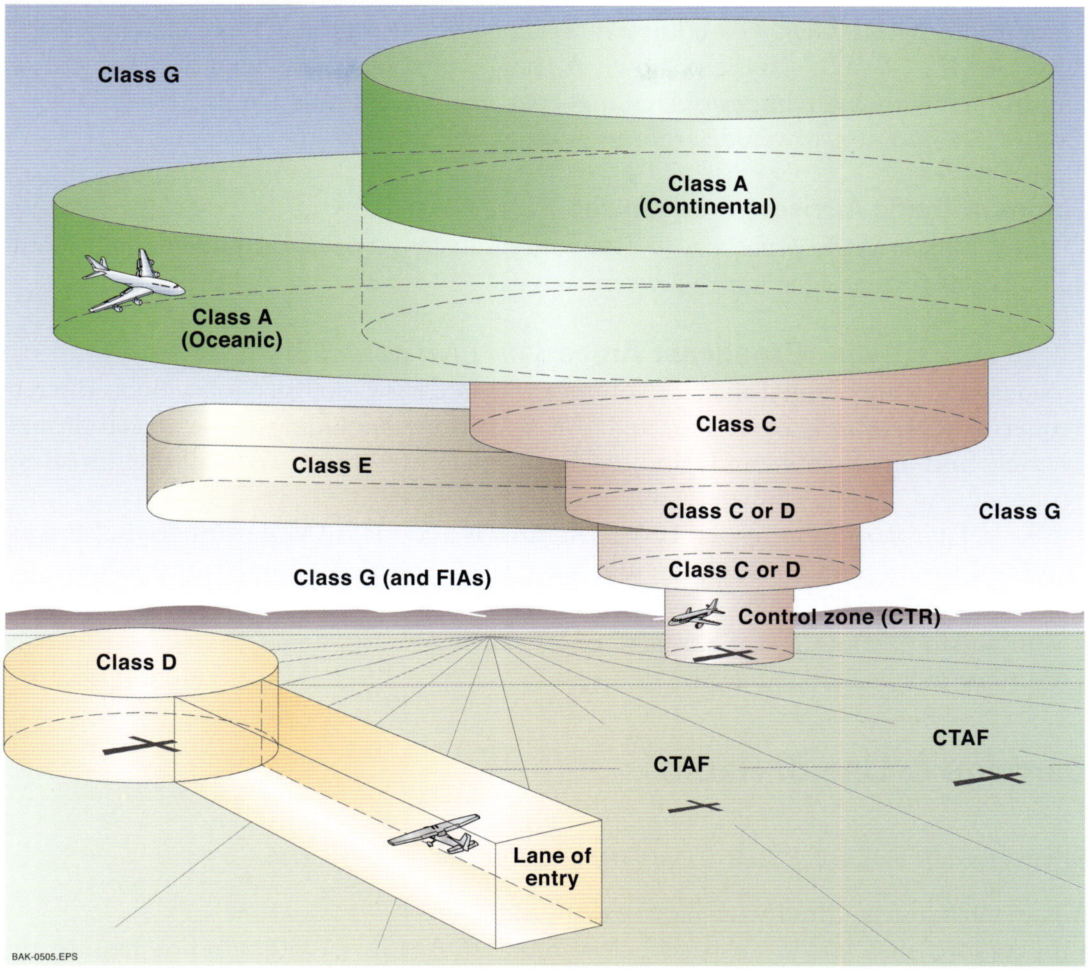

Figure 5-5 Airspace classification.

Non-Controlled Airspace (Class G)

Reference: AIP ENR 1.1-38

Non-controlled airspace is classified as Class G and is subdivided into *flight information areas* (FIA). When operating in Class G airspace, the responsibility for seeing and avoiding other aircraft rests with the pilot-in-command. There is no air traffic control and no requirement for communicating - except near aerodromes.

Flight Information Areas (FIA)

In Class G airspace a *flight information service* (FIS) is provided within defined *flight information areas* (FIAs) within which flight information and *search and rescue* (SAR) alerting services are provided by an *Air Traffic Services* (ATS) unit.

Lane of Entry, Transit Lanes & VFR Corridors

A *lane of entry* (LOE), VFR corridors or transit lanes, can be found near Class D aerodromes which are themselves close to military or Class C capital city airports. They are designed to provide a visual flight path over very obvious ground features to ensure there is no inadvertent penetration of controlled airspace. They are shown on the VTC and also listed in ERSA as Danger areas.

Aerodromes within Class G Airspace

Aerodromes within Class G are known as *non-towered aerodromes*. They may be CERT, REG or MIL - or UNCR (see below). A Danger area may have been declared - as for aerodromes with high intensity training operations (e.g Point Cook). Class D aerodromes become non-towered aerodromes when the tower is not operating.

Common Traffic Advisory Frequencies

Common traffic advisory frequencies (CTAF) are radio frequencies for pilot-to-pilot communications for self separation between aircraft.

Broadcast Areas *(AIP ENR para 3.3)*

Broadcast areas are defined airspace volumes within Class G airspace for which a discrete frequency (CTAF) has been allocated. All operations, including those at aerodromes (charted and uncharted) and landing areas, shall use this CTAF as the broadcast frequency.

The default vertical limit of a Broadcast Area is 5000 FT AMSL. Otherwise, Broadcast Areas where the CTAF applies will have defined vertical boundaries as follows:

- Surface to 5000FT AMSL; or
- Surface to base of CTA if 8,500FT or less; or
- Surface to a nominated level.

Carriage & Use of Radio

Reference: AIP GEN 1.5 Para 1 and AIP ENR 1.2–4

All aircraft must be fitted with radio except that:

- operations in Class G airspace below 5,000 ft AMSL (A050), do not require the installation of VHF radio except in conditions of reduced VMC; and
- recreational aircraft, gliders and balloons may carry an approved hand-held radio.

Note: In remote areas, HF radio is required if no ELB/ELT is carried.

CERT, REG & MIL Aerodromes

A non-towered aerodrome for which a radio and transmissions are mandatory, are designated in ERSA as CERT, REG or MIL. They actually appear with the designation at the top right of the ERSA entry. An aircraft must not approach these aerodromes unless it is radio equipped and the pilot broadcasts on the designated CTAF. As general rule stay clear by 10 nm or fly at least 1,000 feet above circuit height, to avoid conflict.

UNCR Aerodromes

For UNCR aerodromes a radio is not mandatory, but if your aeroplane is radio-equipped, then you should make the same broadcasts - on the CTAF or UNICOM:

- when taxiing;
- entering the runway
- on line-up/take-off;
- transiting;
- joining the circuit;
- within the circuit; and
- if making a straight-in approach

Note: Calls and procedures are described in *Flight Radio for Pilots - VFR Operations*.

Prohibited, Restricted & Danger Areas (PRD)

Reference: ERSA PRD and AIP ENR 1.4

Prohibited, restricted and danger areas are areas in which a potential hazard to aircraft operations may exist. These areas are divided into three types.

Prohibited (P) Areas

You may not enter prohibited areas under any circumstance. There are none in Australia.

Restricted (R) Areas

Restricted areas may only be entered with prior permission and in accordance with specified conditions. For example, the following information is given in ERSA for area R306A:

- the limits specified for this area are 4,500 – FL 200 (this is 4,500 ft to 20,000 ft);
- the hours are NOTAM (that is, the hours of restriction for this area are issued by NOTAM); and
- the authority is military and the activity is military flying.

Danger (D) Areas

You may enter a danger area, but you should enter with caution - it could be busy.

Note: Some PRD areas are only activated by NOTAM.

Approval for flight within an active Danger Area outside controlled airspace is not required. However it is the responsibility of the PIC to be aware of the dangerous activity and take appropriate precautions.

PRD areas may be activated or deactivated at short notice. Access to a Restricted area may be available if the activity for which it has been activated has ceased (early deactivation). It is a pilot's responsibility to check current status with ATS.

Flight within PRD Areas

Flight within a prohibited area is not permitted in any circum- stances. Flight within active Restricted Areas is subject to the conditions published in AIP (ERSA & DAH) and NOTAM. To obtain access to a restricted area or airspace pilots must request approval from the Controlling Authority (see ERSA PRD). When an ATC service is available within that airspace, approval may be requested from ATC directly, in the same manner as a clearance request to enter controlled airspace.

> **Note:** Clearances may be withheld when activities hazardous to the aircraft are taking place, or when those activities require absolute priority. In order to assist with shared use of airspace, all restricted areas have been allocated an RA conditional status. This status will give an indication as to the likelihood of obtaining a clearance to fly through restricted airspace. NOTAMs may be issued to indicate changes to the RA conditional status; which should be checked prior to flight planning.

RA CONDITIONAL STATUS LEGEND:

- Conditional Status RA1: Pilots may flight plan through the Restricted Area and under normal circumstances expect a clearance from ATC.
- Conditional Status RA2: Pilots must not flight plan through the Restricted Area unless on a route specified in ERSA GEN FPR or under agreement with the Department of Defence, however a clearance from ATC is not assured. Other tracking may be offered through the Restricted Area on a tactical basis.

- Conditional Status RA3: Pilots must not flight plan through the Restricted Area and clearances will not be available.

  Note: In a declared emergency, every effort will be made to obtain approval to transit a Restricted Area, irrespective of its conditional status. If the conditional status is uncertain, treat the airspace as conditional status RA3 and avoid the area.

Civil aircraft operating in military Restricted areas or airspace in which a military service is provided will receive a service equivalent to that of Class C airspace unless specified otherwise in ERSA FAC. When compliance with an air traffic clearance requires flight:
- from controlled airspace into an adjoining active restrictedarea or airspace; or
- through an active restricted area or airspace into adjoining controlled airspace; or
- through an active restricted area or airspace within controlled airspace,
- the pilot-in-command may assume that ATC has obtained approval for the flight.

Aerodromes

As a student pilot, you are likely to undergo your flying training at anything from an *aeroplane landing area* (ALA) with a small grass or gravel strip at a flying club, a licensed aerodrome with two or more runways like the Class D aerodromes at Moorabbin and Bankstown, to a capital city airport such as Canberra or Hobart.

Aerodrome, Taxiway & Runway Markings

Reference: AIP AD 1.1

There are standard markings to show you the locations and dimensions of runways and taxiways. They are completely described in the ERSA and AIP.

The important ones to recognise are:
- runway edge markings;
- runway ends, runway threshold and runway number;
- boundary markers (cones and/or gable markers); and
- taxiway and holding point markers.

Taxiway Markings

Taxiway markings are yellow. The taxiway centreline may be marked with two continuous yellow lines. The edges of the taxiway may be marked by two continuous yellow lines to indicate the boundary between high- and low-strength pavements.

Taxiway holding lines, across the width of the taxiway, consist of two continuous yellow lines and two dashed yellow lines. The continuous lines are on the side from which an aeroplane will approach a runway when taxiing, and if instructed to hold short of the runway or if not cleared onto the runway, then you should stop with no part of the aircraft extending beyond the holding line. There may be holding point signs at the edge of the taxiway, with white characters on a red sign face.

An aircraft exiting the runway after landing is not considered clear of the runway until all parts of the aircraft have crossed the holding line (flight strip):
- boundaries of runways, taxiways and aprons may be indicated by cone markers or gable markers, or by solid painted lines;
- holding bays, usually used for engine run-ups, may be marked in the same way as a normal straight taxiway and may include holding point markings; and

- a large white circle marked with H indicates a helipad, i.e. a landing place for helicopters.

Permanent Threshold Markings

Permanent threshold markings are used at the ends of sealed or concrete runways. Where the width of the runway is 30 m or more, this marking is always used; for runways less than 30 m wide, the marking may be used. It consists of a series of parallel longitudinal white lines resembling *piano keys*.

Figure 5-6 Runway threshold.

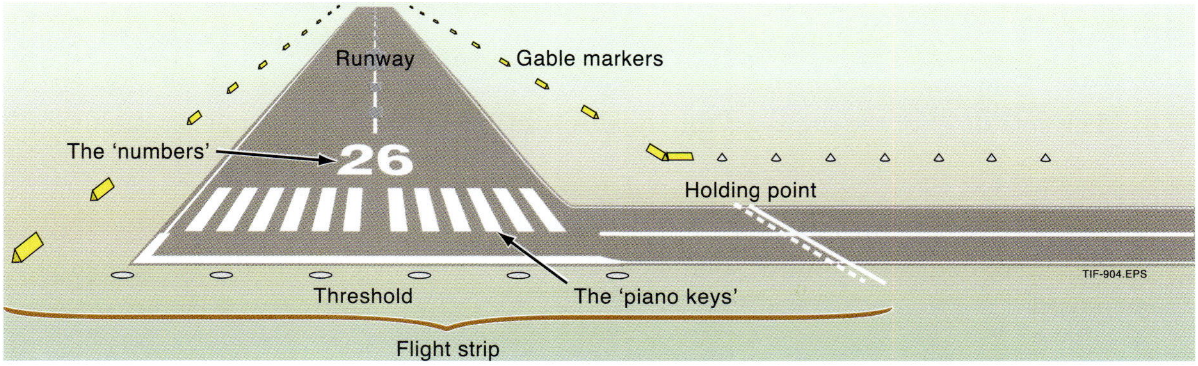

Figure 5-7 Runway and associated boundaries.

Displaced Threshold Markings

Sometimes the full length of the runway is not available – in which case a displaced threshold is marked. A permanently displaced threshold is indicated by arrows leading up to the displaced threshold marking.

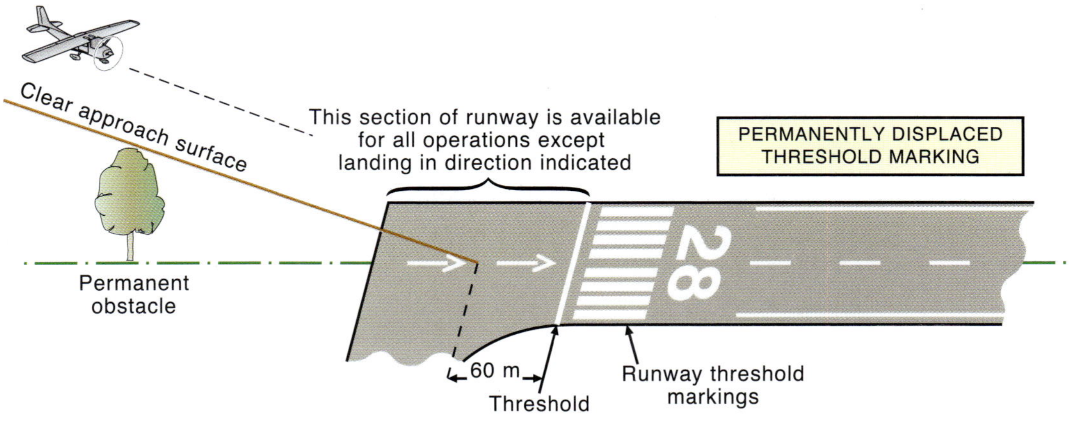

Figure 5-8 Permanently displaced threshold marking.

A temporarily displaced threshold will be indicated by:
- a series of inverted V-markings painted across the runway; or
- V-bar markers situated on both sides of the runway; or
- abbreviated V-bar markers situated on both sides of the runway.

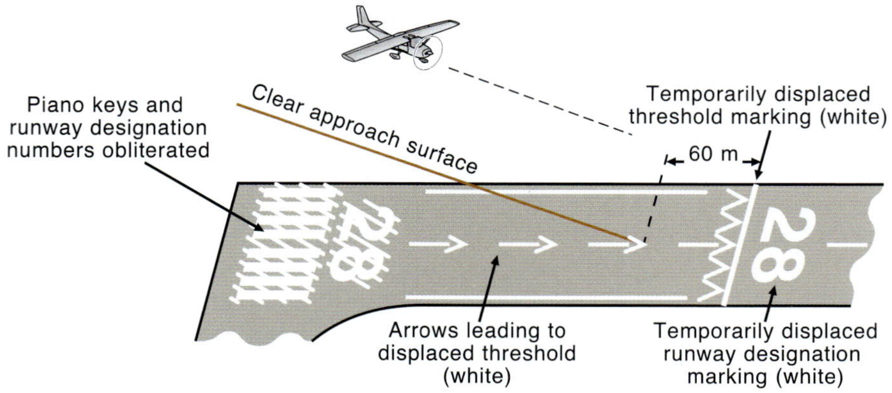

Figure 5-9 Temporarily displaced threshold marking.

The area short of the displaced threshold is available for take-off but not for landing.

Runway Side & End Markings

On sealed or concrete runways, solid white lines delineate the edges of the full-strength pavement.

Windsock

The windsock is a vital indicator to the pilot of wind strength and direction. Your instructor will show you how to read the windsock.

Figure 5-10 Windsocks (the right-hand sock is illuminated).

Ground Signals

Ground signals are displayed within a circle near the windsock to advise the pilot in the air that some limitations apply to the use of the aerodrome.

A horizontal white dumb-bell means that only sealed surfaces should be used.

Figure 5-11 Horizontal white dumb-bell – operate only on sealed surfaces.

A white double vertical cross (++) means that gliding operations are in progress.

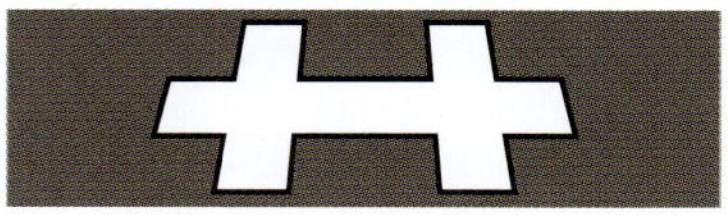

Figure 5-12 Double white cross –

A single white cross (X) by the windsock indicates the complete aerodrome is unserviceable. A cross on a runway indicates that runway is unserviceable.

Figure 5-13 Single white cross – aerodrome unserviceable.

Note: Any specific aerodrome area including a runway, taxiway, parking area displaying a white cross (X) (or crosses) is unfit for use by aircraft.

Figure 5-14 Runway unusable.

Aeroplane Landing Areas (ALA)

Reference: CAAP 92-1(1)

You may use an aeroplane landing area (ALA), which may be grass or gravel runways, during training. Guidelines for the establishment of an ALA are published in the Civil Aviation Advisory Publication (CAAP).

Although an ALA will not have all the markings described for aerodromes, the runways, taxiways and parking areas will normally be marked in outline by cone or gable markers – or painted tyres. Your flying instructor will show you the markings used at your ALA and explain their significance.

Ground Markings

The perimeter of the landing area may be shown by either cone markers spaced not more than 90 m apart or gable markers spaced not more than 180 m apart.

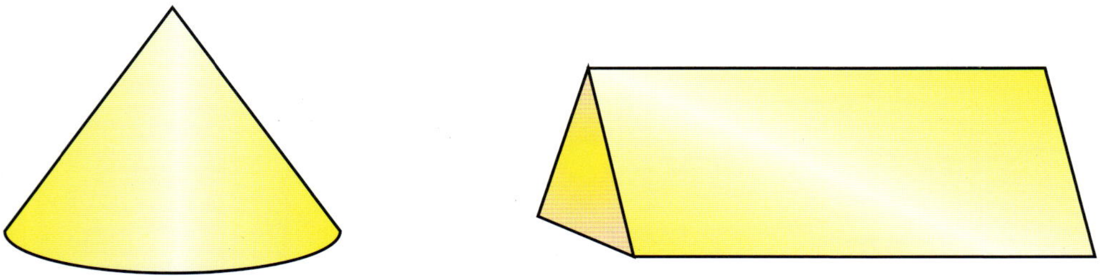

Figure 5-15 A cone marker (left) and a gable marker (right).

The boundaries of taxiways, aprons and parking areas are usually marked with cone markers spaced not more than 15 m apart. Boundary markers are normally white in colour. Where the limits of taxiways or aprons are not clearly defined, yellow cone markers are used. Cone markers also indicate unusable surfaces.

Helicopter Landing Site (Helipad)

There are two types of helicopter landing sites: *basic* and *standard*. The basic HLS should be:

- large enough to accommodate the helicopter safely;
- capable of withstanding the dynamic and static loads; and
- used only for day VMC operations.

The standard HLS must meet all criteria for its intended use for both day and night VMC operations.

Figure 5-16 Helipad symbol.

Standard Circuits

Reference: AIP ENR 1.1 para 54

To maintain safe and orderly flow of traffic at an aerodrome, and to allow easy and safe access to the active runway, aircraft are flown in a traffic pattern called the circuit. As the preferred direction for take-off and landing is into-wind, the same runway direction will generally be used by aircraft both taking-off and landing.

The circuit is a rectangular pattern based on the runway in use. The standard circuit is left-hand with all turns being made to the left. This gives a better view from the pilot's seat than turns to the right. At some aerodromes and on some particular runways, however, the circuits are right-hand to avoid built-up areas, high terrain, restricted airspace or noise-sensitive areas. The circuit is named according to the runway on which it is based, for example, "*join the circuit for Runway 36*" refers to the circuit based on Runway 36.

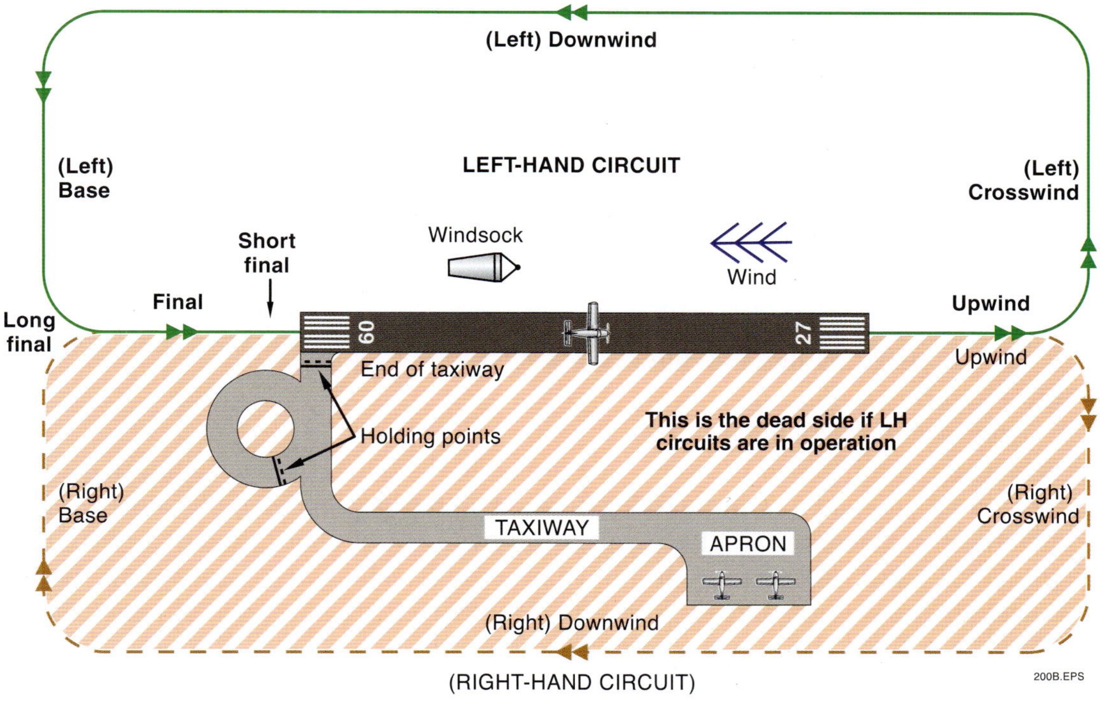

Figure 5-17 The circuit is rectangular.

Legs of a Circuit

Following take-off, aircraft climb straight ahead on the upwind leg. At or above 500 ft (AAL), they may turn onto the crosswind leg to track at 90 degrees to the runway. An allowance is made for wind effect (drift). Then continue the climb to circuit height, which for most aerodromes, is 1,000 ft AAL. At some aerodromes, this may vary (to clear high terrain or remain beneath certain airspace) but will lie in the range of 750 ft to 1,250 ft AAL. Helicopters and ultralights fly the lower height. A turn is made onto the downwind leg and the aeroplane is flown at circuit height to track parallel to the runway.

At the end of the downwind leg, a turn onto base leg is made and a descent commenced. Normally, a turn from base leg onto final approach should be completed by about 500 ft above aerodrome level (AAL) and the final leg should be commenced 500 m or more from the aerodrome boundary.

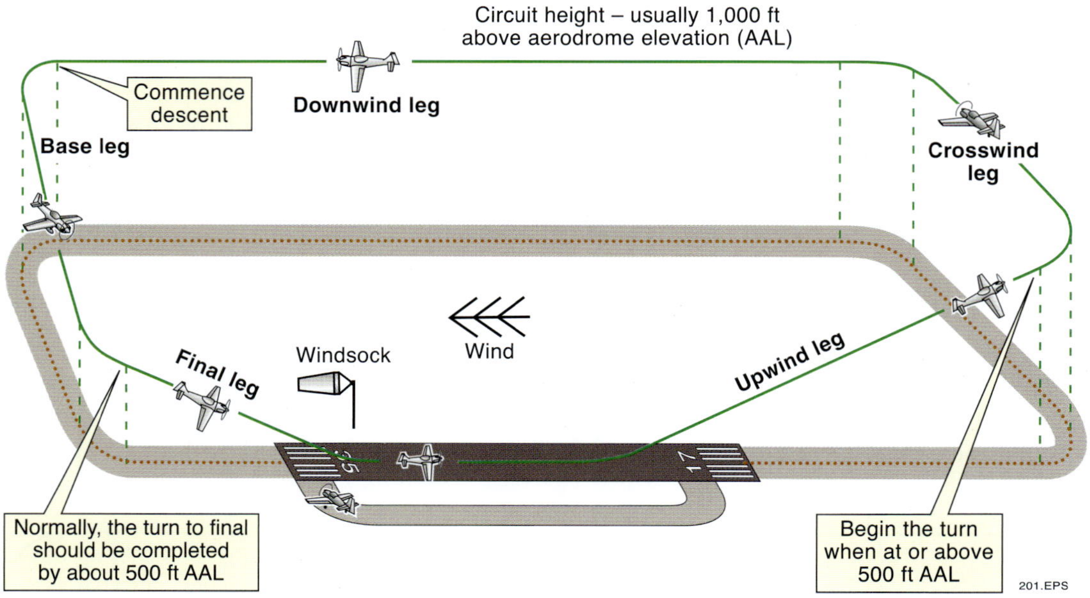

Figure 5-18 The normal circuit is flown at 1,000 ft AGL.

The *dead side* of the circuit refers to the airspace to the side of the runway opposite to the live or active side of the circuit.

Operations on, or close to, an Aerodrome

The rules when operating in the vicinity of an aerodrome are as follows:

- If a CTAF, make an inbound call.
- Observe other traffic.
- Conform with the traffic pattern.
- When approaching a non-towered aerodrome for landing, join the circuit traffic pattern on the upwind or crosswind legs - or via a 45 degree intercept to downwind. If arriving at the aerodrome, it is usual to overfly at 500 ft above the circuit height to check for traffic, and determine the runway in use and surface conditions, before descending to join the circuit. Straight-in approaches are permitted at non-towered aerodromes - you must make a radio call.
- Make all turns to the left in the circuit, unless otherwise directed.
- Final approach must be straight for at least 500 metres from the aerodrome boundary.
- After take-off, climb straight ahead on the runway extended centreline to 500 ft above aerodrome level (AAL).
- Normally land and take off into-wind, or as close to this direction, as possible.

Logbook & Flying Training Records

Reference: CASR PART 61.345 - and PART 141 for the flying school

Prior to commencing your flying training, you should purchase a logbook. It is a requirement that you log all your flights, including the flight details, the aircraft and the crew details specified in the Part 61 regulations.

You should also take pride in it, as you will enjoy looking back on it in years to come. For those of you who are contemplating a career as a pilot, your logbook will form part of your résumé for future interviews.

The Day VFR Syllabus and the Manual of Standards (MOS) outline the sequences you must undertake to qualify for each licence. They also specify the competency standards which you must attain - so that both you and the instructor are clear on what must be achieved. They also outline both the flying sequences and aeronautical knowledge training requirements.

It is a requirement that the school keeps flying training records on your progress in accordance with the Day VFR Syllabus and CASR Part 141. These records must include:

- each training flight, indicating the aircraft type and registration used, the instructor, the training sequence covered and the duration of the flight;
- a progressive total of your aeronautical experience;
- a summary of your progress after each flight; and
- a record of your examination results.

A record of achievement should be kept with your files. This is the responsibility of the flying school. Both you and your instructor, should sign the record of achievement to verify that you have completed each sequence to a satisfactory standard. The record will then be sent to the Civil Aviation Safety Authority with your test form after the completion of a flight test.

Licences, Endorsements & Ratings

Reference: CASR PART 61.

Note: ***The Civil Aviation Safety Authority (CASA) announced that the licensing system was to be changed in December 2013. This was deferred until September 2014 and is now in effect. There is a transition period of three to four years. Students who started training before this date may continue under the old system until they complete a flight test or rating. Then they will be transferred to the new system.***

Licences

The Student Pilot Licence (SPL) is the first licence in the Australian Flight Crew Licensing (FCL) system. You may take dual flying lessons without holding a student pilot licence, but prior to going solo, you must hold both a student pilot licence and a current flight crew medical certificate. The chief flying instructor (CFI) at your flying school issues the student pilot licence. As a student pilot, you may only pilot an aircraft as authorised under the direct supervision of a flying training school.

The list of licences is as follows:

- Student Pilot Licence (SPL);
- Recreational Pilots Licence (RPL)
- Private Pilot Licence - (Aeroplane) (PPL-A);
- Commercial Pilot Licence - (Aeroplane) (CPL-A); and
- Airline Transport Pilot Licence - (Aeroplane) (ATPL-A).

Summary of Changes

The new legislation introduces a new *licence* - the Recreational Pilots Licence (RPL) in addition to the PPL, CPL and ATPL. (Pilots who are current holders of a Recreational Pilots Certificate or have passed the GFPT, may be issued with the RPL after completing a flight review).

Each licence then relates to an aircraft *category* (e.g. aeroplane or helicopter). Within these primary categories, the licence reflects the pilot's competencies by the addition of an aircraft *class rating* or *type rating* (e.g. single-engine, piston or a specified aircraft type). Then there are *operational ratings* such as IR, PIFR and flight instructor.(The previous Command Instrument rating becomes simply an Instrument Rating, (IR).

Each operational rating is then '*endorsed*', e.g. IR for a single-engine aeroplane (SEA) or Low Level rating (LL) for a helicopter (H).

Additionally, there are *design feature endorsements* for items such as a retractable undercarriage or tailwheel - and *flight activity endorsements* for operations such as glider towing, aerobatics or formation flying.

The aircraft class or type rating, operational ratings and endorsements are all displayed on the new licence rather than in the Pilot's Log Book. Over the transition period, records will be transferred from the log book to the new licence when renewed.

Student Pilots Licence

Subpart 61.F Student pilot licences

61.440 Privileges of student pilot licences

Subject to Subpart 61.E and regulations 61.445 and 61.450, the holder of a student pilot licence is authorised to pilot an aircraft when receiving flight training.

Note 1 Subpart 61.E sets out certain limitations that apply to all pilot licences, and ratings and endorsements on pilot licences.

Note 2 The holder of a student pilot licence is also authorised to taxi an aircraft in certain circumstances: see regulation 61.430.

Note 3 The holder of a student pilot licence is also authorised to transmit on a radio frequency of a kind used for the purpose of ensuring the safety of air navigation in certain circumstances: see regulation 61.435.

61.445 Limitations on exercise of privileges of student pilot licences - general

(1) The holder of a student pilot licence is authorised to pilot an aircraft only if the flight is:
  (a) approved by, and conducted under the supervision of, a flight instructor; and
  (b) conducted under the VFR; and
  (c) conducted in accordance with the flight instructor's approval.

(2) For paragraph (1) (a), a flight is conducted under the supervision of a flight instructor if the instructor:
  (a) provides guidance to the pilot in relation to the flight; and
  (b) during the flight:
    (i) is present:
      (A) on board the aircraft; or
      (B) at the aerodrome from which the flight began; or
    (ii) is flying within 15 nautical miles of the aerodrome reference point for the aerodrome; and
  (c) can be contacted during the flight by radio or other electronic means.

(3) The holder of a student pilot licence is not authorised to pilot an aircraft carrying passengers.

(4) The holder of a student pilot licence is authorised to pilot an aircraft on a solo flight in a Contracting State's airspace only if the holder has the permission (however described) of the Contracting State.

61.450 Limitations on exercise of privileges of student pilot licences - recent experience

(1) The holder of a student pilot licence is authorised to conduct a solo flight in an aircraft only if:
- (a) the holder has, within the previous 14 days and in the same type of aircraft, conducted a dual flight; and
- (b) as a result of the flight, his or her accumulated solo flight time since last conducting a dual flight would not exceed 3 hours.

(2) The holder is taken to meet the requirements of paragraph (1) (b) if the holder is enrolled in an integrated training course.

61.455 Requirement for grant of student pilot licences

An applicant for a student pilot licence must be at least 15.

Subpart 61.G Recreational pilot licences

Division 61.G.1 Privileges and grant of licences

61.460 Privileges of recreational pilot licences

Subject to Subpart 61.E and regulations 61.465 and 61.470, the holder of a recreational pilot licence is authorised to pilot a single-engine aircraft as pilot in command or co-pilot if:
- (a) the aircraft is certificated for single-pilot operation; and
- (b) the aircraft has a maximum certificated take-off weight of not more than 1 500 kg; and
- (c) the aircraft is not rocket-powered or turbine-powered; and
- (d) the flight is conducted by day under the VFR; and
- (e) either:
  - (i) the aircraft is engaged in a private operation; or
  - (ii) the holder is receiving flight training.

Note 1 Subpart 61.E sets out certain limitations that apply to all pilot licences, and ratings and endorsements on pilot licences.

Note 2 The holder of a recreational pilot licence is also authorised to taxi an aircraft in certain circumstances: see regulation 61.430.

Note 3 The holder of a recreational pilot licence is also authorised to transmit on a radio frequency of a kind used for the purpose of ensuring the safety of air navigation if the holder also holds a flight radio endorsement: see regulation 61.435.

61.465 Limitations on exercise of privileges of recreational pilot licences - general

(1) The holder of a recreational pilot licence is authorised to pilot an aircraft in a Contracting State's airspace only if the holder has the permission (however described) of the Contracting State to do so.

(2) The holder of a recreational pilot licence is authorised to pilot an aircraft carrying more than one passenger only if the holder:
- (a) also holds a current class 1 or 2 medical certificate; or
- (b) is accompanied by another pilot who:
  - (i) holds a current class 1 or 2 medical certificate; and
  - (ii) occupies a flight control seat in the aircraft; and
  - (iii) is authorised to pilot the aircraft.

(3) The holder of a recreational pilot licence is authorised to pilot an aircraft above 10000 ft above mean sea level only if the holder:
(a) also holds a current class 1 or 2 medical certificate; or
(b) is accompanied by another pilot who:
(i) holds a current class 1 or 2 medical certificate; and
(ii) occupies a flight control seat in the aircraft; and
(iii) is authorised to pilot the aircraft.

61.470 Limitations on exercise of privileges of recreational pilot licences - endorsements

(1) The holder of a recreational pilot licence is authorised to pilot an aircraft in an area that is not:
(a) within:
(i) a 25 nautical mile radius of the aerodrome from which the flight began; or
(ii) a flight training area for the aerodrome; or
(b) along a route between the aerodrome and the flight training area; only if the holder also holds a recreational navigation endorsement.
(2) The holder of a recreational pilot licence is authorised to pilot an aircraft in controlled airspace only if the holder also holds a controlled airspace endorsement.
(3) The holder of a recreational pilot licence is authorised to pilot an aircraft at a controlled aerodrome only if the holder also holds a controlled aerodrome endorsement.

61.475 Requirements for grant of recreational pilot licences

(1) An applicant for a recreational pilot licence must be at least 16.
(2) Subject to regulation 61.480, the applicant must also have:
(a) passed the aeronautical knowledge examination for a recreational pilot licence and the associated aircraft category rating; and
(b) completed flight training for a recreational pilot licence and the associated aircraft category rating; and
(c) passed the flight test mentioned in the Part 61 Manual of Standards for a recreational pilot licence and the associated aircraft category rating; and
(d) completed at least 25 hours of flight time as pilot of an aircraft of the category for which the associated aircraft category rating is sought, including:
(i) at least 20 hours of dual flight; and
(ii) at least 5 hours of flight time as pilot in command.

Note for paragraph (a) For the conduct of aeronautical knowledge examinations, see Division 61.B.3.
Note for paragraph (b) For the requirements for flight training, see Division 61.B.2.
Note for paragraph (c) For the conduct of flight tests, see Division 61.B.4.
Note for paragraph (d) For the determination of a person's flight time and other aeronautical experience, see Division 61.A.2.

(3) Despite paragraph 61.245 (1) (a), the flight test must be conducted in an aircraft.
(4) The applicant is taken to meet the requirements of subregulation (2) if the applicant holds a private pilot licence, commercial pilot licence or air transport pilot licence.

61.480 Grant of recreational pilot licences in recognition of pilot certificates granted by certain organisations

(1) This regulation applies to an applicant for a recreational pilot licence if:
  (a) the applicant holds a pilot certificate, granted by a recreational aviation administration organisation that administers activities involving aircraft of a particular category; and
  (b) the certificate permits the holder to act as the pilot in command of an aircraft of that category.

(2) For subregulation 61.475 (2), the applicant is taken to have passed:
  (a) the aeronautical knowledge examination; and
  (b) the flight test; for the licence and the associated aircraft category rating.

(3) The applicant is also taken to have met the requirements for the grant of:
  (a) the aircraft category rating for each category of aircraft in which the person is permitted by the certificate to act as pilot in command; and
  (b) the aircraft class rating for each class of aircraft in which the person is permitted by the certificate to act as pilot in command; and
  (c) the design feature endorsement for each design feature of an aircraft in which the applicant is permitted by the certificate to act as pilot in command.

Note The holder of an aircraft class rating must successfully complete a flight review for the rating to be authorised to exercise the privileges of the rating, and is not taken to have met the flight review requirement on the basis of being taken to have met the requirements for the grant of the rating under subregulation (3): see subregulation 61.745 (4).

Division 61.G.2 Recreational pilot licence endorsements

61.485 Kinds of recreational pilot licence endorsements

The following are recreational pilot licence endorsements:
  (a) a controlled aerodrome endorsement;
  (b) a controlled airspace endorsement;
  (c) a flight radio endorsement;
  (d) a recreational navigation endorsement.

61.490 Privileges of recreational pilot licence endorsements

(1) Subject to Subpart 61.E, the holder of a recreational pilot licence with a controlled aerodrome endorsement is authorised to pilot an aircraft, as pilot in command, at a controlled aerodrome.

(2) Subject to Subpart 61.E, the holder of a recreational pilot licence with a controlled airspace endorsement is authorised to pilot an aircraft, as pilot in command, in controlled airspace.

(3) Subject to Subpart 61.E, the holder of a recreational pilot licence with a flight radio endorsement is authorised to operate an aircraft radio on the ground or in flight to transmit on a radio frequency of a kind used for the purpose of ensuring the safety of air navigation.

(4) Subject to Subpart 61.E, the holder of a recreational pilot licence with a recreational navigation endorsement is authorised to pilot an aircraft, as pilot in command, on a cross-country flight.

61.495 Requirements for grant of recreational pilot licence endorsements

(1) This regulation applies to a person other than a person who is eligible to be granted a recreational pilot licence endorsement under regulation 61.500.

(2) An applicant for a recreational pilot licence endorsement must:

(a) have passed the aeronautical knowledge examination for the endorsement; and

(b) have completed flight training for the endorsement; and

(c) if the endorsement is a recreational navigation endorsement, have completed, in addition to the flight time mentioned in paragraph 61.475 (2) (d), at least 5 hours of solo cross-country flight time; and

(d) if the endorsement is a flight radio endorsement, have a current aviation English language proficiency assessment.

Note for paragraph (a) For the conduct of aeronautical knowledge examinations, see Division 61.B.3.

Note for paragraph (b) For the requirements for flight training, see Division 61.B.2.

(3) The cross-country flight time required by paragraph (2) (c) must include a flight of at least 100 nautical miles, during which a full-stop landing is made at each of 2 aerodromes or landing areas, other than the one from which the flight began.

61.500 Grant of endorsement in recognition of other qualifications

(1) An applicant for a recreational pilot licence endorsement is eligible to be granted the endorsement if the applicant:

(a) holds a recreational pilot licence; and

(b) holds another flight crew licence that authorises the exercise of the privileges of the endorsement.

(2) An applicant for a controlled aerodrome endorsement is eligible to be granted the endorsement if:

(a) regulation 61.480 applies to the applicant; and

(b) the applicant holds an approval from the recreational aviation administration organisation to pilot an aircraft at a controlled aerodrome.

(3) An applicant for a controlled airspace endorsement is eligible to be granted the endorsement if:

(a) regulation 61.480 applies to the applicant; and

(b) the applicant holds an approval from the recreational aviation administration organisation to pilot an aircraft in controlled airspace.

(4) An applicant for a flight radio endorsement is eligible to be granted the endorsement if:

(a) regulation 61.480 applies to the applicant; and

(b) the applicant holds an approval from the recreational aviation administration organisation to operate an aircraft radio; and

(c) the applicant has a current aviation English language proficiency assessment.

(5) An applicant for a recreational navigation endorsement is eligible to be granted the endorsement if:

(a) regulation 61.480 applies to the applicant; and

(b) the applicant holds a cross-country navigation approval from the recreational aviation administration organisation; and

(c) the applicant has completed at least 5 hours of solo cross-country flight time that complies with subregulation 61.495 (3).

Subpart 61.H Private pilot licences

Division 61.H.1 General

61.505 Privileges of private pilot licences

Subject to Subpart 61.E and regulation 61.510, the holder of a private pilot licence is authorised to pilot an aircraft as pilot in command or co-pilot if:

(a) the aircraft is engaged in a private operation; or

(b) the holder is receiving flight training.

Note 1 Subpart 61.E sets out certain limitations that apply to all pilot licences, and ratings and endorsements on pilot licences.

Note 2 The holder of a private pilot licence is also authorised to taxi an aircraft in certain circumstances: see regulation 61.430.

Note 3 The holder of a private pilot licence is also authorised to transmit on a radio frequency of a kind used for the purpose of ensuring the safety ofair navigation: see regulation 61.435.

61.510 Limitations on exercise of privileges of private pilot licences - multi-crew operations

The holder of a private pilot licence is authorised to exercise the privileges of the licence in a multi-crew operation only if the holder has completed an approved course of training in multi-crew cooperation.

61.515 Requirements for grant of private pilot licences - general

(1) An applicant for a private pilot licence must be at least 17.

(2) The applicant must also have:

(a) passed the aeronautical knowledge examination for the private pilot licence and the associated aircraft category rating; and

(b) completed flight training for the private pilot licence and the associated aircraft category rating; and

(c) passed the flight test mentioned in the Part 61 Manual of Standards for the private pilot licence and the associated aircraft category rating; and

(d) met the aeronautical experience requirements mentioned in Division 61.H.2 or 61.H.3.

(3) Despite paragraph 61.245 (1) (a), the flight test must be conducted in an aircraft.

(4) An applicant who meets the requirements for the grant of a commercial pilot licence is taken to meet the requirements for the grant of a private pilot licence.

Division 61.H.2 Aeronautical experience requirements for private pilot licences - applicants who have completed integrated training courses

61.520 Application of Division 61.H.2

This Division applies to an applicant for a private pilot licence who has completed an integrated training course for the licence and the associated aircraft category rating.

61.525 Aeronautical experience requirements for grant of private pilot licences - aeroplane category

(1) An applicant for a private pilot licence with the aeroplane category rating must have at least 35 hours of aeronautical experience that includes:

(a) at least 30 hours of flight time as a pilot; and

(b) at least 20 hours of flight time as pilot of an aeroplane; and

(c) at least 10 hours of solo flight time in an aeroplane; and
(d) at least 5 hours of solo cross-country flight time in an aeroplane; and
(e) at least 2 hours of dual instrument time; and
(f) at least one hour of dual instrument flight time in an aeroplane.

(2) Any of the required aeronautical experience that is not completed as flight time as a pilot must be completed as simulated flight time in an approved flight simulation training device for the purpose.

(3) The cross-country flight time required by paragraph (1) (d) must include a flight of at least 150 nautical miles during which a full-stop landing is made at each of 2 aerodromes not within the flight training area for the aerodrome from which the flight began.

(4) The flight time in an aeroplane required by subregulation (1) must be completed in a registered or recognised aeroplane.

61.530 Aeronautical experience requirements for grant of private pilot licences - helicopter category

(1) An applicant for a private pilot licence with the helicopter category rating must have at least 35 hours of aeronautical experience that includes:
(a) at least 30 hours of flight time as pilot of a helicopter; and
(b) at least 10 hours of solo flight time in a helicopter; and
(c) at least 5 hours of solo cross-country flight time in a helicopter; and
(d) at least 2 hours of dual instrument time; and
(e) at least one hour of dual instrument flight time in a helicopter.

(2) Any of the required aeronautical experience that is not completed as flight time as a pilot must be completed as:
(a) simulated flight time in an approved flight simulation training device for the purpose; or
(b) tethered flight time.

(3) The cross-country flight time required by paragraph (1) (c) must include a flight of at least 100 nautical miles during which a landing is made at each of 2 landing areas, other than the one from which the flight began.

(4) The flight time in a helicopter required by subregulation (1) must be completed in a registered or recognised helicopter.

Division 61.H.3 Aeronautical experience requirements for private pilot licences - applicants who have not completed integrated training courses

61.540 Application of Division 61.H.3

This Division applies to an applicant for a private pilot licence who has not completed an integrated training course for the licence and the associated aircraft category rating.

61.545 Aeronautical experience requirements for grant of private pilot licences - aeroplane category

(1) An applicant for a private pilot licence with the aeroplane category rating must have at least 40 hours of aeronautical experience that includes:
(a) at least 35 hours of flight time as a pilot; and
(b) at least 20 hours of flight time as pilot of an aeroplane; and
(c) at least 10 hours of solo flight time in an aeroplane; and
(d) at least 5 hours of solo cross-country flight time in an aeroplane; and
(e) at least 2 hours of dual instrument time; and

(f) at least one hour of dual instrument flight time in an aeroplane.

(2) Any of the required aeronautical experience that is not completed as flight time as a pilot must be completed as simulated flight time in an approved flight simulation training device for the purpose.

(3) The cross-country flight time required by paragraph (1) (d) must include a flight of at least 150 nautical miles during which a full-stop landing is made at each of 2 aerodromes not within the flight training area for the aerodrome from which the flight began.

Responsibilities of the Pilot-in-Command

Reference: CAR 224

There must always be one pilot designated as pilot-in-command for each flight. Your responsibilities as pilot in command include the safety of:

- the aircraft throughout its entire flight from startup to shutdown including any diversions; and
- any passengers and/or cargo on board the aircraft, including crew members, and their conduct on board the aircraft.

Reference: CAO 20.2

As the pilot-in-command, you are responsible for ensuring that the checks are carried out before flight. These may be listed in the company operations manual and the flight manual and will include:

- the removal of locking and safety devices, e.g. control locks, the cover on the pitot tube;
- the security of doors, hatches and fuel tank caps;
- that all external surfaces of the aircraft are completely free from frost and ice;
- that the flight controls are functioning correctly (full and free movement, and in the correct sense);
- for aircraft fitted with dual controls (normal for training aircraft), that the spare safety harness and any other articles or equipment which may foul the controls are secure;
- that the engine and flight instruments are functioning properly; and
- prior to the first flight of the day and after refuelling, the fuel system must be checked to ensure that it is free from undissolved water, and if significant water is found, say more than just a small amount of condensation, this should be reported to your flying instructor.

Limitations on Activities

Minimum Heights for Flight

Reference: CAR 157

Legal minimum heights for flight are:

- not lower than 1,000 ft over cities, towns or other populous areas; and
- not lower than 500 ft over any other area.

These heights are above the highest point of the terrain and any object on it within a radius of 600 m from a point vertically below the aeroplane (a radius of 300 m for helicopters). Flights over public gatherings are not permitted unless a special waiver has been issued.

Acrobatic Flight (Aerobatics)

Before engaging in aerobatic flight, you must be trained and approved to perform aerobatic manoeuvres, and your logbook must be endorsed accordingly. The following must also be observed:
- aerobatic flight must be conducted in VMC;
- aerobatic flight must not be conducted at night;
- aerobatic flight must only be conducted in aircraft where the Certificate of Airworthiness, flight manual or the aircraft (through placards) specifies that the aircraft may perform that type of aerobatic manoeuvre; and
- you may not fly over populated areas or public gatherings when conducting aerobatics.

Stalls performed in straight and level flight and steep turns not exceeding 60° angle of bank are not considered to be aerobatic manoeuvres. Unless permission is granted in writing by CASA, aerobatic flight may not take place below 3,000 ft above the highest point of the terrain or any obstacle within a 600 m radius of a line extending vertically below the aircraft. Prior to commencing any aerobatic manoeuvres, you must:
- check that any loose articles are removed or secured in the aircraft;
- all doors and lockers are secured;
- all unused harnesses are secured to avoid interfering with the controls;
- dual controls are removed or made inoperative unless the control seats are operated by qualified pilots who are aerobatic rated or where one pilot is rated and the other is a student under instruction (the dual controls may remain if the other control seat is unoccupied); and
- all persons on board must be properly secured.

Smoking in or Near an Aircraft

Reference: CAR 255

Obviously smoking poses a serious fire hazard to an aircraft and its occupants. Do not smoke on the tarmac, during refuelling, during take-off or landing, or when directed not to by the pilot.

Drugs & Alcohol

Reference: CAR 256

Operating as a pilot when under the influence of any drug or alcohol is prohibited. Alcohol must not be consumed within 8 hours of operating as a flight crew member. This is also applicable to medication which may affect the crew person's abilities. An intoxicated person is prohibited from boarding an aircraft.

Dropping of Articles from Aircraft

Reference: CAR 150

Without special approval, no objects are to be dropped from an aircraft in flight.

Accidents & Incidents

Reference: AIP ENR 1.14

An *accident* is an occurrence related to the operation of an aircraft, resulting in:
- a person dying or suffering a serious injury;
- structural failure or substantial damage to an aircraft; or
- the aircraft becoming inaccessible or going missing.

A *serious incident* is an occurrence related to the operation of an aircraft where an accident almost occurs. Examples of a serious incident include:

- marginally avoiding controlled flight into terrain (CFIT);
- large abnormalities in performance during take-off or initial climb;
- events which require the flight crew to use oxygen or cause flight crew incapacitation;
- take-off or landing occurrences resulting in undershooting, overrunning or running off the side of a runway;
- any fire on board an aircraft;
- aircraft structural failures or engine disintegration not classified as accidents;
- near collisions requiring evasive manoeuvring;
- rejected take-off; and
- landings or attempted landings on a closed or occupied runway.

An *incident* is an occurrence related to the operation of an aircraft affecting or potentially affecting the safety of the aircraft and is not classified as an accident or serious incident.

The agency responsible for investigating the causes of accidents and incidents is the Australian Transport Safety Bureau (ATSB), which is a separate organisation to CASA.

The aim of the ATSB is to promote air safety. Their approach is positive; they investigate causes to avert future accidents and incidents. All accidents and incidents relating to an aircraft, contents or persons on board *must be reported.*

SARTIME

Reference: AIP GEN 3.6-2

Pilots operating away from the departure airfield should nominate a SARTIME. This will alert the appropriate authorities if you fail to cancel your SARTIME on time due to some difficulty or emergency.

A SARTIME is a time nominated by the pilot for the initiation of search and rescue action if the unit does not receive a report to cancel the nominated SARTIME. If you fail to cancel your SARWATCH, your flight watch will enter an emergency phase. There are three emergency phases which have been established for classifying emergency situations.

Uncertainty Phase (INCERFA)

The *uncertainty phase* is initiated when:

- doubt exists as to the safety of the aircraft and its occupants;
- a pilot operating on a SAR procedure (such as a SARTIME) fails to report, and checks fail to reveal any news of the aircraft (this includes calling for the aircraft through air traffic control services and calling any contact numbers provided by the pilot);
- an aircraft is known or believed to be operating irregularly (for example, it is experiencing navigational, altitude or communication difficulties);
- an aircraft is about to make a landing where the position is in doubt or on an unprepared surface or on an aerodrome that is operation unsuitable (not including a forced landing); or
- information is received that an aircraft is missing.

Alert Phase (ALERFA)

The *alert phase* is initiated when:

- apprehension exists as to the safety of the aircraft and its occupants;
- an aircraft fails to land within 5 minutes after having received a landing or approach clearance and communication cannot be reestablished with the pilot;
- after the uncertainty phase, any communication checks fail to reveal any news of the aircraft;

- news is received that the operations of the aircraft have been impaired to the extent that the safety of the aircraft is in doubt;
- there is reason to believe that the aircraft is in jeopardy; or
- the aircraft is operating in conditions below that required for visual flight or at night when the pilot or aircraft is not qualified or should not be operating under these conditions.

Distress Phase (DETRESFA)

The *distress phase* is initiated when:
- there is reasonable certainty that an aircraft an its occupants are in danger and require immediate assistance;
- an aircraft is subject to or believed to be subject to unlawful interference;
- following an alert phase, there is a probability that an aircraft is in distress;
- there is insufficient or no fuel remaining on board an aircraft to allow it to reach safety; or
- an aircraft has made or is about to make a forced landing or has ditched or crashed.

The En Route Supplement Australia (ERSA) has a section at the back on emergencies with the edges of these pages coloured pink to make them easy to locate. The contents of this section includes:
- transponder codes to set in an emergency;
- procedures for a radio failure;
- light signals to aircraft on the ground and in the air;
- actions for before and after an emergency landing;
- what to do if you inadvertently activate your ELT;
- how to activate an ELT;
- air search patterns;
- search and rescue signals;
- recommended contents of a first aid kit in aircraft with a capacity of less than 30 passengers;
- basic first aid;
- information on survival in the sea, desert, jungle and cold water; and
- information on procedures in an air defence identification zone (ADIZ).

Landing before Last Light

Reference: AIP ENR 1.2

You must plan to land at the aerodrome from which you departed at least 10 minutes before the end of daylight. Some schools that you may fly from will have their own company regulations which you must abide by. In the case of landing before last light, they may require you to plan to be back 20 minutes before the end of daylight. These company rules can be found in the company operations manual for the individual school.

Twenty minutes before the end of daylight is not a long time. When planning your arrival time back at the aerodrome, you must consider all the factors which may cause the end of daylight to be sooner. Such factors include:
- the altitude of the observer (the higher the observer, the later the end of daylight will be);
- the amount of cloud cover (with cloud coverage, the end of daylight will be sooner);
- visibility (with poor visibility, the end of daylight will be sooner); and
- terrain (terrain, such as a mountain to the west blocking out the sun as it sets, will result in an earlier end of daylight).

Fuelling of Aircraft

Reference: CAO 20.9

Location of Aircraft

During fuelling operations, the aircraft and ground fuelling equipment shall be located so that no fuel tank filling points or vent outlets lie:

- within 5 m (17 ft) of any sealed building;
- within 6 m (20 ft) of other stationary aircraft;
- within 15 m (50 ft) of any exposed public area;
- within 9 m (30 ft) of any unsealed building in the case of aircraft with a maximum take-off weight not exceeding 5,700 kg.

The drainage of a small quantity of fuel from a fuel system drain point is not considered a fuelling operation. No smoke or naked flame is permitted within 15 m of the aircraft or refuelling equipment.

Safety Precautions

During fuelling operations:

- All engines in the aircraft, shall be stopped with their ignition switches in the OFF position.
- All items of fuelling equipment (including drums, funnels and other loose items of equipment, where used) shall be connected in such a way as to ensure that they are of the same electrical potential and, where a suitable earth point is available at the fuelling site, both the aircraft and the equipment shall be effectively connected to that point.
- Where the fuelling equipment is not mobile, the aircraft shall be so placed that it can be rapidly moved to a place of safety, and a means of ensuring that this can be done shall be readily available. This includes disengaging the park brake and connecting a towbar if needed.
- The person fuelling the aircraft shall not carry any matches, cigarette lighters or other objects which could represent an ignition hazard.
- When a fuelling operation on an aircraft has been completed, the pilot in command of the aircraft shall ensure that all fuel and oil tank caps are securely refitted and carry out a fuel drain for contaminants.

Starting the Engine

The pilot in command or any other person responsible for starting an aircraft shall ensure that where fuel or any other flammable material is spilled within 15 m (50 ft) of an aircraft, the aircraft engines shall not be started or operated until the fire hazard has been removed.

An aircraft engine shall not be started or operated:

- within 5 m (17 ft) of any sealed building;
- within 8 m (25 ft) of other aircraft;
- within 15 m (50 ft) of any exposed public area;
- within 8 m (25 ft) of any unsealed building in the case of an aircraft with a maximum take-off weight not exceeding 5,700 kg (12,566 lb).

Oils

It is the responsibility of the pilot in command to ensure that an aircraft is not flown unless there is sufficient lubricating oil in the engine. The flight manual for the aircraft will specify the correct grade of oil for the engine.

Airworthiness

Reference: CAOs 100 & 101

The documents which specify the airworthiness of the particular aircraft and the limitations governing its operation are contained in the following:
- flight manual;
- certificate of registration;
- certificate of airworthiness; and
- maintenance release.

Aeroplane Flight Manual

Reference: CAR 54, 138, 139

An *aeroplane flight manual* (AFM) is a document containing specific information, limitations and instructions on how the aircraft is to be operated safely. It must be approved by CASA and you must comply with any instructions and limitations within it. It must also be carried on board the aircraft. Most AFMs contain the following information and instructions.
- Limitations:
  - aircraft speeds;
  - weight and balance information;
  - maximum engine rpm;
  - power plant specifications;
  - permissible manoeuvres; and
  - performance data for take-off and landing.
- Operating Procedures:
  - speeds and configurations to achieve the expected or required performance in normal flying situations; and
  - operations for abnormal or emergency situations which may arise.
- Performance:
  - how the take-off, climb and landing performance of the aircraft is affected by weight, runway surface, wind, air pressure and temperature;
  - the minimum climb gradient and associated weight that must be achieved at take-off and for a missed approach.
- Loading: the correct loading and distribution of passengers, cargo and fuel.

Supplemental Information

The AFM will also include supplemental information which may be necessary to the safe operation of the aircraft. In 1975, the General Aviation Manufacturers Association (GAMA) Specification Number 1 *pilot operating handbook* (POH) format was introduced. Most of the new light aircraft produced have had the AFM data produced in this format.

Aircraft Not Requiring a Basic AFM

Some light aircraft do not need a basic AFM. Some light aircraft built between 1953 and the mid 1970s were produced during a time when the manufacturer could provide this information to the pilot via placards in the cockpit. For aircraft produced before and after this period, an AFM is required. For aircraft that do not require an AFM, supplements must be used if there is information relating to modifications, non-standard aircraft configurations, special role equipment or other special purposes. These supplements must be kept in a folder that is conveniently available to the pilot. An amendment record must also be kept within the folder for details of any changes.

Certificate of Registration

An aircraft operating in Australia must be registered (unless it is not intended to be used as an aircraft). The certificate of registration must be in force but does not need to be carried on board the aircraft if the flight is taking place wholly within Australia. The certificate of registration contains details of the owner of the aircraft and the aircraft's registration.

Certificate of Airworthiness

Reference: CASR 21.175

For flights undertaken wholly within Australia, a Certificate of Airworthiness (CoA) must be in force, but it does not have to be carried on board the aircraft. The CoA will stipulate for which category the aircraft is certified. The categories for aircraft include:

- normal;
- utility;
- acrobatic;
- commuter;
- transport; and
- special class of aircraft.

Maintenance Release

Reference: CAR 43(7)

The maintenance release is issued by an authorised person and signed by the person who coordinated the periodic inspection, which was carried out immediately prior to the issuance. The maintenance release is divided into three parts which, in combination, provide the pilot with all the information he or she needs to be assured that all necessary maintenance has been carried out. It also provides maintenance personnel with details of any mandatory work required and when it has to be done. The student pilot:

- does not have the authority to carry out a daily inspection (but must ensure that it has been done);
- does not have the authority to sign off a maintenance release; and
- must report defects (in the manner and to the persons specified by CASA – for the student pilot, the usual means is to report the problem to the flight instructor before any entry is made in the maintenance release).

The pilot will refer to the maintenance release before and after every flight, so it is important that you have a good understanding of it. We will now consider it in detail.

Part 1 of the Maintenance Release

Part 1 of the maintenance release specifies the type and registration of the aeroplane and the operational category for which it is approved.

Part 1 is concerned mainly with routine maintenance requirements and the following:

- certifies that all routine maintenance has been completed;
- specifies the period of validity of the maintenance release (normally 100 hours or 12 months); and
- records any inspections or maintenance tasks required during the period of validity of the maintenance release, such as oil changes, airworthiness directives, time-expired components, etc.

Before flight, the pilot should check that the maintenance release is current by making sure that the period of validity, in either hours flown or elapsed time, has not expired. This is done by checking the expiry date, and comparing the time in service shown in Part 1 with the progressive total shown in Part 3. It is essential to check Part 1 to ensure that maintenance has not become overdue.

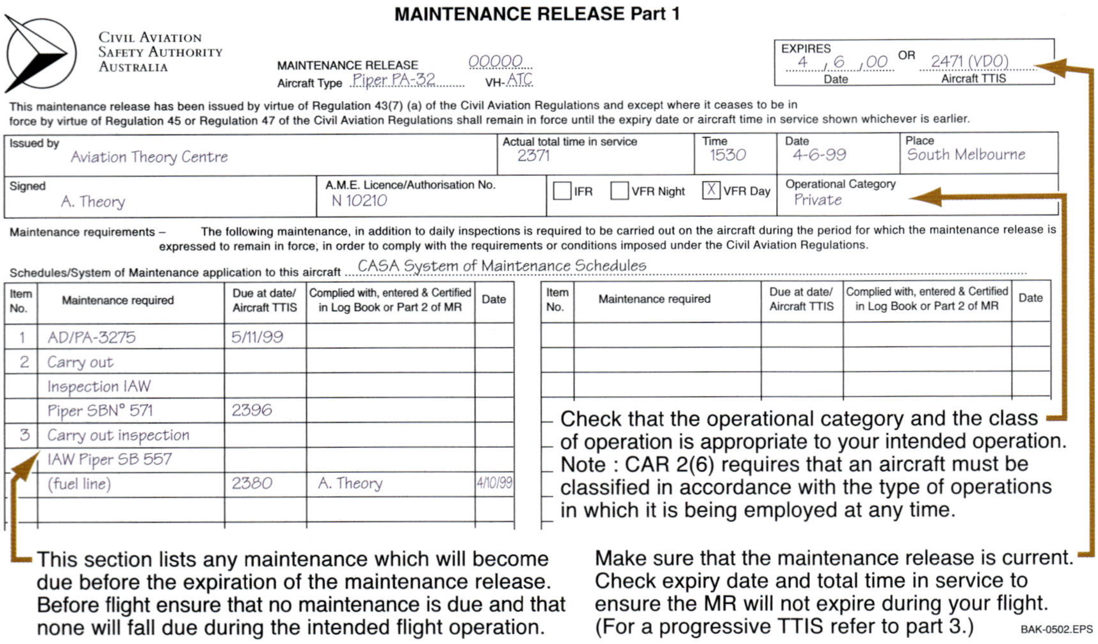

Figure 5-19 Part 1 of the maintenance release.

Part 2 of the Maintenance Release

Part 2 of the maintenance release provides the pilot with the means of reporting defects and indicates whether previously reported defects have been rectified. It provides the pilot with a history of defects on the aircraft for the period of validity of the maintenance release. It is worth stressing that it is required that defects be entered in the maintenance release. These entries are made either by the pilot or an agent on the pilot's behalf (flight instructor, maintenance engineer, etc). Pilots' endorsements must be signed and dated.

Before flight, the pilot should examine Part 2 for endorsements and check that the certification clearing any endorsement is appropriately signed and authenticated with a licence number. The presence of an open endorsement does not necessarily ground the aeroplane. CAOs, supplemented by the aircraft's flight manual, list the aircraft mandatory equipment requirements for various flight categories and classes of operation. An endorsement affecting any of those items or the airworthiness of the aeroplane must obviously be cleared before the aeroplane is flown.

After a flight, any defects should be entered in Part 2 of the maintenance release and endorsed (signed) by the person making the entry. This is an official operational document and gets any defect into the "system" where it must be handled. For a student pilot, the usual means is to report the problem to the flight instructor before any entry is made.

The next pilot to fly the aircraft will refer to Part 2 of the maintenance release to see if any previously reported defects have been rectified unless, that is, they are of a nature that continued operations under certain conditions is permissible.

The entering of appropriate defects into Part 2 of the maintenance release is a legal and moral responsibility – it is a form of protection for the subsequent pilots, ensuring that they will be flying an airworthy machine.

Part 2 of the maintenance release is the interface document between the ground engineers and the pilots. A defect not entered in Part 2 but mentioned casually to someone or scribbled on a piece of loose paper may be forgotten or lost. There is no guarantee that the defect will be picked up in routine maintenance unless it is noted in Part 2. Items such as a heavy landing or an excessive in-flight load on the aircraft (e.g. a hard pull-out from a dive or an inadvertent spin) should be written in, since these can place excessive stress on the aeroplane. For the well-being of the subsequent pilots and passengers, such events, even though possibly embarrassing, must be reported. This is our responsibility.

MAINTENANCE RELEASE Part 2

Item No.	Endorsements	Signature & Date	Item No.	Clearing Endorsements	Clearing Signature Licence No/Authority No and Date
1	Ref Item 3 Part 1	A. Theory 4/10/99	1	SB 557 Carried out - nil defects found	A. Theory 4/10/99
					N102310 4/10/99
2	ADF U/S	T. Centre 30/11/99			

A signature in part 2 of the Maintenance Release certifying for the completion of maintenance shall constitute a certification required by Civil Aviation Regulation 34. Part 2

Check any endorsements to assess their effect on your intended operation and make sure the maintenance release is in force.

Should the defect or damage be major, include the words "the aircraft is unserviceable (U/S)" with your endorsement (CAR 47).

Abnormal flight or ground loads, such as a heavy landing, must also be reported in this manner (CAR 47).

BAK-0503.EPS

Figure 5-20 Part 2 of the maintenance release.

Part 3 of the Maintenance Release

Part 3 of the maintenance release provides a record of the hours flown and certifications for the daily inspections carried out. The record of hours flown is necessary to keep a check on the currency of the maintenance release and to show when maintenance called up in Part 1 is due. It is a requirement that flying hours and number of landings be entered at least at the end of each day's flying for that aircraft.

Before flight, the student pilot should check Part 3 to ensure that the daily inspection has been done and signed off. A student pilot does not have the authority to carry out a daily inspection unaccompanied and so does not have the right to sign this off on the maintenance release. You must hold a PPL at least. As a student pilot, you must not fly an aircraft unless the daily inspection is signed off for that day by a suitable person or unless the pilot in command (the instructor) has taken the responsibility of doing the daily inspection.

Figure 5-21 Part 3 of the maintenance release.

MAINTENANCE RELEASE Part 3
DAILY INSPECTION CERTIFICATION AND AIRCRAFT TIME - IN - SERVICE

Date	Daily Inspection Certification		Aircraft Time-In-Service				Progressive Total of		
			This Flight		Progressive				
	Signature	Licence No	Hrs	Mins	Hrs	Mins	Landings		
	BROUGHT FORWARD				2371	00			
29/9/99	C. Smith	123456	7	00	2378	00	1		
4/10/99	C. Smith	123456	2	00	2380	00	2	3	
1/11/99	W. JONES	246800	4	35	2384	35	1	4	
7/11/99	P. BEAR	130068	3	20	2387	55	6	10	
20/11/99	J. WILSON	196802	2	15	2390	10	1	11	
30/11/99	J. WILSON	196802	3	50	2394	00	2	13	
1/12/99	C. Smith	123456	1	00	2395	00	2	15	

A signature in part 3 of the Maintenance Release certifying for the completion of maintenance shall constitute a certification required by Civil Aviation Regulation 34.

For a 'B' Class aircraft any pilot (not a student pilot) can certify. The person certifying must have performed the daily inspection.

BAK-0504.EPS

Maintenance Schedule

Each aeroplane must have a maintenance schedule approved by CASA. This requires a system of regular checks and inspections by licensed and approved people. A typical maintenance schedule will include:

- scheduled major inspections (in general aviation every 3 years, except for aircraft in the agricultural category which are annual);
- inspections to be carried out every 100 hours (the "100 hourly");
- 25- or 50-hour inspections (not in all cases); and
- the daily inspection.

The maintenance schedule is an airworthiness requirement. The operational document associated with it is the maintenance release.

Flight Documentation & Equipment

Reference: CAR 139

What You Must Carry When You Fly Locally

Pilots are required to carry and have readily accessible the latest editions of aeronautical maps, charts and information. For your training area flights, aeronautical charts with the area boundaries clearly marked should meet the general requirements. Unless specific exemptions are provided you must also carry:

- your licence;
- your current medical certificate;
- the aircraft maintenance release; and
- the aircraft flight manual.

What You Should Carry

The following should be carried at all times:

- headset;
- torch;
- notepad and pencil;
- mobile phone (switched off);
- drinking water;
- chocks, tie-downs, rags, chamois and covers; and
- checklist, VFG and ERSA.

Review 5

Pre-Solo Level of Knowledge

1. If the cloud in the circuit area obscures the ground for half of the circuit pattern, what would you do?
2. You are turning final for Runway 21 left and there is an aircraft ahead crossing the threshold for a full stop landing. You feel that the aircraft will be about to clear the runway just as you are crossing the threshold. What would you say or do?
3. You are given *number two to land* on downwind and then you hear nothing more from the tower. You are now on short final. What do you do?
4. Why do we have to give way to gliders and balloons?
5. You are on final and you notice that an aircraft that is supposed to be lined-up for the parallel runway is ahead of you. What would you do?
6. Explain *see and be seen.*
7. Why is airspace *controlled*?
8. What is the significance of the holding point and its markings?
9. What are the *piano keys?*
10. Name the legs of a standard visual circuit pattern.

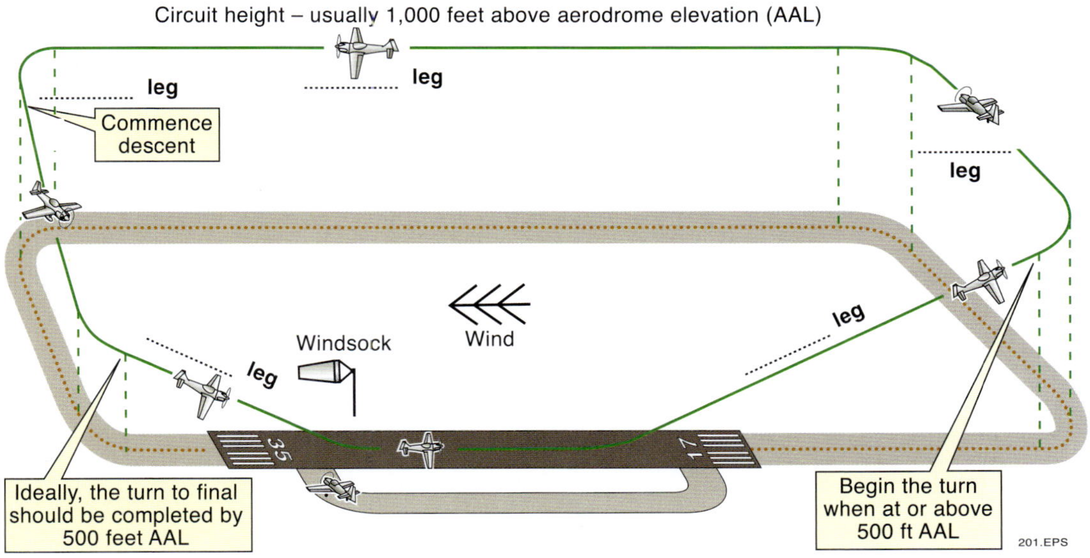

11. What is meant by the *dead* side?
12. What is the minimum height at which to turn crosswind after take-off?
13. Before your RPL flight test, how many consecutive solo hours may you fly before undertaking a dual flight?
14. What flight time do you need to be eligible for a RPL?
15. What is meant by three-axis control?
16. What documents must you carry on every flight?

BAK Level of Knowledge

17. What are VMC below 10,000 ft?
- in Class C, D and E airspace;
- in Class G above 3,000 ft;
- in a Class D aerodrome control zone; and
- in Class G airspace at or below 3,000 ft AMSL or 1,000 ft AGL, whichever is higher?

18. You are in the training area and the cloud builds below you until you cannot fly directly back to the airfield without passing through the cloud. What would you consider?
19. If overtaking another aircraft on the way to the training area, what is the correct and safe way to pass?
20. An aircraft is in your three o'clock high, converging and descending through your level. What flightpath change would you make?
21. Define, in your own terms, *airmanship.*
22. What is the minimum altitude you may fly over cities, towns or populous areas?
23. When, and under what circumstances, may you carry passengers?
24. What weight allowance would you make for children?

Aviation
Theory
Centre

6 - The Theories & Practices of Flight

Aviation Theory Centre

Dynamics

Physical Laws of Motion

A brilliant physicist and mathematician discovered the natural, universal laws that apply to the motion of all objects – whether on the ground, in the air or in space. They are called Newton's *laws of motion*. They are as follows:

- *An object will remain stationary or will rotate at constant speed or continue at a steady speed in a straight line, unless an external force causes it to change speed or direction.*
- *The rate of change of speed or direction is proportional to the applied force and takes place in the direction of the applied force.*
- *To every force there is an equal and opposite reaction.*

In other words, if you leave it alone, it will continue as it is. It will go in the direction that you push it and the harder you push it, the more it will change and the faster it will move. If you push it, you'll be pushed back.

Before we consider an aircraft, let's imagine an object in space where there is no airflow and no gravity to affect the situation. Imagine a space capsule:

- If the capsule is spinning like a top, it will continue spinning indefinitely.
- If the capsule is stationary, it will remain so.
- If it is travelling towards the earth at 10,000 km/hour, it will continue at that speed and in that direction. Incidentally, the mass of the object times its speed is called *momentum*. The greater the momentum, the harder it is to change its direction or speed. This is important, as will be seen later.
- If someone travelling inside the object pushes against the floor, roof or sides, nothing will happen to the speed and direction of the object – although he or she will be pushed away from the wall as a result (the reaction to the push).
- If another spacecraft comes alongside and pushes against the side of the capsule (an external force), the direction of the capsule will change in the direction of the push. If it is exactly at right angles to the direction of travel then the speed won't change. If it slightly forwards or backwards the speed will also change. The rate of change of direction and speed is proportional to the amount of thrust (push) applied and the change will continue until the push is removed. When the push is removed, the capsule will continue in the new direction and speed. As a result of the push, the spacecraft's speed and direction will also change in exactly the opposite way to the capsule (the reaction to the action).
- If instead of the push being applied by another craft, we fire the rocket motor at the rear – which pushes gas particles rearwards – the reaction will cause us to accelerate. The stronger the thrust, the greater the acceleration. If we fire the forward thrusters, we will slow down. If we fire the side thrusters, we will adopt a new direction. The change in speed or direction depends on the amount and duration of the push. The harder the push the more rapid the change. The longer the push lasts, the greater the change. As soon as the push is removed, the capsule will remain in the new steady state.

It's as simple and universal as that, but before we discuss how an aircraft uses these laws, let's clarify a few terms.

Forces, Moments, Work, Energy, Thrust & Power

Let's use the analogy of a person pushing a wheelbarrow loaded with bricks.

- *Force* is how hard you push. The harder you are able to push, the faster the acceleration, the steeper the gradient you can climb or the greater the load of bricks you can move.
- *Thrust* is exactly the same as force.
- *Moment* is simply a turning or twisting force. The torque of an engine shaft is a moment. A see-saw is balanced by two moments. The strength of the moments is the force multiplied by the length of moment arm (the leverage). The longer the arm and the greater the force, the greater the moment. Double the arm but half the force, the moment remains the same.

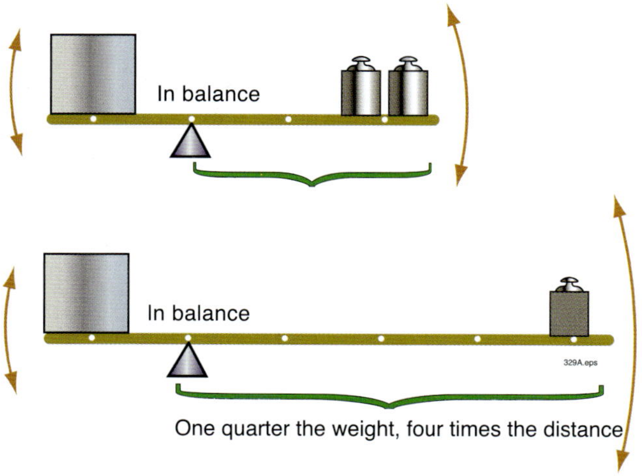

Figure 6-1 Balancing moment depends on weight and moment arm.

- *Work* is done when a force is applied over a distance. No matter how hard you push, if the barrow doesn't move, no work has been done.
- *Energy* is the capacity for doing work. If you have lots of energy, you can do lots of work.
- *Power* is the rate of doing work – how fast you can work. So, it is a combination of force, distance and time. But distance travelled in a certain time is speed, isn't it? So power is force times speed, or in the case of a powered aircraft, we say that power equals thrust multiplied by speed. Thrust is how hard we can push; power is how fast we can push.

$$\textit{Power} = \textit{thrust} \times \textit{speed (velocity)} \text{ or } P = TV$$

Consider the tortoise and the hare, or the Ferrari and the tractor.

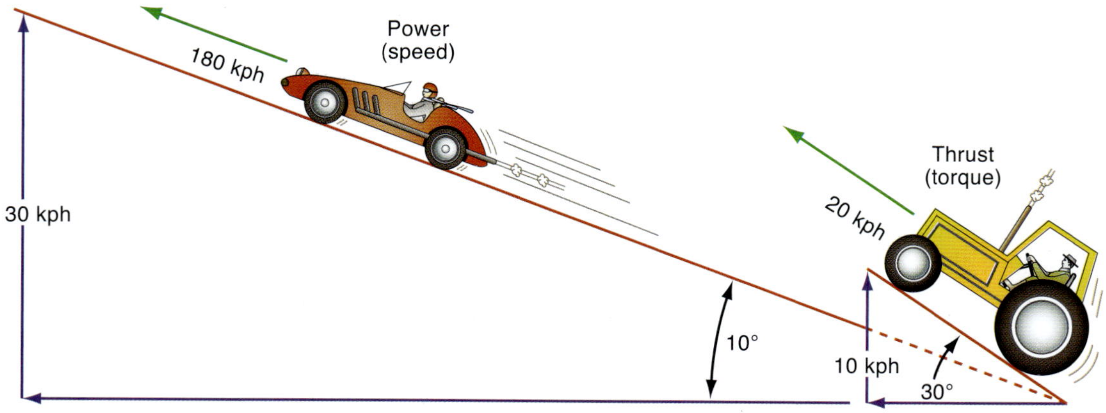

Figure 6-2 The tortoise tractor and the hare Ferrari.

The tractor has more thrust (torque), but it moves slowly. The Ferrari travels faster (travels a greater distance over time and therefore does more work in that time) so it is producing more power. Thrust determines acceleration and angle of climb, and power determines speed and rate of climb.

Power determines how fast we travel, how fast we climb and how fast we consume the fuel. The aircraft has instruments to indicate speed, rate of climb and fuel consumption. An aircraft lined up on the runway at full thrust is producing no power. Because there is no movement, no work is being done. However, the engine is producing power because it is spinning the propeller – but the engine and propeller together are not, because they are not moving the aircraft. The easiest way to remember is to consider that the engine power determines the speed of the propeller – and the propeller produces the thrust. When the aircraft is moving, the thrust times the speed gives the amount of power (and fuel) being consumed. Power is the rate at which work is being done.

Gravity

Gravity is the force of attraction to the earth that is experienced by all objects with *mass* (substance). The force (F) is equal to the mass of the object multiplied by the acceleration, experienced if the object is dropped.

$$F = ma$$

On earth, the force of gravity causes an object to accelerate at 32.2 ft per second. We call this force 1g (1 gravity). The weight of an object measured by a balance is equal to its mass times 1g.

$$W = mg$$

It is gravity that all aircraft have to overcome to be able to rise above the earth. At all times in flight, the aircraft and its contents, including the crew, are subject to this +1g (we call this *positive g* when it is felt from the head down; it is *negative g* if the person is upside down). As well as these complexities, we have to contend with the vagaries of air, without which airborne flight would be impossible.

The Atmosphere

When we discuss the flight of an aircraft (a craft borne by the air), we also need to take into account the effects of the air in which we travel. Firstly, we'll consider average conditions and static air. Then we go further and discuss the effect on flight, of moving air and non-standard, atmospheric conditions.

The Atmosphere – More Specifically, the Troposphere

The atmosphere has several layers. We'll only look at the lower levels in which aerodynamic craft with air-breathing engines operate. This layer is called the *troposphere.* Air is wonderful stuff. It's invisible yet it shields us from ultraviolet (UV) radiation. It's thin enough for us to travel through but dense enough to support us in flight. Air has properties. It has mass (substance), weight (the mass times the force of gravity), volume (space), density (how much mass in how much space), viscosity (thickness or stickiness, whether its like oil, very viscous, or water, not very viscous), temperature (hotness) and static pressure (how much it is compressed in its resting state, i.e. squashed by the molecules above and around it but without pressure due to wind or being pushed against mountains etc.). Air is all of this.

What Does All This Mean?

Air has mass, and because of this, the upper part of the stack weighs down on the lower parts. The lower air is compressed (therefore has a higher static pressure) into a smaller volume (therefore greater density) and because of the higher pressure and proximity to the earth, the lower air is also warmer.

To calculate and predict aircraft performance, we need to use a common environment for a fair comparison so it has been agreed internationally to nominate a standard atmosphere which is typical of average conditions. We then factor this performance for variations from the standard atmosphere.

The International Standard Atmosphere (ISA) is as follows:

- *Surface temperature:* +15°C.
- *Pressure:* 1013.2 hPa (formerly called millibars).
- *Lapse rate* (the reduction in temperature with increasing altitude): 2°C reduction per thousand feet increase in altitude.

Air is wonderful but as well as the benefits, it does cause a few complications in our calculations.

cross reference P.330

1 in.Hg per 1000 ft

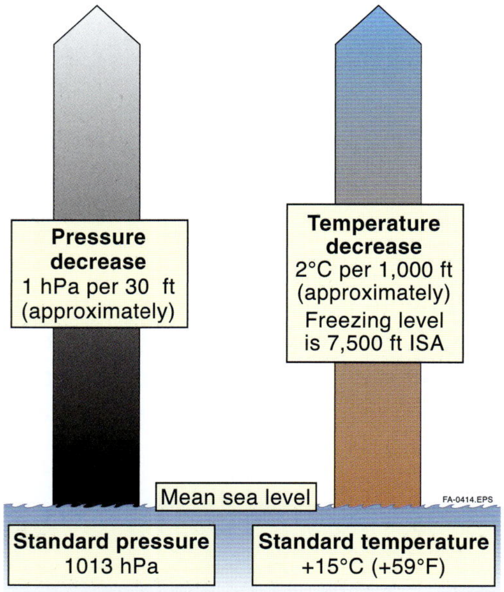

Figure 6-3
International Standard Atmosphere.

Aerodynamics

The science of flight through air is called *aerodynamics* – dynamics (motion) in air. Balloons travel with the air and don't move through it. The science of balloon flight is called *aerostatics. Aeronautics* encompasses both. The path of the aircraft through the air is called its *flightpath*. Its speed through the air is called *airspeed* – more precisely, *true airspeed*. The direction and speed of the air whizzing past the aircraft (because of the aircraft moving through it) is called the *relative airflow* (airflow relative to the aircraft or wing). It is sometimes abbreviated to RAF. It is a result of the aircraft moving through the air and so is exactly equal and opposite to the flightpath. (The path and speed of the aircraft over the ground are different as they also take into account the effect of wind. The path to the runway for landing is called the approach path or the glidepath and is also affected by wind.)

The Aircraft's Forces & Moments

Forces

The four main forces act on the aeroplane in flight:

- *weight* is the force of gravity pulling each part of the aircraft to the centre of the earth;
- *lift* is the force from the wing to overcome the weight and to change flightpath;
- *drag* is the resistance of the air; and
- *thrust* overcomes the drag and maintains or increases speed or altitude.

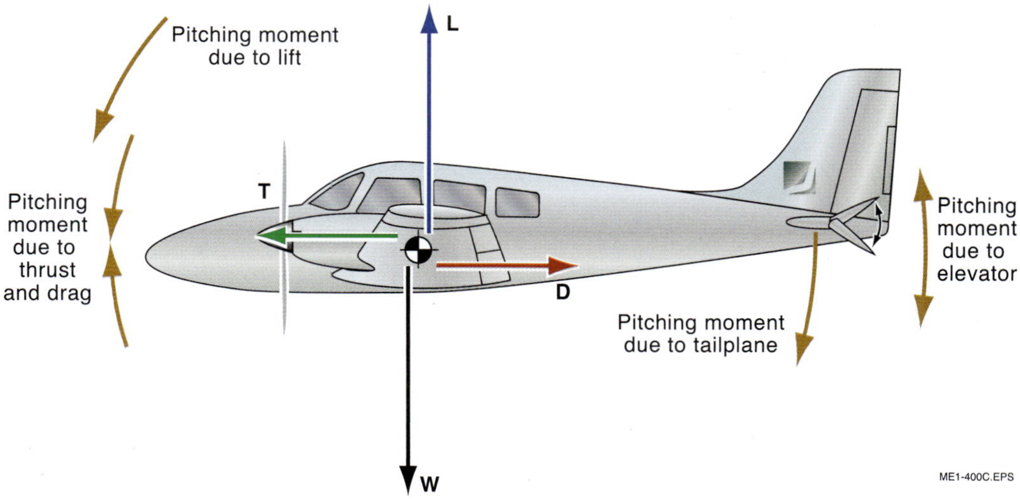

Figure 6-4 Pitching moments.

Moments

Moments about three axes are experienced by the aeroplane in flight:

- *pitching moment* is the twisting force trying to raise or lower the nose caused by the balance of the freight, passengers or fuel, the airflow over the tailplane and the force from the elevators or trim tab;
- *rolling moment* is the twisting force trying to roll the aircraft caused by the ailerons, uneven lift from the wings due to sideslip or propeller slipstream, uneven consumption of fuel from the wing tanks and uneven weight of cargo in the wing lockers; and
- *yawing moment* is the twisting force trying to yaw the aircraft caused by the airflow over the fin due to propeller slipstream, sideslip, rudder deflection or in some aircraft, different drag forces due to aileron deflection.

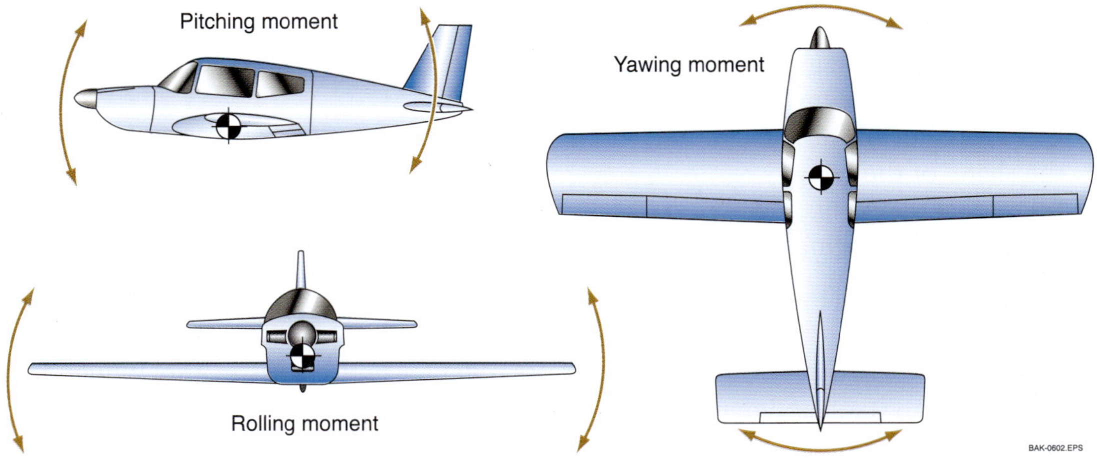

Figure 6-5 Pitching, rolling and yawing moments.

How Lift is Created

All aerial vehicles reduce the pressure of the air above and compress (increase the pressure) the air below. This pressure differential builds the cushion on which they are supported. On average, about two thirds of the lift comes from pressure reduction and one third from pressure increase. However, one comes with the other – the total effect gives lift and some drag. The wing is an efficient shape that generates a much greater upward force in proportion to the rearward force.

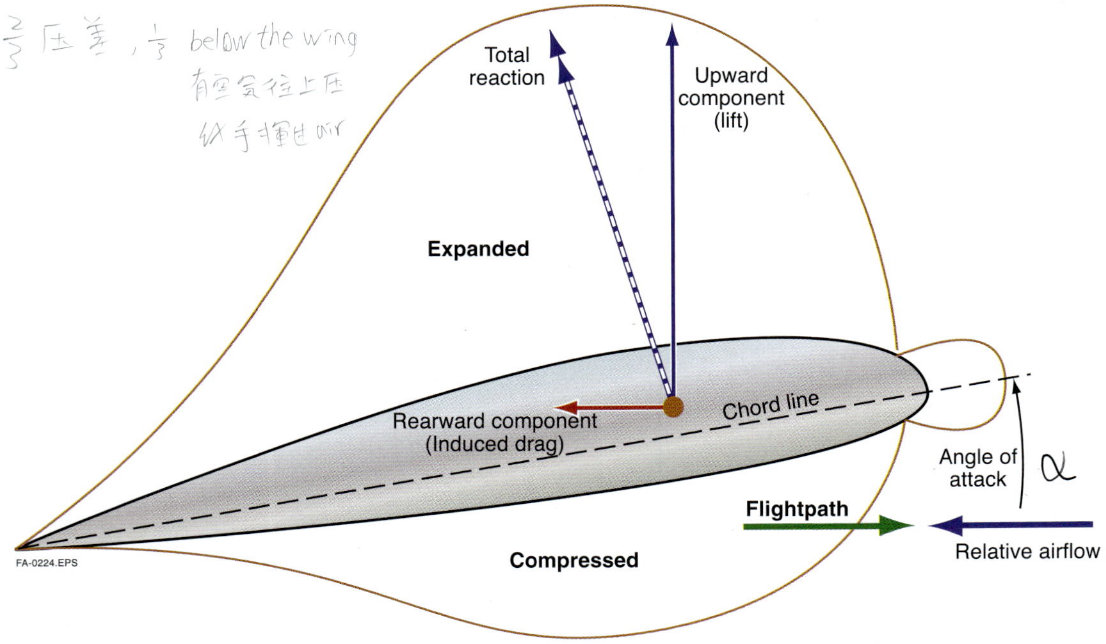

Figure 6-6 Reactions on the wing.

It is actually possible to measure in a wind tunnel what is happening to the wing and to the surrounding air. You would notice the following:

- reduced pressure and increased rush of the air over the top surface of the wing (incidentally the back of your hand will feel cold due to the temperature and pressure drop);
- compression and forward push of the air under the surface of the wing;
- disturbance to the smooth flow of the air around the rear part of the wing's surface; and
- downwash or downward deflection of the air behind the wing as a result of the passage of the wing.

This pressure difference and associated downwash causes lift. The amount of lift (the upward push) and drag (the backward push) is dependent on five elements:

- the speed of the wing through the air;
- the density of the air;
- the shape of the wing;
- the size of the wing; and
- the angle of the wing to the air (the angle of attack).

The production of the lift force by an aerofoil is explained by *Bernoulli's principle*. Daniel Bernoulli (1700–1782) was the Swiss scientist who discovered that the *total energy in a fluid remained constant*. This energy comprises potential and kinetic energy which, in a fluid, equates to static and dynamic pressure. Total pressure is the sum of:

- *static pressure* (compression due to the weight of the molecules); and
- *dynamic pressure* (compression due to motion).

If air is accelerated through a shaped tube called a *venturi* then, at the narrowest point, where the speed of the flow (dynamic pressure) is greatest, the static pressure is least.

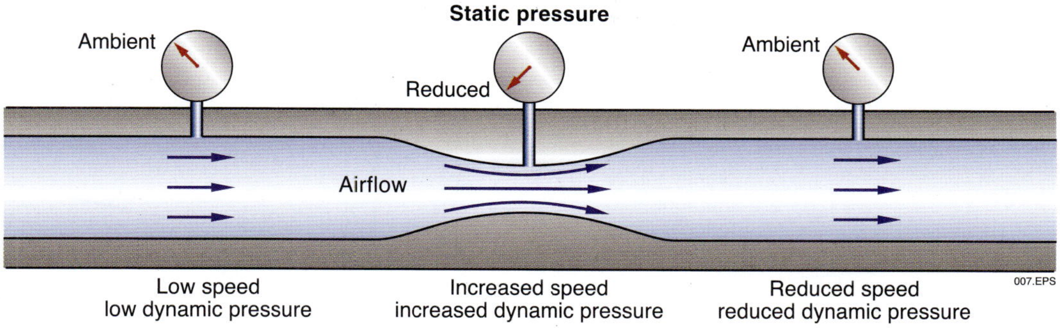

Figure 6-7 The venturi – high flow velocity, low static pressure.

Airflow Around an Aeroplane

The pattern of the airflow past an aeroplane depends mainly upon the shape of the aeroplane and its attitude relative to the freestream airflow. It is the relative velocity of the aeroplane and the airflow that matters, not whether it is the aeroplane moving through the air or the air flowing past the aeroplane. Either situation gives us the same answers.

The most important parts of the aeroplane are the aerofoils. Airflow past the main aerofoils (wings) generates the lift force that enables the aeroplane to fly. The airflow around an aerofoil may be likened to the airflow through a venturi.

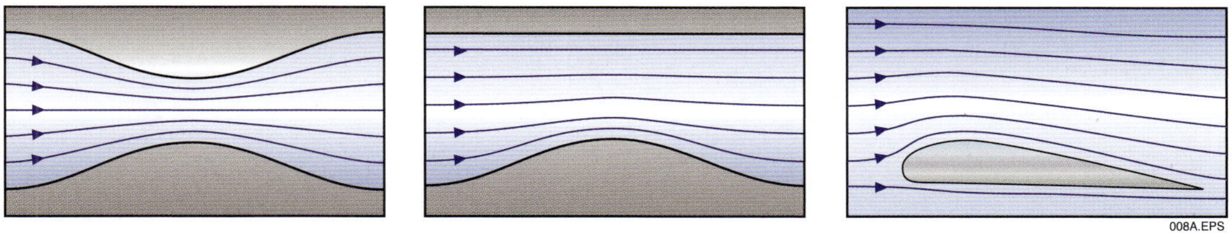

Figure 6-8 The airflow around an aerofoil resembles the flow through a venturi.

Streamline Flow (Laminar Flow)

If succeeding molecules follow the same steady path, then this path can be represented by a *streamline.* There will be no flow across the streamlines, only along them. Streamline flow represents the least air disturbance and so the least drag. Streamlined flow is called *laminar* because it is layered – like sheets of paper sliding over each other. There is no mixing or twisting of the layers. Notice how smoothly they slide. They have a thin layer of air in between; this is the streamlined *boundary layer.*

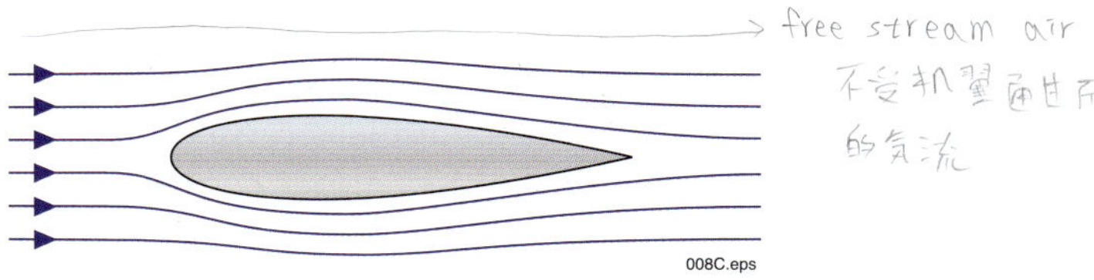

Figure 6-9 Streamline flow.

Turbulent Flow

An object moving through the air eventually causes some turbulence. Succeeding molecules no longer follow a streamlined flow pattern. They mix and tumble. This turbulence is also known as unsteady flow, or eddying – like the water eddies in a river flow. It is caused by an adverse pressure gradient. The point on the surface where the layer of air next to the wing (the *boundary layer*) becomes *turbulent* is called the *transition point.*

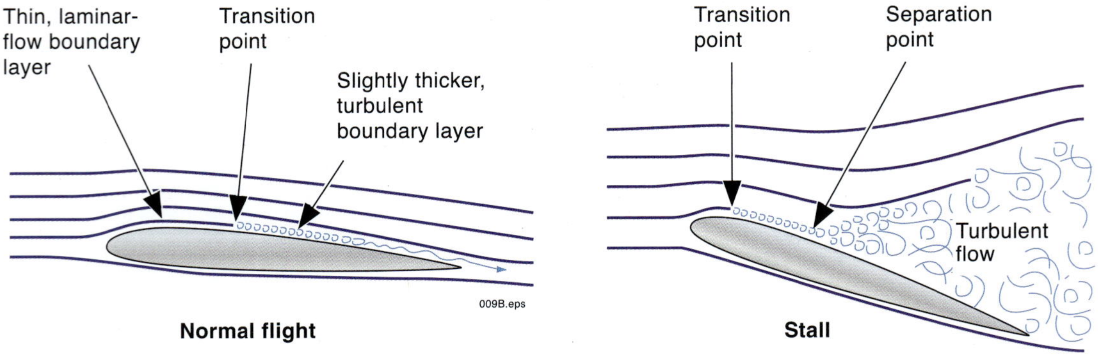

Figure 6-10 Streamline flow is preferable to turbulent flow.

Depending on the shape of the object, the airflow will subsequently not be able to follow the contours and will *separate* causing a wake of disturbed air. The point where this happens is called the *separation point.* The wake contains *vortices* of twisting air.

Angle of Attack

If a thin, flat plate is aligned to the airflow, it causes virtually no alteration to that air mass. It slices through and consequently experiences no reaction (force). If, however, the plate is inclined with respect to the airflow (i.e. it has an *angle of attack*), it will experience a reaction that both tends to lift it and to drag it back. Angle of attack is also represented by the Greek letter α (alpha).

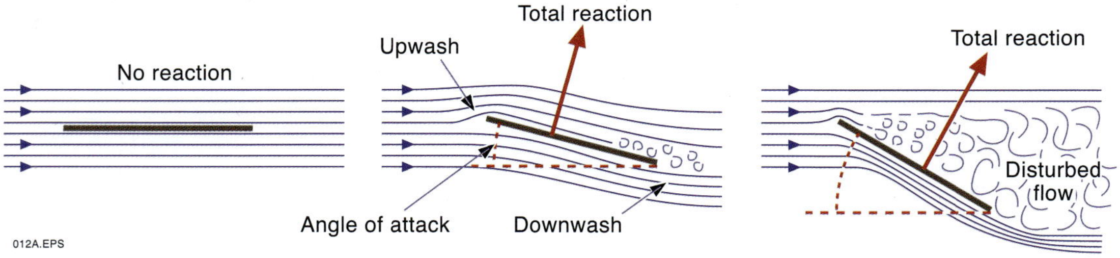

Figure 6-11 Airflow can lift a flat plate.

Due to the angle of attack, the streamline flow is altered. The air is compressed by the lower surface of the plate. The air above the plate experiences a reduction in pressure as it seeks to fill the space. The static pressure above the plate is now lower than the static pressure beneath the plate, causing a net upwards reaction. After passing the plate, there is a downwash of the airstream.

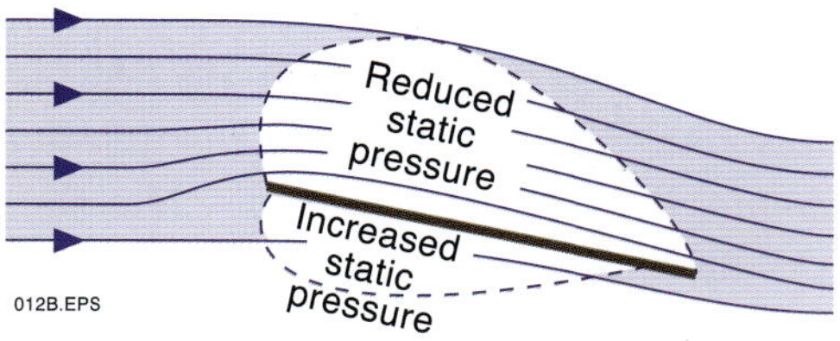

Figure 6-12 Downwash behind the flat plate.

The total reaction on the plate caused by its moving the air has two components:

- one *perpendicular* (at right angles) to the relative airflow known as *lift;* and
- one parallel to the relative airflow, and opposing the relative motion, known as *drag.*

Aerofoil

A flat plate is not the ideal shape because it disturbs the laminar flow, causing vortices and a great increase in drag. It has a sharp leading edge which the air has difficulty in negotiating.

A curved *(cambered)* aerofoil surface generates more lift and less drag compared with a flat plate – with the added benefit that it is stronger than a thin, curved sheet of metal.

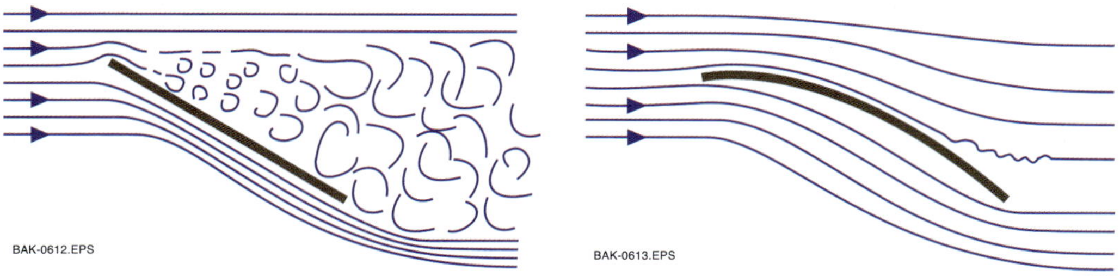

Figure 6-13 The effect of camber.

A shaped "fatter" wing also allows for internal bracing (added strength but less drag) and space for fuel.

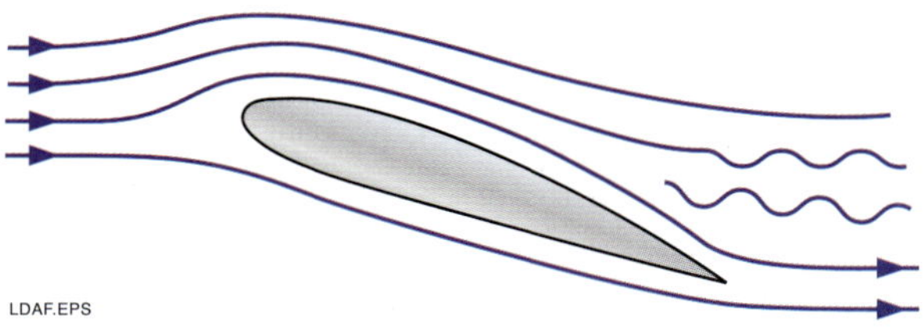

Figure 6-14 Cambered aerofoil.

Even if both surfaces are curved, the wing may still be cambered if the mid-points between the upper and lower surfaces follow a curved line (called the *line of mean camber* or *mean camber line*), i.e. there is more curvature of the upper surface than of the lower. This is called *positive camber.* If the lower surface is more curved, there is *negative camber.* This is sometimes seen on a tailplane which is designed to produce a download.

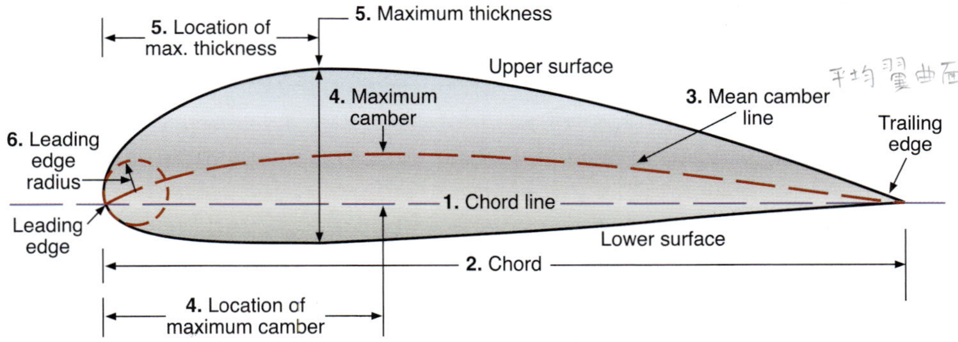

Figure 6-15 Aerofoil terminology.

Wings which are highly cambered produce greater lift, making them suitable for low-speed flight. The point of greatest camber (greatest curvature or greatest distance of the mean camber line from the chord line) is usually about 30% of the chord back from the leading edge. The chord line is the straight line joining the leading edge and the trailing edge of the aerofoil. The chord is the distance from the leading edge to the trailing edge. *Mean chord* is the average chord between the *wingtip* and the *wing root*, where it is attached to the fuselage.

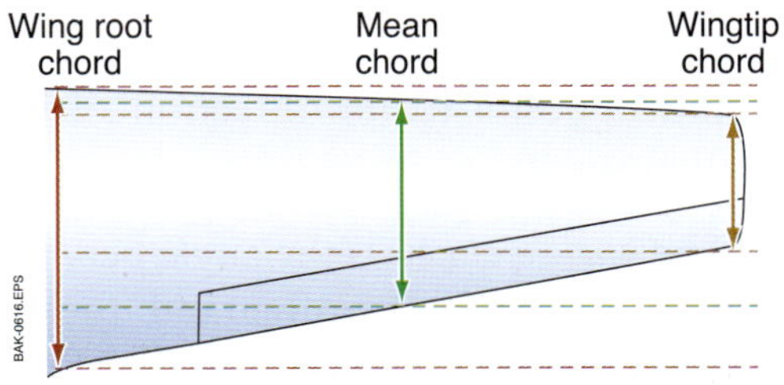

Figure 6-16 Mean (average) chord.

An aerofoil can have many cross-sectional shapes. The aeroplane designer chooses that shape which has the best aerodynamic characteristics to suit his/her purposes. Although most low-speed aerofoils are similar in shape, each section (cross-section) is designed to give certain specific aerodynamic characteristics.

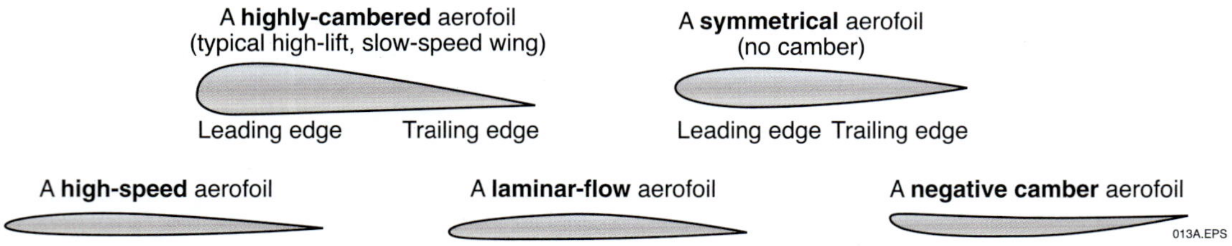

Figure 6-17 Various aerofoil cross-sections.

Low-Speed Wing

At the small positive angles of attack common in normal flight, the static pressure over the upper surface of the aerofoil is reduced when compared with the normal static pressure of the free airstream well away from the aerofoil. At higher angles of attack, the static pressure beneath the lower surface of the aerofoil is greater than that in the free air.

This pressure difference is the origin of the total reaction force exerted on the aerofoil. Generally, the greatest contribution (about two-thirds) comes from the upper surface. The total of all the aerodynamic forces on the aerofoil can be added to make one force, called the *total reaction*. This reaction acts through a point called the *centre of pressure* (CP).

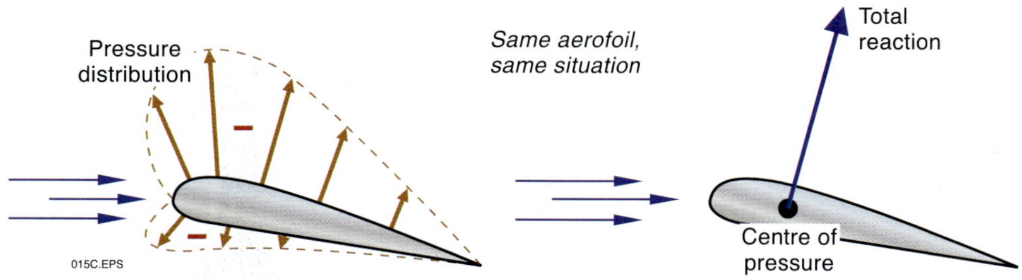

Figure 6-18 Total reaction acts through the centre of pressure.

The total aerodynamic force (the total reaction) has two components:

- *lift*, or the component of the aerodynamic force at right angles, or perpendicular, to the relative airflow (and the flightpath); and
- *induced drag*, or the component of aerodynamic force aligned to the relative airflow and opposite to the direction of motion (flightpath).

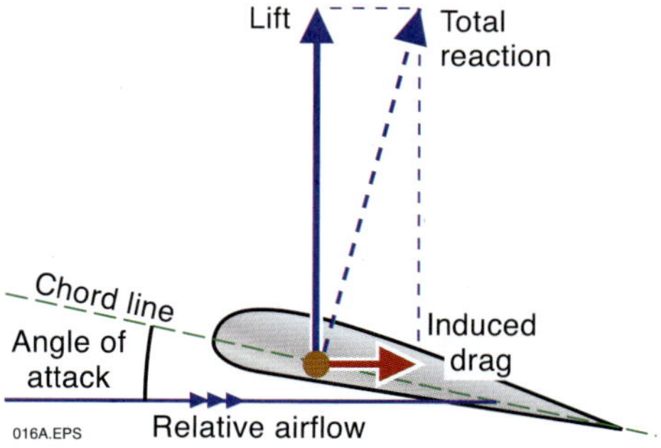

Figure 6-19 Total reaction.

The *angle of attack* is the angle between the chord line of an aerofoil and the undisturbed, relative airflow. The angle of attack is abbreviated by the Greek letter α (alpha). The *relative airflow* refers to the direction and speed between the aircraft and the remote airflow. The relative airflow is exactly equal and opposite to the flightpath of the aeroplane. The *remote airflow,* or freestream airflow, is the airflow sufficiently far away from the body not to be disturbed by it.

Lift from a Typical Wing

The lifting ability of a particular wing depends on its shape but also increases with angle of attack. (The lifting ability is called its *coefficient of lift*, C_L.) The change of lift with angle of attack is called the C_L/α curve. Maximum lifting ability occurs at the *critical angle*, which is also called its *stalling angle* (about 16°).

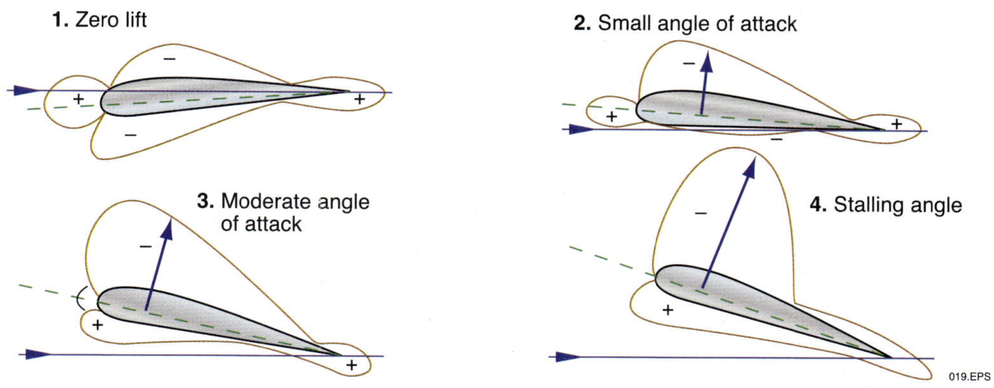

Figure 6-20 Static pressure distribution at various angles of attack.

Also, the centre of pressure (CP) moves forward as the angle of attack is increased. Beyond the stalling angle, the CP moves back, and there is a large reduction in the pressure differential.

The coefficient of lift (C_L) and the angle of attack can be plotted on a graph.

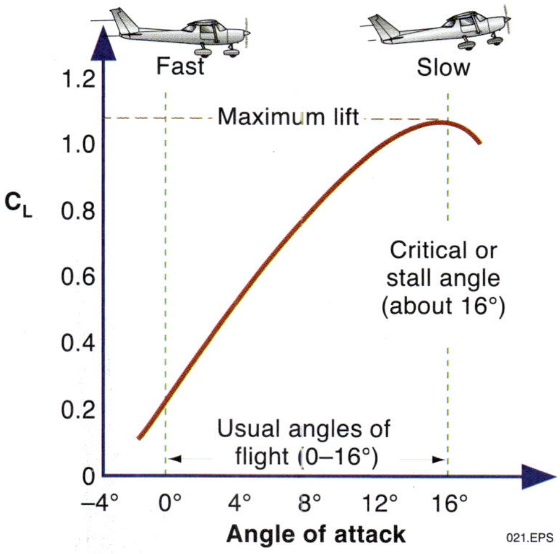

Figure 6-21 Coefficient of lift versus angle of attack. Each angle of attack produces a particular C_L value.

Maximum lift occurs at the critical angle. Once the angle of attack exceeds the critical angle, the streamlined airflow over most of the wing breaks down, becomes turbulent and separates. The lifting ability of the wing is then greatly and suddenly reduced and the wing is said to have *stalled*.

A cambered aerofoil gives higher values of C_L for each angle of attack. Lowering of flaps increases the camber of the wing and has the same effect of increasing the lift coefficient at each angle of attack.

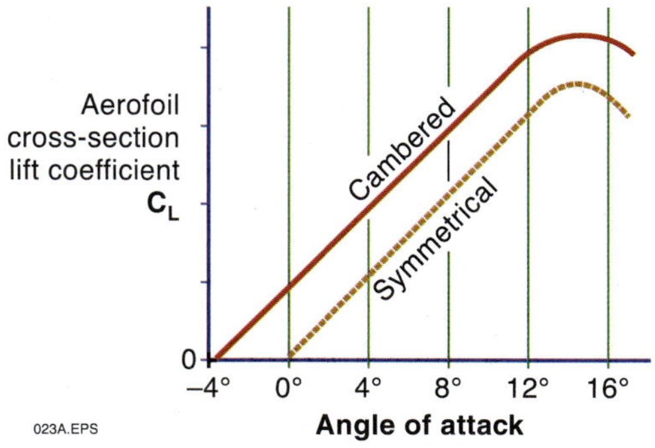

Figure 6-22 Comparison between CL of cambered and symmetrical aerofoils.

Attitude, Flightpath & Angle of Attack

It is vital to distinguish between the terms *attitude, flightpath* and *angle of attack*.

The *attitude* of the aircraft is the position of the nose in relation to the horizon.

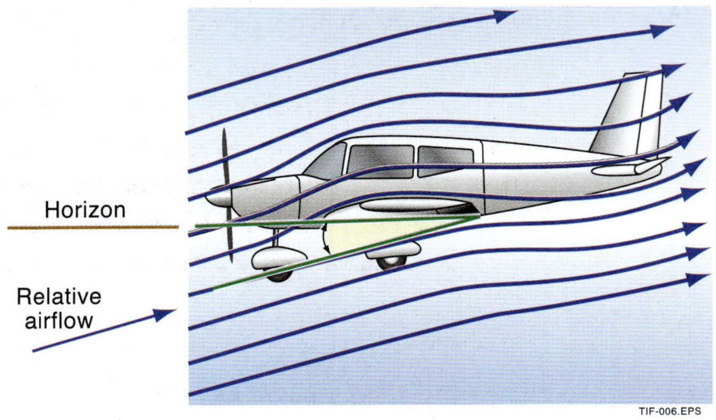

Figure 6-23 Level attitude and descending flightpath.

The *flightpath* of the aircraft is the direction it is travelling relative to the horizon.

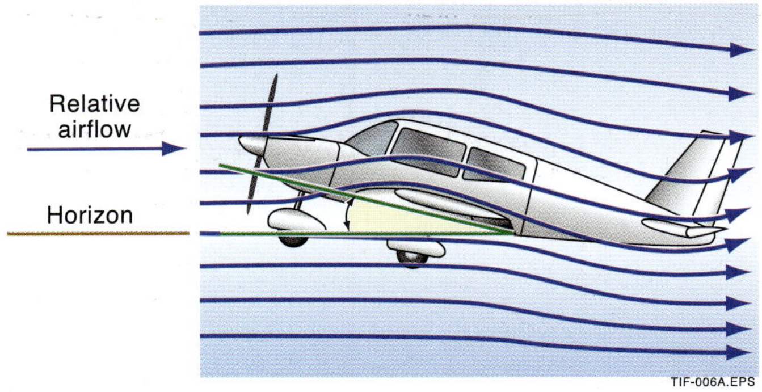

Figure 6-24 Nose-high attitude and level flightpath.

The *angle of attack* is the angle of the wing to the relative airflow:

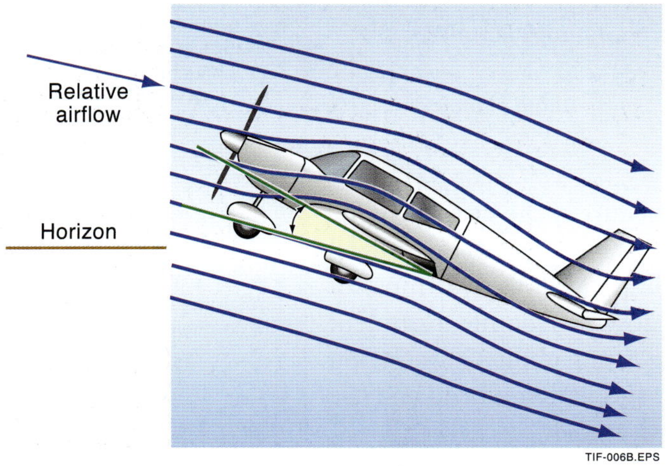

Figure 6-25 Very nose-high attitude and climbing flightpath.

The aircraft shown have the *same angle of attack* with an increasing pitch attitude and with a descending, level and climbing flightpath respectively.

Drag

Drag is the aeronautical term for the air resistance experienced by the aeroplane as it moves through the air. Drag acts in the opposite direction to the motion through the air, i.e. it opposes the motion and acts parallel to, and in the same direction as the relative airflow. Drag is the enemy of high-speed flight. Streamlining of shapes, flush riveting, polishing of surfaces, and many other design features are all attempts to reduce the drag force. The main function of the powerplant-produced thrust is to overcome the drag, and the lower the drag, the less the thrust required to counteract it. The advantages of a lower thrust requirement are smaller engines, possibly even fewer engines (on large aircraft), lower fuel flow, less strain on the engine(s) and associated structures, and lower operating costs.

Figure 6-26 Lift, induced drag and parasite drag.

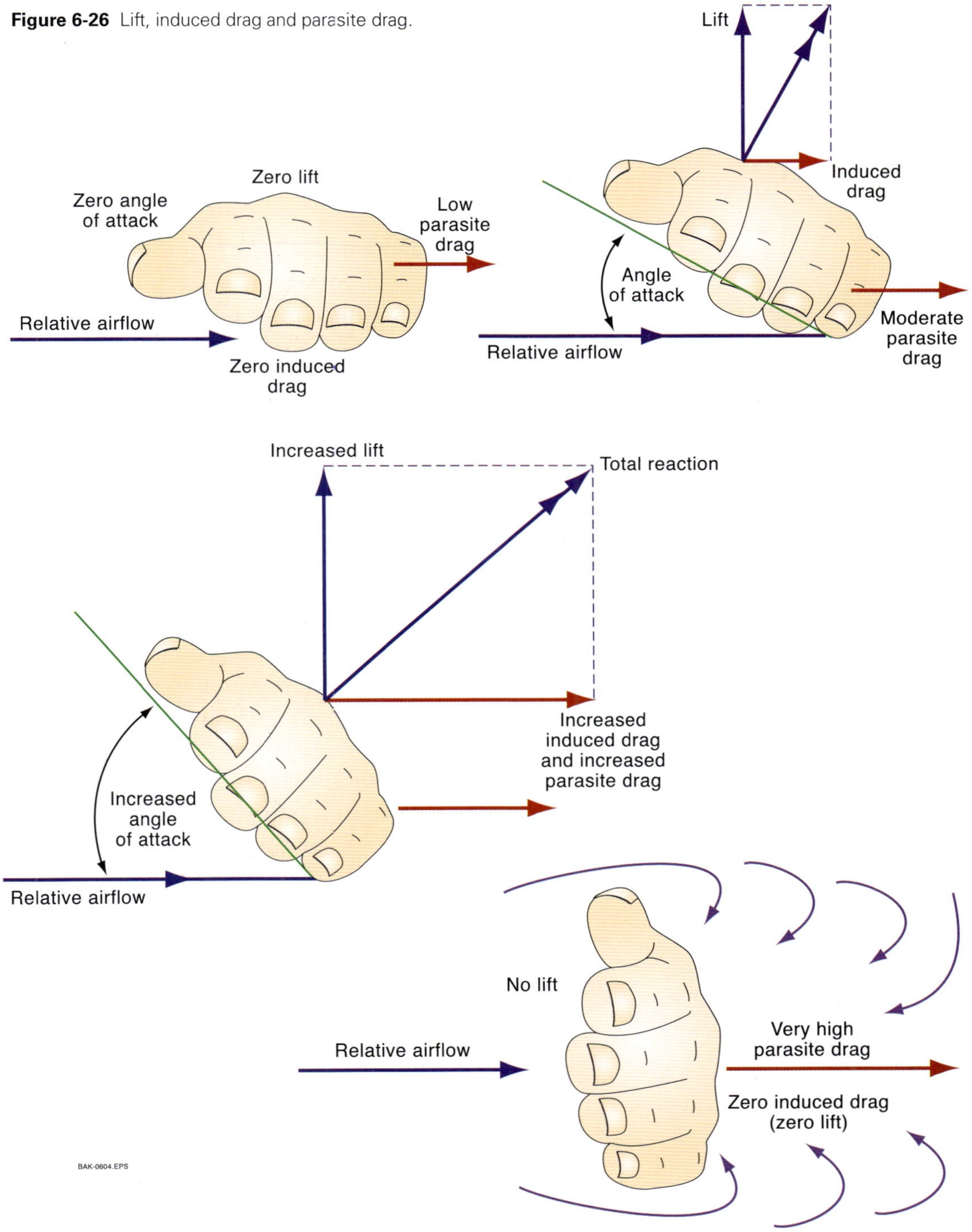

Total Drag

The total drag is the term given to the sum of the various drag forces acting on an aeroplane. A convenient way of studying the various types of drag is to classify them using two categories:

- The total drag force associated with the production of lift, known as *induced drag* (which is manifested as vortices at the trailing edge of the wing and especially at the wingtips).
- The total drag force not directly associated with the development of lift known as *parasite drag.* This includes *form drag* (due to shape and frontal area), *skin friction* (due to the size of the surfaces rubbing against the air) and *interference drag* (due to the mixing of various airflows at the junction of different surfaces).

Induced Drag

Induced drag is a by-product of producing lift and is related to the angle of attack. The greater the angle of attack, the greater the total reaction, and the more it is tilted backwards – thus the more the horizontal component of the total reaction. Induced drag is therefore greatest at low airspeeds. It is inevitable and unavoidable.

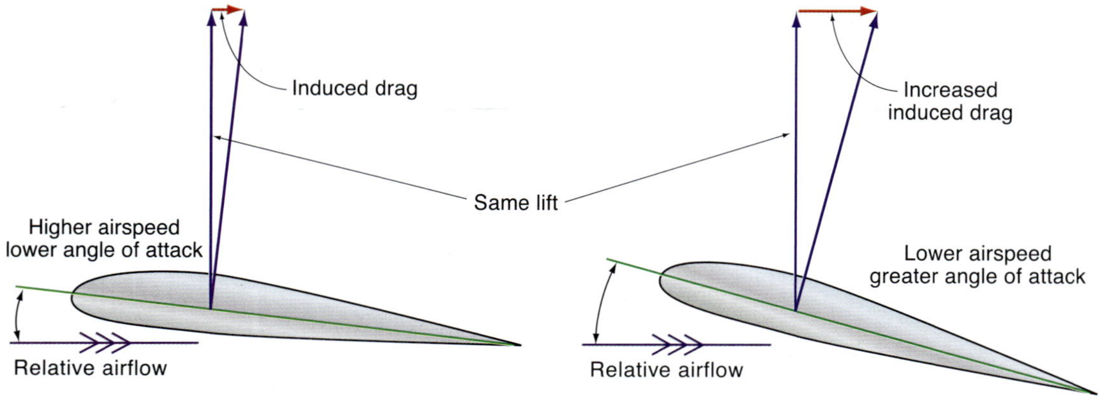

Figure 6-27 Induced drag is greatest at low airspeeds and high angles of attack.

To produce positive (upwards) lift, the static pressure on the upper surface of the wing must be less than that underneath the wing. Due to the pressure differential, some airflow will leak or spill around the wingtip from the high pressure area under the wing to the low pressure area above the wing. This causes a spanwise flow away from the fuselage on the lower surface and a component towards the fuselage on the upper surface. A long, tapered wing can minimised this wingtip vortex. Some aircraft use *winglets* or shaped wingtips to try to minimise the induced drag due to this "leakage" around the wingtip.

The strongest vortices, by far, are formed at the wingtips, where the spanwise flow is greatest. These are known as wingtip vortices. (A vortex is a whirling or twisting flow. Vortices, the plural of vortex, is also sometimes written as *vortexes.*)

Figure 6-28 Wingtip vortex.

The shape can be rectangular, tapered, curved (elliptical) or even triangular (delta).

There is a pressure difference between the upper and lower surface of the wing. There is a loss of this differential by air "leaking" around the wingtip. This wingtip vortex causes a large increase in induced drag.

Induced drag increases at low airspeeds and high angles of attack.

An elliptical distribution of lift, due to wing shape, aerofoil sections or wing twist is best. The famous Spitfire had an elliptically shaped wing.

The shape of the wing and the wingtip is significant. Long, narrow wings with tapered tips or winglets are very efficient at low speed and high altitudes, as is the elliptical wing, because there is minimal ***tip loss***.

Figure 6-29
The Spitfire's elliptical wing.

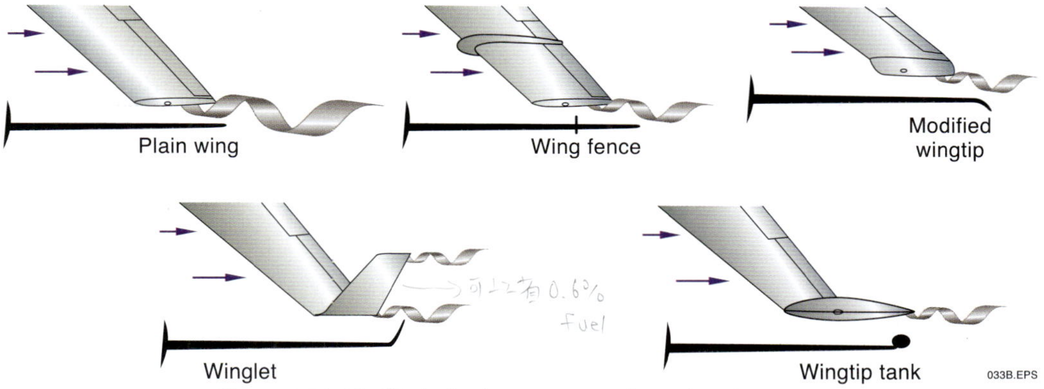

Figure 6-30 Modified wingtips can reduce formation of vortices.

At the trailing edge of the wing the upper and lower airflows meet in a series of vortices which build onto the wingtip vortex to form a *vortex sheet.*

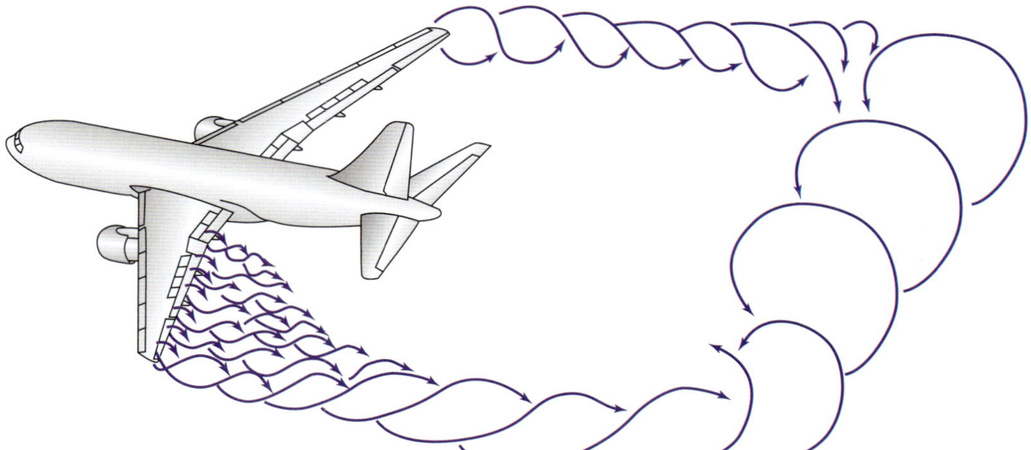

Figure 6-31 Vortex sheet.

For straight and level flight, the lift must remain constant (to counter the force of gravity) as airspeed reduces. At the reduced airspeed, lift is maintained at a constant value by increasing the angle of attack. At the higher angle of attack, the pressure differential and thus the power of the vortices is greatest. The vortex sheet causes the wake turbulence associated with heavy jet aircraft, especially when taking off or landing (lowest airspeed).

Parasite Drag

Parasite drag (from all the parasites – hangers-on – of the wing not contributing to lift) comprises skin friction, form drag and interference drag. Parasite drag is proportional to the speed through the air although some objects also present a greater frontal area to the airflow when the angle of attack is increased.

Parasite drag comprises:

- form drag, which is due to the frontal size and shape of the object;
- skin friction, which depends on the surface area and smoothness of the object (or conversely, the roughness); and
- interference drag, which is caused by the effect of one part on another, can increase the total amount of drag and is one of the reasons why the wings are often blended into the fuselage of high performance aircraft.

Form Drag

Form drag results when the airflow actually separates from the surface, eddies are formed and the streamline flow is disturbed. The turbulent wake so formed increases drag. Perhaps the easiest way to distinguish form drag from skin friction drag is to consider a flat plate in two different attitudes relative to the airflow. At zero angle of attack, the drag is all skin friction. When the flat plate is perpendicular to the airflow, the drag is all form drag.

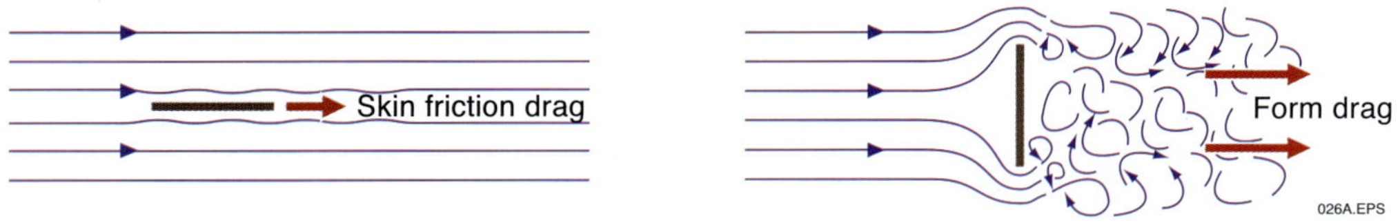

Figure 6-32 Skin friction drag and form drag.

Streamlining of shapes reduces form drag. Streamlining reduces form drag by removing sharp corners, sudden bulges or cavities and discontinuities. Streamlining minimises turbulent flow and delays separation.

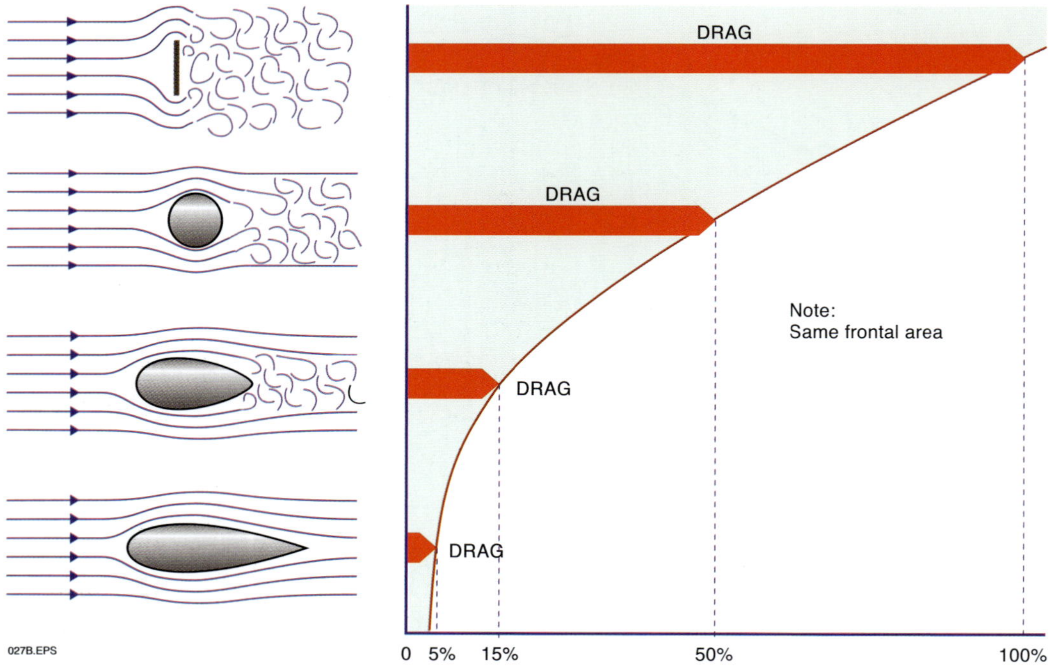

Figure 6-33 Streamlining, especially behind the shape, reduces form drag substantially.

Skin Friction

Skin friction results from the friction forces existing between an object and the air through which it is moving. The magnitude of the skin friction depends upon the following:

- The surface area of the aircraft. The whole surface area of the aircraft experiences surface or skin friction drag as it moves through the air.
- Roughness on a surface (including ice accretion) will increase skin friction drag. Flush riveting and polishing are attempts to smooth the surface and reduce skin friction drag.
- An increase in airspeed increases skin friction drag.

Interference Drag

The total parasite drag produced by an aircraft is greater than the sum of the skin friction and form drag generated by each individual component of the aeroplane that is exposed to the airflow. Additional drag is caused by the mixing, or interference, of converging airflow at the junction of various surfaces, such as between the wing and fuselage, the tail section and fuselage, and the wing and engine nacelle. This additional drag is referred to as interference drag. As it is not directly associated with the production of lift, it is a type of parasite drag.

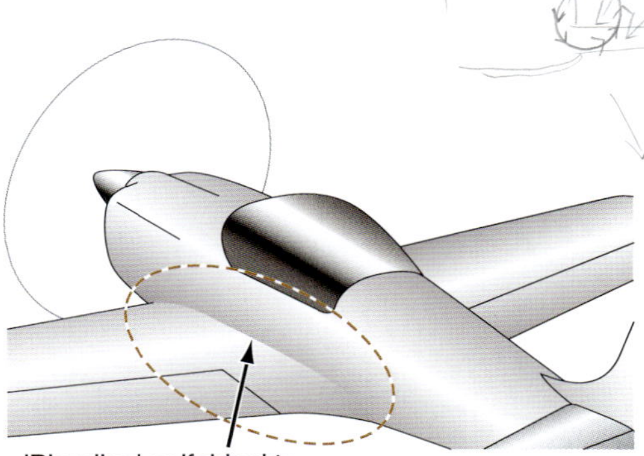

Figure 6-34 Wing-root fairing.

Shaping, blending, fairing and streamlining of shapes minimises interference drag. A fairing is part of the skin of an aeroplane added to encourage laminar flow, thereby reducing eddying and decreasing drag.

Parasite Drag is Greatest at High Speed

At zero airspeed there is no relative motion between the aeroplane and the air. Therefore there is no drag. As the airspeed increases, the skin friction, the form drag and the interference drag (which together make up parasite drag) all increase. Airspeed has a powerful effect on parasite drag. Doubling the airspeed gives four times the parasite drag (2^2 i.e. $2 \times 2 = 4$) . Tripling the airspeed would give $3 \times 3 = 9$ times the parasite drag. We say that the parasite drag is proportional to the square of the airspeed (V^2).

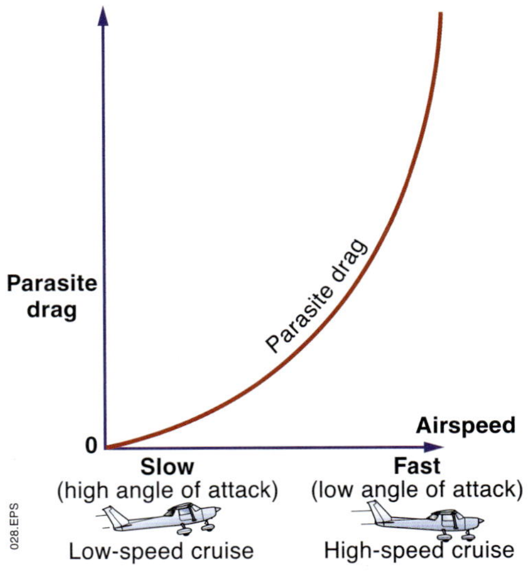

Figure 6-35 Parasite drag versus airspeed.

An aeroplane flying as slowly as possible (at a speed just above the stall) may have only 25% of its total drag due to parasite drag. Most of the drag would be due to induced drag.

At a very high speed, the total drag is due almost entirely to parasite drag. The predominance of parasite drag at high airspeeds emphasises the need for aerodynamic "cleanliness" to obtain high-speed performance.

Incidentally, about half of the parasite drag on some aeroplanes is due to the wings. Consequently, any reduction in skin friction, form drag and interference drag from the wings can have a significant effect in reducing the overall parasite drag.

Drag vs Airspeed

Total drag is the sum total of all the drag forces acting on the aeroplane. As we have seen, the total drag has two components:

- parasite drag; and
- induced drag.

To improve lift and to minimise drag, the designer must keep the airflow smooth (called streamlined or laminar flow) – like the shape of a dolphin.

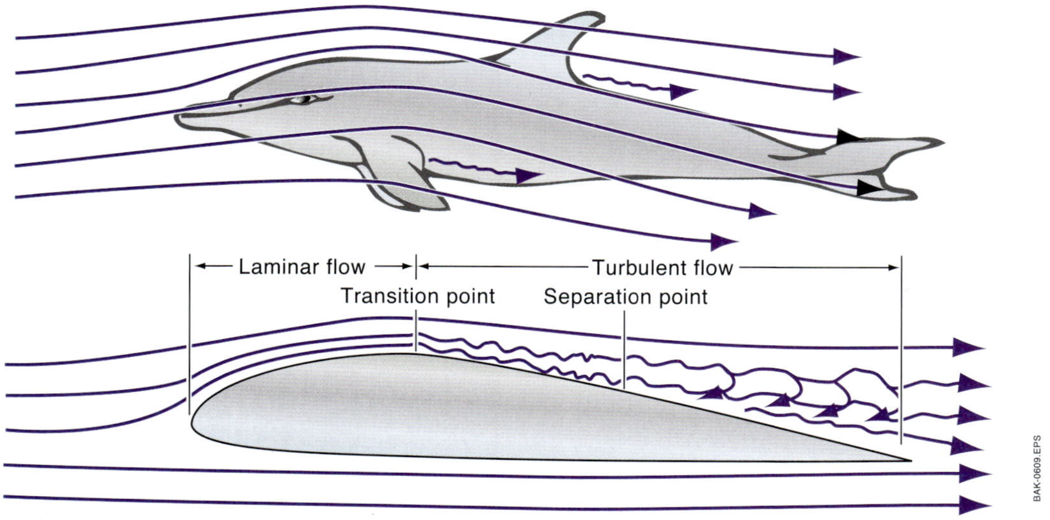

Figure 6-36 Minimising drag.

If the air has to travel around blunt objects, sharp corners or large areas then the flow becomes twisted or turbulent. Eventually the air cannot flow around the corners and separates. This causes a large increase in drag and a large loss of lift. This is what happens when the aircraft is stalled, as we'll discuss in a moment.

Let's now consider an aircraft as the speed increases in level flight. The amount of lift has to remain the same to balance the weight, but as we know, the increase in speed would increase the lift – so the pilot has to reduce the angle of attack as the aircraft accelerates. Therefore, the drag due to angle of attack (the induced drag) decreases as the speed increases in level flight while the form drag increases with the airspeed. The total drag, then, is a balance of the two.

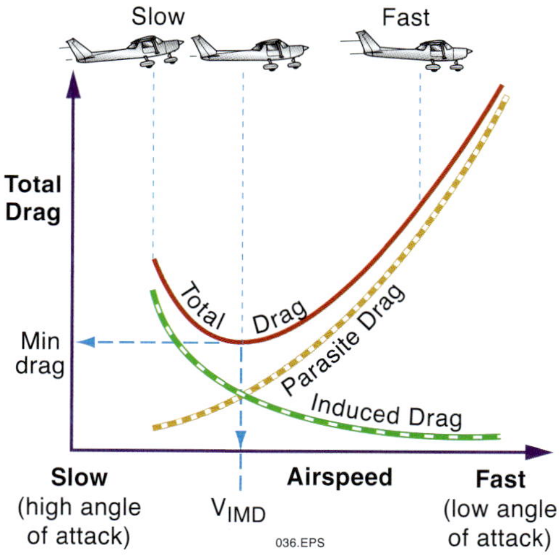

Figure 6-37 Total drag versus airspeed.

If we combine the graphs of each of these drags as they vary with airspeed (figure 6-37), we have a graph that illustrates the variation of total drag with airspeed for a given aeroplane in level flight at a particular weight, configuration and altitude. This curve of drag vs airspeed (angle of attack) is an extremely important relationship. It is really a summary of all we need to know about drag when studying aerodynamics.

Obviously, there is a speed where the drag is least, and this is called, not surprisingly, the *minimum drag speed*, abbreviated V_{IMD} (velocity indicated minimum drag). Notice that total drag is minimum at a medium speed. This airspeed corresponds to an angle of attack of about 4° (the angle for best lift–drag ratio or L/D).

minimum drag and best glide spd

If L/D ratio is 1:9

distance for A to B is 20NM, how high should we fly so we can glide to either point safely?

1NM ≒ 6000' $\frac{10 \times 6000}{9} \doteqdot 6000$

Efficiency & Airflow

If we consider the efficiency of wings, the one that can produce the most lift for the least induced drag is the best. The ratio of the lift versus the drag at any particular angle of attack is called the ***lift–drag ratio***. It is dependent on the design of the wing section (called the aerofoil), which includes thickness–chord ratio (fatness), camber (curvature) and point of maximum thickness (fattest at the front, middle or rear), the radius of the leading edge (roundness) and many other subtle factors. There are specialists and computer programs that focus purely on aerofoil design.

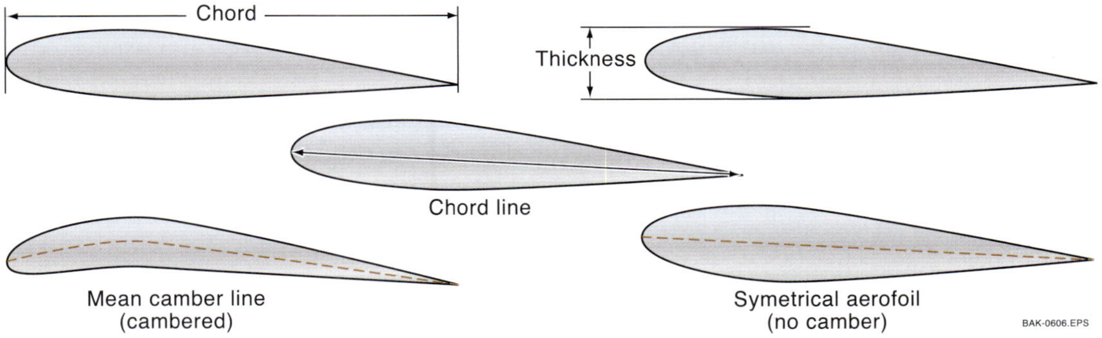

Figure 6-38 Aerofoils for different purposes.

Note: These sections show typical thickness–chord ratios (t/c) for GA aircraft.

If we measure and plot the ratio of lift to drag at each angle of attack, there is an obvious point where we gain the greatest benefit for the least penalty. This is the angle of attack where the wing is most efficient. This is the best lift–drag ratio or best L/D.

Figure 6-39 Best L/D is increased by aspect ratio.

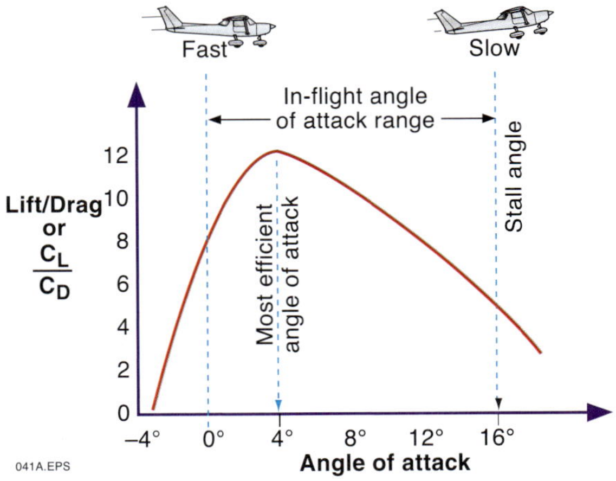

Figure 6-40 Lift–drag ratio versus angle of attack.

A typical aerofoil achieves its best L/D at an angle of attack of about 4° and loses most of its lifting ability after about 16 degrees – it stalls. Because the wing is most efficient at this angle, it is usual to set the wing on the fuselage at an angle of 4 degrees so that in cruising flight, the wing is at 4 degrees and the fuselage is streamlined. The angle at which the wing is set is called the *rigger's angle of incidence.*

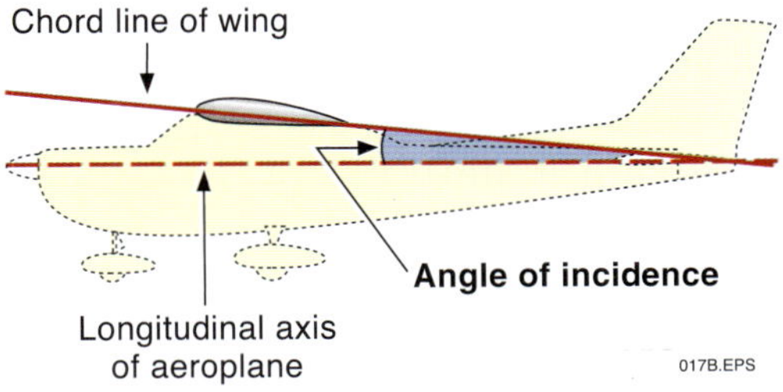

Figure 6-41 Rigger's angle of incidence.

Another influence on the lift–drag ratio is the shape of the wing (the planform of the wing) and the spanwise loading (the spread of the weight over a short or long span). The proportion of the span of the wing to the depth of the chord is called the *aspect ratio*. High aspect ratio means a long, narrow planform and low aspect ratio means short, deeper chord wings. So sailplanes, spy planes and even Jumbos have high aspect ratio wings. However, to reduce the size and therefore the parasite drag for high speed and to increase the strength and the manoeuvrability, fighters have low aspect ratio wings.

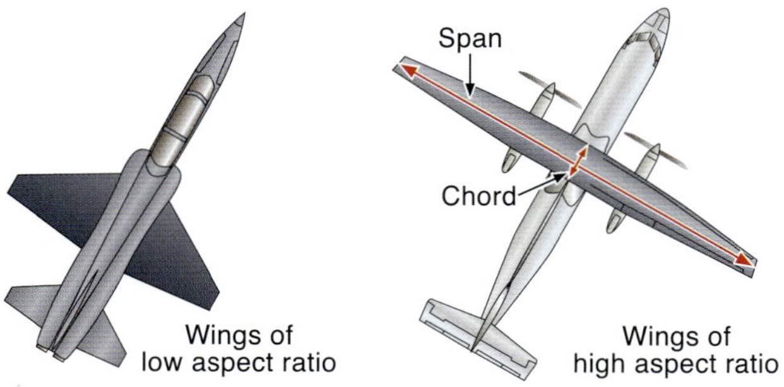

Figure 6-42 Aspect ratio.

A typical training aircraft has an aspect ratio of 8 and a best lift–drag ratio of about 12:1. Once the wing is built, there are only two factors which change the L/D:

- the angle of attack; and
- the extension of flaps.

These are the means by which the pilot flies the aircraft efficiently.

Flappery will get you Everywhere

To support the weight of the aircraft, the wings have to produce the same lift – irrespective of the speed of the aircraft. The pilot manoeuvres the aircraft by changing the lift and does this by changing the angle at which the wing is presented to the airflow – the angle of attack. The pilot uses exactly the same process to maintain level flight at varying airspeeds. As the speed increases, the pilot reduces the angle of attack, and as the aircraft slows down, the angle of attack is increased to maintain the same lift. However, the wing has a minimum speed below which control becomes difficult. There is an analogy with a motorcycle. If the aircraft is flown too slowly, it "loses its balance" just like a motorcycle, and it is more difficult for the pilot to keep it straight and level. This is called ***stalling*** or ***departure from controlled flight***. Modern aircraft are protected against this happening.

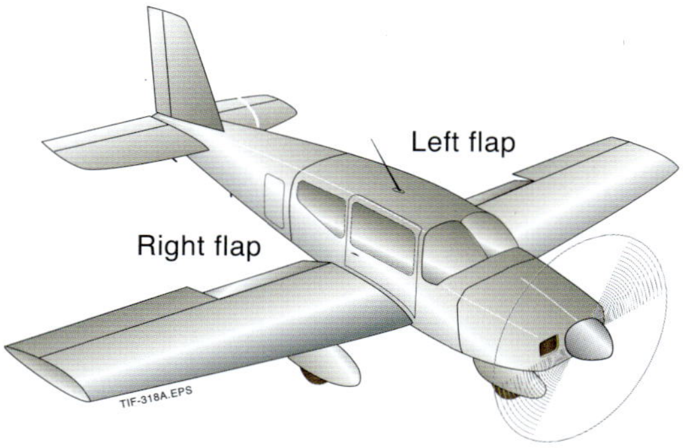

Figure 6-43 Flaps.

Figure 6-44 Flaps extended.

If the aircraft is designed to cruise at an airspeed of approximately 300 kph, this aircraft would reach its stalling angle at a speed of about half this, 150 kph. To reduce the approach speed to enable the aircraft to use a shorter runway, the designer has to reduce the stalling speed by increasing the lift at low speed and by delaying the airflow separation. This is done by the use of flaps. A further advantage of flaps is that they increase the steepness of the approach path, improving the pilot's field of view by lowering the nose attitude on final approach, as well as reducing the approach and landing speed and, therefore, landing distance required. However, although flaps increase lift, they also increase drag (resulting in a reduced L/D).

Control

The pilot has three physical tasks when flying an aircraft:

- control of flightpath and speed (by control of attitude, thrust and configuration);
- balance of the aircraft, during steady and changing conditions; and
- operation of systems such as fuel, electrics and hydraulics.

These three tasks are achieved by use of three types of controls:

- *primary* controls, which are the flight controls and the engine power controls;
- *secondary* controls, the flaps, undercarriage and trim (and speed brakes) which change the configuration of the aircraft; and
- *ancillary* controls, for systems such as carburetor heat, mixture and fuel.

Primary controls directly control the flightpath and speed of the aircraft. Secondary controls assist or fine-tune the control and configuration. Ancillary controls operate the systems such as the brakes, fuel system, electrics and so on. The pilot is continuously balancing the aircraft to maintain the flightpath and occasionally operating the controls to change the flightpath or speed. It is important to realise that, with practice, the balancing becomes automatic – the pilot can focus on navigation, weather and traffic. Conscious control is only needed when the flightpath needs to be changed.

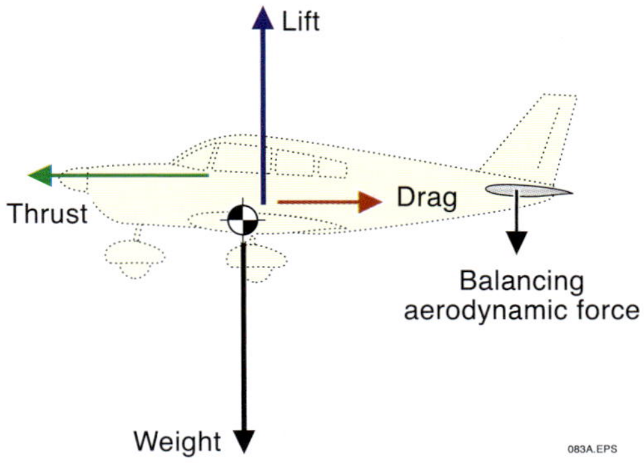

Figure 6-45
The tailplane provides the final balancing moment.

As we have discussed, the primary task of the pilot is to control the aircraft's flightpath. This is achieved by the pilot setting an attitude and thrust. Because the primary controls affect the attitude and the thrust they not only have a direct effect but as a result of the changed flightpath or trim, they also have an indirect effect – which may be quite powerful.

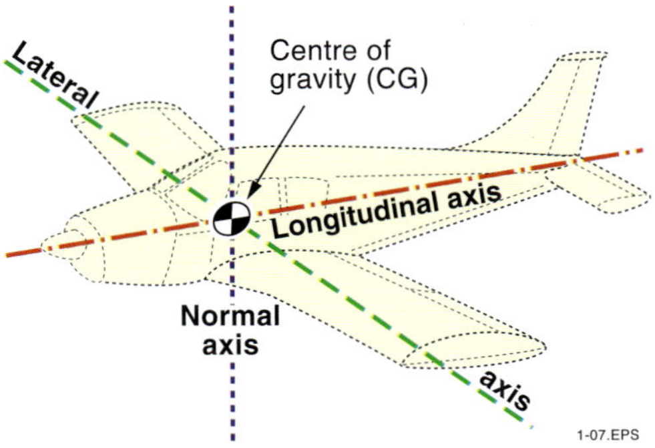

Figure 6-46
Angular movement can occur around three axes.

Direct Effect of the Primary Controls

To describe the type of motion of the aircraft, there is an international convention of terminology. The aircraft is said to move about three *axes* (lines of balance of rotation) which pass through the centre of gravity. The elevators cause a nose-up or a nose-down motion or moment (tendency) called *pitching* (around the *lateral* axis).

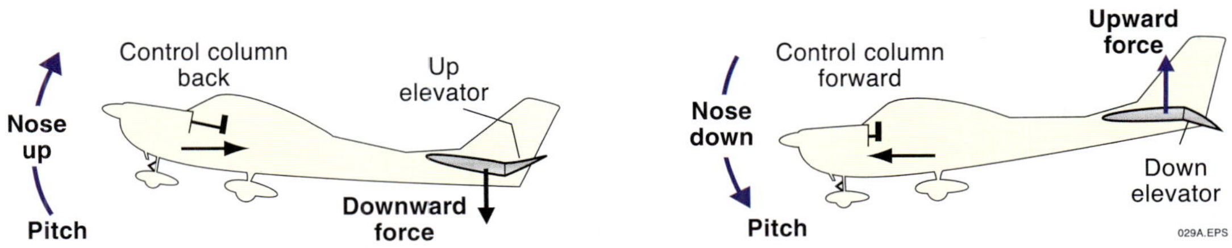

Figure 6-47 The elevator is the primary pitching control.

The ailerons cause a *rolling* moment and motion (about the *longitudinal* axis) – the aircraft is rolled to a certain angle of bank to turn.

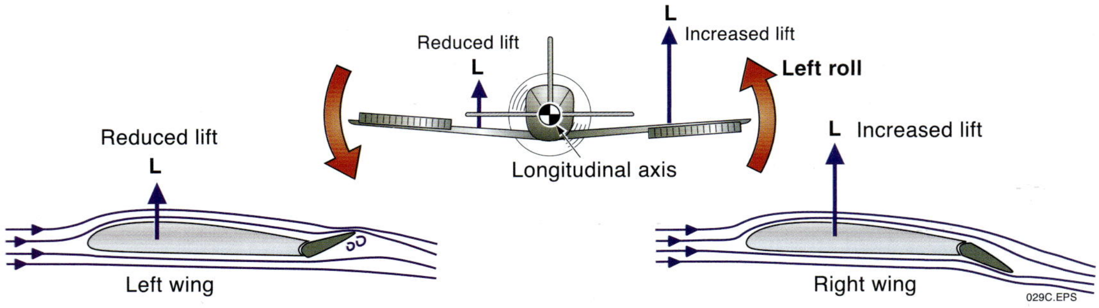

Figure 6-48 Ailerons cause a rolling moment about the longitudinal axis.

The rudder causes a *yawing* moment (about the *normal* or vertical axis) which is used to balance the uneven airflow or engine forces and is used to align the aircraft with the airflow (to prevent sideslip).

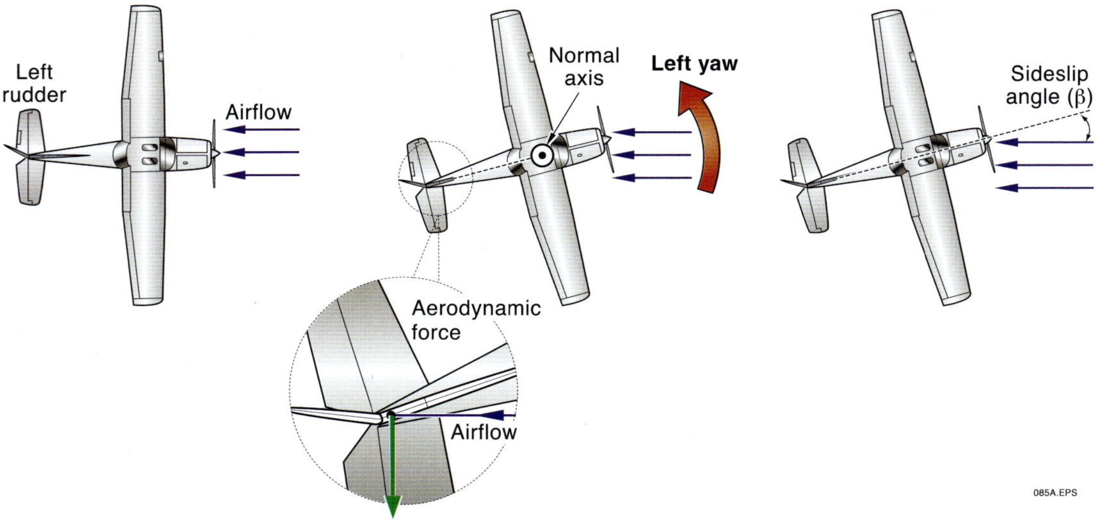

Figure 6-49 Rudder causes a yawing moment about the normal (vertical) axis.

Indirect Effect of the Primary Controls

As well as the direct effect of the control input, the complex relationship of forces and moments will also cause a secondary effect which in some cases is quite noticeable and quite useful. Others are less pronounced and are more of a nuisance. All of these effects will be demonstrated in flight.

Elevators

The elevators cause the aircraft to pitch, and the direct result is a change in angle of attack and attitude of the aircraft. This change causes a change in flightpath, and if the thrust is left constant, the airspeed will vary – like a car encountering a hill and no extra accelerator being applied. It will slow down. Similarly going down, the speed will increase. This indirect effect is used in flying in a climb and in a descent or glide where the thrust is set and the pilot uses small changes in attitude to adjust or maintain a desired airspeed.

Thrust (Power/RPM)

Changing the thrust causes the aircraft to accelerate or decelerate, but more immediately, it causes a pitching moment because of the tailplane. Thus an increase in thrust will cause the nose to rise and the aircraft to climb – until the airspeed reduces and the nose wants to drop again. Also for a given airspeed, the thrust setting determines how steeply and how quickly the aircraft descends. During a descent where the rate of descent is important (as in an instrument approach), the pilot will be using a combination of attitude and thrust to hold a flightpath, airspeed and rate of descent.

Rudder

If the aircraft is yawed with rudder, there is an immediate change in heading, but because the yawing motion causes one wing to advance and one to retard, the difference in speed causes a change in lift and therefore induces a rolling moment. The indirect effect of yaw is roll.

Ailerons – Adverse Aileron Yaw

When the ailerons are deflected, they cause a rolling moment, but also the deflected surface causes a change in the drag on that wing. The downward aileron is in a high pressure area and so has more drag than the upward aileron. The result is a yawing moment opposite to the desired direction of roll. This is called *adverse aileron yaw.* The ailerons can be designed to minimise this effect, but there is usually some noticeable adverse yaw at low airspeeds (high angles of attack). Rudder is needed to balance the adverse yaw. A further effect is when the aircraft is rolled to a bank angle. It will then start to move sideways – to sideslip – and the sideways airflow on the fuselage and fin causes the aircraft to yaw and to turn. However, there is also a degree of shielding of the wing on one side, and the difference in lift due to the sideslip will cause a slight rolling moment back to wings-level flight.

This is accentuated by dihedral (any upward angle of the wing from the root to the tip) and is called ***dihedral effect.***

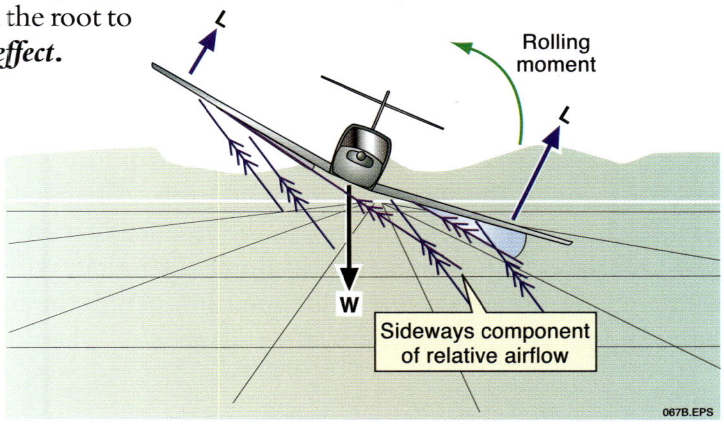

Figure 6-50 Dihedral corrects unwanted roll.

It is more pronounced with a swept wing or a high wing, With a high wing, it is called the *pendulum effect.* Both contribute to lateral stability.

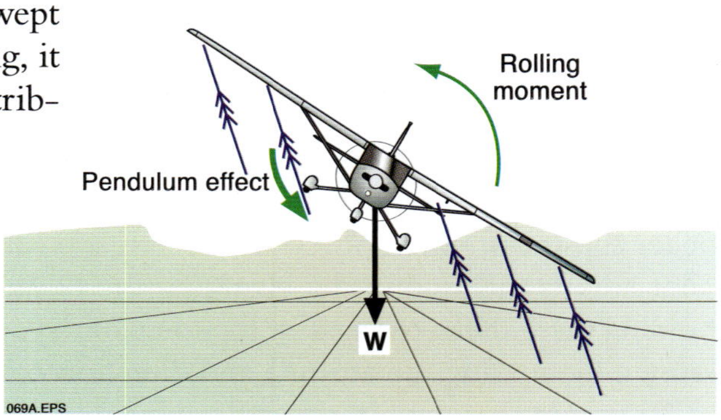

Figure 6-51 Pendulum effect.

In some cases, the rolling moment is dominant. In others, the yawing moment increases the bank.

Balance & Trim

If we consider a typical flight profile, the pilot will control the aircraft through the take-off, and then once the climb is established, the role is one of balancing the aircraft.

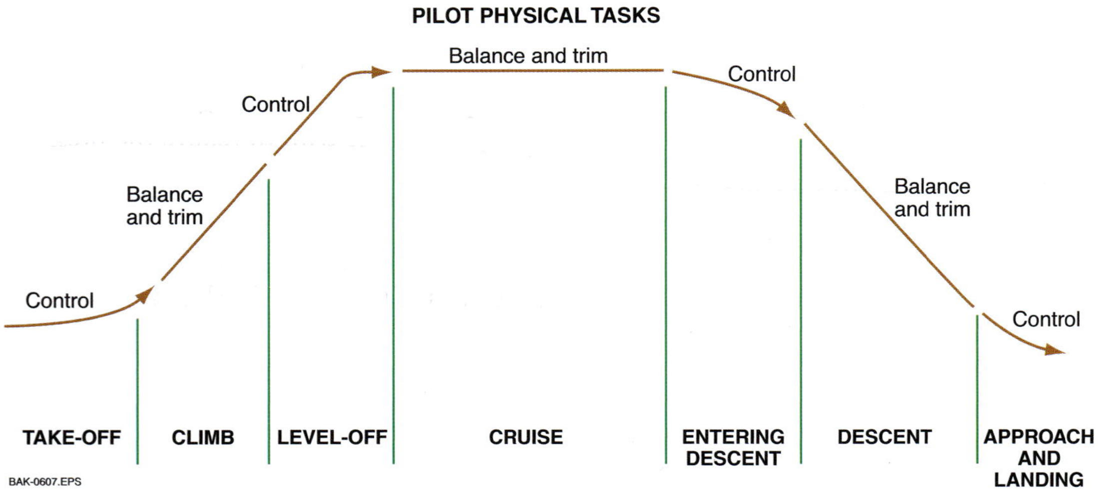

Figure 6-52 Pilot's physical tasks.

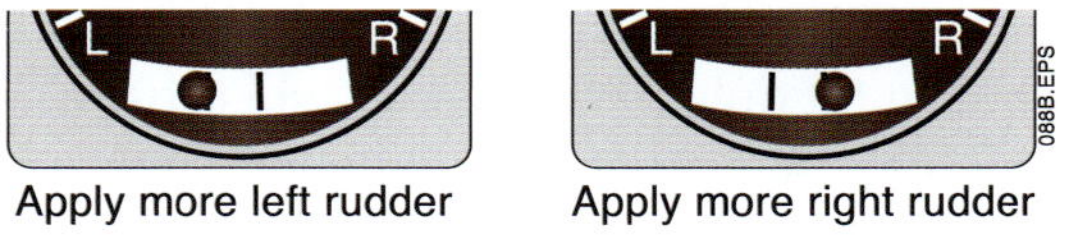

Figure 6-53 Balance ball – indications and responses.

At top of the climb, the pilot will control the aircraft through the level off, and, in the cruise, return to a balancing role. Top of descent brings a control task, as does the approach and landing. Let's examine these. When controlling the aircraft, the pilot is changing the flightpath. Otherwise, the role is balancing the out-of-trim forces either through the primary controls or through the secondary trim controls. All aircraft have an elevator trim. Some have aileron and rudder trim also. In the absence of trim, the pilot uses the primary controls to balance the aircraft – for example, in aircraft without rudder trim, the pilot has to maintain pressure on the rudder pedal to centre the balance ball. This pressure must be varied for all changes in power or airspeed or when the aircraft is turning.

What is Balance?

Stability keeps the aircraft aligned with the relative airflow. It is provided by the fixed parts of the tailplane and fin and by dihedral. Control is provided by the moving parts of the tail, the elevators and rudder, because they change the total force generated by the tail surfaces. In balanced stabilised flight, the forces of lift, weight, thrust and drag cancel each other and the fin and tailplane provide a balancing moment. The moment generated by the tailplane, and the fin changes with speed, angle of attack and the propeller slipstream. Sometimes the force is too much, and sometimes it is too little. The pilot adjusts the amount by changing the position of the elevator and the rudder and holding them deflected against the force of the airflow. How much to deflect it is simply known by holding the attitude and direction constant.

To ensure that the aircraft will maintain the attitude and direction that has been set (once the thrust is set and the speed has stabilised), the pilot uses the primary controls to balance the aircraft and the secondary, trim controls to relieve the pressure.

What is Trim?

Trim is the system that provides the long term relieving force that takes over the task of balancing the aircraft from the pilot.

- The elevators are used to offset imbalances caused by changes in thrust, speed, fuel consumption or passenger and cargo loading. The elevator trim will relieve the backward or forward force on the control column so that the attitude is maintained, "hands-off".
- The ailerons provide lateral balance to counter imbalances caused by fuel or weight differences in the wing lockers. There may be aileron trim to relieve the pressure.
- The rudder provides balance for the propeller slipstream, power setting and even differences in drag caused by the ailerons. There may be rudder trim to relieve the pressure.

By setting the attitude and direction and then removing the push or pull force, the trim helps the pilot, but it is important to remember to have the attitude stable and held with the left hand while the trim is adjusted with the other hand. You wind the trim wheel forward slowly while holding the attitude constant until the left hand is no longer pushing, or you wind the trim wheel back until the left hand is no longer pulling. If the attitude is changing or the trim is used to directly adjust the attitude, the pilot has no "feel" and the trim could be set to a incorrect position.

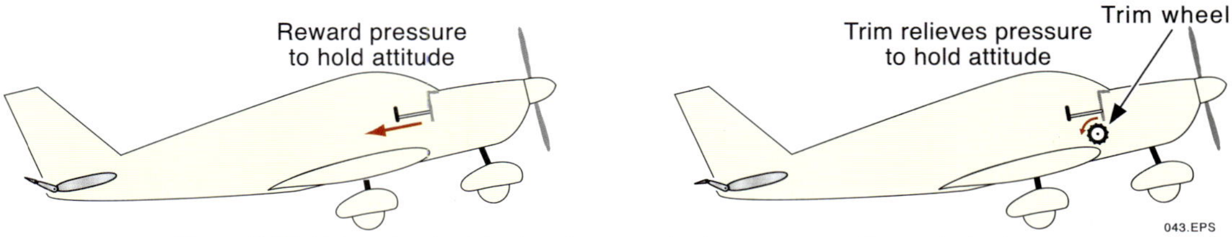

Figure 6-54 Using elevator trim to relieve constant pressures on the control column.

Effect of Thrust & Slipstream on Balance & Trim

Because the airflow from the propeller flows unevenly over the tail surfaces, there is a change in balance with power and speed changes. This does not happen in a jet or in a twin where, in some cases, the tail is clear of the wash and the propellers rotate in opposite directions. In a single engine propeller-driven aircraft, the propwash spirals over the whole aircraft and causes an increased airflow over the tailplane and a force from one side of the fin. In the case of most light aircraft with American, horizontally-opposed engines, the propeller rotates clockwise when viewed from the cockpit.

Figure 6-55 Balance the yawing moment from the slipstream with rudder pressure.

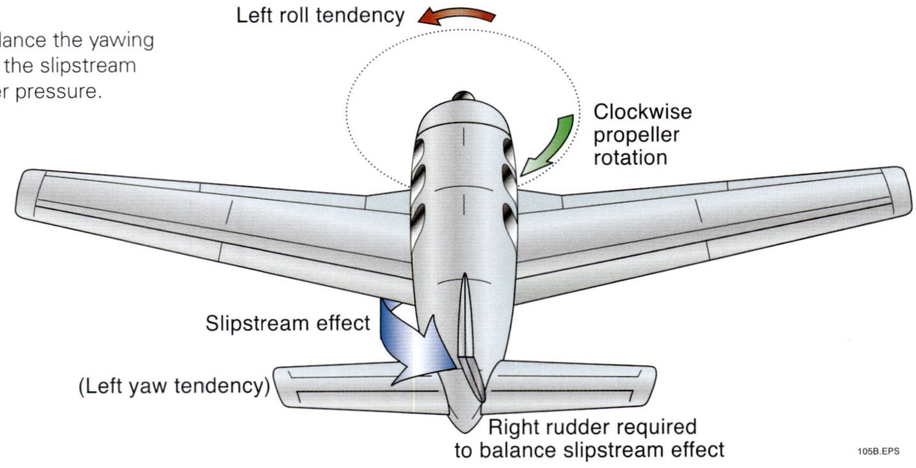

The aircraft yaws left as thrust is increased and right when the thrust is reduced (from its balanced setting). Also, the increased airflow with the thrust increase causes the nose to rise, and conversely, to fall when the thrust is reduced. The pilot compensates by applying right rudder and forward pressure as the thrust is increased and vice versa.

Straight & Level Flight

What is Straight & Level?

Straight and level describes a straight flight-path at a constant height, constant speed and constant heading with the aircraft in trim. There is no tendency to accelerate or to decelerate and no tendency to climb or descend. There is no out-of-balance moment which is tending to change the attitude or trim. The lift counteracts the weight, and the thrust counteracts the drag.

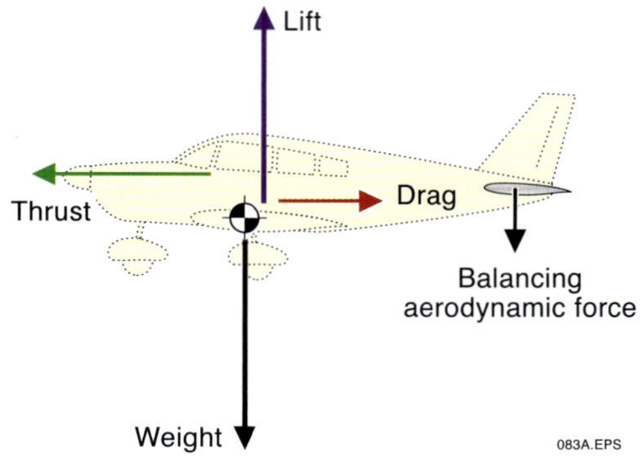

Figure 6-56
The tailplane provides the final balancing moment.

We have mentioned that the pilot adjusts the angle of attack to maintain constant lift at different speeds, so the attitude of the aircraft in straight and level flight changes with speed. Also, because the lift changes with the flap extension, the attitude also has to be adjusted to maintain level flight as the flaps are operated, especially when they are retracted after take-off and the aircraft is still at a low airspeed.

Changing Speed in Level Flight

Increasing thrust will upset the equilibrium of forces. The thrust will now exceed the drag, and there will be a net force forwards to accelerate the aircraft to a higher speed. Also, the increased airflow from the propeller over the tail surfaces will cause a nose-up tendency and a yawing moment.

Remember that in straight and level flight, *lift = weight*, and *lift* $= C_L \frac{1}{2}\rho V^2 S$. The lift coefficient C_L depends directly on angle of attack. Dynamic pressure ($\frac{1}{2}\rho V^2$) depends on the square of the true airspeed.

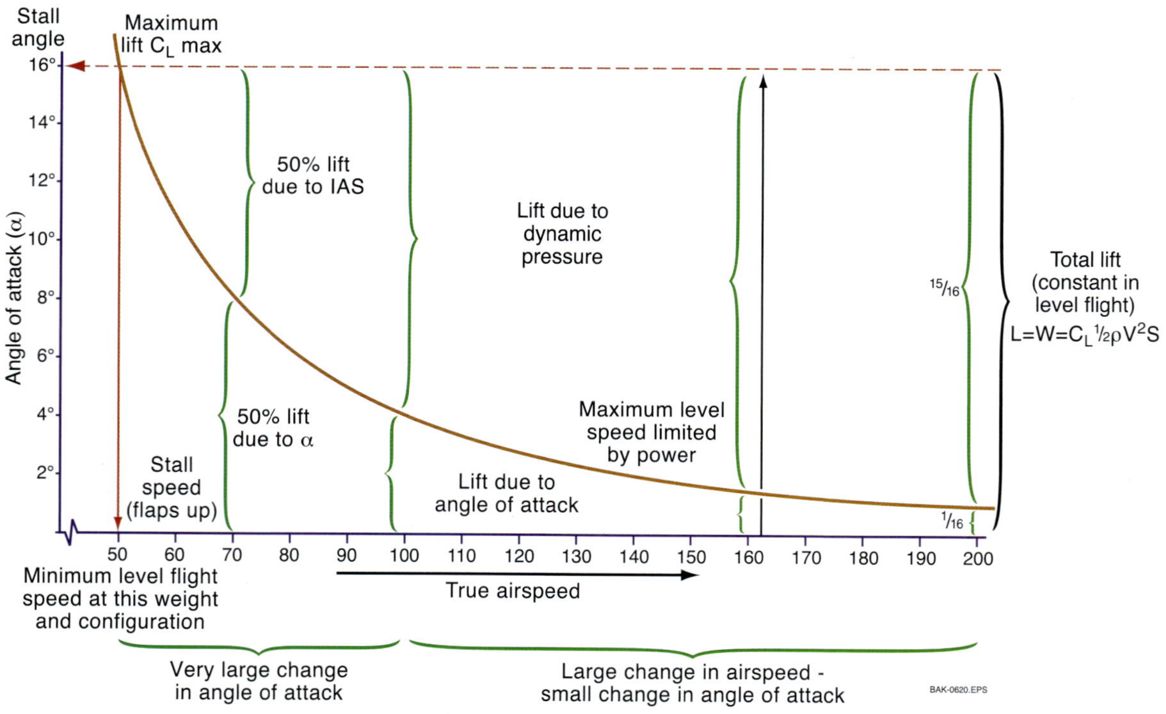

Figure 6-57 The relationship between airspeed and angle of attack in straight and level flight.

If the aircraft is in equilibrium at 100 kt and we increase speed to 200 kt, the lift would increase to four times its previous value. If the angle of attack was 4° at 100 kt, it would have to be reduced to ¼ (1°) at 200 kt.

Conversely, if the aircraft slows from 100 kt to 50 kt, the lift would be ¼ of its previous value. Angle of attack would have to increase to 4 times (16°), which is near the critical angle, to maintain level flight.

Note the required change of attitude from 100 to 200 kt is only 3°, but from 100 kt back to 50 kt there is an increase of 12°. You will notice this need for a large attitude change with reducing airspeed when you start to fly.

As speed increases, the drag will also increase and eventually, when the drag equals the thrust, the system of forces will be in a new equilibrium. However, as the speed increases so would the lift to maintain level flight. The pilot must reduce the angle of attack by lowering the nose attitude. Eventually, lift will again equal weight, and thrust will equal drag. It is a matter of experience and familiarity with your aircraft and seating position to recognise the attitudes you need to set for different speeds and flightpaths.

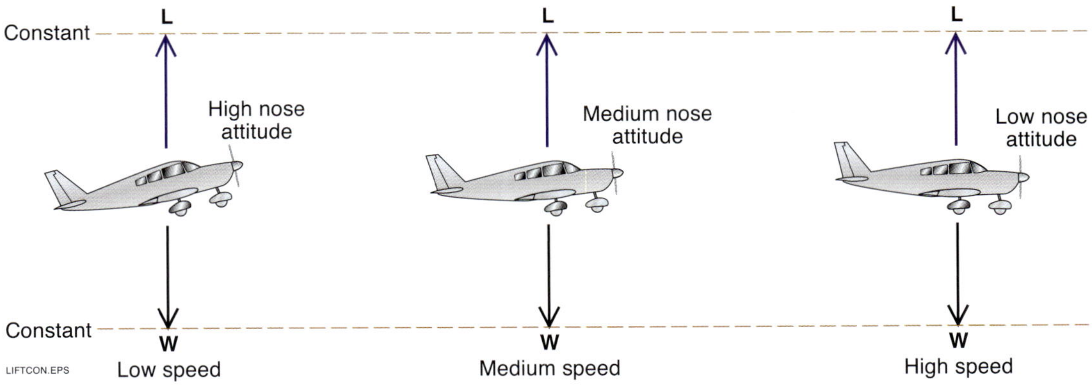

Figure 6-58 Attitude versus airspeed in level flight.

If you are flying fast and wish to slow down, the converse is true: reduce the thrust and allow the drag to slow you down. Raise the nose gradually, increasing the angle of attack and keeping lift constant so that altitude (as shown on the altimeter) is maintained. When the desired airspeed is reached, apply power to maintain it. It is a combination of the power applied and the position of the aeroplane's nose, i.e. the pitch attitude, that determines the performance of the aeroplane. *Power plus attitude equals performance.*

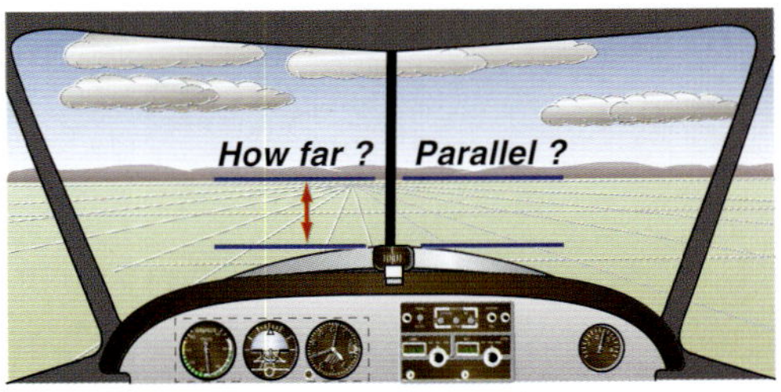

Figure 6-59
Visual attitude.

Climbing

What is a Climb?

A climb is a sustained, upward flightpath at constant airspeed and may be in a straight line or a turn. Most training aeroplanes climb at maximum power, with the pilot setting the nose attitude that provides the optimum airspeed. Some aircraft have a reduced power setting below take-off power. There are different types of climb depending on what we are trying to achieve.

Climb Performance

The climb performance of an aeroplane may be measured by either of the following:

- the time taken, or rate of climb, which is the rate at which it gains altitude in feet per minute, e.g. 300 fpm (feet per minute) as shown on the vertical speed indicator (VSI); or
- the angle of climb, which is the steepness of the flightpath over the ground (for which there is no direct instrument indication in the cockpit).

Types of Climb

Normal Climb (Maximum Rate Climb)

Normally, the aim is to gain altitude in the shortest time. This is known as a *maximum-rate climb* and is achieved by flying at *best rate of climb speed* V_Y. For practical purposes, this speed will be at, or near, the minimum drag speed (i.e. at the best L/D).

Cruise Climb

The cruise climb or en route climb is made at a higher airspeed than the normal climb. It is a compromise which expedites your departure along track and also provides better engine cooling and a better forward view due to the lower nose attitude, but which takes a little longer to reach cruising altitude. The cruise climb will be a shallower climb at a higher airspeed than either V_X or V_Y.

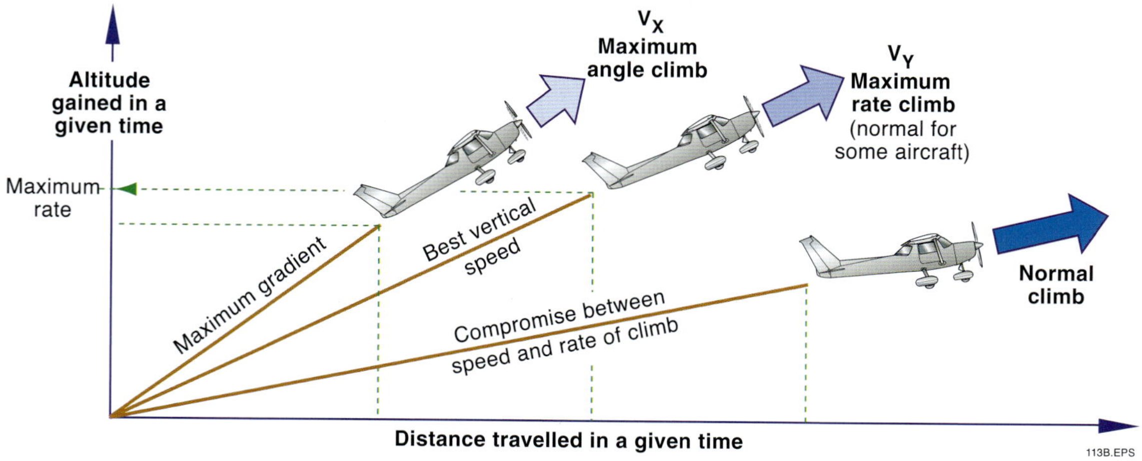

Figure 6-60 Different types of climb.

Maximum Angle Climb

Immediately after take-off, you might want to climb away from the ground at the steepest possible angle, to ensure that you clear any obstacles such as trees in the climb-out path. The speed to achieve this is known as the *best angle of climb speed*, known as V_X, and is the lowest of the three climb speeds. If you climb at V_X with full power set, you will achieve the maximum gradient climb, i.e. the greatest possible altitude gain for horizontal distance travelled. However, the aircraft is at very low airspeed and is very vulnerable to wind gusts and turbulence. The stall warning may be operating intermittently and the passengers may be concerned. The maximum angle climb should only be used when it has to be, and the aircraft should be accelerated to normal climb speed as soon as the obstacles are cleared.

Refer to your pilot's operating handbook for the actual values of the various climb speeds for your particular aeroplane. Typically, the best angle of climb speed, V_X, is 5 to 10 knots above the stalling speed and a similar amount below the best rate of climb speed, V_Y. The cruise climb speed will be another 10 knots or so faster.

Forces Acting in the Climb

In a steady climb, the lift balances a component of the weight but not the total weight. Thus the lift in a climb is less than in level flight. To climb at a constant airspeed, the thrust must be increased to balance not only the drag but also a component of weight which now acts along the flightpath.

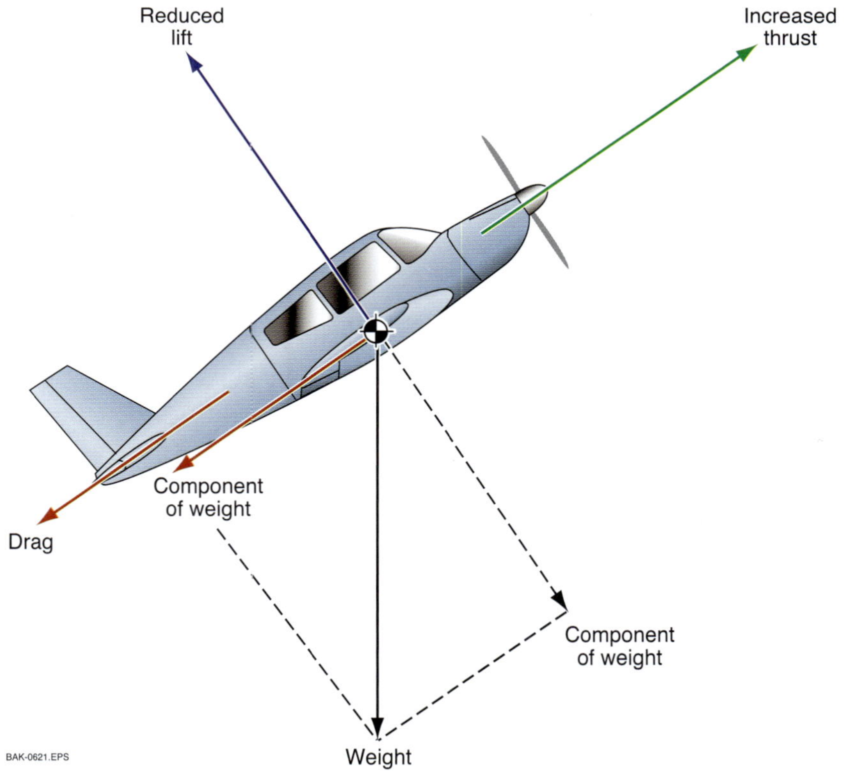

Figure 6-61 forces in a steady climb.

Thrust & Power – What Speed to Fly

Imagine a car climbing a hill. The ground reaction supports all of the weight on level ground. To climb the hill without losing speed, the engine and tyres must counter a downhill component of the weight, but the tyres carry less weight.

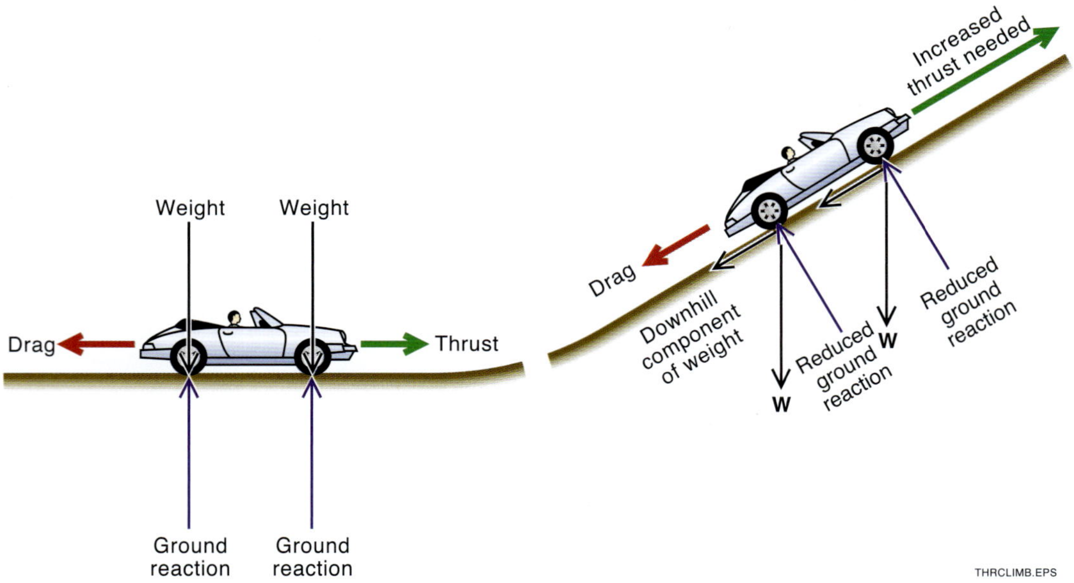

Figure 6-62 Weight resists a climb.

An aeroplane is the same as the car. The wings are the aeroplane's suspension. They produce an air reaction (lift), just as the tyres experience a ground reaction. The wings carry the weight of the aircraft in level flight, absorb shocks and change its flightpath. However, unlike the tyres of a car, the wings do not provide traction. The thrust to climb is provided by the engine and propeller. They overcome drag and the downhill component of the weight.

The more spare thrust (excess thrust) that is available at that airspeed, the steeper we can climb, because we can overcome a greater downhill component of weight.

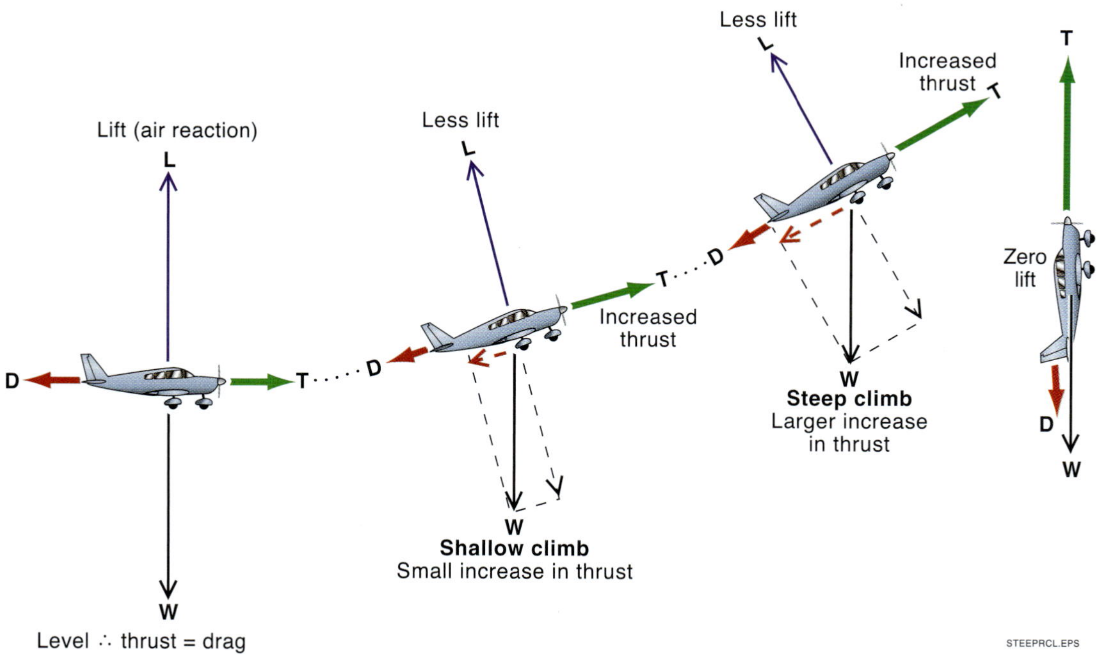

Figure 6-63 Less lift is required but more thrust to climb.

Interestingly, *less* lift is required during the climb because thrust is off-setting some of the weight. If you imagine a vertical climb, no lift is required from the wing as the weight is totally carried by the thrust.

The steepest climb requires the greatest excess thrust (some fighters can climb vertically). However, the amount of excess thrust that the engine can produce reduces as the aircraft flies faster. So the speed for the steepest climb has to be at the slowest safe speed where the thrust is greatest and the drag low.

We mentioned that power is the rate of doing work, and so the best rate of climb occurs at a speed where the spare (excess) power is maximum. Power is a function not only of engine settings but also airspeed. The thrust multiplied by speed tells us the power, but the thrust decreases with speed. So, the speed for best rate of climb is a compromise between the reducing thrust and the increasing speed and the drag. Best rate of climb airspeed is generally about 1.5 times the stall speed.

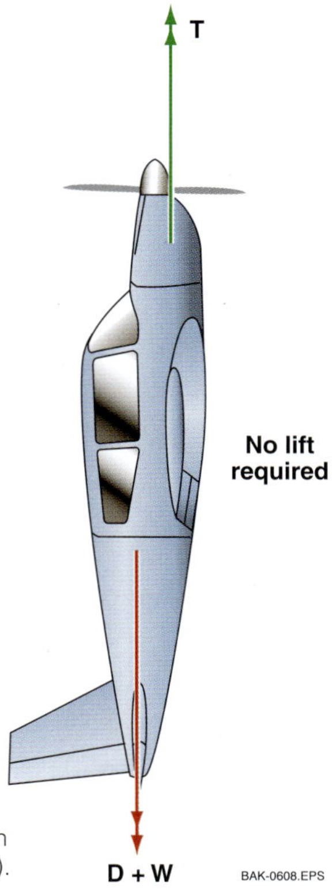

Figure 6-64
Vertical climb (if the engine can produce enough excess thrust).

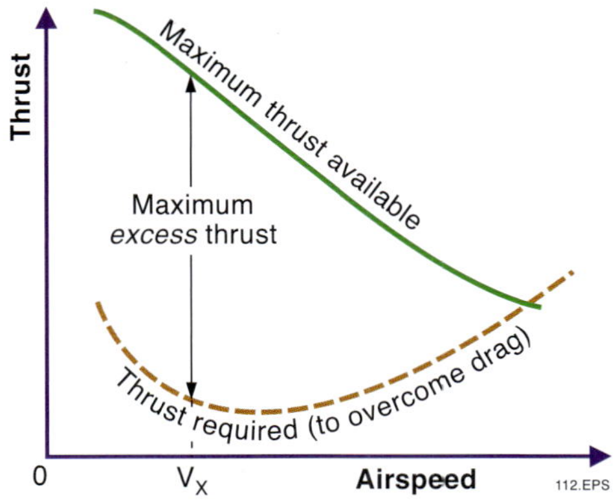

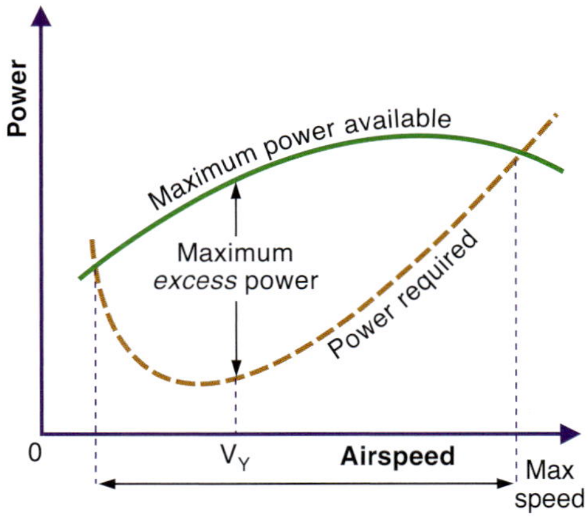

Figure 6-65 (Left) the thrust curve and (right) the power curve. (Climbing is possible in this speed range since power available exceeds that required to maintain straight and level flight at that speed. Outside this speed range there is insufficient power available to climb.)

Factors affecting Climb Performance

Power

Increased power available increases climb performance. Engine power reduces with increasing altitude and higher than normal temperatures.

Airspeed

Flying faster or slower than the recommended airspeed will degrade the climb performance.

Flap Extension

Extended flaps will decrease climb performance due to the higher drag. However, they may produce a shorter take-off run and better obstacle clearance. Check your aircraft's manual.

Weight
An aeroplane that is light will climb better than a heavily laden aeroplane.

Temperature & Pressure (Density Altitude)
Reduced air density caused by aerodrome elevation, higher air temperatures and/or lower pressure (altitude) will cause a decrease in climb performance by decreasing both engine and airframe performance.

Bank Angle
Turning decreases climb performance due to the additional induced drag. The greater the angle of bank, the greater the effect.

Wind
A headwind increases the climb angle and therefore terrain clearance. A tailwind reduces the climb angle. Wind does not affect the rate of climb (time is altitude).

Entering a Climb
In straight and level flight, we use attitude as a reference. All other flight profiles are flown in the same way. To climb, we need to increase power, set the climb attitude, wait for the airspeed to stabilise and set the trim. The rudder is used to balance the change in power and airspeed (keep the ball centred). The sequence of control and balance for entering the climb is power, attitude, trim (PAT).

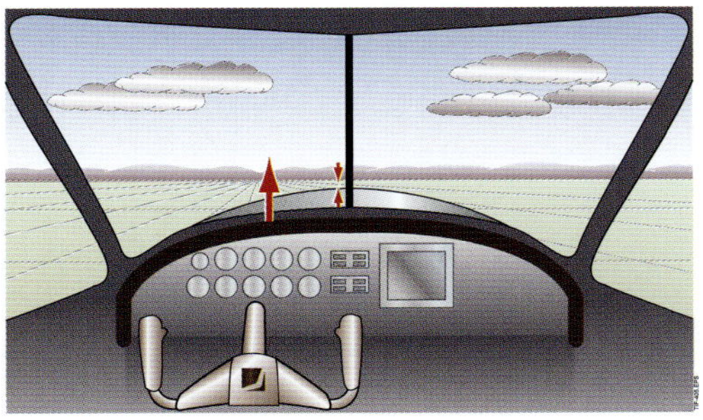

Figure 6-66 Setting the climb attitude.

Maintaining the Climb
During the climb, we need to look out for other aircraft and monitor the engine instruments. We are at low airspeed and high power and the temperatures may increase. Also, with a constant-speed propeller, the manifold pressure (MP) will have to be adjusted as you climb.

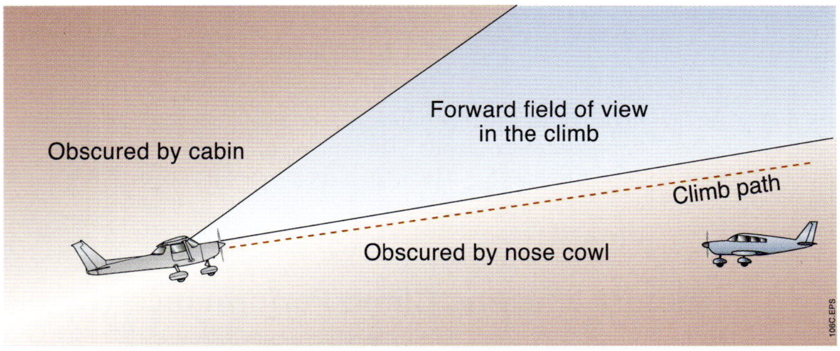

Figure 6-67 Periodically check the area obscured by the nose cowl.

Levelling from a Climb
At about 50 ft before your altitude, slowly reduce the attitude for level flight at low airspeed. It is a very small change. Then allow the aircraft to accelerate and adjust the attitude and balance to maintain straight and level. When you reach normal cruise speed, reduce the power, balance as you do so, and re-trim. The sequence is attitude, *pause,* power, trim (APT).

Descending

While climbing requires increased thrust, descending requires reduced thrust to maintain speed – just like coasting down a hill on your bike.

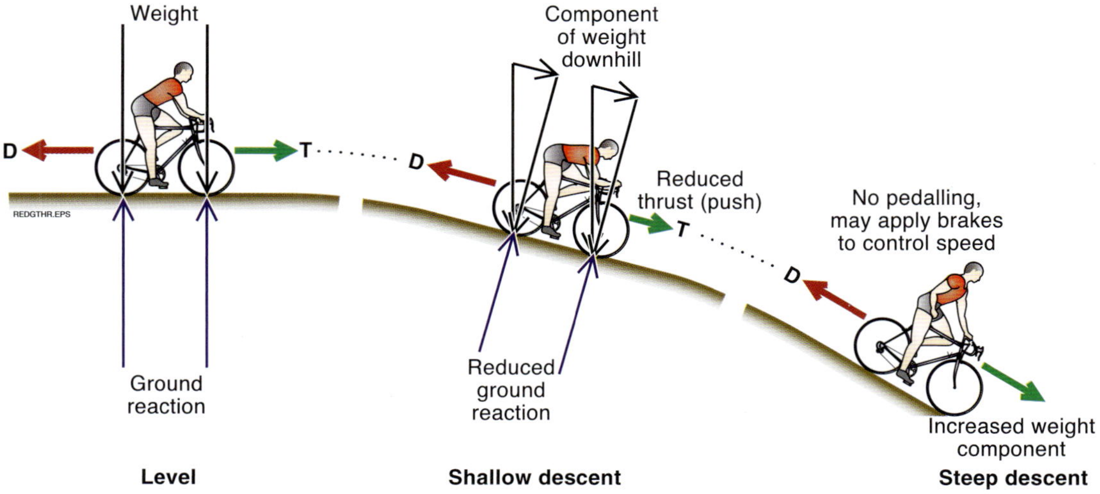

Figure 6-68 Weight assists descent.

The less thrust, the steeper the descent and for a given speed, the faster the descent. When the thrust is reduced to the minimum (called ***idle rpm***) then the aircraft is gliding.

Forces Acting in a Descent

In a descent, lift only balances a component of the weight. Thus lift is less than in level flight. A component of the weight acts along the flightpath and helps overcome drag. Thus to maintain a constant airspeed, thrust is reduced.The more that thrust is reduced or drag is increased (by lowering flaps on extending speed brakes), the steeper the descent path that can be maintained without increasing speed.

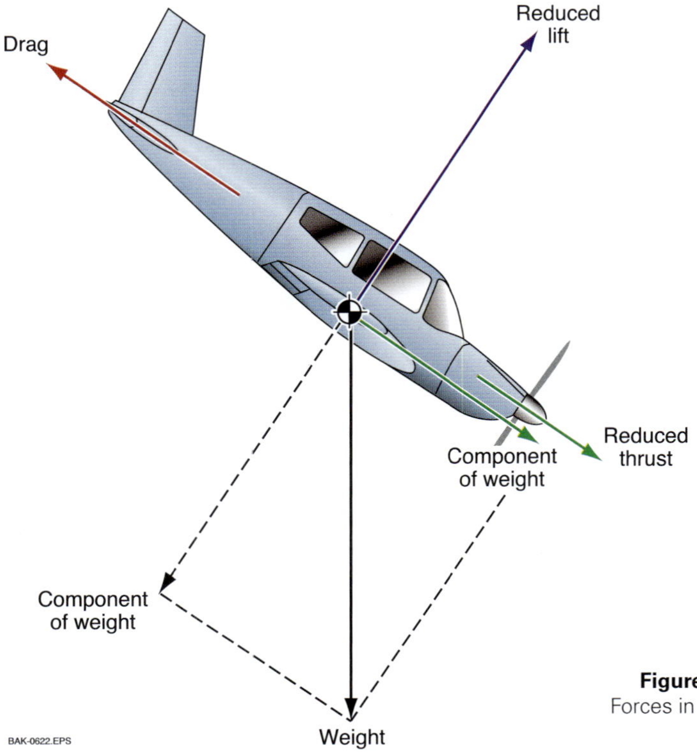

Figure 6-69
Forces in descent.

Types of Descent

The descent profile is chosen to reach a nominated altitude in the following manner:

- in the shortest distance (steepest);
- in the shortest time (maximum rate);
- at a normal rate (normal is about 1,000 fpm); and
- at a very comfortable rate (about 500 fpm) and progression (cruise descent).

The descent profile is a matter of the thrust setting and the attitude. The attitude may be adjusted to maintain an accurate rate of descent or an accurate airspeed, but generally, the descent is not a precise manoeuvre.

Factors Affecting the Descent

Thrust (Power/RPM)

The less thrust, the steeper the descent and the greater the rate of descent for the same airspeed. Conversely, increasing the power produces a reduced descent angle and rate.

Drag

The greater the drag (due to flaps or speed brakes), the steeper the descent and the greater the rate for the same airspeed (also, the lower the nose attitude).

Wind

Horizontal movement of the air (wind) changes the path of the aircraft over the ground. A descent into wind is steeper and downwind is shallower. There is no effect on rate of descent through the air, unless there are vertical air currents.

Weight

The heavier the aircraft, the greater the component of weight along the flightpath. This will lead to increased speed and rate of descent for the same power. For a glide, increased weight gives an increased airspeed for the same glidepath (attitude and angle of attack).

Angle of Bank

If the aircraft is turned while descending, the induced drag is increased, which increases the angle and rate of descent. The greater the bank, the greater the effect.

Entering the Descent or Glide

A descent is entered by reducing the power, balancing with rudder, allowing the nose to fall to the descent attitude, holding it steady and retrimming – power, attitude, trim (PAT). A power reduction of 500 rpm or 5 in. Hg MP gives a rate of descent of approximately 500 fpm while maintaining cruise airspeed.

Figure 6-70 Descent with flaps extended.

A glide is entered in exactly the same way except that the power is reduced to idle and the trim changes are greater. There will be an optimum glide speed which is critical for best performance. In some aircraft, or in some conditions, it is necessary to select carburettor heat to hot before closing the throttle for a glide or even a low-powered descent. Check your aircraft's procedures.

Maintaining the Descent

Again, lift is less in the descent than in level flight as the drag partially offsets the force of gravity (the weight). In a vertical descent, no lift is required from the wing, but you need lots of drag to stop the aircraft accelerating. The WWII dive bombers had massive dive brakes to increase drag and stop the speed increasing.

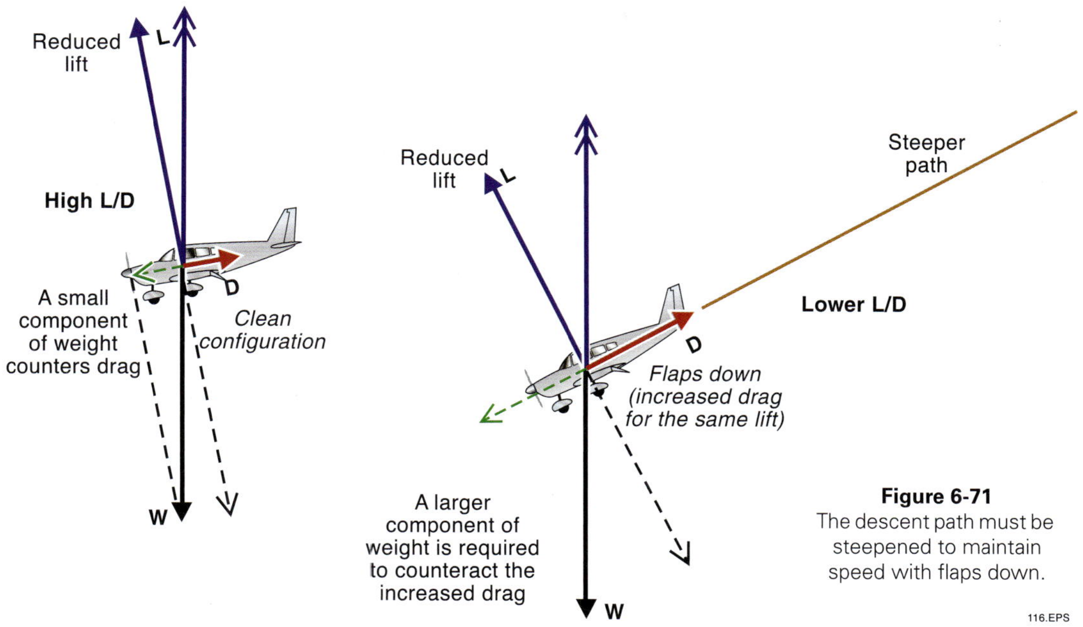

Figure 6-71 The descent path must be steepened to maintain speed with flaps down.

The descent is maintained by setting a constant power and adjusting the attitude to hold the airspeed or rate of descent. If the rate of descent is too high, the power is increased slightly and the attitude raised.

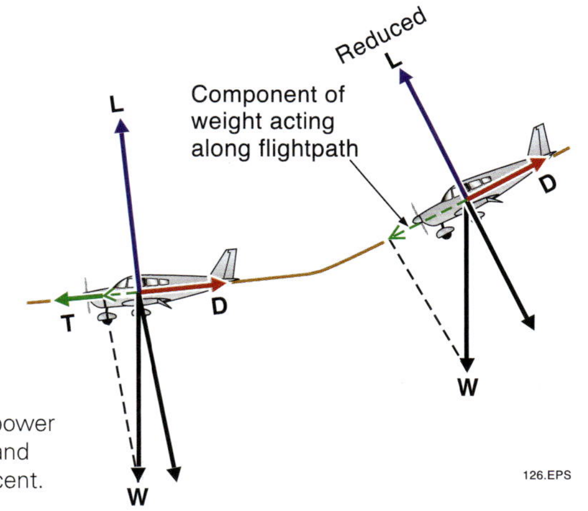

Figure 6-72 Increasing power shallows the descent and reduces the rate of descent.

Gliding

Every aeroplane type has a correct gliding speed which will give the greatest glide distance for the amount of altitude lost in the descent. The gliding airspeed, when maintained, sets the wing at its most efficient angle of attack (usually about 4°). At this angle, the required lift is generated for a minimum cost in drag (i.e. the best ratio of lift to drag, known as the best L/D), and the descent is as shallow as possible. To have this correct angle of attack requires the pilot to make a small adjustment in airspeed to compensate for a heavier or lighter aircraft.

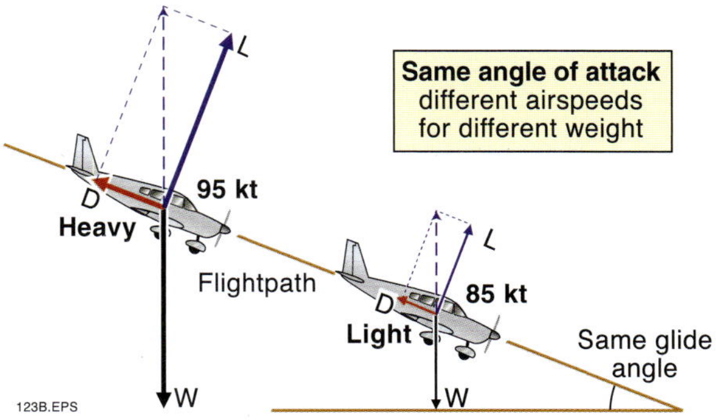

Figure 6-73 Best glide angle is the same at all weights, but airspeed must be lower at lower weights.

Flying at the best L/D airspeed will give the best glide angle. To maintain this best glide angle, the lighter the aeroplane, the slower the best L/D airspeed. If you glide at any other speed than the best glide speed, the required lift will be generated but at a higher cost in drag (i.e. the lift–drag ratio will be poorer), and the result will be a steeper descent and less distance covered through the air for the altitude lost.

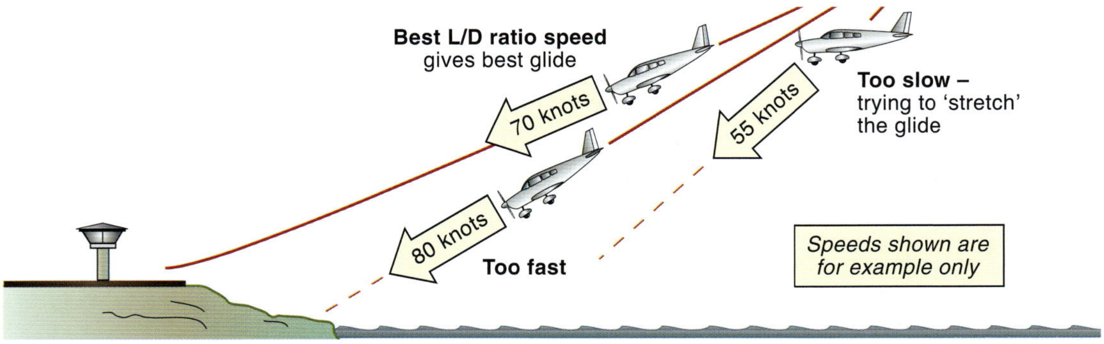

Figure 6-74 The flattest glide is achieved at best L/D airspeed.

This situation applies both to flying faster than the recommended glide speed (which will result in going below the best slope) and flying slower than the recommended glide speed (which will result in the aeroplane "mushing" below the best slope). Raising the nose of an aeroplane too high in an attempt to stretch a glide will, in fact, have the opposite effect! If you are undershooting the desired slope on approach to land, you need to add power and raise the nose to hold the correct airspeed, which will result in a shallower descent. Simply raising the nose without adding power would result in a slower airspeed than desired and an even steeper descent.

Wind has a surprisingly large effect on the glide as it can represent a significant percentage change in your distance travelled over the ground.

Lowering the flaps will reduce the L/D and steepen the glidepath. During a glide approach, you must be sure that you will be able to reach the airfield at the steeper glide angle before you lower the flaps.

During the glide, the engine will cool and the spark plugs may become fouled with oil. Every 1,000 ft warm the engine by momentarily setting climb power and returning the throttle to idle. This will ensure that full power is available when needed at the bottom of the glide.

Descent to an Aim Point

To descend to a specific point on the ground and in a particular direction, as on the centreline to the runway, the pilot uses a combination of attitude, heading and power to achieve lateral positioning, desired approach path and target threshold speed.

Levelling from Descent or Glide

At about 50 ft before the desired altitude (or 10% of the rate of descent), increase the power to cruise or climb and allow the nose to rise with the trim change. Balance with rudder, set the level or climb attitude and re-trim. The sequence is power, attitude, trim (PAT).

Turning

For any object to turn, a force towards the centre of the turn needs to be applied (centripetal force). In the case of an aeroplane, this is achieved simply by banking the wings. This tilts the lift force, and it is the horizontal component of the lift force that pulls the aeroplane into the turn. The steeper the bank angle, the more the lift force is tilted, and the stronger its horizontal component and, therefore, the tighter the turn.

Figure 6-75 Medium bank, level turn.

We know we turn by banking and using part of the lifting force to provide an external force and the reaction causes us to turn; that is, we push the air sideways as well as down and the reaction causes us to turn as well as to stay in level flight. To provide the necessary lifting force at the same speed, we have to increase the angle of attack. So we turn by rolling the aircraft to a desired angle of bank and then hold the attitude with a little back pressure to maintain the slightly increased angle of attack. The tighter we wish to turn, the steeper the bank, and the greater the lifting force, angle of attack and back pressure required.

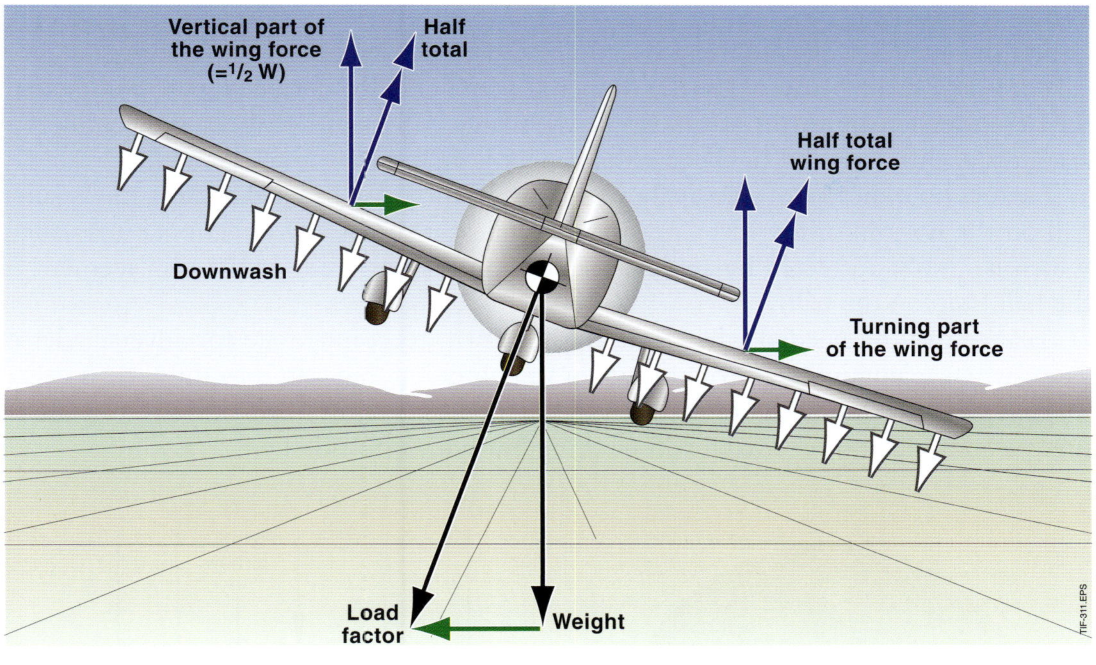

Figure 6-76 Forces in a level turn.

In straight and level flight, the mass of the aircraft, the pilot, the fuel and everything else inside wants to continue in the same direction at the same speed. To change direction (turn), we generate force from the wings and a reaction. So the wings turn but the fuselage and everything else want to keep going as they were. Thus the wings force the rest of the aircraft around the corner. The result is that everything inside the aircraft feels pushed down; in fact, the wings and structure push up, but the result is the same. This push down is called *load factor* or *g* as is measured in multiples of the normal force of gravity. So at 2g we feel twice as heavy, and literally we are. The head pushes down twice as hard. At 4g, it is four times gravity, and at 6g six times. Imagine carrying a head six times its normal weight. It's so heavy you can hardly turn your neck – and this is one of the problems facing the fighter pilots as they manoeuvre. The structure feels it too. The wings want to bend upwards where they join the fuselage, and this *wing root bending moment* is one of the causes of danger in steep turns and the spiral dive.

Types of Turn

There are several types of turn with which you will become familiar:

- medium level turn, which is a turn in level flight with an angle of bank of 20°–30°;
- climbing turn, which is a turn during a steady climb with an angle of bank no more than 15° (to reduced the effect on climb performance);
- descending turn, which is a turn during a steady, powered descent with an angle of bank of up to 30° (to avoid very high rates of descent);
- gliding turn, which is a turn during a glide with up to 30° bank;
- steep turn, which is a turn in level, descending flight with either 45° or 60° of bank; and
- maximum rate turn, which is an emergency turn to avoid a collision.

Steep turns are avoided when gliding or when at low altitude as the stalling speed is increased and high rates of descent can develop.

Balance in the Turn (Countering Sideslip)

What is Sideslip?

When the aircraft is not pointing exactly into the relative airflow, the sideways angle is called *sideslip*. It can be caused by the rudder or trim not being correctly set to compensate for the propeller slipstream; it can occur with large deflections of the ailerons (different amounts of drag, left and right) or if the rudder is deliberately applied and held.

There is no indicator of sideslip, but with experience, you can feel it. Also, the balance ball on the bottom of the turn and balance indicator shows any directional imbalance, which is simply corrected by applying rudder on the same side as the displacement of the ball (step on the ball).

Balance may be needed when entering the turn (to compensate for adverse aileron yaw), when maintaining a turn and when straightening. Sideslip into the turn is called *slipping*, whereas sliding out of the turn is called *skidding* – just like a skid in a car. Turning is a combination of yawing and pitching but with zero sideslip.

Figure 6-77 Imbalance (sideslip).

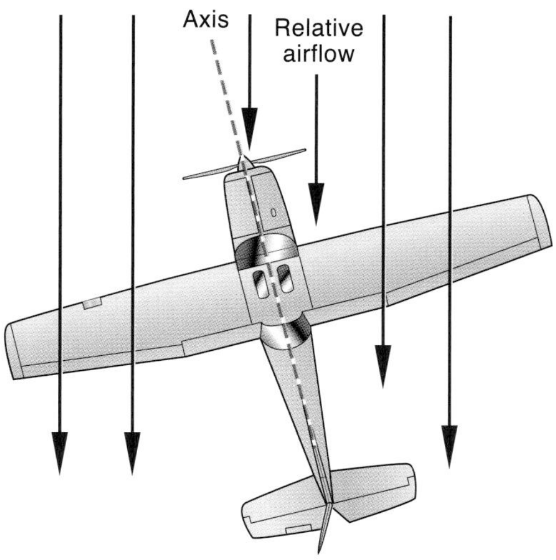

Figure 6-78 Sideslip.

Entering the Turn

As the ailerons are deflected, there will be a difference in drag between them. Depending on their design, this difference may be noticeable or just detectable. It is most noticeable at low airspeed. The effect is called *adverse aileron yaw* and is rare in modern aircraft except ultalights. It is noticeable at low speeds, especially during the final approach, and in this regime, it is important to offset the unbalanced drag with a coordinated application of rudder; that is, when making an aileron input always apply corresponding rudder pressure in the same direction. As the aircraft rolls into the turn, slight back pressure is applied to increase the angle of attack.

Maintaining the Turn

When the angle of bank is established, the ailerons and rudder can be centralised, but this is not quite the most efficient way to fly. If we bank the aircraft, the sideways part of the lift g-force will cause the aircraft to move sideways. If we increase the angle of attack, we will also remain in level flight.

As the aircraft moves sideways, the airflow comes from that side and the sideslip will cause the aircraft to turn (pitch and yaw). But in a sideslip, the aircraft is slightly out of alignment with the air, so the pilot applies a little pressure to balance the turn. The power and trim are not adjusted in a medium turn.

When turning at low altitude and in the circuit pattern, the wind affects the aircraft's path over the ground and can give a false illusion of slipping into the turn or skidding out of the turn. This can be dangerous if the pilot corrects for the false illusion. Also, the speed over the ground can cause the pilot to misinterpret airspeed.

Rolling-out of the Turn

Anticipate the roll out direction by using a visual feature or the heading indicator. As a guide, ⅓ of the angle of bank is a good allowance to commence the roll out. In a medium level turn, anticipate by 10° of heading and roll the wing level. Balance the aileron input with rudder and reduce any back pressure to return to straight and level flight.

Low-Speed Flight

As we decelerate in level flight, the angle of attack has to be increased to offset the reduction in lift due to the reduced speed. Thus the nose attitude has to be increased. Slow flight is first recognised by a high nose attitude – just watch a Jumbo joining final approach as it slows down and before it has lowered full flap.

To hold the nose attitude higher, the pilot has to pull back on the control column so there is a noticeable force and distance back (displacement) of the control. Perhaps most of the rearward trim travel has been used (depending on whether the flaps cause a nose-up or nose-down trim change). The aileron control will be sluggish due to the reduced airspeed.

The elevators will remain powerful if the power has been increased, as in most cases, the elevators are in the propeller slipstream (propwash). Manoeuvring at low speed is characterised by a high nose attitude (unless flaps are lowered), rearward control position, sluggish roll into and out of turns, adverse aileron yaw, higher power to maintain level flight, and more pronounced tendency for the nose attitude to lower in the turn.

Stalling

What is a Stall?

A stall is a condition of flight where the angle of attack is increased (by the pilot) to the point where the airflow over the upper surface of the wing largely separates. There is a loss of lift and increase in drag. If the aircraft was in straight and level flight, it would inevitably descend, and there would be a tendency for the nose to drop or nod and perhaps a tendency for the aircraft to diverge in roll and yaw. It is easily recovered to normal flight unless the stall occurs close to the ground.

Symptoms of approaching Stall

If instead of lowering flaps and increasing power, we continue to decelerate without re-trimming, there will be a very marked pull-force with the rearward control position. There will be some "burbling" or buffeting of the turbulent air around the cockpit, over the tailplane or though the controls. There is a small vane on the leading edge of the wing which flips up just below the stalling angle. This activates the warning buzzer or light.

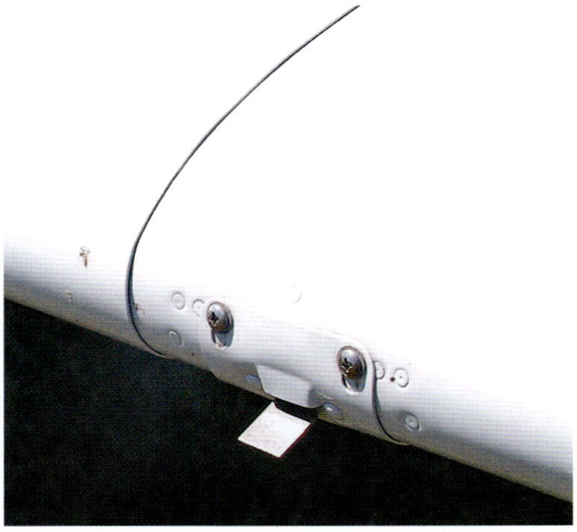

Figure 6-79 Stall warning vane.

As the airspeed decays further and the angle of attack is increased to maintain level flight, the stall warning bell or horn will sound. The nose will be more and more difficult to hold up, and you may actually reach the full-back position. Note here that the aircraft has to be forced to stall. It will not stall by itself unless it is loaded beyond the aft CG limit, if it is trimmed full back and then mishandled, or if it flown at very slow speed and the flaps are suddenly retracted. Even in these cases, the stall itself is quite controllable, but the aircraft will lose altitude in the recovery and this is the cause of the problem.

To avoid stalling at any time, we simply allow the angle of attack to be reduced by the natural stability of the aircraft (by releasing the back pressure) or deliberately reduce the angle by lowering the nose attitude. If we do continue to the minimum level flight speed – the stalling speed – the aerofoil will be at its highest angle of attack (critical angle or stalling angle). If the speed can be reduced beyond this point, then a series of other symptoms appear:

- buffet will increase;
- VSI will indicate a rate of descent which cannot be prevented, and at this point, the airflow over the tailplane will cause the nose to drop;
- the nose will drop or may "nod" down slowly and then come back up; and
- there may be some tendency for the nose to yaw and perhaps for one wing to drop.

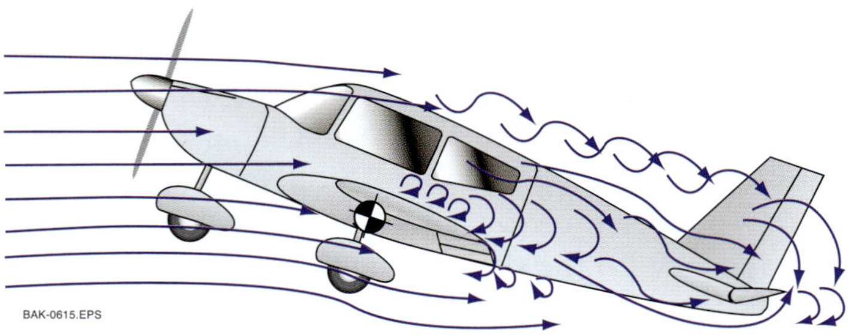

Figure 6-80
Turbulent flow over the tailplane.

If the rearward force is relaxed, the wing will instantly be unstalled and the aircraft will accelerate. If the force is held, the nose will come back up and the aircraft will slow down and stall again. A wing stalls when it exceeds the critical angle of attack.

You can induce a stall at any time by increasing the angle of attack with back pressure on the control column. Note that the stall can occur in any aeroplane attitude.

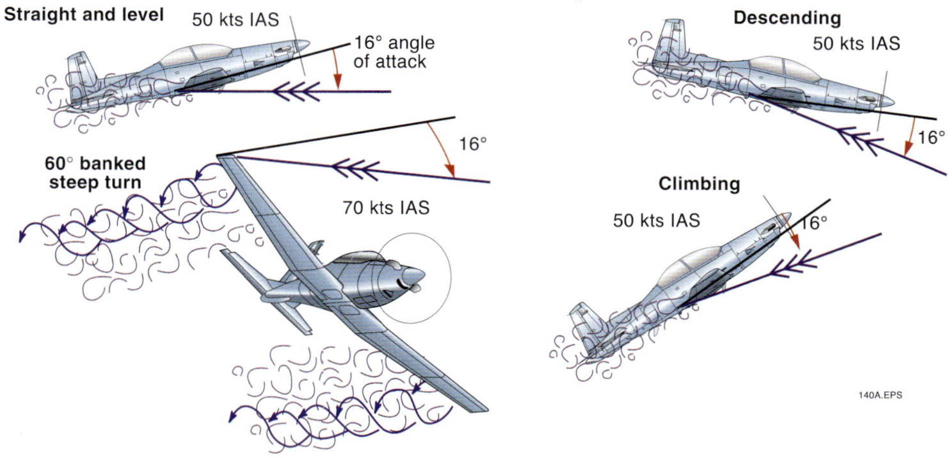

Figure 6-81 Stalling occurs at the same stalling angle irrespective of attitude.

It is very easy both to avoid a stall simply by ensuring that the stalling angle is not approached, and to recover from a stall by releasing the back pressure to decrease the angle of attack.

The stall is associated with a particular angle of attack.

The wing stalls at a particular angle of attack, but not always at a particular airspeed. When pulling positive g-forces in manoeuvres such as steep turns or dives, the stall speed will be greater than when flying straight and level. This is called an accelerated stall.

Angle of attack is not indicated in the cockpit; however, a pilot will not only recognise a stall when it occurs, but will also be able to predict at what airspeed it will occur by knowing the following:

- straight and level stall speed; and
- the multiplying factor due to bank angle (or g-loading).

The stall depends directly upon angle of attack and indirectly upon airspeed.

In level flight, there is a direct relationship between angle of attack and indicated airspeed. Their precise relationship depends upon the following:

- lift produced by the aerofoil;
- weight;
- load factor (the amount of g-force being pulled);
- bank angle;
- power; and
- flap setting (which changes aerofoil shape).

Flight Controls near the Stall

The flight controls are less powerful at low airspeed. A reduced airflow over the controls will cause them to become less powerful as speed reduces and the unaccelerated stall is approached. Control pressures will decrease, and larger movements of the elevator and rudder will be required. It is the wing that stalls. The tailplane remains unstalled (by design) so that during the stall, the elevator and rudder remain effective. The elevator can be used to lower the nose and unstall the wings. The rudder is used to prevent unwanted yaw. The ailerons may or may not remain fully effective during a stall depending upon the aeroplane type. *Be careful using ailerons near the stall.*

A dropping wing can normally be stopped by moving the control column in the opposite direction. This causes the aileron on the dropping wing to deflect downwards, increasing the angle of attack and producing more lift on that wing. If the wing is near the stalling angle, however, the aileron deflection could cause the critical angle to be exceeded on that wing and, instead of rising, the loss of lift would cause the wing to drop further. With any yaw, a spin could develop.

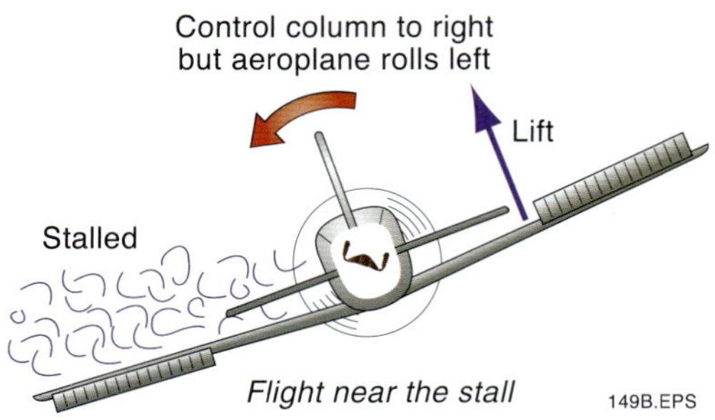

Figure 6-82 Inducing a spin with opposite aileron.

Note that the ailerons on most training aeroplanes are effective right through the stall, and their use, coordinated with rudder, may be possible. This point should be discussed with your flight instructor. Prevent further yaw and wing-drop with opposite rudder.

Near the stall, any tendency for a wing to drop or for the aeroplane to yaw can be prevented with opposite rudder. If the right wing drops, or if the aeroplane yaws right, apply left rudder (and vice versa).

Factors affecting Stalling Speed

In straight and level flight, the lift equals the weight. You will become familiar with the lift formula:

$$L = C_L \tfrac{1}{2} \rho V^2 S$$ ***(Lift equals Cee Ell, Half Rho, v-squared, Ess)***

This formula describes the elements that produce the lift. They include the following:
- the lift coefficient of the wing (C_L) which depends directly upon the angle of attack and camber (due to flap);
- the density of the air (ρ, the greek letter pronounced *rho*);
- the speed through the air (V); and
- the area of the wing (S).

The formula expresses the energy of the air or the energy of the reaction of the air to an object moving through it. Remember kinetic energy = $\tfrac{1}{2}mv^2$. Under normal circumstances, the pilot controls the angle of attack and the speed. The lowest speed at which the aircraft can fly is achieved when the wing is at its maximum angle of attack (the stalling angle). Thus the lowest speed at which the aircraft can fly is its stalling speed.

Stalling occurs at a critical angle of attack, not at any particular airspeed, and the nose attitude may be quite different to the "normal" straight and level stall. If the load factor is doubled, for instance in a 60° banked turn, you will feel 2g (double your normal weight), and the stall speed will be 1.4 times greater. The aerodynamic relationship between stall speed and g-force (load factor) is a square-root relationship. If you pull 2g, the stall speed increases by a factor of 1.4 (the square root of 2), an increase of 40%; instead of 50 kt, the aeroplane will stall at 1.4 × 50 = 70 kt. Stall speed will be increased any time lift from the wings is increased, which will occur in turns, when pulling out of dives, in gusts and in turbulence.

Weight

In straight and level flight, sufficient lift must be generated to counteract the weight. A heavier aeroplane means an increased lift force is required, and this requires a higher angle of attack at any given speed. The stalling angle, however, remains the same. The aeroplane, when it is heavy, will therefore reach the stalling angle of attack at a higher airspeed compared with when it is light.

Stall speed varies directly as weight varies (stall angle of attack stays the same).

The pilot's operating handbook states the stall speed (or the minimum steady-flight speed at which the aeroplane is controllable) at straight and level, power off, for the maximum allowable gross weight. Two stall speeds will be specified: V_{S1}, for the "clean" (flaps up) configuration and V_{S0} for the landing configuration (flaps extended).

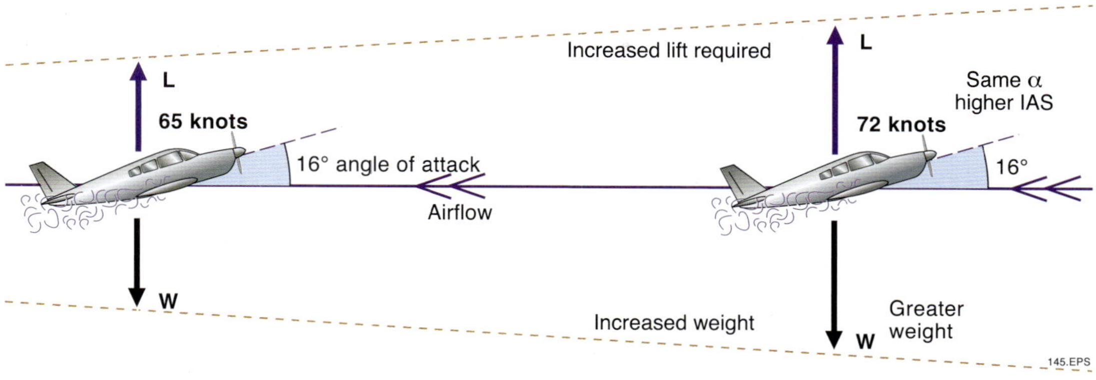

Figure 6-83 Stall speed is a function of weight.

Altitude

The stall angle of attack will be reached (straight and level) at the same stall indicated airspeed irrespective of altitude. If the aeroplane has a stall speed of 45 KIAS at 1,000 ft AMSL (above mean sea level), its stall speed at 5,000 ft AMSL will also be 45 KIAS. (KIAS stands for knots, indicated airspeed – the speed you read on the ASI dial.)

Stall indicated airspeed does not vary with altitude.

Power

With power on, the slipstream adds kinetic energy to the airflow. The separation of the airflow from the upper surface of the inner section of each wing is thereby delayed to a greater angle of attack, and so a more positive stall occurs at a lower indicated airspeed. As the stall angle is approached with power on, the high nose attitude allows the thrust to have a vertical component which will partially support the weight. Therefore, the wings are offloaded a little and less lift is required from them. Less lift means a lowered stall speed.

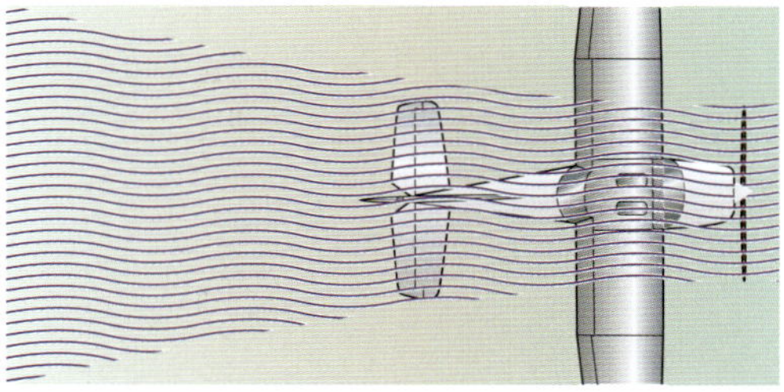

Figure 6-84 Slipstream can lower stalling speed.

Stall speed is less in a power-on stall.

Also, as the power-on stall is approached, the slipstream will provide a fast airflow over the horizontal stabiliser – the rudder and elevator will remain effective, but the ailerons, not being affected by the slipstream, will become "sloppy" or less effective. A power-on stall may be more definite and accompanied by a wing-drop.

If the slipstream encourages the generation of lift from the inner parts of the wing, then the outer sections of the wing may stall first. Any uneven production of lift from the outer sections of the two wings may lead to a rapid roll when the stall occurs. Unwanted yaw and wing-drop can easily be prevented with opposite rudder. Your aircraft design may include stall strips (small wedges on the leading edge of the wing) or twist of the wing (called *wash out*) to ensure that the airflow over the inner section of the wing separates before the outer section.

Flaps

Flap extension decreases the stall speed. Extending the flaps increases the camber and perhaps the area of the wings. The wings can now support the same load at a lower airspeed. The aircraft can fly more slowly before the stall angle is reached. The lowering of stall speed is the main advantage of flaps. They allow safe flight at lower speeds – very useful for take-offs and landings (shorter runways). Also, extending the trailing-edge flaps provides lower nose attitudes – not only is visibility increased, but also the stall angle will be reached at a lower nose attitude.

Ice, frost and mud increases the stall speed. Any build-up has two effects:

- increased weight, and so the stall speed will be increased; and
- contamination on the wings (particularly the front half of the upper surface where most of the lift is generated) will cause separation of the airflow at angles of attack well below the normal stall angle, and so stalling will occur at a higher airspeed.

Load Factor

If the wing has to produce increased lift to manoeuvre the aeroplane at a particular airspeed, such as in a turn or pulling out of a dive, then you will apply back pressure on the control column to increase the angle of attack. Lift will be increased, causing an increased load factor, and you will feel an increase in your g-loading. Turbulence can also increase angle of attack and load factor by changing the direction from which the relative airflow strikes the wing. A sudden upwards gust, for instance, will cause a sudden increase in the angle of attack.

An increased angle of attack in manoeuvres will bring the wing closer to the critical (or stall) angle, even though the airspeed has not changed. In the extreme case, if you increase the angle of attack right to the stalling angle, the wing will stall even though the airspeed is well above the 1g straight and level stall speed. This is known as an *accelerated stall.*

Stall speed increases with load factor, e.g. in manoeuvres.

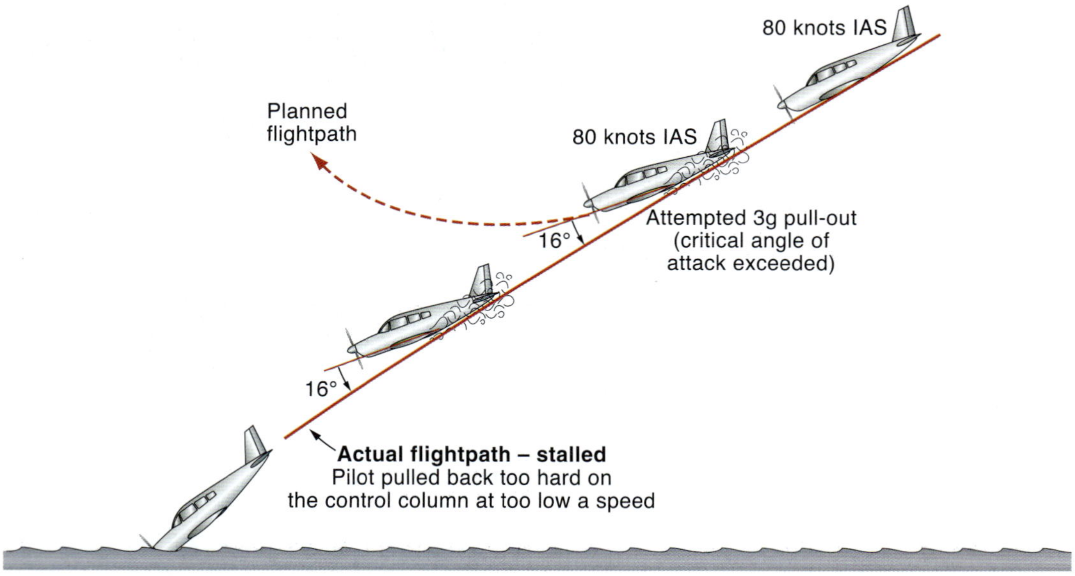

Figure 6-85 Accelerated stall.

Windshear

Windshear, or the significant change in wind from one parcel of air to another, causes a momentary disparity between the aircraft's momentum and its airspeed. If the aircraft is slow and it turns downwind (the wind is from behind), the airspeed drops enough to cause a stall.

Vertical Gusts

A vertical gust, or thermal, changes the angle of attack of the wing. If the aircraft is slow, this may induce a stall above the normal stalling speed.

Bank Angle

The lift force is increased by exerting back pressure on the control column, which increases the angle of attack. This increased angle of attack in a turn brings the wing closer to the stalling (or critical) angle of attack, hence an aeroplane will stall at a higher airspeed in a turn than when flying straight and level. At 30° bank angle, the stalling speed will be approximately 7% greater than the straight and level stalling speed; at 45° bank angle it will be 19% greater; at 60° bank angle it will be 41% greater. For instance, an aeroplane that stalls at 50 kt straight and level will stall at 54 kt in a 30° banked turn and at 71 kt in a 60° banked turn.

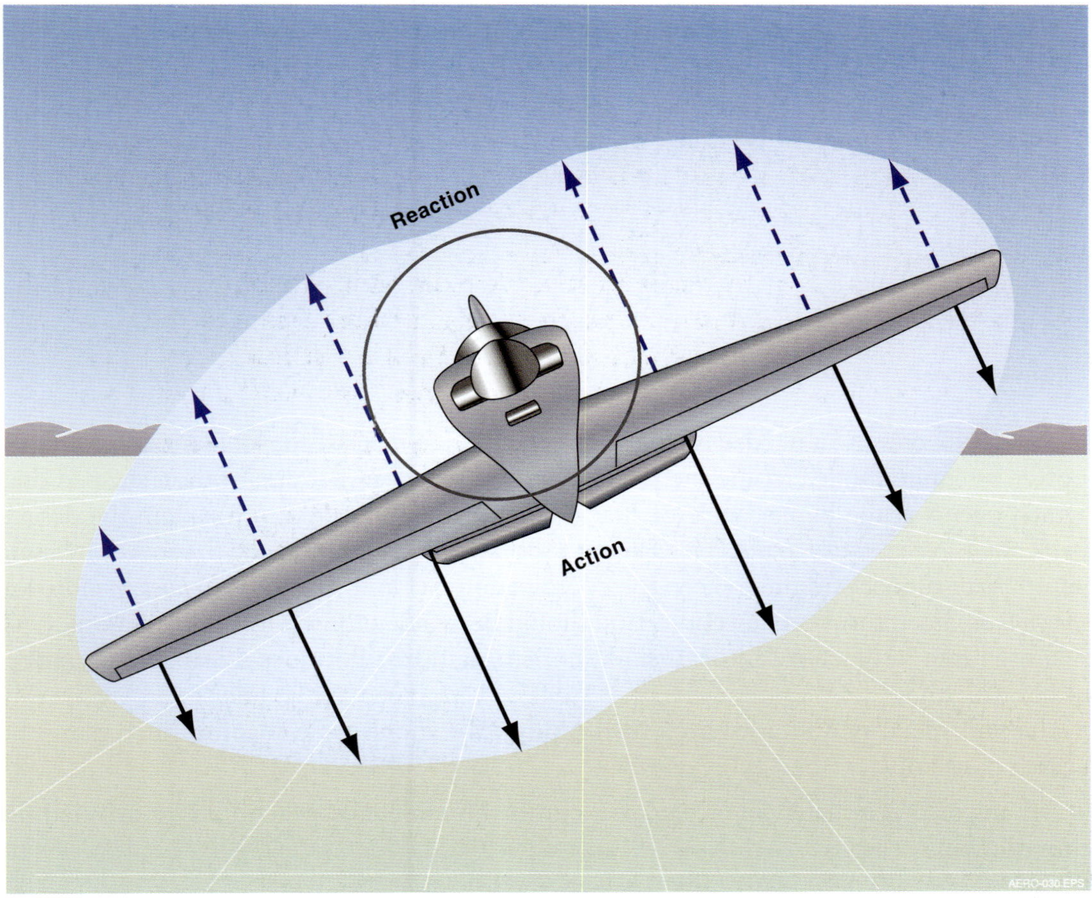

Figure 6-86 The wings provide the force to turn.

Steep Turns

A steep turn is one in which the bank angle exceeds 45°. It is a high-performance manoeuvre which requires good coordination and positive control. A steep level turn requires a significant increase in lift so that:

- a strong horizontal component exists to pull the aeroplane into the turn (the centripetal force); and
- the vertical component is sufficient to support the weight and allow altitude to be maintained.

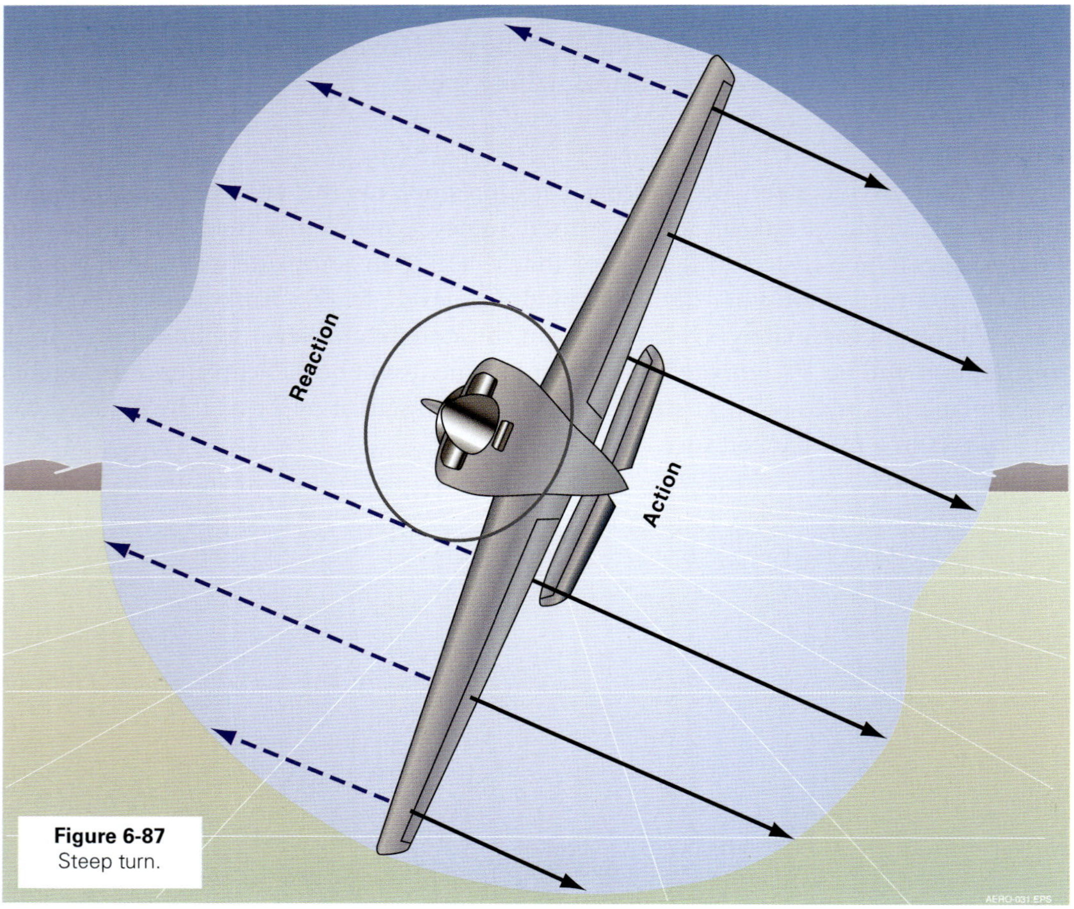

Figure 6-87
Steep turn.

Firm back pressure is needed on the control column to increase the lift force, and increased power is required to overcome the tendency to lose airspeed because of the increased drag which occurs at the higher angle of attack. Ailerons must be used to maintain the desired bank angle as accurately as possible. The turn should be kept coordinated (balanced) by using appropriate rudder pressure to keep the coordination ball in the centre. *Avoid steep turns near the ground.* Steep turns on descent to land should be avoided for the following reasons:

- a high rate of descent can occur in a short time if the pilot does not maintain perfect control; and
- the stall speed will increase in a turn (due to the increased g-loading) increasing the risk of a stall.

Turns of more than 15° of bank on climb-out after take-off should be avoided for the following reasons:

- rate of climb will be drastically reduced;
- the stall speed will increase in a turn (due to the increased g-loading) increasing the risk of a stall; and
- the bank angle could inadvertently increase unless the pilot is very attentive (this is due to a tendency to overbank in a climbing turn).

Steep turns near the ground, if allowed to get out of control, can result in a spiral dive (which, at low altitudes, could end disastrously). In a turn, the angle of attack has to be greater than at the same speed in straight and level flight, to create the additional lift needed to turn the aeroplane as well as support its weight. This means that the stall angle of attack will be reached at a higher speed in a turn. The steeper the bank angle, the higher the airspeed at which the stall angle of attack is reached.

The stall occurs at higher airspeeds in a level turn.

Stalling at higher speeds than the straight and level stalling speed is often referred to as an *accelerated stall.* Any time you experience increased g-loading, the stall speed will be increased – an important point for a pilot to be aware of when manoeuvring.

- At 30° bank angle, the stall speed is increased by 7% over the straight and level stall speed.
- At 45° bank angle, the stall speed is increased by 19%.
- At 60° bank angle, the stall speed is increased by 41%.
- At 75° bank angle, the stall speed is increased by 100%.

If your aeroplane stalls at 50 kt in straight and level, then in a 60° banked turn it will stall at 71 kt (141% of 50 kt) – quite a significant increase. In steep turns, you may feel the onset of the stall buffet even at these high speeds.

The load factor on the wings is increased in a turn.

Flying straight and level, the wing produces a lift force equal to the weight, i.e. L = W. The load factor is said to be 1. The pilot experiences a force from the seat equal to his/her normal weight. He/she feels it as 1g. In a banked turn of 60°, the wings produce a lift force equal to double the weight, i.e. L = 2W. The pilot experiences a force from the seat equal to twice his/her weight, i.e. 2g. The load factor is said to be 2. This is true for all 60° banked turns, irrespective of airspeed or rate of turn or size of aeroplane. The load factor is the ratio of the lift force produced by the wings compared to the weight of the aeroplane.

$$\text{Load factor} = \frac{\text{lift}}{\text{weight}}$$

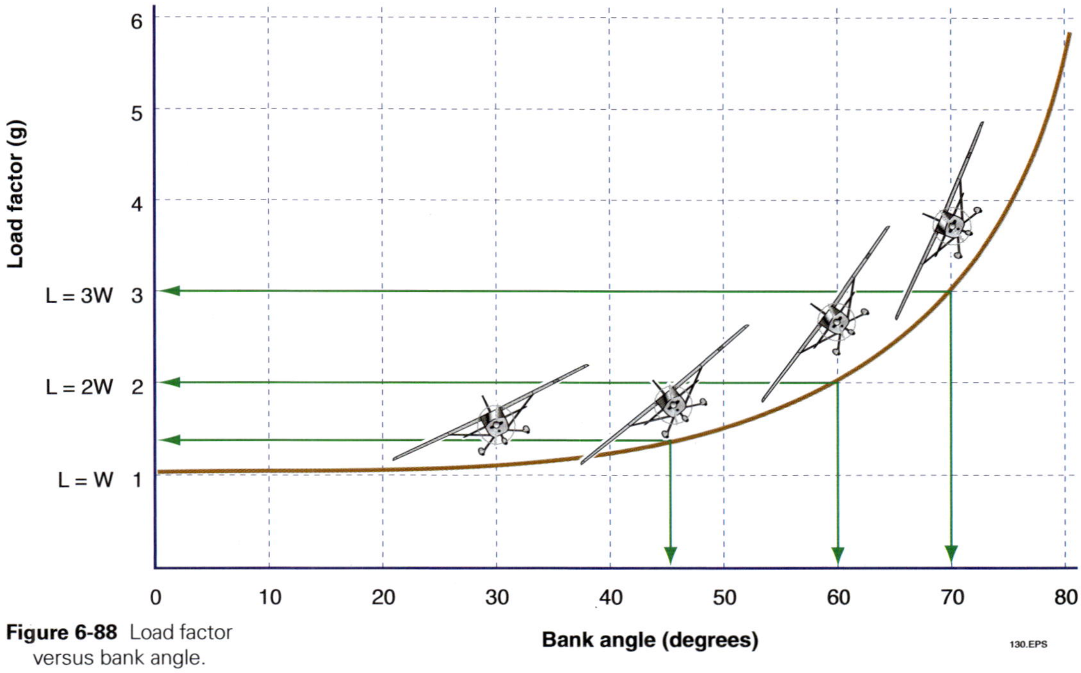

Figure 6-88 Load factor versus bank angle.

At bank angles beyond 60°, the lift force generated by the wings must increase greatly so that its vertical component can counteract the weight – otherwise height will be lost. Increased lift from the wings means increased load factor. We can show this in a curve of load factor vs. bank angle. In a turn, load factor depends on bank angle. Note the following:

- In a 30° banked turn you will experience 1.15g load factor, i.e. the wings will produce 15% more lift than when straight and level, and you will feel 15% heavier.
- At a 45° bank angle, the load factor is 1.4, and so the g-force you would experience will be 1.4 times your normal weight.
- At 60° bank angle, the load factor is 2.

Remember that, if load limits are exceeded, permanent airframe damage is possible.

Departure from Controlled Flight & Spinning

At the point of stall, the aircraft is vulnerable to anything that will cause a lateral imbalance such as the following:

- a gust of wind or a thermal;
- yawing motion that is not stopped;
- power application which gives uneven lift over the wings; and
- control input by rudder or aileron which causes yaw, roll sideslip and changes the relative angle of attack between the left and right wing.

If there is an imbalance, the aircraft will yaw and roll and the motions will become mutually encouraging – yaw leads to more roll and roll leads to more yaw. The aircraft, despite conventional control inputs, will diverge from its path or depart from controlled flight. It was sometimes called "the region of reversed control", because if the wing dropped and the pilot applied opposite aileron control, this would aggravate the situation by causing an increased angle of attack of the dropping (downgoing) wing and by causing an increase in drag of the downward deflected aileron which causes more yaw in the same direction. The result is called *autorotation* – the aircraft rotates by itself. If left to its own devices, the autorotation could lead to a spin.

It is a requirement in the design of training aircraft that they recover from this situation simply by release of the controls. Remember, as soon as the angle of attack is reduced and the wing is unstalled, control is restored. Releasing the controls allows the tailplane to reduce the angle of attack. And of course, the pilot could help more positively by pushing the control column forwards.

If the pilot held the pull force or back pressure on the controls and kept the wing above its critical angle of attack and then did nothing, or worse applied opposite aileron to try to stop the dropping wing, then the aircraft would progressively but quite quickly enter a spin – at first a spin with changing rates and attitudes and ultimately a stable spin with a predictable attitude, rate of turn and rate of descent. This airspeed could be predicted from flight tests, but it is a meaningless figure as the pitot head could cause readings from zero to 100 kt. The airspeed would, however, be low, as distinct from the spiral dive – which we will discuss shortly with its frightening increase in speed, noise, forces and danger.

A spin, like a stall, is not a difficulty if there is sufficient altitude. That's why the practice is only done above 3,000 ft. In the stable spin, the rotation that has built up causes gyroscopic forces to keep the aircraft rotating (Newton again) and to flatten the attitude. The aerodynamic forces are trying to pitch the nose down and reduce the angle of attack to unstall the wings and regain normal stability. A light aircraft won't continue to spin unless it is forced to.

Aircraft vary, but the standard spin recovery includes closing the throttle, centralising the ailerons, applying full rudder opposite to the direction of yaw (to counter the gyroscopic forces) and moving the control column forward (to unstall the wing and reinstate normal control). The dive recovery is then conventional.

Autorotation

There are two elements of the autorotation that occur when a wing drops in stalled flight:

- *autoroll*, where the more-deeply stalled dropping wing generates even less lift and so keeps dropping, causing the aeroplane to continue rolling; and
- *autoyaw*, where the dropping wing generates increased drag and yaws the nose of the aeroplane in the same direction as the roll.

The natural tendency to continue rolling and yawing in the same direction when in the stalled condition is *autorotation*. Autorotation is the basis of the spin. A spin can occur with both wings stalled, or it can occur with only one wing stalled (i.e. the dropping wing) and the rising wing unstalled, producing significant lift.

On some aeroplanes, misuse of ailerons can cause a spin. Trying to raise a dropped wing with opposite aileron may have the reverse effect when the aeroplane is near the stall. If, as the aileron goes down, the stall angle of attack on that wing is exceeded, instead of the wing rising it may drop quickly, resulting in a spin.

This is the spin entry technique used on some older aeroplane types; many modern aeroplanes, however, have ailerons that remain effective right through the stall. (This can be achieved with design features such as wing washout, which results in the inner part of the wing near the fuselage stalling before the wingtip/aileron area.) Application of aileron once a spin has developed may aggravate the spin. Discuss the spin characteristics of your particular aeroplane with your flight instructor.

The Spin

A spin is a condition of stalled flight in which the stalled aeroplane follows a spiral descent path. As well as the aeroplane being in a stalled condition and yawing, one wing is producing more lift than the other, and this results in a roll. The dropping wing is more deeply stalled than the other (which may or may not be stalled). Greater drag from the stalled lower wing results in further yaw, further roll, and so on. Pitching of the nose may also occur. You can induce a spin deliberately by yawing an aeroplane that is stalled, or just on the point of stalling.

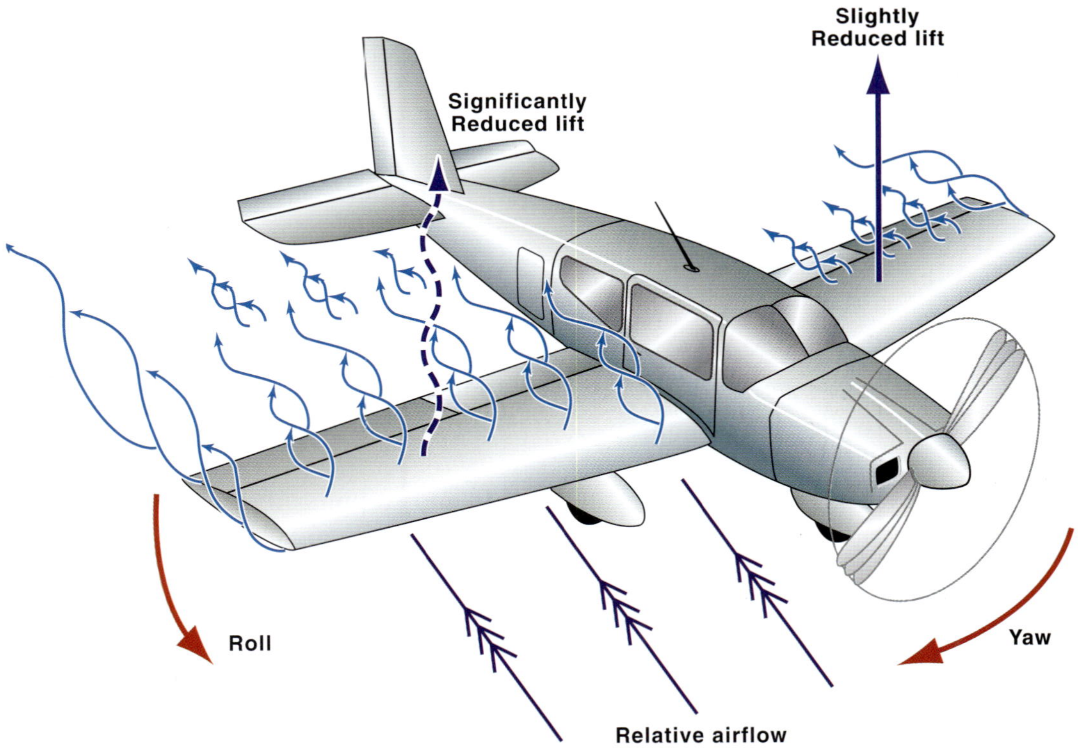

Figure 6-89 The aeroplane entering a spin.

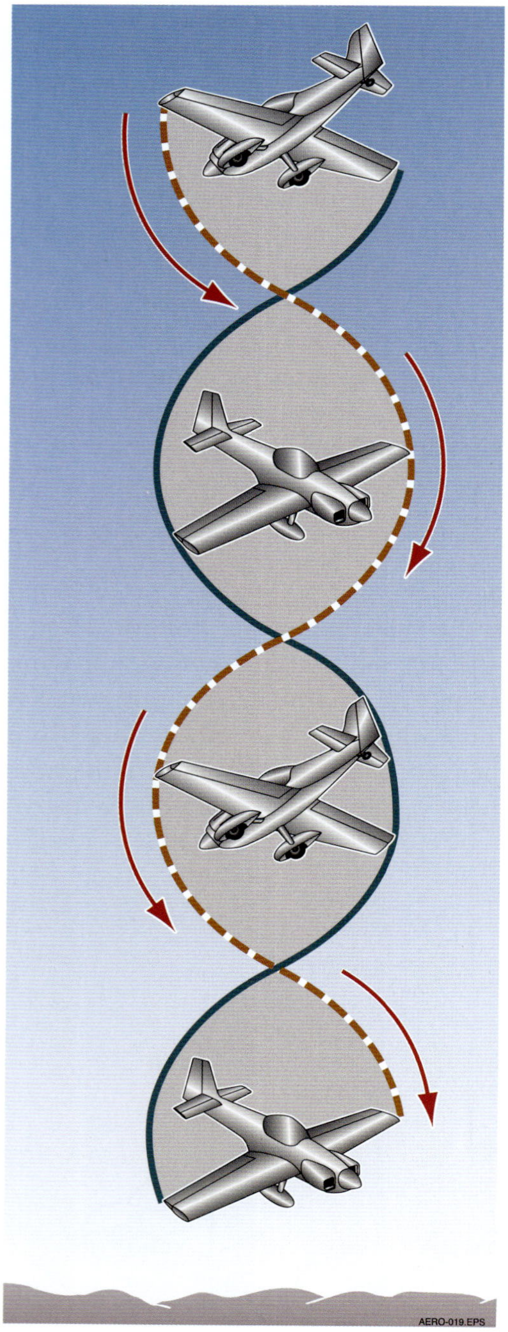

The aeroplane is in motion about all three axes. The aeroplane is:

- rolling;
- yawing;
- pitching;
- slipping; and
- rapidly losing height at a low airspeed.

In a spin, the wings will not produce much lift, since they are stalled. The aeroplane will accelerate downward until it reaches a vertical rate of descent where the greatly increased drag, now acting upward, counteracts the weight. The altitude loss will be rapid as the aeroplane spins downward around the vertical spin axis but, because of the high angle of attack and the stalled condition, the fluctuating airspeed in the spin will remain quite low.

Figure 6-90 The developed spin (steep descent, rapid rotation, low IAS).

Characteristics of a developed spin include a low indicated airspeed (which does not increase until recovery action is initiated) and a high rate of descent. A vital part of the spin recovery is to unstall the wings by lowering the nose (which reduces the angle of attack) and to build up flying speed.

The recovery from a spin involves identifying and stopping the spin rotation using opposite rudder, then moving the control column forward to unstall the wings, and finally easing out of the dive.

The recovery procedure is as follows:

- centre the controls;
- close the throttle;
- apply full rudder opposite to the direction the of yaw;
- apply forward pressure until rotation stops; and
- recover from the dive.

High-Speed Flight

Control surfaces are aerodynamic, that is to say, they generate higher forces at higher speeds. The controls become more powerful, but also the force needed to deflect them increases and so the control column becomes stiff. There is a speed for your aircraft which must never be exceeded (V_{NE}) and a speed that must only be exceeded in smooth air (V_{NO}). The approved flight envelope for the aircraft is shown on a V-n diagram.

V_A is the maximum speed for full deflection of the controls.

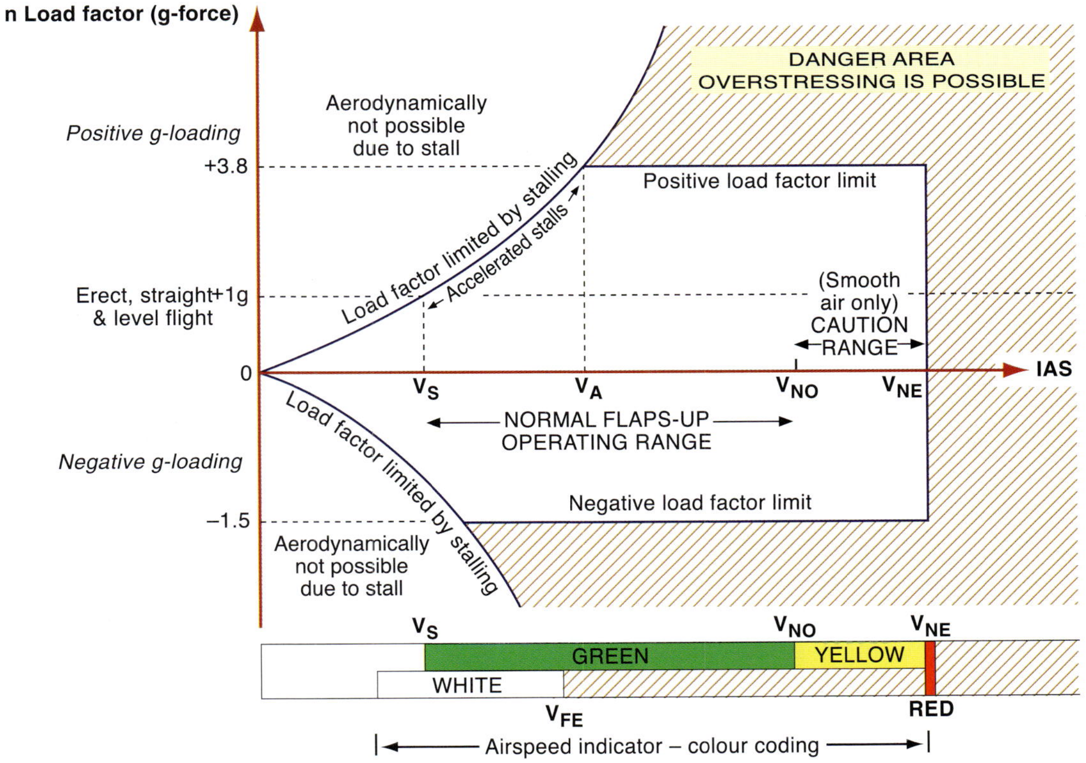

Figure 6-91 A typical V-n diagram related to airspeed indicator colour coding.

At high speeds, make all control inputs smooth. The aircraft will react more firmly to turbulence, so ensure the seat belts are secure, and if there is any discomfort, reduce the power, raise the nose and slow down. Below V_A, the aircraft cannot be damaged. Anticipate turbulence below puffy clouds and near hills on a windy day.

Load Factor

An aircraft is designed to certain strength criteria. For us, FAR 23 requires a design maximum load factor of +3.8g. This figure includes a margin for safety where the ultimate limit load factor where major failure could occur is 1.5 times more.

The Spiral Dive

A manoeuvre that must not be confused with a spin is the spiral dive, which can be thought of as a steep turn that has gone wrong. In a spiral dive, the nose attitude is low, the wings are not stalled (unlike in a spin), the airspeed is rapidly increasing and the rate of descent is high – a spiral dive is really just a steep and steepening descending turn. Because the wings are not stalled, there is no need in the recovery from a spiral dive to move the control column forward like you do when recovering from a spin.

To recover from a spiral dive:

- close the throttle (to reduce speed);
- look for the horizon;
- roll the wings level with ailerons; and
- gently ease out of the dive with elevator (you can expect to feel increased g-loading which must be controlled).

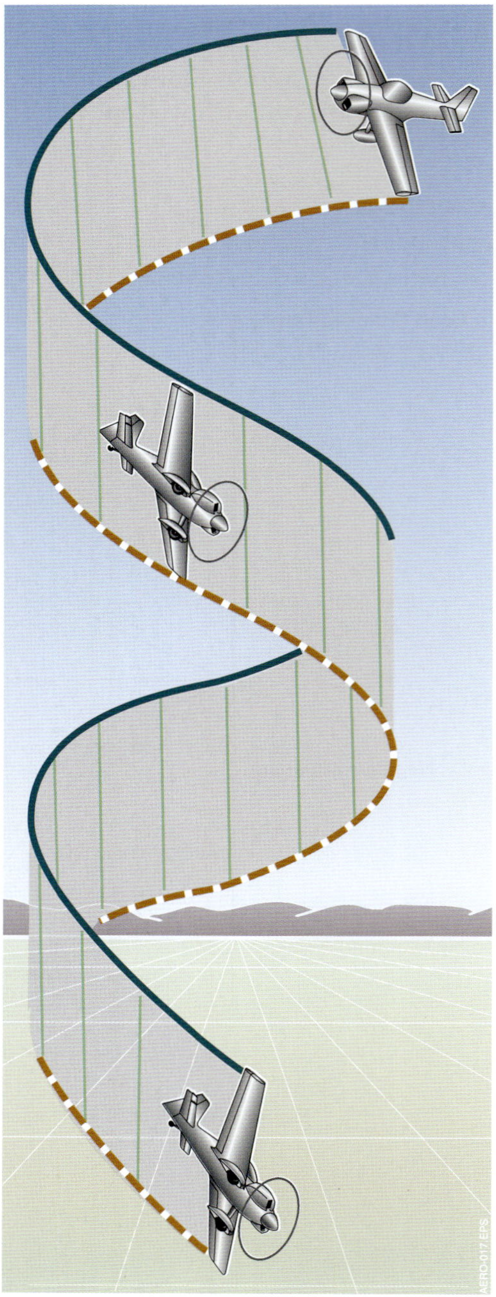

Figure 6-92 Spiral dive (rapid descent, high IAS, increasing bank and load factor).

How Does It Happen?

The aircraft is trimmed for, say, 90 kt straight and level and we are distracted enough to allow the aircraft to start turning very slightly. The bank will slowly and subtly increase then the aircraft's natural stability for once works against it by progressively tightening the turn.

As the bank angle gently increases, the nose lowers and the airspeed starts to increase. As the airspeed increases, the tailplane wants to cause the nose to rise, but because we are banked, it tightens the turn instead. As the turn tightens, the speed increases further, the nose drops and the turn tightens more. The result is an ever-tightening spiral where the aircraft's maximum speed and load factor would be exceeded.

If at any stage the thrust were reduced, the wings were levelled and the nose gently raised to the straight and level attitude, there would be no danger whatsoever. However, in cloud or at night with an inexperienced pilot or a failed attitude indicator, the subtle departure from straight and level is often not detected until it its too late, and at the very high speeds that can result, the dive recovery carries its own risk of structural failure. There is no reason for a spiral dive to develop when there is a clear horizon, and there is no excuse to be flying without a clear horizon – unless the aircraft and pilot are both equipped to do so.

Circuit & Landing

Take-Off & Initial Climb

Take-off is the transition from being ground-boune to being airborne – from wheel-borne to wing-bourne. The aircraft is accelerated through a fast taxi to a point at which flight is possible. At this point (speed), the pilot raises the nose to increase the angle of attack of the wing. At this low speed, a high angle is required. With this angle, the wings lift the aircraft from the ground. The aircraft is then accelerated to a normal climb, and the undercarriage and flaps are retracted.

A short-field take-off and landing is designed to use minimum ground roll. A cross-wind take-off and landing makes allowance for conditions in which the wind is substantially misaligned with the runway.

Closed Circuit

Normally, after establishing a normal climb, the aircraft tracks to the training area. For repetitive practice, we may instead turn onto downwind to fly a closed circuit for training. All aircraft arriving for a landing join via a normal circuit pattern.

Why a Circuit?

The aircraft is established via a circuit for three reasons:

- *Traffic.* The circuit gives the opportunity to identify and locate other traffic and for them to know where you are before you join the standard pattern at the same altitude as the other aircraft;
- *Surface conditions.* It gives the opportunity to assess the wind, drift and turbulence and to choose the appropriate runway; and
- *Base.* It allows the pilot to position the aircraft at the same height, distance, speed and configuration for the approach to provide the best and most consistent start point for the final approach. This is the *base turn position.*

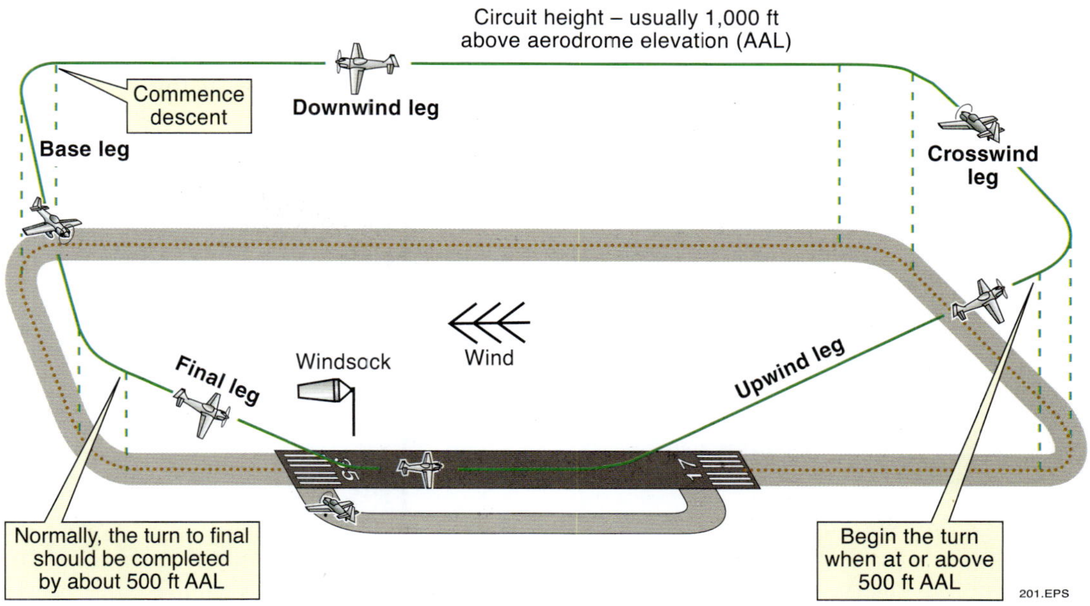

Figure 6-93 Legs of the circuit.

Final Approach

Final approach is different from normal attitude flight in that the primary flightpath reference is now a point on the runway. What is the final approach? It is simply a positioning stage where the landing configuration is established and the aircraft is slowed for landing. The aircraft is aligned with the runway on the centreline, wind is allowed for and the aircraft is stabilised on an approach path of 3–4 degrees.

Flaps are wonderful for the final approach and landing:

- They steepen the glide by increasing the drag, and therefore the descent has to be steeper to maintain speed.
- They require a lower nose attitude for the same speed to compensate for the increased camber and area of the wing and consequent increase in lift. This lower attitude improves the forward view over the nose.
- They reduce the stalling speed and therefore allow the aircraft to be flown more slowly to land with the same margin of safety.
- The increased drag also helps to slow the aircraft on touchdown.

Flapless Approach

If for any reason the flaps are not available, then there are several effects:

- The approach path is more difficult to fly as the nose attitude is higher and the forward field of view may be restricted.
- The airspeed is more difficult to control as there is less drag to slow the aircraft, and so the approach has to be flown at a higher speed to retain a margin above the increased stalling speed.
- Because of the more efficient glide, the aircraft has to follow a shallower approach path and so the circuit pattern has to be extended.
- Visual judgement is different from a normal approach.
- The threshold speed is higher and the reduced drag causes a more prolonged float in the flare.
- The flare itself is very small as the attitude change from the shallower path is less.

Flying the Visual Approach

When you fly an approach, you will notice a significant difference from all other phases of the flight. For the first time, you are flying to a specific point on the ground or trying to maintain a path over the ground, whereas up until now, you just set the attitude and thrust, and they determined the flightpath. The pilot uses attitude as the reference until lined up on final approach and then refers to a visual aim point on the runway, which is held a constant distance below the horizon.

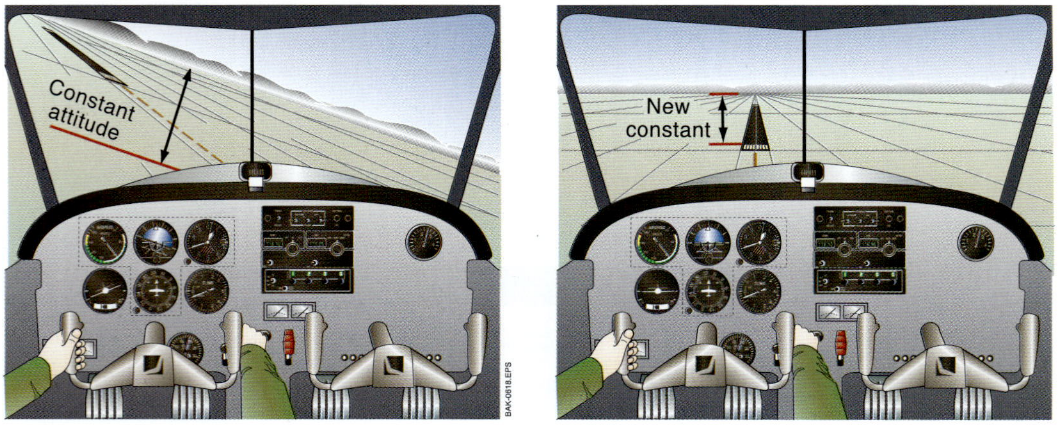

Figure 6-94 Visual approach references.

You will now notice the effects of wind and see that where the aircraft is pointing is not necessarily where it is going. You will make continuous small adjustments to the attitude, direction and thrust to reach the aim point on the runway. This is explained in detail in the *Flying Training Manual*.

It is important to anticipate and to coordinate all aileron inputs with rudder and all elevator inputs with some throttle adjustment. The approach is much easier to judge and fly if the aircraft is stabilised early, in the landing configuration (flaps), at the correct speed and on the centreline.

Flare & Touchdown

The change of flightpath from the approach to the touchdown is called the ***flare*** or ***round out***. The landing flare is judged visually.

When you wish to touch down, there is a need to reduce the thrust so that the landing roll is not extended. However, if the throttle is closed before the aircraft is flared for landing, it makes the landing more difficult. This is due to the following:

- nose down pitching moment when the throttle is closed, just when you want to raise the nose;
- the loss of propeller slipstream causes reduction in lift, just when you need a little extra lift to change the flightpath and to soften the touchdown (remember more lift is needed for level flight than for the descent, and some extra is need to cause the change); and
- a reduction in elevator power because of the reduced slipstream, just when you want the elevators to raise the nose, they have less power.

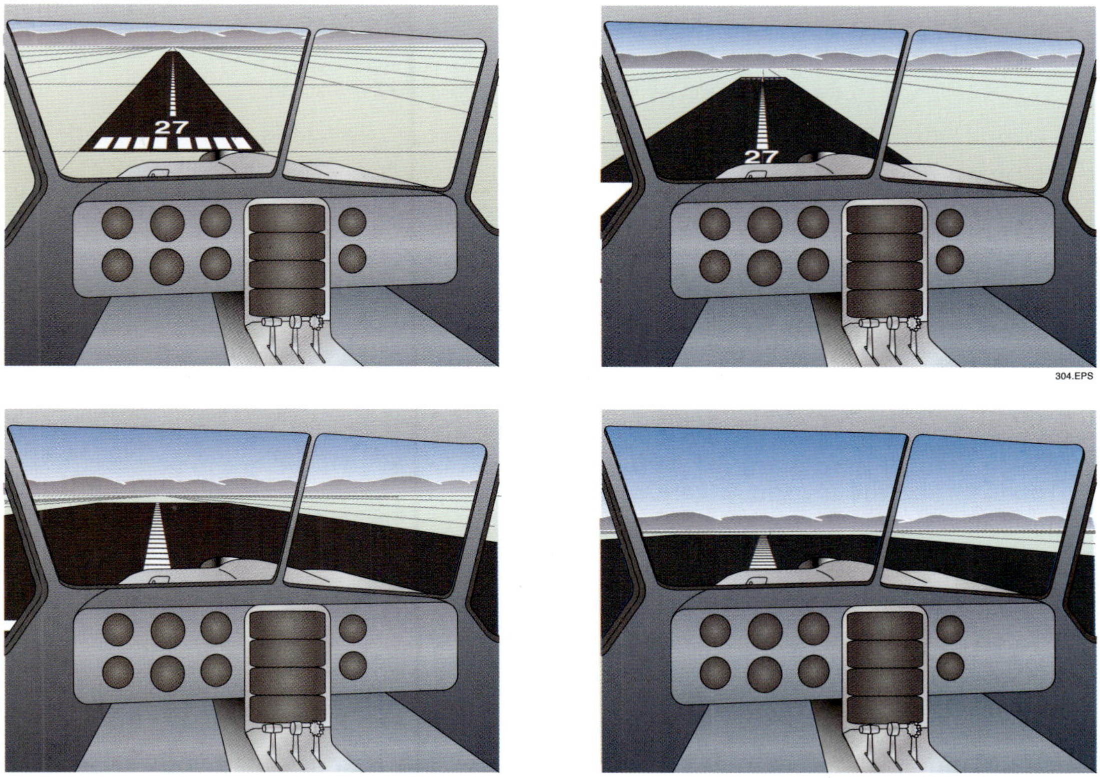

Figure 6-95 Typical attitudes in the approach and flare.

The aeroplane suddenly becomes out of lift, out of balance and out of trim. In some cases, if speed is excessive, it may be necessary to retard the throttle earlier – but be ready for these effects.

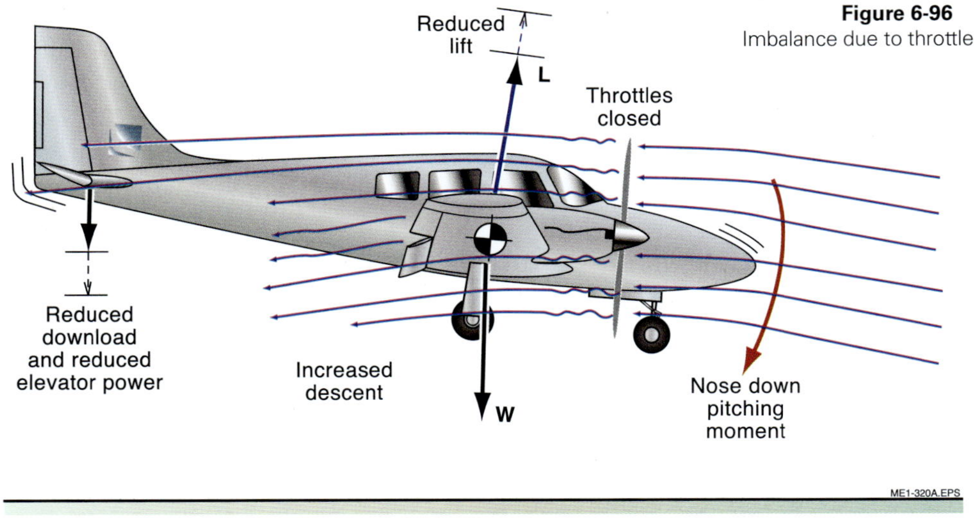

Figure 6-96
Imbalance due to throttle closure.

Ground Effect

When the aircraft is about to land, the downwash behind the wing reaches the surface of the runway. This gives the aircraft added lift or buoyancy and it will tend to "float".

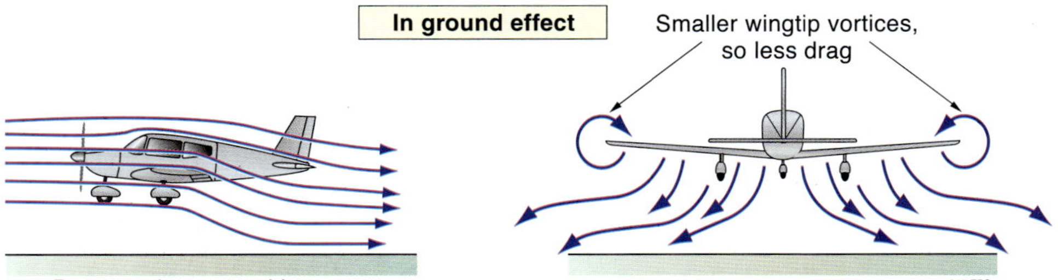

Figure 6-97 Near the ground, the upwash and downwash are restricted and the formation of wingtip vortices is restricted.

Ground effect becomes more significant as the wing gets closer to the ground. It is therefore more noticeable in a low-wing aircraft.

Approach Speed

Your aircraft and school will have recommended approach speed called V_{REF} (reference speed) or will nominate a threshold speed (the speed at which you cross the threshold of the runway). The approach speed is critical.

Figure 6-98 Wheelbarrowing.

- Too slow and the margin of control above the stall is reduced and the aircraft could sink before the runway.
- Too fast and the landing configuration will not be correct. The nosewheel could touch first and control could be very difficult. The nosewheel could even collapse. This is called *wheelbarrowing.*

Also, the greater speed requires a much greater stopping distance.

We have now considered how an aircraft flies within a parcel of air. But what if the air moves or is disturbed?

Review 6

Pre-Solo Level of Knowledge

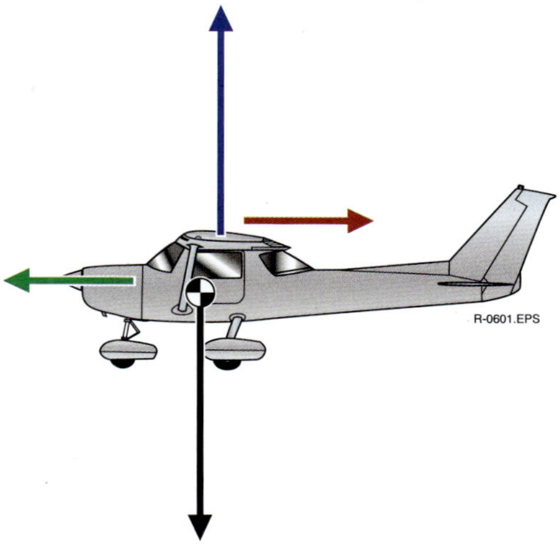

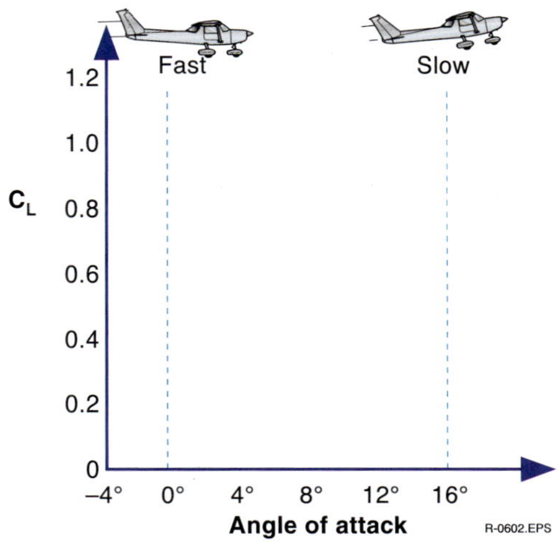

1. To change the speed or direction of a moving object, an . . . . . force must be applied.
2. The change in speed or direction is . . . . . to the applied force.
3. What is a moment?
4. What is gravity?
5. Name the four major forces acting upon an aircraft in flight.
6. Draw the C_L/α curve on the diagram opposite.
7. Define attitude, flightpath and angle of attack.
8. What is balance?
9. How is it indicated?
10. What is trim?
11. How is it adjusted in pitch?
12. What is straight and level flight?
13. What is a climb?
14. How does a pilot enter a climb?
15. What does the pilot need to check in the climb?
16. How does a pilot return to straight and level flight from a climb?
17. How does a pilot enter a climb or a glide?
18. How does a pilot return to straight and level flight from a descent or glide?
19. What force causes the aircraft to turn?
20. What is sideslip and how is it corrected?
21. How does a pilot enter a turn?
22. How is the turn maintained and what reference does the pilot use?
23. How is the aircraft straightened from a turn?
24. What are the general symptoms of an approaching stall?
25. How could the pilot avoid an impending stall?
26. What causes the stall?

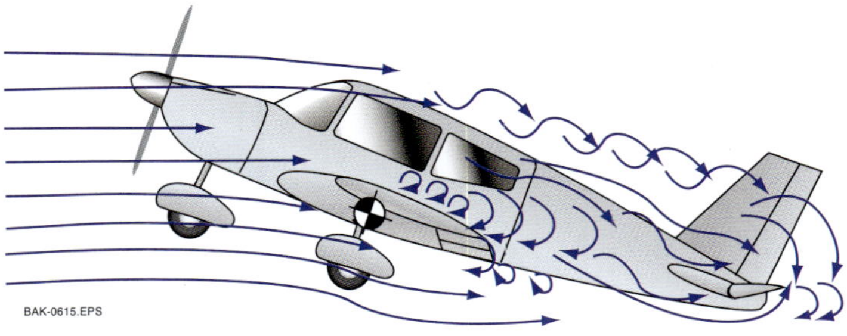

27. Why must the pilot not use the ailerons during the stall recovery?
28. What is meant by flapless?
29. What is the flare?

30. Name the primary controls.

31. List the direct effect of each of the primary controls.

32. Name the axes and the point through which they act.

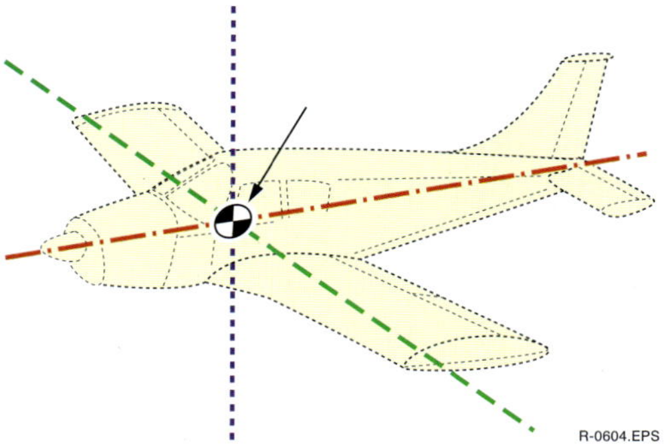

BAK Level of Knowledge

33. Describe the effects of Newton's laws of motion.

34. What two factors determine the size of a moment?

35. What is positive g?

36. What is the temperature at sea level of a standard day (ISA)?

37. What is the standard pressure at sea level in ISA?

38. Name the three moments acting on an aircraft in flight:

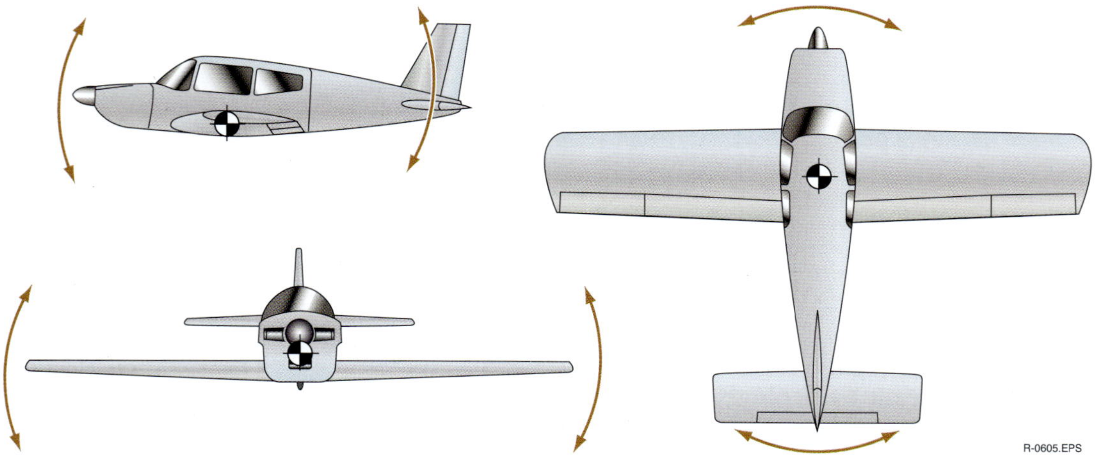

39. What is laminar flow?
40. At what point does the flow change from laminar to turbulent?
41. What was discovered by Bernoulli?
42. Label the following diagram:

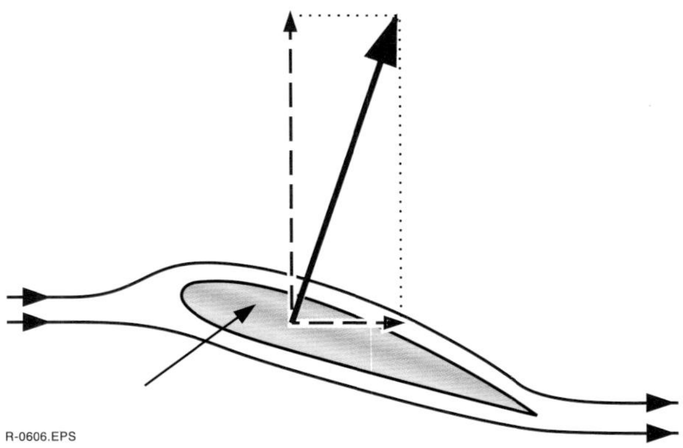

43. Name the types of drag.
44. Plot, on the graph, the total drag curve and its major constituents.

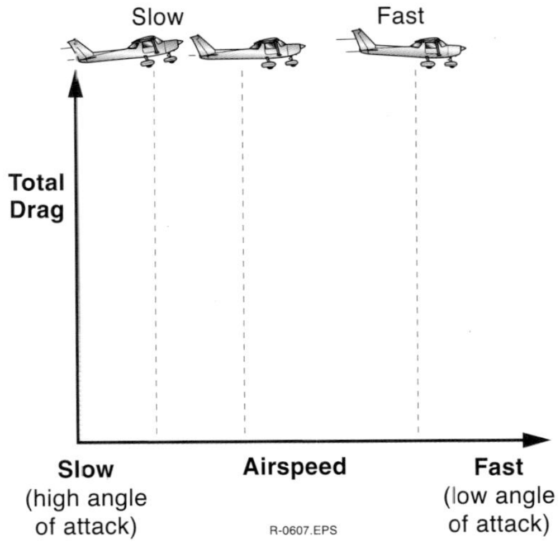

45. Label the following diagram:

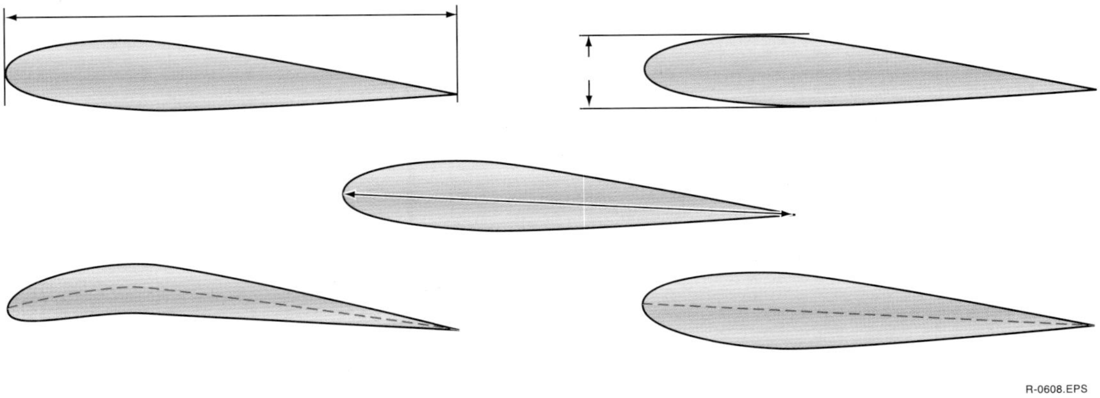

46. Describe the indirect effect of each of the primary controls, including thrust.
47. Describe the types of climb.
48. List the factors which affect climb performance.
49. What is a normal and a comfortable rate of descent.
50. What is a steep turn?
51. What is the correct recovery technique for a stall?
52. Write the equation which explains the relationship between the factors which contribute to the lift in straight and level flight.
53. Over which of these factors does the pilot have control?
54. The stalling speed in straight and level varies with . . . .
55. Describe a spin and the major differences between a spin and a spiral dive.
56. What happens in ground effect?
57. Why it is generally unwise to close the throttle before commencing the landing flare?

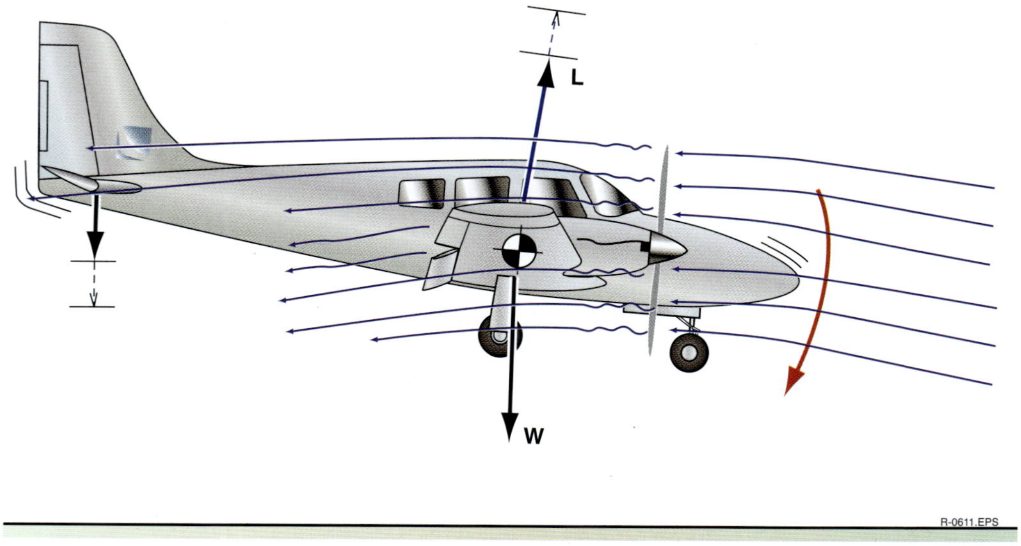

58. Label the following diagrams:

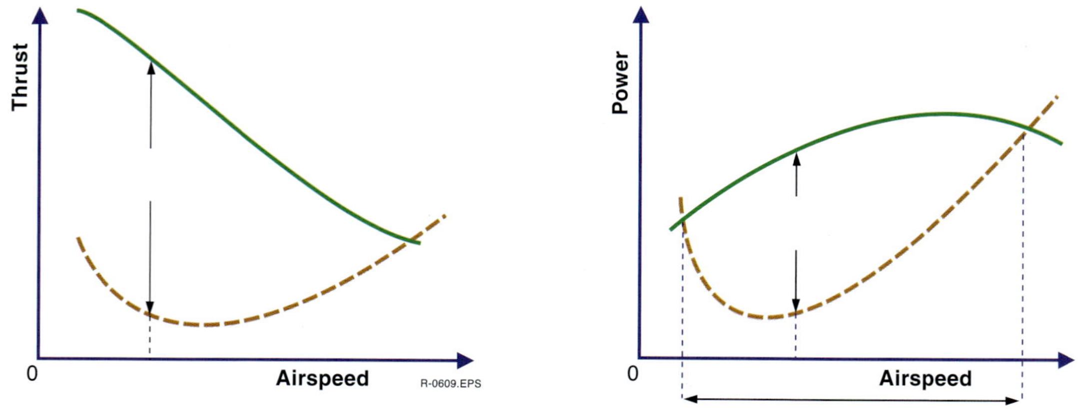

7 - Atmospheric Effects on Flight

Aviation
Theory
Centre

Introduction

We have studied dynamics (motion) and aerodynamics (motion through the air). However, there is a further complication. It is the most important aspect of learning to fly and to navigate. So far, we have considered an aircraft moving through a static parcel of air. But the air itself is rarely stationary. The movement of the aircraft through the air is compounded by the movement of the air itself. This movement obviously is wind. Together they determine the movement of the aircraft relative to the earth.

We'll first examine the effects of a steady wind, then a variable or gusting wind, and then vertical movements of the air. As well as moving, the nature of the air is constantly changing, and despite using the standard atmosphere for comparison, we have to take into account the actual conditions and the effect that the variation, particularly of temperature, humidity, pressure and density, will have on the aircraft's performance. This latter aspect is actually measured when the aircraft is tested and the flight manual has performance charts for the effect of these changes on your aircraft.

Air Density

The "thickness" of the air on which we depend for lift and thrust varies with pressure and temperature. The parameters are intimately interwoven. If we take a parcel of air and squash it, its pressure increases, as does its temperature and its density (same amount of air squeezed into a smaller space). More dense air gives more lift, more drag, greater stability and greater control power. Less dense air gives less.

The engine breathes air and so the pressure, temperature and density also affect its performance. Thrust reduces with reduced density (the propeller has less mass to push) and the engine power output is reduced because there is less mass and less oxygen in each charge that is fired in the cylinders. Also, high outside air temperatures (OAT) mean that there is less temperature rise in combustion and so less power.

To take these factors into account, we need a measure or scale. The performance charts for the aircraft use a parameter, which takes into account the effects of pressure, temperature and density. This is called *density altitude* (DA). It is the equivalent altitude in the standard atmosphere that has the same density of air that corresponds to these values at your elevation. Thus a density altitude of 4,000 ft means that the aircraft will behave as if it is actually at 4,000 ft in the standard atmosphere.

For example, consider that we could be taking off at, say, Canberra, which is nearly 2,000 ft above sea level (your airfield elevation) and the temperature may be 40°C (25°C above ISA and therefore a much lower air density, equivalent to being at about 5,000 ft altitude). Aircraft performance is affected because we now have to travel at a higher TAS to achieve the same IAS and so the take-off run, in particular, will be much longer.

It is very useful to compare the performance of your aircraft in typical summer and winter conditions and from aerodromes of various elevations. It is valuable to know the "ball-park" figures. Your charts may have a direct scale for density altitude, or indirectly for pressure altitude and temperature, which gives the same correction.

Airspeeds

Indicated Airspeed

We use *indicated airspeed* (IAS) as a measure of aircraft performance. Indicated airspeed is not truly a speed at all. It is a measure of the dynamic pressure of the air. This dynamic pressure takes into account both the density of the air and our speed through it. So the same indicated airspeed gives the same aerodynamic forces irrespective of pressure, temperature and density. That is why indicated airspeed is the most important parameter for the pilot. Lift, drag, stability and control depend on it.

True Airspeed

We know that the atmospheric pressure, temperature and density reduce with altitude. Using indicated airspeed accounts for this. An indicated airspeed of 100 kt at 10,000 ft gives the same forces as 100 kt at sea level. However, our actual (true) speed through the air is different as we have to travel faster to build the same dynamic pressure. This *true airspeed* (TAS) can be measured or calculated if we know the pressure (altitude) and outside air temperature (OAT). Some airspeed indicators have a separate scale for this.

Calibrated Airspeed

There is another speed that you will come across called *calibrated airspeed* (CAS). Calibrated airspeed is just the indicated airspeed corrected for errors in the pitot–static sensors and the airspeed indicator itself. CAS may be considered the actual indicated airspeed corrected for specific errors in our aircraft. The flight manual will have both IAS and CAS readings for limiting speeds.

Wind

Wind is moving air. Consider that the aircraft is moving through a parcel of air. If the air itself is moving, then the path of the aircraft as perceived by someone on the ground will be a combination of the two motions.

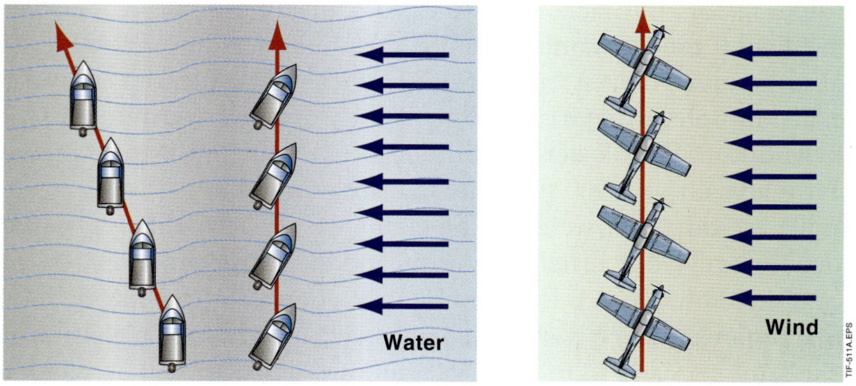

Figure 7-1 Direction – pointing versus travelling.

The path of the aircraft through the air, called the flightpath, is measured by speed (airspeed), direction (attitude and heading = where the aircraft is pointing), altitude and rate of climb or descent. When the air moves and the path relative to the ground is described, the speed is called groundspeed and the direction is called the *track*. The difference between heading and track (the difference between where it is pointing and where it is going) is called *drift*.

Taxiing

When the aircraft is on the ground, it cannot drift and so the only effect is that of the wind trying to lift the aircraft or to damage the control surfaces. Depending on the nature of the aircraft and the strength of the wind, there may be specific control techniques to keep the weight on the wheels and to maximise control on the ground. . .

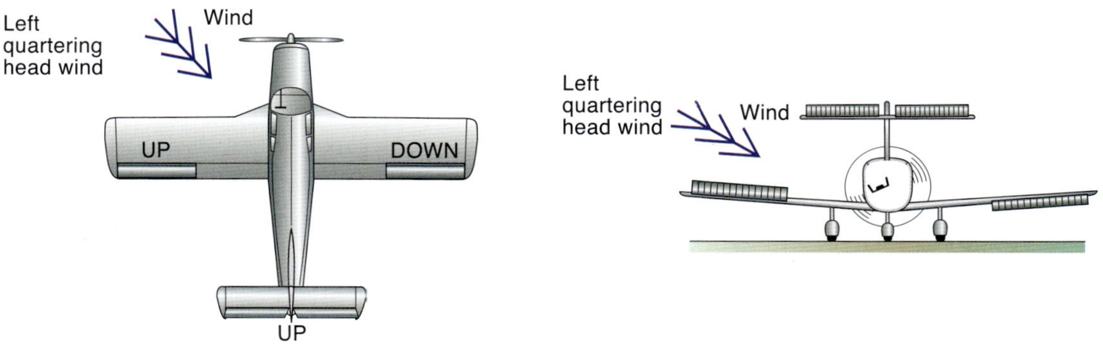

Figure 7-2 Taxiing with a left quartering headwind.

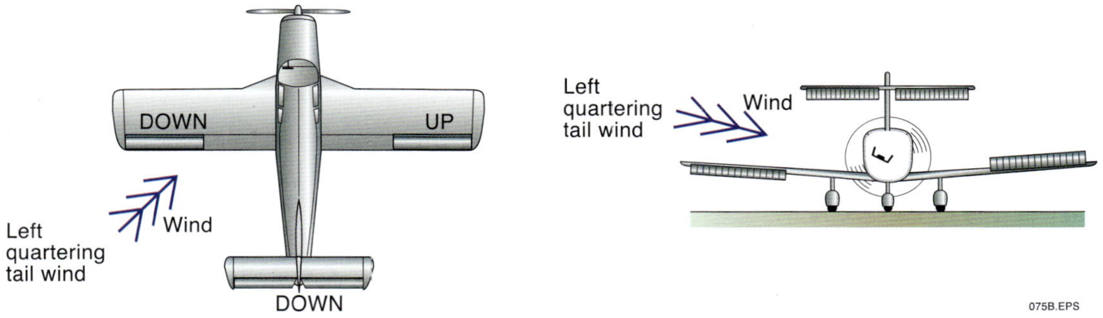

Figure 7-3 Taxiing with a left quartering tailwind.

. . . and to keep straight.

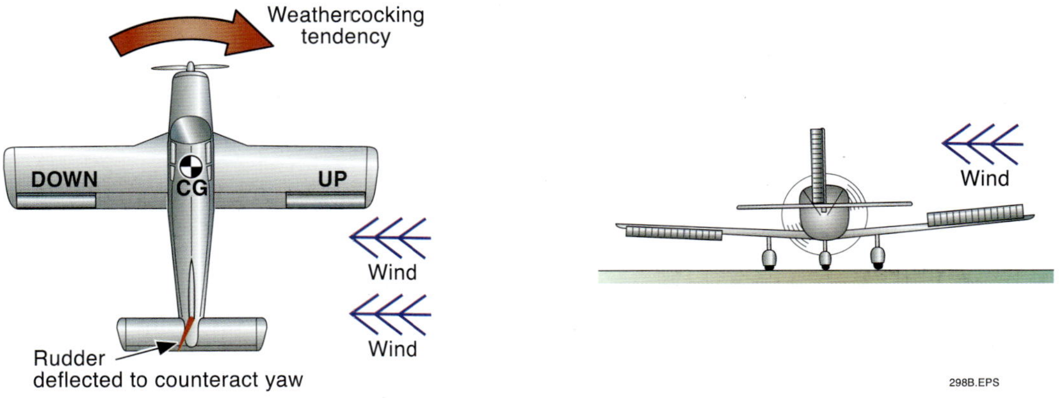

Figure 7-4 Keep straight with rudder and wings level with ailerons.

Also, hold the control column to prevent the wind deflecting the control surfaces.

Take-Off & Initial Climb

On take-off, the aircraft accelerates through the air even though it is on the ground. If it needs an airspeed of 60 kt to lift off then it has to achieve this through the air.

If the air is moving away at 20 kt, then the aircraft has to reach a speed over the ground of 80 kt to achieve 60 kt of speed through this moving parcel of air. It has to catch up by that amount. Acceleration to this speed takes longer and therefore a greater distance is travelled over the ground.

If the air is blowing towards the aircraft at 20 kt, then the aircraft only has to reach 40 kt over the ground to achieve an airspeed of 60 kt – much less time and distance. It has a head start.

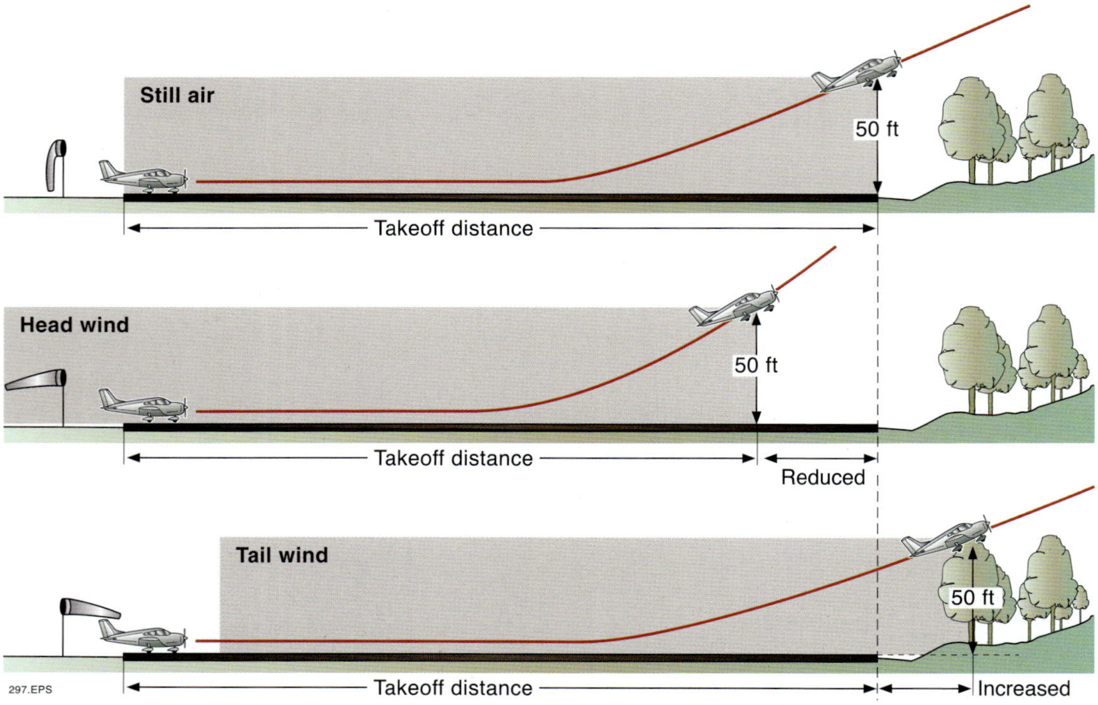

Figure 7-5 Effect of wind on takeoff.

So all aircraft of all sizes take off into the wind (against the wind) if they can.

Wind against us is called headwind and with us is called tailwind. Wind direction is always measured from where the wind is blowing; for example, a wind of 270° is blowing from the west. The speed is measured in knots because the airspeed is indicated in knots and the pilot then can easily calculate the effect of the wind. If the wind is not directly ahead or behind the take-off direction, then there will be part of the wind across the runway (called the cross-wind component or simply crosswind) and a headwind component.

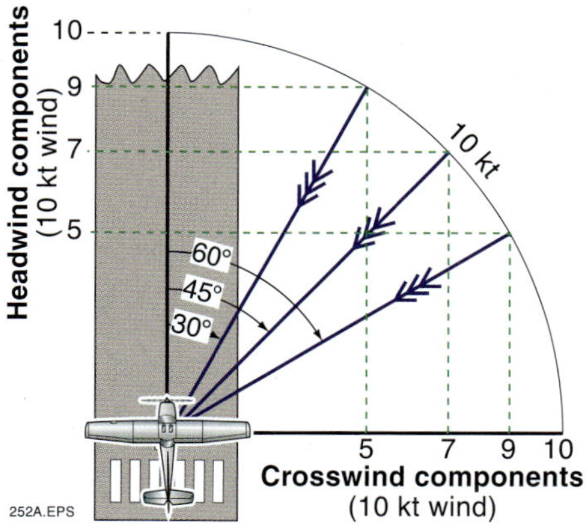

Figure 7-6 Estimating crosswind component.

Only the headwind or tailwind component affects the take-off distance, but the crosswind component causes some control difficulties. Each aircraft has a demonstrated maximum crosswind component that has been established by the test pilots. This is the maximum that a current pilot should accept before changing runways or cancelling the flight.

Climb

The path, speed and rate of climb of the aircraft through the air remain the same, but if the air is moving towards the aircraft, the path will be steeper – when measured from the ground. Conversely, it will be shallower if the wind is blowing from behind the aircraft. So to have the steepest climb after take-off, perhaps to clear high ground, we always climb into wind – until safely clear.

Cruising

When cruising we allow for wind in the planning and the flight. Obviously a headwind will reduce the groundspeed and the flight will take longer. Downwind the speed over the ground is faster and we will get home sooner. Drift is compensated by heading in an offset direction to achieve our desired track. This is the basis of visual navigation.

Descending

Descending into a headwind causes a steeper approach relative to the ground. Descending downwind increases the distance travelled. There is no change to the time taken to descend (the rate of descent).

Flying at Low Altitude

The effect of wind is more noticeable at lower altitudes where the relative movement of objects on the ground is more noticeable. We have examined the effect of drift and the analogy of the boat crossing the river. If we were flying downwind, we would zoom along whereas into wind, everything would seem slow – which it is, relative to the earth. But of course, we have exactly the same airspeed.

Figure 7-7 Low flying.

It is a little more complex when we are turning as both the groundspeed is changing and so is the drift. If we are turning near the ground and we are looking at features, we seem to slide out of the turn – like skidding when we turn from downwind to crosswind, and we seem to drift into the turn when we turn from into wind to crosswind. Again all at the same airspeed and the aircraft is perfectly balanced.

Consider a weight swinging on the end of a string. The speed through the air is constant and equals the speed over the ground (figure 7-8).

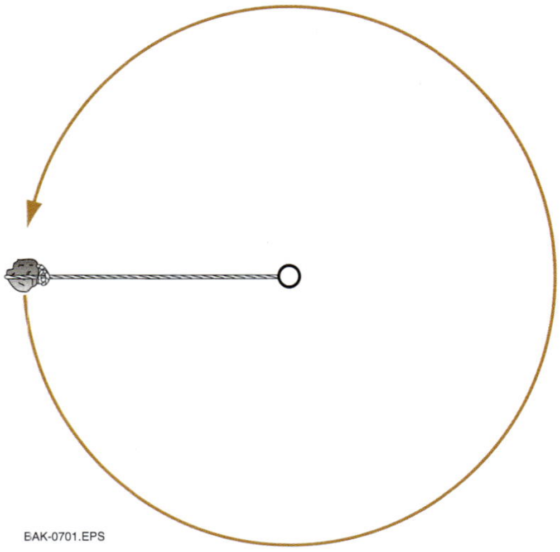

Figure 7-8 Static pivot point.

Let's now swing the weight from a moving platform. If we were standing on the platform, the weight would follow the circle as before – relative to the platform. If we were standing on a hill, looking down at the moving platform, we would see the weight following a spiral path.

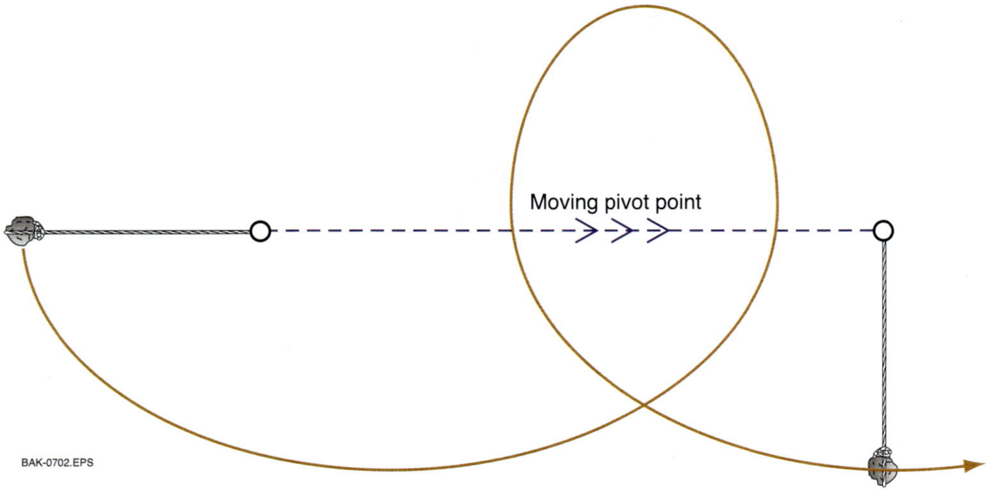

Figure 7-9 Moving pivot.

If we now consider the aircraft flying a circle in a moving parcel of air, the effect is identical. From a balloon moving with the air, the aircraft would appear to follow a circle at a constant speed – as it is.

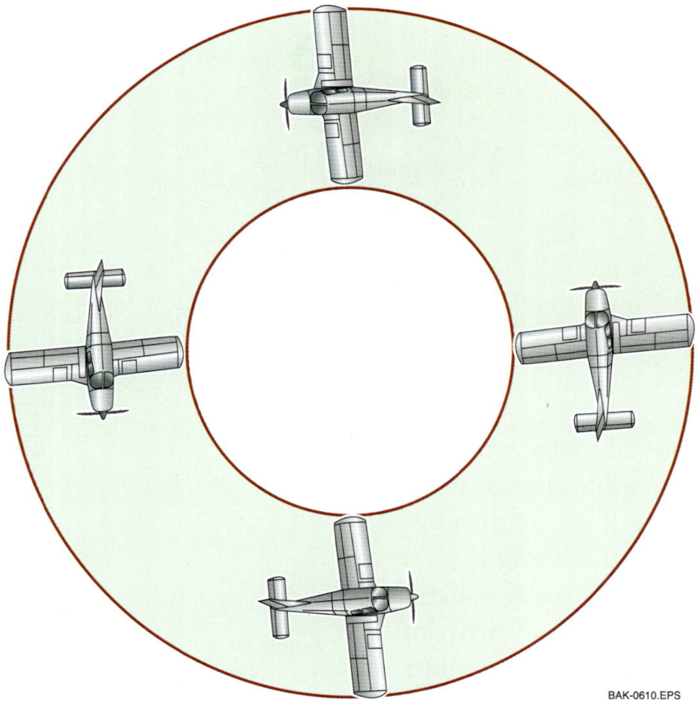

Figure 7-10 Turn in nil wind.

But relative to the ground, the aircraft is changing from an into-wind path (no drift, groundspeed least) to across the wind (maximum drift, groundspeed equalling airspeed) to a downwind path (no drift, groundspeed maximum) to another cross-path with drift now in the opposite direction.

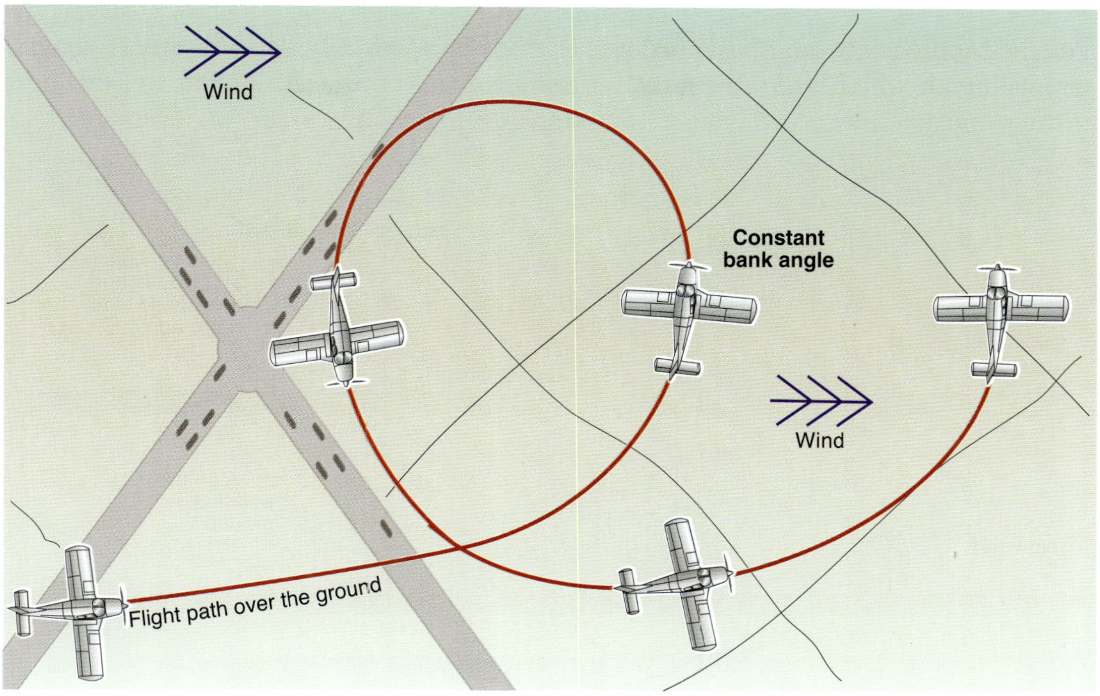

Figure 7-11 Turn relative to the ground.

It can be a trap if the pilot tries to compensate for the apparent drift or speed by making control adjustments. The most dangerous situation is when going from the downwind path to a crosswind path and trying to stay within a feature on the ground. Display pilots know this situation well. There is a great danger of an accelerated stall. There is a further danger on the downwind segment if the pilot feels the speed is too fast (which the speed over the ground will suggest). If the pilot reduces power and speed as the aircraft turns across the wind, there is a further risk of stall. The pilot must cross-refer to the airspeed indicator and be sensitive to any excessive back pressure that may be being applied. If in doubt, or uncomfortable, level the wings, increase power and climb.

Circuit

The effect of wind in the circuit is considerable, and it is the most difficult and most important aspect of flying for the pilot to anticipate and to learn.

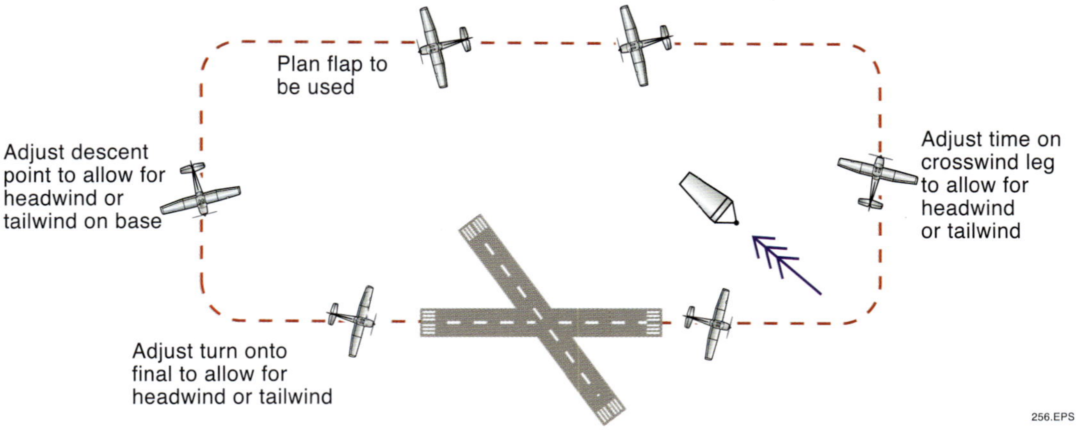

Figure 7-12 Flying the crosswind circuit.

It comes with practice.

Approach

The final approach to land is significantly affected by wind. A headwind causes a steeper approach path which, from the same start point, would cause the aircraft to land short of the runway.

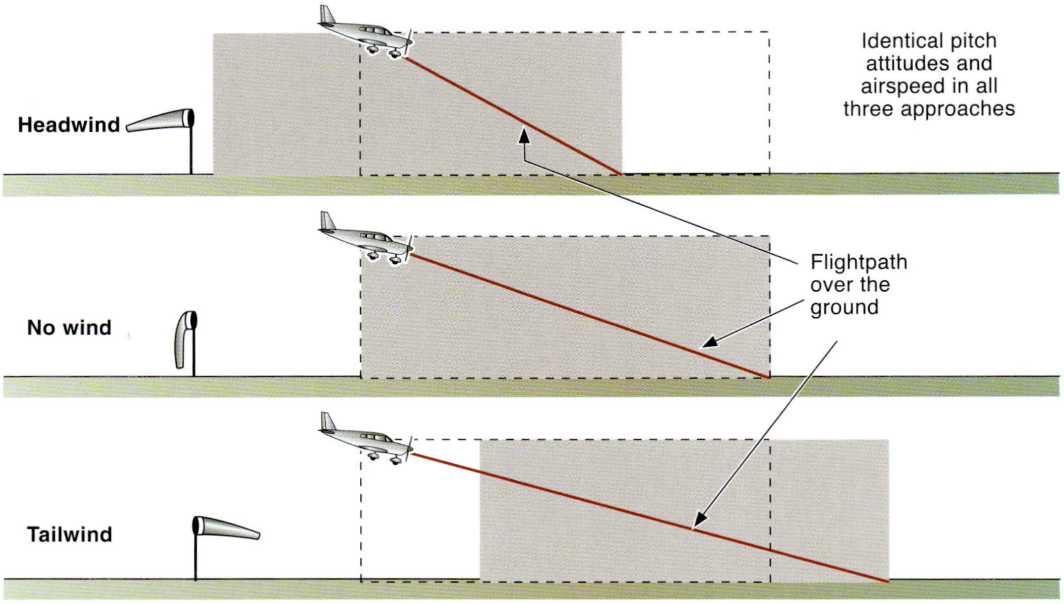

Figure 7-13 Effect of wind on approach.

We could turn base closer and allow for a steeper approach but that upsets the appearance of the runway and affects our judgement. The steeper path also affects the landing flare as the aircraft attitude has to be changed further. It is better to maintain the same approach path by establishing a shallower descent path through the air.

To do this we either increase speed (which would cause a higher approach speed, more difficult flare and a longer landing run) or reduce the rate of descent. Therefore in windy conditions, extra thrust and a slightly higher nose attitude are needed to carry the aircraft to the threshold. A useful rule of thumb is that the rate of descent in feet per minute should be about five times the approach groundspeed in knots. In nil wind, an approach speed of 80 kt then gives a ROD of 400 fpm. With a 20 kt headwind, the groundspeed is reduced to 60 kt and so the ROD should be about 300 fpm (groundspeed is 75% of the normal value, so should be the ROD). It would be useful to establish for your aircraft how much additional rpm or MP is needed to achieve this – it is a guide only, but nevertheless useful.

Figure 7-14 On centreline.

A crosswind component on final also requires the pilot to select an offset point to compensate for drift. The pilot's visual aim point on the runway remains the same but the aircraft has to be pointed to one side to achieve the aim point.

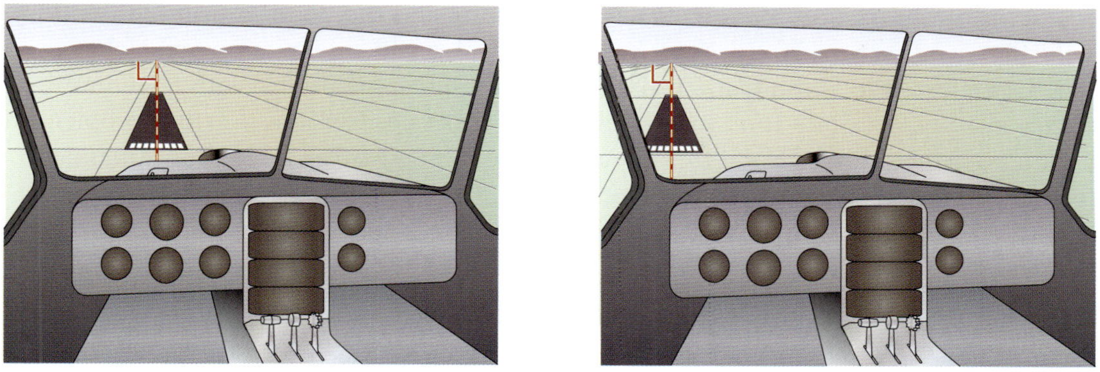

Figure 7-15 Crab technique.

To clarify this, the aim point is the point where the pilot's eyes would impact the runway if the flightpath was maintained with no flare. The aircraft would have to be pointed (aimed) at an offset point to achieve this. This is called a *crabbed* or *crabbing approach* (crabs walk sideways).

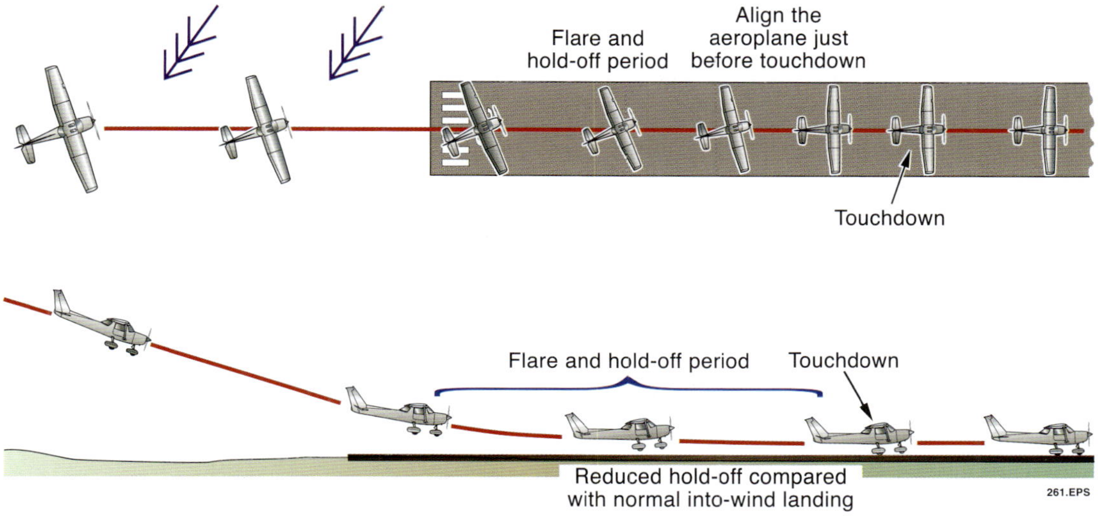

Figure 7-16 Crabbing approach involves aligning the aeroplane just prior to touchdown.

The alternative is to sideslip the aircraft by banking and stopping any turn with opposite rudder (called a *wing-down approach*). The sideways component from the wings causes the aircraft to sideslip through the moving parcel of air at the same rate as the air is moving relative to the ground.

Figure 7-17 Wing-down approach.

Landing

A headwind shortens the ground run because the groundspeed on touchdown is lower – for the same airspeed. The braking distance is proportional to the square of the groundspeed at touchdown and so is very significant.

Windshear & Wind Gradient

The wind usually increases in strength as you move further away from the ground. This is a result of the friction forces between the ground and the wind, causing the wind to slow down near the surface. Any change in wind speed or direction with change in height is referred to as *windshear.* It has the greatest effect on aircraft with large momentum as they take a finite time to accelerate or decelerate. It is a less serious problem in light aeroplanes, although the turbulence and vertical gusts can effect control and performance more severely than a large aircraft.

Take-Off & Climb

Taking off into a headwind would normally mean that you would climb into an increasing headwind, which tends to increase your airspeed and increase the climb gradient (steepness). An increasing headwind leads to increased performance.

Taking off downwind in a windshear situation risks climbing into an increasing tailwind; the effect is a little like trying to catch a bus that is accelerating away from you! The windshear tends to decrease your airspeed, hence the nose must be lowered to retain the desired indicated airspeed. This and the increased movement over the ground cause the climb angle to be degraded. If you are climbing at V_X, there is little airspeed margin above the stall. Another situation to avoid is turning downwind after take-off. If there is a significant crosswind and you turn away from the wind, you risk a momentary loss of airspeed, an increasing groundspeed and a reduced climb gradient. It is better to turn into a crosswind after take-off, if you can. When experiencing windshear, you can only leave full power set and adjust the attitude to restore the desired airspeed and flightpath – but don't "chase" the airspeed fluctuations.

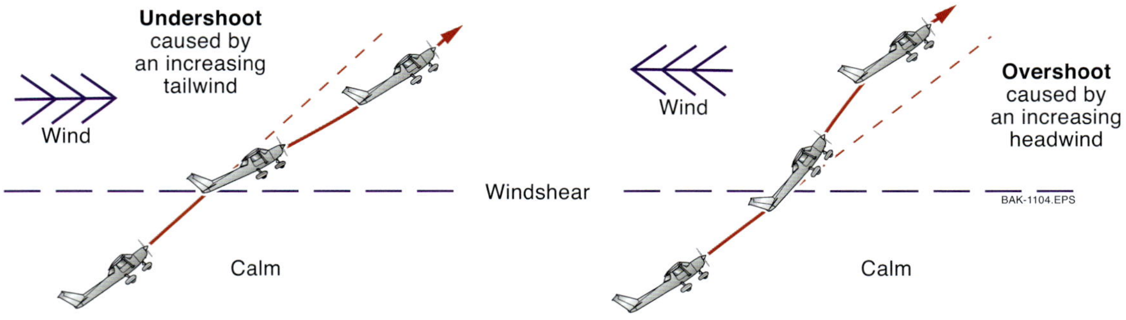

Figure 7-18 Effect of windshear in the climb.

Cruise

Windshear in the cruise is not significant, as you will be cruising within one layer of air. However, it can be a problem near hills, especially on the downwind side.

Figure 7-19
Downdraught near hills.

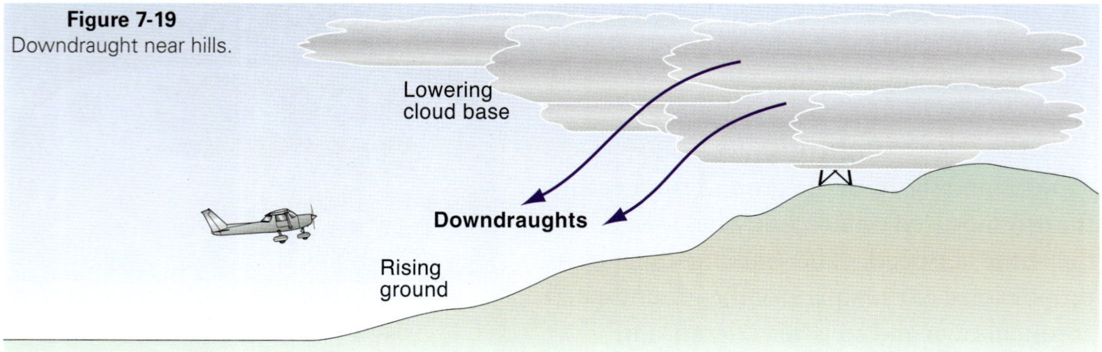

Approach & Landing

On an approach to land, small but virtually continuous changes of power and attitude will be required to maintain the desired flightpath. You will need to be ready to correct any tendency to go above or below the flightpath.

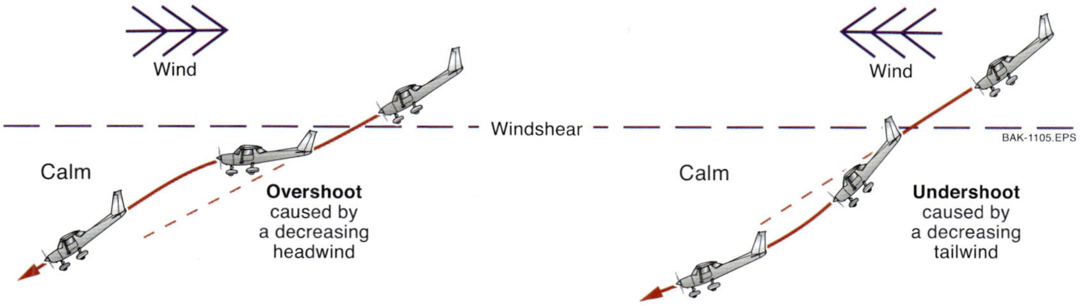

Figure 7-20 Effect of windshear in the descent.

Example 7-1

An aeroplane on approach to land descends from an overlying tailwind into a calm wind. The effect is similar to stepping from a moving train onto a stationary platform. Your body wishes to maintain its original speed (speed of the train or groundspeed) due to its momentum, and your legs will have to move fast when they first touch the platform. No doubt you will act quickly to adjust to the situation (maybe from a run to a walk). In the same way, an aeroplane entering a new parcel of air will initially maintain its groundspeed (due to its inertia). Since the new parcel of air is stationary, the airspeed will show a sudden increase, and the pilot can see this on the airspeed indicator. (Groundspeed is not displayed in light aircraft.)

With the sudden increase in airspeed, the nose of the aeroplane will tend to pitch up, and the temporarily improved performance will cause the aeroplane to move above the desired flightpath. You would reduce power and adjust the pitch attitude to regain the desired airspeed (50 kt on the airspeed indicator) and to regain the desired flightpath. Once back on speed and on slope, further adjustments of power and attitude will most likely be necessary – probably a small increase in power and a higher nose attitude to hold the airspeed and not go below slope.

Since the initial effect of the windshear in the case illustrated is to increase performance, causing an overshoot in the airspeed and/or an overshoot of the flightpath, it is referred to as an *overshoot effect*.

An overshoot effect due to windshear will occur when an aeroplane flies into:

- a decreasing tailwind;
- an increasing headwind; or
- an updraught (e.g. a thermal).

An undershoot effect due to windshear will occur when an aeroplane flies into:

- a decreasing headwind;
- an increasing tailwind (for instance, flying near the ground under a thundercloud); or
- a downdraught, such as just under the base of a mature thunderstorm.

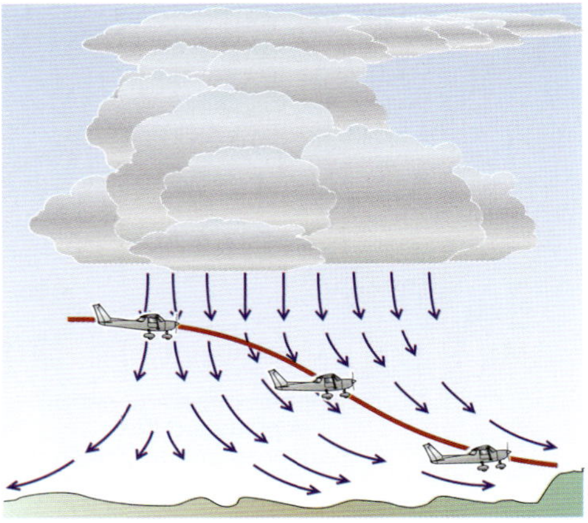

Figure 7-21 Severe downdraughts beneath cumulonimbus (Cb) storm cloud.

Example 7-2

An aeroplane on approach to land descends from an overlying headwind into calm air. In this case, the aeroplane will lose 10 kt of airspeed as it passes through the windshear, its nose will tend to drop, and it will go below the desired flightpath. This is known as *undershoot effect*. Appropriate corrective action would be to add power and raise the nose to regain airspeed and the desired flightpath, and then, when on speed and on slope, adjust the power and attitude as necessary.

Figure 7-22
The aircraft is vulnerable during the approach.

Turbulence

Mechanical

Mechanical turbulence is caused by the wind blowing over, around, through and between various obstructions such as mountains, trees, buildings, valleys and tunnels. The wind is forced up and slowed down as it approaches the object and can be severely disrupted causing eddy currents and vortices. The air is lifted over the object and then pours down and around the lee (downwind) side. There can be significant turbulence and downdraughts on the lee side of the hill, and some smaller aircraft cannot climb as fast as the air is descending. The stronger the wind, the greater the turbulence and the greater the danger. It is best to avoid hilly terrain altogether and especially the lee side on a windy day. It's not very pleasant. Particularly stay away from cliffs, sheer faces, ravines and sudden changes in terrain.

Most of the severe turbulence is in the layers of air closest to the ground and the energy reduces as you get higher. One to two thousand feet of height above the local ground will clear you of the most severe mechanical turbulence – most of the time.

Thermals

Thermals are rising currents of air caused by the uneven heating of the ground. In summer, they can be quite severe and it is sometimes necessary to cruise at seven or eight thousand feet to avoid the worst turbulence. Also, they are most severe if you fly under a developing, or developed, "lumpy" cumulus cloud. The thermal activity is strongest when the heating of the earth is most active. Early mornings and late afternoons are a better time to fly in summer. When flying in turbulence, try to keep the attitude constant and ignore the pressure instruments – otherwise your control inputs may aggravate the situation. In a strong thermal, you may need to reduce power to maintain your selected altitude. Thermals also affect the final approach path.

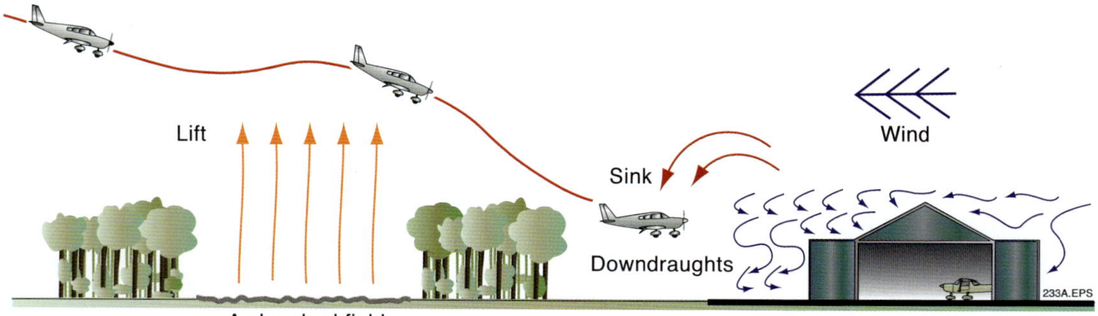

Figure 7-23 Thermals and mechanical turbulence.

Wake Turbulence

As a wing produces lift, the higher static pressure area beneath the wing forces a flow around the wingtip to the lower-pressure area above. The greater the pressure differential (high angle of attack), the greater is this flow around the wingtips.

Figure 7-24 Vortex.

At the high angles of attack necessary to produce the required lift at low speeds, very large and strong *trailing vortices* are formed. As the aeroplane is moving through the air, the wingtip vortices trail behind. Low aspect ratio wings tend to produce stronger wingtip vortices than long, tapered wings, but the greatest influence is the weight in relation to the size of the wing (the wing loading) and the weight in relation to the span of the wing (the spanwise loading).

Figure 7-25 Jets leave large vortices - especially this magnificent aircraft (now retired).

Angle of attack is greatest when an aeroplane is heavy, is flying slowly, and the flaps are retracted. As a large and heavy aeroplane is rotated for take-off or flared for landing, the angle of attack is particularly high. The wingtip vortices can be strong enough to upset a following aeroplane, by inducing a very strong rolling moment or a direct downdraught. This effect is known as *wake turbulence.*

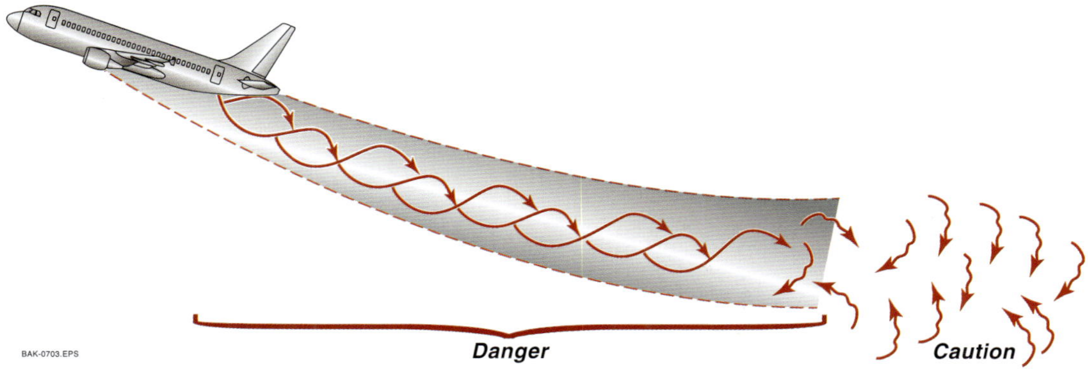

Figure 7-26 Wake turbulence.

The wake turbulence behind a Boeing 747 can even affect a B737 or a DC-9, and can cause a light aeroplane to become uncontrollable. The induced rolling moment may exceed the aileron control power of the aeroplane, making it impossible for the pilot to hold the wings level.

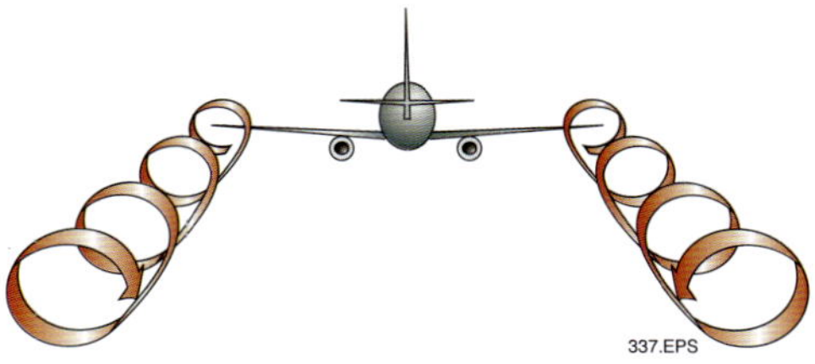

Figure 7-27 Wingtip vortices.

Wake turbulence dissipates to a safe level fairly quickly. However, air traffic control may delay the operation of light aeroplanes behind heavy jets for up to five minutes. Heavy aeroplanes leave strong vortices as they move through a parcel of air.

This parcel then moves with the wind.

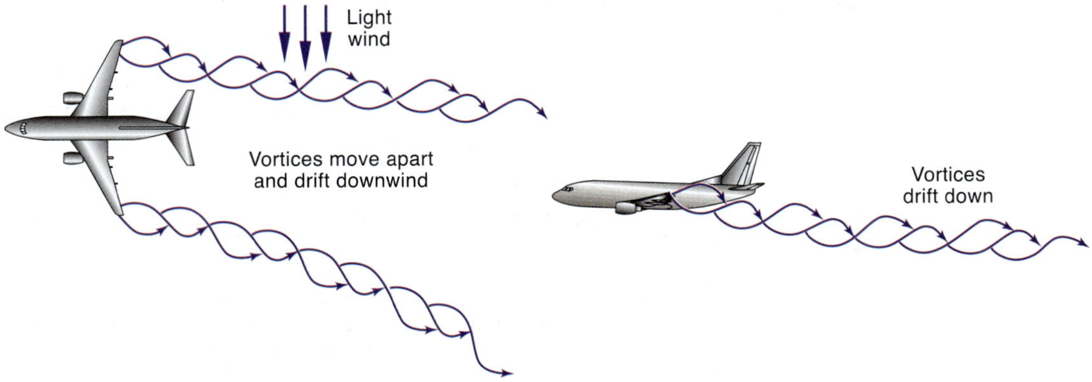

Figure 7-28 Movement of vortices.

A crosswind will cause the vortices to drift off the runway. A light crosswind, however, may move the upwind vortex across the centre of the runway, where it could be most dangerous. A headwind or a tailwind will carry the vortices down the runway in the direction of the wind. In calm or light and variable wind conditions, the vortices will just hang around.

How to Avoid Wake Turbulence

If possible, avoid passing through wake turbulence at all. Fly above and upwind of the flightpath of the aircraft producing wake turbulence. Remember, large aircraft are capable of steep climb gradients after take-off.

On Take-Off

When taking off behind a large aeroplane which has itself just taken off, commence your take-off so that you will become airborne well before the point where the "heavy" rotated or to where its vortices may have drifted. If doubtful, delay your take-off.

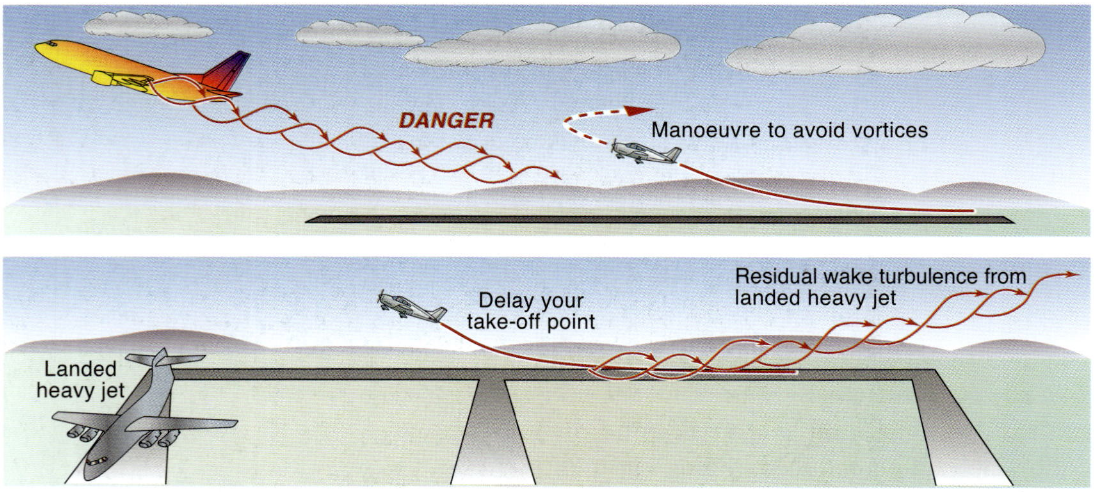

Figure 7-29 Modified take-off.

Avoid an intersection departure (less than the full length of the runway) behind a "heavy", as this will bring your flightpath closer to its wake turbulence.

After take-off, manoeuvre to avoid the vortices by climbing at best rate (but not at maximum angle as speed is a safety factor if you strike wake turbulence). Turn gently away (upwind) from suspected wake turbulence.

Also, be aware that a heavy jet at low weight is capable of a very steep climb gradient – avoid passing above their path, unless you are well clear.

When taking-off after a heavy aeroplane has landed, plan to become airborne well past the point where it flared and landed. If a "heavy" has taken off on a different runway and you expect to be airborne prior to the intersection of the runways, check to ensure that the "heavy" was still on the ground until well past the intersection.

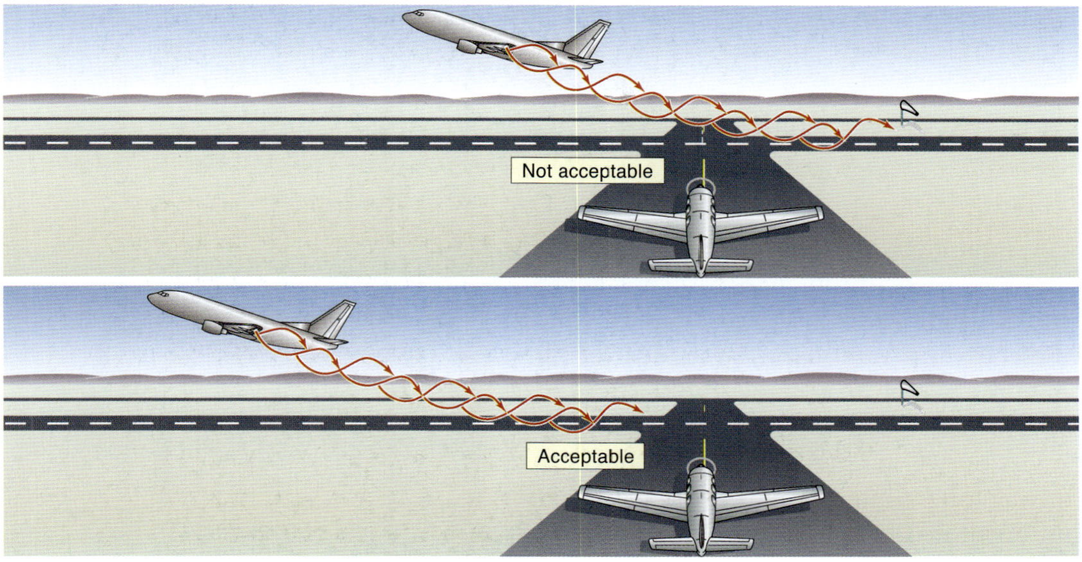

Figure 7-30 Delayed crossing due to wake turbulence.

Always avoid flying through the wake of a heavy aircraft, especially at low speed and low altitude.

In Flight

Avoid flying below and behind large aeroplanes. Fly several hundred feet above them, a thousand feet below them or upwind of them. Calm days, when there is no wind to disperse the vortices, are the most dangerous.

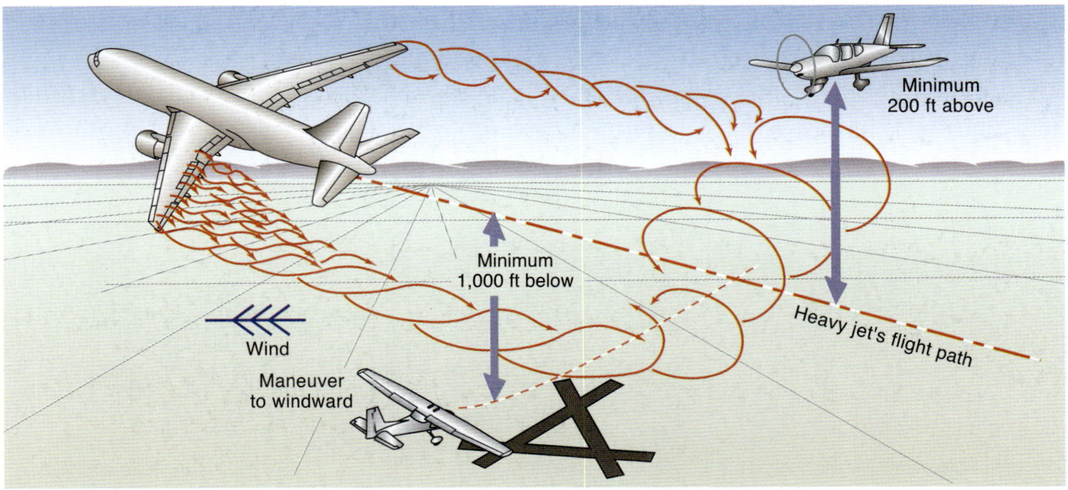

Figure 7-31 Avoiding wake turbulence.

Approach to Land

When following a landing aeroplane, fly above the approach path of the "heavy" and land well beyond its touchdown point. This is usually possible in a light aeroplane landing on a long runway.

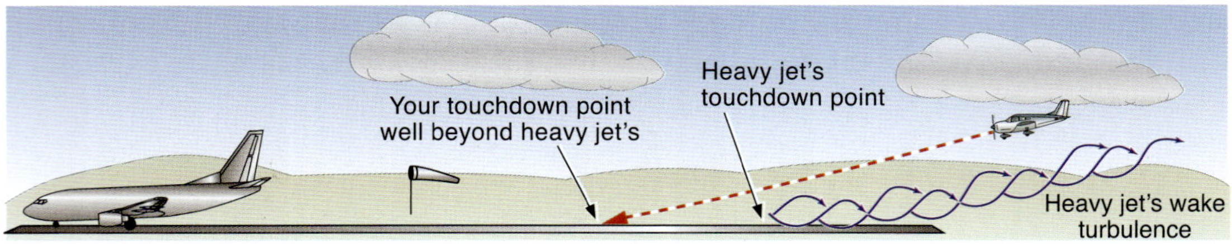

Figure 7-32 Modified approach on a long runway.

A light tailwind on the approach may keep the wake turbulence of a preceding "heavy" right on your approach glideslope. Also, be very cautious in light, quartering tailwinds, which may move the vortices of the preceding aeroplane into your touchdown zone. Consider landing on a separate runway, or delaying your approach to that runway, if no alternative runway available.

Figure 7-33 A landing jet.

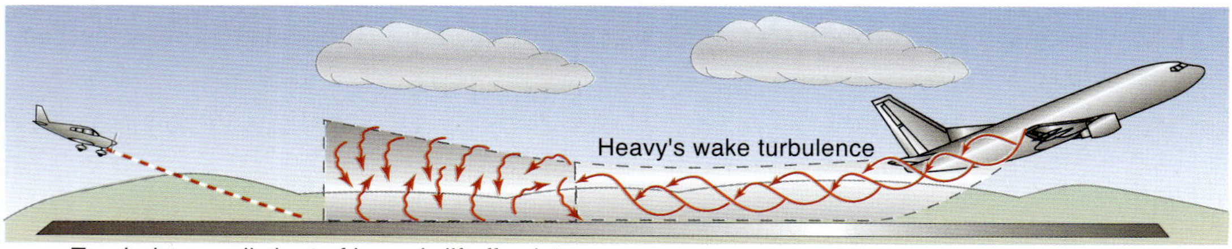

Figure 7-34 Modified approach.

When landing on a runway where a heavy aircraft has just taken off, touch down well before that aircraft's lift-off point or where you think the vortices may have drifted to. Landing in the normal touchdown zone will usually ensure this.

If a preceding "heavy" has discontinued its approach and gone around, its turbulent wake will be a hazard to a following aeroplane. You should consider changing your flightpath or delaying your approach in these circumstances.

Figure 7-35 Wake turbulence – going around.

Thrust-Stream Turbulence

Thrust-stream turbulence is the high velocity air exhausted from a jet engine (jet blast or jet wash) or the slipstream from a propeller (propwash). Thrust-stream turbulence can be dangerous to a light aeroplane taxiing on the ground behind a jet or large propeller-driven aeroplane, so always position your aeroplane when taxiing or when stopped to avoid any potential thrust-stream turbulence.

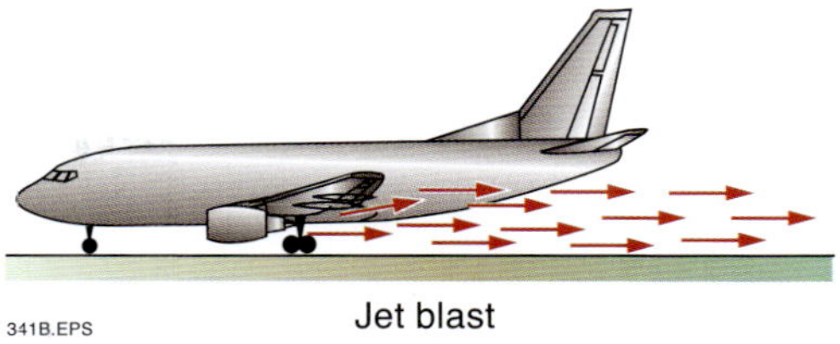

Figure 7-36 Jet blast.

Thrust-stream turbulence varies with engine thrust and distance from the source. If the pilot of the jet or large turboprop adds thrust, you can expect greater thrust-stream turbulence. At 30 m behind a jet aircraft, the thrust-stream may have a speed of 25 kt at idle power and 125 kt at full power. It could possibly be felt out to a distance of 200 m behind a medium jet, and 600 m behind a large jet. Ideally you should position your aircraft so that the thrust-stream from the engines will not blow over you, but if you have to taxi behind a jet or large turboprop, stay several hundred metres back. Thrust-stream turbulence has the potential to overturn a light aircraft on the ground.

Helicopter Downwash

Helicopters also produce wake turbulence. The helicopter blades act as a wing to produce lift and, as the helicopter proceeds, a trail of wingtip vortices will be left behind, just the same as for a fixed-wing aircraft. The heavier and slower the helicopter, the stronger the wake turbulence behind it. A helicopter hovering near the runway is a hazard to small aircraft.

Rotor downwash from a helicopter can be hazardous up to a radius of approximately three times the rotor diameter.

Figure 7-37 Beware rotor wash.

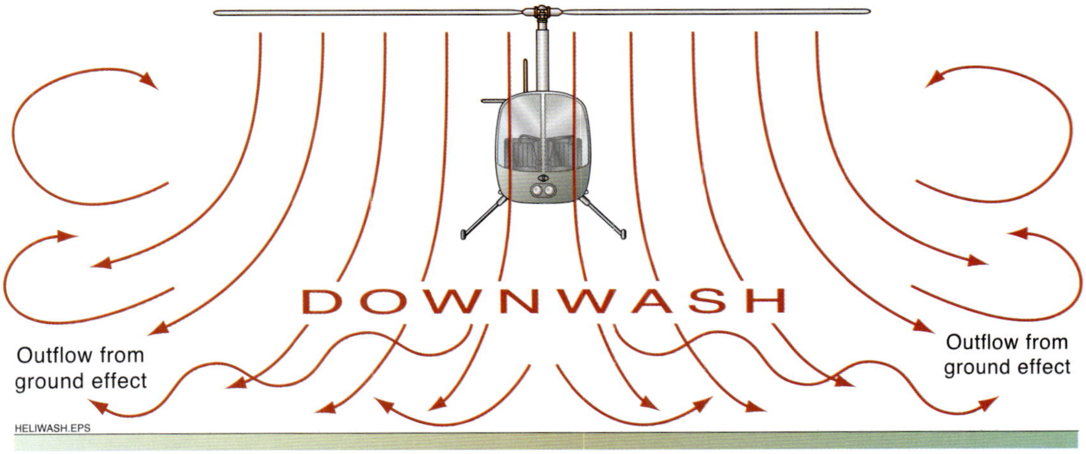

Figure 7-38 Rotorwash.

We have now considered the aircraft, how it flies and the environment in which it operates. But what about the most important element – the pilot?

Review 7

Pre-Solo Level of Knowledge

1. What is drift?
2. Why does an aircraft take off into the wind?
3. Wind against us is called . . . . . and with us is called . . . . .
4. Wind from the side is called a . . . . .
5. The part of the wind that acts across the direction of the runway is called the . . . . .
6. What effect will a headwind have on the descent?
7. What effect will it have on your final approach?
8. How could this be corrected?
9. Which is the best way to correct the effect of headwind on final?
10. What is windshear?
11. What is indicated airspeed?
12. Why is IAS the most important parameter for the pilot to know?
13. What is a thermal?
14. What is wake turbulence?
15. How can a light aircraft avoid the risks associated with wake turbulence?

BAK Level of Knowledge

16. What control deflection would the pilot make to correct a left quartering tailwind while taxiing?
17. A wind of 10 kt from the right at 45° to the runway has a crosswind component of . . . . . kt.
18. An aeroplane on approach has a strong headwind but descends into a region of calm air. What is the likely effect on the flightpath and airspeed?
19. Explain the difference between indicated, true and calibrated airspeeds.
20. What is mechanical turbulence, wake turbulence, and thrust-stream turbulence?
21. Do helicopters produce wake turbulence?
22. What is the crosswind limit for your aircraft?
23. The wind affects the path of the aircraft over the ground. An aircraft in a steady turn to the left turns through 360°. Draw the typical path over the ground when a steady wind is blowing.
24. What is the most dangerous position in this circle?
25. What is the rule of thumb regarding rate of descent and approach speed for a three degree path?
26. Name the two main techniques for correcting a crosswind on final.
27. How far behind a taxiing jet would you stay?

8 - Introduction to Human Factors

Aviation Theory Centre

Introduction

Human factors is the name given to the study of the role and relationship of the human mind and body in the operation of the aircraft. It is the most complex, the most capable and the most prone to error. To operate an aircraft safely we need to develop an awareness of our individual and collective characteristics, strengths and weaknesses.

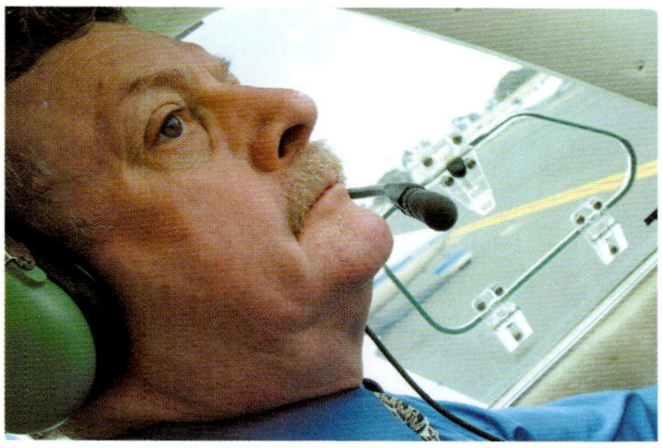

Our Human Condition

While an aircraft is specifically designed for flight, the human body is not. To ensure safe travel by air, we have to develop systems to provide a comfortable travelling environment, we have to develop an awareness of the limitations of the human body (in the case of the crew) and we have to go through a training/learning process to adapt the body to the airborne environment. Let's first look at the characteristics and features of human physiology (the physical aspects of the human body).

The Physical Pilot

The human body is an extraordinarily complex machine. It has the same systems as any complex machine. It consists of:

- the skeletal frame;
- the muscular system to move the frame;
- the nervous system to trigger the muscles;
- the circulatory system to circulate nutrients and oxygen and to carry away waste;
- the digestive system to extract nutrients from food and drink;
- the respiratory system to extract oxygen from the air and to dispose of carbon dioxide;
- the immune system to protect against disease; and
- the sensory system of vision, sound, motion, balance, temperature, stress, humidity and pain.

All of these systems were designed and have evolved to operate within certain parameters and in a particular environment. We will briefly consider the most important of these systems as far as piloting is concerned.

But first let's consider the alien environment in which we will be operating and the effects it can have on this incredible machine.

Environmental Effects

Atmospheric Pressure

The atmosphere in which we live consists of a mixture of gases of which oxygen is vital to sustain all living creatures. The human body is totally dependent on oxygen from the air and the lungs are designed to extract oxygen from the air at the pressure and in the proportion of the atmosphere at sea level.

As the aircraft climbs away from the earth, our bodies are subjected to conditions that are quite different to our normal sea level environment. The temperature decreases which fortunately we can counter by heating the cabin or by simply putting on more clothing. Atmospheric density and pressure also decrease and these have an adverse effect on our ability to breath. The quantity of air we inhale is less and this means our lungs and blood receive less oxygen. We can tolerate this reduced pressure and reduced oxygen intake to an altitude of about 10,000 ft. Above this altitude our mental functions and vision start to deteriorate.

Our ability to function normally is a matter of time. Measurements have been made of this time. It is called *time of useful consciousness*, or *effective performance time* (EPT).

Altitude above sea level	Sudden failure of oxygen supply	
	Moderate activity	Minimal activity
18, 000 ft	20 minutes	30 minutes
22, 000 ft	5 minutes	10 minutes
25, 000 ft	2 minutes	3 minutes
28, 000 ft	1 minute	1½ minutes
30, 000 ft	45 seconds	1 ¼ minutes
35, 000 ft	30 seconds	45 seconds
40, 000 ft	12 seconds	15 seconds

Table 8-1 Time of useful consciousness.

Hypoxia

Hypoxia is a lack of oxygen and may be caused by several factors:

- a lack of oxygen in the air (called *hypoxic hypoxia*); or
- an inability of the blood to carry oxygen (called *anaemic hypoxia*), due to a medical condition (anaemia) or to carbon monoxide poisoning in the blood (from a faulty engine exhaust system or from smoking).

The reduction of the oxygen-carrying capacity of the blood by smoking has the same effect as increasing the cabin altitude by 4,000–5,000 ft; the effect on you will worsen as the aeroplane climbs to higher altitudes. Tolerance to hypoxia can also be reduced by a loss of blood – for instance, after a person has made a blood donation. It is therefore recommended that active pilots do not donate blood. Should you decide that you do want to give blood, it is recommended not to fly for two to three days afterwards.

Barotrauma

Another effect of increasing cabin altitude (decreasing cabin pressure) is that gases trapped in parts of your body – such as the stomach, intestines, sinuses, middle ear, or in a decaying tooth – will want to expand. Either they will be able to escape to the atmosphere, or they may be trapped and possibly cause pain, known as *barotrauma*. Pain is most severe during the climb with teeth and intestines, and on descent with ears and sinus. The only relief is by allowing or assisting the pressure to equalise.

Ears

We hear sound because waves of air pressure move a membrane within our ear (ear drum). The cavity behind the ear drum has a small tube (*Eustachian tube*) which is open through the nose and allows air pressure on the inside to be balanced with outside air pressure. If we have a head cold or sinusitis, this tube can become restricted or even totally blocked.

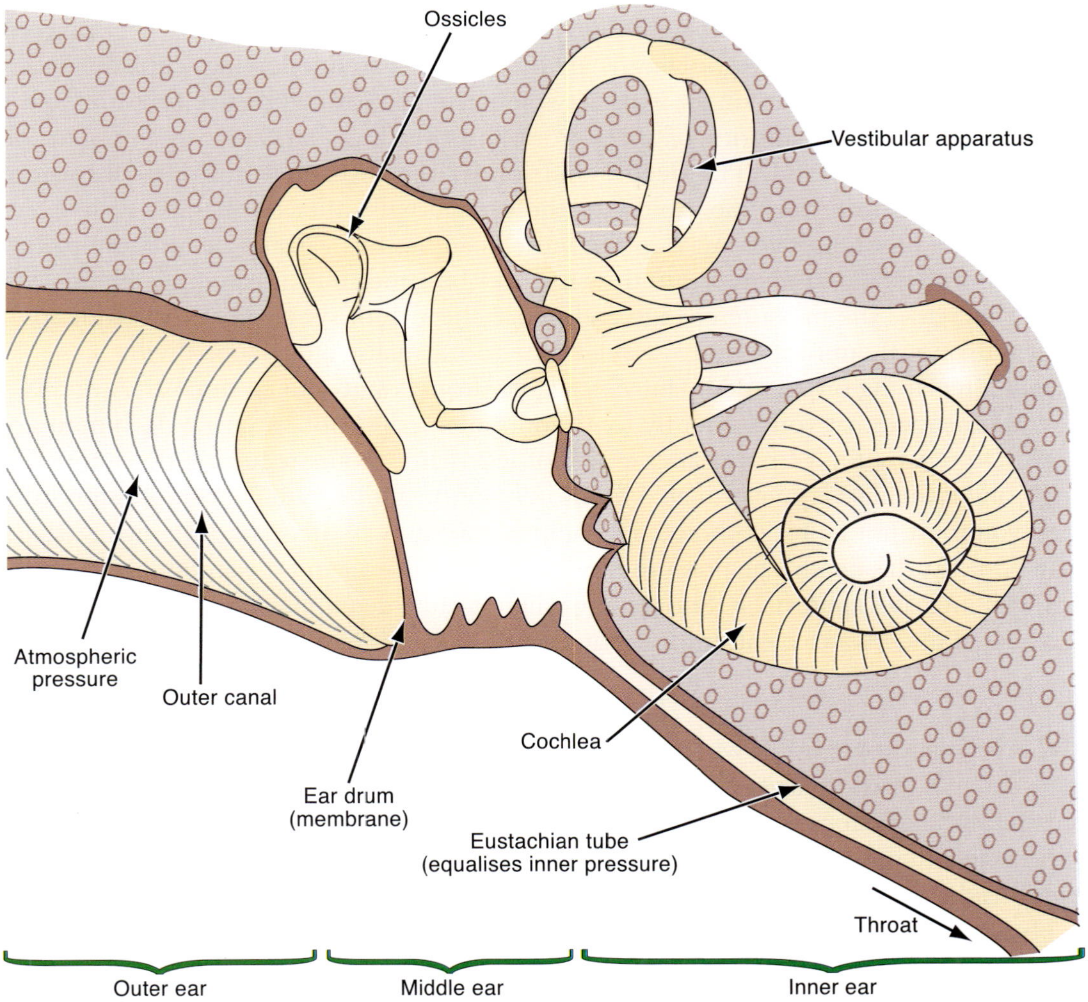

Figure 8-1 Internal ear.

If this is the case, as the aircraft climbs, the air inside the ear easily escapes through the tube because that is the normal direction of fluid movement. However, when we descend again, we end up in a situation where the air on the outside of the drum is at a higher pressure than the air inside. It may collapse the tube. Because of this restriction, air cannot get in to balance the pressure and so the ear drum is pushed in. This can be painful or even damaging. The pressure can usually be helped to equalise and open the Eustachian tube by swallowing, chewing, or by blowing with the mouth and nose held shut.

Circulation

On long flights, you may be seated and stationary for very long periods. You can improve circulation by contracting and relaxing your stomach diaphragm as well as the leg and buttock muscles. Without some physical demand, the heart will go into a dormant mode and the circulation slows down. This leads to sleepiness and loss of concentration. The muscles atrophy and you could suffer cramps. It is important to change your seating position and, if possible, exercise individual muscles by stretching and occasionally shaking a leg or twisting to improve circulation and to straighten the joints.

Decompression

The reduced pressure at altitude has the potential to adversely affect our physical existence. These conditions can be made significantly worse if we allow our bodies to be subjected to a compression before we go flying. Care must be exercised following scuba diving.

When the body is deep under water, it is subjected to strong positive pressures and as a result, additional quantities of gases from the breathing air, such as nitrogen, are absorbed into the blood. The deeper and longer the dive, the more this absorption occurs. A diver returning too rapidly to the surface will suffer the bends as the excess gas from the blood bubbles out into the muscles and joints, causing debilitating pain. If not recompressed and given time, this situation becomes life threatening. Flying after diving increases the pressure change and hence the risk of symptoms. Consequently, a pilot must not fly until the body has had time to normalise after scuba diving.

Rules regarding diving and flying vary slightly from country to country. In Australia, it is recommended that you do not fly for 4 hours after a dive not requiring decompression stops. Do not fly for 12 hours after a dive of less than 4 hours requiring decompression stops, and if the dive is greater than 4 hours in duration and required decompression stops, then you must not fly for 48 hours. Decompression stops are necessary if a dive is deeper than 33 ft. At this depth, the pressure is twice that at sea level and the amount of dissolved nitrogen increases appreciably. Snorkelling will not cause decompression sickness, only the pressurised underwater breathing associated with scuba or deep-sea diving.

Hyperventilation

Hyperventilation can occur when the body "overbreathes" due to some psychological distress such as fear or anxiety. It is a self-perpetuating cycle, in which a feeling of breathlessness develops – one is unable to "catch one's breath" – and continues even if the triggering influence is removed. Even though the person is now overbreathing, the person feels breathless, which tends to add to the anxiety and so promotes the overbreathing.

Hyperventilation flushes the carbon dioxide out of the blood and disturbs its chemical balance; this produces symptoms of numbness and tingling in the lips, fingertips and toes. The further effects may include palpitations, an increased pulse rate, sweating, chest pain, blurred vision, dizziness, fainting and ringing in the ears, muscle spasms, drowsiness and unconsciousness. Donning an oxygen mask will not help treat hyperventilation. If you are under stress and you realise that you are breathing heavily, try to consciously control the breathing – even hold your breath for a few seconds.

Hyperventilation can be remedied by consciously slowing down the breathing rate (talking is a good way of doing this) or by breathing into and out of a bag to increase the carbon dioxide level in the blood. If recovery is not evident, then assume that hypoxia rather than hyperventilation is the problem.

Carbon Monoxide Poisoning

Carbon monoxide (CO) is produced during the combustion of fuel in the engine, so it is present in engine exhaust gases (and cigarette smoke). Carbon monoxide is a colourless, odourless, tasteless and poisonous gas and will sometimes not be noticeable. Haemoglobin in the blood transports oxygen throughout the body to act as "fuel". It has an enormous affinity for CO – even in preference to oxygen. If carbon monoxide molecules are inhaled, then the haemoglobin will transport the carbon monoxide in preference to oxygen, causing the body and the brain to suffer oxygen starvation. The performance of a pilot in an environment contaminated by carbon monoxide will be seriously impaired. Recovery, even on pure oxygen, may take several hours. Carbon monoxide poisoning can be fatal.

Many cabin heating systems use warm air from around the engine and exhaust manifold as their source of heat. Any leaks in the engine exhaust system can allow carbon monoxide to enter the cabin through the heating air and possibly through open windows and cracks. To minimise the effect of any carbon monoxide that enters the cockpit in this way, fresh air should always be used in conjunction with cabin heat.

Even though carbon monoxide is odourless, it may be associated with other exhaust gases that do have an odour. Engine smells in the cabin are a warning that carbon monoxide may be present. Symptoms of carbon monoxide poisoning include the following:

- headache, dizziness and nausea;
- deterioration in vision;
- impaired judgement;
- personality change;
- impaired memory;
- slower breathing rate;
- cherry red complexion;
- loss of muscular power;
- convulsions; and
- coma, and eventually death.

If carbon monoxide is suspected in the cabin:

- shut off the cabin heat;
- stop all smoking;
- increase the supply of fresh air through vents and windows; and
- land as soon as possible.

Some aircraft when flown at low airspeed with the door open or removed can ingest large quantities of exhaust fumes. Many operators place carbon monoxide detectors in the cockpit. The most common type contains crystals that change colour when carbon monoxide is present. These detectors are inexpensive and useful. However, they do have a limited life, so check the expiry date. If the detector is date-expired, it may not indicate the presence of carbon monoxide, and so may lull you into a false sense of security.

Be aware that carbon monoxide is not the only toxic chemical to which you may be exposed in aircraft operation. Vapours and fumes from fuels and lubricants, poorly packed dangerous goods and other products of combustion may produce a range of symptoms including skin, eye and lung irritation, dizziness, drowsiness, confusion and loss of consciousness.

Health & Fitness

Diet & Exercise

A healthy diet and regular exercise is essential for the well being of all persons, not only pilots. However, it is important that pilots maintain a healthy diet and undertake regular exercise to ensure they are operating at peak performance whenever they fly.

There are many benefits to exercise; while these are too numerous to list, some benefits include:

- weight control;
- improved cardiac health;
- lowering of blood pressure;
- improved mental health;
- better sleep;
- control of diabetes;
- increased energy and stamina;
- improved immune system;
- prevention of osteoporosis; and
- enhanced quality of life.

To improve your fitness level and health, you only require 30 minutes of moderate activity over most days of the week; you should exercise at least three times a week. When choosing an exercise, select an activity which you will enjoy. This will make it more interesting for you and easier for you to sustain regular activity. Generally, if you work with a partner or a team, it will be easier to become motivated.

If you are a busy person, try walking for 5–10 minutes several times a day while on errands or on short trips. This can be just as beneficial as structured exercise programmes. During low to moderate activity, you should still be able to talk comfortably during exercise. In moderate to high activity levels, it is difficult to speak during exercise.

There are two types of exercise:

- aerobic; and
- anaerobic.

Aerobic exercise maintains activity (such as jogging or bike riding) at a moderate level or higher for a reasonable period (20–30 minutes or more), and this requires the body to produce and deliver oxygen and nutrients to the cells. Aerobic activity is required to improve your cardiovascular condition, reduce body fat and increase energy and endurance. Anaerobic exercise involves short durations of high intensity activity. Examples of these include climbing stairs quickly, swinging a bat, throwing a ball or sprinting.

If you have any medical condition or if you are over 35 years of age and have not exercised regularly before, you should consult your doctor before commencing any form of exercise programme.

Upper Respiratory Tract Problems

The common cold, hay fever, sinusitis, tonsillitis or any similar condition can lead to blocked ears or sinuses. Also, the feeling of malaise can detract from your normal mental ability. While blocked ears can sometimes be cleared by holding your nose and blowing gently (a technique known as the *Valsalva manoeuvre*), by chewing, swallowing or yawning, the best advice is, if you have a cold, don't fly. Problems can also arise in the sinuses, which are cavities in the head connected by narrow tubes to the nasal and throat passages. Such blockages can cause great pain, especially during descent.

Fatigue & Sleep Deprivation

Fatigue, tiredness and sleep deprivation can lower a pilot's mental and physical capacity quite dramatically. Fatigue can become deep-seated and chronic. If personal, psychological or emotional problems are not resolved, they prevent deep rest and good sleep over a prolonged period. Chronic fatigue won't be cured until the problems are resolved, or at least are being addressed, and the person can relax and unstress. You should prohibit yourself from flying if the distress is distracting. Short-term fatigue can be caused by overwork, mental stress, an uncomfortable body position, a recent lack of sleep, living-it-up a little too much, lack of oxygen or lack of food. To guard against fatigue that is detrimental to flight safety, you should:

- fly only when your psychological and emotional lives are under control;
- maintain a reasonable level of fitness;
- eat regularly and sensibly;
- have adequate and effective sleep;
- ensure that cockpit comfort is optimised and that energy foods and drink are available on long flights; and
- exercise your limbs occasionally and, if practicable, land to stretch your legs at least every four hours.

Dehydration

Dehydration is not only associated with hot days and intense sporting activities when we don't drink enough. It is also a problem when sitting relatively still when flying. As we climb, the atmosphere becomes less dense and is much colder. Both decreased density and temperature means less water is available in the atmosphere. So just by breathing, we are going to lose moisture from our lungs at a greater rate than we would at sea level.

On large aircraft, the pressurisation and air conditioning tend to reduce the moisture content of the air still further. Aircraft manufacturers have to incorporate humidifiers in these systems to keep the cabin environment comfortable. On any flight of more than an hour or so and especially in summer, always carry drinking water and sip it regularly. Don't wait until you are thirsty. Dehydration can quickly affect the brain's ability to function rationally.

Headache

Headaches can compromise safe flight due to stress and lower alertness. Migraine headaches can be totally incapacitating if accompanied by vision impairment, nausea, vomiting and sensitivity to light and sound. Seek advice from your doctor if you are prone to these conditions.

Medication

All drugs affect the body and sometimes the mind. Prescribed drugs may be incompatible with flying – especially sedatives. Also, individual reactions vary. Some drugs may have long half-lives, which means that their residual effects stay for a long time after the drug is administered. Other drugs, called potentiating agents, change or exaggerate the effect of drugs taken in combination. The combination of drugs with alcohol can be serious. Unless cleared by a doctor, it is safest to assume that any drug or medication will temporarily ground you. A list of common medications considered incompatible with flying includes:

- antibiotics (e.g. penicillin) used to combat infection;
- tranquillisers, anti-depressants and sedatives;
- stimulants (caffeine, amphetamines) used to maintain wakefulness or suppress appetite;
- anti-histamines, often used to combat colds and hay fever;
- drugs for the relief of high blood pressure; and
- analgesics to relieve pain.

Anaesthetics (local or dental) require a rest period of 24 hours before returning to flight duties. For general anaesthetics, at least 72 hours are required.

Coronary Risk Factors

Coronary risk factors such as smoking, high cholesterol, obesity and hereditary factors can affect your performance as a pilot, not to mention your general health. If any of these risk factors apply to you, then you should check with your doctor on ways to minimise the risk.

Pregnancy

After becoming pregnant, a pilot should check with a designated aviation medical examiner to ensure that the pregnancy will not in any way interfere with the safe exercise of the privileges of the relevant licence or the health of the mother or the child. A pilot should consider all duties she may be required to undertake as pilot in command and discuss any uncertainties with a medical examiner.

The medical examiner may assess a pilot as being fit to fly only for a specific period. From 30 weeks, all Class 1 and 2 medical certificate holders are deemed temporarily unfit to exercise the privileges of their licence. In some cases, this may occur earlier. After the pregnancy, consult a medical examiner prior to recommencing flying to ensure that it is safe to do so.

Although there are no regulations for pregnancy in terms of the impact on cockpit ergonomics, the pilot should consider how able she is to safely reach all controls in the cockpit. Ensure that all controls can be reached and used to full deflection, as is required for the safe operation of the aircraft being flown.

Ageing

All commercial pilots are required to undergo an aviation medical examination at least once a year to hold a Class 1 medical certificate. Private pilots are only required to hold a Class 2 medical certificate, which remains in force for four years unless you have a condition which requires monitoring at shorter intervals. Since the body tends to degenerate as we get older, it is important to be checked at more regular intervals to ensure we maintain our capacity to exercise the privileges of our licence. As a result, the holder of a Class 2 medical will need to undergo a medical examination every two years once they reach the age of 40.

For the holder of a Class 1 medical certificate, although the medical examinations are required every year, the contents vary and increase with age. For example, an ECG is required for the initial issue of a Class 1 medical examination. After the initial issue, the ECG is then required on the 25th, 30th, 32nd, 34th, 36th, 38th and 40th birthdays. After the 40th birthday, an ECG is required annually.

Food Poisoning

Food poisoning is a term which refers to illness as a result of the consumption of food. This can include any combination of vomiting, nausea, fever, diarrhoea and stomach cramps. Food poisoning occurs when bacteria in a food or a toxin produced by bacteria causes a reaction in the gut. There are other reasons for the above symptoms to occur other than food poisoning. These include gut infections, drugs, allergies, stress, exercises, anxiety and excitement. It is difficult to ascertain whether an individual has food poisoning or the symptoms are a result of any of the above causes. It is much easier to diagnose large groups of people suffering these symptoms that have consumed the same food and are affected simultaneously.

Most cases of food poisoning produce symptoms within the first eight hours of consumption. However, some cases can take up to 24 hours before the symptoms appear. In some cases, blood may be vomited or passed. The foods most susceptible to infection include dairy products, chicken, stale bread, fish, meat that is inadequately refrigerated, reheated meat dishes and foods that have been fried.

The onset of any symptoms are generally very sudden and disappear just as suddenly. Most symptoms clear within six to twelve hours. Clear fluids should be taken if food poisoning has occurred. In severe cases, dehydration may occur and hospitalisation and an intravenous drip may be required. Generally, most cases do not require treatment.

Unless you know the source of your food, avoid reheated food, meals left on display or not refrigerated and opened tins, and be wary about the quality of all drinking water.

Botulism is a condition which requires medical treatment. Symptoms will occur within twelve to thirty six hours after consuming food which is inadequately preserved. The symptoms of botulism include:

- vomiting;
- double vision;
- a dry mouth;
- weak muscles; and
- difficulty talking, swallowing and breathing.

Food poisoning is the most common cause of in-flight incapacitation of flight crew. This is why many airlines adopt a company policy requiring pilots to consume different meals and at different times.

Smoking

Nothing good can be said about smoking. Smoking is detrimental to good health, both in the short term and in the long term. Smoking also significantly decreases a pilot's capacity to perform by reducing the amount of oxygen carried in the blood, replacing it with the useless and potentially poisonous by-products of cigarette smoke. A pilot does not have to be the active smoker to suffer these negative effects; passive smoking has the same affect.

Carbon monoxide is present in cigarette smoke and is absorbed into the blood in preference to oxygen. The maximum blood oxygen concentration for a smoker is 90%. This means that, at sea level, a smoker is already as hypoxic as a non-smoker at several thousand feet. A smoker's night vision is affected by hypoxia at sea level. It is now generally accepted that cigarette smoking plays a significant role in cardiovascular (heart) and other diseases.

Cholesterol

Cholesterol is a yellow-white fatty substance. It is found in foods originating from animals (for example, meat, cheese, eggs and other diary products). Cholesterol is required for the body to function, but as with most things, excess is harmful. Cholesterol is required to build cells (cementing them together), to produce hormones and vitamin D.

Cholesterol is carried in the blood stream. If there are excess amounts, it will be deposited on the walls of the arteries, thereby reducing the blood supply to your heart muscle and may eventually block it. This deposit of fat is called *arteriosclerosis* or hardening of the arteries. If this occurs in an area which supplies blood to the heart, a heart attack will result. If the blockage occurs in an area which supplies blood to the brain, a stroke will result.

There are two types of cholesterol:

- *low density lipoprotein* (LDL), also known as "bad cholesterol"; and
- *high density lipoprotein* (HDL), also known as "good cholesterol".

HDL removes bad cholesterol from the blood and prevents hardening of the arteries.

The people at greatest risk are overweight, middle-aged men, but anyone may be affected. If you feel you are at risk, visit your doctor and have a blood test.

To minimise your risk of excess cholesterol:

- do not smoke;
- limit your alcohol intake;
- exercise; and
- lose weight if you are obese.

These measures may not be sufficient for some people. In these cases, a doctor will recommend a low cholesterol diet and in more severe cases, regular use of tablets or drinks designed to lower the level of fat in your blood. Once these fatty deposits have attached themselves to your arteries, they are permanent. There is a surgical technique which can clean out clogged arteries, but in the late stages, this operation will have little effect.

Your liver manufactures approximately 80% of your cholesterol. You can get cholesterol through your diet or through the cholesterol manufactured by your liver. Hereditary factors affect the amount of cholesterol that is produced in your body and how much is removed from your blood stream. If your diet includes no cholesterol at all, your body would still produce cholesterol. It will produce as much as your body requires and even more if it is in your genes.

To control your cholesterol, minimise saturated fats, including fatty meats, dairy products, sausages, fried foods, nuts, egg yolk, liver and shrimp. Polyunsaturated fats are better. Monounsaturated fats such as olive oil and peanut oil are the best of the fats for human consumption.

Obesity

Obesity occurs if you eat more than your body needs for its energy requirements. In some instances, it occurs due to a problem with an organ in your body which controls how your body functions, such as an under-active thyroid. The factors that determine your weight include:

- food intake;
- exercise; and
- your genes.

Obesity increases the risk of:

- strokes;
- heart attacks;
- diabetes;
- liver disease;
- arthritis;
- poor circulation;
- strain on the lungs;
- strain on joints;
- rashes in skin folds;
- hernias;
- indigestion;
- complications from surgery; and
- gynaecological problems.

If you believe you are obese, consult your doctor to learn the options you have available to you. In general you should:

- eat a balanced diet;
- do not eat too much;
- drink plenty of water; and
- exercise daily (check with your doctor to determine the level of exercise that is appropriate for you).

A combination of regular exercise and a healthy diet is the ideal way of maintaining your body in a fit status to fly. Drugs are available to suppress appetite, but avoid these if you can. Always check with your doctor if you are unsure.

Deep Vein Thrombosis (DVT)

Deep vein thrombosis is the formation of a clot in the veins. Generally, it is the lower legs that are affected and the clot forms in the larger veins in this area. Apart from restricting circulation, a clot may break off and move through the blood stream to an area which will cause blockage and severe damage to vital organs, such as the brain, lungs or heart.

While travelling for long periods, exercise during the flight, particularly your legs, in order to avoid DVT. If you cannot go for a walk on the aircraft, then exercise your legs any way you can. You should move or wiggle your legs, feet and toes in some form of exercise at least once every hour.

The risk of DVT is increased through dehydration, so ensure that you drink plenty of fluids, particularly water. The regular walk to the toilet also helps circulation. Avoid alcohol and coffee.

Alcohol

Even small quantities of alcohol in the blood impair a pilot's immediate performance and severely affect judgment. It takes time for the body to remove alcohol. A pilot must not fly for at least 8 hours after drinking the last of any alcohol. This time interval must be increased if greater quantities are consumed. You must allow at least an extra hour per standard glass.

Sleep will not speed up the removal process; in fact it slows down the body processes and the elimination of alcohol may take even longer. The long term effects of alcohol consumption include dependency, social and family breakdown, and physical damage to kidneys, liver and brain.

Alcohol is absorbed directly into the bloodstream through the stomach and the small intestine. The rate at which alcohol is absorbed can be slowed down by food in the stomach, but this does not prevent intoxication or drunkenness. All alcohol that has been consumed will reach the blood at some point. In excess of 90% of all alcohol consumed is transported from the blood to the liver where it is metabolised.

Any remaining alcohol is eliminated unchanged in breath, sweat, tears, urine and faeces, or metabolised in the stomach. It takes time to sober up, and the following will *not* assist this process: cold showers, exercise, black coffee, fresh air or vomiting.

Alcohol is a depressant, and therefore its primary effect is to slow down the brain and nervous system. As a result, your judgement and comprehension of situations will be affected. It also suppresses social inhibitions, caution, shyness and fear and may generate over-confidence. Coordination, judgement and reflexes deteriorate.

People who have consumed large amounts of alcohol can become aggressive or engage in risky behaviour. Excessive drinking will lead to confusion, nausea, vomiting and unconsciousness. In extreme cases, you may even stop breathing. Drinking copious amounts of alcohol can result in hangovers, memory loss and blackouts.

The dangers of alcohol include:

- impairment of judgement;
- release from inhibitions;
- slowed reaction time;
- impaired performance;
- compounding of the detrimental effects of hypoxia;
- reduced attention to detail; and
- increased probability of being involved in an accident or an incident.

Sadly, high residual blood alcohol levels have been documented in many pilots who have been involved in fatal aircraft accidents.

The Functional Pilot

We have considered the physiological make-up of the human pilot and the environment in which a pilot operates. Let's now consider the pilot's role and how the human has limitations in this role.

What Do Pilots Do?

The pilot's task is to process information – that is to receive information, analyse it, decide on a course of action, make a control input, check the response, make an adjustment if necessary – and to keep doing this as the flight progresses.

This cycle is called a *control loop.*

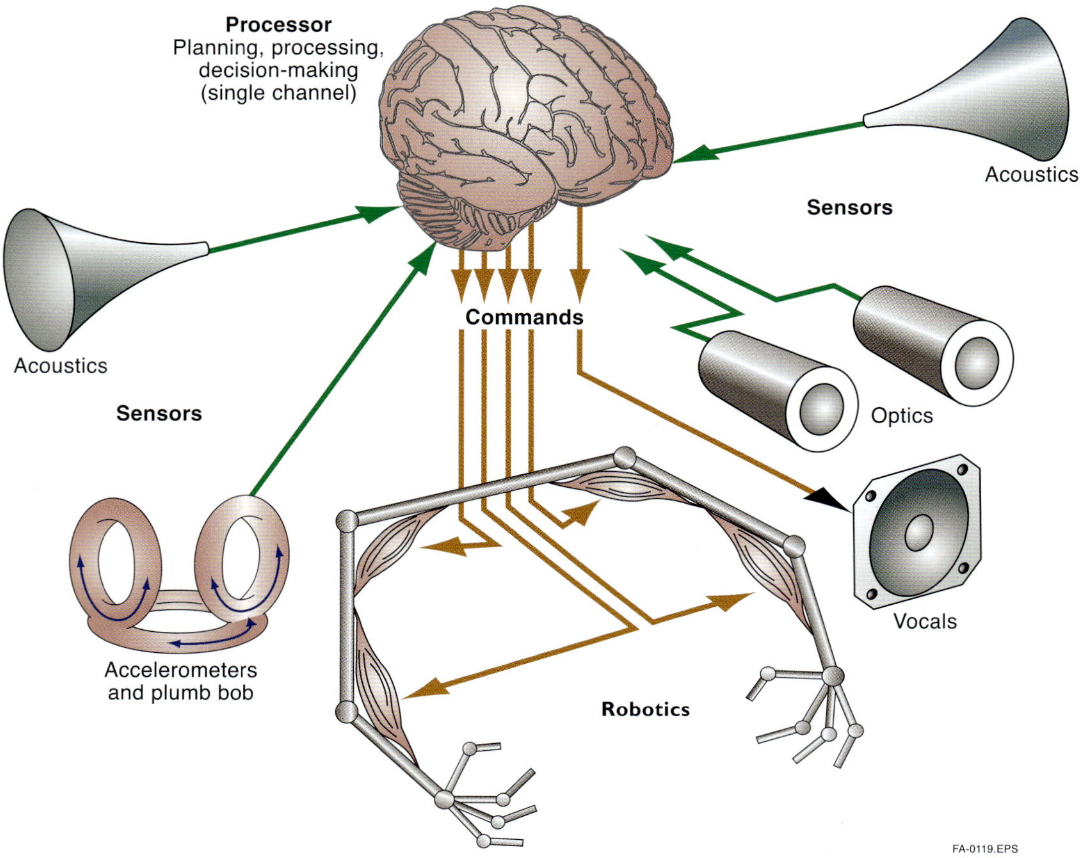

Figure 8-2 Inputs/processor/outputs.

The pilot can only function as the controller of the aircraft, and the decision maker (commander), if he or she can take the information and if he or she possesses:

- the knowledge to interpret and process the information;
- the training and skill to make the correct control inputs and to anticipate and assess the outcome; and
- the discipline and attitude to make further changes to achieve a safe, correct and accurate result.

The first stage is the sensations that the body receives. These are designed to assist in the tasks of walking upright upon the earth and being ready to fight or flee. In flight, they can become confused.

Vision & Illusions

The eyes provide us with a visual image of the environment. Each eye acts as a natural and very sophisticated digital camera. Its basic function is to collect light rays reflected from an object, using the lens to focus these rays into an image on a screen (the retina). The brain then matches the image to previously stored data so we then "recognise" the object. Seeing is both a visual and a mental process.

The Structure of the Eye

The main components of the eye are the cornea, the lens, the retina, and the optic nerve. Light passes into the eye through the cornea and the lens, which focus the light rays onto the retina. The retina converts the image made by the received light into electrical signals which are then sent via the optic nerve to the brain – and so we see.

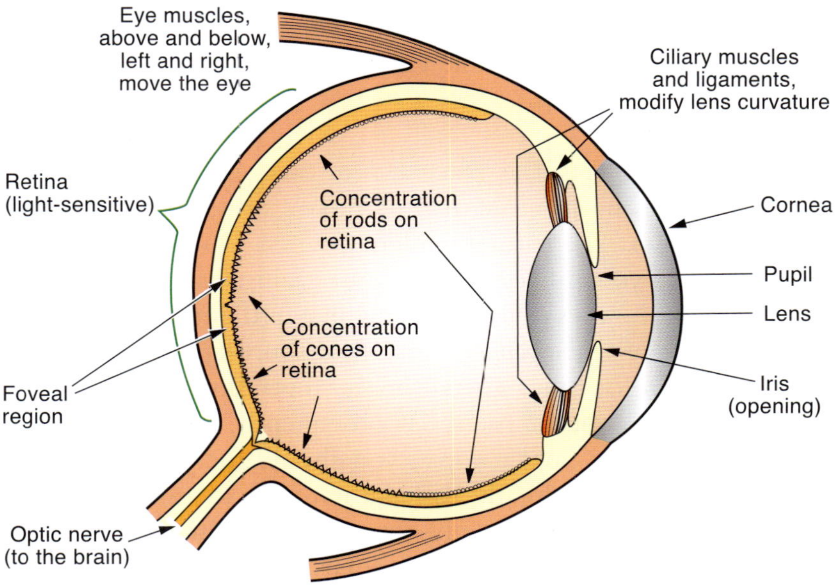

Figure 8-3 Cross-section of the eye.

Retina

The retina is the light-sensitive layer located at the back of the eye. It is the screen onto which the lens focuses images, and these are converted to electrical signals that pass along the optic nerve to the brain. The retina contains two types of light-sensitive (or photo-sensitive) cells: cones and rods.

Cones

Cone are concentrated around the central section of the retina, especially the foveal region directly opposite the lens. Cones are sensitive to colour, small details and distant objects, and are most effective in daylight and less effective in darkness. They provide the best visual acuity (the ability to resolve fine detail). The foveal region is where we focus most objects and it is this area of the retina which provides our central vision in good light conditions. Objects focused on the foveal region in very dim light (as at night) will not stimulate the cones to transmit a message along the optic nerve, so the image will therefore not be seen by us.

Rods

Rods are concentrated in a band outside the central foveal area. They are sensitive to movement, but not to detail or colour, and so "see" only in shades of black, white, and grey, rather than the colours seen by the cones. Rods are effective in both daylight and darkness and are responsible for our peripheral vision (i.e. off-centre vision), which helps our orientation and night vision.

Objects in dim light, such as at night, are therefore most easily noticed when their image falls somewhere on the peripheral area of the retina where the rods are concentrated. You can achieve this by looking slightly to the side of an object at night, rather than directly at it as you would during daylight.

Characteristics of Vision

Binocular Vision

Binocular vision describes the process whereby optical information is received and processed from two eyes. To track a moving object with both eyes, the eyes need to move in harmony, and this means coordinated control of the two sets of muscles by the brain. In a fatigued person, this coordination sometimes fails, and the result is quite different images from each eye, resulting in double vision.

Empty-Field Myopia

When focusing on near objects, the visual axis of each eye will be turned-in slightly; when focusing on distant objects more than six metres away, the visual axes of your two eyes will be nearly parallel. The natural tendency, when you are not trying to focus on any particular object and you are, for instance, just gazing (lazing) out the window into an empty blue sky, is for the eyes to focus somewhere in the range of one to two metres. This is referred to as *empty-field myopia* (empty-field short-sightedness).

When trying to search for other aircraft in an empty sky, the natural tendency of a resting eye is to focus at about 2 metres. Consequently, distant aircraft may not be noticed. To avoid this empty-field myopia, you should focus on any available distant object, such as a cloud or a landmark, to lengthen your focus. If the sky is empty of clouds or other objects, then focus briefly on a relatively distant part of the aeroplane, like a wingtip, as a means of lengthening your focus. Having spotted an aeroplane in an otherwise empty sky, be aware that it could be closer to you than it appears to be, because you have no other object with which to compare its size.

Unless you have a distant object in view at night, your eyes will tend to focus at a point about one to two metres ahead of you, especially if you are an older person with "tired eyes", and you may miss sighting distant objects. This empty-field myopia or night myopia (short-sightedness) can be combated by searching for distant lights and focusing briefly on them. Beware also of false horizons at night (see later in this chapter).

Blind Spot

A pilot flying visually must continually scan the sky for other aircraft and for obstacles, then focus on any that are observed. In an empty sky, it requires effort to focus on distant objects, since the eyes tend to focus on a much closer point. It is very important, therefore, that the eyes are fit and healthy, and that you are not flying when fatigued.

Absolute distance can only be judged by triangulation (the convergence of sight lines) and this is the prime reason for binocular vision. The other reason is to compensate for the blind spot in each eye. The blind spot is the small area on the retina of the eye where the nerve fibres from the light-sensitive cells (rods and cones) on the retina lead into the optic nerve. At this point, there is no coating of light-sensitive cells, and hence any light falling here will not register, that is, it is literally a "blind" spot.

However, it is not possible for an image to fall on the blind spot of both eyes simultaneously because it will be in different relative position to each. Even when an image falls on the blind spot of one eye, and is therefore not registered, the brain will receive a message from the other, and so the object will be seen.

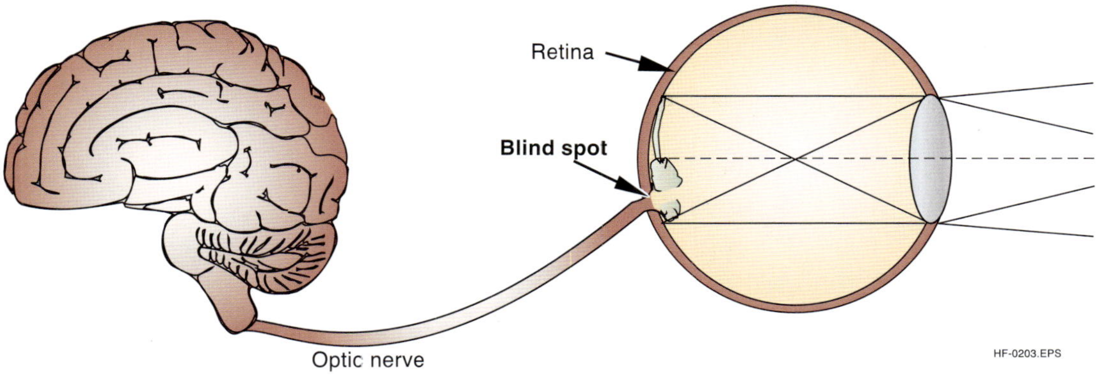

Figure 8-4 The blind spot.

You can observe the existence of the blind spot in each eye by viewing figure 8-5. Hold the page at arm's length, cover your right eye, and then with your left eye focus on the aeroplane on the right. It will be clearly recognisable as a biplane because it will be focused on your retina. Move the page closer and as you still focus on the biplane, you will notice that the helicopter will eventually disappear. Its image has reached the position on the retina occupied by the optic nerve. In practice, you must be careful when you are scanning the sky that another aircraft is not blocked from view by the magnetic compass or some part of the windscreen structure. If it is blocked from the view of both eyes, you will not see it at all; if it is blocked from the view of only one eye, you will lose the blind spot protection provided by binocular vision.

Figure 8-5 Example of a blind spot.

Visual Scanning by Day

The central (foveal) region of the retina provides the best vision, and in full colour, but only during reasonable daylight. Objects are best seen by day if you can focus their image on the foveal region, and you do this by looking directly at them.

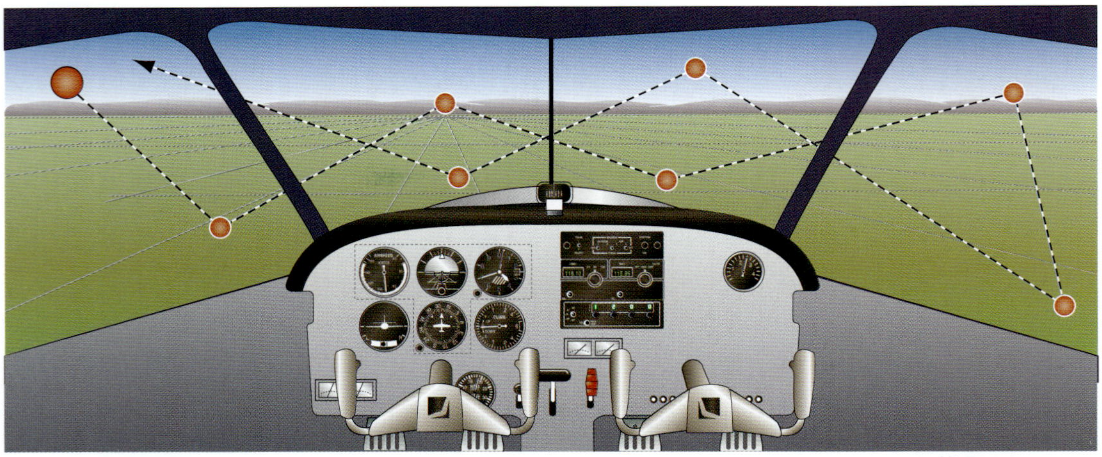

Figure 8-6 Methodical scan.

The most effective method of scanning for other aircraft for collision avoidance in daylight is to use a series of short, regularly spaced eye movements to search each 10° sector of the sky. Systematically focusing on different segments of the sky for short intervals is a better technique than continuously sweeping the sky. This is sometimes called the *saccade–fixation cycle* where each move/look cycle takes about one-third of a second.

Relative Movement

You may be on a collision course with another aircraft if there is no apparent relative motion between you and the other aircraft, especially if the other aircraft appears to be getting bigger and bigger in the windscreen. Because of the lack of movement across your windscreen, an aircraft on a collision course with you will be more difficult to spot than one that is not on a collision course.

Any relative movement of an object against its background usually makes it easier to notice in your peripheral vision. The image of the other aircraft may not increase in size much at first, but, shortly before impact, it would rapidly increase in size. The time available for you to avoid a collision may be quite brief, depending upon when you see the other aircraft and the rate of closure. If you are flying at 100 kt and it is flying at 500 kt in the opposite direction, the rate of closure is 600 kt, i.e. 10 nm/minute.

If you spot the other aircraft at a distance of 1 nm, you only have one tenth of a minute (6 seconds) to potential impact. If you are a vigilant pilot and spot it at 3 nm, you have 18 seconds in which to act. In hazy or low-visibility conditions, your ability to see other aircraft and objects, the edges of which might be blurred, will be diminished and, if you can see them, they may appear to be further away than their actual distance – you might be closer than you think.

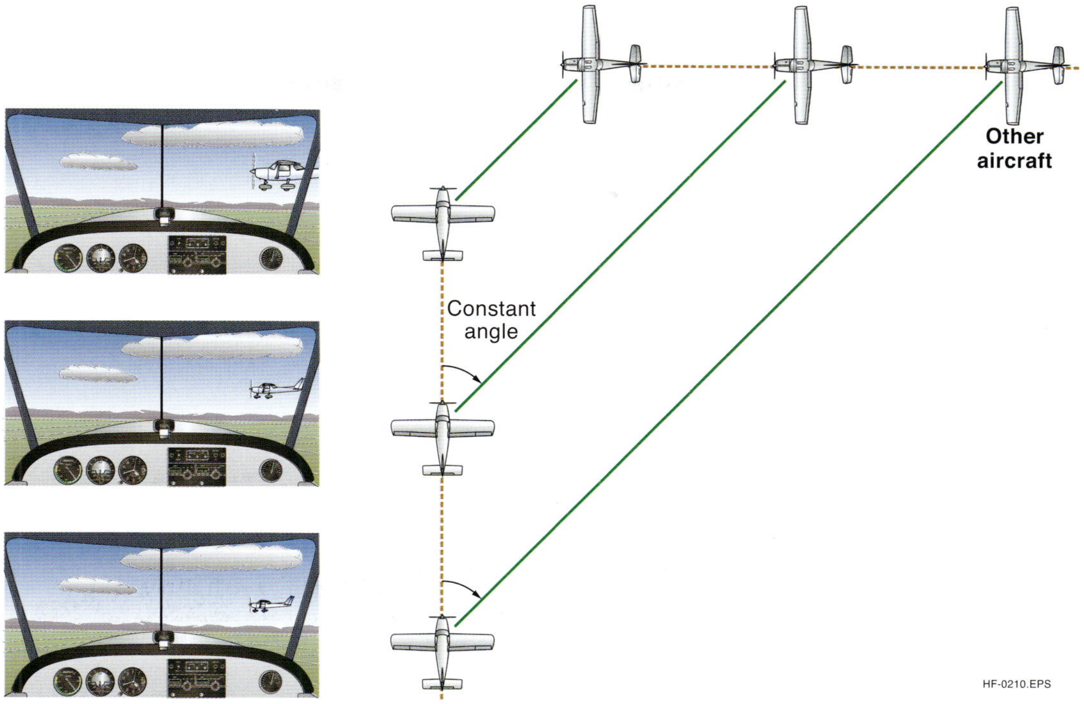

Figure 8-7 Constant relative position.

Specks

A small, dark image formed on the retina could be a distant, but rapidly approaching aircraft, or it could be a speck of dirt or dust, or an insect spot, on the windscreen. Specks or sometimes a dust particle, a scratch, or an insect on the windscreen might be mistaken for a distant aeroplane. Simply moving your head will allow you to discriminate between marks on the windscreen and distant objects.

Figure 8-8 Specks?

Visual Scanning by Night

The central foveal region of the retina containing mainly cones is not effective by night, causing an area of reduced visual sensitivity in your central vision. You need to rely on your peripheral vision which is provided by the rods in the outer band of the retina. An object at night is more readily visible when you are looking to the side of it, rather than directly at it. Look out of the side of your eye.

Vision on Approach

The eyes and brain use many clues and stored images of known objects to help in judging distance, size and height. Some items are mathematical, such as the relative size of objects – a bigger object assumed to be nearer than a smaller object. Also, binocular vision (the slightly different images of a nearby object relative to its background seen by each eye) assists in depth perception when the object is near. Texture also assists in depth perception – the more visible the texture, the closer the object appears to be.

On final approach as you near the aim point, the surface texture will appear to flow outwards in all directions from the point on which you are focused. This is one means by which you can visually maintain the flightpath to the aim point – adjusting attitude and heading, and so that the point from which the texture appears to be moving outwards remains the desired aim point.

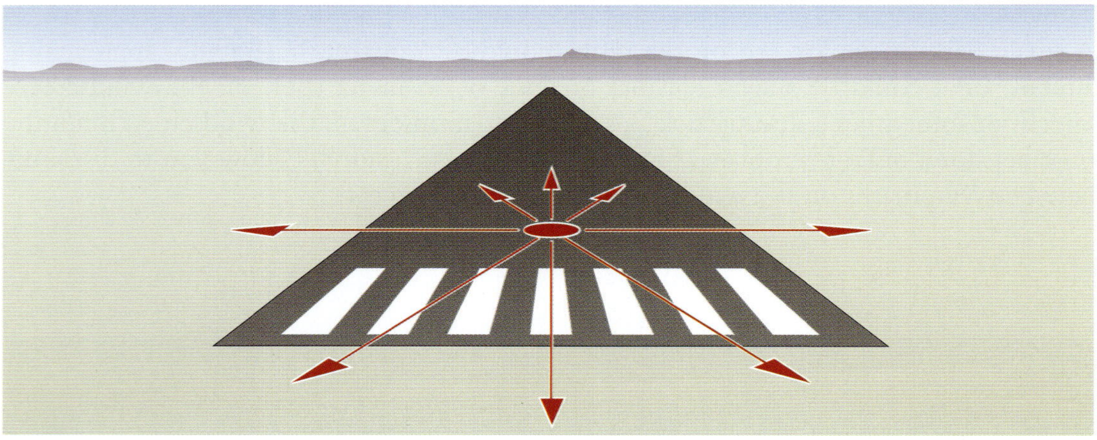

Figure 8-9 Centre of radiating texture.

Texture is also used for the estimation of distance – for instance, as you approach flare height for a landing, the actual texture of the runway or the grass becomes increasingly noticeable and texture is used as an indirect cue for flare height.

Relative motion also aids in depth perception. Near objects generally appear to pass by the windscreen faster than more distant objects. This helps a visual pilot estimate height above the runway before and during the flare – the closer the aeroplane is to the runway, the faster the runway surface and the surrounding environment appears to pass by.

Depth perception can also be difficult in hazy or misty conditions, where edges are blurred, colours are muted, and light rays may be refracted unusually. This gives the impression of greater distance, an impression reinforced by the fact that we often have to look at distant objects through a smoggy or hazy atmosphere. This illusion is referred to as *environmental perspective.*

In hazy conditions, the object might be closer than it seems; in very clear conditions, the object might be further away than it seems. On hazy days, you might touch down earlier than expected; on very clear nights, you might flare a little too soon.

Make use of approach lights if available.

Visual Illusions

Sometimes what we "see" in our brain (what we think we see) is not actual because images sent from the eyes can sometimes be misinterpreted by the brain.

Relative Movement

We are all familiar with the effect that movement of an adjacent vehicle causes the occupants of a stationary one to think that they are moving. An aircraft moving slowly into an air bridge may feel that they have speeded up if an adjacent aircraft is pushed back.

Autokinesis

The visual illusion of autokinesis (self-motion) can occur at night if you stare continuously at a single light against a generally dark background. It will appear to move, perhaps in an oscillating fashion, after only a few seconds of staring at it, even though in fact it is stationary. You could lose spatial orientation if you use it as your single point of reference. The more you try to concentrate on it, the more it may appear to oscillate. You can guard against autokinesis at night by maintaining movement of your eyes in normal scanning, and by monitoring the flight instruments frequently to ensure correct attitude.

False Expectations

We expect that a pencil will be smaller than a tree, so when we see the image of a pencil beside the image of a tree that is occupying the same angular area on the retina, we assume that the tree is further away. This is usually the case, but need not be, e.g. if the tree is a miniature one.

Environmental Perspective

From birth we learn that anything that is indistinct is far away and anything that is clear is closer. This is not always so, as atmospheric conditions, which alter visibility, vary. This can cause pilots to underestimate distances on approach or from hazards, such as mountains and trees.

Haze

In hazy conditions, you may be closer to the runway than you appear to be, an illusion that may lead to an unnecessarily hard landing if you are not prepared for the effect of haze on your vision.

Judgement of Distance & Angles

The brain often has to make sense of a pattern of lines, and the interpretation may not always be correct. Does a stick bend upwards as you put it into a bucket of water? No, it does not, but it certainly looks as though it does because our brain and eyes assume light travels in straight lines, which is not always the case, as we know from an understanding of refraction.

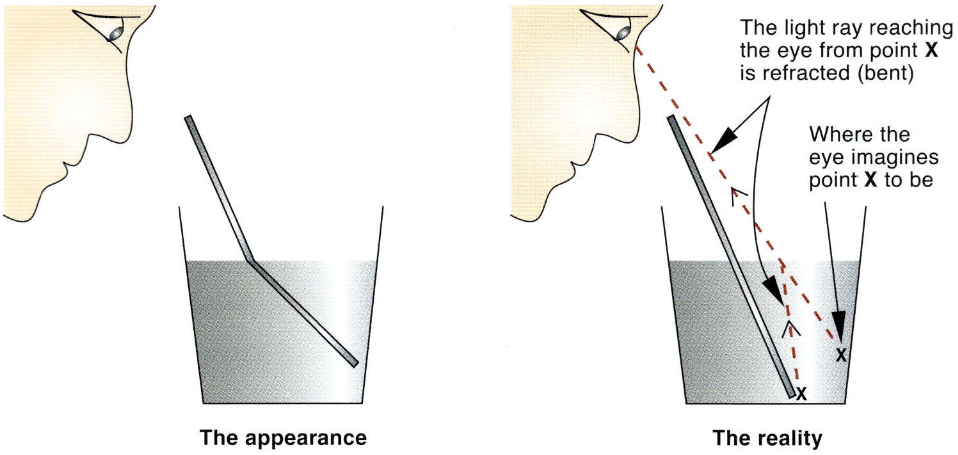

Figure 8-10 Refraction.

An aeroplane on approach through heavy rain can sometimes experience quite a build-up of water on the windscreen, which refracts the light rays on their way to the pilot's eyes, perhaps causing an illusion like the "bent stick". Knowledge of this effect can be some protection for the pilot.

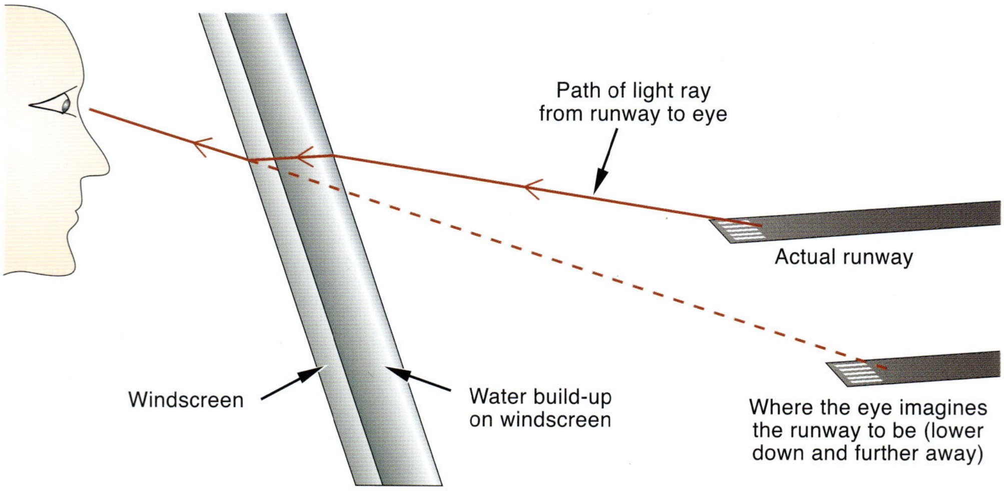

Figure 8-11 Refraction through a wet windscreen.

False Horizons

Sloping cloud layers by day, or angled lines or areas of lights by night, can sometimes present a pilot with a false horizon that can be very misleading. This is not uncommon with a ragged, lowering cloudbase, and associated drizzle or rain obscuring the horizon. Make use of the flight instruments to confirm your flight attitude.

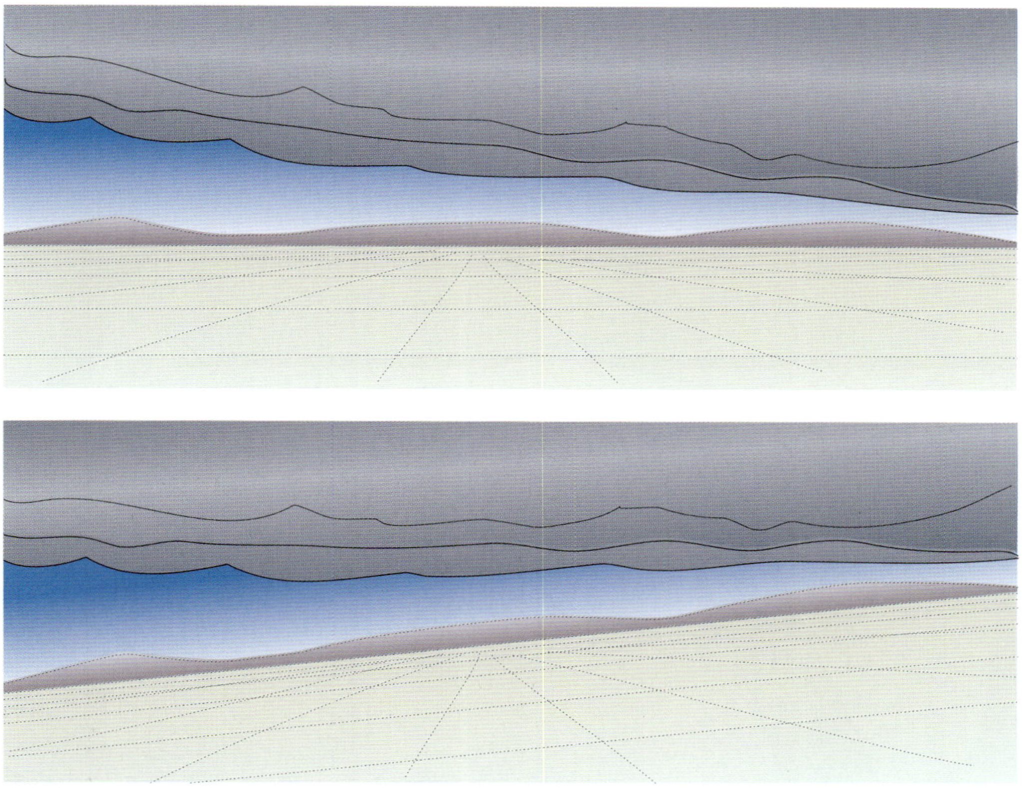

Figure 8-12 False horizon.

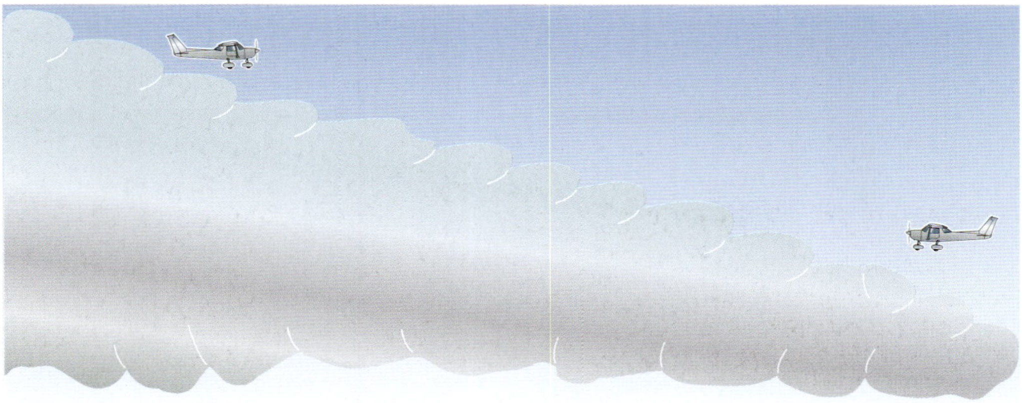

Figure 8-13 False level.

The perceived horizon, real or imagined, is so important.

Visual Illusions in the Circuit

Visual Estimation of Height

A pilot flying a right circuit may get the impression that the aircraft is higher than normal. This illusion could occur to a pilot who has developed the habit of visually judging circuit height and position by relating the position of the runway lights to some feature of the aircraft, such as a particular position in a side window. Such a rule of thumb which worked satisfactorily for the more typical left circuits could lead a pilot to descend lower to achieve the same picture when making right circuits. Like most habits, such a practice could happen unconsciously.

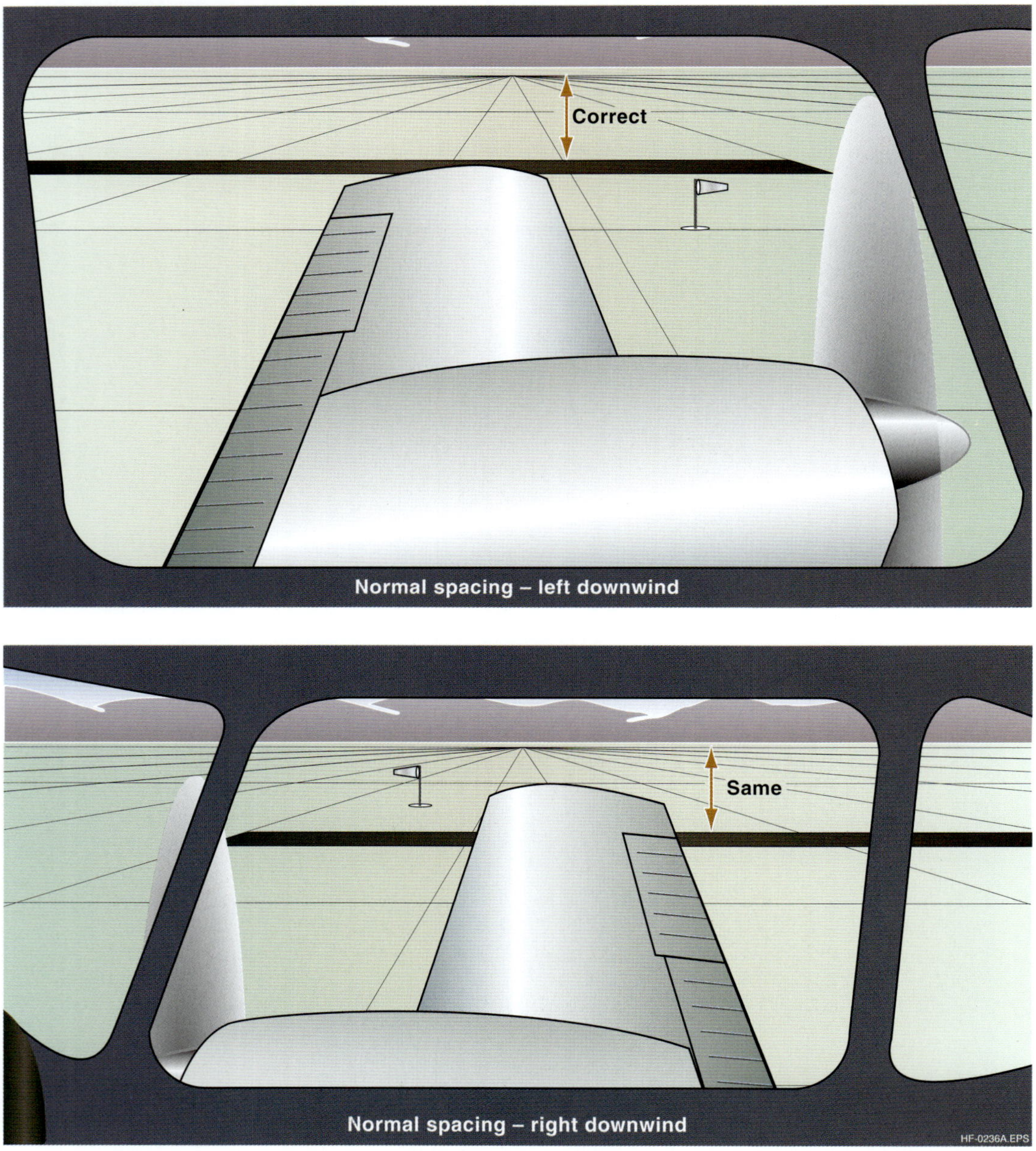

Figure 8-14 Downwind spacing – day.

Visual Illusions on Approach

Runway Slope

Most runways are of known width and on level ground. On every approach, you should try to achieve the same flightpath angle to the horizontal, and your eyes will become accustomed to this, allowing consistent approaches along an acceptable approach slope merely by keeping your view of the runway through the windscreen in a standard perspective.

If approaching a sloping runway, the perspective will be different. A runway that slopes upwards will look longer, and you will feel that you are high, when in fact you are on slope. The temptation will be for you to go lower and make a shallower approach. If you know that the runway does have an upslope, you can avoid this tendency.

Figure 8-15 Runway upslope.

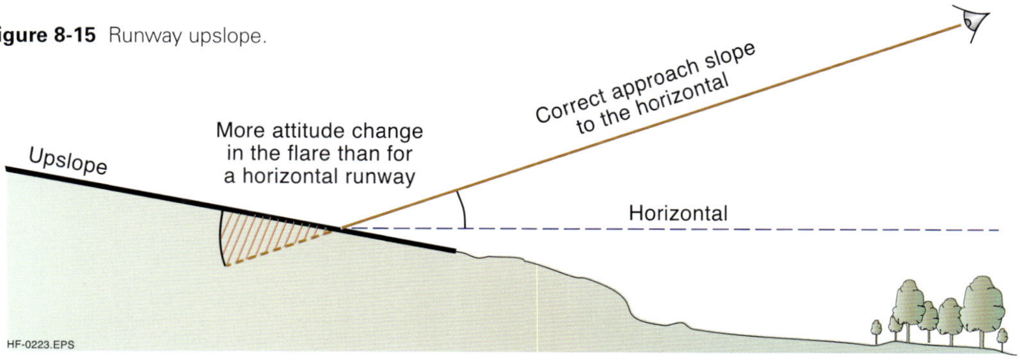

A runway that slopes downwards will look shorter, and you will feel that you are low, when in fact you are on slope. The tendency will be for you to go higher and make a steeper approach. If you know that the runway does have a downslope, you can anticipate and avoid this tendency.

Figure 8-16 Runway downslope.

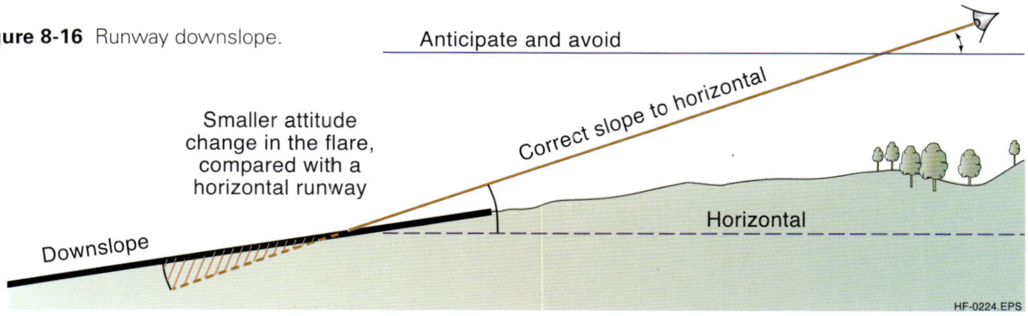

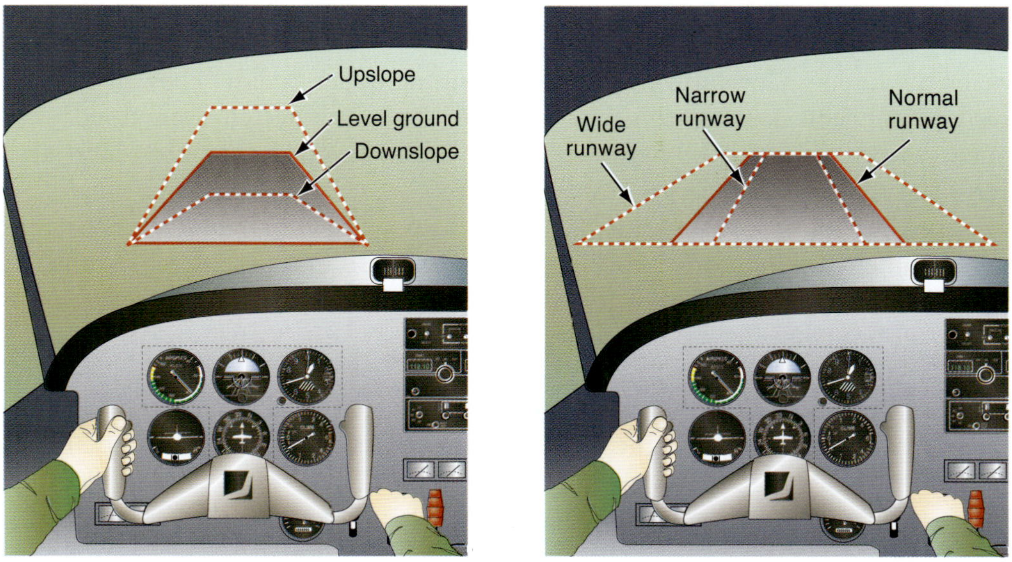

Figure 8-17 (Left) runway aspect and (right) runway width.

Runway Size

A runway that is larger than usual will appear to be closer than it really is. Conversely, a runway that is smaller than usual will appear to be further away than it really is. A wide runway, because of the angle at which you view it peripherally in the final stages of the approach and landing, will cause an illusion of being too low, and you may flare and hold-off too high as a result. This may lead to "dropping-in" for a heavy landing. Conversely, a narrow runway will cause an illusion of being too high, and you may delay the flare and make contact with the runway earlier (and harder) than expected. If you know that the runway is wider or narrower than what you are familiar with, then you can allow for this in your visual judgement of flare height and hold-off prior to touchdown.

A variety of atmospheric and terrain conditions can produce visual illusions. When you encounter these situations, you can anticipate and compensate for them.

Situation	Illusion	Result	
Upslope rwy or terrain	Greater height	Lower approaches	Shallower
Narrower than usual rwy	Greater height	Lower approaches	
Featureless terrain	Greater height	Lower approaches	
Rain on the windscreen	Greater height	Lower approaches	
Haze	Greater height	Lower approaches	
Downsloping rwy or terrain	Less height	Higher approaches	Steeper
Wider-than usual rwy	Less height	Higher approaches	
Bright rwy and approach lights	Less distance	Higher approaches	

Table 8-2 Visual illusions.

Correction and Protection of Vision

Spectacles and Contact Lenses

Spectacles are used to correct short or long sightedness. If required for flying, you may need to carry a spare pair.

Safety Glasses

A pilot's vision is precious. Always wear eye protection for sport, when using tools or when gardening.

Sun Glasses

When flying into a rising or setting sun or above cloud layers, the pilot is exposed to very high intensity light coming from all angles. The eyes are protected from light coming from above by the forehead, eyebrows, eyelashes and strong upper eyelids. They are not so well protected from light coming from below. Bright sunlight reflected from cloud tops, for instance, can be particularly bothersome because of this lack of natural protection. In conditions of glare, it is advisable to protect your eyes by using high-quality sunglasses that reduce glare but not your visual acuity. The contrast between the glare of a very bright outside environment and the darker cockpit interior may also make it difficult for the eyes to adjust quickly enough to read instruments and charts inside the cockpit. Sunglasses should:

- be impact resistant – have thin metal frames;
- transmit 10% to 15% of the light;
- filter out damaging ultraviolet rays; and
- not be worn in decreased light (polarised sunglasses may produce some areas with total loss of vision).

When landing towards the sun, 100% of your vision is lost at the moment of flare. Even when the sun is 40° to the side, vision is reduced by 42%.

Hearing

Ears

The ears provide two senses – hearing and balance. Hearing allows us to perceive sounds and to interpret them; the sense of balance lets us know which way is up and whether we are accelerating or not. Balance is the next most important sense for a pilot after vision.

Sound

Sound is defined as energy that we can detect with our ears. It is often very useful and pleasant, as with voice messages and music, but excessive sound may be annoying and fatiguing, and can even lead to damage within the ear. Irregular, unwanted and unpleasant sound is called noise, and it is best filtered out if we can find a means to do it.

Sound signals are caused by pressure variations travelling through the air as pressure waves, and these cause the sensitive membrane of the eardrum to vibrate. The inner ear translates these pressure vibrations into electrical signals which are sent via the auditory nerve to the brain. Sounds (vibrations) are also felt through the bone structure.

Balance and Acceleration

Similarly, balance and acceleration signals from the balance mechanism in the inner ear pass to the brain as electrical signals for interpretation. The interpretation is sometimes tricky in the case of an airborne pilot, since the brain is used to the person generally being upright on the earth's surface.

Structure of the Ear

The ear is divided into three areas: the outer, middle, and inner ear.

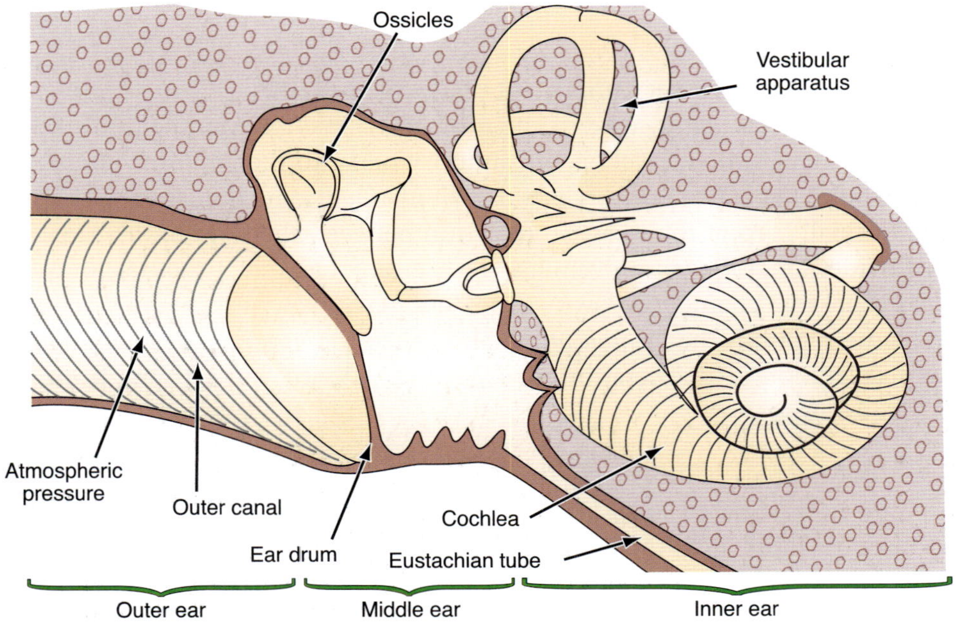

Figure 8-18 The ear.

The Outer Ear

The *outer ear* includes:

- the external ear (known medically as the pinna or auricle), which is used to gather the sound signals;
- the outer canal through which the pressure waves pass; and
- the eardrum, which is caused to vibrate in harmony with the pressure waves.

Any obstruction to the outer canal, such as earplugs or an excess of wax, can reduce the sound pressure waves reaching the eardrum.

Similarly a padded cover over the external ear will reduce the sound waves entering the ear, unless the cover is a headset that blocks external noise, but has a small speaker for radio and interphone messages.

The Middle Ear

The middle ear is an air-filled cavity containing three small bones, known as ossicles, which are forced to move by the vibrating eardrum, converting the pressure wave energy into mechanical energy of motion. The ossicles are arranged like a series of levers to increase the effect of the initial movement. Together with the eardrum, they constitute the conductive tissue. This energy then passes on to the cochlea in the inner ear.

The air in the middle ear is maintained at ambient pressure via the Eustachian tube, which connects the interior of the middle ear to the nasal passages. There is (or should be) no leakage of air across the eardrum, and there should be easy passage of air through the Eustachian tube, when needed, to equalise pressures – for instance, when climbing or descending. This is sometimes hindered by swelling and inflammation when a person has a cold, and can lead to serious consequences (this is explained later) if a person flies with a cold or similar infection. Interference to the movement of the three small ossicles or their joints will reduce or distort the sound signal. This can be caused by ear infections, damage to the bones or joints, or a blocked ear with air trapped inside the middle ear (barotitis).

The Inner Ear

The *inner ear* contains two very important pieces of apparatus:

- The cochlea for hearing; it converts the mechanical energy from the ossicles into electrical signals which then travel via the auditory nerve to the brain for interpretation.
- The vestibular apparatus consists of three fluid-filled semicircular canals. Each has a cluster of small hairs at their base. Interaction between the fluid in the canals and the hairs provides sensations of movement. The sensing hairs sit at the base of each semicircular canal in a chamber known as the "cupula".
- In the same region is the *otolithic organ* (also called the *utricle*), a device which detects linear acceleration or deceleration. It is co-located with, but separate from, the vestibular apparatus.

Fluid in the cochlea is moved by the mechanical energy from the ossicles, and this causes a wavy movement of small hairs protruding into the fluid. The movement is converted to electrical signals at the bottom of each hair, and these signals are sent along the auditory nerve to the brain.

Excessive noise can lead to damage of the hairs in the cochlea, and infection or injury can damage the auditory nerve, possibly causing ringing in the ears (*tinnitus*).

Aural Sensations

The ear is never switched off, and loud or particular noises to which we have a conditioned response can always help stir us from even the deepest sleep. For this reason, a quiet room is best if you want to sleep soundly. It is interesting to note how you can extract messages important for you out of a noisy background – for instance, a radio message directed at you, the sound of your own child on a crowded beach, or your own name mentioned in a distant conversation – known as "the cocktail party effect".

The region of the middle ear has much to do with your sensations of movement and balance. It is for that reason that people with middle ear infections often lose their sense of balance. Further, disturbed signals from these sensors lead to feeling of nausea. In extreme cases, vertigo – total loss of balance, massive and disturbing disorientation – results. The comments that follow apply to the hearing aspects of the ear.

Sound is what we hear, and each sound can be defined by:

- *Frequency or pitch:* the number of pressure waves per second (or hertz, Hz) that the sound source produces. Perfect human hearing is in the range of 20 Hz to 20,000 Hz, and voices use the frequency range 500 Hz to 3,000 Hz.
- *Loudness:* the perception of loudness is not the same value as pressure. Pressure waves are measured in decibels (dB): this is a logarithmic scale where an increase of 10 dB signifies a doubling of loudness (a pressure level of 10 dB is twice as loud as 0 dB, the threshold of hearing; 20 dB is 2 times louder again, i.e. four times as loud as 0 dB).
- *Duration:* how long the sound lasts.

Fatigue & Damage From Noise

Unwanted sound, especially if it is loud and disagreeable, is noise. It can be mentally fatiguing through its effect on our ears, but it also affects the rest of our body, especially if it is associated with vibration as is often the case. Noise can interfere with communications, and with our concentration.

130 dB	Standing near a jet aircraft (noise becoming painful)
120 dB	Standing near a piston-engined aircraft (noise becoming uncomfortable). Several hours per day for 3 months could lead to deafness.
110 dB	Maximum recommended for up to 30 minutes exposure
100 dB	Maximum recommended for 2 hours exposure
90 dB	Maximum recommended for 8 hours exposure (a working day)
80 dB	Standing near heavy machinery. Above 80 dB for long periods can lead to temporary or permanent hearing loss.
60 dB	Loud street noise, trucks, etc.
50 dB	Conversation in a noisy factory
40 dB	Office noise
30 dB	Quiet conversation
20 dB	Whispering
0 dB	The threshold of hearing

Table 8-3 Noise levels of typical sounds.

Extreme noise levels can also do permanent damage to our ears, with duration of exposure being as important as loudness.

Aircraft Type	Take-Off	Cruise	Landing
Aero Commander 680	102	92	83
Beechcraft A 36	97	86	75
Cessna 172	94	89	75
Piper Pawnee	103	102	89
Bell 206	91	92	89

Table 8-4 Indicative cockpit noise levels (decibels).

Loss of Hearing

A person can experience a temporary hearing loss after exposure to noise. The noise of an engine, for instance, may no longer be heard after a while even though the engine noise is still there. Some factory workers lose the ability to hear frequencies that they are subjected to all day long. A temporary hearing loss may disappear after a few hours or after a few days.

Exposure to high noise levels greater than 80 dB for long periods can also lead to a permanent hearing loss, especially in the high-frequency range. This is a risk area for pilots who are exposed to a noisy work environment for long periods. Put it together with visits to the car races, noisy discotheques, plus a top set of loudspeakers at home, and you are in a high risk environment from the point of view of your hearing.

Very, very gradually, and imperceptibly, a person can lose the ability to hear certain sounds clearly, speech becomes more difficult to comprehend, and radio communications become more difficult. Sudden, unexpected loud noises greater than about 130 dB, such as an explosion or the sound of an impact, can cause damage to hearing, possibly even physical damage to the eardrum or to the small and delicate ossicle bones behind the eardrum. Hearing loss can also result from:

- problems in the conduction of the sound, through a blocked outer canal (ear wax), fluid or pressure problems in the middle ear (barotrauma caused by a cold, for instance), or faulty ossicle bones and joints – this is known as *conductive hearing loss*;
- loss of sensitivity of the hair cells in the cochlea, through exposure to noise, infection, or age – this is known as a sensory or noise-induced hearing loss;
- presbycusis, a natural loss of hearing ability with increasing age, especially in the higher frequencies – down about 5% by age 60 and 10% by age 70; or
- alcoholism, or excessive use of medications.

Precautions for Minimising Hearing Loss

A noise-induced hearing loss may develop gradually over a period of years without the person noticing – something which cannot be reversed, hence the need for prevention rather than cure. As pilots, we are lucky in that we have regular audiometry tests which can be monitored over the years to look for any gradual loss of hearing, especially in the higher frequencies. Wear hearing protection when in noisy areas. A good noise-cancelling headset is highly recommended for the cockpit, and earplugs or earmuffs for when you are moving around outside the aircraft. Earplugs can reduce noise by about 20 dB, and good earmuffs by about 40 dB. The radio headset, especially if it is well sealed, will block out background noise. The squelch control on the radio will reduce background hash, and you should keep the volume turned down as much as possible without disturbing your comprehension of voice messages. Unprotected close exposure to jet-engine noise can be hazardous to the balance mechanism in the ears also – another reason to wear hearing protection on the tarmac.

Balance

The human body balances on earth by a combination of visual observation, sense of weight (on the soles of the feet or the buttocks, if you are seated) and a balance mechanism called the *vestibular apparatus* in the inner ear. When there is a visual horizon or vertical reference, it is powerfully dominant. If we remove the visual reference (at night, in cloud or even in the aircraft cabin) then the body tries to orient itself using these other inputs.

Rotary Acceleration

The mechanism in the inner ear consists of three orthogonal (90° to each other) circular tubes, within which fluid moves due to rotary acceleration. Fine hairs sense the motion of the fluid. The three canals therefore sense acceleration in pitch, roll and yaw.

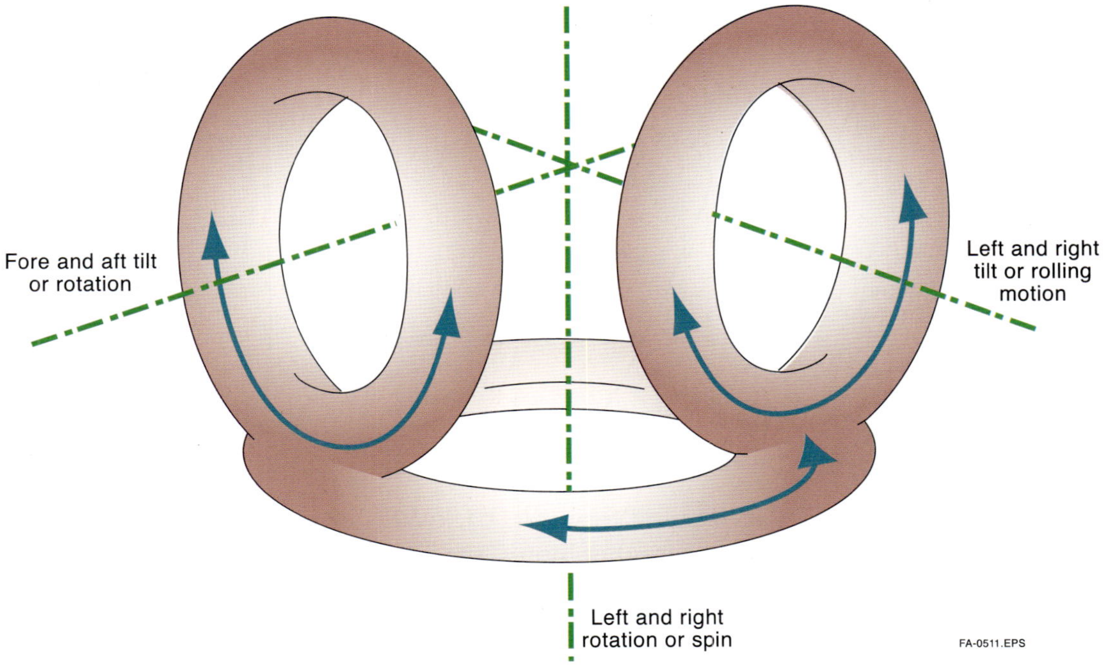

Figure 8-19 Semi-circular canals.

The hairs do not sense very slow or steady motion. It is possible when flying in cloud to enter a gentle turn which the vestibular apparatus does not sense. If the pilot now rolls out of the turn, at a normal rate, it is detected and the brain computes this as a roll to the right from level. The aircraft has actually rolled to level flight but the brain thinks that it has rolled from level into a right hand turn. There is now a dilemma. The brain is being told that the aircraft is tilted to the right but the pilot's eyes looking at the attitude indicator tell the brain that the aircraft is level. This conflict causes an unnerving condition called *the leans*. Pilots are trained to discipline themselves to believe their eyes and ignore their inner sensations. It is not a nice feeling and takes some getting used to.

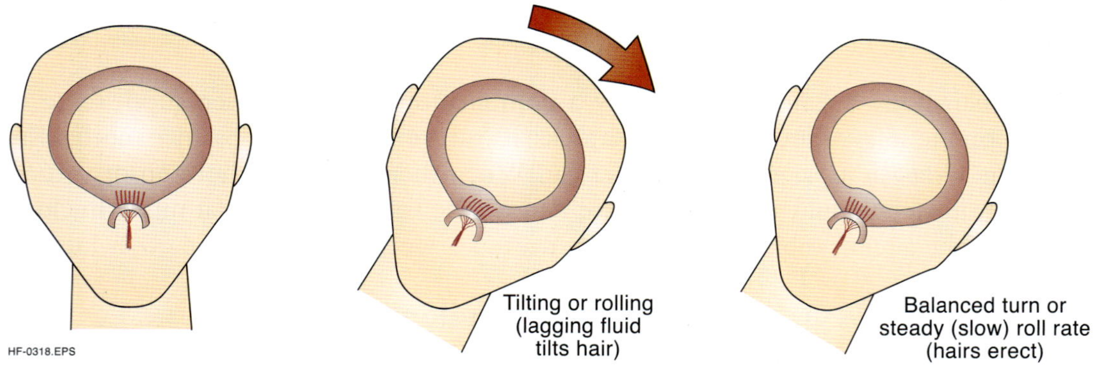

Figure 8-20 Erect, rolling and balanced.

Linear Acceleration & Tilt

The other element of the inner ear (the utricle) senses linear (straight line) acceleration or tilt. It consists of a gelatinous bubble enclosing small crystals which are balanced on hairs. If the head is tilted, the crystals bend the hairs.

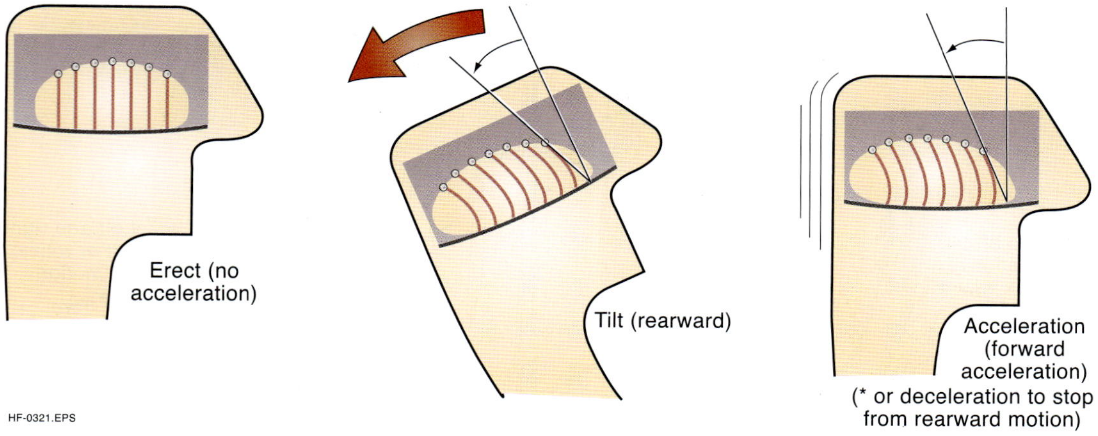

Figure 8-21 Tilt or acceleration?

Similarly, if the head is accelerated forwards, backwards or sideways, the crystals are temporarily "left behind". Without other inputs, the utricle cannot distinguish between tilt and acceleration.

It's just like a glass of wine.

Figure 8-22 Tilt or acceleration?

This misleading condition is particularly important to pilots on a night take-off when the acceleration can be sensed as tilting backwards and the body wants to lower the nose of the aircraft to compensate.

Stress

In the course of normal activity we respond to stimuli, or demands, placed on us in response to our actions and by our environment. These demands can be mental or physical, and if they create a pressure overload, we are adversely affected and stress results.

Exposure to constant stress can bring about changes in the balance of hormones in the body, which threatens the health. Also, the existence of one form of stress tends to diminish the resistance to other forms. A potential stressor can be acute in the sense that it is immediate and disappears after a short time; another can be chronic, long lasting and fatiguing. It is important for general health, and for longevity, that all pressures and demands are managed so as not to be stressful for us as much as possible.

Stressors

An experience causing stress is known as a stressor. Stressors can be divided into two classes:

- environmental or physical stressors, which include such items as noise and physical contact; and
- intellectual, psychological, and emotional stressors, which are often related to problems at home and at work.

Environmental or Physical Stressors

If you are working in an environment that differs from the ideal environment for humans – for instance in an environment which is excessively hot, cold, noisy, damp, dry, turbulent, vibrating, dark, light, smelly or lacking in oxygen – you can become tired and stressed more quickly than otherwise.

Stress Caused by Heat (Hyperthermia) and Lack of Humidity

In very high environmental temperatures, say 35°C and above, the body struggles to keep its internal temperature at just under 37°C and prevent itself from overheating (known as *hyperthermia*). The perspiration rate, heart rate and blood pressure all increase. In a humid atmosphere, as opposed to a dry atmosphere, your perspiration will tend not to evaporate, hence no latent heat is absorbed into the air from your skin and the underlying blood, so there is a greater tendency for your body to overheat. Your attention becomes narrowed and restricted affecting your decision-making.

Try to take a drink before you actually become thirsty, since thirst is a sign that you are already on the way to becoming dehydrated. In fact you should drink 250 ml of water every 30 minutes to prevent dehydration when air temperatures are above 30°C. Above 30°, say, heart rate and blood pressure increase.

To minimise heat stress you should try to control the environmental temperature, and, most importantly, drink enough fluids. Water is ideal. Thirst is a sign that you are already on the way to becoming dehydrated. Don't wait until you feel thirsty.

Remember that tasks outside the cockpit prior to flight, such as loading the aircraft or flight planning, or even just standing or sitting in high temperatures, may cause your body to overheat and/or dehydrate. Take appropriate measures by drinking fluids, staying under shade, and not rushing.

Humidity levels also effect our stress levels. Humidity in a cockpit can fall as low as 5%. The human body's comfort range is normally 40%–60%.

Stress Caused by Cold (Hypothermia)

In a cold environment, the body automatically sends more blood to the body core, rather than to the extremities. This is an attempt to keep the internal temperature at about 37°C by minimising heat loss from the skin. Heat loss can occur by:

- radiation from exposed areas of skin, especially from your head which has many blood vessels near the surface of your scalp;
- conduction as wind flows across your skin and carries heat away, which is known as the *wind chill factor*; and
- evaporation of perspiration or other moisture from your skin, which causes cooling by absorbing heat from the skin and underlying blood vessels, and using it to change the state of the moisture from liquid to vapour (latent heat).

In low temperatures, your toes and fingers may feel cold, your muscles might feel stiff and weak, you may feel tired and drowsy, and you might start to shiver – this is an attempt by your body to generate warmth by muscle activity. It is said that "if your hands and feet feel comfortable, then all is well". Most people normally clothed are comfortable around 20°C.

Stress Caused by Vibration

Vibrations transmitted to the body from the aircraft via the seat, seat-belts and the floor can make you feel uncomfortable, distract you from your main tasks, and lead to fatigue.

A vibrating instrument panel may make the instruments difficult to read. Severe vibration may even cause your eyeballs to vibrate, making it almost impossible to read your flight instruments or your navigation charts, or to scan for other aircraft. Even though it might be impossible to reduce the vibration from the aircraft itself, the vibration reaching your body can be reduced by well-mounted and well-cushioned seats.

Stress Caused by Turbulence

Turbulence will cause irregular movements of the aircraft, varying from fairly small movements when flying through slight turbulence to unbelievably strong movements associated with severe turbulence that may even damage the aircraft. Turbulence can cause discomfort to the pilot and passengers by shaking them around, exerting unusual g-forces on them, and perhaps causing motion sickness. It may cause the instrument panel to vibrate or the eyeballs to judder, making it difficult to read the instruments, and it may make the aircraft very difficult to control.

Stress Caused by Noise

Excessive noise in the cockpit, especially if it is high-pitched and loud, can cause stress and fatigue. An industry limit for continuous noise is 85 dB (decibels), with ear protection required above this level. Noise levels in a typical cockpit are in the range 75–80 dB, but this is only background noise, with noise from radio messages superimposed on it. Noise above about 90 dB will cause stress that raises your arousal into the poor performance area, making you irritable, and leading to fatigue. Your attention becomes narrowed and restricted. Above about 80 dB, you should wear protection to avoid stress damage to your ears. Stress can also be caused by having to strain to understand radio messages against a high background noise level. With your ears protected from background engine and air noise by a high-quality headset, you should be able to hear radio messages even when the volume is quite low.

Stress Caused by Being Uncomfortable

The nature of our job as pilots is that we are confined to sitting in small cockpits for long periods of time. The stress of sitting in a noisy, vibrating aircraft for long periods, and having to cope with the usual problems of flight, such as turbulence, navigation, radio calls, and so on, can lead to an accumulation of stress and fatigue. The best means of combating this form of stress is to keep yourself fit, be well rested prior to flight, maintain a good posture (sit well back into the seat and ensure your lower back is well supported), and exercise periodically by wriggling your toes and feet and stretching your arms.

It is also important to be appropriately dressed for the job. Wearing too much or too little clothing will make you uncomfortable and is therefore distracting. You should also make sure that your clothes fit well. There are few things worse than a tight shirt collar, tight trousers, or tight shoes.

Stress Caused by Feeling Unwell

If feeling unwell, you may be easily overloaded and prone to becoming fatigued. Your body will be using up energy to combat the illness, and so you will have less energy available for other tasks. Your general performance will be much lower than normal. If you have a headache, an upper respiratory tract infection (such as a cold), a sporting or other injury, a stomach upset, hay fever or a sneezing attack, you should consider whether to commence your flight. If you feel unwell in flight, then you should consider landing and resting.

Motion sickness (feeling airsick) can make a person feel very low and uninterested in events. It is not confined to new student pilots and passengers – on rare occasions even experienced pilots feel airsick. Their knowledge that it might cause them to feel apathetic, however, is some protection against lowered performance.

A pilot will also be subject to stress unnecessarily if not eating regularly or eating well, the result possibly being hypoglycemia, a low blood sugar level. Its symptoms are headache, stomach pain, lack of energy, nervousness and shaking, and can be relieved in the short term by eating a snack, such as a banana or some chocolate.

Stress Caused by Eye Strain

Eye strain due to impaired vision or poor lighting can cause stress and fatigue. Impaired vision can be remedied with glasses or contact lenses. The solution to bad lighting is obvious. This need not mean that the whole cockpit be brightly lit when all you need to see are the instruments and your charts – simply turn the instrument lights up and use a small spotlight, if available, for your charts. If the main cabin lights are turned up too brightly at night, you may have to strain your eyes to scan outside for other aircraft and weather.

Stress Caused by Flashing or Strobing Lights

A flashing light is designed to attract attention, usually to other vehicles or aircraft. Seeing a flashing light will raise your level of alertness. If, however, the warning does not apply to you, the flashing light may be very distracting and even fatiguing. For instance, a flashing amber light from a fuel truck parked right in front of your cockpit at night can be very distracting if you are trying to complete your flight preparation tasks. Reflected light from your own strobe lights when flying in cloud at night can be highly distracting, so turn the strobes off temporarily – other aircraft will not be able to see them while you are in cloud anyway.

Stress Caused by Concentration

Skill stress which leads to fatigue can result if you have to maintain a high level of performance for an extended period – for instance, hand-flying on instruments in turbulent IFR conditions, or for a student pilot even straight and level, visual flying.

Stress Caused by Lack of Sleep

A lack of restful sleep leaves a pilot fatigued, and needing to struggle to stay awake to handle the demands of flying. The pilot has to fight off sleep, and really force concentration, leading to a high stress level and even deeper fatigue. It is a vicious circle. The solution to this is, of course, not to fly unless well rested.

Psychological & Emotional Stressors

Psychological or emotional stress can arise from a number of sources and constitutes a major source of overload. It could be work related (a difficult flight about to begin, or a strained relationship with management or colleagues), or it could have a domestic cause (marital or financial problems).

The result of psychological stress is that a pilot may be overaroused and move into the area of poor performance:

- concentrating on a single problem and not maintaining a good overview of the flight;
- exhibiting poor judgement;
- becoming disoriented quite easily;
- being distracted from prime tasks;
- taking a resigned attitude to problems that arise ("*why does this always happen to me?*"); and
- becoming fatigued at an early stage.

Work-Related Psychological Stress

Most pilots experience a certain amount of apprehension regarding a forthcoming flight, but this is quite normal and can raise the level of arousal into the optimum area for good performance. A pilot who is stressed and over-anxious, however, may be too highly aroused to perform well – a common situation with inexperienced student pilots, and in many experienced pilots who are facing a demanding flight.

Psychological & Emotional Stress

Psychological and emotional stress can be caused by problems at home. Domestic-related stress can be very damaging to a pilot. If distracted by emotional problems during highly charged periods such as following the death of a spouse or child (considered the most stressful life experience), a divorce, or when experiencing severe financial difficulties, a responsible pilot should consider grounding himself or herself. Domestic-related problems can lead to lack of sleep, chronic fatigue, emotional instability, and a dangerous flight operation.

Anxiety, depression or fear may cause emotional instability. Some anxiety can be considered normal. For example, if you are about to undertake an exam or a flight test, you many feel a little anxious or nervous. If, however, this anxiety is affecting you physically, then you should consider cancelling your flight. If you become nauseous, get stomach cramps or become ill in some other way, the stress is too much for your flight to be a safe one. Also, if a pilot is learning something for the first time, they may feel a little anxious, but they will feel less stress the next time they attempt the same exercise.

Depression will affect your judgement and your ability to think logically. If you are feeling depressed about a situation, whether it be domestic or some other situation, you should keep your feet firmly planted on the ground. Flying requires your full attention to ensure that you do not encounter a dangerous situation. If your mind is diverted to a problem, it cannot be focused on the many tasks associated with flying an aeroplane.

Fear will provoke an anxiety response and diminish your ability to function effectively in the cockpit. Again, your mind will be preoccupied if it is in a state of fear and will take you away from your ability to safely carry out tasks in the cockpit. Deal with your fear before embarking on any flight.

Managing Stress

To some extent, the pilot has some control over the stress level, and can often reduce the pressures. Some ways in which this can be done are:

- make early decisions – turn back or divert before flying into bad conditions, or land well before last light if necessary;
- do not accept an a track or climb leading into clouds – keep clear of cloud and request a new clearance;
- do not be distracted from checklists: request your passengers, flight instructor, or examiner not to interrupt;
- do not interrupt or change your usual routines unnecessarily; and
- request ATC to stand by if you are busy coping with an emergency or having trouble handling the aeroplane – flightpath and airspeed always come first.

Be prepared for delays – weather may force a delay, as can refuelling and aircraft unserviceabilities; always allow a time buffer, even for the drive to the airport. There is no such thing as a stress free environment, the pilot must learn to minimise and manage the associated stresses so he or she is fit to act as a decision maker.

Allow time to manage time. Do not be pushed into anything.

Reflexes & Reactions

The brain exerts control by sending electrical signals via channels of nerve cells to the various parts of the body. These channels are referred to simply as *nerves,* and each muscle, organ or sense in the body has one or more nerves connecting it to the brain.

As well as sending out signals to the various parts of the body, the brain also receives signals from them, which it then processes, perhaps sending out another signal in response. For instance, a finger having touched the object you are looking at sends back a "tactile" message to the brain saying, "*We've arrived at where you sent us, what now?*". The brain may follow up with signals to the various muscles involved in picking up the object and throwing it – or drinking from it. This is an example of the feedback function.

A sudden and unexpected noise may cause fright, to which the brain responds by quickly preparing the body for action – electrical signals are transmitted to appropriate muscles, and certain chemicals are released (adrenalin, for instance) to speed up the rate of metabolism and prepare the body to "fight or flee". The constant interplay of transmitted signals and reception of feedback signals is a never-ending activity of the brain throughout life, even when we sleep.

The brain is also involved in the many automatic bodily functions carried out in the autonomic nervous system (such as control of the senses, body temperature, breathing rate and depth, pulse rate, the digestive process, and blood pressure). We will use the term *autonomic,* which refers to responses to stimuli that are wholly automatic, and not consciously controlled, such as salivating when you smell food, or secretion of hormones when exposed to bright light or entering into a new relationship. Learned or autonomous (self-contained) functions are also spontaneously activated, but they comprise thinking and physical movement patterns – e.g. attitudes and walking – that, while being automatic, can also be subjected to conscious control or management. That is, they are learned, trained or conditioned habits.

Reflexes are mainly autonomic, but may also be subject to control, to the extent that they can be subordinated to management – e.g. your ability not to flinch at a loud noise or not to drop a cup of coffee even though it's burning your hand – they become "reactions". If you knock a bottle from a table, your automatic response is such that you will catch it before it hits the floor, without conscious thought. If it is a sharp knife, while you may start to move your hands towards it, conscious control intervenes and you let it drop to the floor. That is a reaction, and in the latter case one that is consciously overridden.

The Emotional Pilot

Decision-Making

Decisions are mostly emotional. The pilot's primary task is control. Being in control implies processing information and making decisions. The pilot needs to know what control input to make and when, to monitor the outcome of the control input and to then adjust the input to achieve the desired result. The control input is a function of the sensory data received and the training to know what to do with the sensory information. Knowing what to do and when and then doing it are the processes in making a decision. This is ultimately the pilot's role.

The body contains a vast network of cells which carry information in the form of nerve impulses to and from all of its parts. These impulses are the means by which all bodily activity occurs. The brain – the master controller – and the spinal chord together form the central nervous system, which is responsible for the integration of virtually all nervous activity in the body. The remaining nervous tissue – the peripheral nervous system – includes the autonomic nervous system, which controls various bodily functions that are not consciously directed, including:

- the regular beating of the heart;
- digestion and intestinal movements;
- respiration;
- sweating; and
- salivation.

Other functions, such as the need to move an arm, hand and fingers to turn the pages of this book, require our conscious intervention if repetitive, or could be a learned unconscious response. An activity such as flying an aeroplane requires conscious intervention. Although training and experience can reduce the amount of conscious effort we need to make in conducting a flight, it can never become an entirely automatic activity like the heartbeat.

Almost every accident situation and potential accident situation can be traced back to a poor decision or a deferral of a decision until it was to late. There are no simple rules except to say that in aviation, we must err on the safe side. If uncertain about the outcome, don't do it. Don't press on. Don't assume.

The essence is to objectively look at ourselves, out fitness, our skill, training, recency, familiarity with the aircraft, the aerodrome, terrain and weather. Objectively means honesty, warts and all. We gain far more respect as a pilot by saying no to situations with which we are uncomfortable. There is no shame by insisting on a delay until the situation is more comfortable and manageable.

This leads us to the topic of '*Threat & Error Management*'.

Threat & Error Management

Threat & Error Management (TEM) is a holistic safety concept which specifically addresses potential weaknesses in human performance in the aviation environment – when threatened by external influences. It is primarily the result of observations from airline operations and is now being considered for smaller commercial and private operations – and single pilot operations.

TEM evolved from a *Line Oriented Safety Audit* (LOSA). This was a program to observe flight operations by volunteer airlines to identify and categorise threats to safety, errors performed by the crew, resulting in undesired aircraft states and possible accident outcomes. The program was most effective in identifying links in the chain of events that could lead to an accident.There is a great deal of information available but it is well summarised herein:

- Captain Dan Maurino (www.flightsafety.org/doc/tem/maurino.doc);
- Ashleigh Merrit Ph.D. & James Klinect Ph.D. (www.psy.utexas.edu/HumanFactors);
- Robert Helmreich Ph.D. FRAeS, also University of Texas; and
- GAPAN (www.gapan.org.au).

ICAO has now adopted the system and it will be introduced world-wide. The Guild of Air Pilots and Navigators (GAPAN), has conducted pilot seminars around Australia to introduce the scheme. It will not only apply to airlines but all facets of aviation, including GA – and the pilot training syllabus (the CASA Day VFR syllabus), was amended to include TEM training. Further the *Manual of Standards* (MOS) released as part of the new CASR PART61 legislation, includes TEM in addition to BAK - as part of the knowledge base for the Recreational Pilot Licence.

Background

Previous research of human performance in aviation had overlooked the most important factor, i.e. the interaction between people and their operational environment (the organization, the regulations and the environmental factors within which flight crew worked).

What is Threat & Error Management?

In considering the environment in which aircrews worked, the researchers identified factors that *threat*ened the safe conduct of the flight.

They next classified inappropriate crew actions (errors) which were a result of, or independent of, the threat situation but which could lead to the aircraft being placed in a less than desirable situation. These *undesired aircraft states* could lead to an accident or incident outcome. Thus the *TEM model* was developed – which sorts the complex factors in the aviation world into these categories and also examines the links between them and how the chain of events could be interrupted.

The Threat & Error Management Model

The TEM model is a theoretical framework that categorises the major factors in the accident chain of events and, within each, highlights the inter-relationship between external influences and human response. TEM categorises external factors, human errors, crew responses, undesired aircraft states and likely outcomes and identifies opportunities for countermeasures.

Components of the TEM model

From the flight crews' perspective, there are three basic components in the TEM model. These are described as:

- threats;
- errors; and
- undesired aircraft states.

Threats and errors are part of everyday operations that carry the potential to generate undesired aircraft states. These states may lead to an outcome such as an aircraft accident. At various stages in the chain of events, the flight crew may interrupt the process and avoid the development of an accident scenario such that a potentially threatening situation becomes a non-event. In fact, the crew is doing this as a matter of course but sometimes the stress, workload and other factors, break the crew's concentration. This model is not to check the crew but to highlight the importance of crew actions in the control process and to illustrate why vigilance and cross-checking has become even more important in what are more complex flight environments. The crew interruptions are called *countermeasures*.

At each stage the crew may initiate countermeasures in the form of:

- anticipation of, avoidance or counters to *threats*;
- recognition and prevention of *errors;*
- correction or recovery from *undesired aircraft states;* and
- final avoidance of an accident *outcome.*

So that the model can be used on an international basis, there are strictly agreed definitions of the various stages and categories within each.

Threats

Threats are defined as *events or errors made by others, that occur beyond the influence of the flight crew, increase operational complexity, and which must be managed to maintain the margins of safety.* A threat is something beyond the control of the crew but something that may be anticipated, avoided, countered or made ineffective.

Various complexities or events arise during normal flight operations, for example, weather, terrain, traffic, aircraft malfunctions, or mistakes made by other people outside of the cockpit, such as air traffic controllers, flight attendants or LAMEs. The TEM model considers these complexities as threats because they all have the potential to negatively affect flight operations by reducing margins of safety.

There are three types of threat:

- **expected threats** – that can be anticipated, since they are expected or known to the flight crew, e.g. thunderstorm activity, windshear, intense traffic in a terminal area,
- **unexpected threats** – that can occur unexpectedly, such as an in-flight aircraft malfunction; and
- **latent threats** – that are not immediately obvious or observable, such as equipment design issues, optical illusions, or shortened turn-around schedules.

Regardless of whether threats are expected, unexpected, or latent, one measure of the effectiveness of a flight crew's ability to manage threats is whether they are detected in time for the flight crew to respond.

Categories of Threat

Threats are grouped under two basic categories derived from the TEM model:
- environmental threats; and
- organisational threats.

Environmental threats – occur due to the environment in which flight operations take place. Some environmental threats can be anticipated and some will arise without warning. All have to be addressed by flight crews and not be allowed to lead to errors. Environmental threats include:
- weather: thunderstorms, turbulence, icing, wind shear, cross/tailwind, very low/high temperatures.
- ATS – traffic congestion, TCAS RA/TA, ATC command, ATC error, language difficulty, ATS non-standard phraseology, similar call-signs, runway change, ATIS communication, units of measurement.
- airport – contaminated/short runway; contaminated taxiway, lack of/confusing/faded signage/markings, birds, aids U/S, complex surface navigation procedures, airport constructions.
- terrain – high ground, slope, lack of visual references, “black hole”.
- operational pressures – delays, late arrivals, equipment changes; or
- aircraft malfunction, automation event/anomaly.

Organisational threats – are deficiencies or errors within the infrastructure of flight operations, that can lead to aircrew errors. Organisational threats may arise from a:
- flight attendant error – cabin event, distraction, interruption, cabin door insecurity;
- maintenance event or error;
- ground handling event or error;
- dispatch error;
- documentation error – data entry, manual or chart error; or
- crew scheduling error.

Threat Management

Threat management is a stepping stone to error management and undesired aircraft state management. Mismanaged threats normally lead to errors, which in turn, are often linked to undesired aircraft states – if the error is not recognised and not corrected.

Threat management provides the most proactive option to maintain margins of safety in flight operations, by anticipating and avoiding the threat altogether – e.g. by track diversion, change of flight timing, change of flight profile or by carrying additional fuel.

Management of threats, errors and undesired aircraft states is discussed later under *countermeasures*.

Errors

Errors are ***actions*** *or* ***inactions*** *by the flight crew that lead to deviations from organisational or flight crew intentions or expectations.* Errors that are not corrected or are mis-handled, frequently lead to undesired aircraft states. Errors reduce the margins of safety and increase the probability of an adverse outcome.

Errors can be:

- spontaneous and independent of a threat, e.g mis-setting an altitude;
- induced by a threat which was not countered, e.g. missing a checklist item due to a radio call interruption; or
- be a link in a chain of errors – each compounding the problem, e.g. iced pitot head leading to airspeed error, leading to incorrect pilot actions, leading to an extreme attitude and airspeed.

Regardless of the type of error, its effect on safety depends on whether the flight crew detects and responds to the error before it leads to a UAS and to a potentially unsafe outcome.

There are three primary categories of error in the TEM model:

- aircraft handling error;
- procedural error; or
- communication error.

Aircraft handling errors include:

- manual flight: altitude, track or speed deviations, exceeding airspeed limitations (V_S, V_{FE}, V_{NO}, V_B, M_{MO}), incorrect attitude, heading or power setting, wrong configuration – flaps, speedbrakes, autobrake or undercarriage;
- auto flight: incorrect autopilot mode, incorrect GPS/FMS data entry or autothrottle setting;
- systems/radio/instruments: any incorrect setting such as airspeed bug, altimeter subscale, fuel selection, NAVAID or radio frequency or waypoint;
- ground navigation: choosing wrong taxiway/runway, taxiing too fast, failing to hold short.

Procedural errors include:

- SOPs: failure to cross-check settings and clearance limits.
- checklists: wrong challenge and response; items missed, checklist performed late or at the wrong time.
- callouts: omitted/incorrect callouts
- briefings: omitted briefings; items missed.
- documentation: incorrect weight or CG, incorrect fuel calculation and quantity, ATIS, or clearance information, incorrect logbook or maintenance release entries, incorrect application of MEL procedures.

Communication errors include:

- external: missed calls, misinterpretations of instructions, incorrect read-back, incorrectly stated or misread clearance.
- internal: misunderstood or interrupted communications.

Note: In the TEM concept, errors have to be observable and therefore, the TEM model classifies errors based upon the primary interaction of the pilot or flight crew – at the moment the error is committed. Thus, in order to be classified as aircraft handling error, the pilot or flight crew must be interacting with the aircraft (e.g. through its controls, autopilot or systems). In order to be classified as procedural error, the pilot or flight crew must be interacting with a procedure (e.g. checklists; SOPs; etc.). In order to be classified as communication error, the pilot or flight crew must be interacting with people (ATC; groundcrew; other crew members, etc.).

Aircraft handling errors, procedural errors and communication errors may be unintentional or involve intentional non-compliance with clearance limits, regulations or SOPs. Pilot proficiency, i.e. skill or knowledge deficiencies, and personality, may underlie all three categories of error.

Note: For simplicity and to avoid confusion, the TEM model does not consider intentional non-compliance and proficiency as separate categories of error, but rather as sub-sets of the three major categories of error.

Human Error

Error is inevitable because of human limitations – limited memory capacity, limited mental processing capacity, negative effects of stress, tunnel vision, and the negative influence of physiological factors such as fatigue, hunger and thirst. Technology was seen as a way of improving accuracy, compensating for human limitations and reducing error. However, technology itself is a source of threat and error. Technology does not eliminate error but changes the type and potential consequences of some errors.

Error Management

One of the objectives of TEM is to understand *error management* (i.e. error detection and correction), rather than solely focusing on error causes and committal. Operational errors that are detected and responded to in a timely manner (i.e. properly managed), and therefore do not lead to undesired aircraft states, do not reduce safety margins. Thus they become operational non-events. This is part of routine flight operations – error detection and correction.

Some errors are quickly detected and resolved, thus becoming operationally inconsequential, while others go undetected or are mismanaged. *A mis-managed error is an error that is linked to or induces an additional error or an undesired aircraft state.*

Note: COMMITTED ERRORS

The CASA Day VFR Syllabus specifically mentions committed errors, as follows:

- 'Give an example of a committed error and how action could be taken to ensure safe flight'.

We have been unable to locate a definition of *committed error* but, in 'Human Factors for Pilots', Roger Green refers to an *Error of Commission* (Page 43 para 2.a.8 d), as follows:

- 'If we expect a stimulus and prepare the appropriate response, we will respond more rapidly if the expected stimulus occurs. If however, an unexpected stimulus occurs we will be more likely under pressure to make the prepared response, ie to make an error of commission.'

I suppose a classic example is a pilot who, towards the end of the landing roll and being asked to turn off early, retracted the undercarriage instead of the flaps. On shorter runways, he had always retracted the flaps towards the end of the roll to increase weight on the wheels - to improve braking. Therefore he was comitted to an action but *committed* it incorrectly (rather than *omitting* an action). This was a pre-learned, rehearsed and practised action. The distraction caused him to select the gear lever instead of the flap lever.

Undesired Aircraft States

Undesired aircraft states are *flight crew-induced aircraft position or speed deviations, misapplication of flight controls, or incorrect systems configuration, associated with a reduction in margins of safety.* Undesired aircraft states that result from ineffective threat and/or error management may lead to compromising situations and reduced safety margins. Undesired aircraft states are the critical final event in the pilots management of a situation. The threat and errors have not been countered and the correction of the aircraft state is the last chance for the pilot to avoid an accident outcome. An undesired aircraft state may also arise spontaneously and directly from a threat – e.g a vertical gust may cause an attitude upset or load factor exceedence, windshear may cause an airspeed excursion beyond V_S or V_{FE}.

Further examples of undesired aircraft states would include lining-up for the incorrect runway during approach (as a result of communications error or autopilot setting error), exceeding ATC speed restrictions during an approach (deliberate or error due to not checking ATC instruction), or landing long on a short runway requiring maximum braking (error of judgement). Threats such as equipment malfunctions or air traffic control errors can also place the aircraft in a UAS without the crew having made an error – although it implies that the crew did not detect and counter the threat.

Undesired aircraft states can be managed effectively, restoring margins of safety, or incorrectly, can inducing an additional error, an incident, or an accident.

Undesired aircraft states are categorised as:

- aircraft handling;
- ground navigation; or
- incorrect aircraft configuration.

Aircraft handling states – include:

- aircraft control (attitude or heading deviations).
- altitude, track or speed deviations.
- unnecessary weather penetration.
- unauthorised airspace penetration.
- exceeding aircraft limitations.
- non-stabilised approach.
- continued landing after a non-stabilised approach, incorrect threshold speed or approach path.
- long, bounced, firm or off-centreline touchdown.

Ground navigation states – include:

- taxiing for wrong runway.
- excess taxiing speed.
- positioned on wrong taxiway, ramp, gate or holding point.

Incorrect aircraft configurations – include:

- incorrect systems configuration.
- incorrect flight controls configuration.
- incorrect autopilot mode or value.
- incorrect NAVAID or GPS setting.
- incorrect power setting.
- incorrect fuel quantity or distribution.
- incorrect loading.

Error Management vs. UAS Management

An important learning and training point is the timely switching from error management to undesired aircraft state management. An example would be as follows: a flight crew selects a wrong approach in the *flight management computer* (FMC). The flight crew subsequently identifies the error during a crosscheck prior to the *final approach fix* (FAF). However, instead of selecting the heading mode or manually flying the desired track, both flight crew become involved in attempting to reprogram the correct approach prior to reaching the FAF. As a result, the aircraft overshoots the centreline and descent point, descends late, and develops an unstable approach. The aircraft is now in a UAS. This is an example of flight crew getting locked-onto error management, instead of correcting the undesired aircraft state.

The model assists in training flight crews that, when the aircraft is in an undesired state, the primary task is to correct the UAS and return to controlled, stabilised flight.

UAS Management & Outcomes

From a learning and training perspective, it is important to establish a clear differentiation between undesired aircraft states and outcomes.

- undesired aircraft states are *transitional states* where a normal operational state has been compromised. They lie between a normal state (i.e. a stabilised approach) and an outcome (e.g. an undershoot).
- outcomes are *end states*, most notably, reportable occurrences (i.e., incidents and accidents).

An example of the difference would be: a stabilised approach (normal operational state) is allowed to develop into an unstabilised approach (an error) leading to an undesired aircraft state, due to turbulence (threat). The UAS results in a touchdown short of the threshold (incident/accident outcome). The pilot could have anticipated and countered the threat (the turbulence), avoided the error (not allowed the approach to become destabilised) or recovered the undesired aircraft state (brought the aircraft back under control) – but didn't.

UAS Management

At the stage of a UAS, the flight crew has the possibility of recovering the situation, returning to a normal operational state, and restoring safe flight. If the undesired aircraft state is allowed to develop into an outcome, recovery to a normal operational state and restoration of safe flight is not possible.

Countermeasures

Mention has been made of threat management, error management and undesired aircraft state management. The means of managing these is by use of *countermeasures*.

As part of their normal operational duties, pilots employ countermeasures to keep threats, errors and undesired aircraft states from reducing margins of safety in flight operations. They employ *countermeasures*. Examples of countermeasures include checklists, briefings, call-outs and SOPs, as well as personal strategies and tactics.

Empirical observations during airline checking and training flights suggest that as much as 70% of flight crew activities may be countermeasures-related.

All countermeasures are flight crew actions. However, some countermeasures to threats, errors and undesired aircraft states are based upon 'hard' resources. These are preventative systems, checks and procedures. They are *systemic-based countermeasures* (they are part of the total flight safety system). The following are examples:

- stall warning system;
- systems failure warnings;
- airborne collision avoidance system (ACAS);
- ground proximity warning system (GPWS),
- standard operation procedures (SOPs);
- checklists;
- briefings; and
- training.

Other countermeasures are intrinsic to the human crew. These are personal strategies and tactics, and formal individual and team countermeasures, that typically include skills, knowledge and attitudes. These attributes are further developed by training such as *Crew Resource Management* (CRM) training.

There are basically three categories of individual and team countermeasures:
- planning countermeasures: essential for managing anticipated and unexpected threats;
- execution countermeasures: essential for error detection and error response; and
- review countermeasures: essential for managing the changing conditions of a flight.

Enhanced TEM is the product of the combined use of systemic-based and individual and team countermeasures.

The Role of the Pilot in TEM

Pilot Intervention

As mentioned in the Introduction to this book, the pilot is not the weakest link in the chain of events that may lead to an accident. On the contrary, the sharp pilot is usually the strong link that prevents the succession of events. Remember:

threat (uncountered or unavoided) and/or error (undetected or uncorrected) and/or undesired aircraft state (unrecovered) = outcome (accident or incident)

If the pilot intervenes at any stage and takes appropriate action, the outcome is a non-event – a safe, routine and more likely enjoyable flight.

The pilot does not weaken the chain – he or she breaks the chain. The pilot breaks the chain not because of weakness but because the accident chain is destructive.

The pilot offers countermeasures to break the sequence of events leading to an accident.

The pilot's countermeasures include:
- anticipating threats and consequences;
- weighing options to reduce, counter or avoid threats;
- making safe decisions;
- detecting, reporting and correcting errors;
- intervening or recovering from undesired aircraft states; and
- practising recovery techniques for UAS.

How can TEM make GA Single-Pilot Operations Safer?

In many ways, an RPT flight is much easier than a GA non-scheduled flight. The crew is very current and rested, the aircraft is known, its maintenance is carefully monitored, ATS is fully available, fuelling is separately supervised and checked, loading and passenger care is delegated and data is gathered for the crew.

The GA pilot-in-command is a one-person band.

Let's go through a flight from go to whoa, and describe what most pilots probably do informally but may not strictly or consciously follow. If we make a check-list we can see where there are potential threats to safety and how best to counter them.

A flight is scheduled............

Data Gathering

The first stage is gathering data:

- destination airfield/heliport – terrain, runway, navaids, lighting, local weather effects;
- terrain en route;
- NAVAIDS available;
- Track, altitude, airspace limitations and tolerances;
- possible/probable weather;
- direction, distance, time, fuel margins;
- cargo/passenger constraints and requirements; and
- weight, balance, performance margins.

Threat Analysis

Threats are risks. Any risk is weighed against two aspects:

- the probability of it happening; and
- the consequences of it happening.

Pilot attitude (self discipline and training) and motivation, now determines the thoroughness of the consideration of potential threats. Are you carrying precious cargo e.g. your family? Does your life/job depend on this flight? Does the life of a patient or persons on the ground or in the water, depend on this flight? Do you have to reach the destination today?

The analysis is not to delay the flight but to increase the probability of successfully completing the flight and the mission objectives.

What threats are probable?

- Is weather a threat – turbulence, icing?
- Is terrain a threat?
- Is lack of daylight a threat?
- Is lack of recent experience in this aircraft, on this flight, to this destination, a threat?
- Is engine or systems failure a threat?
- Am I a threat? – fatigue, health, stress, anxiety, distractions, dehydration, hunger, low blood sugar, hang-over, lack of sleep

Decision-Making

Anticipation – consideration of threats and the potential errors they may induce and undesired aircraft states.

What-iffing:

- what errors could I make as a result of the above threats?
- what if an engine fails/
- what if fuel consumption or headwind is higher than planned?
- what if there is icing?
- what if electrics fail, comms fail, lighting fails?
- what if it is too turbulent?
- what if I am sick or tired half way there?

Options:

- cancel;
- defer/delay;
- select different aircraft with autopilot, more navaids, more engines, more range;
- continue with precautions/alternatives;
- proceed part way or to an intermediate airfield and reassess situation;
- carry more fuel;

- take an extra torch, hand-held radio or GPS;
- take a safety pilot; or
- mentally prepare more thoroughly e.g re-read the anti-icing procedures, the fuel management and leaning techniques, check the forced landing speeds and profiles, recall the no-comms procedure, check the turbulence penetration speed and configuration.

Countermeasures/Escape Routes/Back-up (relevant for all flights but perhaps accentuated for this flight):

- carry charts and log (to back-up GPS) -check they are up to date;
- note landing fields/pads en route – for possible engine failure, fuel, electrics, hydraulic failure, escape routes;
- lighting failure – carry a spare torch etc. or perhaps, night vision goggles; or
- carry a spare pilot.

Flight Planning & Notification

The *Nitty-Gritty:*

- Weather forecast and actual – does it change the threat analysis?
- NOTAMS
- selection of route – airspace, PRD areas, weather, daylight, terrain, diversion
- alternatives, escape routes for engine failure and systems malfunctions
- single-engine service ceiling if appropriate
- IFR or VFR?
- flight notification or SAR watch.
- fuel calculations and reserves
- weight and balance
- take-off and landing performance and margins.

When all of these elements have been taken into account, all that remains is unexpected arisals which your experience, maturity, judgment, skill and training (the airmanship package/toolkit) will take care of – won't it?

Unless you are flying alone, prepare and provide a thorough briefing for the crew and the passengers. What are the threats, what are you countering with, who is responsible for what duties, what are your expectations for cross-checks and monitoring.

If you are alone, it is great value to think through the flight in your head.

Now a thorough pre-flight, fuel check and steady progress – one step at a time (no rush no short-cuts). Organise the cockpit and the paperwork, *leapfrog* the NAVAIDS, get comfortable, have drinking water handy and a torch, pencils etc.

Now enjoy the flight. You've earned the right!

There are two more things you can do *post-operatively*:

- After shutting-down, complete a thorough post-flight inspection of the aircraft before securing it. The reason is that, if there are leaks, fluid losses, flap, leading-edge and underside damage due to stones, a birdstrike or heavy landing, over-heated brakes, mud build-up, worn tyres, etc. they can be reported and fixed before the aircraft is presented for the next flight. You save yourself delays, stress and added threats or if you are not flying the aircraft next, you save stressing your colleagues who find these items by surprise. This is teamwork and pride in the profession and the organisation – isn't it?
- When you are comfortably home and rested, don't forget the flight. While it is fresh in your mind, recall and review the entire flight – the good, the bad and the ugly points, the threats that arose, the errors that were made and corrected and even UASs that were recovered. This review is to highlight the symptoms of the threat and the appropriate counters for next time, the errors and how they could have been detected

and corrected and the UAS recovery techniques and how they could have been better handled. These steps make a good pilot exceptional and exceptionally well prepared for the next flight. This is how to correctly build on experience.

TEM in Everyday Life

You are planning a long drive over the Easter weekend. You are taking your family – spouse and two children – one young, one still a baby. You are visiting friends who have recently moved. You have not been to their city before. It's a 16 hour drive – within speed limits and no stops. The long-range forecast is for rain.

Let's consider both environmental and organisational threats in the context of their likelihood:

Expected threats (definite or very likely) – wet roads, steep hills and inclines at one point, fatigue, reduced visibility, heavy traffic at times;

Unexpected threats (possible) – it is possible that booze buses and delays will be experienced causing a much longer drive, the forecast could be wrong and it could be quite hot, petrol prices will escalate before the break, the child and baby will get tired and bored after a couple of hours, road repairs and maintenance are possible, diverted traffic, unsealed roads; and

Latent threats (not obvious but inherent deficiencies you know about) – your car is getting old, front tyres are worn, the car needs a service, your street directory is out of date, accommodation en-route is booked-out, rest areas are a long way apart.

We now have a picture of the hazard matrix. What can we do?

- plan a stop and book accommodation in advance;
- buy petrol a week before;
- have the car serviced, replace the worn tyres, have a safety check of brakes etc;
- wash the car and check the lights, wipers and cleanliness of windows;
- get a current chart, SATNAV or ring the owner service group for advice on road condition and possible diversions;
- check rest areas and find some where kids can play for while and you can stretch etc;
- plan and early departure so that the children sleep the first several hours;
- have a selection of music and games for the kids;
- carry drinking water and light snacks; and
- share the driving.

So, in effect, we have undertaken a risk minimisation program. If we have covered everything, there are only unexpected, unexpected threats, errors and UVSs (undesired vehicle states).

Now complete a self analysis. Ask yourself are you *au fait* with interstate road rules and limits, are you current at vehicle handling on a wet road, are you guilty of becoming impatient behind slower vehicles and would you be better letting your partner do the majority of the driving in the high density areas?

Perhaps review the route to use multi-lane highways. Take a longer route that doesn't have unsealed sections nor single lanes on steep inclines where you could be trapped for hours behind slow trucks. Make sure you a rested, sober, and relaxed. Pack the car the night before and spend a few minutes reviewing the road map so you don't have to read it while driving.

Have a safe trip and on arrival, don't forget the post-drive vehicle check and the review – for the trip back.

Review 8A

Pre-Solo Level of Knowledge

1. Name two of the human body's systems.
2. What is the function of the lungs?
3. What effect does reduced oxygen have on the brain?
4. How can pain in the ear during a descent be relieved?
5. If you are flying at 2,000 ft and you feel light-headed or dizzy, what would you suspect and what would you do?
6. What condition would you be careful to avoid – not only on hot days?
7. What is the minimum time that should elapse after the last alcoholic drink before flying.
8. What does the blood absorb in preference to oxygen?
9. What is the blind spot in the pilot's vision?
10. What is the most effective technique for scanning visually for other aircraft?
11. If the eye has no object on which to focus what happens?
12. What is the most important function of the pilot in the conduct of a flight?
13. What is the function of the otolithic organ or utricle?
14. What two sensations can the utricle confuse?

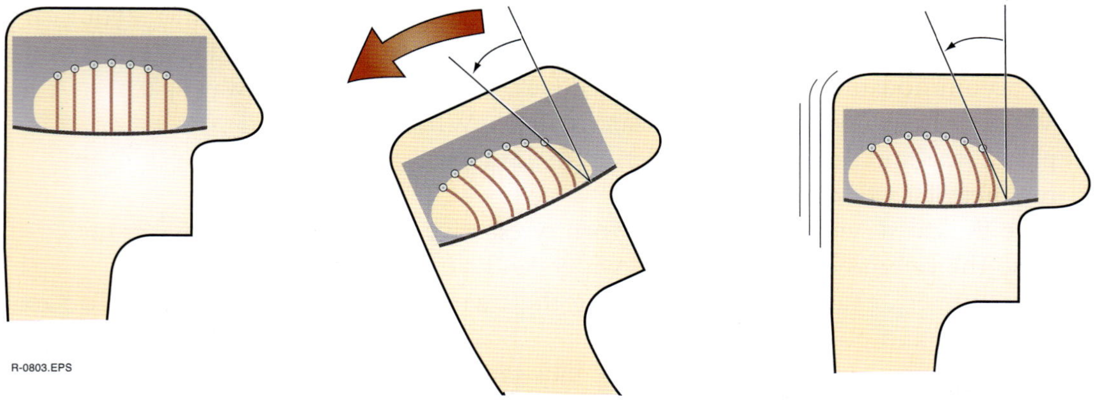

R-0803.EPS

BAK Level of Knowledge

15. Define hypoxia.
16. How long should you allow after a blood donation before flying an aircraft.
17. What is barotrauma?
18. List two of the factors that can contribute to short-term fatigue.
19. List three medications that are considered incompatible with flying.
20. What is, or are, the bends?
21. If you scuba dive for more than 4 hours and the dive required decompression stops, for how long should you not fly?
22. What does a pilot do?
23. What is the retina?
24. What two types of light sensitive cells are contained in the retina?
25. Which are colour sensitive?
26. To scan for other aircraft at night you should look . . . . .
27. If you stare at a single light, or star, at night, it may appear to move. The name of this phenomenon is . . . . .
28. A downward sloping runway may cause the pilot to believe that the aircraft is on a . . . . . approach than normal.

29. What is the name of the tube which balances pressure on the inside of the ear drum?

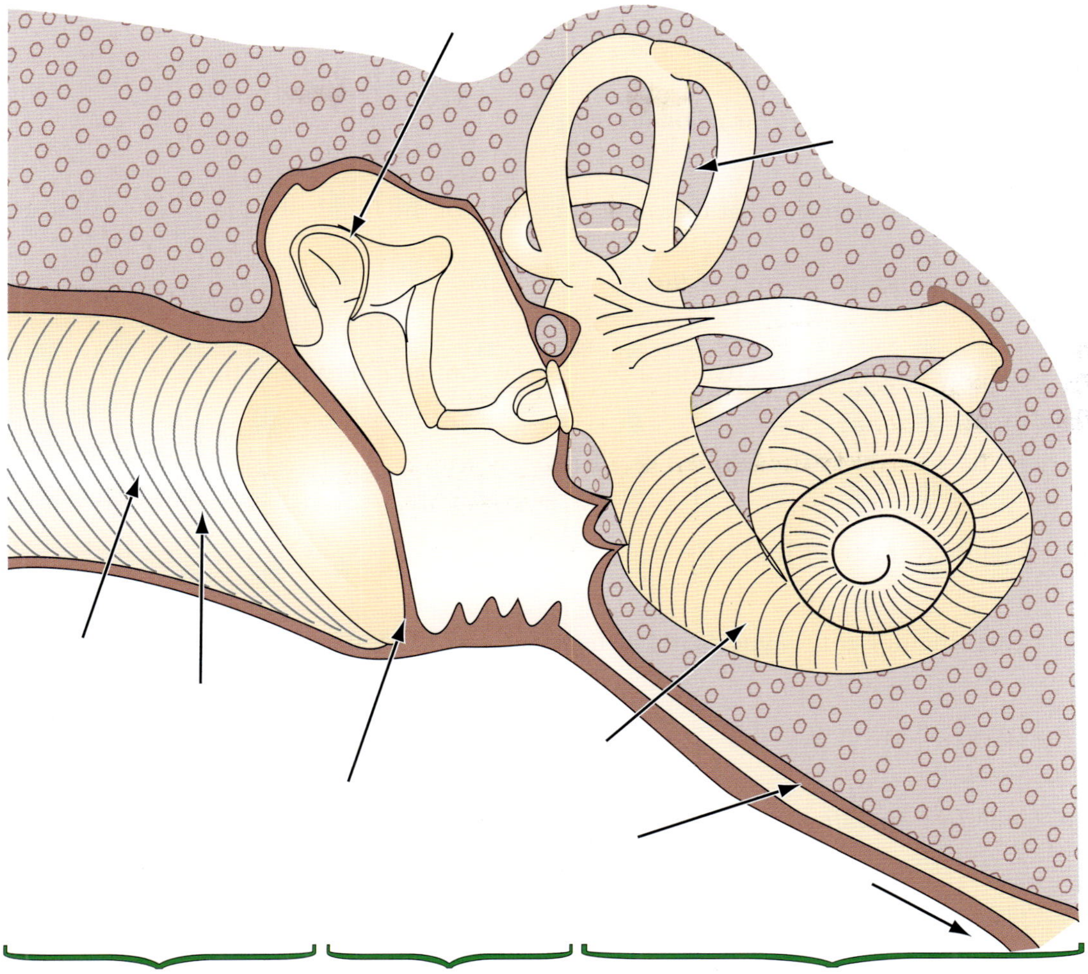

30. What is the name of the manoeuvre used to assist unblocking this tube?
31. Name two environmental stressors.
32. What two senses are provided by the ear?
33. What is the aim point?

34. How do you know if you are on a steady path to the aim point?

Review 8B: Threat & Error Management

1. What does the abbreviation TEM stand for?

2. Define ***Threat and Error Management***.

3. A threat is something that threatens the safety of the flight. It is . . . . to the crew.

4. What are the three types of ***threat***?.

5. What are the two proactive measures a crew can take regarding threats?

6. Define an ***error*** in the context of TEM.

7. What may an error lead to?

8. Errors include three types; aircraft handling, procedural and

9. Error management includes

10. ***Undesired aircraft states*** are categorised as

11. Name three incorrect aircraft 'configurations'.

9 - Introduction to Meteorology

The Atmosphere

The atmosphere is full of wonderful life-sustaining features. Oxygen to breathe, water vapour to condense as clouds and precipitation to water our plants and animals, ozone to protect us from the sun's ultraviolet and infrared rays, wind to carry seeds and insects, to fill the sails of our boats and to lift our kites, and miraculously this fluid we call air is thick enough to carry us but not too thick to prevent travel through it.

The atmosphere is layered from ground level up as follows:

- the troposphere;
- the tropopause;
- the stratosphere; and
- the ionosphere.

The *troposphere* is the layer nearest the surface of the earth. Most of our weather occurs here. Also it contains high winds and pronounced vertical currents. It consists of air of varying density and temperature – because the little particles, called molecules, are stacked on top. Ninety percent of the mass of air is squashed below about 50,000 ft. And almost all of it below 150,000 ft. The temperature reduction with altitude is called the lapse rate. Because the earth rotates, there is a centrifugal reaction which tends to push the air away at the equator so the troposphere is thickest in depth here. Also, it is lower in winter and higher in summer.

The *tropopause* is the upper layer of the troposphere. It occurs at around 36,000 ft in temperate latitudes and up to more than 50,000 ft in the tropics. The atmospheric temperature decreases as we climb; consequently, the tropopause represents the lowest temperature, and above this, the temperature remains fairly constant throughout the stratosphere. The tropopause is a very important level for pilots because optimum performance for a jet aircraft occurs here. Weather phenomena such as thunderstorms, jetstreams and clear air turbulence all occur in the tropopause. The tropopause also separates the troposphere and the relatively stable and uniform stratosphere.

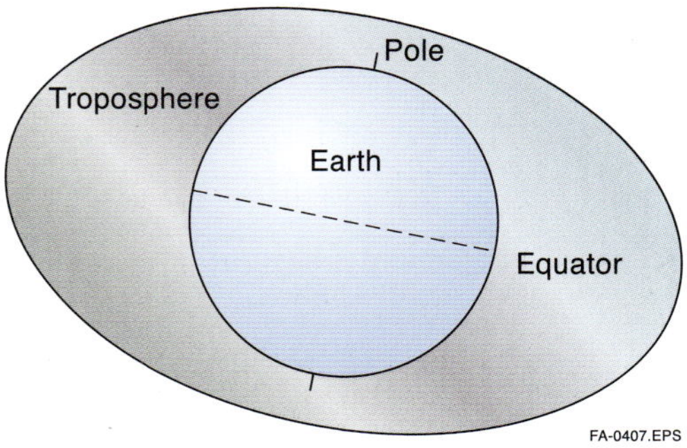

Figure 9-1 The troposphere.

The tropopause also "caps" the vertical development of thunderstorms, and when you see the classic anvil-shaped cloud, it is the top of the cloud having reached the tropopause being blown along by upper level winds.

The *stratosphere* is a cold, thin but uniform layer of air where there is virtually no cloud or weather. Flight at these altitudes has to be at very high speeds – several times the speed of sound or ballistic like the trajectory of a projectile. Jet engines cannot breathe here and thrust must be provided by a rocket motor. The ozone layer is contained in the lower stratosphere.

The *ionosphere* is above the stratosphere and is the layer of charged particles which reflects or "skips" radio waves. It is affected by sun-spot activity as any ham radio enthusiast will tell you.

International Standard Atmosphere

So that we can compare notes around the world, scientists have agreed on average atmospheric conditions called the International Standard Atmosphere. Like the average person, it never exists but it is a useful yardstick for comparisons. For those who dabble in numbers, the International Standard Atmosphere is as follows:

- Surface temperature: +15°C.
- Lapse rate: 2° per 1,000 ft (up to the tropopause, then constant).
- Freezing level (0°): 7,500 ft.
- Pressure: 1,013.2 hPa.
- Tropopause: 36,000 ft.
- Temperature at and above the troposphere: –56°C.

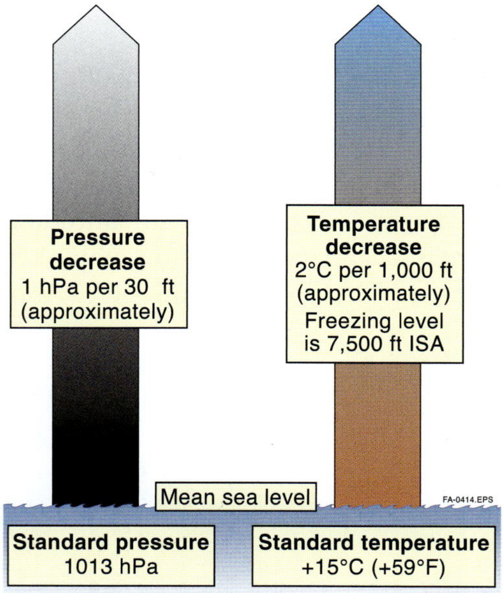

Figure 9-2 The International Standard Atmosphere.

As you can see, our space capsule is keeping us alive in what is an alien atmosphere for humans, –56°C, almost as cold as Siberia (or North Dakota) in winter! It can be as low as –80°C in the atmosphere above the tropics. Also, there is a pressure drop as altitude increases, and the air at the tropopause is about half the density of sea level air. Thus there is not enough oxygen to sustain life. Fighter pilots breathe oxygen through the masks. We have a pressurised cabin which replicates a near sea level pressure and so there is sufficient oxygen crammed into the cabin for us to breathe normally. Also, because the air at this altitude is so thin, we have to fly twice as fast to generate the same amount of lift.

Weather & Climate

In the troposphere, the horizontal and vertical currents and the presence of water vapour causes all of our weather – from fogs to clouds, to thunderstorms, to high level mare's tails, to rain, hail, ice and snow.

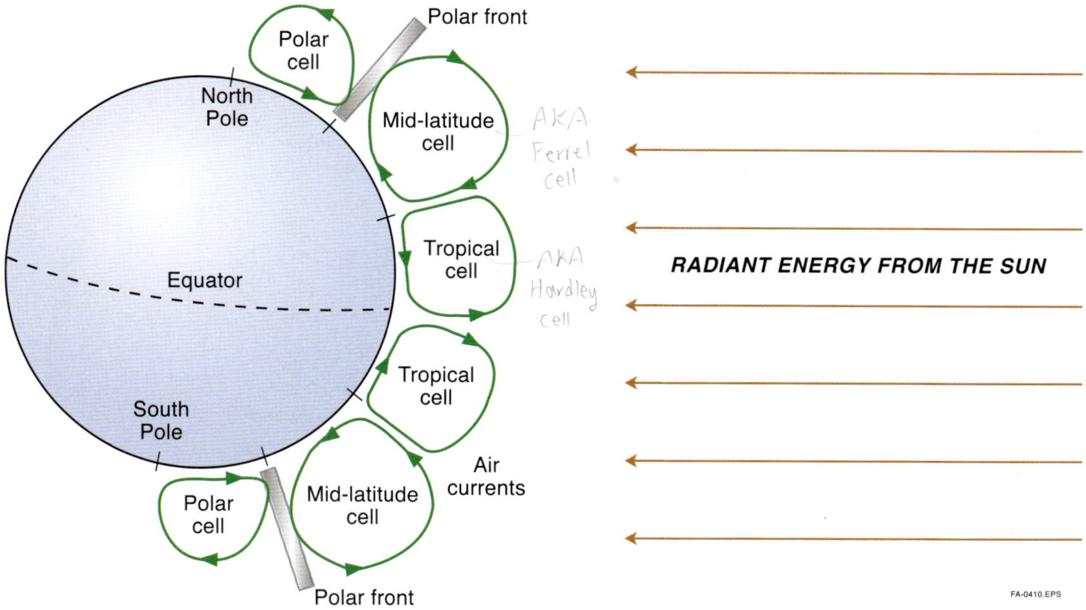

Figure 9-3 A cross-section of the circulation pattern.

The currents are nominally in the direction shown, but of course there is interaction between the horizontal and vertical currents and there are areas of *shear* where the adjacent layers are moving at different direction and speeds. It is these areas where turbulence is felt and where *jetstreams* predominate.

As well as these major flows, there are considerable local influences by physical features such as mountain ranges and coastlines.

Figure 9-4 General circulation in the troposphere.

Figure 9-5
Prevailing winds and currents.

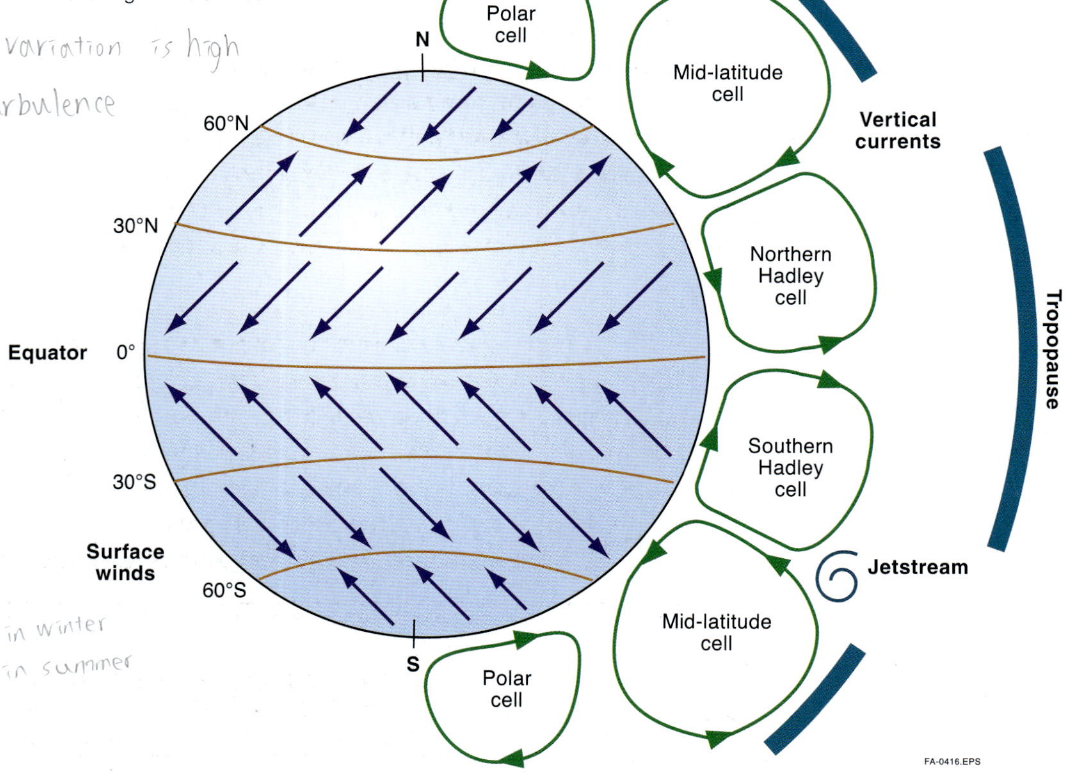

When SAT variation is high that means turbulence is imminent

Jet stream move south in winter move north in summer

These interactions together with daily heating and cooling, the effect of local terrain and the differences in atmospheric pressure, cause the cyclones and anti-cyclones (low and high pressure cells respectively) we see on the weather forecasts.

Figure 9-6
Cyclonic patterns.

Local Weather

Weather plays a very important role in the life of a pilot, since it determines the conditions in which he or she will be flying, or, indeed, if we will be flying at all on a particular day. The main features of weather for a pilot are wind direction and speed, visibility, and clouds, in particular cloud base and sky coverage as well as the possibility of cumulonimbus thunderclouds. The temperature of the atmosphere is also important. High temperatures reduce air density and, consequently, reduce aeroplane performance, while low temperatures below freezing may lead to ice forming on the aeroplane, which will reduce its performance and controllability significantly.

Wind

Wind direction and strength generally determine our choice of runway, since taking off and landing into wind has many advantages, such as a shorter take-off ground run. A steady wind over flat ground, or no wind at all, may provide us with smooth flying conditions, whereas a gusty wind might cause more turbulent flying conditions.

Strong winds underneath and near thunderstorms can also cause turbulence and windshear (windshear being large changes in wind speed and/or direction), as can obstructions such as hangars, hills or trees by breaking up the flow of the wind.

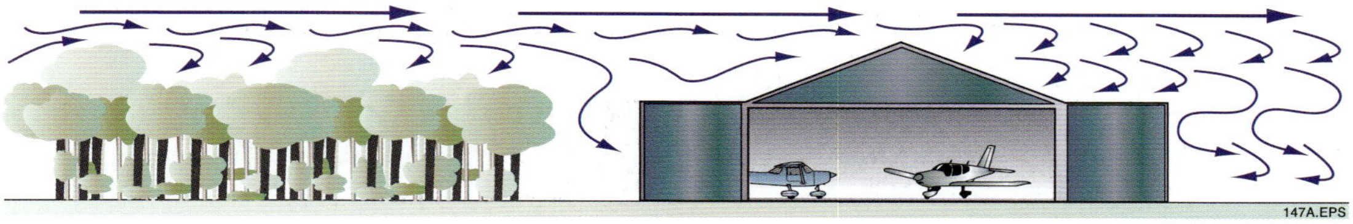

Figure 9-7 Friction and obstacles affect the surface wind.

Visibility

Visibility is very important to a pilot because it determines how far you can see. Unlimited visibility on a clear day makes flying and navigating much easier than on a day with poor visibility when you cannot see the horizon (making it more difficult to hold the aeroplane's attitude) or distant landmarks (making visual navigation more difficult). Poor visibility can be caused by small particles in the atmosphere, such as water droplets (mist or fog), dust, pollen, smoke, sand, sea spray, and so on. Rain may reduce visibility somewhat, but visual flight may still be possible. Be careful of ice forming on the aeroplane in sub-zero conditions.

Clouds

Clouds are a very important aspect of weather since they restrict visibility and cause precipitation. Visual pilots are not permitted to fly in cloud, including fog. Cloud base above the ground determines if visual flight operations are possible. Cloud coverage of the sky is usually expressed in oktas (i.e. eighths), with 8 oktas being complete coverage of the sky, 5 oktas being more than half, and 1 okta being not very much cloud at all.

Thunderstorms

Thunderstorms are a hazard to all aeroplanes, and should be avoided by all pilots, including instrument-rated pilots. Thunderstorms, so-called because of the clap of thunder that accompanies the electrical discharge we call lightning, originate in large cumulonimbus clouds.

Figure 9-8 A developing storm.

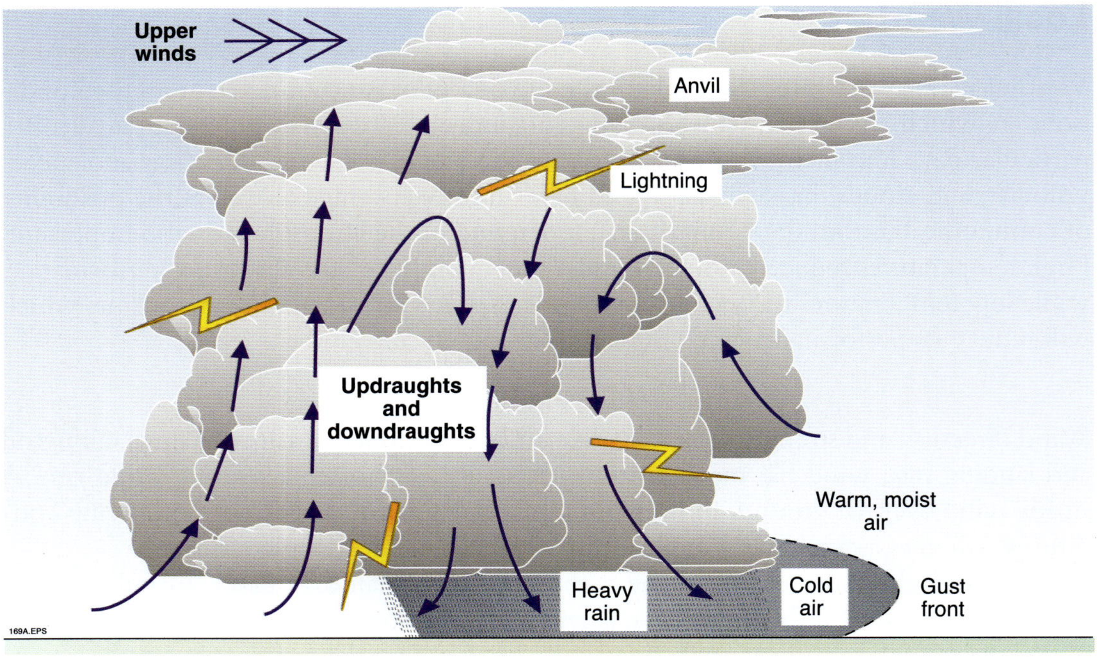

Figure 9-9 The mature stage of a thunderstorm.

They can cause severe turbulence, severe windshear, reduced visibility, severe icing, damage from hail or lightning strikes, as well as interference with radio communications and navigation aids. You should avoid thunderstorms by at least 10 nm. The good news is that, generally, they are easy to see and avoid.

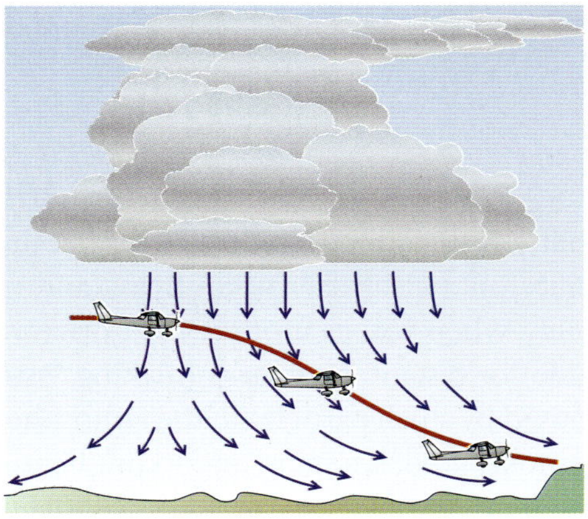

Figure 9-10 Downdraughts beneath storm cloud.

Fog

Fog is especially dangerous since it restricts visibility near the ground. You can sometimes be flying in a beautiful, clear sky and have a good, if somewhat misty, view of ground features beneath you (such as the runway below), but on approach to land, lose sight of the runway due to the greater slant distance through the fog or mist.

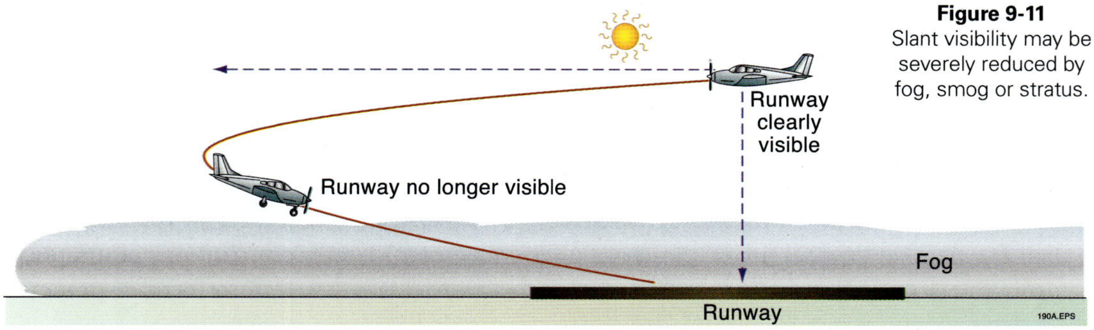

Figure 9-11 Slant visibility may be severely reduced by fog, smog or stratus.

Heating Effects in the Atmosphere

All weather is caused by heating, the initial source of the heat energy being the sun. The sun's rays are of such wavelengths that they penetrate the atmosphere and heat the earth's surface. The amount of heating depends upon the season (summer or winter), the time of day (day or night), and local conditions (cloud coverage, mountain shadows, etc.).

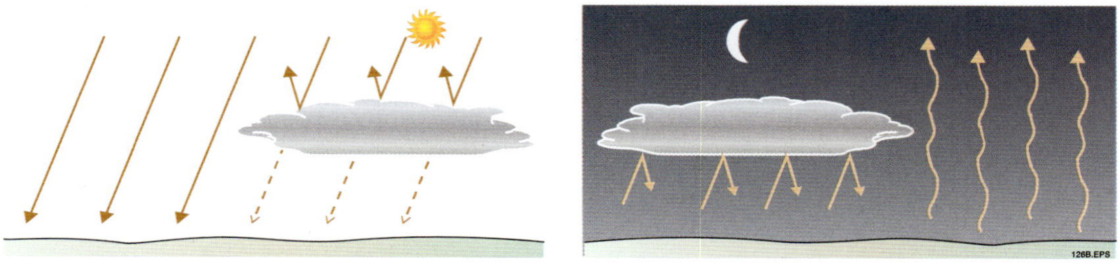

Figure 9-12 Cloud reduces surface heating by day and cooling by night.

The earth's surface, having been heated by the sun's rays, then gives off heat energy of a different wavelength that can be absorbed by the air, and so, surprisingly, the earth's atmosphere is heated from below. Land tends to absorb and emit heat energy more readily than the oceans or green-forested areas, so greater temperature variations, such as hot days and cold nights, are more likely over open land (for example, in inland desert areas). A parcel of hot air will rise through cooler air surrounding it and, as it rises, it will become cooler. Providing it contains sufficient vapour, it will reach a temperature (known as its *dewpoint temperature*), at which the water vapour will condense out as droplets and so a cloud will form.

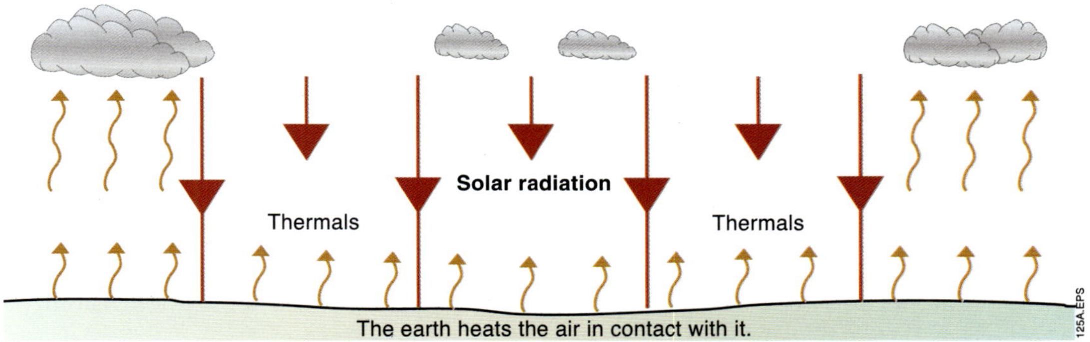

Figure 9-13 Indirect heating of the accomplisher by the sun.

The rising hot air is known as a *thermal*, and can be detected by cumulus clouds forming above it, and sometimes by birds hovering in it. Thermals are good news for glider pilots since they allow a glider, which doesn't have the advantage of an engine, to gain altitude.

Figure 9-14
Thermals forming for weather cumulus clouds.

If the air is dry, no cloud will form in the rising air due to the lack of moisture. The nature of any cloud that does form will depend upon the stability of the atmosphere – unstable air will continue to rise, forming lumpy, cauliflower-shaped *cumulus* clouds (also known as *cumuliform* clouds); stable air, however, will tend not to rise further, causing any cloud that forms to be of a layer type, known as *stratus* or *stratiform* cloud.

The characteristics of unstable air are:

- turbulence in the rising air;
- the formation of cumuliform (cauliflower) clouds;
- showery rain from these clouds (if there is precipitation); and
- good visibility between the showers (due to the rising air carrying any obscuring particles away).

The characteristics of stable air are:

- the formation of stratiform (smooth layers) cloud with little vertical development;
- steady rain (if any);
- poor visibility if there are any obscuring particles; and
- possibly smooth flying conditions with little or no turbulence.

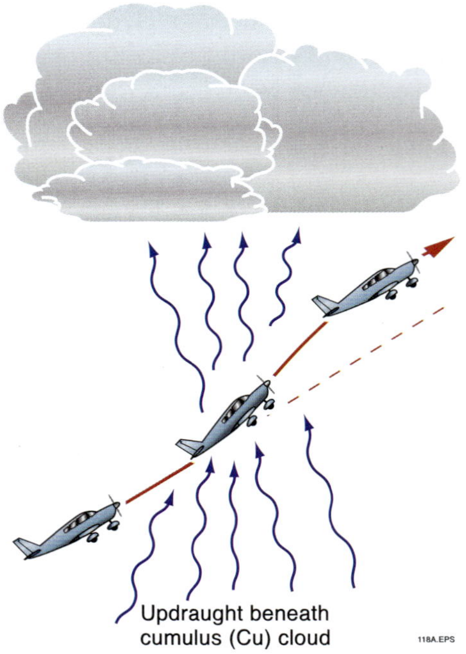

Figure 9-15
Updraught beneath cumulus (Cu) cloud.

Inversion

An extreme case of stable air is a temperature inversion where, instead of temperature decreasing with altitude, it increases. This can happen on a cold, clear night when the land cools by giving off heat, and so the lower level of the atmosphere, usually below 1,000 ft, becomes very cool (sometimes causing fog to form). There will be no tendency for the cooler air to rise, and so flying conditions may be smooth with poor visibility.

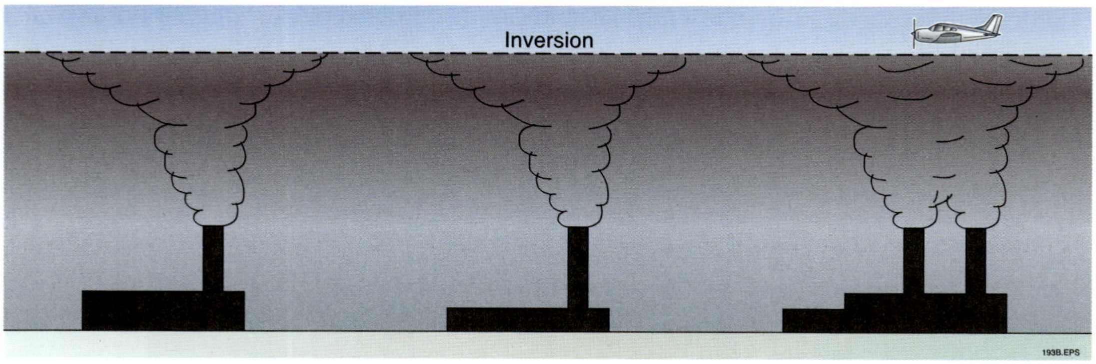

Figure 9-16 Inversions can lead to reduced visibility.

Winds

The term *wind* refers to the flow of air over the earth's surface. We describe it in terms of:

- the direction from which it is blowing, for instance a north wind blows from the north (i.e. from 360°); and
- its strength in knots.

Meteorologists relate wind direction to true north, and so a wind appearing on a meteorological forecast as 32015 kt means a wind strength of 15 kt from a direction of 320°T. When taking off or landing, however, you will be using a runway described in terms of its magnetic direction, and so winds passed to you over the radio by the tower or on an automatic terminal information service (ATIS) will be expressed in degrees magnetic.

Wind is caused to blow by pressure differences resulting from uneven heating of the earth. Air will want to flow from a high-pressure area to a low-pressure area, but other effects resulting from the rotation of the earth modify its direction of flow. The result is that air flows anticlockwise around high-pressure areas and clockwise around low-pressure areas in the southern hemisphere. (The direction of flow is reversed in the northern hemisphere.)

The surface wind is important to a pilot because of its effect on take-offs and landings. It is usually measured at about 30 ft above ground level. Friction effects between the flow of air and the earth's surface may cause the surface wind to be less strong and different in direction from the wind at altitude. The resulting effect for a pilot taking off or landing may be some turbulence and/or windshear.

Sea Breeze

The sea breeze, which occurs usually in the afternoon in coastal areas, is the result of uneven heating of the land and sea. On sunny afternoons after the land has warmed, the hot air above it rises. Cool air from over the sea moves in, causing an onshore breeze and lower temperatures on the beach. These are called *anabatic winds*, and examples of these include the "gully winds" in Adelaide and the "Fremantle doctor". A small circulation pattern is set up, possibly only up to 1,000 or 2,000 ft, causing a very different wind at circuit altitude compared to ground level.

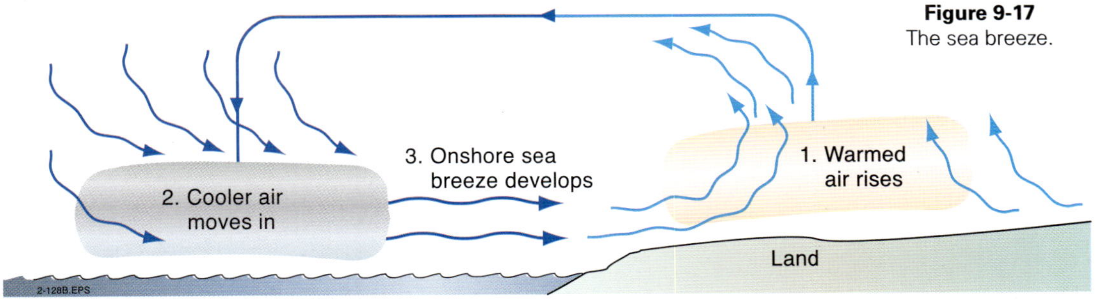

Figure 9-17
The sea breeze.

Katabatic Winds

Katabatic winds are winds that flow down mountain slopes and out of valleys at night and in the early mornings. They are caused by cooling of the earth's surface at night and the cooling of the air in contact with it. The cooler and heavier air tends to sink, and strong winds could be flowing down the slopes by the end of the night and maybe causing problems for pilots at nearby aerodromes.

Figure 9-18
Katabatic winds.

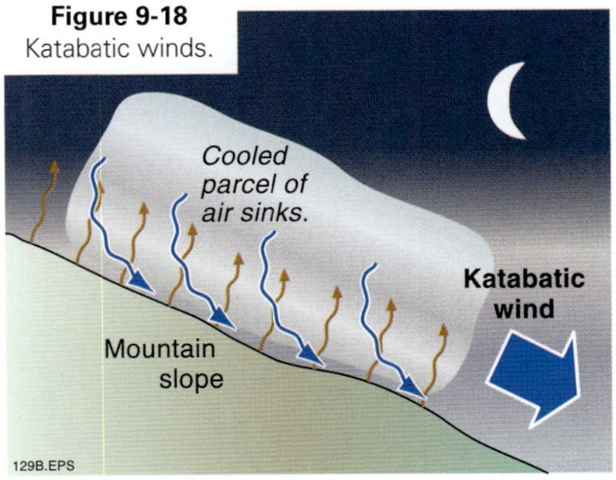

Turbulence

Some degree of turbulence is almost always present in the atmosphere and pilots quickly become accustomed to slight turbulence. Moderate or severe turbulence, however, is uncomfortable and can even overstress the aeroplane.

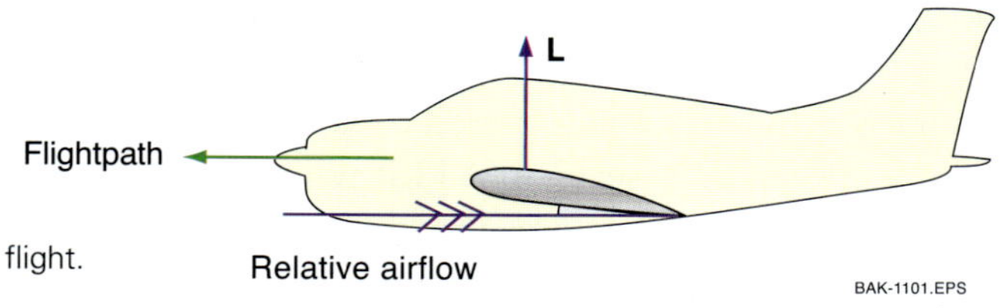

Figure 9-19 Cruise flight.

Vertical gusts increase the angle of attack, causing an increase in the lift generated at that particular airspeed and therefore an increased load factor. Of course, if the angle of attack is increased beyond the critical angle, the wing will stall and this can occur at a speed well above the published 1g stall speed.

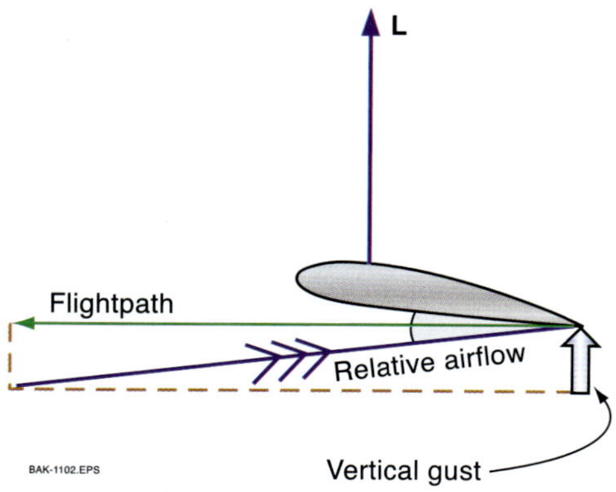

Figure 9-20 Small vertical gust.

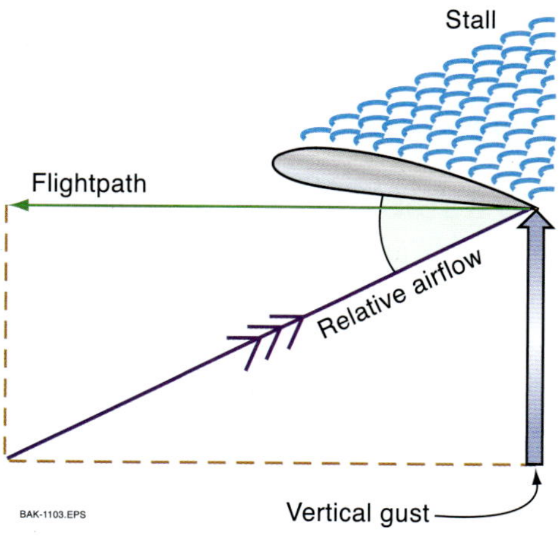

Figure 9-21 Large vertical gust.

Load factor (or g-force) is a measure of the stress on the aeroplane, and each category of aeroplane is built to accept specified maximum load factors. It is important that these load factors are not exceeded.

One means of achieving this is to fly the aeroplane at or below the turbulence penetration speed (V_B) which is usually slower by some 10%–20% than normal cruise speed, but not so slow as to allow the aeroplane to stall, remembering that in turbulence the aeroplane may stall at a speed higher than that published.

When encountering turbulence:
- fasten seat belts;
- hold the level flight attitude for the desired flight phase (i.e. climb, cruise, descent) using whatever aileron movements are needed to retain lateral control, but being fairly gentle on the elevator to avoid overstressing the airframe structurally through large changes in angle of attack and lift produced, and being prepared to accept variations in altitude; and
- since the airspeed indicator will probably be fluctuating, it will be less useful than normal, so aim to have the airspeed fluctuate around the selected turbulence penetration speed, which may require reduced power, by using power to maintain speed.

It is, of course, better to avoid turbulence, and to some extent this is possible by:
- avoiding flying underneath, in or near thunderstorms where changes to airflow can be enormous;
- avoiding flying under large cumulus clouds, because of the large updraughts that cause them;
- avoiding flying in the lee of hills when strong winds are blowing, since they will tumble over the ridges and possibly be quite turbulent as well as flowing down and into valleys at a rate which your aeroplane may not be able to outclimb; and
- avoiding flying at a low level over rough ground in strong-wind conditions.

Classification of Turbulence

So that pilots and air traffic controllers can communicate efficiently regarding turbulence, turbulence is given three basic classifications.

Light

In light turbulence, there is no significant changes to the aircraft attitude and/or altitude.

Moderate

In moderate turbulence, there may be moderate changes in aircraft attitude and/or altitude, but the aircraft remains under positive control at all times. Usually, there are small variations in airspeed and changes in accelerometer readings of 0.5g to 1.0g at the aircraft's centre of gravity. Occupants feel a strain against seat belts. Loose objects move about.

Severe

In severe turbulence, there are abrupt changes in aircraft attitude and/or altitude; the aircraft may be out of control for short periods. Usually, there are large variations in airspeed, and changes in accelerometer readings greater than 1.0g at the aircraft's centre of gravity. Occupants are forced violently against seat belts. Loose objects are tossed about.

Windshear

If two parcels of air are moving relative to one another, which is the same as saying that the wind speed and/or direction of each parcel is different, then a windshear exists between them. The greater the difference over a short distance, the stronger the shear.

Windshear affects the climb path. . .

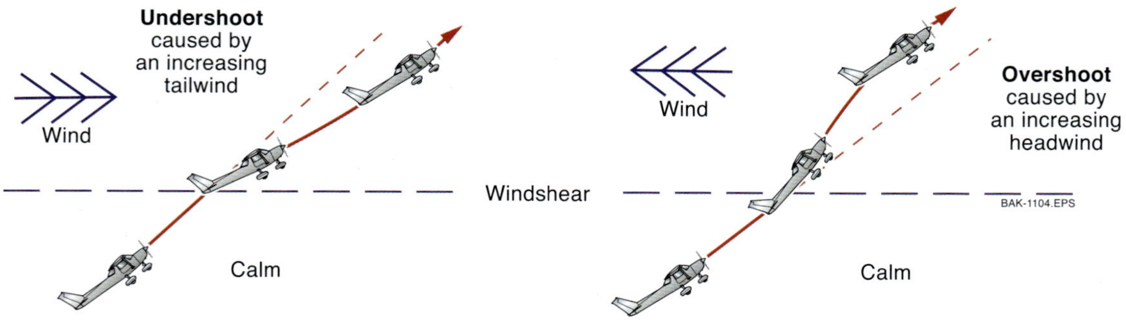

Figure 9-22 Effect of windshear on the climb path.

. . . but it affects more seriously, the descent and approach path.

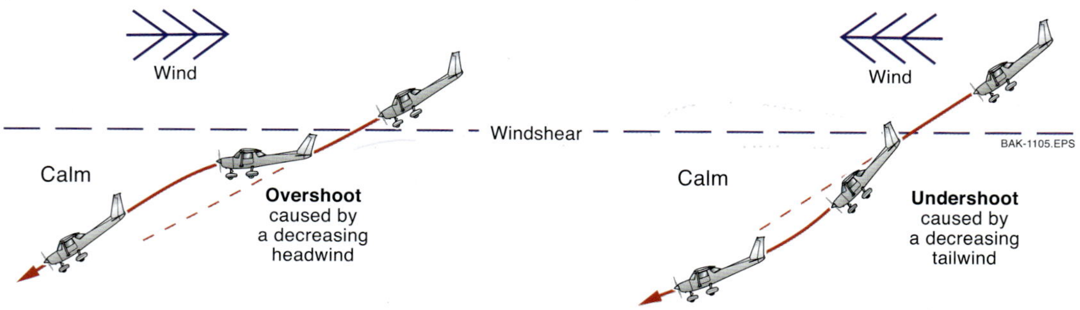

Figure 9-23 Effect of windshear on the descent path.

As well as the effect of wind, there are vertical currents that directly change the flightpath. . .

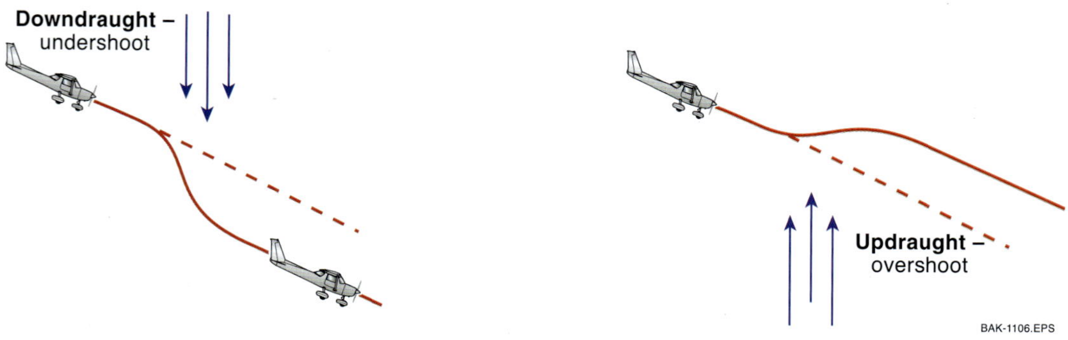

Figure 9-24 Common windshear situations.

. . . and a combination of both:

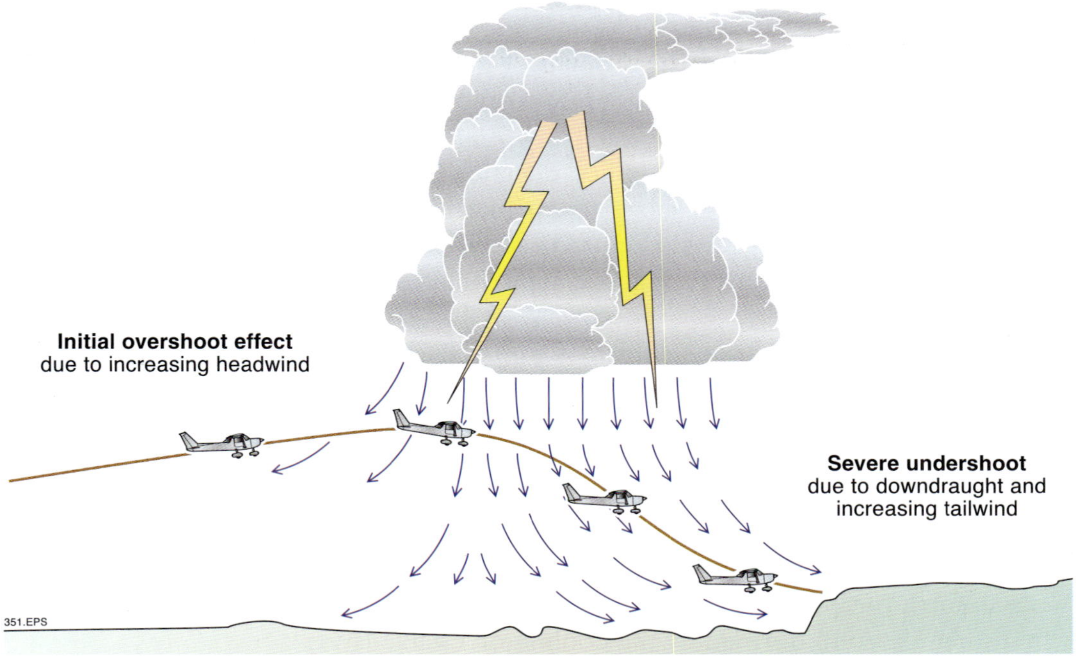

Figure 9-25 Avoid thunderstorms and cumulonimbus clouds.

The most significant effects seen by a pilot as the aeroplane passes suddenly from one parcel of air into the other are:

- a sudden change in airspeed;
- a tendency for the nose to pitch and the flightpath to change; and
- possibly some turbulence.

Figure 9-26 Potential hazard.

The sudden loss or gain of airspeed, if it is great enough and if it lasts more than a few seconds, will affect the performance of the aeroplane, since performance is determined to a large extent by the aeroplane's speed through the air. An increase in airspeed will improve performance, whereas a decrease in airspeed will degrade performance.

Turbulence is often associated with windshear due to friction between the two parcels of air moving relative to each other. There will be some form of wind gradient (wind change with distance) between the two parcels, with windshear and turbulence often being stronger in direct proportion to the wind gradient. Be very careful on final approach.

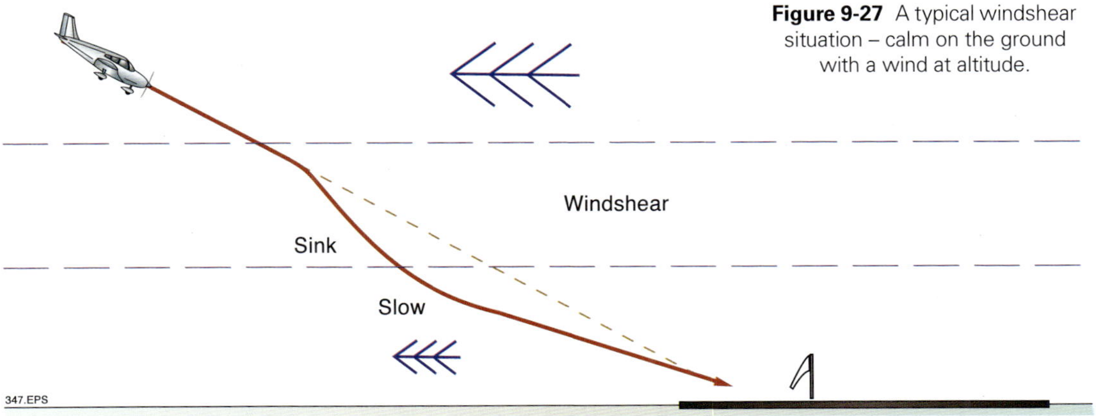

Figure 9-27 A typical windshear situation – calm on the ground with a wind at altitude.

Clouds

Clouds are made up of small water droplets or ice particles and take many forms. They are classified into many families according to the height of their base, and are named individually according to their nature.

Clouds belong to one of four families, depending upon height. These are:

- high-level clouds with a base above approximately 20,000 ft, and composed mainly of ice crystals in the below-freezing upper atmosphere (cirrus, cirrocumulus, cirrostratus);
- middle-level clouds with a base above approximately 7,500 ft (altocumulus, altostratus, nimbostratus);
- low-level clouds with a base below approximately 7,500 ft (stratocumulus, stratus, fair weather cumulus, nimbostratus); and
- clouds with extensive vertical development (towering cumulus, cumulonimbus).

Cloud Types

Clouds are named according to the following types:

- cirriform (fibrous), consisting mainly of ice crystals;
- cumuliform (heaped), formed by unstable air rising and cooling;
- stratiform (layered), formed by the cooling of a stable layer;
- nimbus (rain-bearing);
- mammatus (bulging downwinds);
- fractus (fragmented);
- castellanus (common base with separate vertical development – like towers on a castle – often in lines); and
- lenticularis (lens-shaped, often formed in strong winds over mountainous areas).

For example, nimbostratus means stratified clouds from which rain is falling. Altocumulus are middle-level heaped clouds. Cumulus fractus are fragmented cumulus clouds. Cirrostratus are high-level stratified clouds consisting of ice crystals. Standing lenticular altocumulus clouds are lens-shaped middle-level clouds standing in the one position, usually over a mountain range in strong winds. Nimbostratus is a hybrid cloud in terms of classification since its base can be low level or middle level, and it can have great vertical depth. Sometimes nimbostratus is 10,000 ft or even 15,000 ft thick, making it very dark when seen from underneath and capable of causing heavy rain for many hours. The abbreviations for the various cloud types in table 9-1 are used in weather forecasts and reports.

Abbr.	Type	Height
Ci	cirrus	high
Cc	cirrocumulus	high
Cs	cirrostratus	high
Ac	altocumulus	medium (base)
As	altostratus	medium (base)
Ns	nimbostratus	low (base)
Sc	stratocumulus	low (base)
St	stratus	low (base)
Cb	cumulonimbus	low (base)
Cu	cumulus	low (base)
TCu	towering cumulus	low (base)

Table 9-1 Cloud types.

Formation of Clouds

Clouds are formed by air cooling to below its dewpoint temperature and the water vapour condensing as water droplets (or ice crystals). The air can be cooled by rising to higher altitudes (hence clouds form above thermals and where the air is forced to rise above mountains), or by lying over a cold surface (which is how fog can form on cold nights with clear skies and little or no wind). The air can be caused to rise by being heated, or by being forced aloft by a mountain range (a process known as orographic uplift).

If the air is unstable, it will continue to rise, and any cloud that forms will be cumuliform. Stable air has no tendency to rise further, and so stratiform cloud will form. Unstable conditions can lead to thunderstorm development. Whether the air is stable or unstable depends upon conditions in that part of the atmosphere at the time.

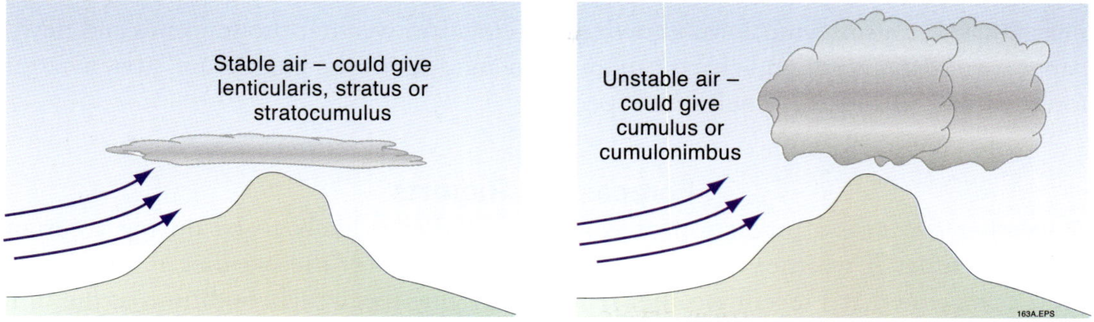

Figure 9-28 Orographic uplift can lead to cloud formation.

Large cumuliform clouds can also develop when cold air moves in at the surface and forces warmer air aloft.

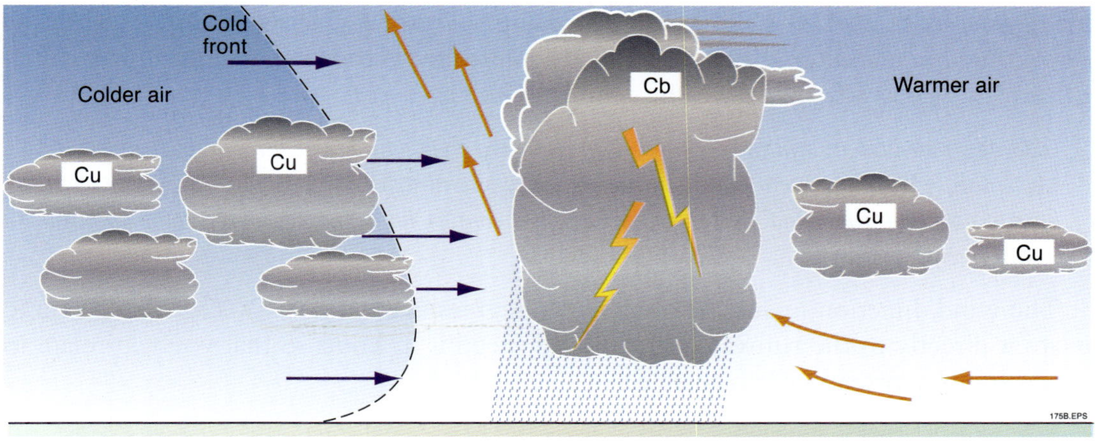

Figure 9-29 Cross-section of a cold front.

This is known as a cold front, and the passage of a fast-moving cold front can be quite dramatic (as people who live in Melbourne well know).

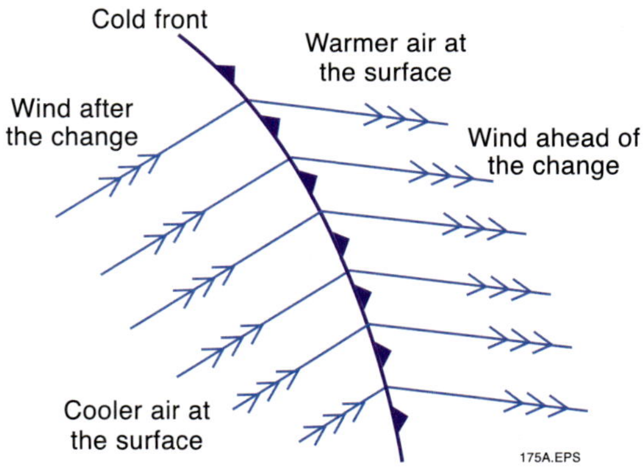

Figure 9-30 Depiction of a cold front on a weather chart.

Precipitation

Precipitation refers to falling water that reaches the ground, including:

- rain, consisting of liquid water drops;
- drizzle, consisting of fine water droplets;
- snow, consisting of branched and star-shaped ice crystals (snap-frozen);
- hail, consisting of small balls of ice;
- freezing rain or drizzle, which are liquid drops or droplets that freeze on contact with a cold surface (such as the ground or an aircraft in flight); and
- dew, frost or ice.

Steady precipitation and drizzle is typical from stratiform clouds, whereas precipitation from cumuliform clouds is likely to consist of showers and large droplets.

Weather Data

Weather conditions vary from time to time and from place to place. You can observe the weather around your local aerodrome and then assess the likely conditions over the next few hours using your local knowledge. Television weather programmes and newspaper weather forecasts and charts can give you an idea of "the big picture", but aviation forecasts and reports are much more specific.

Forecasts & Reports

A weather *forecast* is a prediction of what the weather is likely to be during a certain period of time. A weather *report* is an actual observation of the weather at a particular time. It may be that a recent weather report specifying the actual conditions at the time of observation has a trend forecast attached to it, which is a prediction of what the weather is likely to be over the following few hours. A most useful weather report is the information passed to you by air traffic control, either directly or in the form of an automatic terminal information service (ATIS) broadcast on a specific COM, VOR or NDB frequency. (These are radio communications and radio navigation aid frequencies.) Normally you listen to the ATIS prior to taxiing for take-off or when approaching an aerodrome for a landing. A typical ATIS at a controlled aerodrome will nominate a duty runway as well as advise the weather conditions, e.g.:

> *Camden terminal information Bravo, Runway two four, wind two three zero degrees, one two knots, QNH one zero zero four, temperature one nine, visibility eight kilometres, cloud four oktas three thousand five hundred, on first contact with Camden Tower or Ground, notify receipt of Bravo.*

The wind direction in an ATIS is given as degrees magnetic (°M). This allows you to relate it directly to the runway in use. Wind speed is in knots so that you can relate its effects to your aircraft's performance.

Preflight Weather (Meteorological) Briefing

The provision of weather briefing information (and other necessary briefing material such as NOTAM) is now automated. There are three basic ways in which you can obtain a preflight briefing via:

- *DECTALK*, an automated national weather service available from a synthesised voice on selected 008 telephone numbers in Brisbane and Melbourne;
- *AVFAX*, which has all meteorological products, including charts, plus NOTAM information, available by facsimile; and
- *Telephone Briefing Service* from the Weather Service Office (WSO) or the Regional Forecasting Centre (RFC) servicing the area.

Full details of the various briefing facilities available are contained in the En Route Supplement Australia (ERSA) and Visual Flight Guide (VFG), which your flying school will have for you to study. At this stage of your flying career, it will be the responsibility of your flight instructor to ensure that the weather is suitable for your flight. However, it is in your own interest to become familiar with the systems, and learn to interpret the different types of weather forecast that you may see. It's also fascinating. The two basic meteorological forecasts that you will use are:

- the area forecast (ARFOR) for the general areas in which you intend flying; and
- the terminal area forecast (TAF) for the specific aerodromes that are appropriate to your planned flight.

Forecasts

Forecast Abbreviations

To read weather forecasts and reports, you will need to become familiar with some new abbreviations and terms.

Cloud Coverage

To describe the amount of cloud cover, we use the term *okta*, which means an eighth. For example, 4 oktas means that half the sky is covered by cloud, while 8 oktas means complete cloud cover, i.e. overcast. In reports, forecasts and low-level area forecasts, however, rather than referring to oktas, the amount of cloud will be indicated by the following abbreviations:

SKC (sky clear)	0 oktas
FEW (few) 稀雲	1-2 oktas
SCT (scattered) 疏雲	3-4 oktas
BKN (broken) 裂雲	5-7 oktas
OVC (overcast) 密雲	8 oktas

Table 9-2 Cloud amount abbreviations.

Figure 9-31
Scattered cloud.

These terms are not particularly precise since they refer to large areas. SKC is seldom used, since a completely clear sky is relatively rare. Similarly, OVC is seldom used, since a completely overcast sky without a single break is also rare.

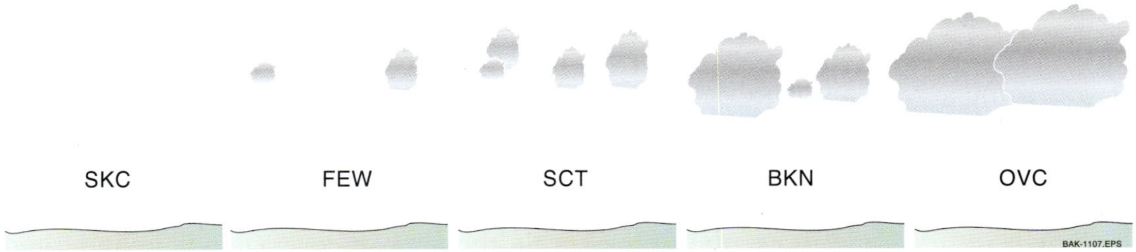

Figure 9-32 Cloud amount abbreviations.

Thunderstorms

Thunderstorms, which you should avoid, are associated with cumulonimbus (Cb) clouds. The amount of Cb cloud in an area is indicated by:

- ISOL (isolated), for individual Cbs;
- OCNL (occasional), for well-separated Cbs; and
- FREQ (frequent), for Cbs with little or no separation.

These three terms are also used to describe the concentration of showers (not necessarily thunderstorms or Cb clouds) in an area. In practical terms, ISOL Cbs should not cause you much trouble unless they are situated near the aerodrome, since they should be easy to see and to avoid. OCNL Cbs will be more difficult to avoid of course, since there will be more of them, and be vary wary of Cbs being hidden in a layer of stratocumulus. FRQ Cbs should encourage you to stay on the ground or choose another route.

Cloud Heights

In an *area forecast (ARFOR)*, the heights of the cloud bases and tops are given above mean sea level (AMSL). A typical example of how cloud is reported in an ARFOR is:

BKN ACAS 10000/20000

This means that there will be 5–7 oktas of altocumulus/altostratus with a base at 10,000 ft AMSL and tops at 20,000 ft AMSL.

In *terminal area forecasts* (TAF) and reports (METAR/SPECI), only the cloud base is given. It is shown as a three-figure group of tens of thousands, thousands, and hundreds of feet, and is measured above aerodrome level (AAL). This means that we must add the aerodrome elevation to the reported cloud base so that we can relate it to our altitude on QNH. It is done this way as it gives the actual vertical space between the cloud and the ground.

CAVOK

You will sometimes see the term CAVOK used in a TAF to indicate that "ceiling and visibility are OK". In practice, it means slightly more than this:

- visibility of 10 km or more;
- no cloud below 5,000 ft AAL, and no cumulonimbus clouds; and
- no precipitation, thunderstorms, shallow fog, low drifting snow, or dust devils.

TEMPO & INTER

TEMPO and INTER are used to indicate significant variations of a temporary or intermittent nature in aerodrome and landing forecasts:

- TEMPO is used to indicate change in prevailing conditions expected to last for a period of more than 30 minutes and less than 60 minutes in each instance; and
- INTER is used to indicate changes expected to occur frequently for periods of less than 30 minutes duration, the conditions fluctuating almost constantly, between the times specified in the forecast.

FM

If you come across this abbreviation, which means "from", in a forecast, it indicates there will be a change in the forecast conditions. The change will last from the time quoted, e.g. FM 0830 means from 0830, until the end of the forecast validity period, or until the start of another significant change. If turbulence is forecast, its start time will be shown as "FM" and its cessation time within the forecast coverage will be indicated by the word "TILL", e.g. "FM 02 MOD TURB TILL 08".

Area Forecast (ARFOR)

An area forecast (ARFOR) is issued routinely every 6 hours for each MET area as specified by number on the PCA planning chart (see graphic below). Area forecasts comprise a statement of the meteorological conditions expected to prevail in the designated area. Each area forecast usually has a validity period of 12 hours from the time that it is issued and you should *ensure that the ARFOR is valid for the period of your flight.*

Forecast areas may be subdivided if there are significant differences in weather within the one forecast area. To specify each of the subdivisions, locations with identifiers shown on the PCA planning chart will be used by the MET officers. These identifiers usually consist of three or four letters.

If you are unfamiliar with the area and the various locations within it, you can refer to the PCA planning chart or some other chart to find their exact location.

The location identifier for an aerodrome can be found in the FAC section of ERSA. For example, the location identifier for Albury is YMAY, which consists of:

- Y – Australia;
- M – Melbourne Flight Information Region (FIR); and
- AY – Albury.

For example:

AREA50(50)

ARFOR AREA FORECAST 0200400 TO 201400 AREA 50

AMEND OVERVIEW:
SURFACE TROUGH EXTENDING FROM PORT AUGUSTA THROUGH KINGSCOTE AT 05Z MOVING EASTWARD EXPECTED AT RENMARK / MT GAMBIER AT 13Z
AREAS OF RAIN AND BROKEN LOW CLOUD WEST OF TROUGH
AREAS OF RAISED DUST EAST OF PORT AUGUSTA TO ADELAIDE TILL 10Z

SUBDIVISIONS:
A: EAST OF TROUGH
B: WEST OF TROUGH

WIND:

	2000	5000	7000	10000	14000	18500
A:	330/30	340/35	340/35	330/35 PS01	310/35 MS07	300/40 MS17
B:	270/25	280/30	290/35	290/35 MS01	310/40 MS10	310/45 MS19

CLOUD:
SCT ST 1000 / 2500 IN RA BECOMING BKN WITH BASE 800 AFTER 10 AREAS OF BKN SC 2500 / 6000 IN RA
BKN AC / AS 10000 / 20000 W OF PORT AUGUSTA EXTENDING THROUGHOUT BY 13Z

AMD WEATHER:
RA
AREAS RAISED DU E OF PORT AUGUSTA TO ADELAIDE TILL12Z

VISIBILITY:
5000M IN RA
4000M IN DU

FREEZING LEVEL:
9000

ICING:
MOD IN AC / AS

TURBULANCE:
MOD IN AC
MOD BLW 5000FT

AQNH AREA QNH 04/07
AREA 50: EAST PORT AUGUSTA 1012 REST 1008

BAK-1108.EPS

Figure 9-33 Example of an ARFOR.

The interpretation of the area forecast is relatively simple. It starts with an overview of the general weather situation in the area, and follows this with details of the winds and temperatures for different altitudes (i.e. height above mean sea level) from 2,000 ft to 18,500 ft. The next items cover information on the clouds to be expected (showing cloud type, amount, base and tops), weather, visibility, freezing level, icing and turbulence.

Terminal Area Forecast (TAF)

A terminal area forecast (TAF) is a statement of meteorological conditions expected for a specified period of time. The area covered by the TAF extends for a radius of 8 kilometres from the centre of the aerodrome or runway complex. AIP MET provides complete details of the composition of a TAF, and a simple graphic explaining the sequence of information in a TAF. There is also a complete decode of weather details used in forecasts and reports. However, you will not normally have to concern yourself with these details since, in a TAF received by AVFAX, the weather details will be spelt out in plain language.

Composition of the TAF

The TAF comprises:

- message identification, location indicator, time of origin and validity period;
- forecast surface wind in degrees true and knots;
- forecast visibility in metres – a visibility in excess of 10 km is shown as "9999";
- forecast significant weather;
- forecast cloud amount and height;
- forecast significant changes and variations;
- any probability of poor visibility;
- statement of turbulence; and
- forecast temperatures and QNH.

In forecasts, the time of origin is a six-figure date–time group. All times are in GMT (same as UTC) but symbolised as "Z" for the GMT time zone "Zulu".

For example:

TAF YMMB 290650Z 0820 15004KT CAVOK
FM14 00000KT 3000 HAZE PROB40 1720 0400FOG
T 14 15 17 14 Q 1016 1014 1013 1014

This decodes as follows:

- The TAF for Moorabbin (YMMB) issued at 0650Z on the 29th of the current month (290650Z), and valid for the period from 0800Z (i.e. 1 hour and 10 minutes after the time of issue) to 2000Z (0820).
- The surface wind is forecast to be 150°T/04 kt (15004KT).
- The weather is CAVOK.
- The conditions are expected to change significantly from 1400Z (FM14) for the remainder of the period, with the wind dropping to calm (00000KT) and the visibility reducing to 3,000 m in haze (3000 HAZE); there is a 40% probability (PROB 40) of fog with visibility reduced to 400 m between 1700 and 2000 (1720 0400FOG).
- The temperatures (T) and QNH (Q) at three-hourly intervals from the commencement of the period of validity of the TAF are:
    - 0800Z, 14°C, 1016 hPa;
    - 1100Z, 15°C, 1014 hPa;
    - 1400Z, 17°C, 1013 hPa; and
    - 1700Z, 14°C, 1014 hPa.

Note that the temperature and QNH do not appear for the end of the forecast period at 2000Z.

Provisional Forecasts

A forecast is prefixed with PROV when it is compiled from insufficient synoptic information. Therefore, there is less confidence in the predictions. When later or revised data is received, MET will confirm or amend the provisional part of the forecast.

Aerodrome Weather Reports

Aerodrome weather reports are actual observations (not forecasts) of meteorological conditions at aerodromes, made by approved observers.

Routine Reports (METAR)

METARs are issued at fixed times, hourly or half-hourly, and are available on request to aircraft in-flight.

Special Reports (SPECI)

SPECIs are aerodrome weather reports issued whenever the actual conditions fluctuate about, or are below, specified criteria. For example, if a cold front had just passed through the vicinity of an aerodrome, a SPECI would be issued. As with METARs, SPECIs are available on request.

Composition of METAR/SPECI

A METAR/SPECI comprises:

- message identification, location indicator, and time;
- surface wind, with gusts if appropriate;
- visibility, including sector variations;
- present weather;
- cloud;
- temperature and dewpoint temperature;
- pressure setting; and
- supplementary information, including recent weather.

METAR YPPH 0600Z 27020KT 8000 SCT025 SCT060 12/06 Q1019

This is a METAR for Perth, issued at 0600 UTC, at which time:

- the surface wind was 270°T at 20 kt;
- the visibility was 8,000 m; true north
- there were 3–4 oktas of cloud, base 2,500 ft AAL and, 3-4 oktas, base 6,000 ft AAL;
- the temperature was +12°C and dewpoint +06°C; and
- the QNH was 1019 hPa.

Trend Type Forecast (TTF)

At some aerodromes, specific forecasts known as *trend type forecasts* (TTFs) are issued. The TTF is an aerodrome weather report (METAR/SPECI) with a trend statement added. The TTF relates to weather conditions expected to affect the aerodrome of origin for three hours following the time of the report. Because it is more accurate and precise, the TTF supersedes the TAF for its validity period which is three hours commencing from the time the observation is made. It becomes the current forecast for pilots of aircraft with an arrival time falling within this three-hour period.

Composition of a TTF

As a TTF is only issued with a METAR/SPECI, it includes the same information, and uses the same abbreviations and weather code details as a TAF. For example:

TTF SPECI YBBN 2000Z 02001KT 0400S 8000N PATCHES
FOG 18/17 Q1022 FM2030 02003KT 8000 NO SIG WX SKC

This example, for Brisbane, indicates that there will be a significant change in the conditions from 2030Z. The visibility will increase from a minimum of 400 m to the south, maximum of 8 km to the north, patches of fog to 8 km visibility in all directions. The observed weather will change from patches of fog to no significant weather and the sky clear.

Automatic Terminal Information Service (ATIS)

At aerodromes where air traffic services are provided by a tower (see ERSA FAC for details), there is usually a tape-recorded radio message of the current aerodrome terminal information. It is transmitted on a specific frequency in either the COM or NAV groups, and sometimes on both. The message runs continuously and is updated periodically as conditions change. This service is known as the automatic terminal information service or ATIS (pronounced ay-tiss).

The information provided on the ATIS will usually include:

- runway in use details;
- wind direction and strength;
- cloud (amount and base), plus visibility and other conditions as appropriate;
- aerodrome QNH; and
- temperature.

An example of an ATIS broadcast is:
Essendon terminal information Delta
Runway three five
wind three five zero degrees one three knots
QNH one zero one seven
temperature two six
cloud few two thousand
Essendon terminal information Delta

There is quite a bit of information, so you should jot down the important aspects as you listen to the ATIS for later reference to avoid having to listen to it again. (Once familiar with the procedures, you may find it unnecessary to write down simple ATIS messages.)

The ATIS is prepared by air traffic control personnel, and includes details from the latest meteorological reports. To signify changes in the information, the ATIS code letter will be changed, e.g. from information Alfa to information Bravo, or from information Echo to information Foxtrot, etc.

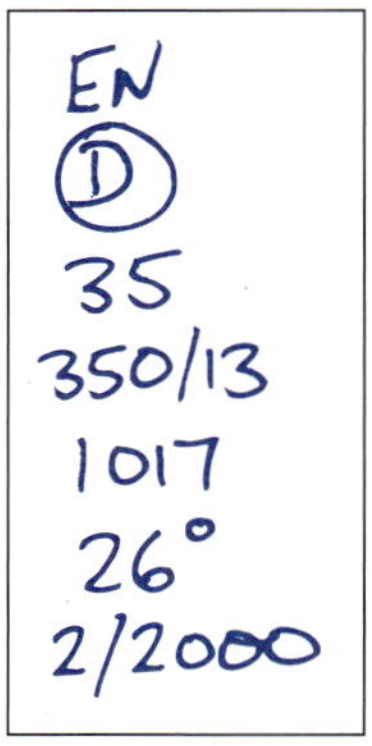

Figure 9-34
Note down the ATIS.

Note: At certain non-towered aerodromes at which a CTAF has been established, an aerodrome weather information broadcast (AWIB) may be available on the VOR or NDB frequency. At this time some of the aerodromes with this facility are as follows: Canberra, Devonport, East Sale and Wynyard.

ATIS may be Transmitted on a Discrete (Separate) VHF Frequency

At many of the busier aerodromes, where there may be many basic training aeroplanes with just VHF communication radio equipment, a discrete VHF-COM frequency is made available purely for broadcasting the tape-recorded ATIS. At Class D aerodromes – Melbourne/Moorabbin, Perth/Jandakot, Brisbane/Archerfield, Sydney/Bankstown and Adelaide/Parafield – the ATIS is broadcast on 120.9 MHz, a discrete VHF-COM frequency reserved exclusively for this purpose. You can select the discrete ATIS frequency on your VHF-COM and obtain the ATIS whenever you want. (Only the VHF-COM set can be used to receive this, as it is outside the range of frequencies that the VHF-NAV can be tuned to.) Consequently, unless you have two separate VHF-COM radios you will have to break your listening watch on the COM frequency.

ATIS is often Transmitted on a Radio Navaid Frequency

When you are about to use a radio navaid, the first thing you must do after tuning the frequency is to identify the aid. This is done by listening to a two- or three-letter Morse code group (e.g. PF for Parafield) transmitted at regular intervals with the navigation signals from the radio navaid. The Morse code table that is printed on each VTC and ERC.

Alternatively a taped voice message, the ATIS, containing the current terminal information for the aerodrome, will be broadcast as the station identification.

The aircraft equipment that receives the VOR is the VHF-NAV and that which receives signals from the NDB is the ADF. Thus:

- a VOR frequency is selected on your VHF-NAV set; and
- an NDB frequency is selected on your ADF.

A	• ▬	N	▬ •
B	▬ • • •	O	▬ ▬ ▬
C	▬ • ▬ •	P	• ▬ ▬ •
D	▬ • •	Q	▬ ▬ • ▬
E	•	R	• ▬ •
F	• • ▬ •	S	• • •
G	▬ ▬ •	T	▬
H	• • • •	U	• • ▬
I	• •	V	• • • ▬
J	• ▬ ▬ ▬	W	• ▬ ▬
K	▬ • ▬	X	▬ • • ▬
L	• ▬ • •	Y	▬ • ▬ ▬
M	▬ ▬	Z	▬ ▬ • •

Figure 9-35 The Morse code.

You can obtain the ATIS on these radio navaids simply by listening to them – there is no need to know how to use them for navigation to do this.

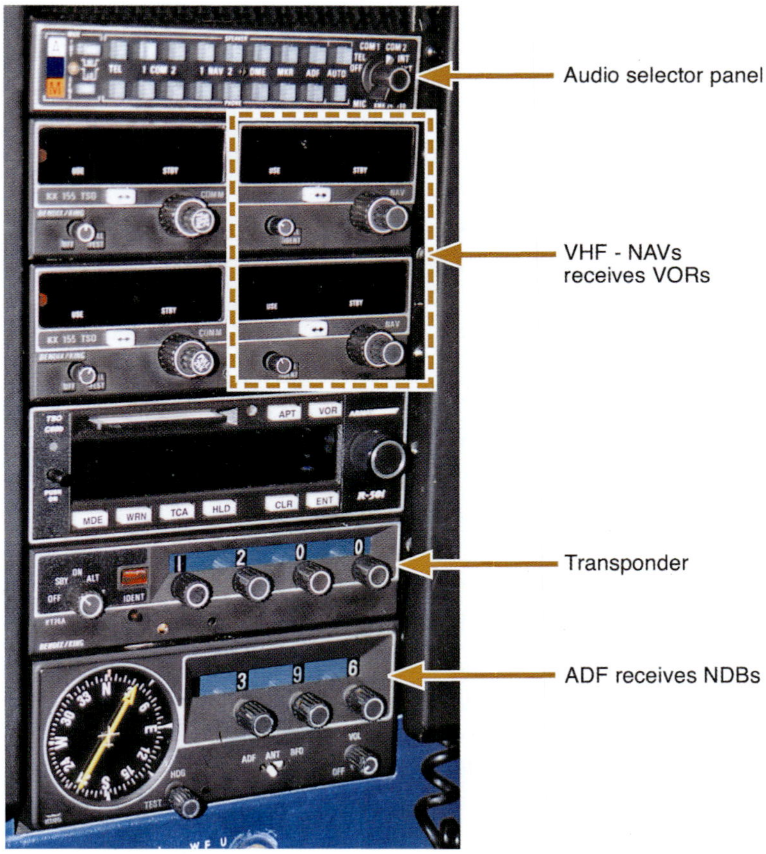

Figure 9-36 Some NDBs and VORs carry the ATIS.

The ADF (for NDBs) and the VHF-NAV (for VORs) are different radios from the VHF-COM, and at certain aerodromes you may listen to the ATIS on them without interrupting your listening watch on the VHF-COM frequency.

To listen to the ATIS being transmitted on the voice channel of a radio navaid, you must ensure that the volume control of the appropriate radio receiver is turned up, and that it is selected to the headset or speakers via a switch on the audio selector panel, as desired. This is the small panel immediately above the no. 1 VHF-NAV/COM in the radio stack pictured above.

Not all training aeroplanes have the same audio selector panels. Ask your flying instructor for details on your specific aircraft type.

ATIS at Controlled Aerodromes

The major difference in the ATIS at controlled aerodromes compared with that at uncontrolled aerodromes is that the duty runway is nominated. An example of such an ATIS is the following:

Camden terminal information Echo
Runway two four
wind two one zero degrees eight knots
QNH one zero zero eight
temperature two eight
cloud scattered four thousand five hundred
Camden terminal information Echo

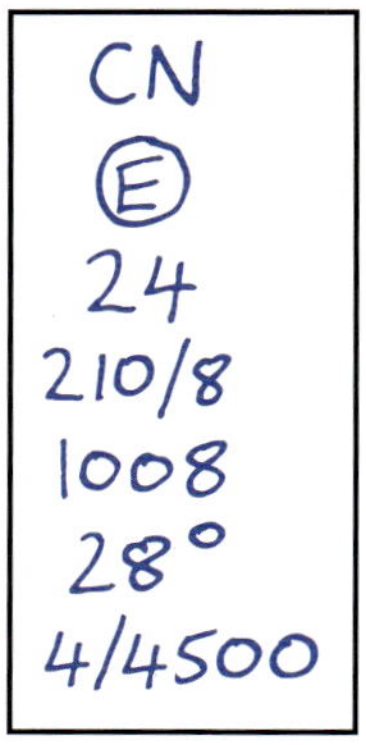

Figure 9-37 Example of noted down ATIS details.

This could be jotted down as in figure 9-37.

Some of the Class D aerodromes have many runways and taxiways, and a lot of aeroplanes operating in the vicinity, both in the circuit and the local training area. The radio at these aerodromes can be very busy at times so, to minimise messages on the VHF-COM frequency, as many general operational instructions as appropriate are placed on the ATIS, along with the standard weather and runway information.

To simplify operations at these aerodromes, the traffic is directed to use different runways and different circuit directions (depending upon the intentions of the pilot in command). Detailed information on this is provided in AIP ENR 1.1, as well as the En Route Supplement Australia (ERSA) FAC listing for the aerodrome. At Class D aerodromes, the ATIS may contain more operating instructions than the ATIS at a less busy aerodrome.

If you are unfamiliar with the aerodrome, you may have to listen to the ATIS a number of times before you have absorbed and/or noted down all the vital details. Below is an example of such an ATIS.

Moorabbin terminal information Papa
Runway one seven
wind two two zero degrees up to one two knots crosswind at times eight knots
QNH one zero one nine
temperature one eight
CAVOK
arrivals and departures east and circuits, Runway one seven left frequency one one eight decimal one
arrivals and departures west, Runway one seven right frequency one two three decimal zero
northern part of taxiway Golf closed due works in progress
aircraft taxiing for Runway left, obtain clearance to cross Runway right
Moorabbin terminal information Papa

And this could be jotted down as in figure 9-38.

MB
Ⓟ 17
220/12 X/W 8
1019
18°
CAVOK
17L EAST + CCTS 118.1
17R WEST 123.0

Figure 9-38 Example of notes for more complex ATIS.

ERSA is your reference for how to navigate around an aerodrome. The runways and taxiways are clearly marked on the aerodrome diagrams contained in the FAC section. Always ensure you obtain a clearance to cross an active runway.

Note: There may be other messages appended towards the end of the ATIS such as "*aircraft calling ready, nominate their first tracking point*", "*when taxiing or reporting inbound, notify receipt of information Papa*" or "*parachuting in progress at Lower Light*".

ATIS at aerodromes in Class C CTRs can be received up to a radius of 90 nm, and up to 30 nm for Class D aerodromes.

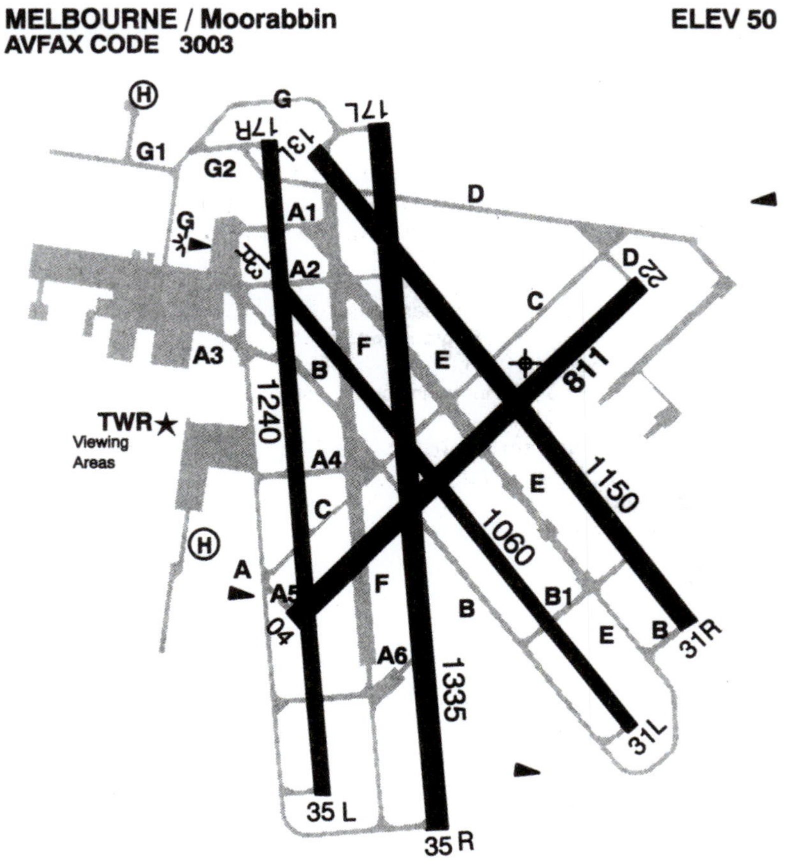

Figure 9-39 Runway layout at Melbourne/Moorabbin Airport from ERSA.

Weather Details in an ATIS

The term CAVOK (pronounced kav-oh-kay) will be encountered frequently on the ATIS. For VFR operations, CAVOK indicates that the visibility, cloud and present weather are all better than:

- visibility 10 kilometres or more;
- no cloud below 5,000 ft AAL (above aerodrome level); and
- no precipitation, thunderstorm, shallow fog, low drifting snow or dust devils.

Where CAVOK conditions do not exist, the met report on the ATIS will include cloud, visibility and any significant weather, e.g.

cloud broken one thousand
overcast one zero thousand
visibility three thousand metres
light rain
patches of fog in valleys adjacent to the aerodrome

Listen to the ATIS prior to Taxiing

At controlled aerodrome, you should listen to the ATIS broadcast before taxiing for take-off, and notify receipt of it in your taxi call, e.g.

Parafield Ground
Delta Alfa November, Warrior
received Bravo, VFR
for the training area
*Runway two one right**

Note: If more than one runway is in use at a Class D aerodrome, the runway to be used should be nominated by the pilot, to advise the tower and other taxiing aircraft.

This is an example of a taxi report at a Class D aerodrome.

A typical request for taxi clearance at an aerodrome in a Class C or D CTR is:
Townsville Ground
Papa November Romeo, Tobago
received Uniform
for the training area
request taxi

Listen to the ATIS prior to making your inbound call

When about to enter a control zone (Class C, Class D), your inbound report is normally made at a designated VFR approach point to the zone. You should listen to the ATIS several minutes prior to reaching the approach point, and when making your inbound report, notify receipt of the ATIS broadcast, in the same way as you did before taxiing.

Do not forget to listen to the ATIS, as failure to do so will require the controller to transmit the aerodrome information to you. This unnecessarily increases his or her work-load and clutters up the COM frequency for everyone. Try and organise yourself to listen to the ATIS at an appropriate time; however, keep your priorities and think ahead.

What if you do not receive the ATIS?

Sometimes you do not have the radio equipment to receive the ATIS, or perhaps it is difficult to read. In these cases, at controlled aerodromes, the controller will pass you the relevant information on the communications frequency when you make your initial contact. If this is not forthcoming, then simply "request terminal information" if departing, or "request landing information" for an arrival.

ATIS at Deactivated Control Zones

When a control zone is deactivated outside normal (i.e. published) hours of operation, the zone becomes an CTAF. When this happens, the ATIS may be used to broadcast operational information of an unchanging nature. This might include confirmation of the CTAF frequency, preferred runways or expected re-opening time of the zone. These outside-hours broadcasts use the code letter ***Zulu***. You are encouraged to monitor the ATIS outside normal operating hours, but do not need to nominate receipt of Zulu in your inbound report. ATIS Zulu will advise if AWIB is available for that airfield.

Aerodrome Weather Information Broadcasts (AWIB)

Broadcasts of actual weather conditions may be made on navigation aids from automated weather station (AWS) sites that use Bureau of Meteorology AWS equipment. Basic AWSs provide wind direction and speed, temperature, humidity, pressure setting and rainfall. Advanced AWSs provide automated cloud and visibility elements, which will be appended to the meteorological report as remarks for guidance only.

Information provided in AWIB broadcasts is in similar format to that of an ATIS broadcast and will contain some of the following additional items:

- test transmissions identified as "Test";
- station identifier as a plain language station name;
- identifier "AWS Aerodrome Weather";
- wind direction in degrees magnetic and speed in knots;
- altimeter settings (QNH);
- temperature in whole degrees Celsius;
- low cloud below 12,500 ft;*
- visibility;*
- dew point in whole degrees Celsius;**
- percentage relative humidity;** and
- rainfall over previous ten minutes.**

* Provided from advanced AWS as guidance material
** Provided as supplementary information.

Information broadcast from AWS is considered to be "real-time" data. When information is not available about a particular item, either because of invalid data or an inoperative sensor, the element of the broadcast will be identified as "currently not available", e.g. "temperature currently not available". The integrity of the barometric system is such that they are an approved source of QNH. The QNH may be used as the actual aerodrome QNH. The wind and temperature information does not have the same degree of integrity and should be used at pilot discretion. The AWIB is transmitted on the VOR or NDB frequencies and is available by phone; details in ERSA and Jeppesen.

Review 9

BAK Level of Knowledge Only

1. Name the layers of the atmosphere.
2. At what altitude is the tropopause in ISA?
3. Wind velocity has two elements. They are . . . . . and . . . . .
4. What is meant by an okta?
5. By how many nautical miles should we avoid a thunderstorm?
6. What happens if the air is cooled to below dewpoint temperature?
7. What causes thermals?
8. Turbulence and vertical wind gusts can cause the wing to stall or can overstress the aircraft. What is the speed below which the aircraft should be flown in turbulence?
9. What are the three levels of severity of turbulence?
10. When air is forced to lift over a mountain range, the phenomenon has a special name. It is called . . . . . lift.
11. List three types of precipitation.
12. What is the difference between a weather forecast and a weather report?
13. What is meant by stratiform?
14. AVFAX is . . . . .
15. DECTALK is . . . . .
16. BROKEN cloud means a certain sky coverage. What is the range of oktas in this case?
17. What is meant by CAVOK?
18. The terms TEMPO and INTER mean a deterioration in conditions for certain periods. What is the period of time in each case?
19. What is meant by ARFOR and TAF?
20. When is a forecast considered provisional (PROV)?

10 - Loading

Aviation
Theory
Centre

Introduction

Before the aircraft is loaded, consider the following definitions:

- *Mass* is the amount of matter or material in an object.
- *Gravity* is the force of attraction between objects. The force of gravity is directly proportional to the mass of the objects and inversely proportional to the distance between them. For our purposes, since the mass of the earth does not change and we remain comparatively the same distance from the earth's centre, we consider the acceleration due to the gravitational force of earth to be the constant g equal to 9.807 metres per second squared.
- *Weight* is the measure of the force of gravity on a body – in units of 1g or kilograms.

The terms *weight* and *mass* are often mistakenly interchanged – they are not the same thing. Mass, the amount of material in a body, does not consider the effect of gravity. Since weight is a measure of the gravitational force on a mass, it takes into consideration the effect of gravity acting on the mass – thus the effect of weightlessness in space where the gravitational forces are minimal. The imperial unit for weight is the pound-force – the mass in pounds × the force on the mass in feet per second^2. The metric unit is the newton – 1 newton being a force which would give a one kilogram mass an acceleration of one metre per second^2.

To find the mass of an object, divide its weight by the gravity constant:

$$\text{mass in pounds} = \frac{\text{weight in pounds-force}}{\text{gravity constant 32.2 feet per second}^2}$$

or

$$\text{mass in kilograms} = \frac{\text{weight in newtons}}{\text{gravity constant 9.807 metres per second}^2}$$

It is technically correct to use the term *mass*. However, as we operate small aircraft near the earth's surface where gravity is constant, it is traditional to use the term *weight* when loading light aircraft.

An aeroplane must only be flown within certificated limits of weight and balance to ensure that it remains controllable, performs adequately, and is not overstressed. The correct loading of an aeroplane ensures that:

- the maximum weight is not exceeded for that take-off and landing; and
- the centre of gravity (CG) remains within the manufacturer's specified range during all stages of flight.

Weight & Balance

Weight

Let's first consider the weight-only implication when operating an aeroplane. The thrust available from the aircraft engine and the lift available from the wings are combined to create the force which must overcome the total weight of the aircraft so it can fly. Clearly, if an aircraft weighed too much it could not take-off at all. The weight could be reduced so the aircraft could just take-off. In this case, a very long, level and smooth runway would be required. At excessive weights, the aircraft hitting bumps on the runway or turbulence in the air could suffer mechanical damage (overstressing) and perhaps structural failure.

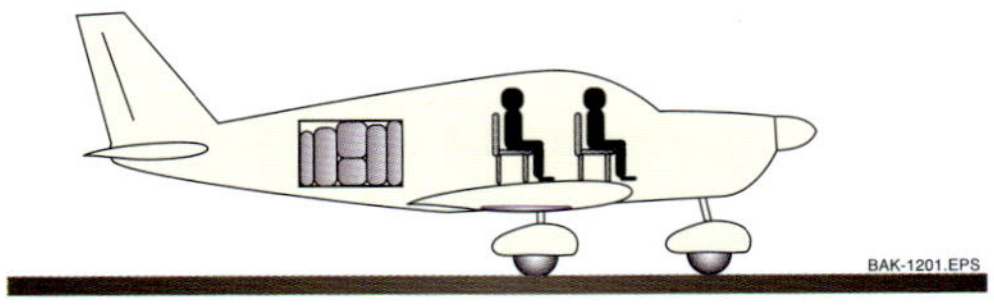

Figure 10-1 Correct weight and distribution.

Typically, the design weight of an aircraft will be such so as not to risk structural damage and to allow the aircraft to perform satisfactorily. This means take-off, climb, cruise and land in a safe and efficient manner. Controlling the aircraft weight (aircraft and equipment) and the added weight (fuel and cargo) is only half the story.

Balance

An aircraft is exactly like a see-saw, a weight-bearing structure with a balance point. The balance point when the aircraft is on the ground is the main wheels. If the aircraft were loaded incorrectly (static balance), it could be tipped up.

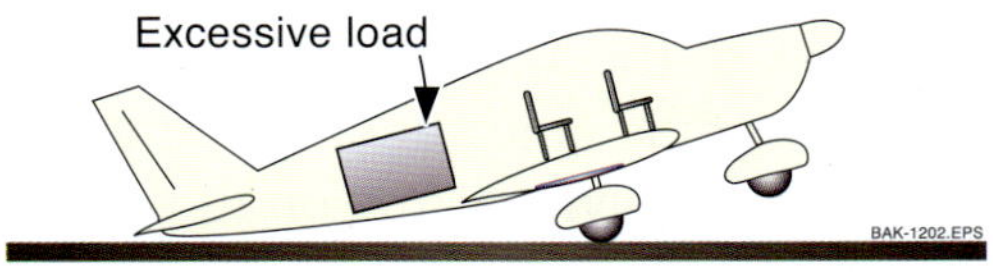

Figure 10-2 Excess weight – too far aft.

While this could damage the aircraft, the far more critical function of balance relates to the inflight balance of the aircraft. In flight, the balance of the aircraft may change. Aircraft weight acts through the centre of gravity (CG), which may move significantly as the aircraft weight reduces with fuel consumption or drops parachutists, water etc.

This CG change must remain within design limits. These limits are determined by the size of the control surface available and the length of the arm available to the CG, which in turn will enable the pilot to control the aircraft. Hence the main function of correct balance is to maintain aircraft stability and controllability. At maximum weight, the aeroplane performance will be not as good as when it loses weight with fuel burn-off, and it will be less responsive to the controls. From a performance point of view, a heavy aeroplane will have poorer performance, such as:

- higher stall speed;
- higher take-off speed and a longer take-off run;
- poorer climb performance (poorer climb angle and climb rate);
- lower service ceiling;
- less manoeuvrability;
- higher fuel consumption, and less range and endurance;
- reduced cruise speed for a given power setting;
- higher landing speed and a longer landing distance; and
- greater braking requirements when stopping.

Similarly, an aeroplane balanced near its forward or rear limits will begin to show some adverse handling characteristics. However, if the weight and balance is within limits, the aeroplane will be safe to fly.

Do not fly an aeroplane that is outside its CG limits.

You must take particular care never to exceed either the maximum certificated take-off weight or maximum permissible take-off weight. Apart from a severe degradation in performance and handling, and the fact that it is illegal to fly under these circumstances, an overloaded aeroplane may render your insurance invalid.

Do not fly an aeroplane that is above any of its maximum allowable weights.

Weight Terminology

Empty Weight (EW)

Empty weight includes the airframe, engine and fixed equipment as necessary for flight. Empty weight also *includes* unusable fuel and undrainable oil. Empty weight *does not include* pilot and payload, and ballast or *usable* fuel.

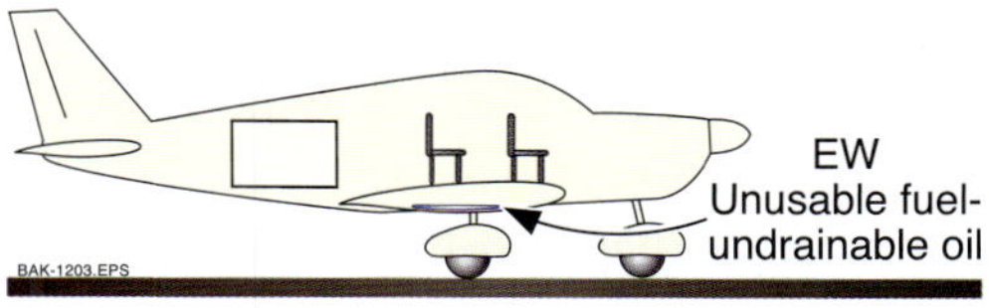

Figure 10-3 Empty weight.

Basic Empty Weight (BEW)

Basic empty weight includes the airframe, engine, fixed equipment, unusable fuel, *full oil* and other items necessary for all flights. The basic empty weight *does not include* pilot, payload (passengers and freight), or ballast (for balance) or *usable* fuel. The basic empty weight (and moment arm, which we will consider later) will be different for each individual aeroplane, and is always specified in that particular aeroplane's flight manual.

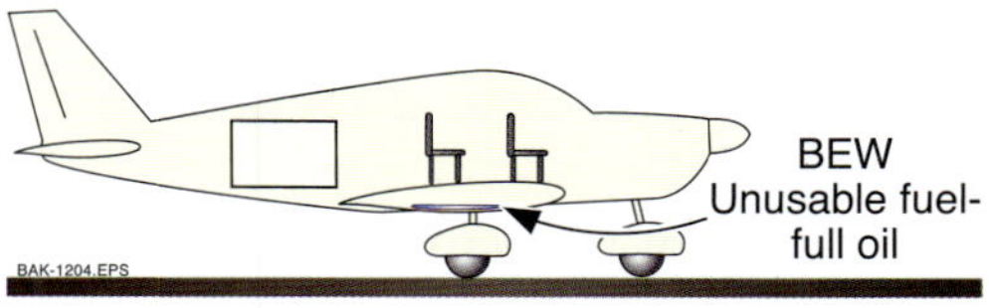

Figure 10-4 Basic empty weight.

Zero Fuel Weight (ZFW)

The *zero-fuel weight* is the basic empty weight of the aeroplane *plus the pilot, plus passengers, plus baggage and cargo.* Usable fuel is *not* included.

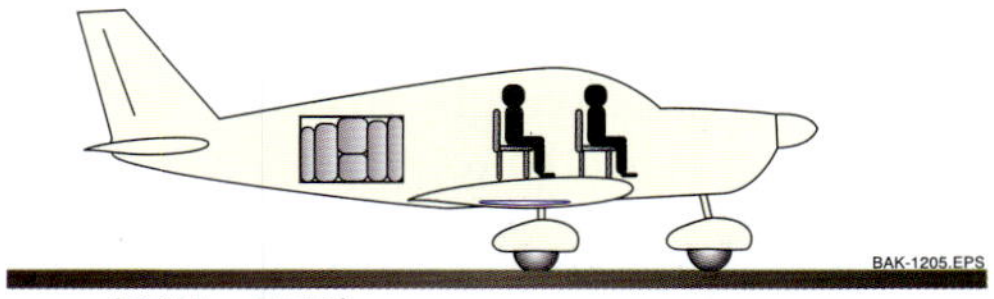

ZFW = BEW + cargo + passengers + crew

Figure 10-5 Zero fuel weight.

Gross Weight (GW)

The *gross weight,* also called *all up weight* (AUW), is the total weight of the aircraft (and its contents) at any particular time. It is the basic weight plus pilot plus passengers and cargo, plus ballast (if any) and fuel load. The gross weight must not exceed the maximum weight permissible for any given manoeuvre. For take-off, GW must not exceed the certificated MTOW or the performance-limited TOW. On landing, GW must not exceed the certificated MLW or the performance-limited LW. Each aircraft has weight limitations placed upon it depending upon the structural strength of the aircraft, the operations for which it is designed, and the manoeuvre being considered.

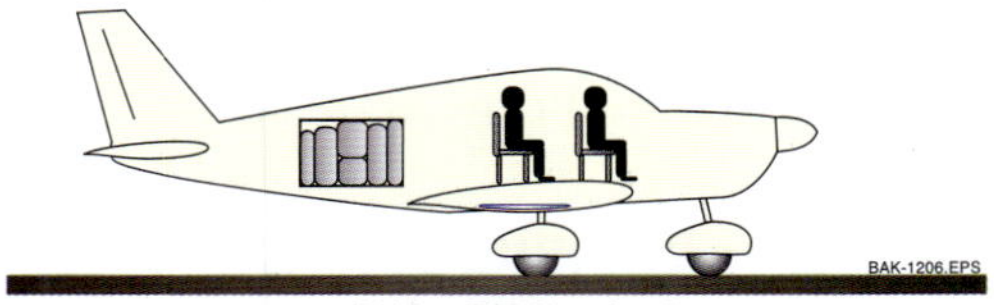

GW = ZFW + fuel

Figure 10-6 Gross weight.

Maximum Ramp Weight

The *maximum ramp weight* is the maximum gross weight permitted prior to taxiing. It may exceed the MTOW by the start-up and taxi fuel allowance. While this is not specified for many light aircraft, it is specified for some, and so you should be aware of ramp weight. For example, an aeroplane may have a 3 kg start-up and taxi allowance (fuel burn-off during the taxi), so in this case the ramp weight may exceed the maximum permissible take-off weight by 3 kg.

Maximum Take-Off Weight (MTOW) – Structural
The MTOW is the maximum certificated gross weight permitted for take-off.

Performance-Limited Take-Off Weight (TOW-P)
Sometimes an additional limitation such as a short runway, obstacle in the take-off path, unfavourable wind or slope, high temperature or a high density altitude, will limit that particular take-off to a maximum weight less than the MTOW.

Maximum Landing Weight (MLW) – Structural
The MLW is the maximum certificated gross weight for landing. For many light aircraft, the MLW is the same as the MTOW, and you can take-off at maximum weight and return for an immediate landing without exceeding the limitations. The MLW of other aircraft may, for structural reasons, be less than the MTOW. In this case, the fuel burn-off must be sufficient to reduce the actual take-off gross weight to a figure less than the MLW.

Performance-Limited Landing Weight (LW-P)
Sometimes a performance limitation (short runway, high obstacle in the approach path making a long touchdown necessary, unfavourable wind or slope, high density height) may limit that particular landing to a maximum permissible weight less than the MLW.

The Weight of Fuel
Piston-engine fuel (100/130 or 100LL AVGAS) has a specific gravity (SG) of 0.71. This means that a volume unit of AVGAS weighs only 0.71 times as much as an equal volume of water. As 1 litre of water weighs 1 kg, 1 litre of AVGAS will weigh 0.71 kg.

Ballast
Ballast is a *dead* weight (usually lead shot or sand bags) used for balance. Ballast is used to position the CG within its moment limits at or below its ZFW weight limit.

Flight Fuel
Flight fuel is the amount of fuel planned to be used during the flight. It is sometimes called *fuel burn off* (FBO). Flight fuel does *not* include any variable reserve (if applicable), fixed reserves or taxi allowance. It does include fuel to divert to an alternate aerodrome if one is required due to weather or aerodrome lighting.

Familiarity with your Aeroplane's Weight Limitations
The more familiar you are with the weight limitations applicable to your aeroplane, the easier weight and balance problems will become. You should now go ahead and fill in the following details for your aeroplane, and then memorise them.

MTOW (structural)	=. . . kg	Taxi allowance (if any)	=. . . kg
MLW (structural)	=. . . kg	Maximum number of passengers	=. . . kg =. . . kg
Basic empty weight	=. . . kg (with/without full oil)	Maximum baggage compartment load	=. . . kg
Maximum fuel load	=. . . litres=. . . kg	Fuel tank capacities	Mains. . . litres =. . . kg Aux. . . litres =. . . kg

Table 10-1 Aeroplane weight limitations.

Moment of a Force

The moment of a force is its leverage, which depends upon two things:

- the strength (magnitude) of the force; and
- its moment arm, which is the distance from the point at which the force is applied to the pivot point (or *fulcrum*).

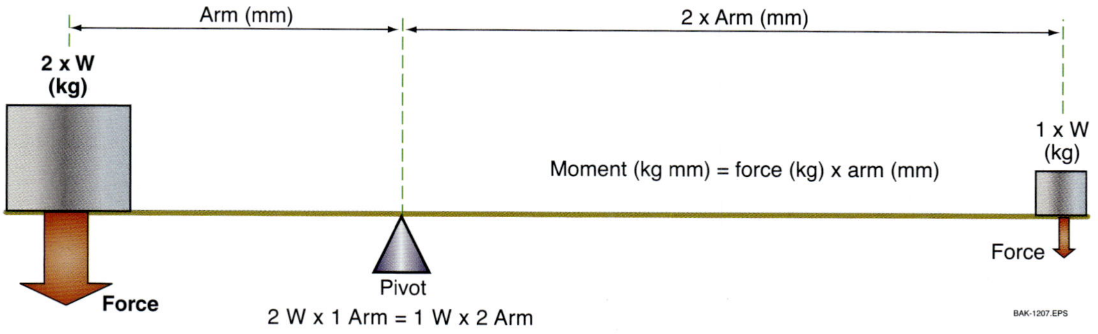

Figure 10-7 Balance of moments.

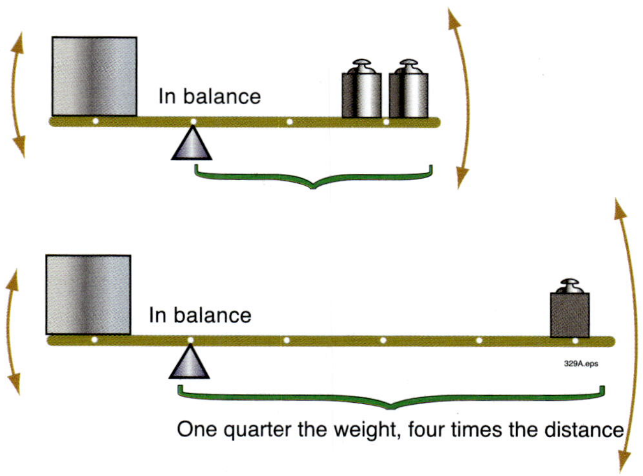

Figure 10-8 Same moments.

We are all familiar with the effect of a lever – the longer the lever arm, the smaller the force required to achieve the same turning effect. In the case of an aeroplane, we are trying to balance it, i.e. stop it rotating (or pitching). This is like a balanced beam, where the moments trying to turn it clockwise are perfectly balanced by the moments wanting to turn it anticlockwise.

In the lower of the two balance beams illustrated in figure 10-8, the same turning effect (moment) is achieved by half the original weight at double the distance. If the force being applied (weight) is measured in kilograms (kg) and the arm is in millimetres, then the moment is expressed in kilogram millimetres (kg mm).

A weight of 2 kg with arm 200 mm has a moment of 2 kg × 200 mm = 400 kg mm.
A weight of 1 kg with arm 400 mm has a moment of 1 kg × 400 mm = 400 kg mm.

Balancing a Loaded Beam (or Aeroplane)

To balance a beam, we need to provide a supporting force at its central position, i.e. the point where the total weight may be considered to be concentrated. This is the point where the anticlockwise turning moments are balanced by the clockwise turning moments, and this is called the centre of gravity (CG).

The magnitude of the supporting force will need to equal the total weight. For a beam, the supporting force may be provided by a pivot or by a rope; for an aeroplane, the supporting force is provided by the lift from the wings.

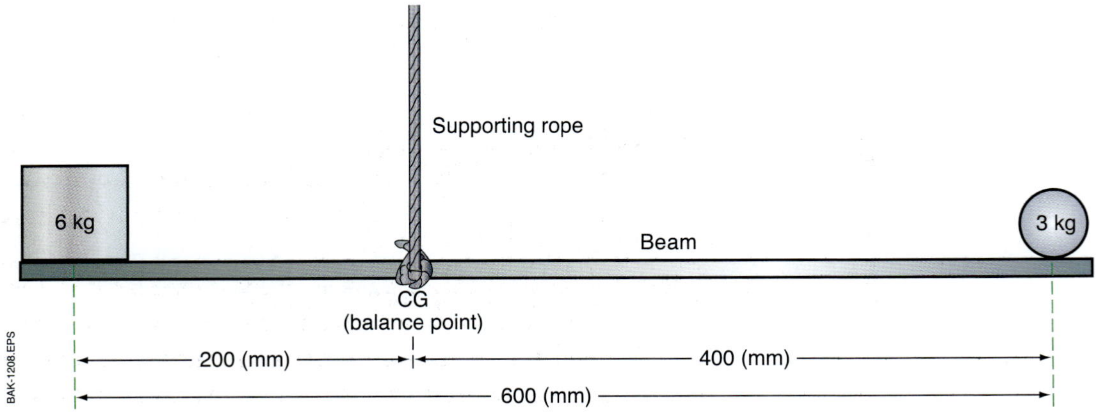

Figure 10-9 Centre of gravity (balance point).

In the simple case of a loaded beam, you have probably already estimated the position of the CG to be closer to the 6 kg weight, in fact about 200 mm from it. If the supporting force is provided at this CG position, the beam will balance. For an aeroplane to be in balance and stable, its CG must lie ahead of and close to the point where the lift is produced by the wings.

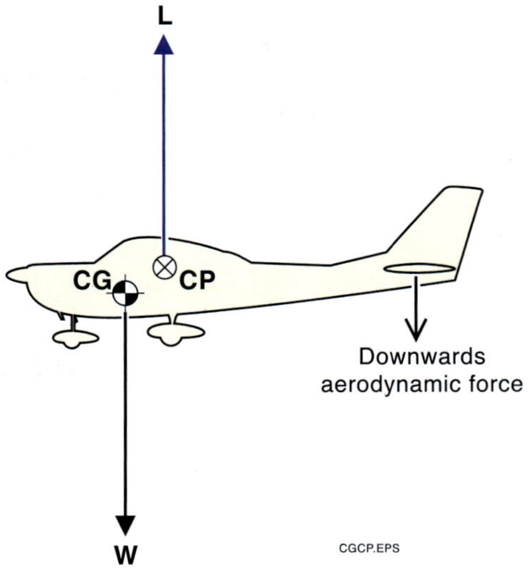

Figure 10-10 Balance of forces.

Aeroplane Balance

The CG of an aeroplane must be within the manufacturer's limits so it remains controlled. The centre of gravity of an aeroplane is computed along its longitudinal axis, and it must lie within a specified range for the aeroplane to be controllable and to fly safely (and legally).

The main supporting force in flight counteracting the total weight of the loaded aeroplane is, of course, the lift generated by the wings. It is considered to be concentrated at the centre of pressure (CP), usually situated somewhere on the forward section of the wings – its position varies depending upon angle of attack and other factors. The balancing force (usually downward) is provided by the horizontal stabiliser. If loaded with the CG well forward, the horizontal stabiliser has a long moment arm, and the aeroplane will be very stable longitudinally; that is, the aeroplane will resist any pitching moment. The forward position of the CG is limited to ensure that the elevator has sufficient pitching moment to overcome the nose-heaviness, and greater longitudinal stability so that you are able to rotate the aeroplane for take-off and flare it for landing at relatively low airspeeds.

If the CG is aft, the aeroplane will be tail-heavy and less stable longitudinally, because of the shorter moment arm from the CG to the horizontal stabiliser, and the shorter moment arm between the CG and the CP. The aft position of the CG is limited to ensure that the aeroplane remains sufficiently stable to hold a reasonably steady nose position without excessive and frequent control movements by the pilot being necessary, and so that the elevator feel experienced by the pilot through the control wheel remains satisfactory. If the CG were outside the aft limit, the aeroplane would be very tail-heavy, difficult to control, and would tend to stall and/or spin more easily, from which it might be difficult, or even impossible, to recover.

Finding the Position of the CG

To calculate the position of the centre of gravity (rather than just estimate it), we need to calculate the total moment, i.e. the sum of the turning effects of the individual weights. Then we find the position where a single weight (equal to the sum of the individual weights) will have the same total moment; that is, find CG arm so that total weight × CG arm = total moment.

To do this we need to know the individual moment arms as measured from an appropriate datum. As it turns out, it does not matter which point we choose as the datum – the results for CG position will always be the same. This fact is important, because different aeroplane manufacturers choose different datums. By convention, moment arms to the left of the chosen datum are negative; those to the right of the datum are positive.

Datums

Aeroplane manufacturers specify a datum point for CG calculations. Some choose the nose of the aeroplane as the datum, others choose the firewall behind the engine and others choose an external point along the extended longitudinal axis ahead of the nose. The datum point for your particular aeroplane will be stated in its weight and balance documents.

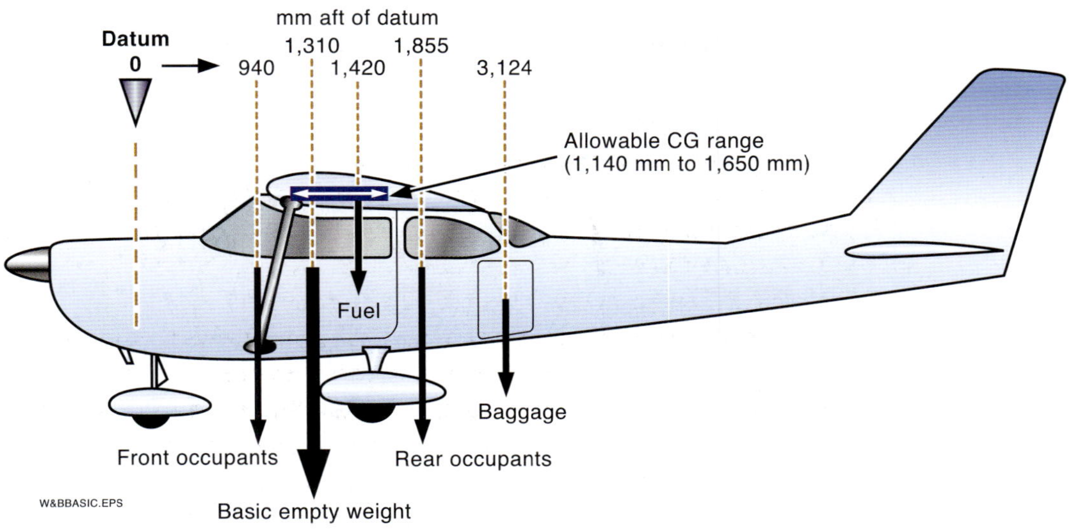

Figure 10-11 Common datum (reference point).

It doesn't matter which datum is used for CG calculations. We simply compare the positive and negative moments about that point. The point where they cancel is the CG position – relative to the chosen datum. What we are doing is adding all of the small components of the total weight of the aircraft and finding what and where a single weight would have the same effect. The position of the datum is often referred to as *station zero* (i.e. STA 0). Other positions may be specified relative to the station zero datum – for instance, a point 940 mm aft of the datum is called STA 940. If the datum is aft of the nose, then all weights forward of this datum will have a negative arm and a negative moment. The advantage of having a datum at or forward of the nose is that all moments are positive, making the calculations simpler. This is the case for VH registered aircraft.

Simple Layout for Weight & Balance Calculations

The CG is the position through which all of the weights, combined into a gross weight (or total weight), may be considered to act. The total weight must have the same turning moment as the sum of the individual moments.

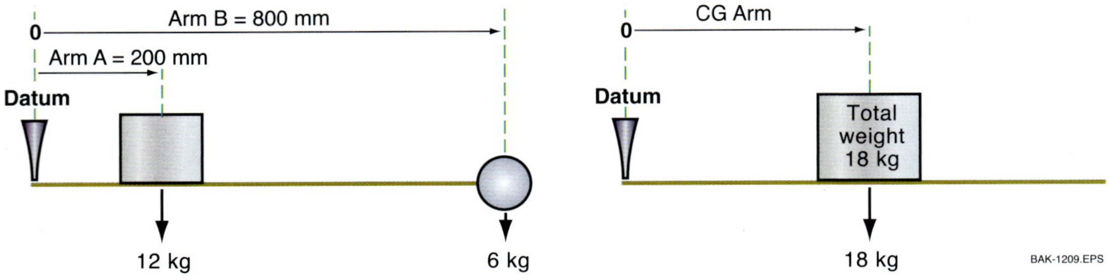

Figure 10-12 Equivalent moments.

$$
\begin{aligned}
\text{Sum of individual moments} &= \text{total moment} \\
&= \text{total weight} \times \text{moment arm} \\
&= (12 \times 200) + (6 \times 800) \\
&= 7{,}200 \text{ kg mm} \\
&= 18 \text{ kg} \times \text{CG arm}
\end{aligned}
$$

The CG position can now be found by dividing total moment by total weight:

$$\text{CG arm} = \frac{\text{total moment}}{\text{total weight}} = \frac{7{,}200 \text{ kg mm}}{18 \text{ kg}} = 400 \text{ mm}$$

Therefore, the CG position is 400 mm aft of datum. This can be neatly laid out in tabular form.

	Weight (kg)	Arm (mm)	Moment (kg-mm)
	12	x 200	= 2, 400
	6	x 800	= 4, 800
Total	18	400 CG position	7, 200

BAK-TABLE12.EPS

Figure 10-13 Sample tabulation.

To Find the Position of CG

Step 1
Calculate individual moments.

Step 2
Calculate total weight and total moment.

Step 3
Calculate $\text{CG arm} = \frac{\text{total moment}}{\text{total weight}}$

Take particular note when doing these problems that you cannot add the individual arms to obtain the location of the CG. This answer can be found only by dividing the sum of all the moments by the total weight.

Finding the CG for a Loaded Aeroplane

Now that we have seen how to calculate the total moment and hence the location of the CG, we can apply this to an aeroplane. Remember, "station" is abbreviated to STA.

Note that you may use an electronic calculator to help in weight and balance calculations. Set your working out in tabular form; this will possibly be supplied.

Example 10-1

Given the following information about a loaded aeroplane, calculate the total moment and position of the CG.

- Data given in the flight manual (will always be supplied):
  - maximum take-off weight (MTOW): 1,150 kg;
  - CG limits are: 1,140 mm to 1,650 mm aft of datum;
  - basic empty weight: 690 kg at 1,310 mm aft of datum (i.e. STA 1,310).
- Pilot and passenger in front seat: 140 kg at STA 940.
- Passengers in rear seat: 180 kg at STA 1,855.
- Baggage in baggage compartment: 20 kg at STA 3,124.
- Fuel: 100 litres @ 0.71 SG at STA 1,420.

Item	Weight (kg) X	Arm (mm) =	Moment (kg-mm)
Basic empty weight	690	1,310	903,900
Pilot + front passenger	140	940	131,600
Rear passengers	180	1,855	333,900
Baggage	20	3,124	62,480
Fuel 100 litres @ 0.71	71	1,420	100,820
Total	1,101	1,392	1,532,700

BAK-1210.EPS

Figure 10-14 Aircraft loading table.

We calculate the location (arm) of the CG by using the formula derived previously (see opposite). We now see that the gross weight of 1,101 kg is less than the MTOW of 1,150 kg, and the location of the CG at 1,392 mm aft of the datum lies within the allowable CG range of 1,140 to 1,650 mm. If you had found that the aeroplane was too heavy or the CG outside the allowable limits, you would have to reorganise the loading to bring the weight and balance within limits. You will learn how to do this during your private pilot licence (PPL) training.

$$\text{CG arm} = \frac{\text{total moment}}{\text{total weight}} = \frac{1{,}532{,}700}{1{,}101} = 1{,}392 \text{ mm aft of the datum}$$

Index Units

When calculating the weight and balance of an aeroplane, the moments are often quite large numbers as can be seen from example 1, i.e. 1,532,700. The size of these numbers can be reduced by dividing them by 10,000 to give the value in index units, e.g. moment/10,000 index units where 1 index unit = 10,000 kg mm.

Example 10-2

If you are given a moment of 550 IU:

$$550 \text{ IU} = 550 \times 10{,}000 \text{ kg mm} = 5{,}500{,}000 \text{ kg mm}$$

As an alternative, you may find the moment divided by 1,000 (rather than ten thousand) to give moment/1,000 index units, where 1 index unit = 1,000 kg mm.

Example 10-3

If you are given 1,240,000 kg mm:

$$1{,}240{,}000 \text{ kg mm} = \frac{1{,}240{,}000 \text{ kg mm}}{1{,}000} = 1240 \text{ IU}$$

Loading Systems

Rather than having to compute the moment by multiplying the weight by the arm for each station, and then calculating the location of the CG, manufacturers have developed various loading graphs to help us in our weight and balance problems.

In figure 10-15, you will see that the units for weight and moment are metric units (kg and mm). For US-manufactured aeroplanes, the graphs will also show the weight in pounds (lb) and moment in inches.

Note that, on the loading graph for your aeroplane, you may find figures plotted along the fuel line showing the fuel tank capacity versus weight. These figures will be based on the fuel having a specific gravity of 0.71 or weighing 6 lb/USG. These figures must not be used in Australia because the specific gravity of AVGAS 100/130 or 100 LL is 0.71 or 0.71 kg/litre (SG 0.71). This value must be used to calculate the weight of the fuel with which you enter the loading graph.

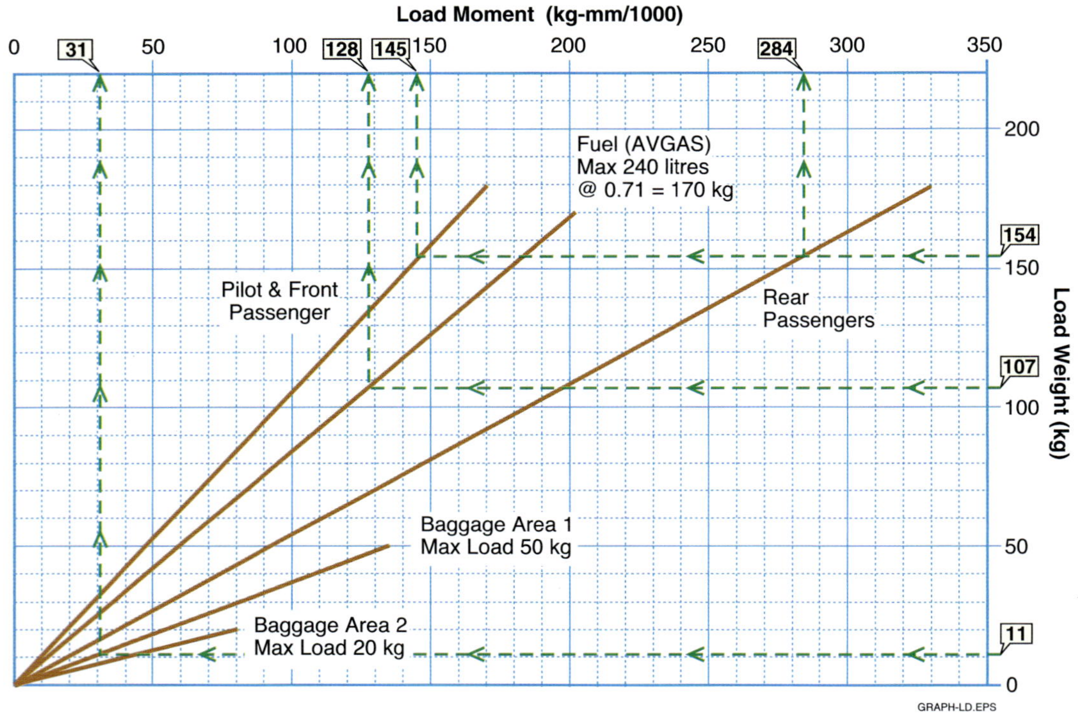

Figure 10-15 Loading graph.

Sample Loading Calculation

Example 10-4

Using the loading graph, determine the take-off weight and moment for an aeroplane loaded as follows, and check whether it is loaded within its weight and balance limits.

Maximum take-off weight (MTOW)	1,090 kg
Basic empty weight and moment	665 kg; 660 kg mm/1,000
Pilot and front seat passengers	154 kg
Rear passengers	154 kg
Baggage area	11 kg
Baggage area 2	Nil
Usable fuel (151 litres @ 0·71 SG)	107 kg
Allowance for engine start, taxi and run-up	3 kg; 3 kg mm/1,000

Step 1

To find the moments for each station, we enter with the weight on the vertical axis, e.g. fuel 107 kg. We now read horizontally across to the sloping line marked "Fuel (AVGAS)", and then move vertically up to read off the moment, 128 kg mm/1,000. This process is repeated for each station as shown in the table below. Once complete, we add up the two columns and find the take-off weight and moment.

Loading Details	Weight kg	Arm (mm)	Moment kg mm/1,000
Flight Manual Basic Empty Weight (incl. unusable fuel and oil)	665		660
Usable fuel (151 litres; SG 0.71)	107		128
Pilot and front passenger	154		145
Rear passenger(s)	154		284
Baggage area 1	11		31
Baggage area 2	—		—
RAMP WEIGHT and MOMENT	1,091		1,248
less Fuel allowance for engine start, taxi and run-up	–3		–3
TAKE-OFF WEIGHT and MOMENT	1,088		1,245

Table 10-2 Loading table.

Note: Shaded areas show values of moment extracted from graph.

Step 2

Having found the total weight and moment (1,088 kg and 1,245 index units), we check to ensure that the weight is within limits and that the aeroplane is balanced correctly (CG is within limits). Using the following CG/moment graph, find the intersection of the weight of 1,088 kg and the moment 1,245 kg mm/1,000. The CG is where the two lines meet. This point must be within the CG envelope for the loading to be acceptable.

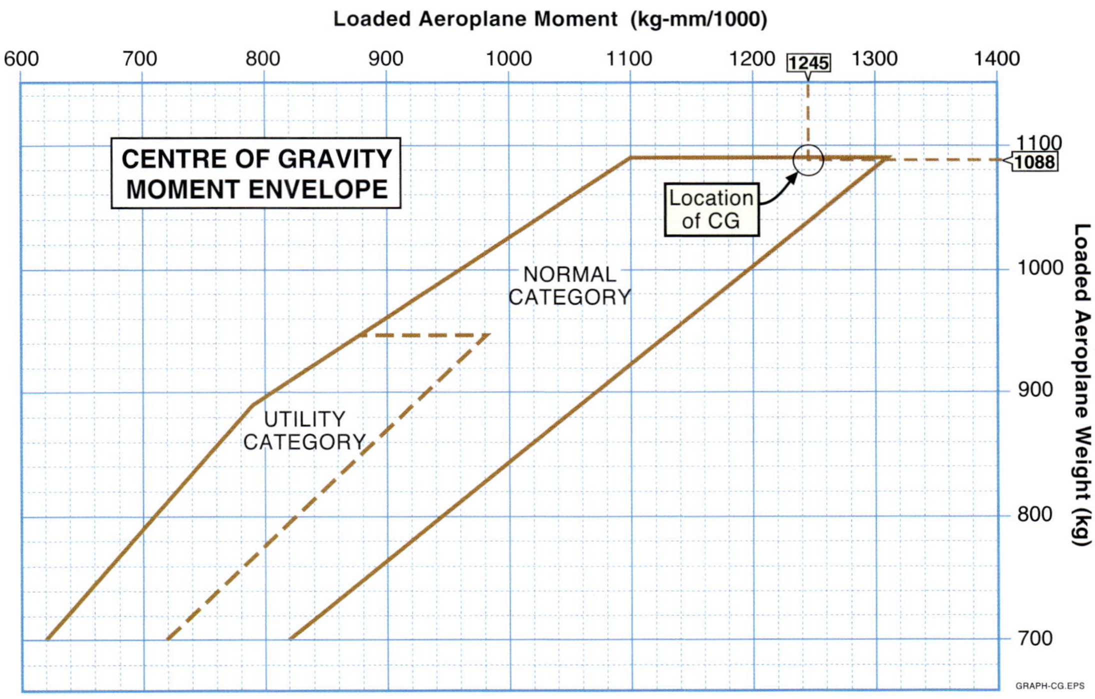

Figure 10-16 Sample CG/moment graph.

Should you find that the aeroplane is loaded incorrectly, then you would be obliged to reorganise the loading so that it is within the weight and CG limits for the aeroplane.

If the aeroplane is too heavy, then you must remove some of the load, which is baggage, passenger(s) or fuel. You choose. If the aeroplane is out of balance, i.e. the CG does not lie within the specified limits, then you must alter the CG position.

As previously mentioned, you will be taught how to recalculate the location of the CG during your training for the private pilot licence (PPL).

Remember that many graphs cater for both metric (kilograms and millimetres) and non-metric (pounds and inches) units. When using the weight and balance graphs, be sure that you enter each graph using the correct scale units.

Alternative Graph for Plotting CG Position

As an alternative to the CG moment envelope graph, you may sometimes find a graph, like the one that follows, showing CG limits. When using this graph, you will have to calculate the CG arm using the weight and the moment, derived from the loading calculation, as shown previously.

Example 10-5

Using the previous sample loading calculation (TOW 1,088 kg and index moment 1,245 IU):

Step 1

Convert index units to moments: 1,245 × 1,000 = 1,245,000 kg mm;

Step 2

Find the CG arm: $\frac{\text{moment}}{\text{weight}} = \frac{1,245,000}{1,088} = 1,144 \text{ mm}$

Step 3

Plot position of CG on graph, and check it is within the envelope.

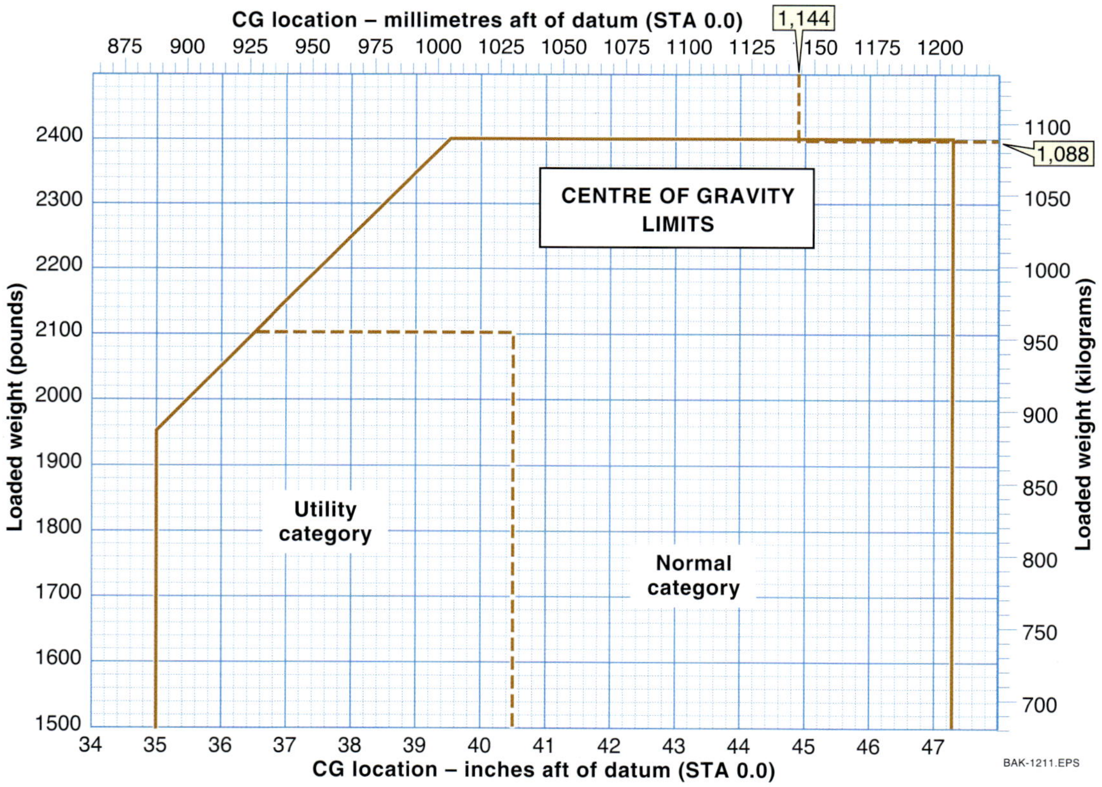

Figure 10-17 Weight/CG graph.

You will notice on the graph that there is a dashed outline marked "utility category", as well as the words "normal category" to the right of the dashed outline. These refer to different categories of aeroplane which you are likely to operate during your student pilot training.

- A normal category aeroplane has an MTOW below 5,700 kg, is certificated for non-aerobatic manoeuvres (normally limited to stalls and 60° steep turns), and typically has load factor limits from +3.8g to –1.5g.
- A utility category aeroplane is fundamentally the same as a normal category aeroplane, but is certificated for limited aerobatic manoeuvres, which will be detailed in the flight manual, and typically has load factor limits from +4.5g to –1.8g.

Note that some aeroplanes in the normal category may be allowed to operate in the utility category subject to weight and balance limitations. Utility limitations usually include a maximum of two crew, no baggage and a limited fuel load.

These limitations will be shown on the aeroplane loading graphs. As you can see, for this particular aeroplane to be allowed to operate in the utility category, its maximum weight is reduced to 955 kg. This means that the aft limit of the CG moment envelope moves forward from 1,310 kg mm/1,000 to approximately 982 kg mm/1,000. The actual location of the aft limit of the CG moves forward from STA 1,230 to approx. STA 1,028.

Great care must be exercised when operating a normal category aeroplane in the utility category, to ensure that the weight and balance limits are not exceeded.

Adjusting the CG Position

Load to Shift

To find the load to shift to achieve a required movement of the CG:

$$\text{load to shift} = \frac{\text{GW} \times \text{change of CG (mm)}}{\text{distance moved (mm)}}$$

- GW does not change.
- Distance moved is from one station to another.

Load to Remove or Ballast to Add

To remove or add weight to achieve a required movement of the CG:

$$\text{load to add or remove} = \frac{\text{GW} \times \text{change of CG}}{\text{distance between old and new stations}}$$

- Old STA could be hold, row, tank.
- New STA is required CG.
- Calculate at original GW.

Other Methods to Vary the Load

$$\frac{w}{W} = \frac{\Delta}{D}$$

w = weight moved, added etc.

W = Gross Weight (GW)

Δ = distance, change of CG

D = distance between old and new station (distance the weight is moved)

$$\text{CG} = \frac{\text{total moments}}{\text{total weight}}$$

$$\therefore \text{new CG} = \frac{\text{original moments} \pm \text{new moments}}{\text{total weight} \pm \text{weight added or removed}}$$

Sample Calculations

There are three loading systems which "represent" common aircraft types that you will need to be aware of. These are load systems Alpha, Bravo and Charlie. An example problem and solution is provided after each system is presented.

Units

- *Weights*: kilograms (kg) or pounds (lb)
- *Distances*: millimetres (mm) or inches (in)
- *Fuel*: litres (L), US gallons (USG) *(*must be converted to weight)*
- *Index Units*: $\frac{\text{moment}}{10,000}$ or $\frac{\text{moment}}{1,000}$

Load System Alpha – Working

(Refer to figure 10-18, page 374.) Given the information opposite, what is the maximum weight of fuel, in kg, which may be carried at take-off?

Basic index units = –300
Basic empty weight = 998 kg
Row 1: pilot and passenger = 135 kg
Row 2: forward-facing passengers = 142 kg
Row 3 = 120 kg
Baggage (total weight) = 85 kg

Follow the instructions completing the weights in the right side boxes. You must be aware of the limitations of each loading area, ZFW and GTOW. Your answer should be 153 kg. The same question could be asked but the answer may be required in litres or some other unit.

Now your conditions have changed, you require 150 kg of fuel and you are performance limited to 1,600 kg for take-off. Under these conditions, what is the maximum weight of baggage that may be carried in the rear compartment? If you apply basic discipline to your work, these graphs work well (10 kg).

Load System Bravo – Working

(Refer to figure 10-19, page 375.) Find the maximum weight which may be carried on the rear seat:

Aircraft empty weight = 1,270
Arm = 80 in
Oil = 15 lb
Pilot and passenger = 340 lb
Baggage = 120 lb
Fuel = 141 litres

	Weight	Arm (in)	
EW	1270	80	101600
Oil	15	32	480
Fuel (ltr)	222	91	20202
PLT & PAX	340	91	30940
Baggage	120	151	18120
	1967		171342

Table 10-3 Table for Bravo.

The initial loaded weight is 1,967 lb. The maximum take-off weight is 2,200 lb; therefore the difference is 233 lb. It is important now to rework the load sheet to ensure the CG stays within the balance limits (which is weight against moment for load system Bravo).

Load System Charlie – Working

(Refer to the figures, 10-20 and 10-21, pages 376 and 377.) Given:

Aircraft empty weight = 689 kg
Empty aircraft index units = 19,522
Oil = 7 kg
Row 1: pilot and passenger = 110 kg
Baggage (baggage compartment) = 75 kg
Fuel = 140 litres

What is the maximum passenger weight, in kg, that may be carried in row 2 at take-off?

	Weight (kg)	**Arm (mm)**	**Index units**
EW	689		19,522
Oil	7		86
Row 1 Pilot + Pax	110		3,025
Row 2			
Baggage	75		3,157
ZFW	881	2,927	25,790
Fuel	99	2,950	2,920
TOW	980	2,930	28,710

Table 10-4 Table for Charlie.

Ballast to add formula:

$$\frac{\text{GW (kg)} \times \text{distance to move CG (mm)}}{\text{new STA} - \text{current STA}}$$

$$\text{GW} = 980$$

$$\text{Distance to move} = \text{AFT limit} - \text{current STA} = 3{,}004 - 2{,}930 = 74 \text{ mm}$$

$$\text{New STA} = 3600$$

$$\text{Current STA} = 2930$$

$$\therefore \text{ballast to add} = \frac{980 \times 74}{3{,}600 - 2{,}930} \quad 108 \text{ kg}$$

∴ 108 kg is max. passenger weight for row 2 with ZFW and take-off limits checked. Finally, the key to loading an aircraft is not to exceed any limit. You are advised to check-plot weight moment or weight arm at both ZFW and TOW to ensure compliance.

Loading System Alpha Configuration: 6/7 Seats

Instructions for Use of Loading System

1. Obtain Basic Empty Weight and Index Units from current Section of 6.2 of Flight Manual.
2. Mark Basic Empty Weight Index Units on top scale. Enter Basic Empty Weight at top of right-hand column.
3. Enter Weights of load items required for flight in appropriate squares of right-hand column. Maximum weights for load items are indicated on Index Unit scales.
4. Total weights in right-hand column to obtain Zero Fuel Weight and Take-Off Weight. **
5. Draw horizontal lines on C.G. Envelope graph corresponding to Zero Fuel Weight and Take-Off weight.
6. Draw a line vertically down from point marked on Basic Empty Weight Index Units scale to first load item scale.
   *Move to the left or right on this load item index scale as per arrow direction, and mark point as appropriate to the load indicated in the right-hand column (e.g. 154kg load @ 77kg dive. = 2 div.)
7. Draw a line vertically down from the point marked on the first load item index scale to the second load item index scale and continue as per* above. Continue down the scales to "Rear Baggage". Draw a line vertically from the "Rear Baggage" point down to intersect the Zero Fuel Weight line and Take-Off Weight line previously marked on the C. G. envelope graph.
8. The two intersection points as per 7. Above must not exceed the boundaries of the C. G. envelope graph. If they do, reorganise the load in the aircraft and start with steps 3. to 7.

****Do not exceed the maximum take-off weight as shown on C.G. envelope diagram of this loading system.**

Example:

Basic Empty Weight	1050kg
Empty index units	-260
Row 1	150kg (2 persons)
Row 2 (forward facing)	160kg (2 persons)
Row 3	120kg (2 persons)
Nose baggage	40kg ⟶ Zero Fuel Wt = 1520kg
Rear baggage	Nil
Fuel	113kg ⟶ Take-Off Wt = 1633kg

Note: Basic Empty Weight includes unusable fuel and full oil.

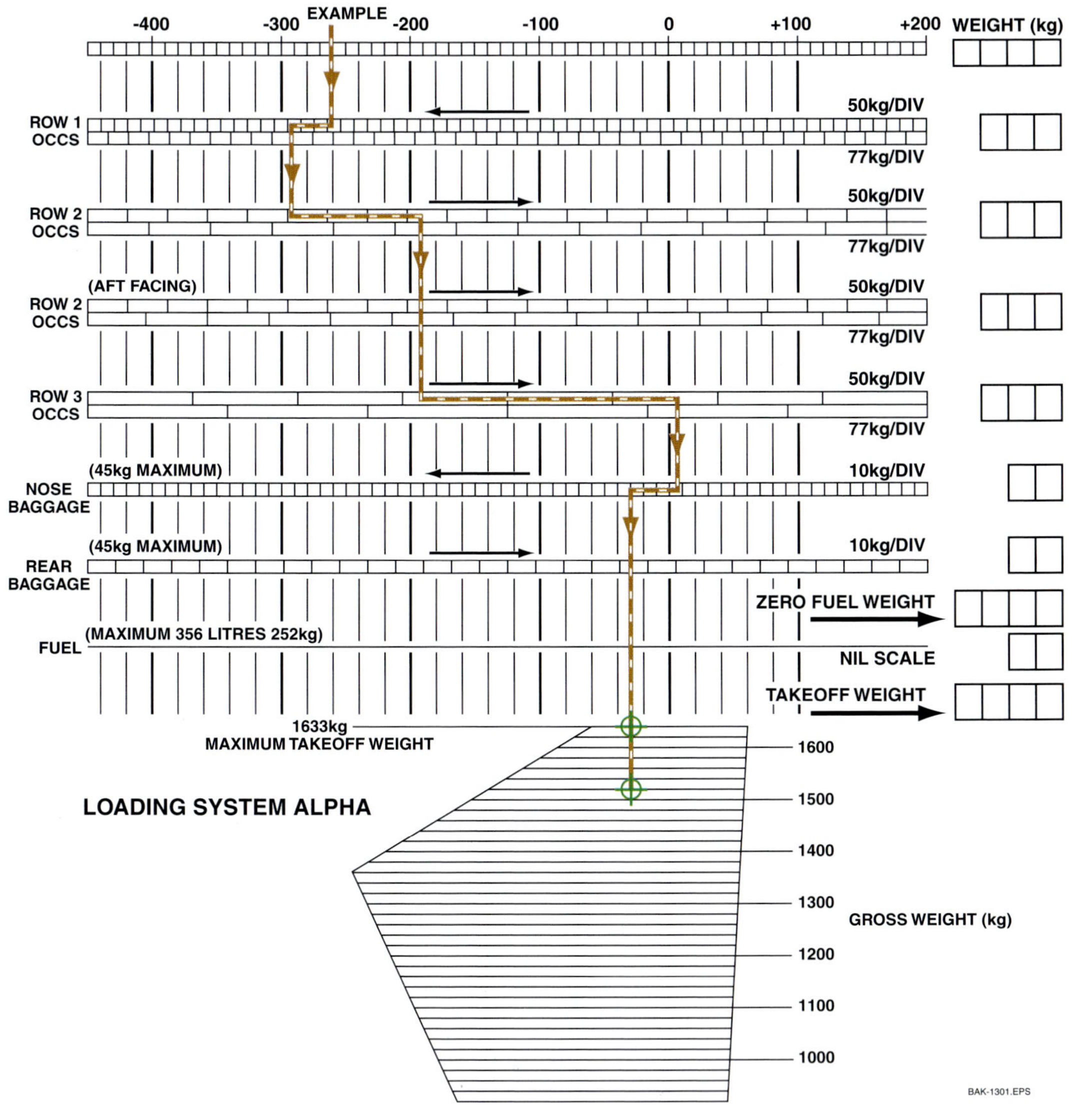

Figure 10-18 Loading system Alpha.

Loading System Bravo Configuration: 4 Seats

Instructions for Use of Loading System

To check the loading of the aircraft before take-off, calculate the total weight and total moments as shown in the example below.

Plot the total weight and moment on the "Centre of Gravity Envelope" chart, and if the intersection point is within the envelope, the loading is acceptable.

Aircraft Limitations

Maximum take-off weight
- Normal category: 1000 kg/2200 lbs
- Utility category: 841 kg/1850 lbs

Maximum baggage compartment baggage: 53 kg/120 lbs

Notes:
1. The aircraft is fitted with standard tanks (37 US Gallons at 6 lbs/gallon)
2. Empty weight includes unusable fuel and undrainable oil
3. Obtain Moment/1000 inch pounds from the loading graph

Example:

	Weight (lbs)	Arm (in)	Moment/ 1000 in lb
Empty Weight	1260	80	100.80
Oil	15	32	.48
Fuel (141 litres)	222	91	20.02
Pilot & Co-pilot	320	91	29.12
Rear Seat Passengers	350	126	44.10
Baggage	25	151	3.78
Takeoff Weight	2192		

Check C.G is within the envelope

BAK-1302.EPS

LOADING SYSTEM BRAVO

**Add weight of items to be carried to aeroplane licensed empty weight.
Add moment/1000 of items to be carried to total aeroplane moment/1000.
Use Center of Gravity Envelope to determine acceptability.**

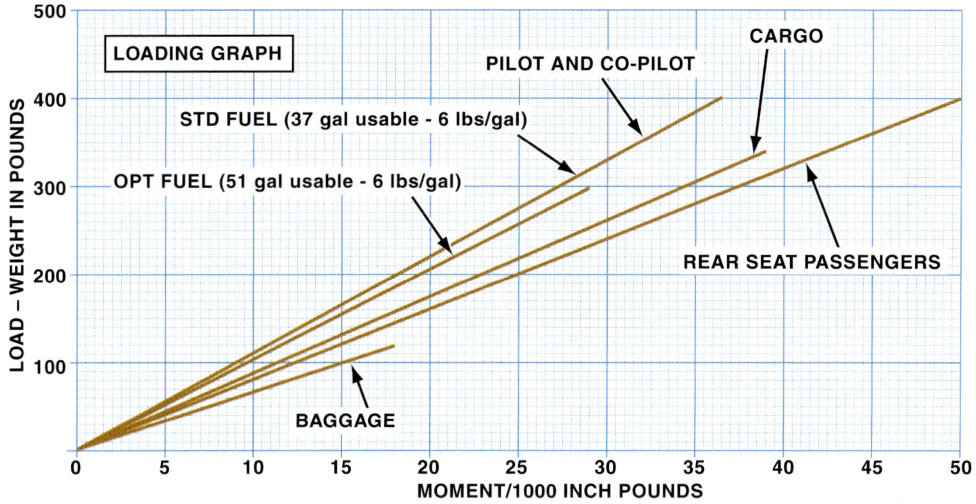

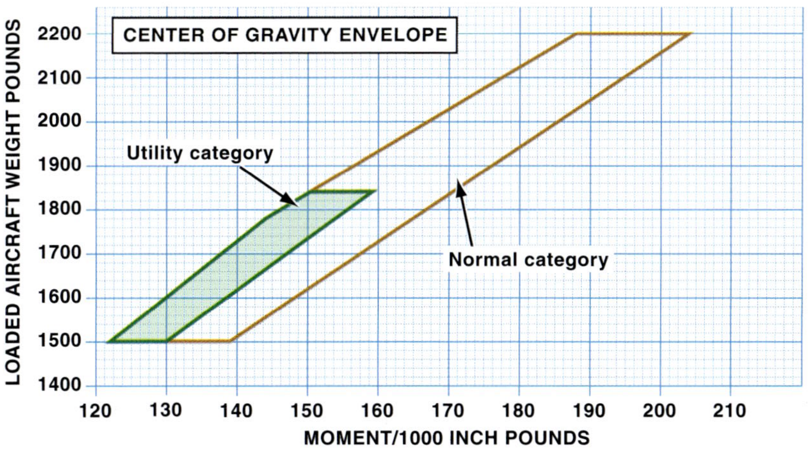

Figure 10-19 Loading system Bravo.

Loading System Charlie Configuration: 4 seats

Instructions for Use of Loading System

To check the loading of the aircraft before take-off, carry out a summation of weight and index units as shown in the example below. Check the centre of gravity of the aircraft at Zero Fuel Weight and Take-Off Weight by use of the formula:

$$\text{C. G. (mm aft of datum)} = \frac{\text{index unit} \times 100}{\text{Weight}}$$

The C. G. must be within the envelope given at all times.

Aircraft Limitations

Maximum take-off weight

Normal category:	1115 kgs
Utility category:	925 kgs
Maximum baggage compartment baggage:	122 kgs

Notes:
1. Aircraft empty weight includes unusable fuel and undrainable oil
2. All arms are in mm aft of datum
3. 1 index unit = 100 kg mm

Example:

	KG	IU
Aircraft Empty Weight	687	19,522
Full Oil	7	86
1 Pilot & 1 Passenger	140	3,850
2 Passengers	160	5,760
Baggage	20	842
Zero Fuel Weight	1014	30,060
Fuel (140 Litres)	99	2,920
Takeoff Weight	1113	32,980

C. G. check:
1. At Zero Fuel Weight = (30,060 x 100) ÷ 1014 = 2965 mm OK
2. At Take-Off Weight = (32,980 x 100) ÷ 1113 = 2963 mm OK

Loading System Charlie

Index Units

FUEL ARM: 2950

20	14	413
40	28	826
60	43	1268
80	57	1682
100	71	2095
120	85	2507
140	99	2920
160	114	3363
180	129	3806
200	142	4189
216	153	4513

BAGGAGE	ARM: 4210
10	421
20	842
30	1,263
40	1,684
50	2,105
60	2,526
70	2,947
80	3,368
90	3,789
100	4,210
110	4,631
122	5,136

OCCUPANTS

KG	Row 1 ARM: 2750	Row 2 ARM: 3600
40	1,100	1,440
45	1,237	1,620
50	1,375	1,800
55	1,512	1,980
60	1,650	2,160
65	1,786	2,340
70	1,925	2,520
75	2,062	2,700
80	2,200	2,880
85	2,338	3,060
90	2,475	3,240

OIL ARM: 1230

US Quarts	Litres	KG	Index Units
6	5.7	5.0	62
7	6.6	6.0	74
8	7.6	7.0	86

BAK-1303.EPS

Figure 10-20 Loading system Charlie.

CONVERSION FACTORS

1 inch	=	25.4mm
1 foot	=	0.305 metre
1 lb	=	0.454 kg
1 Imp gal	=	1.201 US gal = 4.546 litres

Avgas 100 (100/130) : Specific Gravity = .71

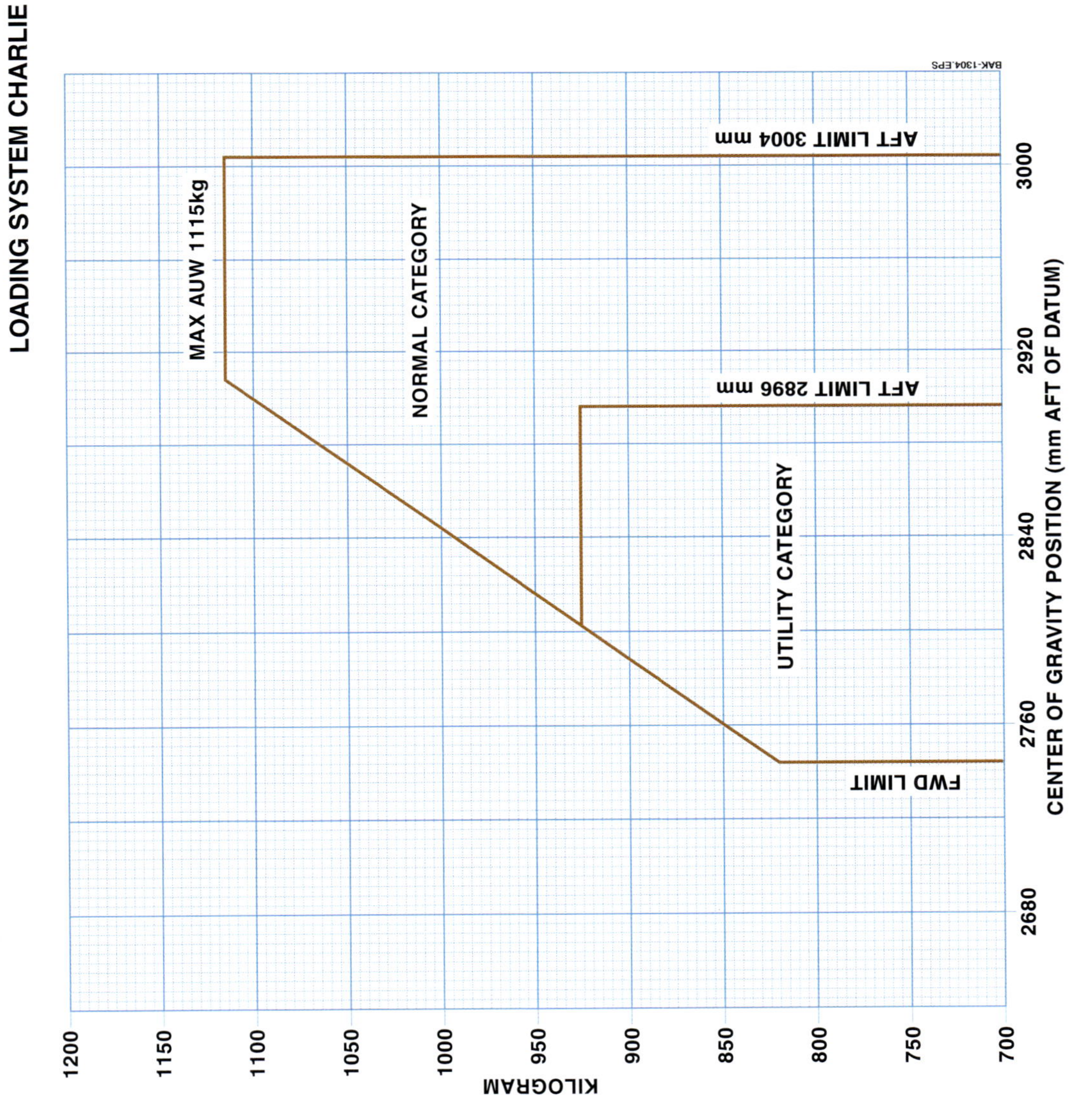

Figure 10-21 Loading system Charlie.

Review 10

BAK Level of Knowledge Only

1. What is the difference between the terms *weight* and *balance?*
2. Basic empty weight includes an extra item over empty weight. What is this item?
3. What is then added to achieve zero fuel weight?
4. The volume of fuel is converted to weight by multiplying by the . . . . .
5. In the case of AVGAS, this conversion factor is 0 . . . . .
6. The aircraft may have fuel quantities and gauges in US gallons. What is the ratio of litres to US gallons?
7. A moment has two elements, ... and . . . . .
8. The balance point is called the . . . . . of . . . . .
9. Why are there limits on the position of the CG for an aircraft?
10. The distance from the allowable forward position of the CG to the allowable rear-most position is called the CG . . . . .
11. What is the relationship between the moment, moment arm and weight?
12. What is meant by the datum?
13. What is the AUW/CG envelope?
14. What is the normal category?
15. What is the utility category? Why is it different from the normal category?

11 - Performance

Aviation
Theory
Centre

Introduction

After the weight and balance limits have been satisfied, the aircraft must be able to take-off and land within the runway distance available. If it cannot, you must reduce your weight, wait until the environmental conditions change to permit safe flight, or use an alternative runway. After take-off, the aircraft must have the ability to climb at a specified gradient (usually 6% for small aircraft). Again, the aeroplane weight and the environment will affect this part of your flight, the climb both after take-off and at landing.

And at landing? If you approach to land and the runway is occupied by another aircraft, you aircraft must have the ability to *climb* to complete a circuit or to depart to an alternate airfield. This is the climb weight limit.

International Standard Atmosphere

The International Standard Atmosphere (ISA) was established to provide a yardstick for aircraft performance. It enables very accurate performance calculations and charts to be drawn under "ideal" conditions. The fundamentals of ISA are:

- sea level pressure 1,013.2 hPa;
- sea level temperature +15°C; and
- temperature lapse rate of 2°C/1,000 ft (lower atmosphere).

For convenience, we also consider that one hectopascal (1 hPa) pressure change is equivalent to 30 ft altitude change.

A temperature change of 1°C is equivalent to a density change of 120 ft of altitude. These will be used later to calculate pressure and density altitudes.

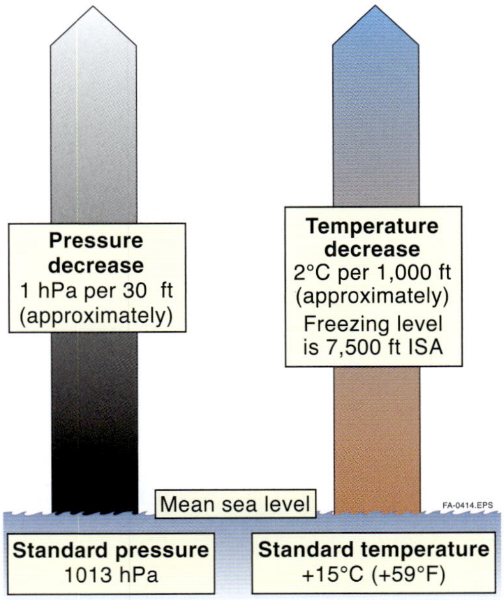

Figure 11-1 International Standard Atmosphere.

Pressure Altitude & Density Altitude

Pressure altitude (PA) (or pressure height (PH)) is the equivalent altitude in the International Standard Atmosphere. If the datum (QNH) is 1013.2 hPa, then the altimeter indicates pressure altitude. If the actual QNH is different from standard, a correction is made.

Density altitude (DA) is that altitude which corresponds to density in the ISA. Density altitude is pressure altitude corrected for temperature (i.e. temperature variation from the ISA). If the sea level temperature and pressure were ISA and the actual temperature lapse rate equalled the ISA lapse rate, then an altimeter would indicate the density altitude. In simple terms, atmospheric density has a huge effect on aircraft performance. If the atmosphere is "thin", it is more difficult for an aircraft to take-off and climb. Later, we will calculate pressure and density altitude.

"V" Speed Definitions

There are some important speed definitions that relate to aircraft performance.

V_{FE}

Flaps extended maximum speed, to prevent overstressing the flap structure. It is the higher end of the white arc on the ASI.

V_{FO}

Maximum speed when the flaps are moving (operating).

V_S

Stall speed.

V_{LO}

Landing gear operating speed. Speed not to exceed while undercarriage is being extended or retracted.

V_{LE}

Maximum landing gear extended speed. When gear is down and locked it is stronger than when not locked and so V_{LE} may be higher than V_{LO}.

V_{NE}

Never exceed speed. Maximum speed under *any* circumstances. It is shown on the ASI as a red line.

V_{NO}

Maximum speed for normal operating conditions which may only be exceeded in smooth air and when justified by operational requirements. This is the speed when the green arc changes to the yellow arc.

V_A

Manoeuvre speed. The highest speed at which a full control deflection and therefore increased load factor will not overstress the aircraft. At or below V_A the aircraft will stall before the load factor can increase sufficiently to cause permanent damage to the aircraft.

V_B

Turbulence (rough air) penetration speed. Slow enough to avoid overstressing but fast enough to prevent a gust causing a low speed stall.

V_{REF}

Reference speed for final approach. The constant speed flown on finals.

Take-Off Performance

Take-off charts provided by the aircraft manufacturer allow you to calculate the minimum take-off distance required (TODR). This is the distance you require from the start of your take-off run to reach lift-off speed and then climb at the take-off safety speed to 50 ft above the runway surface. This distance must not exceed the take-off distance available (TODA) of the runway you are about to use.

Take-Off Safety Speed

The take-off safety speed (TOSS) is used as a reference speed that is to be achieved at a height of 50 ft after take-off. It must give a safe margin over the stalling speed (not less than 1.2 V_{STALL}). On multi-engine aircraft, the TOSS is referred to as V_2.

Take-Off Distance Required

The take-off distance required (TODR) is obtained from measurements made during flight testing, measured from stationary to 50 ft AAL (screen height) at TOSS. These results are sometimes factored to provide a safety margin to allow for average piloting skills. This margin in take-off distance is usually 15%. For a 15% increase over the test distance, it will be expressed as 1.15.

Not all performance charts are factored. It is a pilot's responsibility to ensure that sufficient take-off distance is available for the safe operation of the aircraft.

Factors affecting Take-Off Performance

Weight

The heavier an aeroplane is, the greater the take-off distance required. This is because of slower acceleration on the runway (due to increased mass and friction), increased stalling speed and therefore an increased TOSS to provide the required safety margin (20%) above the stall speed. A 10% increase in weight may increase the take-off distance required by as much as 25%.

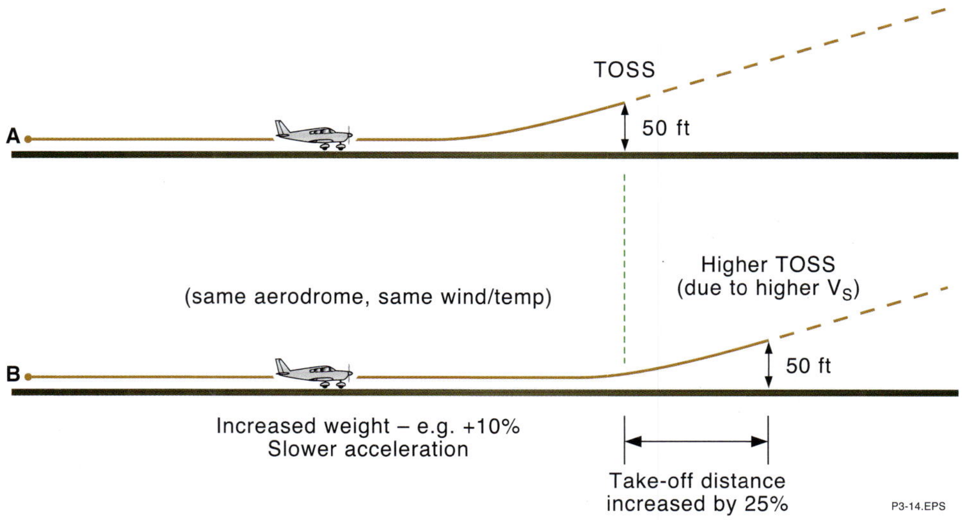

Figure 11-2 A 10% increase in weight increases take-off distance by 25%.

Wind Effect

Wind is the most important consideration for take-off and climb. A headwind will reduce the take-off distance required, since it will take less time for the aeroplane to reach TOSS. Conversely, a tailwind will cause an aeroplane to take a longer time and greater distance to reach take-off speed.

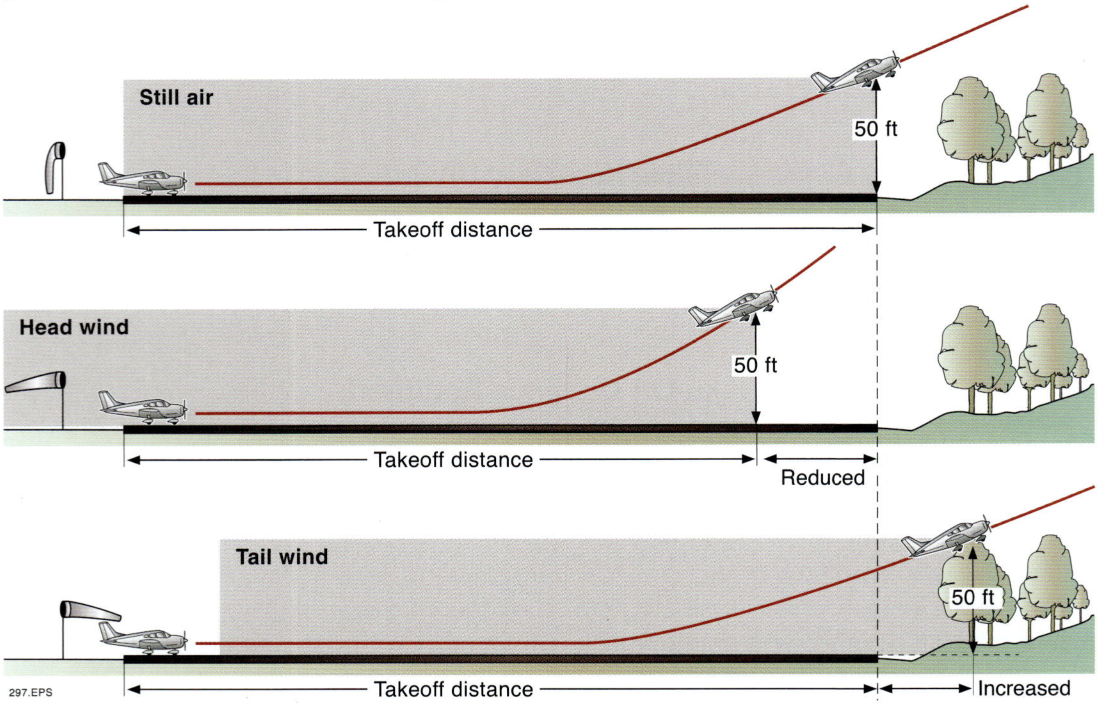

Figure 11-3 Effect of wind on takeoff distance.

Note that the adverse effect of a tailwind on climb angle (gradient) is not considered in take-off charts. When the wind is gusting, you must use only the lowest gust figure as a headwind component. However, to consider the crosswind component, the highest gust speed must be used.

Air Density

Reduced air density results in a greater take-off distance required because of poorer performance of the engine and airframe. It will also decrease the climb performance of the aeroplane. The take-off chart will indicate a climb-weight limit, which will ensure adequate climb performance after take-off. Lower air density will occur:

- at high-elevation airports;
- on hot days; and
- on low-pressure days (low QNH).

Figure 11-4 Hot, high and humid means decreased performance.

Air density is allowed for on performance charts under the headings of pressure altitude and temperature, or density altitude (which is a combination of the two). Humidity of the air is not allowed for on these charts, but high humidity will also decrease take-off performance.

High aerodrome elevations decrease aeroplane and engine performance.
High temperatures decrease aeroplane performance.
High humidity decreases aeroplane and engine performance.

Runway Slope

Runway slope will affect take-off distance required. An up-sloping runway will reduce acceleration and so necessitate a longer take-off run than a flat or down-sloping runway. Slope and wind can offset each other. It is important to consider taking-off down-slope if you have a tail wind of 5 kt or less.

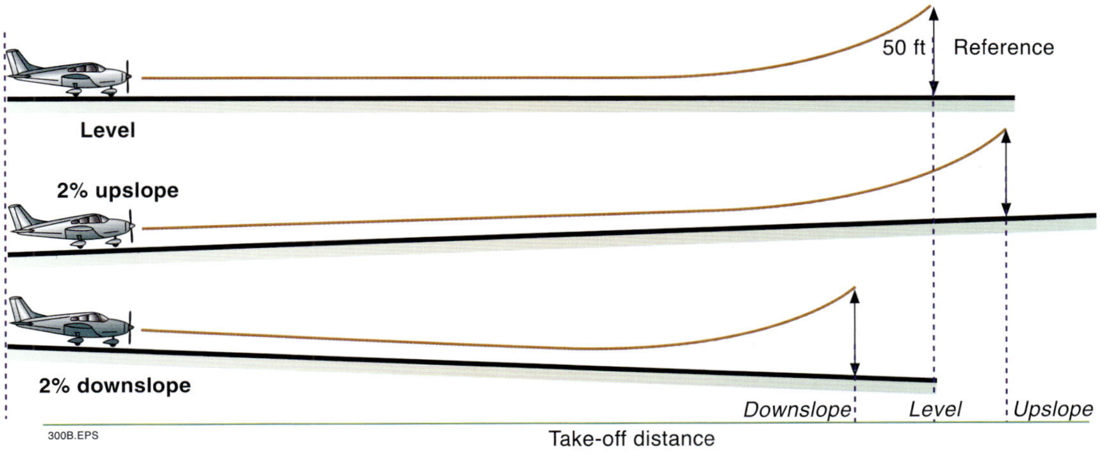

Figure 11-5 An upward sloping runway will increase take-off distance.

Runway Surface

Runway surface will affect take-off distance required. A wet, slushy or sandy runway, a gravel or long-grass surface, or a strip with wheel ruts will reduce the acceleration of the aeroplane and result in a greater take-off distance required.

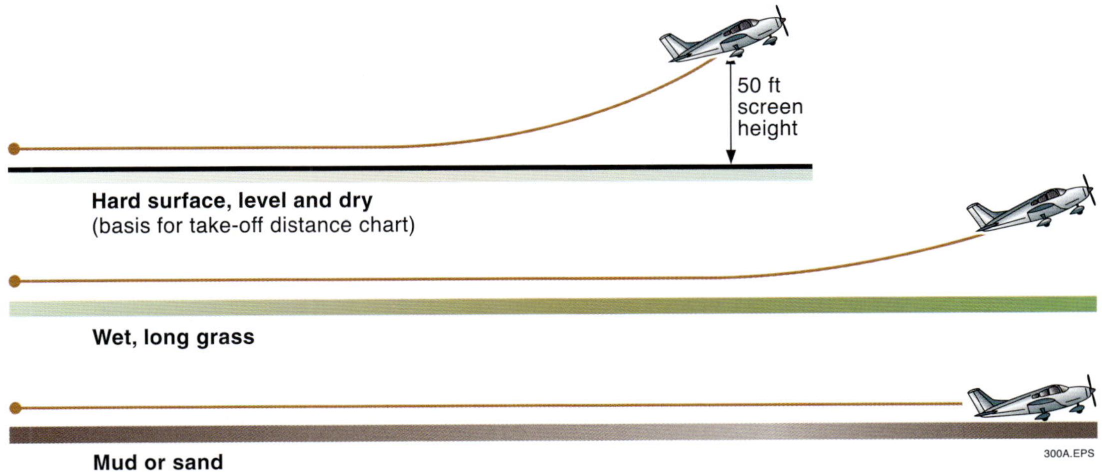

Figure 11-6 Poor surfaces can increase take-off distance.

Other Factors

Frost or other contamination on an aircraft, particularly on the wings, will diminish take-off and climb performance by disturbing smooth airflow over the upper surface of the wings where most of the lift should be produced. Be sure to remove frost or other contamination prior to flight.

Summary of Factors affecting Take-Off Performance

The performance of an aeroplane during take-off is assisted by:

- high thrust (new engine, new propeller);
- low weight;
- low friction forces (correct tyre inflation, good runway surface);
- low aerodynamic drag;
- down slope; and
- high density (low temperature, high pressure).

The performance of an aeroplane during take-off is degraded by:

- low thrust (tired engine, poor propeller condition);
- high weight;
- high friction forces (poor runway surface, incorrect tyre inflation, dragging brakes);
- high aerodynamic drag;
- upslope; and
- low density (high temperature, low pressure).

Landing Performance

Landing charts provided by the aircraft manufacturer allow you to calculate the landing distance required (LDR). This is the distance from a point 50 ft over the runway at the correct approach speed (1.3 V_S), with full flaps and power off, to the point where the aircraft reaches a full stop using maximum braking. This distance must not exceed the landing distance available (LDA) of the chosen runway. Some charts are factored to allow a 15% increase in LDR as a safety allowance.

Factors affecting Landing Performance

Weight

The heavier an aeroplane is, the greater the landing distance required. This is because of the extra mass and the faster approach speed necessary to provide the required safety margin (30%) above the increased stall speed and the slower deceleration on the runway.

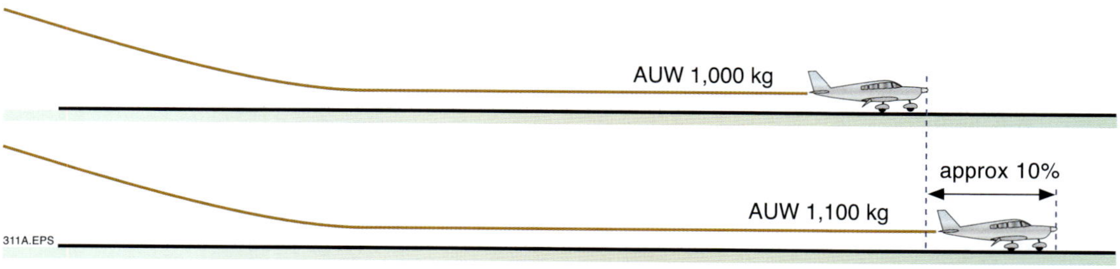

Figure 11-7 A 10% increase in weight requires an approximate 10% increase in landing distance.

Air Density

Low air density results in a greater landing distance required because of the higher true speed of the aeroplane and consequently higher groundspeed on the approach and landing. Lower air density will occur:

- at high-elevation airports;
- on hot days; and
- on low-pressure days (low QNH).

As with take-off performance charts, air density is allowed for on landing performance charts under the headings of pressure height and temperature, or density altitude (which is a combination of the two).

Runway Slope

Runway slope will affect landing distance required. A downslope will require more landing distance than a level or upsloping runway.

Runway Surface

A slippery or wet runway surface will reduce braking action and result in an increased landing distance. However, deep puddles will rapidly slow the aircraft.

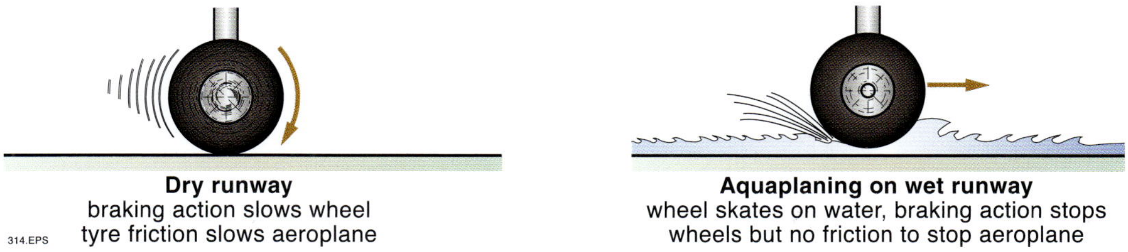

Figure 11-8 Low-friction surfaces increase landing distance.

Wind Effect

A headwind will reduce the landing distance required, since the aeroplane, at the correct approach airspeed, will touch down at a lower groundspeed and so take less distance to stop. A tailwind will cause an aeroplane to land at a faster groundspeed and thus take more distance to stop. Ten percent additional speed equates to 40 percent extra energy.

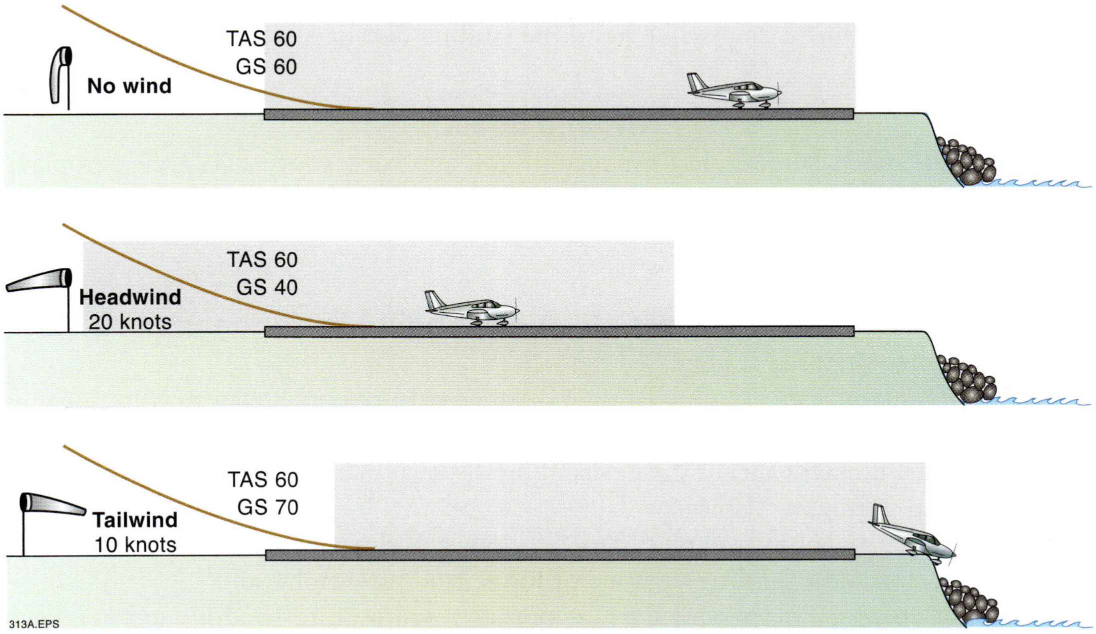

Figure 11-9 A headwind reduces landing distance.

Figure 11-10
Wind has a significant effect on landing performance

A crosswind effect can occur when wind direction is different between the two parcels of air, requiring the pilot to make heading changes to stay on the extended runway centreline when on approach to land. The crosswind component itself does not affect landing performance.

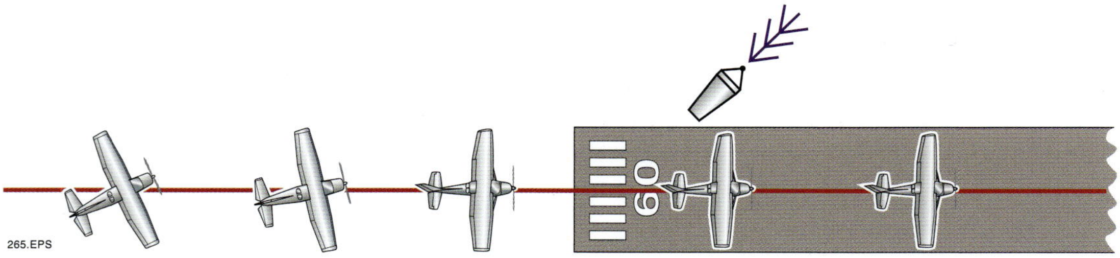

Figure 11-11 Crosswind approach and landing.

It is usual to factor the final approach speed (V_{REF}) according to the intensity of wind gusts or the presence of windshear (add half the gust factor to the normal approach speed). The increased airspeed directly increases the landing distance by extending the flare (float) and roll-out distance. Some aircraft use a reduced flap setting in crosswind conditions. The reduced drag will extend the landing distance.

Ground Effect

Ground effect affects landing performance. If you approach above $1.3V_S$ the aeroplane will tend to float longer in ground effect before touching down, resulting in a longer landing distance.

Summary of Factors affecting Landing Performance

Landing distance required is increased by:

- higher temperatures mean more landing distance required or a lower maximum landing weight;
- higher pressure height means greater landing distance or reduced landing weight;
- reduced flap setting, or flapless;
- downslope means more landing distance or lower landing weight;
- tailwind means more landing distance or lower landing weight; and
- constantly changing crosswind during approach will require heading and approach speed changes.

Calculating Pressure Altitude & Density Altitude

One of the factors affecting aeroplane performance is the atmospheric density. This air density is a function of both pressure and temperature. We will consider pressure altitude first. Since aeroplane performance charts are based on standard conditions (ISA), we need to be able to determine what we call pressure altitude, which is the vertical distance above the 1,013 hPa pressure level. There are two methods of determining pressure altitude:

- we can set 1,013 hPa on the altimeter subscale and read off directly the value of pressure altitude; or
- we can make a simple calculation using our knowledge that, up to 5,000 ft, the approximate rate of fall of pressure is 1 hPa per 30 ft.

Calculating Pressure Altitude

To calculate pressure altitude, calculate the difference in hPa between the QNH and the ISA MSL pressure of 1,013 hPa. This is then converted to feet by multiplying by 30. This correction amount is then added to, or subtracted from, as appropriate, the aerodrome elevation to obtain pressure altitude.

Example 11-1

Determine the pressure altitude on the surface of an airfield which has an elevation of 1,875 ft if the QNH is 1,020 hPa.

Method:

$$\begin{aligned}\text{Difference between ISA MSL pressure and QNH} &= 1{,}013 - 1{,}020\\ &= -7 \text{ hPa}\\ \text{Difference in pressure altitude} &= -7 \times 30 \text{ ft/hPa}\\ &= -210 \text{ ft}\\ \text{Aerodrome elevation} &= 1{,}875\\ \therefore \text{pressure altitude} &= 1{,}875 - 210 = 1{,}665 \text{ ft}\end{aligned}$$

Answer: Pressure altitude = 1,665 ft.

From these two examples, we can now derive the following rule of thumb:

When QNH is greater than ISA MSL pressure of 1,013 hPa, pressure altitude is less than elevation.

When QNH is less than ISA MSL pressure of 1,013 hPa, pressure altitude is greater than elevation.

Example 11-2

Determine the pressure altitude on the surface of Cooma aerodrome which has an elevation of 3,106 ft, if the QNH is 1,000 hPa.

Method:

$$\begin{aligned}\text{Difference between ISA MSL pressure and QNH} &= 1{,}013 - 1{,}000\\ &= 13 \text{ hPa}\\ \text{Difference in pressure altitude} &= 13 \times 30 \text{ ft/hPa}\\ &= 390 \text{ ft}\\ \text{Aerodrome elevation} &= 3{,}106\\ \therefore \text{pressure altitude} &= 3{,}106 + 390 = 3{,}496 \text{ ft}\end{aligned}$$

Answer: Pressure altitude at Cooma = 3,496 ft.

Calculating Density Altitude

To calculate density altitude, you must first calculate the pressure altitude. In example 11-2, Cooma had a pressure height of 3,496 ft. To find the density altitude, we need to know the surface temperature at Cooma – in this case, +12°C. In ISA, the temperature at 3, 500 feet would be +15 – (2 degrees per thousand feet) = 15 – 7 = +8 degrees.

Compare the actual temperature to the ISA temperature (12 is 4 degrees above ISA), multiply this temperature difference (+4 degrees) by 120 feet per degree, then add or subtract this height from the pressure altitude (depending on whether the temperature is more or less than ISA). In this case it is warmer, so less dense – the density altitude is 480 feet higher than the 3,496 pressure altitude. The density altitude, then, is 3,496 + 480 = 3,976 feet. This is the altitude that the aircraft and engine actually feel.

Cooma

ISA temperature @ 3,500 ft	=	15°C – (3.5 × 2°C)
	=	+8°C
Actual temperature @ 3,500 ft	=	+12°C
Difference	=	12 – 8
	=	+4°C
Conversion to height	=	+4°C × 120
	=	+480 ft
Temperature is hotter than ISA, correction to PA	=	+480 + 3496
	=	3,976 ft

∴ The density altitude at Cooma is 3,976 ft

Often the use of a diagram will help you to quickly and accurately calculate pressure and density altitudes. To visualise this Cooma example:

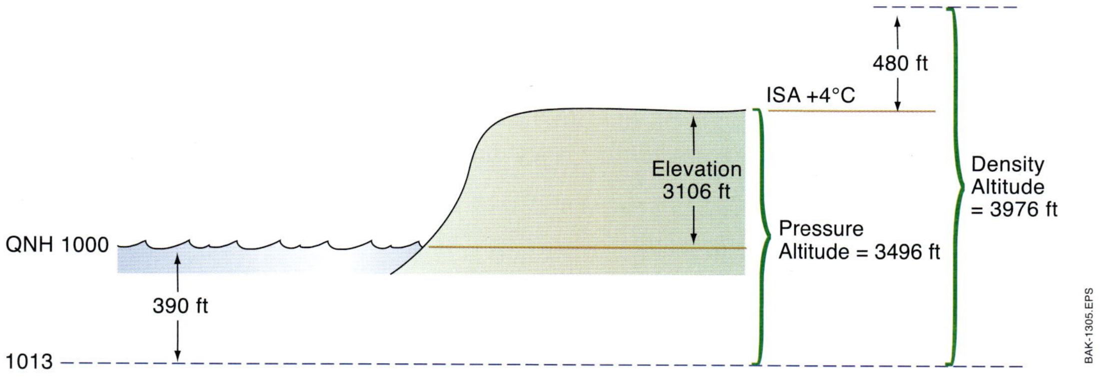

Figure 11-12 Pressure altitude and density altitude.

Finally, this example confirms:

- When the temperature is ISA plus (ISA+) at the PA, the DA is higher than the PA.
- When the temperature is ISA minus (ISA–) at the PA, the DA is lower than the PA.

If ambient or forecast conditions of pressure and temperature are not available, the pilot must calculate take-off and landing performance on the basis of seasonal Declared Density Altitude charts contained in appendices to CAO 20.7.0.

Take-Off Charts

Presentation

As a student pilot, the most usual training aeroplanes you are likely to operate are those manufactured by Piper and Cessna, and each of these manufacturers presents performance data for take-off in different ways.

In both cases, the take-off charts allow you to enter temperature and pressure height (to give density height), and then proceed through the charts taking account of the known factors that affect the take-off performance: size of propeller (not applicable in all cases), runway surface and slope, wind component (head or tail), and take-off distance available. You then end up with the maximum permissible take-off weight for the current (ambient) conditions at the time of your planned departure.

Take-off performance has two aspects that must be satisfied:

- *Runway performance.* Is the take-off distance available (TODA) sufficient? If not, reduce the take-off weight.
- *Climb performance.* Is the aeroplane's climb performance adequate to achieve the required climb gradient? If not, reduce the take-off weight.

The maximum permissible take-off weight for a particular set of conditions is the lesser of these two and must not exceed the structural MTOW.

To achieve the distances given in the aeroplane P-charts, you must fly the aeroplane using correct techniques. This means having the flaps set in the recommended position, and the engine operating at the maximum take-off power (static MAP and/or rpm) limits.

Be sure that you select the appropriate P-chart for the flap setting you will be using for that particular take-off.

Take-Off Performance Limit

Earlier in this chapter, we discussed the take-off distance required and the various factors which affect take-off performance. The take-off weight charts allow us to determine the take-off distance required (TODR). Provided this distance is equal to, or less than, the take-off distance available (TODA), we have no runway performance limit. If we find that the TODR exceeds the TODA, then we have a runway performance limit, and our take-off weight will have to be reduced.

Climb Performance Limit

Aeroplanes of less than 5,700 kg maximum take-off weight (MTOW) must be able to achieve a climb gradient of at least 6% at take-off safety speed, without ground effect, and with all engines operating at take-off power, in the take-off configuration with landing gear extended. This gradient is then used to determine airfield and runway suitability.

We already know that under conditions of high temperatures and therefore a density height greater than the aerodrome elevation, aeroplane performance is degraded.

If the 6% climb gradient cannot be achieved at the runway performance weight limit found from the P-chart, say because of high gross weight, high temperature, high pressure altitude or some other factor, then a climb weight limit must be imposed so that the 6% can be achieved. Where such a situation applies to a particular aeroplane type, then a climb-limit graph will be provided either separately or associated directly with the take-off weight chart.

As a general rule, most light aeroplanes can achieve the 6% climb gradient, and climb weight limits do not apply. However, you should always be alert for the possibility if the data is supplied on the take-off charts.

Practical Use of P-Charts – Take-Off

Cessna

A typical Cessna-type of P-chart is provided (see figure 11-13, page 394). When using this type of chart, simply enter with the appropriate data and follow the guidelines through the boxes. Verify that the different effects of slope, wind etc. are having the expected effect.

Example 11-3

Using the Cessna take-off weight chart (page 394), determine the maximum permissible take-off weight for the following conditions.

Aerodrome elevation	4,400 ft
QNH	993 hPa
Temperature	+10°C
Take-off distance available (TODA)	900 m
Surface	Short, wet grass
Slope	2% down
Wind component	nil (still air)

Step 1
Calculate pressure altitude.

$$
\begin{aligned}
\text{Difference between ISA MSL pressure and QNH} &= 1{,}013 - 993 \\
&= 20 \text{ hPa} \\
\text{Difference in pressure altitude} &= 20 \times 30 \text{ ft/hPa} \\
&= 600 \text{ ft} \\
\text{Aerodrome elevation} &= 4{,}400 \text{ ft} \\
\therefore \text{pressure altitude} &= 4{,}400 + 600 = 5{,}000 \text{ ft}
\end{aligned}
$$

Step 2
Enter with 5,000 on the airfield pressure altitude scale, and draw a horizontal line across to intersect the +10°C line.

Step 3
From this point, draw a vertical line up to the TODA 900 m line. Where this line intercepts the climb-weight limit line from below, draw a horizontal line out to the right. This gives us a climb weight limit of 1,080 kg (point B). The significance of the climb-limit weight will be discussed shortly.

Step 4
From the intersection of the TODA 900 m line, draw a horizontal line to the reference line. From the reference line follow the guidelines down to the particular surface line (short, wet grass in this example), and then move across horizontally to the slope graph.

Step 5
From the intersection with the appropriate slope line, draw a vertical line down to intersect the headwind or tailwind component.

Step 6
From this point, draw a horizontal line to give you a take-off weight of 1,015 kg (point A). This is the runway performance weight limit.

Answer: the maximum permissible take-off weight on this runway in these conditions is 1,015 kg – the lesser of the runway performance weight (A) and the climb performance weight (B).

Example 11-4

Refer to the Cessna take-off weight chart (page 395). Calculate the take-off distance required given:

Pressure altitude	4,000 ft
Temperature	+25°C
Surface	long dry grass
Slope	level
Wind	nil
Take-off weight	maximum possible

Step 1
Enter with 4,000 ft pressure altitude to intersect the +25°C temperature line.

Step 2
Draw a vertical line upwards through the take-off distance available box. Notice this take-off has a climb weight limit.

Step 3
Project a horizontal line to the right to establish the climb weight limit of 1,050 kg which is therefore the take-off weight, because to answer the question we must look at the maximum possible take-off weight.

Step 4
Continue the horizontal line to meet the "nil wind" line then draw a vertical line to meet the "level runway" line.

Step 5
Now project a horizontal line to the left to meet the "long dry grass" factor line. Parallel a line up to the left to meet the reference line.

> **Note:** When moving backwards on the graph (counter clockwise), you must meet the "factor lines" *then* move to the reference line. It is more common to work the graph forward (clockwise) where the reference line is met then the factor adjustment made.

Step 6
From the reference line project left to intersect your original vertical line.

Answer: Take-off distance required: 1,140 m.

This is very much a worst case example, and the take-off distance required for a small aircraft is excessive. It does demonstrate that, for poor environmental conditions, the take-off distance may be much greater than you think.

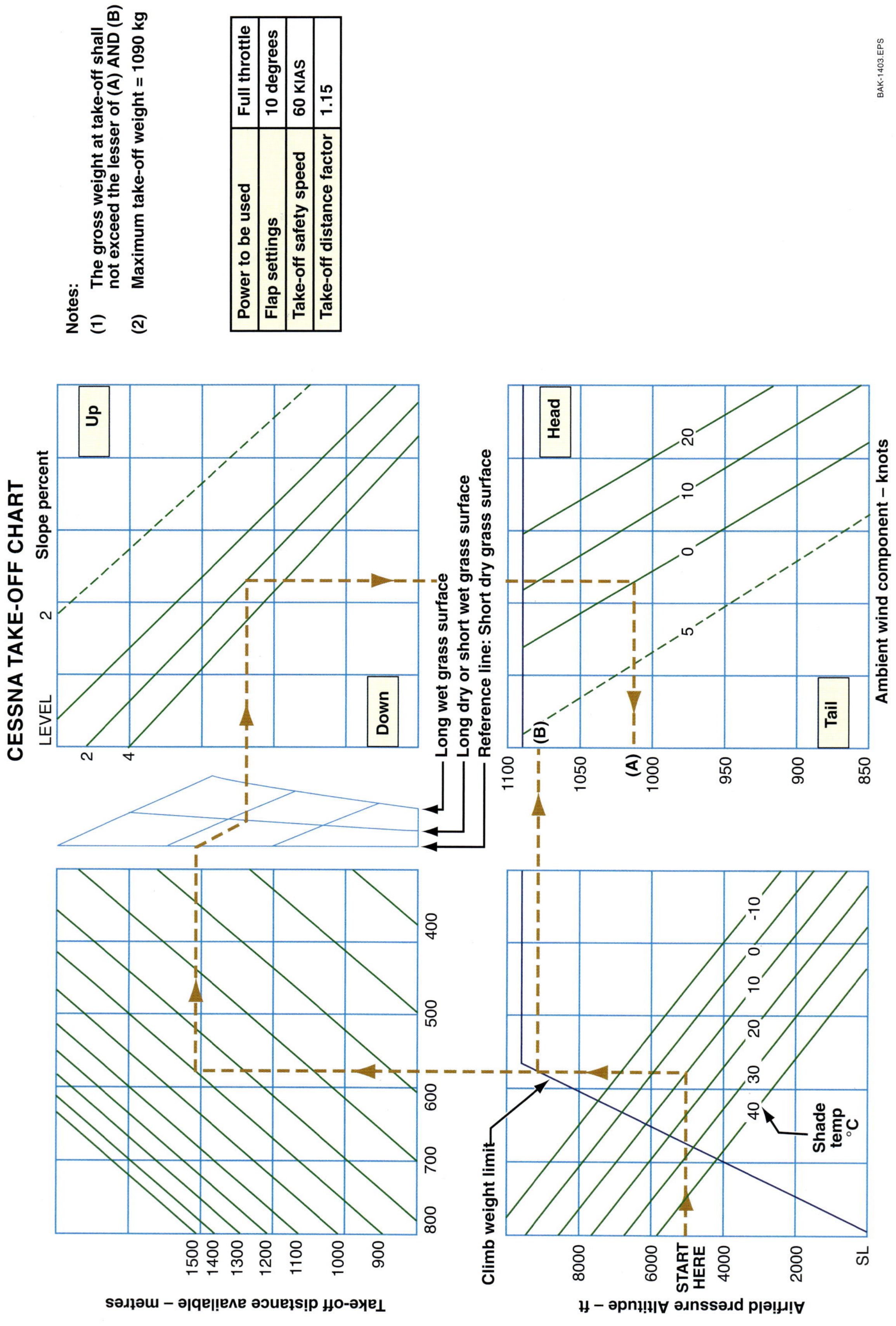

Figure 11-13 Cessna take-off chart.

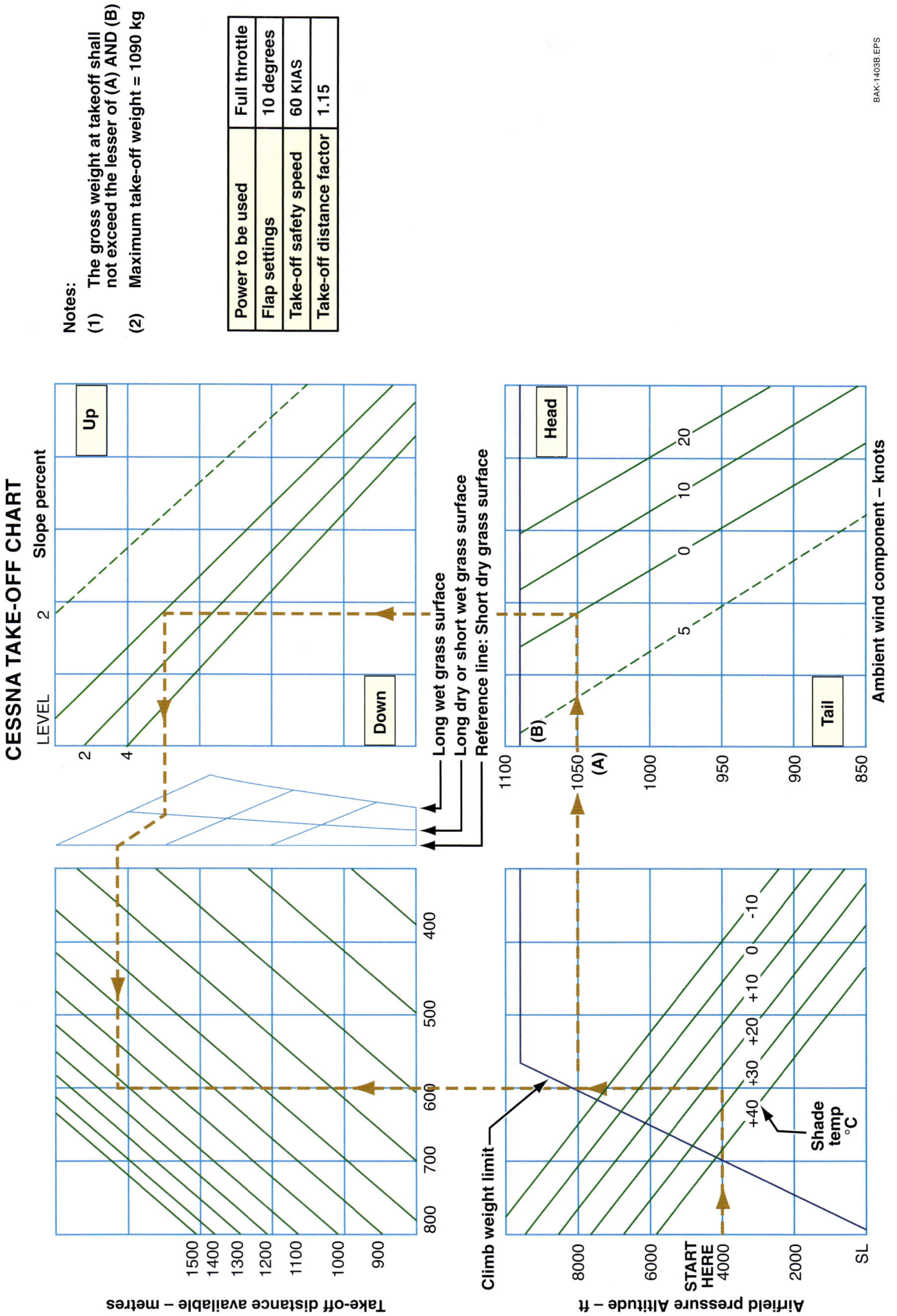

Power to be used	Full throttle
Flap settings	10 degrees
Take-off safety speed	60 KIAS
Take-off distance factor	1.15

Figure 11-14 Cessna take-off chart

Piper

The Piper P-chart shown on page 397 is typical of the other common method of presenting take-off performance data. The data used to enter this type of chart is the same as before, and is clearly explained in the following example.

Example 11-5

Using the procedures recommended on the Piper-take-off chart (i.e. flap setting zero, full power, not less than 2,350 rpm, take-off safety speed 64 kt IAS), determine the maximum permissible take-off weight for the following conditions.

Temperature	+16°C
Pressure altitude	6,000 ft
Surface	Short dry grass
Slope	2% down
Wind component	10 kt head
Take-off distance available	850 metres

Step 1

As shown on the Piper chart, we enter with a temperature of +16°C, and proceed vertically up to intercept the airfield pressure altitude of 6,000 ft.

Step 2

From this point, proceed horizontally to the surface reference line, following the guide lines up from it to the short dry grass line.

Step 3

Now proceed horizontally to the slope reference line, and since our surface has a 2% downslope, we follow the guide lines down to the 2% down line.

Step 4

Continue across to the wind reference line and follow the guide lines down to the 10 kt headwind line. With reference lines, you proceed to them first, before following the guide lines on or back as required. You will see that the guidelines may not be parallel to each other and care must be taken when following them.

Step 5

Proceed horizontally until you intercept the 850 m TODA line (take-off distance available), and then drop vertically and read off the take-off weight of 960 kg. This is the runway performance weight limit.

Step 6

We now need to check that this runway weight limit does not exceed the climb-weight limit. To do this, we return to step 1, and extend the temperature line of +16°C vertically until it intercepts the 6,000 ft pressure altitude line in the small climb-weight limit graph.

Step 7

From this point, proceed horizontally to the left and read off the weight of 990 kg. This is the climb-weight limit.

Answer: The maximum permissible take-off weight on this runway in the given conditions is 960 kg – the lesser of the runway performance weight and the climb performance weight.

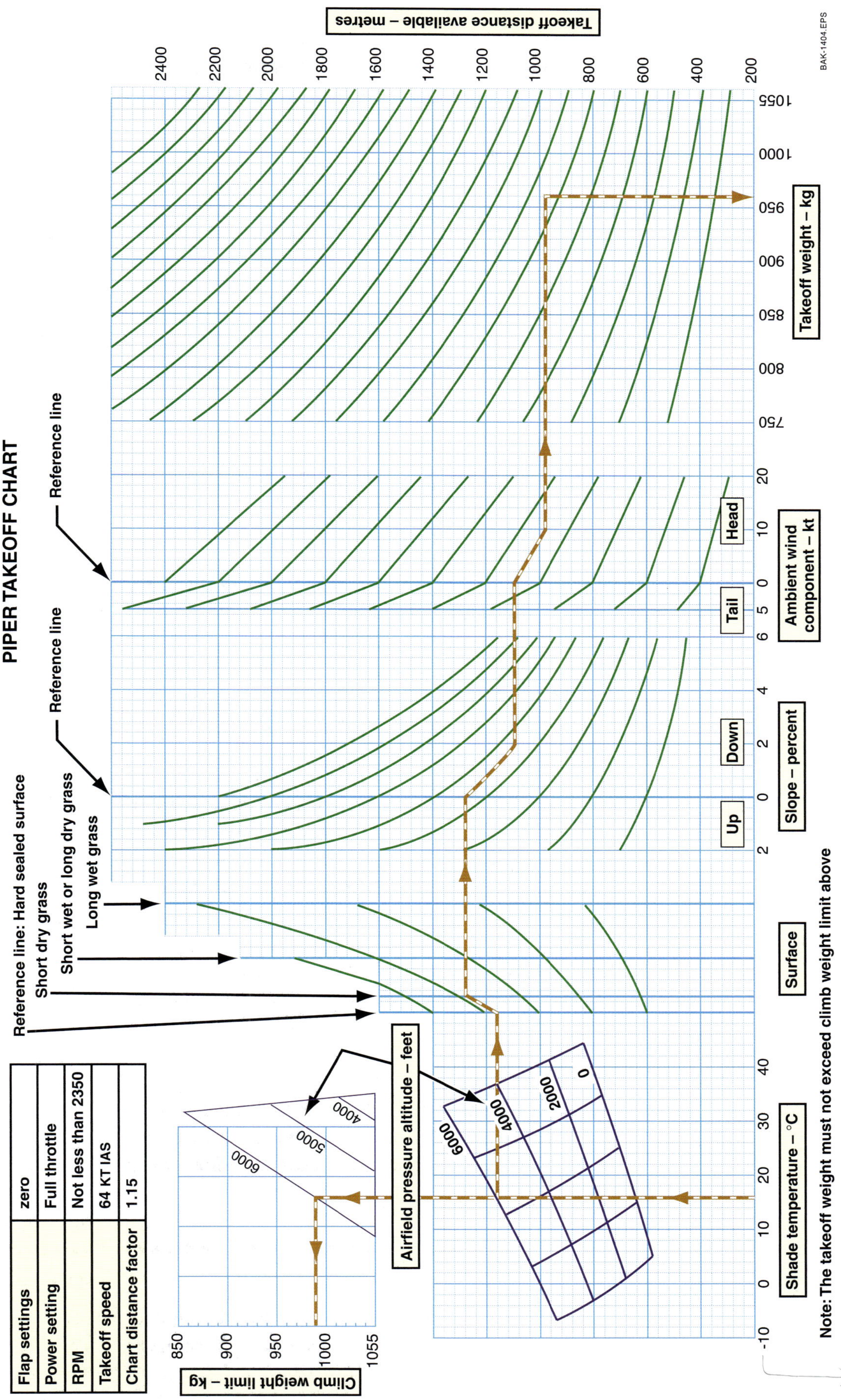

Flap settings	zero
Power setting	Full throttle
RPM	Not less than 2350
Takeoff speed	64 KT IAS
Chart distance factor	1.15

Figure 11-15 Piper take-off chart.

Landing Charts

Presentation

Landing charts provide information in a similar fashion to the take-off P-charts, except that normally there is no allowance for different runway surfaces. Make sure you use the correct chart for the conditions, and in particular, check the following which are displayed on the chart:

- flap setting for landing;
- landing distance factor; and
- approach speed.

As with the take-off charts, there are different presentations for landing performance. The two most usual are the "round the houses" for Cessna, and the "horizontal with reference lines" for Piper. The methods of using the various charts are fundamentally the same as for the take-off charts.

Landing Climb Performance Limit

Even though the aim of an approach is to achieve a landing, the aeroplane must be capable of going-around if required. There are many reasons why you might decide to go-around on an approach, e.g. another aeroplane blocking the runway, a poor approach from which a safe landing might not be made, excessive crosswind or other unsatisfactory conditions.

Before it is approved by CASA, an aeroplane must demonstrate the ability to achieve a certain minimum landing climb performance. Landing climb performance requirements mean that, for a given weight, the aeroplane must be capable of achieving a 3.2% climb gradient in ISA conditions, at maximum take-off power on all engines, at a speed (IAS) not exceeding 1.3 V_S in the landing configuration.

The climb performance of an aeroplane depends to some extent upon its gross weight. If the landing climb performance is not adequate, this will put a limit on the allowable landing weight. Aeroplanes which are limited by the landing climb consideration will have a landing climb limit line marked somewhere on the landing chart.

The landing climb requirements apply to the landing configuration situation (i.e. landing flap and landing gear extended). Once you have initiated the go-around, "cleaning-up" the aeroplane (raising gear and flaps as required) will improve the climb performance.

Practical Use of P-Charts – Landing

Cessna

Example 11-6

Using the Cessna-type landing chart (page 400), determine the maximum permissible landing weight and landing distance for the following conditions.

Aerodrome elevation	5,050 ft
Temperature	0°C
QNH	998 hPa
LDA	500 m
Slope	2% UP
Wind component	6 kt head

Step 1
Calculate pressure altitude as before (see opposite).

Difference between ISA MSL pressure and QNH	= 1,013 – 998
	= 15 hPa
Difference in pressure altitude	= 15 × 30 ft/hPa
	= 450 ft
Aerodrome elevation	= 5,050 ft
∴ pressure altitude	= 5,050 + 450 = 5,500 ft

Step 2
Enter with 5,500 on the airfield pressure altitude scale, and draw a horizontal line across to intersect the +0°C line. To check the climb weight limit (for a go-around) continue the horizontal line to meet climb limit line then drop vertically and note 1,020 kg (A).

Step 3
Now from the 5,500 ft and 0°C intersection, draw a vertical line up through the distance required box.

Step 4
The other data we have available is a wind and slope. From the 6 kt headwind point project upwards to the 2% upslope line.

Step 5
Project to the left to intercept your original vertical line and you will find the landing distance required is 480 metres. For this example, we have used some fairly extreme conditions to illustrate the use of the graph. Note that this aircraft is climb weight limited, and therefore its landing weight is limited to 1,020 kg.

Piper

The Piper-type landing chart shown on page 401 is based upon an approach with a flap setting of 40°, and an approach speed of 65 kt IAS. In this particular chart for the Piper Warrior, the landing distance required does not vary significantly with landing weight, so weight is not factored into the graph. For larger aircraft, landing weight is a factor in determining the landing distance available.

Example 11-7

Using the Piper landing chart provided, determine the landing distance required for the conditions given opposite:

Aerodrome elevation	4,000 ft
QNH	1,013 hPa (so elevation equals pressure altitude)
Temperature	+14°C
Slope	4% up
Wind component	10 kt head

Step 1
Enter at +14°C and move vertically to intercept the pressure altitude 4,000 ft line.

Step 2
Move horizontally to the slope reference line and from there follow the guide lines down to the 4% up line (notice by a quick glance to the landing distance scale on the right-hand side that this has the effect of reducing it).

Step 3
Next, proceed to the wind reference line, and follow the guidelines down to the 10 kt headwind line.

Step 4
Move horizontally to the right and read off the landing distance required of 510 m. Although unlikely to apply, you should get into the habit of checking the climb weight limit. In this case you would use the small graph in the top left-hand corner of the main graph. There is no climb weight limit here, so landing at maximum weight is appropriate.

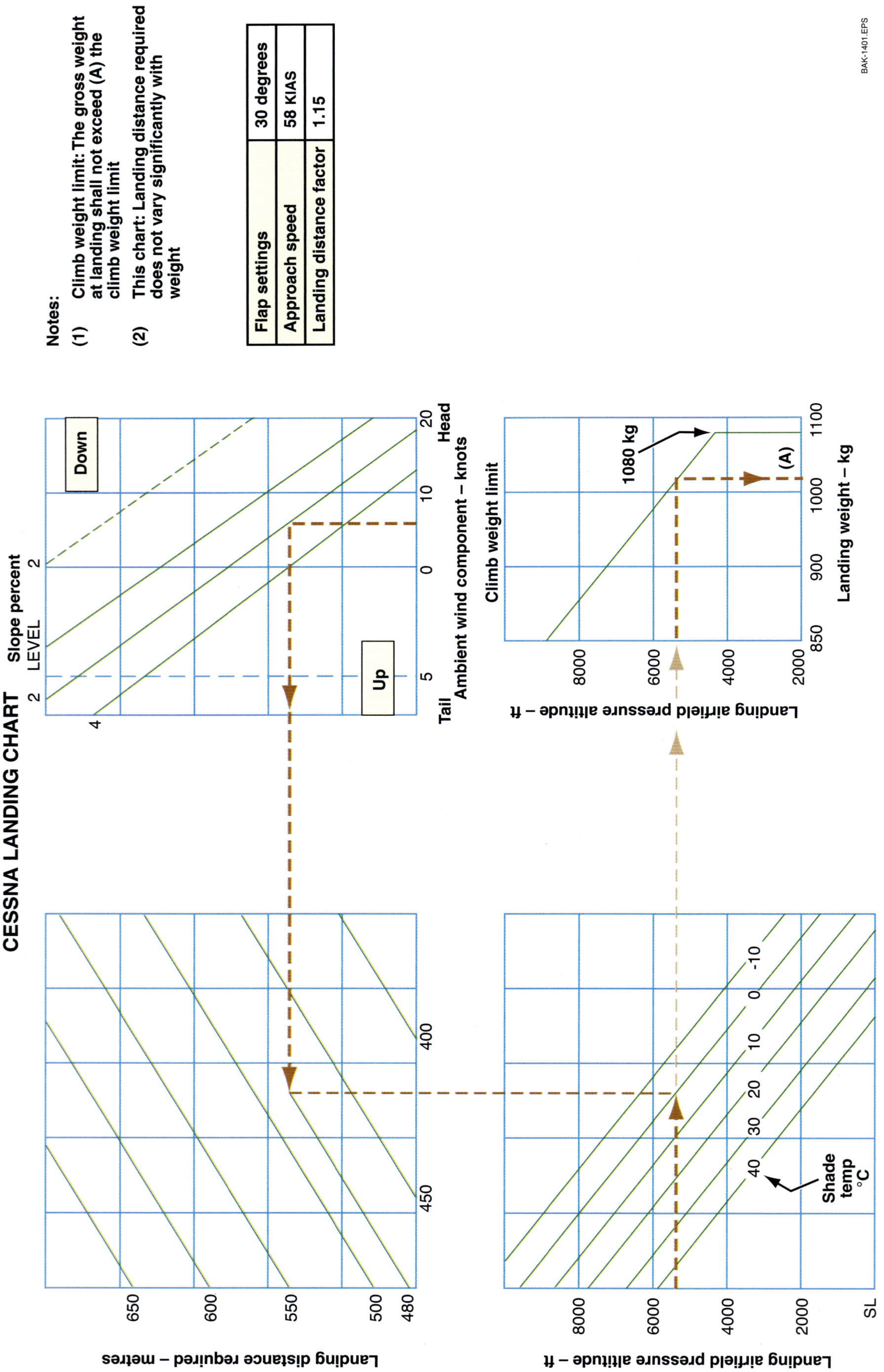

Figure 11-16 Cessna landing chart.

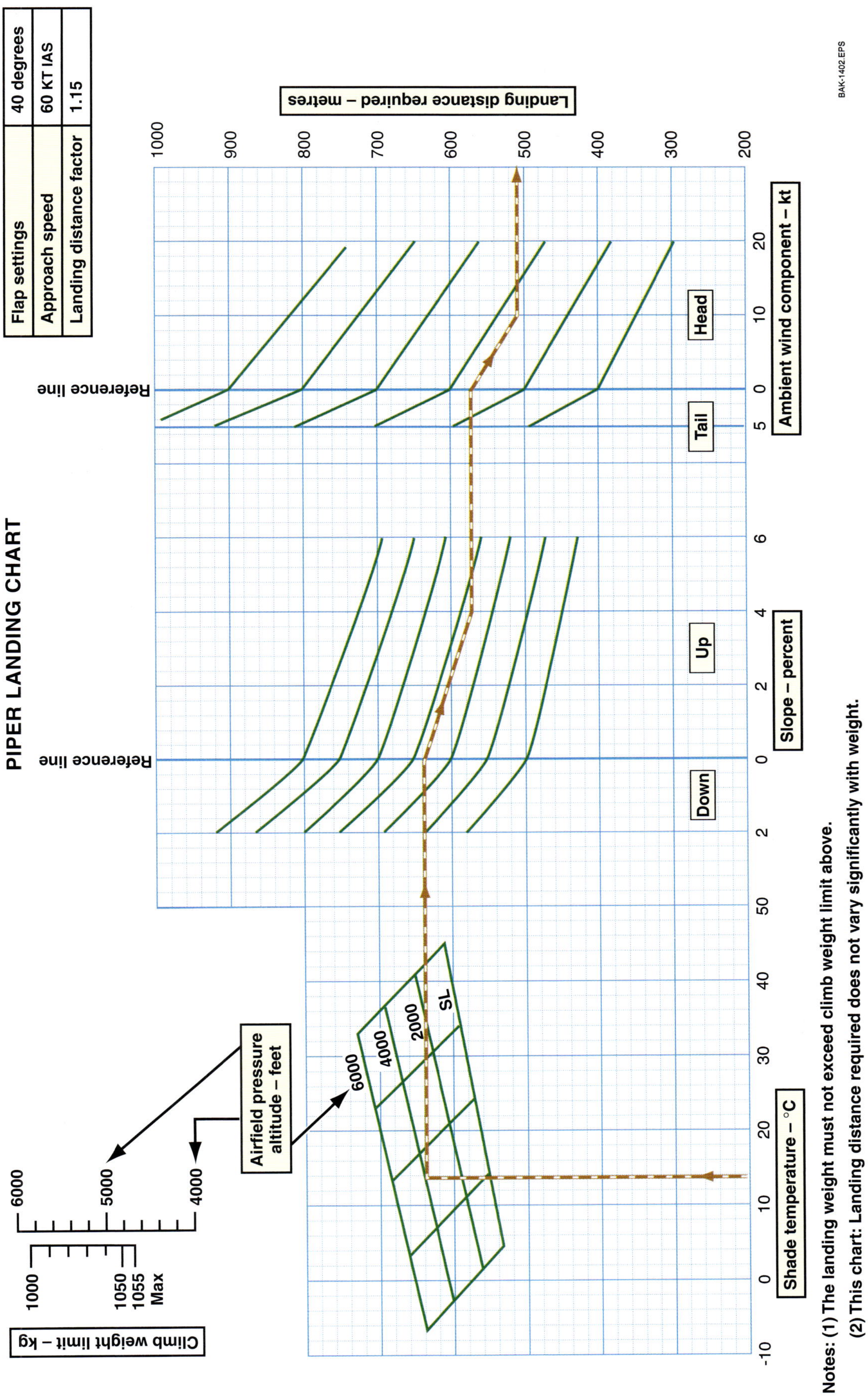

Figure 11-17 Piper landing chart.

Review 11

BAK Level of Knowledge Only

1. State the ISA sea level temperature and pressure.
2. What would ISA plus 15 degrees mean?
3. What is meant by QNH?
4. Density altitude is not a simple measure of height. What extra parameter does it account for?
5. Define V_S, V_{NO}, V_{NE}, and V_{FE}.
6. What is meant by TODR and TODA?
7. What is TOSS?
8. List six factors which affect take-off performance – 3 favourable and 3 unfavourable.
9. What is aquaplaning?
10. List three factors which adversely affect landing performance.
11. Given a pressure altitude of an aerodrome of 2,500 ft and a temperature of 30°C, what would be the density altitude?
12. What effect would this have on the take-off performance of your aircraft?

12 - Introduction to Navigation

How does a Pilot Navigate?

The pilot's primary task is managing the flight. This is done by:

- piloting the aircraft (aviation);
- being responsible for its progress and position (navigation);
- talking and listening to air traffic services and other aircraft (communication); and
- supervising the systems, passengers and crew (supervision).

Thus the task of a pilot in command requires being an aviator, navigator, communicator and supervisor. Navigation is the aspect relating to the geographic position of the aircraft.

Once piloting the aircraft has become automatic to the extent that the pilot can devote attention to other tasks, then the lessons will include navigation. Flying is very like learning to ride a bicycle. It does become second nature and your conscious mind can attend to other things. Navigation consists of planning a flight to a destination, conducting the flight accurately while making allowances for wind and weather, avoiding conflict with other traffic and restricted airspace, as well as adjusting time and fuel calculations to achieve a safe arrival within time and fuel constraints. The pilot does this by reference to maps and charts and, in poor weather, by reference to navigation instruments, called *navigation aids* or *navaids*.

Navigation is a complex subject in its own right. In principle, the pilot controls the direction the aircraft is pointing (called *heading*) and its speed. The progress of the aircraft is monitored by reference to features on the ground, taking into account the effect of the wind. This path over the ground is called the *track* of the aircraft. The elapsed time is monitored to assess the rate of progress (called *groundspeed*) and then adjustments are made to the estimated time of arrival and fuel calculations. Navigation is a simple but fascinating art and worthy of separate study.

At this stage of training, flying is restricted to local flights within sight of known features and airfields. The flights will be conducted in approved training areas, and the instructor will show you these features. Navigation is simply a matter, then, of pointing where you wish to go and making adjustments in direction to allow for wind and to achieve the flightpath you desire in relation to those features. You will notice that, because of wind, you may have to point left or right of the desired direction to actually reach it. What we know as wind is simply a mass of moving air, and now that we are flying within that mass, our path over the ground (track) is modified by the movement of the air.

It is like a boat crossing a river – you have to point upstream to track directly across. Similarly, the boat moving downstream moves faster relative to the shore (groundspeed) than one moving upstream – although both may have the same water speed (airspeed in our case). You will recognise this allowance after a while. It is noticeable close to the ground when you are taking off or landing, and you will be taught later in your training how to compensate for the conditions.

Where the aircraft is pointing is called its *heading*. Where the aircraft is going is called its *track*. This is a very, very important difference.

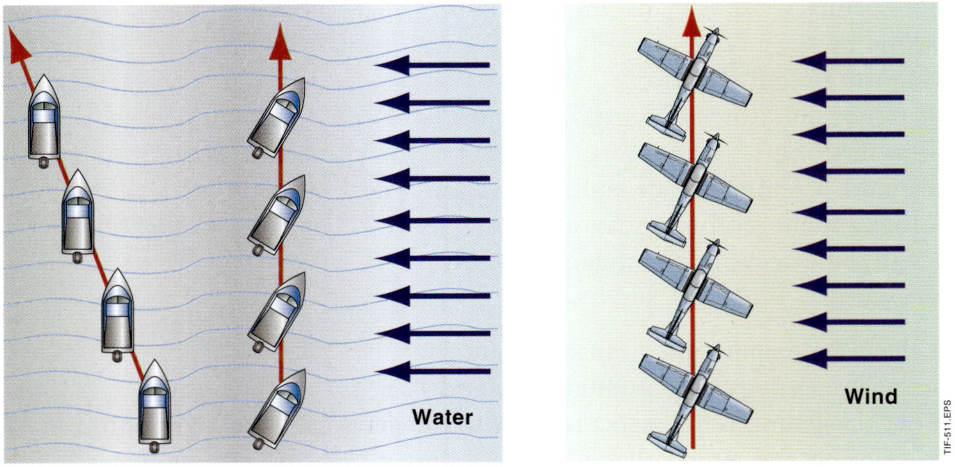

Figure 12-1 Heading and tracking.

During training, you will need to transit from the circuit area to a training area in order to practise basic flight sequences. Some training is conducted from airfields that use Class D aerodrome procedures. These airfields always have an associated training area which is not necessarily nearby. You will learn to find your way to and from the training area. While this is easy, you will become a safer and more competent pilot if you learn the basic navigation principles at this stage.

Which Heading?

After take-off, we must climb our aircraft to a safe altitude and distance from the field before making a turn. If we are turning with the circuit direction, we can start the turn at 500 ft AGL, but onto which heading do we turn? When planning the flight, take a look at your VTC. In figure 12-2, the training area is exactly west of the airfield. You can tell this because a line marked "latitude S35°00′"runs through the airfield and the training area.

All maps use true north as the direction reference. This means that if a protractor is placed on the start of the track line and aligned with true north, i.e. along a line of longitude, it will measure an angle of 260°T to the training area, so our planned track to the training area is 260°T.

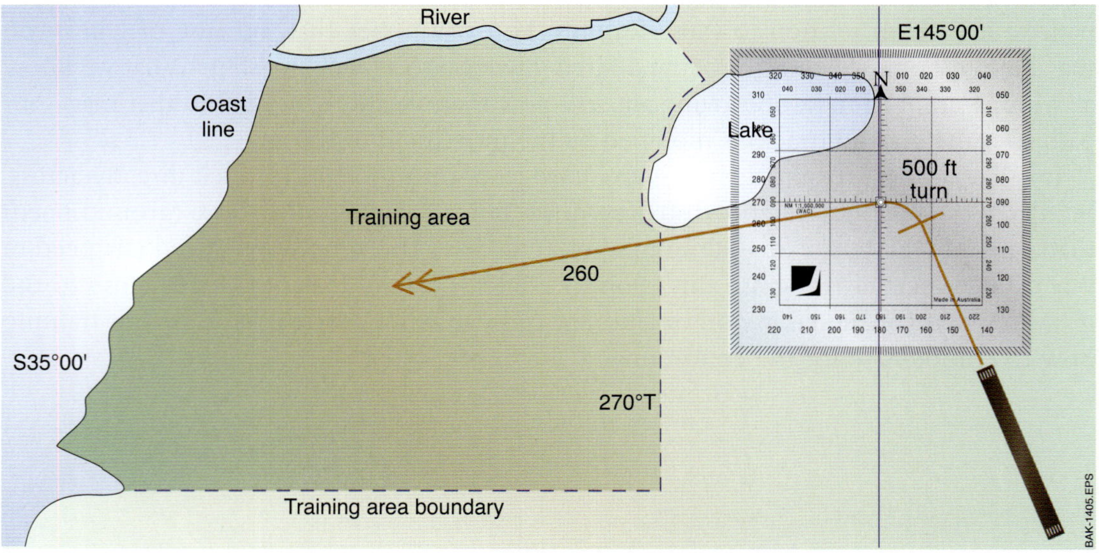

Figure 12-2 Planned track to the training area.

Magnetic Variation

The only direction reference in most small aircraft is by a magnetic compass. Here, a magnet senses magnetic north, so during flight the *direction reference used* is *magnetic north*. As the earth's magnetic field changes and rarely lines up with the true reference, there is usually a significant difference between true north and magnetic north, and this is called *variation*. Variation can be left or right of true north, so variation is always stated as E or W. This is explained later, so for now remember: "*variation east, magnetic least; variation west, magnetic best*".

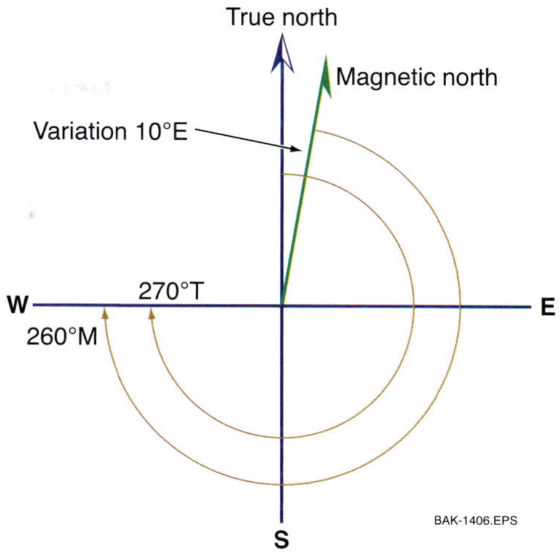

Figure 12-3 Magnetic variation.

Check the chart and find the variation is quoted in this example as 10°E. The true track we measured as 270°T so our magnetic track is 260°M; the variation is 10°E so the magnetic track is least (less than the true track). In small aircraft, it is usual to convert tracks to magnetic for the flight plan. This means we must convert the wind direction to magnetic (the forecast wind is provided in degrees true), so when the heading is calculated it will be presented in degrees magnetic. All this seems a little complex at first, but it really is fairly straight forward. Before we calculate the wind, it is helpful to know a little about distance and true airspeed (TAS).

Deviation

The magnetic compass aligns to the earth's magnetic field and *should* indicate magnetic heading (direction). However, the compass is vulnerable to errors due to ferreous metals and electrical fields caused by the aircraft. This error is called *deviation* and is measured by a technique called a *compass swing*. For this, the compass reading is taken with the engine running and systems operating, and the error is noted on various headings. A deviation card then displays the compass error and correction to be applied so that the correct magnetic heading can be read:

- compass heading (°C) ± deviation = magnetic heading (°M); and
- magnetic heading (°M) ± variation = true heading (°T).

Distance

A scale ruler is available for both the VTC and WAC. Distance can be measured with a scale rule, the chart scale or use a set of dividers to step off nautical miles as minutes of latitude along a line of longitude (vertical line). One degree (60 minutes) of latitude represents 60 nm; therefore one minute of latitude equals one nautical mile. Note that the minutes of longitude marked on the parallels of latitude (horizontal lines) do not represent nautical miles.

TAS

The aircraft airspeed indicator provides indicated airspeed (IAS). While this speed is very close to TAS at low level, there is a large separation in value as the aircraft climbs. The density at altitude will determine the TAS, which you will learn to calculate for now; for the same IAS at a higher altitude (reduced density), the TAS is always greater than the IAS. The aircraft flight manual will provide altitude and IAS figures. However, for most training aircraft, a practical TAS will be provided.

Navigation Triangle

We know enough to draw the triangle and start using a circular slide rule to calculate the missing pieces. To ensure calculation results are accurate, three facts are to be remembered:

- heading (HDG) and true airspeed (TAS) form one vector;
- track (TR) and groundspeed (GS) form a vector; and
- wind direction and speed (W\V) form the other.

The unknowns of a typical navigation problem are heading and groundspeed.

Example 12-1

Given the following, calculate heading and groundspeed:

Track 270°T; TAS 110KT; W/V 320/20; VAR 10°E

Convert the track and wind to magnetic. Whenever possible, layout the navigation data in the same order as the standard flight plan so you will not have to relearn the process later. Complete the details you know:

TAS	TR(M)	W/V(M)	HDG(M)	GS
110	260	310/20	......	......

- *Set TAS and mark W/V.* Using an ASA E6-B flight computer, mark the wind on the wind face – set 310 against the "true index". Remember we are working with magnetic north as our reference. All directions, HDG, TR and WIND are expressed as magnetic. Move the slide to put the TAS of 110 kt under the centre grommet then mark a small dot 20 kt below the grommet (at the 90 kt point) to represent the W/V.
- *Drift and HDG.* Rotate the transparent face (inner direction ring) to set the TR of 260 against the true index. Read the drift; it is 9° left. We know the wind is from 310 so from our track of 260 turn the 9° into wind (towards 310). The heading looks like 269 but because we have turned the direction ring, the indicated drift is now 8°. So the refined HDG is 268; the drift is 8° left.
- *Track and groundspeed.* The track is known as 260. To find the G/S, read it off under the wind mark; it is 96 kt. Note that there are other types of navigation computers that do this calculation equally well, but the E6-B is recommended.

To help understand this calculation, each vector can be plotted. Keep it simple by basing the plot on a one hour time scale. If you plot on a piece of paper, you can decide your own scale and make the direction reference magnetic like the plot that follows. To plot on a map, all the direction references must be in degrees true.

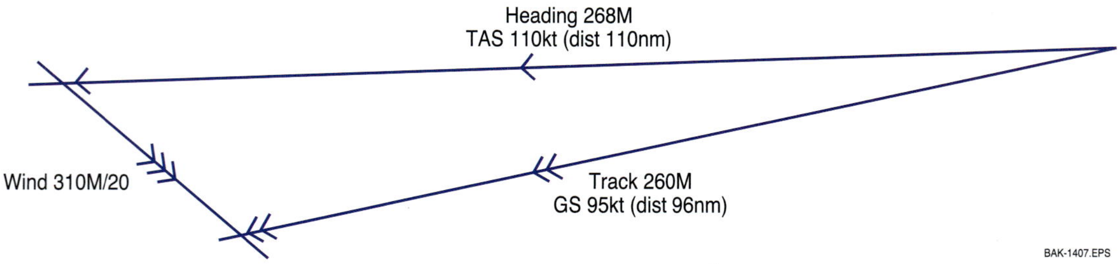

Figure 12-4 Triangle of vectors used for navigation planning.

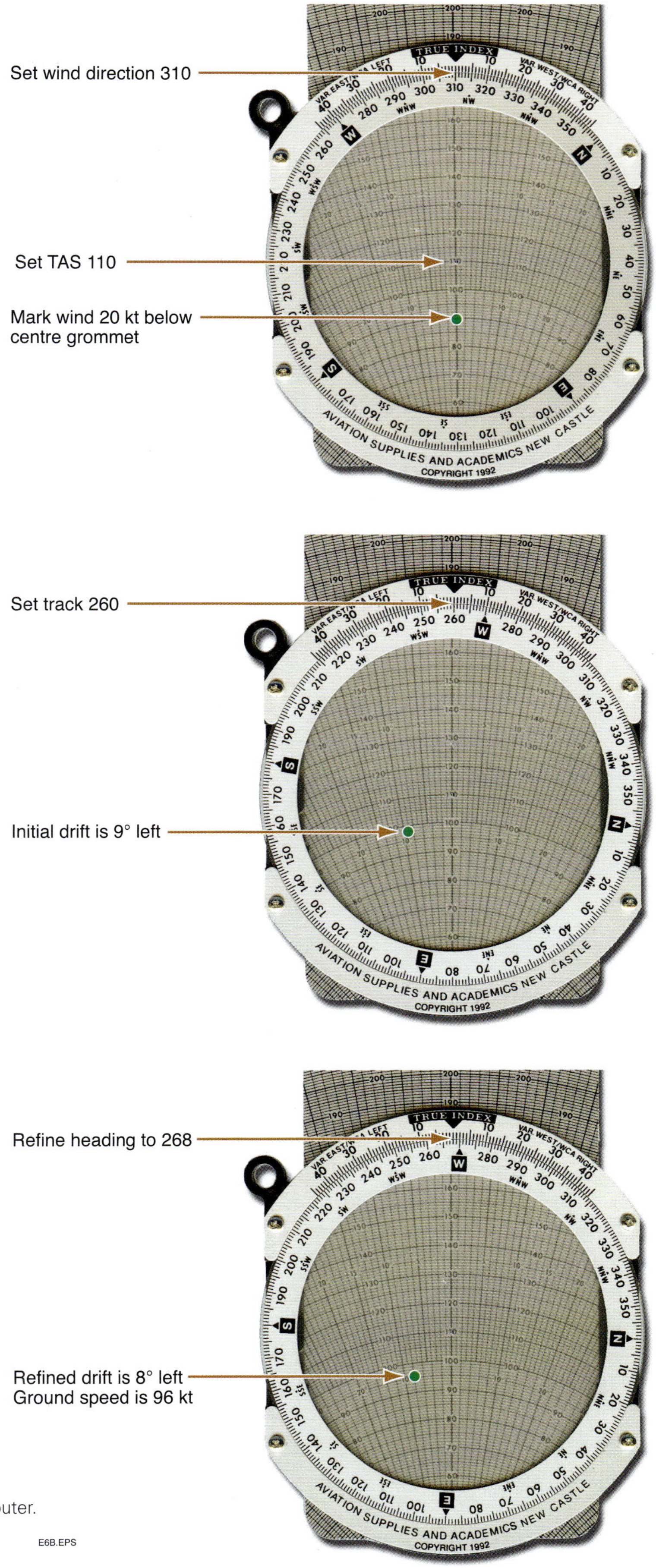

Figure 12-5
Using the slide computer.

E6B.EPS

Crosswind

To determine crosswind, headwind or tailwind components quickly and easily, you must know the angle between your track and the reported wind direction. You must also know the reported wind velocity. This will be especially helpful in anticipating the effect of wind when landing, because wind reported by a tower or ATIS is surface wind. Wind direction is given in magnetic direction so it can be compared to the heading indicator without correction. To determine the wind vectors at altitude, remember forecast winds are provided in relation to true north, and you must apply variation before comparing them to the heading or track.

CROSSWIND CORRECTION

Angle between wind direction and track (both °M or °T)

Wind speed – knots	0°	10°	20°	30°	40°	50°	60°	70°	80°	90°
10	10/0	10/2	9/3	9/5	8/6	6/8	5/9	3/9	2/10	0/10
20	20/0	20/3	19/7	17/10	15/13	13/15	10/17	7/19	3/20	0/20
30	30/0	30/5	28/10	26/15	23/19	19/23	15/26	10/28	5/30	0/30
40	40/0	39/7	38/14	35/20	31/26	26/31	20/35	14/38	7/39	0/40
50	50/0	49/9	47/17	43/25	38/32	32/38	25/43	17/47	9/49	0/50
60	60/0	59/10	56/21	52/30	46/39	39/46	30/52	21/56	10/59	0/60
70	70/0	69/12	66/24	61/35	54/45	45/54	35/61	24/66	12/69	0/70

Headwind 0/0 Crosswind

BAK-1109.EPS

Figure 12-6 Crosswind correction.

Terminology

Direction Reference

Earlier in this chapter the true and magnetic system of referencing was mentioned. Magnetic variation (degrees east or west), either subtracted from or added to the reference. In simple terms, the difference between true and magnetic north is *variation* at your position. In a similar way, when we put a compass in an aircraft, it does not exactly read magnetic heading. The heading indication is distorted slightly by the magnetic field of the aircraft, so we call the reading *compass heading* and it is written as, for example, 216°C. The error is caused by magnetic *deviation*, which is an aircraft environment error. As with variation we say "*deviation east, compass least*", so we check the deviation card next to the compass and adjust the compass reading to obtain an accurate magnetic heading.

Direction

Direction is described in three ways:

- Bearings, headings and tracks are stated using the three figure method: "*After take-off I'll turn onto a heading 268°M*" (pronounced "two six eight"). Heading and tracks are always the direction from where you are to where you want to go, whereas a bearing may be from you to the station, or where you are from the station.

- Bearings are measured to or from the station and are usually the magnetic track to or from the station. The magnetic bearing from the station is also known as the *radial*. Another way of describing the bearing of something from your aircraft is relative to your axis, e.g. 10° right, or more commonly using the clock code, e.g. an aircraft off the right wingtip is at "three o'clock" (refer to figure 3-1, page 57).
- Runways are referred to by using a two-figure group. This is the runway direction in degrees magnetic rounded up or down. If a runway direction were 213°M then the runway would be 21 (said *two one*). This is correct when the runway is first constructed but as the earth's magnetic field changes its alignment might measure 216°M; the runway is likely to be called 21 for some years as its magnetic reference might shift back.

Distance, Speed & Velocity

When describing distance in aviation we use the term nautical miles (nm). One nautical mile is a precise distance determined by describing an angle of one minute of latitude from the centre of the earth – it's about 6,080 ft. Take a look at the calculator side of your computer; it will show that 100 nm equals 115 statute miles equals 185 km (kilometres).

- Distance for the purpose of describing visibility is given in metres, usually kilometres and is the horizontal distance you can see until smoke, haze or cloud interferes with your vision.
- Speed is stated in knot (kt) which is the number of nautical miles travelled in one hour.
- The wind vector is stated as "030/15", meaning 030 degrees true at 15 kt. In area and route forecasts, the wind is always given in degrees true from where it comes. The ATIS, runway and ATC headings are given in degrees magnetic.

Time

The time used in aviation is universal co-ordinated time (UTC) previously known as Greenwich Mean Time (GMT) which has been redesignated as ***Zulu*** time. Mostly we use only the minutes by saying the time is 42, meaning forty-two minutes after the hour. We can write time in three ways:

- hour-minute, e.g. 1442 (HHMM);
- day-hour-minute, e.g. 301442; and
- month-day-hour-minute, e.g. 10301442.

Zulu time is fine for flying but many ground activities require standard times. These include airfield operating hours and services available at some fields at first and last light.

When you first need to convert times, it is fairly important to write the time down in an eight figure time group. So if you cross over the 2400 hour mark, you increase or decrease the date by one day. Be careful at the end of the month, as you might also have to change months. All clocks in given areas, known as time zones, are set to a common local time, which is based on longitude.

- Eastern Standard Time (EST) = Zulu + 10 hours.
- Central Standard Time (CST) = Zulu + 9 hours 30 minutes.
- Western Standard Time (WST) = Zulu + 8 hours.

(Refer to figure 12-7, page 412).

Example 12-2

What is the Zulu time if the local time in Sydney is 0830 on 1 November?

The answer is 2230 the day before. Time conversions are usually simpler than this so it is important to be careful and correct. If you find any reference to coordinated universal time (UTC), it is the same as Zulu time and GMT.

```
 11010830
    -1000
 10312230
```

Summer Time

To make things more challenging for you, some states advance their clocks during summer and this is known as summer time. The summer time period is not standardised across Australia but generally starts on the last Saturday in October and ends about mid March:

- Eastern Summer Time (ESuT) is EST + 1 hour and so equals Zulu + 11; and
- Central Summer Time (CSuT) is CST + 1 hour and so equals Zulu + 10:30.

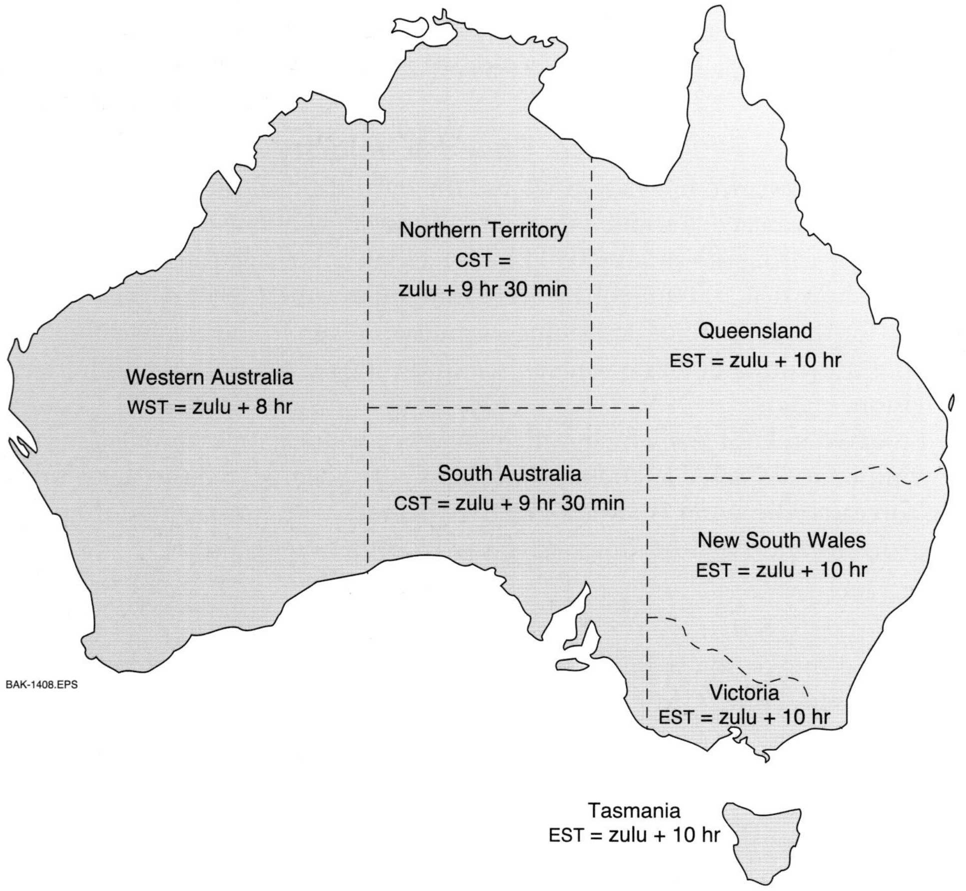

Figure 12-7 Time zones in Australia.

Vertical Measurement

The vertical measurements of height, altitude and elevation are all measured in feet. It is important to understand the differences between these terms:

- *height* is the vertical distance of the aircraft above ground level (AGL). This is not always the best way to manage the aircraft for vertical flight as the ground level changes;
- *altitude* is the vertical distance above mean sea level (MSL); this is read from the altimeter when the QNH is set. The QNH is the code for the sea level pressure that makes sea level the reference datum;
- *elevation* is the vertical distance of the earth's surface above mean sea level. It is essential you know the elevation of your airfield so when you do your altimeter check during preflight, the instrument is within 60 ft of that elevation and so is serviceable for flight; and
- *flight level* is the pressure altitude which is equivalent to the vertical distance above the 1,013 hPa datum above 10,000 ft when certain conditions are met, e.g. 15,000 ft becomes FL150.

Defining your position on the Earth

The position of any point on the earth can be specified by:

- its *latitude*, which is its angular position N or S of the plane of the equator; together with
- its *longitude*, which is its angular position E or W of the prime meridian through Greenwich.

Usually, it is sufficiently accurate to specify the latitude as a four-figure group, and longitude as a five figure group, of a place in degrees and minutes only (although for accuracy each minute can be divided into 60 seconds of arc). The inception of electronic (digital) navigation systems means that positions are usually expressed in degrees, minutes and decimal minutes, such as Mangalore (YMNG) which is South 36°53'. East 145°11' is expressed S3653.3: E14511.1.

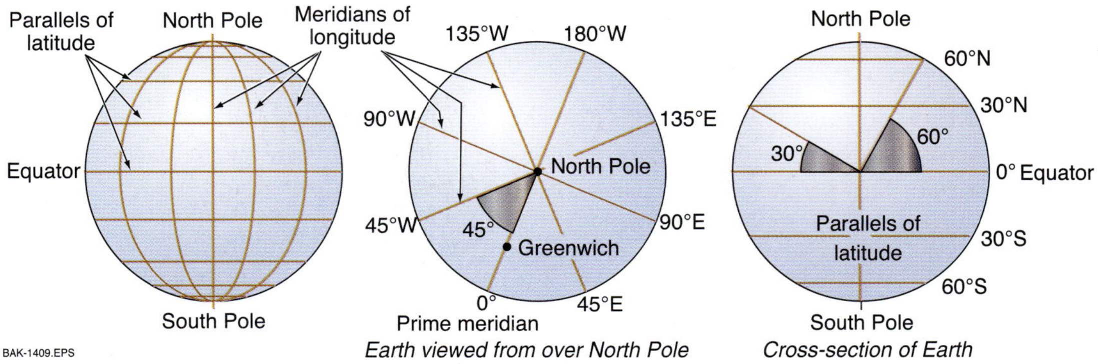

Figure 12-8 Latitude and longitude.

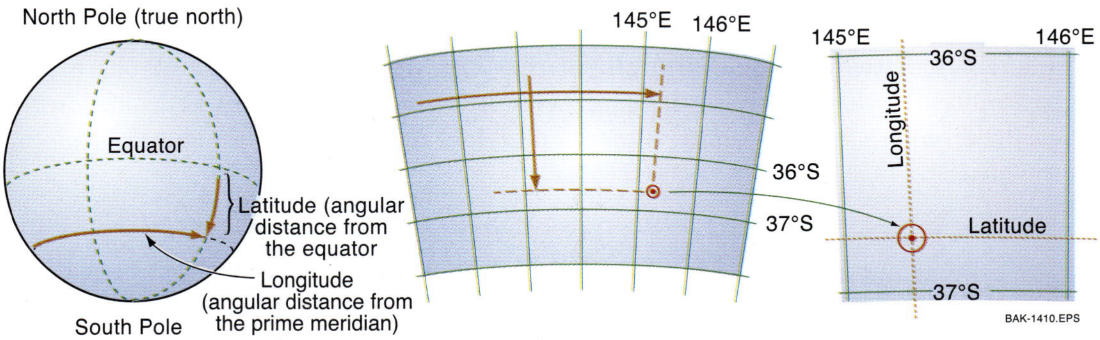

Figure 12-9 The position of Mangalore (YMNG) is S3653.3: E14511.1.

Latitude and longitude is the normal method of specifying position on earth and is the one that pilots most commonly use at the flight planning stage when they are preparing their charts and flight plan. Once in flight, however, there are other means of specifying the position of the aircraft:

- by position over a landmark or radio beacon, e.g. over the Harbour Bridge; or
- by range (distance) and bearing from a landmark or radio beacon, e.g. ten nautical miles (10 nm) on a bearing of 290° from Mackay.

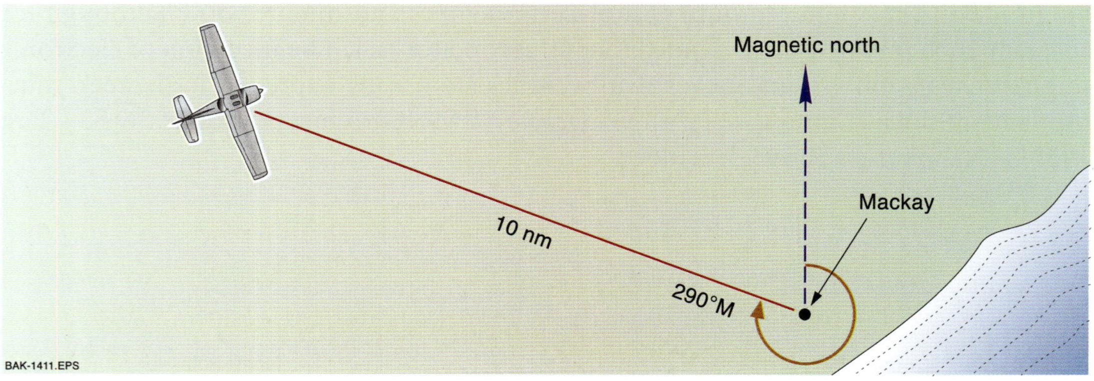

Figure 12-10 Specifying aircraft position.

The latitude–longitude graticule is translated onto charts by cartographers (mapmakers) whose major problem is representing the spherical surface of the earth on a flat sheet of paper. This process always leads to some distortion.

Scale

Scale is defined as the ratio of the chart length compared to the earth distance that it represents. The larger the chart length for a given earth length, the larger the scale and the more detail that can be shown. This means that large-scale charts cover small areas in detail. For example, a Visual Terminal Chart (VTC) has a larger scale and shows more detail than a World Aeronautical Chart (WAC).

Scale can be expressed in various ways:

- as a graduated scale line, usually situated at the bottom of the chart. A graduated scale line allows you to measure off the distance between two points on the chart and match it against the scale line; and
- as a representative fraction. For example, the WAC series are 1:1,000,000 charts (one to a million), where 1 cm on the chart will represent 1,000,000 cm or 10 km on the earth, or where 1 nm on earth is represented by one millionth of a nautical mile on the chart.

Aeronautical Charts for VFR Pilots

The charts described below will mainly be used when you are flying within the confines of the local training area associated with your flying school. You should obtain a VTC, WAC and PCA (the VNC and ERC can come later). There is much to learn about the charts, in particular what information they present to you. Study the chart legend.

Visual Terminal Chart (VTC)

The VTC is produced to a scale 1:250,000, and shows detailed information surrounding the local terminal area. It should be used whenever available, but other charts described below can be used in those areas for which a VTC has not been produced. The VTC shows both topographical (e.g. hill contours, rivers, reservoirs) and cultural (e.g. towns, roads, railways) information, as well as aeronautical information.

The aeronautical information shown on the chart includes the following:

- prohibited, restricted and danger areas within the terminal area;
- control zones and associated control areas at an enlarged scale;
- lanes of entry;
- aeronautical beacons, lights and obstructions;
- air traffic control (ATC) checkpoints and en route reporting points;
- visual flight rules (VFR) approach points and routes – over which pilots should plan to fly when making a VFR entry to control zones and general aviation control zones;
- an approximate runway layout for the major aerodromes that the VTC covers;
- VFR approach points for Class D aerodromes; and
- colour-shaded areas where less than 500 ft clearance exists between terrain and the overlying CTA.

World Aeronautical Chart (WAC) Series

The WAC is produced to a scale of 1:1,000,000. It is the primary chart for use in en route navigation. We use WACs to provide us mainly with topographical information (mountains, lakes, rivers, coastlines, etc.) and cultural information (cities, towns, highways, railway lines, etc.) for visual en route navigation. Each WAC has an identification number displayed at the top beside the name of that particular chart.

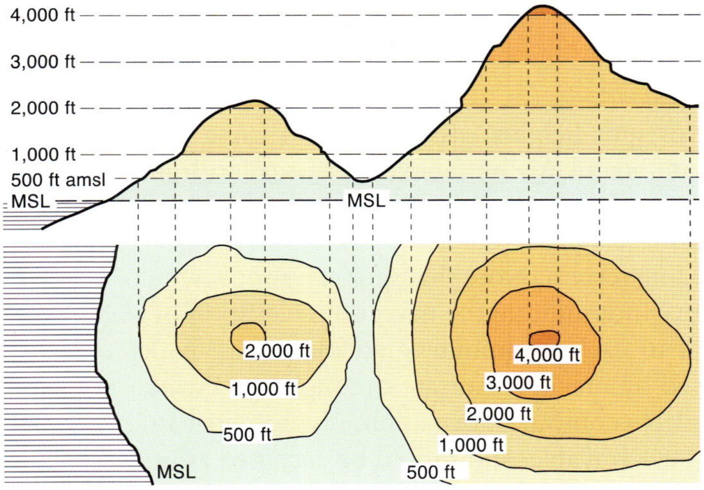

Figure 12-11 Contour lines and hypsometric tinting are used to present relief (terrain) on WACs.

Such things as radio towers, irrigation channels, roads and railway lines change, so WACs are continually updated. Interim amendments are issued for users to update charts by hand (known as manuscript amendments). This information is distributed to all holders of the AIP in the form of AIP supplements (on yellow pages). The information is then incorporated in new editions as they are published. The WAC is the primary chart used by VFR pilots in Australia to navigate when well away from busy terminal areas. Aeronautical information (e.g. controlled airspace and restricted areas) will then be obtained from the ERC, and the VTC when close to a terminal area where one is provided. The topographic information shown on a WAC is that which is considered to be of most use to the pilot.

Drainage & Water Features

Drainage and water features (hydrographic features) are usually depicted on the WAC in blue. This includes creeks, streams, rivers, canals, lakes, swamps, waterholes, wells and bores, shorelines, tidal flats, dry lakes, etc. Just how they are depicted is explained by the legend – but bear in mind that after a flood, for instance, what might be shown as a dry river bed on the chart might in fact be a raging torrent. Right throughout aviation, commonsense is necessary. One water feature not depicted in blue is the mangrove swamp, which is usually near a coastline and is depicted in green.

Relief

There are various ways of bringing the ground into relief, so that an impression of hills, mountains, valleys, etc, is obtained when you look at the chart. The WAC uses contours, which are lines joining places of equal height above sea level, and the closer the contour lines are together on the map, the steeper the hill on the ground.

- Colour or layer tinting is used in conjunction with the contour lines to give even more relief. The colours or tints used for the various ground elevations are shown on a hypsometric tint table at the side of the WAC. (Hypsometric means establishment of vertical heights or elevations.) The shades of colour on the WAC start with green for low land, then go through yellow and into brown, gradually darkening as ground height increases.
- Hachuring and hill shading are used to give a three dimensional relief effect. Hachuring consists of very short lines radiating from high ground and is commonly used to portray bluffs, cliffs and escarpments. Hill shading shows darkened areas on the low side of high ground where you would expect to see shadows at certain times of the day.

Spot Elevations

Spot elevations (or spot heights) are also shown using a black spot with an adjacent number to indicate height AMSL (above mean sea level) in feet. These heights can be assumed to be accurately measured (unless amended by NOTAM). Spot heights are normally used to show local peaks and other critical elevations that are significantly higher than the surrounding terrain. Note that spot elevations, which denote ground level, not tree top height, may not indicate the maximum elevation of land in any area. The highest spot elevation in each 30-minute graticule square is depicted in bold type. Spot elevations enclosed by brackets indicate the highest elevation of terrain (not surveyed) based on best available contour information. Hypsometric information is accurate to the extent of the surveys available, and should be accepted as only indicative of elevation.

Cultural Features

Cultural features are of great help to the pilot. It is not possible to show every town or every house on the chart, so a choice is made to show what is significant and of value for visual air navigation. A group of say 100 houses is of little significance if it lies in the middle of a city the size of Sydney and so will not be specifically depicted on the map, yet in the outback, it is extremely significant and will certainly be shown. In remote areas, the chart will even show isolated homesteads, outstations and water tanks.

Roads & Railways

Roads and railways can be of great assistance in visual navigation. Those that will be most significant for air navigation will be clearly shown. Distinctive patterns such as curves, roads running parallel to railway lines and then crossing over, junctions, forks, overpasses, tunnels, etc are especially useful.

Other Information

Many other useful cultural features may also be shown such as wheat silos, telegraph lines, etc. Become familiar with the legend and the symbols.

Limited aeronautical information is also shown on WACs, such as aerodromes (civil, military, or joint use), aerodrome beacons and landing grounds. The date at which this aeronautical information was still considered to be current is specified on the chart. The division of airspace is not shown on WACs – this information is shown on ERCs and VTCs.

The latitude–longitude graticule is clearly marked on WACs:

- the east–west parallels of latitude indicating degrees north or south of the equator (south in Australia of course) are labelled at either side of the chart; and
- the north–south meridians of longitude gradually converging as they near the south pole are labelled at the top and bottom in degrees east or west of the Greenwich meridian (in Australia, longitudes are east).

This makes the WACs ideal for measuring the latitude and longitude of a position.

Planning Chart Australia (PCA)

The PCA is useful when preparing for a cross-country flight and for en route communications in more remote areas:

- area forecast areas depicted in circled red area forecast identification numbers and shaded red dividing lines;
- World Aeronautical Chart (WAC) coverage shown as a black grid with WAC numbers in black, e.g. 3221, plus a WAC decode table at the foot the chart;
- locations shown in coded groups of purple letters and an encode table which codes the places, is included on the back, e.g. BWN for Bowen, YMMB for Moorabbin; and
- communications coverage OCTA – purple tints for VHF coverage at 5,000 ft and 10,000 ft, plus 10,000 ft red shaded areas with ATC frequencies for emergency use only – frequencies for the HF radio network, in red, with dashed-red borders.

Visual Navigation Chart (VNC)

The VNC is a new series of charts designed for visual navigation, with the added benefit of aeronautical information overprinted (such as airspace). VNCs have a scale of 1:500,000 on a Lambert conformal conic projection. Like the WAC, the VNC also provides:

- topographic information (e.g. mountains, cliffs, sand ridges, rivers, lakes, contours and coastlines); and
- cultural information (e.g. cities, towns, railway lines, and other significant man-made landmarks).

En Route Chart (ERC) Series

The En Route Chart (ERC) Low is designed for use in both VFR and IFR operations. This chart series provides complete details of aeronautical information over a large area, covering such items as airspace dimensions, location of aerodromes, and radio navigation aid details. As a student pilot, you will not need to be familiar with the ERC, but you will have to use it when you begin cross-country navigation exercises.

Currency of Charts

It is important to have current editions of charts when you fly. Latest charts are obtainable from the Airservices Publications Centre or your local pilot's shop. You may also purchase charts over the web at *www.airservices.gov.au/publications*.

Directional Information

The prime source of directional information in the aeroplane is the magnetic compass, which is aligned to *magnetic north*. However, the charts are all aligned to *true north*. Measurement of bearings and tracks from a chart needs to be converted by the *variation* between magnetic north and true north in the area in which you are planning to fly. *Isogonals* (lines joining places of equal magnetic variation) are indicated on the WAC by dashed purple-coloured lines. The eastern states of Australia experience easterly variation (magnetic track is less than true track by this amount – 'magnetic is least'), while in Western Australia, the variation is westerly ('magnetic is best'). The *agonic line* (variation zero, where true north and magnetic north are the same) lies in between.

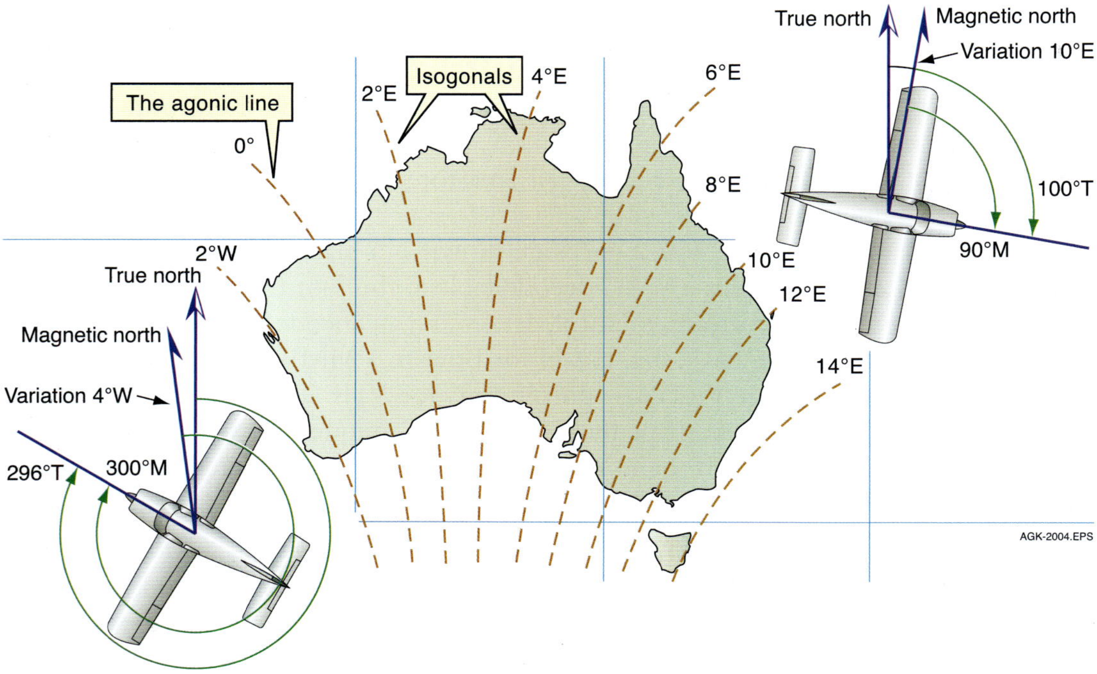

Figure 12-12 Magnetic variation.

Estimating Tracks & Distances

Estimating Track

The direction of a track can be measured accurately with a protractor. However, direction can be estimated reasonably accurately from a chart without the use of any equipment.

Estimation of track is surprisingly easy and, with a bit of practice, you can achieve a ±10° accuracy. In fact, it is a good idea to always estimate track direction before measuring it with a protractor – this will avoid making 180° or 90° errors, as has happened from time to time. Estimating before measuring will also develop faith in your ability to estimate to a practical degree of accuracy, as you gain experience.

Halving known angles is the simplest means of estimating angles. Halving the angle between a quadrantal point and a cardinal point will give you an angle of 22.5°, say 22°, and halving this again will give you 11°. An accuracy of ±10° will be achieved with practice. Remember, the estimated track from the map is in degrees true; you will have to adjust it for magnetic variation.

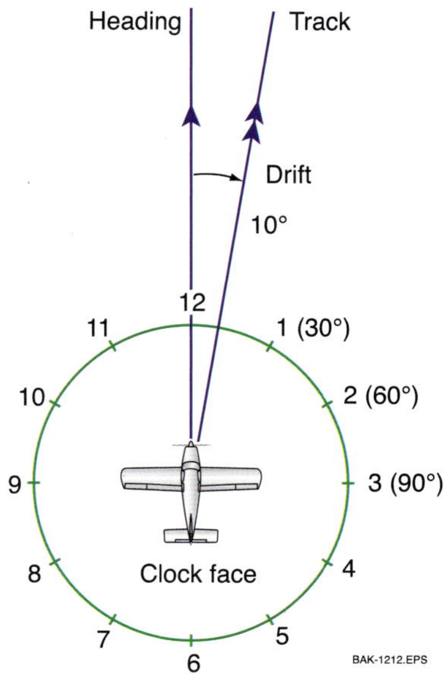

Figure 12-13
Using the clock code to estimate track and drift (R. Mackay).

Estimating Distance

Distance on a chart can be measured accurately using the scale line on the chart or a suitable scale rule. However it can also be estimated to within about 5 nm using other means.

The average top thumb-joint will cover about 20 nm on a 1:1,000,000 (WAC) chart and 5 nm on 1:250,000 Visual Terminal Chart. Check yours! This makes it very easy to estimate short distances.

A full hand span might measure 120 nm on a 1:1,000,000 chart. Check yours!

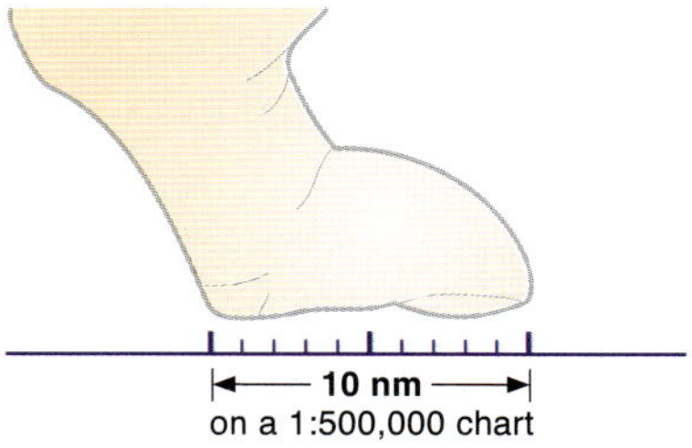

Figure 12-14
The top thumb joint covers approximately 10 nm on a 1:500,000 chart.

Chart Orientation in the Cockpit

In flight, the pilot must relate the land features and their relative bearing from the aeroplane to their representations on the chart. To do this, it is best to place the chart so that it is orientated with the heading of the aeroplane. This process can be aided by making the chart into a "stripmap", so only track and its immediate surroundings are displayed.

If, according to the chart, a landmark is 30° off-track to the right (from the present position of the aeroplane), then the pilot should be able to spot it by directing attention out of the cockpit window approximately 30° to the right of track.

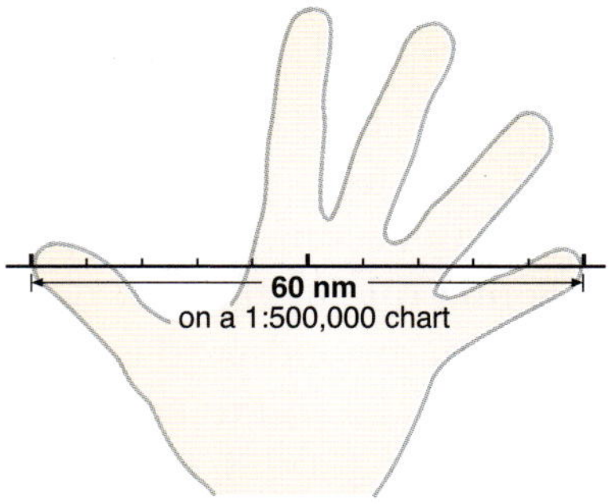

Figure 12-15
Full hand span is approximately 60 nm on a 1:500,000 chart.

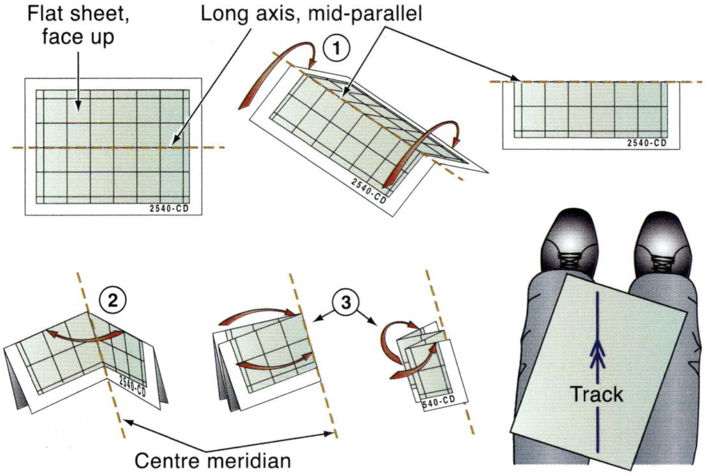

Figure 12-16 Fold charts so that you "fly up the page".

Useful Navigation Publications & Calculations

In addition to the various aeronautical charts, there are other very useful publications such as the *En Route Supplement Australia* (ERSA) and the *Visual Flight Guide* (VFG), which provide important information for VFR pilots.

This information includes:

- facilities:
  - aerodrome details, with simple diagrams showing runway layout, length and direction, windsock position, etc (detailed runway distance information is included in a supplement to ERSA;
  - radio navigation aids;
  - Air Traffic Services, e.g. the responsible FIS (Flight Information Service) centre and frequency;
  - any special procedures, such as Class D procedures, and noise abatement procedures;
- prohibited, restricted and danger (PRD) areas;
- conversion of units and wind component tables;
- light signals;
- other special procedures not associated with an aerodrome;
- pilot briefing services;
- met forecast code/decode;
- radio broadcasting stations; and
- emergency procedures.

Units of Measurement/Conversion of Units

Navigation Calculations

When you are going for the full private or commercial licence and proceed onto cross-country flying (over longer distances than what you have covered in navigating to/from the local training area), you will use a navigation computer for flight planning and when en route.

The traditional mechanical navigation computers have a wind side for calculating the effect of the wind on your track and groundspeed, and a calculator side for carrying out arithmetic-type problems, such as conversions, or calculating estimated time intervals.

At this stage, you can do many of the simpler navigation calculations mentally, but once you become familiar with doing these on the navigation computer, you will probably find this an efficient way to work.

- If your groundspeed is 120 kt (a knot is a speed of 1 nautical mile per hour), how long will it take you to cover 30 nautical miles (nm)?
  120 kt = 120 nm in 60 minutes = 2 nm/minute.
  To cover 30 nm will take 30 ÷ 2 = 15 minutes.
- If your groundspeed is 90 kt, how long will it take to cover 24 nm?
  90 kt = 90 nm in 60 minutes = 1.5 nm/minute.
  To cover 24 nm will take 24 ÷ 1.5 = 16 minutes.
- If your aeroplane burns 30 litres of fuel per hour (i.e. 30 L/hour), what endurance do you have (excluding reserves) with 75 litres on board?

  Endurance = fuel amount over consumption rate = $^{75}/_{30} = 2\frac{1}{2}$ = 2 hours and 30 minutes.

Speeds

You will encounter a number of different airspeeds. The basic airspeed indicated on the airspeed indicator is, naturally enough, the indicated airspeed (IAS). Unfortunately, there are small errors in the pitot–static system which senses the pressures used by the airspeed indicator. These vary with airspeed and are especially related to the position of the pitot tube on the airframe. Correcting the IAS for this position error gives us a new airspeed known as *calibrated airspeed* (CAS). The amount of correction for each aeroplane type will be found in the pilot's operating handbook and is usually only one or two knots (subtracted from the IAS).

In practical flying, the calibrated airspeed is rarely referred to because of its small difference from the IAS at normal flight speeds. However, to be theoretically correct, CAS is one step on the road from the indicated airspeed towards calculating a true airspeed. A much bigger correction is required to cover the density error due to a non-standard air density, compared with the pitot–static system error correction.

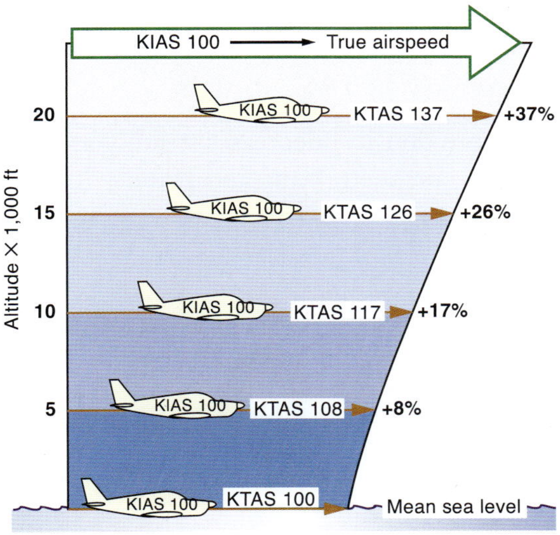

Figure 12-17 Indicate airspeed at 100 kt – true airspeed increases at altitude.

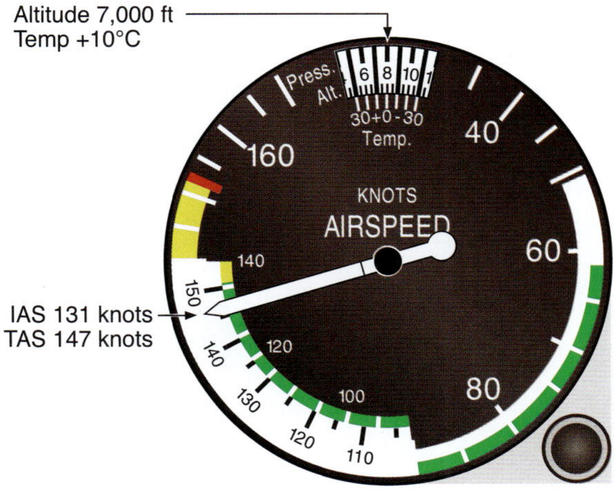

Figure 12-18 Airspeed indicator with a true airspeed correction scale.

To use the airspeed indicator as a measure of the aeroplane's actual speed through the air for navigation purposes, we have to make a correction to the IAS due to the fact that the temperature and pressure (density) in the atmosphere vary from place to place, and particularly because pressure decreases with altitude. Every ASI is calibrated to indicate the true airspeed under conditions where the air density is the same as under ISA MSL conditions, i.e. pressure 1,013.2 hPa and temperature +15°C. As temperature increases, or as pressure decreases (for instance, with a change in altitude), air density will fall. To meet the same number of air molecules in the same time (and so indicate the same IAS), the aeroplane will have to travel faster through the thinner air; that is, the true airspeed will be a little greater than the indicated airspeed. This difference will increase the lower the density of the air.

The two factors which determine density are temperature and pressure, and so to obtain the true airspeed (TAS) these two factors must be applied to the IAS (CAS). This can be done by setting temperature against pressure height (altitude corrected for ISA pressure deviation) on the navigation computer, or some airspeed indicators have a built-in correction scale which cleverly enables a display of both IAS and TAS.

From the point of view of practical handling of the aeroplane, for instance when taking off and landing, it is indicated airspeed that is of the greatest importance. If your approach speed is 60 kt indicated airspeed (sometimes written 60 KIAS), this is the approach speed irrespective of the air density, even at very hot and/or high-elevation aerodromes. True airspeed (TAS) is only of importance when carrying out navigation calculations, such as determining the expected groundspeed and time intervals.

Calculating TAS on the Navigation Computer

Step 1
In the true-airspeed window, set *pressure altitude* against temperature (finding pressure altitude was explained in the chapter on performance).

Step 2
Against IAS on the inner (of the two outer) scales, read TAS on the outer scale.

Remember that many navigation computers have the term pressure altitude engraved on them. This has the same meaning as pressure height:

- Temperature +10°C at pressure altitude 7,000 ft.
- IAS 131 kt IAS (knots of indicated airspeed) gives 147 kt TAS.

In normal circumstances, air pressure (and therefore density) decreases steadily as you climb and so, if climbing with a constant indicated airspeed, your aeroplane's "true" speed will gradually increase.

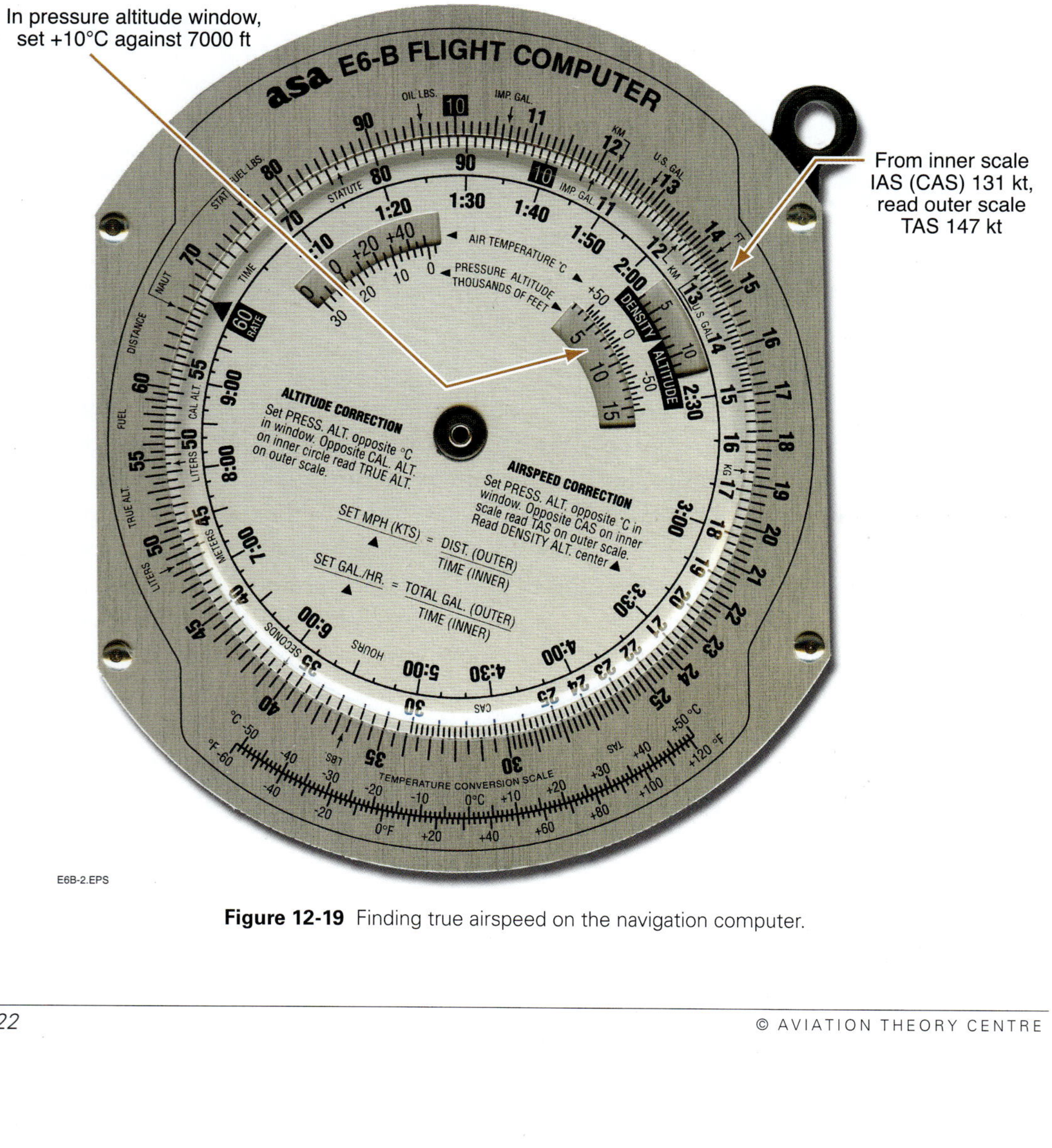

E6B-2.EPS

Figure 12-19 Finding true airspeed on the navigation computer.

The Effect of Wind

As you fly over the ground at a known true airspeed, the air itself is usually moving. This, as we know, is called the wind. The effect of the wind on the aeroplane causes the speed relative to the earth, known as groundspeed (GS), to differ from the true airspeed. For example, flying due north at a true airspeed (TAS) of 120 kt with a 30 kt tailwind (a southerly) will mean that our groundspeed is 150 kt. If we have a 20 kt headwind component, our GS will be 100 kt.

Figure 12-20 All flights must take wind into account.

Calculating the wind component (headwind or tailwind) on a particular track is another function of the navigation computer, usually done at the flight planning stage using forecast winds before setting out on a navigation "cross-country". This procedure is covered fully in the theory preparation for the private pilot licence (vol. 2 of our Pilot's Manual series, *Meteorology and Navigation*). Another way of finding groundspeed is to time how long it takes to fly between two known landmarks on a cross-country flight. If the landmarks are 12 nm apart, and it takes 6 minutes to cross them, then our groundspeed is 12/6 = 2 nm/minute = 2 × 60 nm/hour = 120 kt.

Summary

- The airspeed indicator reads *indicated airspeed* (IAS);
- IAS corrected for position error gives *calibrated airspeed* (CAS);
- CAS (IAS for practical purposes) corrected for density (pressure and temperature) variation from ISA MSL conditions gives *true airspeed* (TAS); and
- *Groundspeed* (GS) is determined by applying the headwind or tailwind component to the TAS.

Review 12

BAK Level of Knowledge Only

1. What is the difference in meaning between heading and track?
2. What is the angular difference?
3. What is the difference in meaning between true airspeed and groundspeed?
4. What is the mathematical difference?

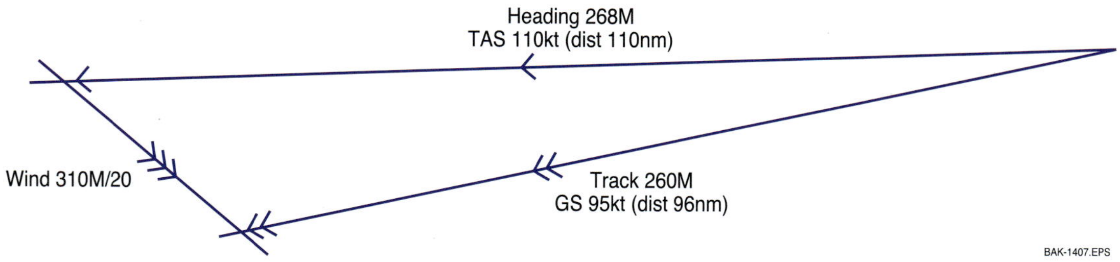

5. What is the reference for magnetic track?
6. What is the difference in reference between track magnetic and track true?
7. What is the angular difference called?
8. What is the angular difference between magnetic heading and compass heading?
9. Variation east is (added/subtracted) from true track to achieve magnetic track.
10. Given heading with airspeed, and track with groundspeed, what is the third vector in the navigation triangle?
11. What is Zulu time?
12. What is UTC and GMT?
13. What is the difference in time between UTC and Australian EST?
14. What is meant by the scale of a chart?
15. Give two examples of defining position on the earth.
16. What is a WAC?
17. What scale does it use?
18. The VTC is a (larger/smaller) scale than the WAC.
19. An isogonal joins areas of equal . . . . .
20. The magnetic variation for Melbourne is approximately . . . . .

Appendix

Aviation
Theory
Centre

Appendix 1

Practice Exams

Pre-Circuit Solo Practice Examination

Questions:	20
Marks:	20
Pass Mark:	70%
Time Allowed:	40 minutes

1. Seat belts/safety harnesses must be worn, at all stages of flight, by:
a. the pilot when he/she is the sole pilot.
b. the occupants of both control seats.
c. all on board during climb and descent.
d. two children when they occupy a single seat. *(1 mark)*

2. Civil Aviation Regulations require that turns onto final approach must:
a. commence not below 500 ft AGL.
b. be completed not closer than 500 metres from the threshold.
c. be completed not closer than 500 metres from the aerodrome perimeter.
d. be completed not closer than 500 metres from any displaced threshold. *(1 mark)*

3. A pilot in command shall not consume any alcoholic liquor:
a. 12 hours before the departure of the flight.
b. 24 hours before reporting for duty.
c. 8 hours before reporting for duty.
d. 8 hours before the departure of the flight. *(1 mark)*

4. The minimum horizontal distance from cloud for a fixed-wing aircraft, operating in Class G airspace, is:
a. 1,500 metres.
b. 1,500 ft.
c. 1,000 ft.
d. clear of cloud. *(1 mark)*

5. The fuel system in an aircraft must be checked for water contamination:
a. before each flight.
b. before the first flight of the day and after each refuelling.
c. before the first flight of the day and after the last flight of the day.
d. at least once a day. *(1 mark)*

6. One restriction placed on VFR aircraft, operating at or below 2,000 ft, is:
a. minimum horizontal distance from cloud is 2,000 metres.
b. minimum flight visibility is 6 km.
c. navigation must be by visual reference to the ground or water.
d. minimum vertical distance from cloud is 1,000 ft. *(1 mark)*

7. A student pilot is not permitted to carry passengers unless:
- **a.** he/she has completed 2 hours as pilot in command.
- **b.** he/she has passed the General Flying Progress Test and flies within the student pilot area limits.
- **c.** he/she has completed 5 hours of cross-country flying.
- **d.** he/she has had a dual flight within the last 30 days. *(1 mark)*

8. With local QNH set on the subscale, an altimeter will always read:
- **a.** pressure height.
- **b.** density height.
- **c.** height above mean sea level.
- **d.** height above ground level. *(1 mark)*

9. At a non-towered aerodrome, you should not continue an approach beyond the threshold until a preceding light aeroplane, using the same runway, has:
- **a.** landed, and has vacated the runway, irrespective of the runway length, and is taxiing away.
- **b.** landed, and is at least 1,800 metres from the landing threshold.
- **c.** taken off and is at least 200 AGL.
- **d.** taken off and is at least 600 metres ahead of the landing threshold.

(1 mark)

10. You are to operate from a non-towered aerodrome where there is no ATIS and no other way of knowing the latest QNH. Before take-off, you should:
- **a.** set the altimeter to read the aerodrome elevation.
- **b.** set the altimeter to read zero feet.
- **c.** set an approximate aerodrome pressure in the subscale.
- **d.** set 1013 hPa on the subscale. *(1 mark)*

11. One item which must be included in a passenger briefing prior to take-off is:
- **a.** a demonstration of the correct crash landing position.
- **b.** the use and location of fire extinguishers.
- **c.** the use and adjustment of seat belts.
- **d.** the demonstration of evacuation procedures. *(1 mark)*

12. With regard to the rules of the air in the CAR, which statement is correct?
- **a.** An aircraft that is overtaking another aeroplane, has the right of way.
- **b.** If an aeroplane and a glider are approaching head-on at approximately the same height the aeroplane must give way to the glider.
- **c.** An aircraft that is within 70° of the astern position of an aircraft ahead is considered an overtaking aircraft, if its speed is greater.
- **d.** An aircraft that is overtaking another aircraft must do so by altering its heading to the left.

(1 mark)

13. On which of the following types of flying is a passenger not permitted to be carried?
- **a.** An aircraft engaged in aerobatic flying.
- **b.** Flying training given to a person who has not passed the General Flying Progress Test (GPFT).
- **c.** An aircraft carrying out formation flying.
- **d.** An aircraft engaged in search and rescue (SAR) operations. *(1 mark)*

14. You are to carry out a flight from Parafield to the training area in a Piper Arrow – XYG. You are also in receipt of ATIS information "Charlie", indicating Runway 21 Right is being used. Your pre-taxi radio call will be:
- **a.** "Parafield Ground, X-ray Yankee Golf, Piper Arrow, received Charlie, VFR for the Training Area, Runway 21 Right".
- **b.** "Parafield Ground, Piper Arrow X-ray Yankee Golf, for the Training Area, Runway 21 Right, taxi clearance, received Charlie".
- **c.** "Parafield Ground, X-ray Yankee Golf, Runway 21 Right, for the Training Area, received Charlie".
- **d.** "Parafield Ground, Piper Arrow X-Ray Yankee Golf, taxi clearance for the Training Area, Runway 21 Right, received Charlie".

(1 mark)

15. Area QNH is:
- **a.** the aerodrome pressure set in the altimeter before taxiing.
- **b.** the mean sea level pressure set in the altimeter before taxiing.
- **c.** the local aerodrome pressure set in the altimeter while on a navigation or cross-country flight.
- **d.** the mean sea level pressure set in the altimeter of the area over which the aircraft is flying while on a navigation or cross-country exercise.

(1 mark)

16. When the aerodrome QNH is set, during taxi, the altimeter should read:
- **a.** zero.
- **b.** airfield elevation.
- **c.** vertical distance AGL.
- **d.** vertical distance AAL. *(1 mark)*

17. One of the basic rules following an engine failure immediately after take-off is:
- **a.** always try to restart the engine.
- **b.** immediately make a distress call.
- **c.** never turn back to the runway. *(1 mark)*

18. A hard pull up on the control column can cause a aeroplane to stall at almost any speed because:
- **a.** of reduced control effectiveness.
- **b.** the critical angle of attack can be exceeded.
- **c.** of decreased angle of attack.
- **d.** of reduced airspeed. *(1 mark)*

19. A white dumb-bell symbol has been placed adjacent the primary wind indicator on your airfield. This means:
- **a.** the airfield is completely unserviceable.
- **b.** poor surface this area, do not taxi here.
- **c.** parachute operations in progress.
- **d.** use hard surfaces only. *(1 mark)*

20. An aircraft stall-warning device will:
- **a.** indicate that a stall has occurred.
- **b.** cause a light to come on and a horn to sound after the aircraft stalls.
- **c.** indicate that the aircraft is approaching the stall at any attitude. *(1 mark)*

Pre-Area Solo Practice Examination

(Answer in addition to the previous questions)

Questions:	30
Marks:	30
Pass Mark:	70%
Time Allowed:	60 minutes

1. An aircraft fitted with a piston engine must be fuelled with:
a. AVTUR fuel.
b. Unleaded fuel.
c. Leaded fuel.
d. MOGAS.
e. AVGAS. *(1 mark)*

2. What colour is AVGAS 100LL?
a. Clear or straw colour.
b. Blue.
c. Red or purple.
d. Green. *(1 mark)*

3. The carburettor heat can be used as:
a. an anti-icing action (ice prevention).
b. a de-icing action (ice removal).
c. an alternate supply of air to the engine.
d. all the above. *(1 mark)*

4. Should ice form in your carburettor and you have a small reduction in MP, rpm, or airspeed, you should:
a. keep adjusting power by opening the throttle.
b. apply carburettor heat, full on.
c. use alternate static. *(1 mark)*

5. Ice that forms on the engine air filter is known as:
a. throttle ice.
b. fuel evaporation ice.
c. impact ice. *(1 mark)*

6. What common action should be taken if impact or throttle icing occurs?
a. Reduce power.
b. Increase power.
c. Apply carburettor heat.
d. Warm the engine. *(1 mark)*

7. After flying for some time, the centre-zero ammeter shows almost zero (just a small positive indication). This would mean:
a. that the aircraft alternator has failed and the battery is providing all the power.
b. insufficient electrical output is being produced by the alternator.
c. that the battery is being recharged.
d. that the battery is fully charged and the system is working normally. *(1 mark)*

8. If the alternator fails, the electrical system will receive its power from:
a. an emergency generator.
b. the battery.
c. a wind driven electrical generating device. *(1 mark)*

9. Should the alternator fail and the battery power be consumed:
a. the engine-driven fuel pump would stop working.
b. the fuel boost pump would still be available.
c. most of the engine instruments would stop working.
d. the engine would malfunction. *(1 mark)*

10. Excessive priming of an engine for start can:
a. cause the spark to occur at the incorrect time.
b. increase the risk of a manifold fire during start.
c. reduce the amount of fuel available in the manifold.
d. adversely effect the oil pressure. *(1 mark)*

11. Aircraft fuel tanks require a vent, the purpose of which is to:
a. avoid a build-up of dangerous fumes.
b. allow condensation inside the tank to escape.
c. allow the pressure inside the tank to equalise with the outside pressure.
(1 mark)

12. Aircraft spark plugs may become fouled with a build-up of lead from the fuel, if the engine is operated for any length of time at a:
a. high power setting with a lean mixture.
b. low power setting with a lean mixture.
c. high power setting with a rich mixture.
d. low power setting with a rich mixture. *(1 mark)*

13. If you set the altimeter to QNH, the instrument should read:
a. zero feet.
b. density altitude.
c. pressure altitude.
d. vertical distance AMSL. *(1 mark)*

14. The red radial line on the airspeed indicator represents the:
a. structural cruising speed.
b. landing gear lowering speed.
c. normal operating speed range.
d. never exceed speed. *(1 mark)*

15. Rotation about the longitudinal axis is referred to as:
a. yawing, and is effected by the rudder.
b. yawing, and is effected by the ailerons.
c. rolling, and is effected by the ailerons.
d. pitching, and is effected by the elevator. *(1 mark)*

16. The tendency of an aircraft to return to its original condition when disturbed from straight and level flight is known as:

a. controllability.
b. manoeuvreability.
c. stability.
d. balance. *(1 mark)*

17. During a climbing turn you must be careful of:

a. the tendency to over-bank the aircraft as the horizon is not always obvious.
b. decreasing your rate of climb.
c. the tendency to under-bank the aircraft as the horizon is not always obvious. *(1 mark)*

18. How is the aircraft's performance affected by mud or minor damage on the surface of the wings?

a. Lift is decreased; drag is decreased.
b. Lift is increased; drag is decreased.
c. Lift is increased; drag is increased.
d. Lift is decreased; drag is increased. *(1 mark)*

19. A blockage of the static system would likely be corrected by applying:

a. alternate air on.
b. pitot heat on.
c. alternate static on.
d. carburettor heat on. *(1 mark)*

20. During your take-off roll, the airspeed indicator remains at zero. You should:

a. abort the take-off.
b. try to work out why the ASI is not working.
c. estimate your rotate speed.
d. select alternate static and pitot heat on. *(1 mark)*

21. If after landing, you find one brake is not working, you should:

a. stop on the runway.
b. taxi back to the parking tarmac as the nosewheel steering will still be functional.
c. allow your aircraft to slow using most of the runway, taxi clear of the landing area and radio for assistance on the ground frequency. *(1 mark)*

22. For proper internal cooling the engine must have:

a. a functioning oil cooler thermostat.
b. a correctly leaned mixture setting.
c. circulating oil at a pressure within the permissible range.
d. proper airflow over the exhaust manifold. *(1 mark)*

23. If you encounter gusting wind in the circuit, what speed would you try to maintain on the final approach?

a. About 5 kt above the stall to minimise the impact of the gusts.
b. Normal approach speed because it is chosen to account for such conditions.
c. About 5 to 10 kt above normal approach speed depending upon the strength of the gusts.
d. Manoeuvre speed. *(1 mark)*

24. After start, engine oil pressure must reach normal operating pressure (the green sector) within:
- **a.** 30 minutes.
- **b.** 10 minutes.
- **c.** 15 seconds.
- **d.** 30 seconds.

(1 mark)

25. While taxiing, you notice another aircraft is approaching you on the same taxiway from the opposite direction. Should you:
- **a.** continue straight ahead and be prepared to stop.
- **b.** move to the left and stop if necessary.
- **c.** move to the right and stop if necessary.
- **d.** stop immediately.

(1 mark)

26. An aircraft will stall:
- **a.** at a higher speed if power is increased.
- **b.** at the same indicated airspeed as altitude increases.
- **c.** when the aircraft's weight exceeds lift.
- **d.** at a lower indicated airspeed as altitude decreases.

(1 mark)

27. When considering the hazards of wake turbulence, the wingtip vortices trailing behind large aeroplanes in flight:
- **a.** will present no hazard when the vortices are encountered in level cruising flight.
- **b.** will increase in intensity and violence as the speed of the large aeroplane increases.
- **c.** are most severe when the large aeroplane is at low speed during climbs or approaches for landings.

(1 mark)

28. For proper cooling the engine must have:
- **a.** the correct mixture setting for that operation.
- **b.** the correct quantity of oil in the engine.
- **c.** the correct amount of cooling airflow around the engine.
- **d.** all of the above.

(1 mark)

29. Detonation occurs in a reciprocating engine when:
- **a.** a spark plug is fouled and shorts out.
- **b.** the mixture is too rich.
- **c.** the charge explodes instead of just burning.
- **d.** hot spots ignite the mixture too soon.

(1 mark)

30. Although the master switch is off, before leaving an aircraft a pilot must also ensure that the magneto switch is off. The reason for this is:
- **a.** the magneto system is independent of aircraft power and the engine could start if the propeller was turned.
- **b.** so the key can be removed.
- **c.** the magneto system will have no earth and cannot be energised.
- **d.** so the battery will not discharge over night.

(1 mark)

Basic Aeronautical Knowledge (BAK) Practice Examination

Questions:	60
Marks:	70
Pass Mark:	70%
Time Allowed:	1 hour and 40 minutes

1. Where the refuelling equipment is not mobile, the Civil Aviation Orders require that an aeroplane being refuelled shall:
   a. have no persons on board.
   b. have a fire extinguisher on board.
   c. have all electrical systems switched off.
   d. be so placed that it can rapidly be moved to a place of safety if needed. *(1 mark)*

2. An aeroplane's fuel must be checked for the presence of water:
   a. prior to every flight.
   b. prior to the first flight of the day and at each change of pilots.
   c. prior to the first flight of the day and following each refuelling.
   d. after each refuelling and/or change of pilots. *(1 mark)*

3. Following an incident, an Air Safety Incident Report shall be submitted:
   a. within 48 hours of the completion of the flight.
   b. within 48 hours of the incident occurring.
   c. within 24 hours of the incident occurring.
   d. immediately. *(1 mark)*

4. Which of the following would justify the use of a Mayday call?
   a. You need navigational assistance.
   b. You sight a capsized yacht off the coast.
   c. A passenger becomes ill and you need to land for medical assistance.
   d. You have an engine failure on a training flight. *(1 mark)*

5. An aeroplane must not fly over a populated area at a height lower than:
   a. 1,500 ft AMSL.
   b. 1,000 ft on the area QNH.
   c. 1,000 ft AGL.
   d. 500 ft AGL. *(1 mark)*

6. Increasing power when flying straight and level at normal cruise speed will cause?
   a. an increase in airspeed and a decrease in drag.
   b. an increase in airspeed and an increase in drag.
   c. a decrease in airspeed and a decrease in drag.
   d. a decrease in airspeed and an increase in drag. *(1 mark)*

7. What is the effect of lowering full flap?
   a. An increase in lift and a decrease in drag.
   b. A decrease in lift and a decrease in drag.
   c. A decrease in lift and an increase in drag.
   d. An increase in lift and an increase in drag. *(1 mark)*

8. Stalling speed is increased if:
  a. weight is increased.
  b. weight is decreased.
  c. load factor is decreased.
  d. angle of attack is increased. *(1 mark)*

9. What do we call the angle between the chord line of an aerofoil and the relative airflow?
  a. Angle of incidence.
  b. Stalling angle.
  c. Sweepback.
  d. Angle of attack. *(1 mark)*

10. Increasing the load factor will:
  a. decrease the stalling speed.
  b. increase the stalling speed.
  c. increase the stalling angle.
  d. decrease the stalling angle. *(1 mark)*

11. What happens to lift and drag as the angle of attack approaches the stalling angle?
  a. Lift increases and drag increases.
  b. Lift increases and drag decreases.
  c. Lift decreases and drag decreases.
  d. Lift decreases and drag increases. *(1 mark)*

12. An aeroplane is descending at the best gliding speed. Raising the nose will:
  a. increase the gliding range.
  b. decrease the gliding range.
  c. decrease the glide angle.
  d. decrease the rate of descent. *(1 mark)*

13. When compared to the stall IAS at 1,000 ft, the stall IAS at 10,000 ft will:
  a. increase by approximately 40%.
  b. decrease by approximately 40%.
  c. be the same.
  d. vary according to the actual density at 10,000 ft. *(1 mark)*

14. If a tailwind is encountered during a glide descent, when compared with a glide in still-air conditions, the:
  a. aeroplane pitch angle will be shallower.
  b. flightpath over the ground will be steeper.
  c. distance over the ground will be greater.
  d. rate of descent will be less. *(1 mark)*

15. When in a 30° banked level turn, the load factor:
  a. is the same as in straight and level flight.
  b. decreases by a factor of 15%.
  c. will increase to 1.15g.
  d. will be limited by the airspeed. *(1 mark)*

16. What are the VMC requirements for a VFR flight conducted in Class G airspace between 3,000 ft AMSL (or 1,000 ft AGL if higher), and 10,000 ft AMSL?
  a. Visibility 5 km, clear of cloud.
  b. Visibility 8 km, 1,000 metres horizontally from cloud, 1,000 ft above or below cloud.
  c. Visibility 5,000 metres, 1,500 metres horizontally from cloud, and 1,000 ft vertically from cloud.
  d. Visibility 8,000 metres, clear of cloud. *(1 mark)*

17. A cold front is likely to produce:
- **a.** cumiliform clouds with smooth flying conditions.
- **b.** stratiform clouds with smooth flying conditions.
- **c.** cumiliform clouds with turbulent conditions.
- **d.** stratiform clouds with turbulent conditions. *(1 mark)*

18. The term INTER on a forecast means that the weather will be:
- **a.** interminable in nature.
- **b.** expected to last for at least 60 minutes.
- **c.** interrupted every 30 minutes.
- **d.** expected to last for less than 30 minutes. *(1 mark)*

19. The cloud base in a TAF is given as a height above:
- **a.** the 1013.2 hPa level.
- **b.** the highest ground within 10 km of the aerodrome.
- **c.** mean sea level.
- **d.** aerodrome level. *(1 mark)*

20. The wind direction in the ATIS is given in:
- **a.** degrees true from the wind direction.
- **b.** degrees magnetic to the wind direction.
- **c.** degrees magnetic from the wind direction.
- **d.** degrees true to the wind direction. *(1 mark)*

21. Using your navigation computer, determine the true airspeed (TAS) if you are flying at 120 kt IAS, with a temperature of +15°C at a pressure altitude of 8,000 ft.
- **a.** 139 kt.
- **b.** 132 kt.
- **c.** 127 kt.
- **d.** 120 kt. *(1 mark)*

22. If the time in Sydney on 23 March is 0628 EST, what is the UTC time?
- **a.** 231628 UTC.
- **b.** 222028 UTC.
- **c.** 232028 UTC.
- **d.** 221628 UTC. *(1 mark)*

23. The track to your training area is 270°M. If the wind is from the south and is causing 10 degrees of drift, your heading would be closest to:
- **a.** 270°T.
- **b.** 280°M.
- **c.** 290°T.
- **d.** 260°M. *(1 mark)*

24. Magnetic variation is:
- **a.** the angular difference between magnetic north and compass north.
- **b.** the direction in which all compass errors occur.
- **c.** always expressed in degrees, either east or west.
- **d.** the angular difference between true north and compass north. *(1 mark)*

25. A line of longitude on a WAC is:
- **a.** drawn north-south and represents true north and true south.
- **b.** drawn east-west and represents magnetic north and magnetic south.
- **c.** sometimes referred to as an isogonal.
- **d.** drawn parallel to the next meridian. *(1 mark)*

26. On a day when the temperature is 30°C and the relative humidity is 30%, carburettor ice:
- **a.** is unlikely to form.
- **b.** will form with maximum power set.
- **c.** is likely to form with normal cruise power set.
- **d.** is highly likely to form with low power set. *(1 mark)*

27. Why do most aeroplane piston engines have dual ignition systems?
- **a.** For the sole reason of safety in the event of the failure of one magneto.
- **b.** For safety and for improved combustion.
- **c.** For improved combustion even though safety is not increased.
- **d.** To spread the load between each of the spark plugs in a cylinder. *(1 mark)*

28. If, following combustion, there is unburned fuel remaining in the cylinders, then the mixture is described as:
- **a.** rich.
- **b.** chemically correct for the power setting being used.
- **c.** lean.
- **d.** having a fuel/air ratio of 100%. *(1 mark)*

29. What do we call explosive, spontaneous combustion in the cylinders?
- **a.** Run-on.
- **b.** Detonation.
- **c.** Pre-ignition.
- **d.** Normal combustion. *(1 mark)*

30. What is one effect of applying carburettor heat?
- **a.** It will result in more air immediately going through the carburettor.
- **b.** It will not affect the fuel-air mixture.
- **c.** It will enrich the mixture.
- **d.** It will lean the mixture. *(1 mark)*

31. Which flight instrument gives a pilot a direct reading of the bank angle?
- **a.** Direction indicator.
- **b.** Attitude indicator.
- **c.** Turn coordinator.
- **d.** Magnetic compass. *(1 mark)*

32. You are cruising in an aeroplane with a fixed-pitch propeller and notice a slight drop in engine rpm. You suspect carburettor icing and apply full carburettor heat. Which one of the following statements most correctly indicates that ice was present?
- **a.** There will be an immediate increase in engine rpm as soon as carburettor heat is applied.
- **b.** The engine will start to run roughly with a further decrease in engine rpm.
- **c.** The engine rpm will remain constant.
- **d.** The engine rpm will decrease and then increase. *(1 mark)*

33. When compared with an engine fitted with a carburettor, which of the following applies to a fuel-injected engine?
- **a.** It is more prone to starting problems and is less susceptible to fuel contamination.
- **b.** It is easier to start when hot and is more responsive to throttle movement.
- **c.** It is less likely to have to icing problems and is more efficient.
- **d.** It requires greater care in throttle handling and is more susceptible to fuel contamination.

(1 mark)

34. Fuel that appears to be uncoloured or a very pale yellow is:
- **a.** 100LL low-lead AVGAS for piston engines.
- **b.** 100/130 AVGAS for piston engines.
- **c.** MOGAS.
- **d.** AVTUR (kerosene) for turbine engines (i.e. jet or prop-jet engines). *(1 mark)*

35. To improve engine cooling during a maximum power climb, you should:
- **a.** fly at a higher IAS.
- **b.** fly at a lower IAS.
- **c.** lean the fuel-air mixture.
- **d.** apply carburettor heat. *(1 mark)*

36. The correct sequence of the various strokes in a four-stroke engine is:
- **a.** intake, compression, power, exhaust.
- **b.** intake, exhaust, power, compression.
- **c.** intake, power, compression, exhaust.
- **d.** intake, power, exhaust, compression. *(1 mark)*

37. Which statement concerning carburettor ice do you consider most accurate?
- **a.** Carburettor ice is most likely to form when the air temperature is in the range –10°C to +20°C with visible moisture or high humidity.
- **b.** The carburettor heater is a de-icing device that heats the air after it leaves the carburettor.
- **c.** Carburettor ice will always form when the temperature is below freezing.
- **d.** The first indication of carburettor icing in an aeroplane with a fixed-pitch propeller is an increase in rpm.

(1 mark)

38. If the static vent ices over during a descent, the airspeed indicator will then read:
- **a.** zero.
- **b.** higher than the actual IAS.
- **c.** lower than the actual IAS.
- **d.** correctly. *(1 mark)*

39. With battery and generator switches ON, what is the probable reason for a zero reading on a left-zero ammeter?
- **a.** The battery is fully charged.
- **b.** The alternator is still charging the battery.
- **c.** The battery is completely flat.
- **d.** The alternator has failed. *(1 mark)*

40. The pitot-static system supplies pressure for:
- **a.** the ASI only.
- **b.** the ASI, artificial horizon and VSI.
- **c.** the ASI, turn and slip indicator and altimeter.
- **d.** the ASI, VSI and altimeter. *(1 mark)*

41. If you decide to fly when you have a cold or flu, you put yourself at risk of:
- **a.** being too tired to concentrate.
- **b.** having balance difficulties and sinus pain.
- **c.** becoming dehydrated.
- **d.** developing hypoxia. *(1 mark)*

42. Atmospheric pressure variations affect the human body. These pressure changes are:
- **a.** minimum at low level so we generally don't need to worry about them.
- **b.** minimum at high altitude.
- **c.** maximum at high altitude so we need pressurisation and oxygen supplied.
- **d.** maximum at low level so we need to understand their adverse effects.

(1 mark)

43. Which of the following drugs are considered acceptable for flying?
- **a.** Antibiotics.
- **b.** Analgesics.
- **c.** Antihistamines.
- **d.** Amphetamines.
- **e.** None of the above. *(1 mark)*

44. If an aeroplane is loaded in such a way that the centre of gravity is outside the forward limit, it will:
- **a.** be very unstable longitudinally.
- **b.** have a very short moment arm.
- **c.** be very unstable about the normal axis.
- **d.** be very nose heavy and difficult to rotate on take-off. *(1 mark)*

45. Along which axis of the aeroplane is the centre of gravity computed?
- **a.** Lateral.
- **b.** Normal.
- **c.** Longitudinal.
- **d.** All of the above. *(1 mark)*

46. An aeroplane must not be operated at a weight in excess of the maximum certificated gross weight because:
- **a.** structural limitations will be exceeded.
- **b.** an overloaded aeroplane is excessively stable in flight.
- **c.** flight in excess of certificated weights is not possible.
- **d.** fuel consumption will be greater. *(1 mark)*

47. Which of the following factors improves take-off performance?
- **a.** The runway sloping upwards.
- **b.** A tailwind.
- **c.** A crosswind.
- **d.** Low atmospheric pressure.
- **e.** Low atmospheric temperature. *(1 mark)*

48. V_{NO} is defined as the:
- **a.** maximum indicated airspeed for extending flaps.
- **b.** true airspeed beyond which flight is not permitted.
- **c.** maximum indicated airspeed for normal operations in smooth conditions.
- **d.** indicated airspeed beyond which flight is not permitted.

(1 mark)

49. Strong wake turbulence produced by wingtip vortices is most likely to form:
- **a.** behind a heavy aeroplane which is flying slowly just after take-off.
- **b.** behind any aeroplane which is flying slowly with full flap extended.
- **c.** behind any aeroplane which is flying at high speed.
- **d.** only behind aeroplanes powered by turbo-jet engines. *(1 mark)*

50. As you approach to land the wind is gusting. You increase your approach speed by 5 kt to ensure a margin of safety. This means:
- **a.** the approach path flown will be steeper.
- **b.** climbing for a go-around would not be possible.
- **c.** the LDR will be greater.
- **d.** descent will be much more rapid. *(1 mark)*

51. To load an aeroplane, where would you find the weight and balance details for that aircraft?
- **a.** In the maintenance release.
- **b.** On the passenger manifest.
- **c.** In your flight instructors handbook.
- **d.** In the aircraft flight manual. *(1 mark)*

52. The weight of 230 litres of AVGAS is closest to:
- **a.** 128 kg.
- **b.** 145 kg.
- **c.** 163 kg.
- **d.** 172 kg.
- **e.** 180 kg. *(1 mark)*

Use Load System Charlie, page 376 for question 53. Given:

EW 695 kg
IU 19,788
The student pilot weighs 60 kg and the instructor weighs 75 kg

53. The maximum amount of fuel on board that will allow "utility category" operations immediately after take-off is closest to:
- **a.** 62 litres.
- **b.** 88 litres.
- **c.** 100 litres.
- **d.** 123 litres.
- **e.** 135 litres. *(3 marks)*

Use Load System Charlie, page 376 for questions 54 and 55. Given:

EW 695 kg
IU 19,788
The student pilot weighs 60 kg and the instructor weighs 75 kg
Load the aircraft with 95 kg weight of baggage and load 170 litres of fuel.

54. The zero fuel weight condition is closest to:
- **a.** weight 824 kg, arm 2821 mm.
- **b.** weight 890 kg, arm 2933 mm.
- **c.** weight 932 kg, arm 2960 mm.
- **d.** weight 990 kg, arm 3004 mm. *(2 marks)*

55. The take-off condition is closest to:
- **a.** weight 932 kg, arm 2,960 mm.
- **b.** weight 1,013 kg, arm 2,999 mm.
- **c.** weight 1,035 kg, arm 3,004 mm.
- **d.** weight 1,053 kg, arm 2,960 mm.
- **e.** weight 1,102 kg, arm 2,999 mm. *(2 marks)*

Use the following performance data to answer questions 56 to 60. Airfield:

Elevation: 1,890 ft
Runways: 17/35 sealed TODA 3,000 metres (slope: level)
12/30 short grass TODA 1,000 metres (slope: 1% down to SE)
ATIS
Terminal Information Delta
Runway 12
Wind: 150/15
QNH 1,010
Temperature: 15°C
Cloud FEW 3000
Runway wet.
Works in progress Runway 17/35.

56. The pressure altitude of this airfield is:
- **a.** 1,800 ft.
- **b.** 1,980 ft.
- **c.** 2,260 ft.
- **d.** 2,440 ft. *(2 marks)*

57. The density altitude of this airfield is:
- **a.** 1,800 ft.
- **b.** 1,980 ft.
- **c.** 2,260 ft.
- **d.** 2,460 ft. *(2 marks)*

58. The headwind component on the duty runway is closest to:
- **a.** 5 kt.
- **b.** 8 kt.
- **c.** 10 kt.
- **d.** 12 kt. *(1 mark)*

59. Use the Cessna take-off chart: page 346. At the MTOW, the take-off distance required on Runway 12 is closest to:
- **a.** 550 m.
- **b.** 730 m.
- **c.** 890 m.
- **d.** 980 m. *(3 marks)*

60. Use the Piper Landing chart: page 353. Under the conditions given the landing distance required for this aircraft is closest to:
- **a.** 310 m.
- **b.** 420 m.
- **c.** 530 m.
- **d.** 640 m. *(3 marks)*

Answers

Pre-Circuit Solo Practice Examination

1. a.	**11.**c.
2. d.	**12.**c.
3. d.	**13.**b.
4. a.	**14.**a.
5. b.	**15.**d.
6. c.	**16.**b.
7. b.	**17.**c.
8. c.	**18.**b.
9. a.	**19.**d.
10.a.	**20.**c.

Pre-Area Solo Practice Examination

1. e.	**11.**c.	**21.**c.
2. b.	**12.**d.	**22.**c.
3. d.	**13.**d.	**23.**c.
4. b.	**14.**d.	**24.**d.
5. c.	**15.**c.	**25.**c.
6. c.	**16.**c.	**26.**b.
7. d.	**17.**a.	**27.**c.
8. b.	**18.**d.	**28.**d.
9. c.	**19.**c.	**29.**c.
10.b.	**20.**a.	**30.**a.

Basic Aeronautical Knowledge (BAK) Practice Examination

1. d.	**16.**c.	**31.**b.	**46.**a.
2. c.	**17.**c.	**32.**d.	**47.**e.
3. b.	**18.**d.	**33.**c.	**48.**c.
4. d.	**19.**d.	**34.**d.	**49.**a.
5. c.	**20.**c.	**35.**a.	**50.**c.
6. b.	**21.**a.	**36.**a.	**51.**d.
7. d.	**22.**b.	**37.**a.	**52.**c.
8. a.	**23.**d.	**38.**b.	**53.**d.
9. d.	**24.**c.	**39.**d.	**54.**c.
10.b.	**25.**a.	**40.**d.	**55.**d.
11.a.	**26.**a.	**41.**b.	**56.**b.
12.b.	**27.**b.	**42.**d.	**57.**d.
13.c.	**28.**a.	**43.**e.	**58.**d.
14.c.	**29.**b.	**44.**d.	**59.**b.
15.c.	**30.**c.	**45.**c.	**60.**c.

Appendix 2

Answers to Review Questions

Review 1

1. Air is a mixture of gases, mostly nitrogen and oxygen.
2. Thrust is the reaction to propelling air rearwards.
3. An equal and opposite reaction.
4. The left foot.
5. Clears fences, easier to load, better downward view.
6. Directional control – especially in a crosswind.
7. Retractable.
8. Cowls.
9. Flightpath.
10. Less or reduced compared to the pressure beneath the wing and the local static pressure.
11. Angle of attack.
12. The fuselage is the primary structure joining the wings, engine and tail assemblies and which contains the passengers, crew and cargo.
13. The fin.
14. Attitude (pitch and roll or bank).
15. Horizon.
16. By banking the aircraft a sideways component of lift is used to turn.
17. To roll one wing up and the other down – simultaneously.
18. They are not control surfaces – they increase the curvature of the wing and so increase lift.
19. To increase lift for take-off and to increase both lift and drag for approach and landing.
20. Down or away from the pilot.
21. It works in the same sense relative to the pilot.
22. "You have control".
23. One knot is a speed of one nautical mile per hour.
24. Pitch and bank. How far the nose is above or below the horizon and whether the coaming is parallel to the horizon or at the desired angle.
25. Airspeed indicator, attitude indicator, altimeter, vertical speed indicator, heading indicator and turn coordinator with balance ball.
26. Relative airflow.
27. Propeller, air.
28. Total reaction.
29. Lift and induced drag.
30. Airspeed, angle of attack and camber.
31. Induced drag.
32. The downward movement imparted to the air after the passage of the wing.
33. The tendency of the aircraft to continue or return to its trimmed state and flightpath.
34. The centre of gravity.
35. Yes. The increased stability reduces the degree of control response.
36. The elevators.
37. Flightpath.
38. By tilting the total reaction from the wing.
39. The leading edge.
40. The trailing edge.
41. Attitude and power determine the sustained flightpath of the aircraft.
42. Rate of turn and balance by the balance ball.
43. The direction that the aircraft is pointing in relation to magnetic north.
44. A unit of distance used for altitude. A foot is approximately 30 cm.
45. It indicates that a rate one turn produces a 360 degree turn taking 2 minutes.
46. The right hand pedal is depressed.
47. It indicates not only speed through the air but is also an indirect indication of angle of attack in straight and level flight. Low airspeed equals increased

angle of attack; minimum airspeed equals stalling angle of attack.

48. The throttle.
49. Radio/electronic aids to navigation.
50. The nose.
51. The part of the total force that is acting in the particular direction.

Review 2

1. Radio telephony.
2. To avoid misunderstanding (see table 2-3, page 43).
3. 30–300 MHz.
4. Megahertz – signal frequency in millions of cycles per second.
5. The magnitude of the peaks and troughs of an oscillation.
6. In between – to respond to signals without admitting excess hash.
7. So the pilot's hands remain free to control the aircraft while transmitting.
8. Yes.
9. It is the international prelude to a distress message.
10. Alpha Tango Charlie.
11. Standby.
12. Continue a normal circuit, make normal transmissions, look for a green light on final approach, look for traffic on the runway.
13. Emergency locator transmitter.
14. VHF COM is the radio transmitter/receiver. VHF NAV is the navigation (VOR) receiver.
15. 60 nm maximum.
16. There are no pros for the hand-held. It is a back-up only.
17. India Hotel Tango Foxtrot Papa.
18. Strength 2 readability 3.
19. Otherwise there are spurious transmissions as it passes through other selected codes.
20. Not if all other indications were normal. I would turn for home and if there were any other unusual indications a pan-pan would be declared.
21. Return via normal reporting points and lanes of entry. Make normal calls. Select 7600 on the transponder. Enter the circuit form 500 ft above on the dead side and look for traffic. Follow a normal circuit for landing.
22. Reset the connections. Check radio and intercom turned on, volumes and squelch adjusted. If still quiet try the hand-held mike.
23. 121.5 MHz.
24. Over your left shoulder – nearly behind.
25. Go around for another normal circuit.

Review 3

1. α is the Greek symbol for angle of attack.
2. A maintenance release is a document telling the pilot that the aircraft is serviceable for the flight. It is vital to flight safety because it tells the pilot if the aircraft is fit to fly and when it is due for its next servicing.
3. The *numbers* are indications of runway direction to the nearest 10°.
4. •ASI: airspeed indicator;
   - IAS: indicated airspeed;
   - VFR: visual flight rules;
   - VMC: visual meteorological conditions;
   - VSI: vertical speed indicator;
   - CFI: chief flying instructor;
   - RPM: revolutions per minute;
   - MAP: manifold absolute pressure;
   - AVGAS: aviation gasoline; and
   - GFPT: General Flying Progress Test.
5. Magnetic north is the direction to the north magnetic pole.
6. β is the Greek symbol used to represent sideslip angle.
7. The term wake turbulence refers to the disturbed air behind large aircraft.
8. •AMSL: above mean sea level.
   - TAS: true airspeed.
   - NDB: non-directional beacon.
   - LAME: licensed aircraft maintenance engineer.
   - NOTAM: notice to airmen.
   - VTC: visual terminal chart.
   - WAC: World Aeronautical Chart.

- CAVOK: ceiling and visibility OK.
- AGL: above ground level.

9. Radial is the magnetic bearing of an aircraft *from* a point.
10. The difference between true north and magnetic north is called magnetic variation.
11. The significance of this is that charts are aligned to true north, whereas the magnetic compass is aligned to magnetic north. The pilot must allow for variation.
12. The time difference between Australian EST and UTC is 10 hours.
13. Zulu time is Greenwich Mean Time.
14. Altitude is the vertical distance above mean sea level, and height is the vertical distance above terrain.
15. Groundspeed is the speed of the aircraft relative to the ground.
16. Drift is the difference between heading and track.
17. The specific gravity of AVGAS is 0.71.

Review 4

1. The structure transfers lift from the wings to support the load. It also protects the cargo and passengers (payload) from the environment.
2. The tail surfaces provide the balancing force about the lateral and vertical axes. The tail incorporates rudder and elevator controls and pitch trim.
3. Two.
4. A yoke is the Y-type control handle provided for the pilot. It activates both elevator and aileron controls.
5. Most light aircraft are *trikes*, there undercarriage configuration is a pair of main wheels with either a nosewheel or a tailwheel.
6. The lower portion of the foot pedals activates rudder.
7. About 95% of existing piston engine aeroplanes have engines, and therefore propellers that rotate "clockwise viewed from behind".
8. Lubrication:
   - reduces friction;
   - provides cooling; and
   - provides protection.
9. Engine oil.
10. Before flight the pilot must check the quantity of oil in the engine is sufficient.
11. Aero 100, an ashless dispersant oil for normal operations, but "red band", a straight mineral oil, is used in new engines or when some parts are new to allow wearing in.
12. Two magnetos are provided primarily for safety reasons, if one fails the other will keep the engine running. A secondary effect of having two magnetos is the engine combustion is more complete and there is a small power gain.
13. To prevent engine failure in the case of one magneto failing.
14. During circuit and early flight training the student pilot is expected the change power settings frequently, A rich mixture reduces the risk of damage to the engine if power was increased rapidly with a lean mixture.
15. The more chips and dents the poorer the propeller performance. If you have any doubt about the acceptability check with an engineer.
16. The pilot carries out a fuel drain to check for visible signs of water, impurities and colour to ensure safe operation with that fuel.
17. The law requires a fuel drain before the first flight of the day and after each refuelling. I check it before every flight.
18. The fuel drain sample is taken from each of the aircraft drain points and then should be tested in one of two methods:
    - Use fuel testing paste.
    - Put a small quantity of AVGAS in the container before taking the sample. This way, if the sample is all water, you will see the problem.
19. Visible signs of water, any impurities and ensure the colour indicates the correct fuel.
20. When you suspect icing and often

during descent.

21. The pitot tube will be blocked and the airspeed indication will remain at zero. You would not take off.

22. The flaps operating range.

23. In straight and level non-accelerating flight read the compass and immediately set the HI to that heading. This should be done about every 20 minutes.

24. A canard is the forward wing found on some aircraft only. It functions with or instead of a horizontal stabiliser.

25. Most light aircraft have the engine at the front so they use tractor or puller propellers.

26. The angle of incidence is that angle between the fuselage and a line through the main plane and the tail plane. This angle is set during manufacturing and does not change during any condition of flight.

27. On a conventional aircraft the horizontal portion of the tail plane consists of the horizontal stabiliser and the elevator. Some modern aircraft combine the function of both these aerodynamic devices, the whole tail moves with the pitch control and this is called a stabilator.

28. Fowler flaps move back and down, which means they significantly increase the chord of the wing as well as the curvature.

29. Chocks are used to prevent the aircraft moving when parked. Park breaks can lose pressure. There are occasions where it is preferable to have the brakes off, such as when the aircraft is in the hanger.

30. Nothing, the ignition system and the electrical system are entirely independent.

31. During any descent.

32. De-ice.

33. The carburettor mixes the fuel with the air in the correct proportions and provides control over the quantity of this mixture reaching the engine.

34. The fuel air mixture is set at sea level at a ratio of 10:1 (10 parts air 1 part fuel). As the aircraft climbs less air is available for the engine so the amount of fuel provided to the mixture is reduced. Pulling the mixture control rearwards achieves this. To lean an engine the fuel is reduced so the new ratio is about 13:1.

35. The mixture lever controls the fuel air ratio, the throttle controls the quantity of mixture reaching the engine.

36. Reducing the throttle first when reducing power ensures you do not over-charge or over-boost the engine, which can cause detonation.

37. A nosewheel aircraft to veer left during take-off because of propeller torque reaction and the slipstream effect on the tail, a tail-dragger has two extra reasons to swing left, the down going propeller blade is more effective and the gyroscopic effect that occurs when the tail rises.

38. Safety. Engine driven mechanical pumps can supply all the fuel needed, but if it were to fail, the engine would stop almost immediately. With the electric boost pump on, a mechanical pump failure will not be noticed until you turn the boost pump off. For this reason when you turn the boost pump off keep your hand on the switch for a few seconds, if the engine does anything but run perfectly put the boost pump back on.

39. Many high wing aircraft have gravity feed fuel systems so they don't necessarily need a boost pump. However, they often have both an engine driven pump and an electric boost pump.

40. Stop as soon as you can. Preferably not on the runway or taxiway. Park on the grass where you are, radio for assistance or walk for help. There is no point in taxing to where people or other aircraft are if you do not have full control of you aircraft.

41. Static pressure is that pressure applied by the atmosphere; it is about 1013 hPA (14.7 psi). Dynamic pressure is that pressure caused by the movement of a body through the air or by the air moving against that body. Pitot and total pressure are the same. They consist of both dynamic and static pressures together and total pressure is measured at the pitot tube.

42. We use pitot pressure (D+S) then measure static (S) at a static vent or port to separate the dynamic pressure, (D+S) – S = D, which we use to indicate airspeed.

43. At different airspeeds, the aircraft flies at different attitudes meaning the pitot tube is not at the most efficient angle to measure accurately all the time. This is called position error.

44. The angle of attack of an aeroplane in straight and level flight directly relates to its airspeed. A fast aircraft will have an angle of attack of about 4° and a slow aircraft an angle of attack of about 12°. Don't forget a conventional aircraft will stall at about 16° angle of attack.

45. With the static port blocked an altimeter will indicate that altitude at which the blockage occurred.

46. With the static port blocked VSI will indicate zero climb or descent because there is no longer any change of static pressure.

47. Vacuum pressure is simply used as an alternative source of energy to rotate some gyros. The law states that the second attitude indication must be driven by a separate and independent power supply; one supply is vacuum pressure and the other is electricity.

48. Using air pressure means the air would have to pass through the pump before it is used in the gyros. Air provided like this is far more likely to be contaminated by pump lubricants. A vacuum system has the pump on the exit line.

49. Electricity is reliable and it is a separate and independent power supply.

50. The numbers on the card of the direct reading compass are positioned to indicate correctly by the aircraft turning around the compass card. Unfortunately, the card oscillates a little and the indications from the rotating card can be confusing. Take your time.

Review 5

1. Make the next landing a full stop.

2. If asked, advise that you have that aircraft sighted. Continue your approach keeping the aircraft in sight, if the aircraft clears the runway, land. If the aircraft does not or may not clear the runway, go around.

3. Remain clear of the other aircraft. Try to contact the tower by radio and watch the tower for light signals. Obey any signal received, however, if no signal is seen, and you can see the other aircraft and the runway is clear, you may decide to land. If there is any doubt go around, make the radio calls at the normal places advise "transmitting blind" and try again. Don't rush – the runway will still be there next time.

4. A powered aircraft has more manoeuvring options than balloons or gliders.

5. Keep clear of that aircraft. If the situation is likely to become dangerous, move to the live side and go around.

6. See and be seen is the concept used when no procedural or radar separation is provided by air traffic control. It means lookout, communicate and remain clear of other aircraft.

7. Airspace that is used by large numbers of aircraft and by aircraft of very different performance characteristics is controlled for both safety and efficiency.

8. The holding point is the boundary between the taxiway and the runway. At controlled aerodromes a clearance is required to cross the holding point. In all cases the holding point is marked with continuous lines and should serve to remind all pilots to look for approaching aircraft.

9. The threshold is painted a little like large black and white piano keys.
10. From the runway:
    - Upwind.
    - Crosswind.
    - Downwind.
    - Base.
    - Final.
11. When there is only one runway the side of the runway inside the circuit is the live side and the side outside the circuit is the dead side.
12. 500 ft AGL.
13. 3 hours.
14. 20 hours.
15. Three-axis control means using all controls:
    - elevator for pitch (about the lateral axis);
    - ailerons for roll (about the longitudinal axis); and
    - rudder for yaw (about the vertical axis).
16. Licence, medical certificate, maintenance release and flight manual.
17. VMC below 10,000 ft in:
    - Class C, D and E airspace is vis 5,000 m distance from cloud 1,000 ft vertically and 1,500 m horizontally.
    - Class G airspace 3,000 to 10,000 ft . . . same.
    - Class D CTR vis 5,000 m and clear of cloud.
    - Class G airspace > 3,000 ft. V is 5,000 m clear of cloud insight of ground or water.
18. Advise air traffic control and request a clearance through controlled airspace if necessary. If the cloud is prohibitive land at the nearest suitable airfield. As a last resort land in a paddock. Any airfield is better than a paddock as paddocks aren't surveyed.
19. Remain at the same level, turn right to overtake, remain well clear.
20. Make a right turn, remain level and pass behind that aircraft. When safe turn left to regain track.
21. Airmanship: common sense, a high level of self discipline, good manners, good preparation, consideration for others all put together.
22. 1,000 ft above the highest object within a radius of 600 m of the aircraft.
23. As a student pilot may carry passengers:
    - When authorise by an instructor.
    - Flight is permitted only within the student area limit.
    - Must have passed GFPT or RPL test.
    - Must have passed BAK on aircraft type.
24. Actual weights should be used.

Review 6

1. External.
2. Proportional.
3. A twisting or turning force.
4. The force of attraction of the earth.
5. Lift, weight, thrust and drag.
6. The walking stick – tilted and upside down – peak at 16 degrees angle of attack.
7. Attitude is the direction, left-right, up-down, that the aircraft is pointing in relation to the horizon. Flightpath is the path the aircraft is following or is going relative to the horizon. Angle of attack is the angle of the chord line to the relative airflow irrespective of attitude and flightpath.
8. Straightness to the airflow (left-right).
9. Balance is indicated by the balance ball being centralised.
10. Trim is longitudinal (nose-up nose-down) balance.
11. By setting the attitude, holding it constant and operating the trim wheel to remove any hand pressure on the control column.
12. No climb or descent, no turn – constant altitude, constant direction.
13. A steady ascending flightpath at constant airspeed.
14. Set Power, Set Attitude, hold and then Trim.
15. Look out and check engine temperatures and pressures and adjust power if necessary.

16. Attitude, pause, Power, Trim.
17. Power reduced, Attitude adjusted, hold and Trim.
18. Power, Attitude, Trim.
19. A centripetal force caused by tilting the lift from the wing.
20. A sideways motion through the air corrected by centring the balance ball with rudder.
21. By rolling to the desired bank angle and applying back pressure to maintain the desired attitude.
22. By holding a constant attitude with a set bank angle. Elevators, ailerons and rudder are used normally.
23. By rolling to level and relaxing back pressure to the straight and level attitude.
24. Reducing airspeed, increasing attitude, back pressure and movement, sloppy controls, buffet, stall warning horn.
25. Reduce the angle of attack or cease increasing the angle of attack.
26. Exceeding the critical angle of attack of the wing.
27. It can cause a wing drop in the direction opposite to the desired direction of roll.
28. An approach with the flaps retracted.
29. The change of flightpath from the descending approach to almost level for touchdown.
30. Elevators, ailerons, rudder – and power.
31. Pitch, roll and yaw respectively.
32. Lateral, longitudinal and normal axes – through the centre of gravity.
33. A body continues at rest or in motion in a straight line unless pushed by an external force. The change in direction or speed is proportional to the applied force. There is an equal and opposite reaction to the applied force.
34. The magnitude of the force and the lever arm.
35. Acceleration which is felt from the pilot's head to toes.
36. +15°C.
37. 1013.2 HPa.
38. Pitching, rolling and yawing moments.
39. Layered smooth flow – like sheets of paper sliding over each other.
40. At the transition point.
41. The total pressure in a fluid remains constant.
42. Total reaction, lift and drag (induced drag).
43. Induced and parasite drag (which includes form, skin friction and interference drag).
44. A U-shaped curve with minimum drag at the lowest point. Below this the induced drag increases and is dominant and above this the parasite drag increases and is dominant.
45. Chord, thickness, chord line, line of mean camber, symmetrical aerofoil.
46. Airspeed is the indirect effect of elevator, roll is the indirect effect of rudder, yaw is the indirect effect of aileron (and sideslip) and rate of descent is the indirect effect of thrust. Some would argue that airspeed is the indirect effect of thrust and that rate of descent is the direct effect.
47. Normal climb, maximum rate climb, maximum angle climb and cruise climb.
48. Thrust, power, airspeed, density altitude, weight, wind (climb angle only).
49. 500 fpm.
50. 45 degrees bank or more.
51. Reduce the angle of attack, apply full power, prevent yaw and roll with opposite rudder. Establish a climb when the airspeed increases.
52. Weight = lift = $C_L \frac{1}{2} \rho V^2 S$.
53. Angle of attack and airspeed. The pilot can also change C_L, and, in some case, S by extending the flaps.
54. Weight.
55. A spin is a low airspeed, low g, stalled condition with rotation in yaw, pitch and roll and perhaps oscillations in pitch. A spiral is a high airspeed, accelerating, high g condition which risks structural failure.
56. The aircraft is cushioned and there is a reduction in induced drag.
57. There is a reduction in slipstream over the elevators, there is a nose-

down pitching moment, and there is a loss of lift.

58. Maximum excess thrust (best angle of climb speed), maximum excess power (best rate of climb speed).

Review 7

1. Drift is the difference between heading and track – where the aircraft is pointing versus where it is going.
2. Shorter run, better directional control, lower groundspeed, steeper climb.
3. Headwind and tailwind respectively.
4. Crosswind.
5. Crosswind component.
6. No change to time or rate but steeper path relative to the ground.
7. Same. Power will need to be added to maintain the same approach path. This will reduce the rate of descent for the same airspeed.
8. By adding power.
9. Increasing power.
10. A change in wind direction or speed with differing altitudes.
11. The airspeed displayed on the ASI – a measure of dynamic pressure.
12. It shows the margin above the stall in straight and level flight and acts as a guide to the angle of attack.
13. A rising current of warm air.
14. The turbulent wake behind a heavy aircraft – primarily from the wing-tip vortices at high angles of attack (low airspeed).
15. Fly behind and above heavy jets or wait several minutes.
16. Control column forward and right.
17. 7 kt.
18. Flightpath would become shallower and the airspeed would reduce.
19. Indicated is displayed on the ASI, Calibrated is corrected for pressure error and True airspeed is the actual speed relative to the air.
20. Mechanical is due to wind over terrain, wake is due to wing-tip vortices, and thrust stream is due to propeller or jet efflux.
21. Yes – from the rotor tips.
22. Check your flight manual – type specific.
23. The circle becomes a stretched spiral with the centre of the circle moving downwind.
24. Turning from the downwind direction to across the wind.
25. Rate of descent in fpm should be about 5 times the groundspeed in knots.
26. Crab and wing-down.
27. 150 m.

Review 8A

1. Circulatory and Nervous.
2. To inhale air and extract the oxygen and to exhale waste carbon dioxide.
3. Reduced processing, disorientation, dizziness, euphoria, loss of consciousness.
4. By the Valsalva manoeuvre, by chewing or swallowing.
5. Hyperventilation. Consciously slow down the rate of breathing.
6. Dehydration.
7. Eight hours.
8. Carbon monoxide.
9. The part of the retina where the optic nerve passes through.
10. Saccade/rest cycle.
11. It rests at about 1–2 metres.
12. Decision-making.
13. To sense acceleration or tilt.
14. Acceleration and tilt.
15. A reduction in oxygen to the blood stream.
16. 24 hours.
17. Trapped gases in the blood, intestines, joints or cavities (sinuses).
18. Lack of sleep, noise.
19. Antihistamines, sedatives, antibiotics.
20. Decompression sickness – nitrogen coming out of solution especially around the joints.
21. 24 hours.
22. Aviates, navigates, communicates –

but most of all decision-makes.

23. The rear coating of the eyeball containing light sensitive rods and cones.
24. Rods and cones.
25. The cones in the central foveal region.
26. Slightly to one side of the anticipated direction.
27. Autokinesis.
28. Shallower.
29. Eustachian Tube.
30. Valsalva manoeuvre.
31. Noise, heat.
32. Hearing and balance.
33. The point of the runway where the pilot's eyes would ideally impact – with no flare.
34. It remains a constant distance below the horizon and a constant position in the windscreen if the aircraft's on a constant approach path at a constant speed in a set configuration.

Review 8B - TEM

1. Threat and Error Management
2. Threat and Error Management is a holistic safety concept which specifically addresses potential weaknesses in human performance in the aviation environment.
3. External.
4. Expected threats, unexpected threats and latent threats.
5. Anticipate and avoid the threat.
6. An error is an action or inaction by the flight crew that lead to deviations form organisational or flight crew intentions or expectations.
7. An undesired aircraft state.
8. Communication.
9. Error detection and correction.
10. Aircraft handling, ground navigation or incorrect aircraft configuration.
11. Incorrect autopilot mode, incorrect power setting, incorrect NAVAID setting, incorrect loading, incorrect fuel quantity or distribution, etc.

Review 9

1. Troposphere, stratosphere, ionosphere.
2. 36,000 ft.
3. Direction (330°T) and speed (20 kt).
4. Okta is the number of "eights" of cloud cover. 4 oktas = 4/8 cover.
5. Ten nautical miles, preferably upwind.
6. Condensation occurs thereby forming cloud.
7. Air that is heated by the earth's surface rises causing a thermal.
8. V_B is the turbulence penetration speed. If this is not known, use V_A.
9. Lights, moderate and severe.
10. Mechanical lift.
11. Frost, rain, hail.
12. A forecast is a prediction of likely weather over some period in the future. A report is a statement of observed weather at a particular time past.
13. Stratiform is layered cloud.
14. AVFAX is a self-help system that delivers meteorological and NOTAM information.
15. DECTALK is a self-help system which delivers meteorological information via telephone using a computer generated voice.
16. BKN cloud → 5 to 7 oktas.
17. CAVOK – ceiling and visibility OK. To use this abbreviation, visibility must be more than 1 km; no Cb visible; no cloud below 5,000 AAL; and no precipitation, TS, fog, snow or dust devils.
18. TEMPO 30 minutes; INTER 60 minutes.
19. ARFOR is an area forecast. TAF is a terminal area forecast.
20. A forecast is declared provisional (PROV) when it is compiled from incomplete information – it may have errors.

Review 10

1. Weight concerns the amount of mass or load we can put on an aircraft, while balance is the position within the aircraft that weight can be located.
2. BEW is the empty weight plus full oil.
3. ZFW includes BEW and the weight of the:
   - pilot;
   - passengers;
   - payload; and
   - ballast.
4. Specific gravity.
5. To convert AVGAS from volume to weight multiply by 0.71.
6. To convert Litres to USG divide by 3.8.
7. Weight (force) and arm (lever).
8. Centre of Gravity (Fulcrum).
9. To ensure adequate stability, and at the same time provide a sufficient degree of control.
10. Allowable CG range.
11. Moment = weight multiplied by the arm.
12. The datum is the point from which all measurements are taken.
13. A graphical representation of the allowable CG range and all weights.
14. The "normal category" is specified limits within which an aircraft is permitted to carry out normal manoeuvres.
15. The "utility category" is a specified range, usually a lower weight with a forward CG that allows manoeuvres not permitted in the normal category. This might include some aerobatic manoeuvres.

Review 11

1. 15°C and 1013.2 hPa.
2. This means that the temperature is 15°C greater than the ISA temperature at that point. ISA plus 15°C at sea level is 30°C.
3. QNH is a code (not an abbreviation) which indicates the atmospheric pressure datum in use. QNH is the mean sea level datum pressure.
4. Density altitude is pressure altitude adjusted for temperature, which takes density into account.
5. •V_S – Stall speed, the speed where the angle of attack will exceed the stall angle.
   - V_{NO} – Normal operating speed, the normal speed operating range is indicated by the green arc on the ASI.
   - V_{NE} – Never exceed speed, the maximum speed under any circumstance, the risk of structural damage is great if exceeded.
   - V_{FE} – Flap extension speed. The white arc on the ASI indicates the speed at which full flap can be used. Flap settings of less than full flap may be used consistent with the flight manual speeds.
6. TODR, take-off distance required. TODA, take-off distance available.
7. TOSS, take-off safety speed – that speed not less than 1.2 V_S which provides safety margin above the stall.
8. Take-off considerations, favourable:
   - Long runway.
   - Low airfield elevation.
   - High pressure.

   Take-off considerations, unfavourable:
   - High humidity.
   - High temperature.
   - Soft runway surface.
9. Aquaplaning or hydroplaning is where the tyre loses contact with the runway surface because water has formed a planning surface above the runway. It means poor braking and possible loss of directional control.
10. Landing considerations, adverse:
    - Wet runway.
    - Tail or cross wind.
    - Down slope.
11. Density altitude 4,900 ft. Temperature at 2,500 ft in ISA is 10°C. Actual temperature is 30°C. This is ISA plus 20. Therefore 20 × 120 = 2,400 ft, add this to 2,500 ft.
12. This very high density altitude will

significantly reduce take-off and climb performance.

Review 12

1. Heading is where the aircraft is pointing. Track is the actual path of the aircraft over the ground.
2. Drift.
3. True airspeed is the actual speed of the aircraft through the air; it is almost always faster than indicated airspeed which only takes into consideration the local dynamic effects. Groundspeed is the true airspeed corrected for wind effect along track.
4. Add the tail wind component to TAS to get groundspeed. Subtract the headwind component to get groundspeed.
5. Magnetic north.
6. True track is referenced to (measured from) true north. This is the process that takes place when we measure a track on a map. Magnetic track is referenced to magnetic north.
7. Magnetic variation.
8. Magnetic deviation.
9. Variation east, magnetic least. . . therefore variation is subtracted from true to give magnetic.
10. Wind velocity W/V.
11. The time zone "Zulu" is the verbal manner use to describe UTC and GMT.
12. Coordinated universal time (UTC) is the same as Greenwich mean time (GMT).
13. +10 hours.
14. The actual distance as represented by chart distance (1:1,000,000).
15. Latitude and longitude, bearing and distance.
16. World Aeronautical Chart (WAC) – a topographical map.
17. WAC scale is 1:1,000,000.
18. VTC scale is 1:250,000 and is a larger scale.
19. Equal magnetic variation.
20. 12°E.

Aviation
Theory
Centre

Index

B

C

D

E

N

O

P

T

Y

Z

Aviation
Theory
Centre